INTERNATIONAL RELATIONS IN POLITICAL THOUGHT

*Texts from the Ancient Greeks
to the First World War*

This unique collection presents texts in international relations from ancient Greece to the First World War. Major writers such as Thucydides, Augustine, Aquinas, Machiavelli, Grotius, Kant, and John Stuart Mill are represented by extracts of their key works; less-well-known international theorists such as John of Paris, Cornelius van Bynkershoek, and Friedrich List are also included. Fifty writers are anthologized in what is the largest such collection currently available. The texts, most of which are substantial extracts, are organized into broadly chronological chapters, each of which is headed by an introduction that places the work in its historical and philosophical context. Ideal for both students and scholars, the volume also includes biographies and guides to further reading.

CHRIS BROWN is Professor of International Relations at the London School of Economics. His publications include *International Relations Theory: New Normative Approaches* (1992), *Understanding International Relations* (2nd edn., 2001), and *Sovereignty Rights and Justice,* (2002). He also edited *Political Restructuring in Europe: Ethical Perspectives* (1994).

TERRY NARDIN is Professor of Political Science at the University of Wisconsin-Milwaukee. He is the author of *Law, Morality, and the Relations of States* (1983) and *The Philosophy of Michael Oakeshott* (2001), editor of *The Ethics of War and Peace* (1996), and coeditor (with David Mapel) of *Traditions of International Ethics* (1992) and *International Society* (1998).

NICHOLAS RENGGER is Professor of Political Theory and International Relations at St. Andrews University. His publications include *International Relations, Political Theory and the Problem of Order* (1999), *Retreat from the Modern?* (1996), and *Political Theory, Modernity and Postmodernity: Beyond Enlightenment and Critique* (1995). He has edited *Treaties and Alliances of the World* (6th edn., 1995) and *Dilemmas of World Politics: International Issues in a Changing World* (with John Baylis, 1992).

INTERNATIONAL RELATIONS IN POLITICAL THOUGHT

Texts from the Ancient Greeks to the First World War

Edited by

CHRIS BROWN
London School of Economics and Political Science

TERRY NARDIN
University of Wisconsin-Milwaukee

NICHOLAS RENGGER
University of St. Andrews, Scotland

CAMBRIDGE
UNIVERSITY PRESS

PUBLISHED BY THE PRESS SYNDICATE OF THE UNIVERSITY OF CAMBRIDGE
The Pitt Building, Trumpington Street, Cambridge, United Kingdom

CAMBRIDGE UNIVERSITY PRESS
The Edinburgh Building, Cambridge CB2 2RU, UK
40 West 20th Street, New York, NY 10011-4211, USA
477 Williamstown Road, Port Melbourne, VIC 3207, Australia
Ruiz de Alarcón 13, 28014 Madrid, Spain
Dock House, The Waterfront, Cape Town 8001, South Africa

http://www.cambridge.org

In the editorial matter,

First published 2002
Reprinted 2003

Printed in the United Kingdom at the University Press, Cambridge

Typeface Golden Cockerell 11/13 pt. and Perpetua   *System* LATEX 2$_\varepsilon$ [TB]

A catalogue record for this book is available from the British Library

Library of Congress Cataloguing in Publication data
Texts in international relations : from ancient Greece to the First World War / edited by
Chris Brown, Terry Nardin, Nicholas Rengger.
    p.   cm.
Includes bibliographical references and index.
ISBN 0 521 57330 0 (hardback) – ISBN 0 521 57570 2 (pbk.)
1. International relations – History – Sources.   2. International relations – Philosophy –
History – Sources.   I. Brown, Chris, 1945–   II. Nardin, Terry, 1942–   III. Rengger,
N. J. (Nicholas J.)
JZ 1305. T45   2002
327 – dc21   2001037928

ISBN 0 521 57330 0 hardback
ISBN 0 521 57570 2 paperback

Contents

Acknowledgements .... *page* ix

1 Introduction 1

2 Ancient thought (500 BCE–312 CE) 17

THUCYDIDES
From *History of the Peloponnesian War* 34

ARISTOTLE
From *The Politics* 61

CICERO
From *On Duties* 83

MARCUS AURELIUS
From *Meditations* 86

PLATO
From *The Epistles* 90

3 Late antiquity and the early middle ages (312–1000) 95

ANONYMOUS
From *The Teaching of the Lord to the Gentiles through
the Twelve Apostles* or *The Didache* 111

EUSEBIUS
From *Tricennial Orations* 115

AUGUSTINE OF HIPPO
From *The City of God against the Pagans* 119

CONSTANTINE PORPHYROGENITUS
From *De Administrando Imperio* 136

AL-FARABI
From *The Political Regime* 148

v

AVICENNA
From *The Healing* 170

MOSES MAIMONIDES
From *Logic* 174

4 International relations in Christendom 177

JOHN OF PARIS
From *On Royal and Papal Power* 191

DANTE ALIGHIERI
From *Monarchy* 198

MARTIN LUTHER
From *On Secular Authority* 204

THOMAS AQUINAS
From *Summa Theologiae* 213

DESIDERIUS ERASMUS
From "Dulce Bellum Inexpertis" 221

FRANCISCO DE VITORIA
From "On the American Indians" 231

5 The modern European state and system of states 243

NICCOLÒ MACHIAVELLI
From *The Prince* 257
From *The Discourses* 262

JEAN BODIN
From *Six Books of the Commonwealth* 270

FRANÇOIS DE CALLIÈRES
From *On the Manner of Negotiating with Princes* 276

CORNELIUS VAN BYNKERSHOEK
From *On Questions of Public Law* 281

ALEXANDER HAMILTON
From *Letters of Pacificus* 286

EDMUND BURKE
From *Letters on a Regicide Peace* 292

FRANÇOIS DE SALIGNAC DE LA MOTHE FÉNELON
From "On the Necessity of Forming Alliances" 301

FRIEDRICH VON GENTZ
"The True Concept of a Balance of Power" 307

6 The emergence of international law 311

HUGO GROTIUS
From *The Law of War and Peace* 325

THOMAS HOBBES
From *Leviathan* 335

SAMUEL PUFENDORF
From *On the Duties of Man and Citizen* 341

SAMUEL RACHEL
From "On the Law of Nations" 349

CHRISTIAN VON WOLFF
From *The Law of Nations Treated According
to a Scientific Method* 356

EMMERICH DE VATTEL
From *The Law of Nations or Principles of Natural Law* 370

7 The Enlightenment 379

THE ABBÉ DE SAINT-PIERRE
From *A Project for Settling an Everlasting Peace in Europe* 394

MONTESQUIEU
From *The Spirit of the Laws* 399

DAVID HUME
From *Of the Balance of Power* 407

ADAM SMITH
From *The Wealth of Nations* 410

JEAN-JACQUES ROUSSEAU
From *The State of War* 416
From *Abstract and Judgement of Saint-Pierre's Project
for Perpetual Peace* 425

IMMANUEL KANT
From *Essay on Theory and Practice* 428
From *Perpetual Peace* 432
From *The Metaphysical Elements of Right* 450

8 State and nation in nineteenth-century international
political theory 457

G. W. F. HEGEL
From *Elements of the Philosophy of Right* 470

G. MAZZINI
From *On the Duties of Man* 476

JOHN STUART MILL
From "A Few Words on Non-Intervention" 486

H. VON TREITSCHKE
From *Politics* 494

B. BOSANQUET
From "Patriotism in the Perfect State" 506

9   International relations and industrial society 519

ADAM SMITH
From *The Wealth of Nations* 532

DAVID RICARDO
From "On the Principles of Political Economy
and Taxation" 535

RICHARD COBDEN
From *The Political Writings of Richard Cobden* 538

FRIEDRICH LIST
From *The National System of Political Economy* 550

RUDOLF HILFERDING
From *Finance Capital* 561

KARL MARX AND FRIEDRICH ENGELS
From "The Communist Manifesto" 572

JOSEPH SCHUMPETER
From "The Sociology of Imperialisms" 575

List of references 585

Index 596

Acknowledgements

The authors are grateful to John Haslam of Cambridge University Press for his encouragement and advice, and to the many reviewers for the Press who have commented anonymously and helpfully on our work. Chris Brown is grateful for comments and advice from colleagues at the University of Southampton and the London School of Economics, especially Russell Bentley and David Owen at Southampton, and to Tim Dunne from the University of Wales, Aberystwyth. Terry Nardin thanks Susan Rosa for translating Fénelon, Roger Epp for help with Luther, Frederick Whelan for help with Burke, and Cecelia Lynch and Jeff Holzgrefe for helpful criticism and advice generally. Nick Rengger would like to thank Chris Smith, Tony Black, and Onora O'Neill for very helpful discussions.

The publishers and editors are grateful for permission to reproduce the extracts found in this book:

Thucydides, from *History of the Peloponnesian War*, trans. and ed. Rex Warner (Harmondsworth: Penguin Books, 1954), Book 1, 21–3, pp. 47–9; Book 2, 34–46, pp. 143–51, 50–4, pp. 150–6; Book 3, 36–49, pp. 212–23; Book 5, 84–116, pp. 400–8.

Aristotle, from *The Politics*, ed. Steven Everson (Cambridge: Cambridge University Press, 1988), Book 1, chapters 1–6, pp. 1–9; Book 3, chapters 6–12, pp. 59–73; Book 7, chapters 1–3, pp. 156–61. Reprinted by permission of Princeton University Press.

Cicero, from *On Duties*, ed. Miriam Griffin and Margaret Atkins (Cambridge: Cambridge University Press, 1988), Book 1, sections 53–60, pp. 22–5.

Marcus Aurelius, from *Meditations*, Book 2 (17), pp. 41 and 43; Book 6 (36), pp. 149 and 151 and Book 6 (44), pp. 155 and 157; Book 9(1), pp. 231 and 233, and (9), p. 239; Book 12 (36), pp. 341 and 343. Reprinted by permission of the publishers and the Trustees of the Loeb Classical Library from *Marcus Aurelius*, Loeb Classical Library Volume L058, trans. C. R. Haines (Cambridge,

Mass.: Harvard University Press, 1916, revised 1930). The Loeb Classical Library ® is a registered trademark of the President and Fellows of Harvard College.

Eusebius, from *Tricennial Orations*, ed. and trans. H. A. Drake (Berkeley: University of California Press, 1976), Part I, "In Praise of Constantine," IX, 8–19, pp. 99–101.

Augustine of Hippo, from *The City of God against the Pagans*, ed. and trans. Robert W. Dyson (Cambridge: Cambridge University Press, 1988), Book 4, chapters 1–5, pp. 143–9; Book 19, chapters 11–14 and 17, pp. 932–47.

Constantine Porphyrogenitus, from *De Administrando Imperio*, ed. G. Moravscik and R. J. H. Jenkins (Dumbarton Oaks, 1949), proem and secs. 1–8, 13, 15, pp. 46–55, 65–77. Reprinted by permission of Dumbarton Oaks.

Al-Farabi, *The Political Regime*, from *Medieval Political Philosophy*, ed. Ralph Lerner and Mushin Mahdi (Ithaca: Cornell University Press, 1963), pp. 32–56.

John of Paris, from *On Royal and Papal Power* in *Medieval Political Theory – A Reader*, ed. Cary J. Nederman and Kate Langdon Forhan (London: Routledge, 1993), chapters 1, 5, and 7, pp. 161–3 and 164–7. Reprinted by permission of Routledge.

Dante Alighieri, from *Monarchy*, ed. Prue Shaw (Cambridge: Cambridge University Press), Book 1, sections 2, 3, 5, 10, and 16, pp. 4–8, 9–11, 14–15, and 28–9. Most editor's notes have been omitted.

Martin Luther, from *On Secular Authority*, in *Luther and Calvin on Secular Authority*, ed. and trans. Harro Höpfl (Cambridge: Cambridge University Press, 1996), Book 1, pp. 6–12, 13–14, 15, 17, 20–2.

Thomas Aquinas, from *Summa Theologiae*, in St. Thomas Aquinas, *On Law, Morality, and Politics*, ed. William P. Baumgarth and Richard J. Regan, SJ (Indianapolis: Hackett, 1988), II–II, Q. 40, a. 1 and Q. 64, a. 6–8, pp. 220–8. Reprinted by permission of Hackett.

Francisco de Vitoria, from "On the American Indians", in *Political Writings*, ed. Anthony Pagden and Jeremy Lawrance (Cambridge: Cambridge University Press, 1991), pp. 233, 239–40, 249–51, 277–8, 279–80, 281–4, 285–6, 287–8, and 290–2.

Niccolò Machiavelli, from *The Prince*, ed. Quentin Skinner and Russell Price (Cambridge: Cambridge University Press, 1988), chapters 1, 2, 3 (parts), and 15, pp. 5–10, 54–5.

Niccolò Machiavelli, from *The Discourses*, trans. Leslie J. Walker (London: Routledge, 1950), Book 1, Chapters 6, 9, 26, and Book 3, Chapter 41 [reprinted in *The Discourses*, ed. Bernard Crick, with revisions by Brian Richardson (Harmondsworth: Penguin, 1970), pp. 118–24, 131–4, 176–7, and 514–15]. Reprinted by permission of Routledge. Originally published by Routledge and Kegan Paul.

Jean Bodin, from *Six Books of the Commonwealth*, in *On Sovereignty*, ed. Julian H. Franklin (Cambridge: Cambridge University Press, 1992), Book 1, chapter 8 (parts), pp. 1–2, 4–5, 7–8, 11, 13–14, and 15. Most editor's notes have been omitted.

Cornelius van Bynkershoek, *Quaestionum Juris Publici Libri Dui* (1737), trans. Tenney Frank (Oxford: Clarendon Press, 1930), Book II, Chapter 10 (parts), pp. 190–4. Reprinted by permission of Oxford University Press.

Friedrich von Gentz, from "The True Concept of a Balance of Power" (1806), trans. Patricia M. Sherwood, in *Theory and Practice of the Balance of Power*, ed. Moorhead Wright (London: J. M. Dent, 1975), pp. 94–8. Reprinted by permission of J. M. Dent.

Thomas Hobbes, from *Leviathan*, ed. Richard Tuck (Cambridge: Cambridge University Press, 1996), chapters 13 and 14, pp. 86–92. Hobbes' spelling has been modernized and his marginal headings omitted.

Samuel Pufendorf, from *On the Duties of Man and Citizen*, ed. James Tully (Cambridge: Cambridge University Press, 1991), Book 2, chapters 1 and 16, pp. 115–19 and 168–72.

Christian Wolff, from *Jus Gentium Methodo Scientifica Petractatum* (1748), trans. Joseph H. Drake (Oxford: Clarendon Press, 1934), Prolegomena, pp. 9–19. Reprinted by permission of Oxford University Press. The translator's notes have been omitted.

The Abbé de Saint-Pierre, *A Project for Settling an Everlasting Peace in Europe* (1712–13), from *Basic Texts in International Relations*, ed. Evan Luard (London: Macmillan, 1992), pp. 411–14. Reprinted by permission of Macmillan Ltd.

Montesquieu, from *The Spirit of the Laws*, ed. and trans. Anne M. Cohler, Basia Carolyn Miller, and Harold Samuel Stone (Cambridge: Cambridge University Press, 1989), Part 1, Book 1, chapter 3, pp. 7–9; Part 2, Book 10, chapters 1–4, pp. 138–9; Part 5, Book 26, chapters 20–1, pp. 514–15.

Jean Jacques Rousseau, *Abstracts and Judgement of Saint-Pierre's Project of Peace*, taken from *A Lasting Peace through the Federation of Europe and the State of War*, trans. C. E. Vaughan. Reprinted with the permission of Constable & Robinson. Copyright © Constable & Co., London 1917. Reprinted in *Rousseau on International Relations*, ed. Stanley Hoffman and David P. Fidler (Oxford: Clarendon Press, 1991).

Immanuel Kant, selections from *Essay on Theory and Practice, Perpetual Peace* (removing all footnotes), and *The Metaphysical Elements of Right*, in *Kant's Political Writings*, ed. Hans Reiss (Cambridge: Cambridge University Press, 1970), pp. 89–92, 93–109, 112–30, 164–5, 168–9, 172–5.

G. W. F. Hegel, from *Elements of the Philosophy of Right*, ed. Allen Wood (Cambridge: Cambridge University Press, 1991), 330–40, pp. 366–71.

John Stuart Mill, from "A Few Words on Non-Intervention", in *Collected Works of John Stuart Mill*, vol XXI: *Essays on Equality, Law and Education* (Toronto: University of Toronto Press, 1984), pp. 376–84. Reprinted by permission of Toronto University Press.

H. von Treitschke, from *Politics* (Constable, 1916), vol. II, pp. 587–620. Reprinted by permission of Constable & Robinson.

David Ricardo, from "On the Principles of Political Economy and Taxation," in *The Works and Correspondence of David Ricardo*, vol. I, ed. Piero Sraffa (Cambridge: Cambridge University Press, 1951), pp. 133–7.

Friedrich List, from *The National System of Political Economy* (London: Frank Cass & Co., 1966), pp. 119–32. Reprinted by permission of Frank Cass & Co., Reprints of Economic Classics.

Rudolf Hilferding, from *Finance Capital*, ed. Tom Bottomore (London: Routledge and Kegan Paul, 1981), pp. 307, 308, 310, 321–5, 326–8, 331, 332, 334–6. Reprinted by permission of Routledge and Kegan Paul.

Karl Marx and Friedrich Engels, from "The Communist Manifesto," in *Marx: Later Political Writings*, ed. Terrell Carver (Cambridge: Cambridge University Press, 1996), pp. 2–5 and 17–18.

Joseph Schumpeter, *Imperialism and Social Classes* (New York: Augustus M. Kelly Inc., 1951), pp. 97–9, 104–7, 110, 111, and 120–30. Reprinted by permission of Augustus M. Kelly.

Every effort has been made to secure necessary permissions to reproduce copyright material in this work, though in some cases it has proved impossible to trace copyright holders. It would be appreciated if any errors or omissions could be brought to the attention of the publisher; we will be happy to include appropriate acknowledgements on reprinting.

1

Introduction

In recent years there has been a revival of interest in the classical theory of international relations, or, as we will call it here, "international political theory." We define international political theory as that aspect of the discourse of International Relations which addresses explicitly issues concerning norms, interpretation, and the ontological foundations of the discipline; it could be argued that all theories of International Relations necessarily address this agenda, but international political theory does so explicitly (Neufeld, 1995; Frost, 1996). One way of looking at this revival is in terms of a renewed engagement between "International Relations" and "Political Theory," two modes of thinking about the world that, for much of this century, have developed in isolation – "renewed" because, as will be demonstrated in the rest of this book, there have been many periods in the past when the idea of a clear-cut distinction between the "international" and the "domestic" has not existed. Part of this renewed engagement has involved a re-examination of the classics of the field, but this re-examination has been hampered by the fact that many of the texts which might be thought of as central to the emergence of a historical approach to international political theory have not been available, or at least not in convenient, accessible editions or translations. It should also be added that there is little in the way of consensus as to which, actually, are the most important texts in international political theory, precisely because of the lack of a clear-cut distinction between the international and the domestic referred to above.

Our aim in this book is to remedy the first problem by making available substantial extracts from texts on international political theory from classical Greece to the First World War, that is, from the beginnings of "Western" thinking on the subject up to the point where, after 1914–18, the academic discipline of International Relations emerged; in performing this task we will, of necessity, be obliged also to address the second issue. The purpose of this general introduction is to explain the principles we have employed in making our selections and in organizing the collection, and to set out,

1

in brief, a number of themes which, although they do not all appear in every era, will, we hope, be helpful in assisting readers to navigate their way through the wealth of material presented below. Before proceeding to this task, however, it may be helpful to dispose of one issue; we do not propose to provide an extended defense of the worth of international political theory or to relate its past to current debates in International Relations concerning "positivism," "constructivism," "post-modernism," and similar contemporary ideas (Smith, Booth, and Zalewski, 1996; Wendt, 1999). Although our sympathies are (in different ways) broadly "post-positivist," we see no reason why our readers need agree with us on this. The writers represented in this collection can be made to address contemporary debates in International Relations theory, but the significance of what they have to say about the world is unrelated to those debates; they have to be understood in their own terms and their own context before they can be turned into our contemporaries. Our aim in this collection is, as far as is possible, to allow the authors we select to speak for themselves rather than to respond to our agenda. We believe that what they have to say will remain relevant long after the academic debates of the end of the twentieth century have been superseded.

Delineating the international political theory "canon"

Obviously, before classical writers can "speak for themselves" they have to be selected as suitable for inclusion in a collection of this nature – unless, in some sense, they can be said to choose themselves. On the face of it this seems a rather strange idea, but, in fact, in some similar circumstances, it is supported by our intuitions; for example, it is fairly uncontroversial that any collection of plays purporting to represent dramatic works in English through the ages would have to include some works by Shakespeare; in this context, Shakespeare, as it were, chooses himself. Another way of putting this would be to say that Shakespeare is part of the *canon* of English literature. The notion of a canon is derived from the study of religion. The canonical texts of a religion are those that meet the rules and criteria governing the authenticity of its scriptures, as it might be the rules which established which books are to be included in the Old and New Testaments in the case of the Christian religion. By extension, the "canon" has come to be a term applied in other areas of intellectual life to works which are paradigmatic, exemplary within a particular field. Of particular relevance here is the use of the term in Western political philosophy to refer to the masterpieces, the great achievements, of that discourse by writers such as Plato, Aristotle, Augustine,

Aquinas, Machiavelli, Hobbes, Locke, Spinoza, Montesquieu, Rousseau, Kant, Hegel, Bentham, Mill, and Marx.

Clearly this is a controversial notion. The presence of several names on this list could be contested, and others substituted, simply on the basis of a dispute over the quality of the work in question. Moreover, determining which writers are candidates for the canon becomes more and more difficult as one gets closer to the present day, because one feature of canonical status is precisely the longevity that no modern can demonstrate, and, *a fortiori*, because the relevant criteria can change on the basis of current fashions – thus, for example, the fact that all the writers named above are white male Europeans might, or might not, be regarded a legitimate criticism. Nonetheless, the idea of establishing a canon of exemplary texts in a field has much to be said for it as an educational device. Some thinkers clearly have produced more significant work than others and it seems right that this should be recognized in an informal way, always assuming that the canon is never fixed once and for all, and is always open to revision in the way that, for example, in recent years, albeit for different reasons, the names of Wollstencroft and Nietzsche have been added to the above list.

What can be said of the canon in international political theory, if indeed there is one? This question needs to be approached with caution. Clearly there are a number of classical authors who are as unavoidable in this context as Shakespeare is in his. It would be very difficult to imagine a collection of this sort which did not contain work by Thucydides, Machiavelli, Hobbes, Grotius, and Kant – and these authors are, indeed, substantially represented herein – but it is important to stress that their canonical status represents a judgement about the quality of their thought in general, and does not depend on their role in contemporary debates in International Relations theory. These authors are indeed employed by contemporary theorists to articulate particular positions (see, for example, the construction of a Grotian tradition by "English School" writers, and the use of Kant to buttress the Democratic Peace hypothesis by Michael Doyle) but there is a danger that if they are studied only for this reason or in this context a misleading picture of their thought will emerge (Bull, 1966; Doyle, 1983).

The best illustration of this danger comes in the appropriation of figures such as Thucydides and Machiavelli by realist International Relations theorists. When Barry Buzan writes of "the timeless wisdom of realism" (albeit with a question mark), he is drawing attention to a particularly troubling cast of mind here (Buzan, 1996). If realism is a timeless doctrine this means, first, that its tenets can be illustrated by texts drawn from any period past or present, but, second, all of these texts can be treated as though they were written by our contemporaries. Thus it is that a canon of texts by pre-modern "realists" who are taken to be addressing our agenda – once a few allowances are made for turns of phrase, different vocabularies and the like – can be constructed, and books written with titles such as *Thucydides and the Politics of Bipolarity* explicitly linking the Peloponnesian War of the fifth century BCE with the Cold War of the 1960s (Fliess, 1966). The problem with this approach to the canon is not so much that it necessarily results in absurdities – Peter Fliess' book is actually a sensitive reading of *The Peloponnesian War* – as that it relies on a pre-determined account of international relations. In effect, international relations becomes defined by the concerns of the dominant theories of the post-1945 discipline of International Relations, and the historical record is then searched to find instances when thinkers from another time and another place can, plausibly, be taken to be responding to similar concerns. In a circular argument, the work of these thinkers is then employed to reinforce the initial definition of the field. Thus, Thucydides is taken to be a realist because he appears to employ characteristically realist concepts such as power and interest in his account of the causes and conduct of the Peloponnesian war. Extracts from his book, such as his account of the underlying causes of the war or his rendition of the dialogue between the Athenians and the Melians, are then held up as classic texts of realism, which can be employed to buttress modern theories of international relations by demonstrating that they have a distinguished past. In fact, it can just as well be argued that this reading of Thucydides is a projection of modern concerns and that the way in which he, and virtually all other classical Greeks, thought about these matters cannot be conveyed by using these modern categories of thought. For example, both the Melians and the Athenians think about their relationship to their fellow citizens in ways that are shaped by the religious ceremonies and rites of the *polis*, which means that their dialogue is resistant to the kind of a-historical reading that would see it as an early case study in statesmanship and moral choice (the introduction to the first collection of readings in this book, on classical thought, discusses these problems at length).

The use made of Thucydides by realists is but one example of the difficulties which arise when a canon is constructed with reference to current concerns. As "contextualists" such as Skinner have stressed, it is a mistake to think that there is a timeless agenda of political questions that thinkers from all ages can be taken to be addressing; instead each thinker addresses the agenda of his or her own age in his or her own terms (Tully, 1988). It may be that their agendas can, in certain circumstances, be seen to be not dissimilar to ours, but this identification cannot be taken for granted; it has to be argued for on a case by case basis. However, a determination to avoid the unsubtle reading of past thinkers in terms of our current agendas brings with it a major problem of its own. The advantage of approaching matters a-historically is that the criteria for selecting the canon can be reasonably clear cut. Thinkers are included if they can be made to say things that appear to relate to our problems, and, if not, not. Once it is decided to present texts in their own terms and not in ours, deciding which texts are important and why becomes a decidedly difficult task. If the "international" has no predetermined meaning, if it is a notion that is negotiated afresh by every age then it is difficult to think of establishing criteria upon which a canon of texts in international political theory could be constructed.

To illustrate this danger consider the state of international political theory in the European middle ages. For most of this period – bounded by the fall of the Roman empire and the modern European state-system – there were no states in the modern sense of the term, nor were there territorial political units which could with any plausibility be equated with states, as was the case with the *polis* in classical Greece. "Political" authority was divided amongst a number of different kinds of entities, ranging from territorial magnates and incorporated bodies such as towns or universities to universal entities such as the Holy Roman Empire or the papacy. Each of these bodies exercised some authority, none exercised sovereignty in the modern sense of the term. This is a state of affairs that leads realists to draw a veil over much of the period between St. Augustine (who can be seen as anticipating some modern realist thinking on human nature and the contingent quality of political authority) and Machiavelli (whose alleged advocacy of *raison d'état* marks for realists the beginning of the modern international order).

It should be clear that this is an extremely unsatisfactory approach to medieval thought. People in the middle ages thought about social life in different ways from the ways that we do, but they thought deeply and with great theoretical sophistication; it is inherently implausible that they would have nothing interesting to say about relations between political communities. What is less clear is what the right approach to medieval thought would be. The danger here is that presenting medieval thought in its own terms leads to problems in two directions. First, the texts chosen to illustrate medieval conceptions of the "international" are liable to amount to an overview of medieval thought as a whole, since the idea of the international as a separate sphere of social life is not one that medievals would accept, and this is simply too large and unmanageable an undertaking. But second, and perhaps more important, it would be difficult to draw connections between this body of thought and that which preceded and followed it. In effect, this strategy would leave one with a series of self-contained accounts of the thought of particular ages with too few points of contact between them. Clearly this would not be acceptable.

To summarize, although it would be a mistake to look for a common agenda of problems persisting over the ages, it is necessary to try to establish points of contact between one period and another. Unless family resemblances can be identified to link the writings of the classical Greeks, medieval theologians, early modern natural lawyers, and nineteenth-century political philosophers, the question of a canon of international political theorists cannot arise. In fact, such family resemblances can be found; there are a number of themes which although they do not recur in all periods and are by no means addressed by all classical writers do, nonetheless, establish points of contact across time and between very different sets of political circumstances.

Themes in international political theory

While there is no common agenda that all the classics of international political theory address, there are a number of themes, or clusters of themes, that recur over time – not all of the writers we present later in this collection address all of these themes, but most address some of them, and they would hardly be recognizable as international political theorists if they did not. The most important themes are, first, "*inside/outside*" – international political theory addresses relations between collectivities, and how collective identities are forged, where the "domestic/international" line is to be drawn, if drawn at all, is a recurrent theme. Second, "*universalist/particularist*" – this theme refers to the normative orientation of individuals towards "their" collectivity and its relationship to the wider whole. Third, "*system/society*" – at a minimum the idea of International Relations presumes the existence of regular contacts between collectivities, and this theme concerns the quality of those contacts, the role of norms and power, the possibility that relations can be managed, even governed. Each of these themes warrants further elaboration.

The first theme raises the most fundamental questions. That this collection addresses specifically "international" political theory and not simply "political theory" suggests immediately that relations between collectivities are at the heart of the matter. The term international itself is a convenient coinage of Jeremy Bentham in the context of a discussion of the "law of nations" (*ius gentium*) which he was the first to give its modern English name, international law (Bentham, 1789/1960: 426). In the Roman Law origins of the *ius gentium*, the nations in question were peoples within the Roman empire – within, that is, one wider political authority – and the law that governed the relations between these peoples was originally concerned primarily with commercial matters of one kind or another, the sort of legal relationships covered by the modern discourse of *Private* International Law. This original sense of the "law of nations" gradually became superseded, in a process that will be illustrated at length in chapters 4, 5, and 6 below, by the modern usage that identifies international law as governing legal relationships among politically autonomous units, *Public* International Law. However, the earlier meaning of "inter-national" raises interesting issues about the nature of the inside/outside distinction.

An obvious point is that although international political theory addresses relations between separate collective entities, such entities are not necessarily autonomous, territorial political units. "International" relations can take place between the inhabitants of cities in classical Greece and between papacy, emperor, corporation, and prince in the middle ages as well as between modern nation-states. Perhaps something akin to international relations can exist within empires, or, for that matter, within medieval universities where, at Paris, for example, scholars were organized in "national" groupings and the politics of the university were, in this sense, "inter-national." The key notion here is that individuals find themselves part of a collectivity with an identity which distinguishes them from others; international political theory emerges when the nature of this identity and its relationship to others becomes a matter for reflection.

This may seem obvious, but an inference that can be drawn from the same starting point is less intuitively appealing, namely that there is a sense in which *all* politics is "international." This is a proposition that contradicts the distinction between the "domestic" and the "international" which is fundamental to both conventional Political Science and conventional International Relations. The model on which these disciplines are based posits a clear separation between politics within the collectivity (city, empire, dynastic state, nation-state, or whatever) and politics between collectivities; as the Roman roots of the term "international" remind us, the problem with this model is that it is clear that almost every collectivity is itself an ensemble of other collectivities. Such is clearly the case with the ancient city: cities such as Athens and Rome were founded as associations of families, and the lineage groups of the original families, the tribes, continued to play an important role in the politics of the city throughout the classical period – under the republic, the Romans always voted with the tribe as the constituency rather than any territorial sub-division of the city, and tribal identities were equally important amongst the Athenians, where the large number of resident aliens – some of second or third generation or more – testified to the near impossibility of non-descendants of the founders achieving citizenship. Rome had a more open policy in this respect, but under the Republic the notion of descent as the basis for citizenship was preserved by the policy of adopting naturalized citizens into a particular tribe. Within the modern "nation-state" the link to lineage groups is less obvious, if present at all, but it remains the case that virtually all modern states are actually multi-national in composition. The number of mono-national states is very small, and in even these exceptions other kinds of deeply felt collective identities divide the people – see, for example, the importance of clan membership in Somalia, the only African state that is not multi-ethnic (Lewis and Mayall, 1996).

What this near-universal phenomenon suggests is that while any particular collective entity is engaging in relationships with other collective identities, its component collectivities are engaging in relationships with each other. The unitary actor which plays such a large part in the assumptions of a great deal of international theory can only come into existence as the result of a successful negotiation of internal collective identities to create a new meta-identity, in the manner of the Athenian or Roman tribes, or, by the suppression of such different collective identities by one dominant faction, a process often seen in modern nation-states. The first theme which is addressed by a number of authors collected in this anthology involves the elaboration of this kind of intra-collectivity "international relations" as well as the more conventional notion of relations between collectivities.

This theme amounts to an exploration of the politics of "inside/outside" (Walker, 1992). Whereas conventional political theory explores the development of community within a collective context which is taken for granted, international political theory focuses more self-consciously on the way in which one particular notion of collective identity comes to dominate others in the creation of separate communities, and the relationship between this process and the process of relating to external others. To what extent does the "outside" constitute the inside? The origins of the Greek *polis* appear to have been defensive; it seems the word *polis* itself originally meant "fortified place," which indicates that the families that came together to create cities did so as a means of collective self-defense. Thus, at the very beginning of Western experience of these matters, the presence of an external enemy, outsiders, is crucial to the constitution of insiders, fellow citizens (and their dependent subjects). Putting it like this suggests that the foundation of this particular kind of polity was the product of voluntary acts, which has often not been the case, even if it was in pre-classical Greece. However, whether the clash between insiders and outsiders reflects real experience or is contrived in the interests of dominant groups is, in this context, neither here not there. What is important is that a collection of texts in international political theory should not be restricted to writings on the external relations of collectivities; there is a place also for the study of the internal constitution of collectivities by these external relations. This means, for example, that the common view that empires, universal political orders, do not have international relations does not stand up to close examination, as will be demonstrated below.

The first theme, or perhaps cluster of themes, thus both establishes and questions the inside/outside distinction. The second cluster of themes relates to characteristic normative orientations towards this distinction. There are a number of possible different accounts of where the moral center of the individual ought to be located, what rights and duties individuals who inhabit different collectivities can claim of each other, and an obvious contrast here is between *universalist* and *particularist* thinking. Universalists regard their identity as part of a local collective body – state, city, or whatever – as less significant than their identity as part of the wider whole, which is often, but not always, defined in religious terms. This seems to have been the attitude of most medievals towards their identity as, say, bondsmen or guildsmen or local fief-holders as opposed to their identity as part of the wider world of Christendom. It is the attitude of, for example, Christian pacifists or Islamicists and, indeed, in principle, though often not in practice, of all followers of Christ or the Prophet. It was the attitude of the post-classical Greek philosophy/religion of the Stoics, who contributed their word for the universe (*cosmos*) towards the creation of a synonym for universalist: cosmopolitan. Sometimes universalists have desired to create a universal political order, a world government of some kind, but others (including the Stoics) have defined their universalism in moral rather than institutional terms. On the other side of the divide, particularists give their primary allegiance to local as opposed to universal notions of identity, or, more accurately, refuse to see the claims of the universal as, even potentially, in opposition to the claims of the local. This was the orientation of most of the Greeks in the era of the *polis* and has been the position of the majority of nationalists in the modern era; in modern times its best non-nationalist advocates have been Hegel and later neoHegelians.

The universalist/particularist divide captures a large part of the content of this cluster of themes, but it undervalues the importance that some thinkers have placed on what might be termed the "civilizational." The Greeks of the classical age gave their primary allegiance to their fellow citizens with whom they shared the rites and ceremonies of their *polis*, but many also drew a clear distinction between fellow Greeks – with whom they shared a common language, the Olympic games, some common shrines and oracles, most particularly at Delphi, and, in the realm of mythology, the Homeric Pantheon – and the "barbarians" who, as their (onomatopoeic) name suggests, could not speak Greek and thus were not part of Greek civilization. The world of Islam makes a primary distinction between lands governed by believers, the Dar al Islam, and the realm of war, the Dar al Harb, but also a secondary division of considerable importance between those non-Muslims who are, nonetheless, peoples of the Book (Jews and Christians) and unbelievers such as Hindus and Buddhists. The former have rights, the latter do not; they may not be forcibly converted and may practice their religions subject to payment of a poll-tax and agreement not to evangelize. Similarly, in the European middle ages, universalism meant commitment to Christendom, which although, in principle, a universal religion, in fact covered only part of the world and was regularly

in conflict with its neighbors. Thus, this second theme, the orientation of
the individual towards the distinction between inside and outside which is
common to all political arrangements, is more complex that at first sight
might be thought.

A third theme which recurs in this collection is less oriented towards
the individual, more towards different conceptions of the rights and duties owed to one another by the collective entities themselves rather than
by their members. As with the orientations of individuals, there is a range
of possible positions here, each of which has been advocated at one time
or another. One position is that collectivities have responsibilities only towards their own members and that relations with other collectivities rest
simply on the contingencies of power and interest. These relations may be
regular and patterned, that is, they may form a system, but they are not
normatively grounded. This is sometimes described as the realist position,
although not all of those usually thought of as realists actually subscribe to it
in this blunt form. It appears to be the position advocated by the Athenians at
Melos as presented by Thucydides – although whether Thucydides himself
subscribed to it is another matter – and described, but again not necessarily
advocated, by Machiavelli. The classical twentieth-century realists – Niebuhr,
Morgenthau, Kennan – for the most part would not have subscribed to this
position, but some neorealists may; their emphasis on the international system as the creation of an interplay of objective forces lends itself to this
interpretation.

On the basis of the historical record, it seems a reasonable to say that
any international order whose members do not acknowledge some kind of
obligation towards one another will be unstable and short-lived. Those orders that have persisted for substantial periods of time – in particular, of
course, the modern states-system – have been based on a normative framework which involves collectivities acknowledging each other's rights and
duties. In the medieval world this framework was provided by the universal
church and the memory of the unity of the Roman empire; in the modern world, the international relations of the absolutist state were to an
extent based on reciprocity, with rulers recognizing each other's rights as
a way of promoting their own which is the basis of, for example, modern diplomacy; but, more fundamentally, the rights and duties of modern
states have been conceived in legal terms. In so far as there is today, or has
been in the recent past, an international *society* in which relations have been
norm-governed, it has been international law that has been the critical force
in its creation. One aspect of this theme which will recur in this collection concerns the extent to which international law is *sui generis* – is this a
unique achievement of the modern system, the secret of its longevity, or can
institutions performing the same function be found in other international

orders? Is international law *law* in the same sense that a domestic legal code is law?

The contrast between an international *system*, held together, if at all, by a balance of forces, and an international *society* based on law, does not of itself define the possible positions that might be held on the obligations of collectivities towards one another. The nature of the legal ties between collectivities can vary dramatically, from the minimum required for coexistence to the far more extensive networks of rights and duties often held to be in force in the late twentieth century. There is dispute as to whether an international society exists simply to allow coexistence or to promote positive goals (Dunne, 1998; Mapel and Nardin, 1998). It may be that to the duality of system and society should be added a third term, community – although whether a genuine international community composed of modern states is possible, and how it might be characterized, is contentious (C. Brown, 1995).

This third theme, the international political theory of the rights and duties of collectivities is obviously related to the second, the rights and duties of individuals, but there is no one-for-one correspondence here. It might be thought that universalists would be oriented towards the idea of an international society but such is not always the case. Some universalists, Christian pacifists for example, reject the idea of an international society because they take it to amount to the legitimization of a divided human race, which is unacceptable to them, although, as suggested above, even a universal community would be, in some sense, "international." Conversely, some particularists, Mazzini and other early theorists of the nation, for example, stress the value of the local and particular but do not regard this as incompatible with a norm-governed relationship between societies. As suggested above, one of the points of this collection is to draw out these sorts of complexity.

The system/society distinction addressed by this theme cross-references also to the inside/outside distinction raised earlier. The latter is often cast in terms of the distinction between a power-oriented, anarchic, international realm, and a normatively integrated, governed, domestic society. It was noted above that the so-called domestic realm is frequently characterized by conflict and the exercise of power, but one of the possibilities pointed to by the third theme is that of an "anarchical society" (Bull, 1977). The extent to which a "society of states" can come to resemble a kind of universal republic is an issue addressed by a number of the authors who developed these ideas – see, in particular, chapter 6 below.

These then are three themes which recur over time. There is no intention here to suggest that they constitute a kind of cross-temporal agenda, a set of questions that all the authors we have anthologized must address; rather that it will be found that one or more of these themes, expressed in the languages of, and with the characteristic coloring of, their own time and place, turns up with great regularity and that each of our authors has something to say about at least one of them. However, it must be stressed that this collection is not organized on thematic lines, and the next step in this introduction is to set out more clearly the actual organizing principles employed.

Organizing the collection

This is a collection of texts and not a history of international thought, still less a history of the discipline of international relations. A history of international thought – whether it focuses on a particular text, author, or idea or treats many texts, authors, and ideas over an extended period – presents and defends a thesis. David Boucher's recent *Political Theories of International Relations* is a case in point (Boucher, 1998). Boucher organizes his book around three traditions of thought which he terms "empirical realism," "universal moral order," and "historical reason." Each tradition appears as a chronological series of works; thus empirical realism covers selected writers from Thucydides to Hobbes, universal moral order begins with the Stoics and ends with Kant, and historical reason takes us from Rousseau to Marx (and on into late twentieth-century international political theory). This is an interesting and fruitful way of organizing a text, and the three categories he employs work rather better than, for example, Martin Wight's "realism," "rationalism," and "revolutionism," categories developed in his celebrated lectures at the London School of Economics, later published as *International Theory: The Three Traditions* (Wight, 1991). However, the key point here is that Boucher is presenting a thesis about possible or characteristic modes of international thought, and this inevitably involves emphasizing some arguments and de-emphasizing others – in this case, for example, the position of "non-empirical" realists such as St. Augustine is marginalized as is that of Manchester School liberals such as Richard Cobden. This effect is one that as far as possible we wish to avoid. Similarly, histories of the discipline – Tim Dunne's recent exploration of the English School, *Inventing International Society*, and Brian Schmidt's more ambitious study of the modern discipline of International Relations, *The Political Discourse of Anarchy*, come to mind as two recent, excellent, examples – are more or less obliged to construct a story about how the various figures they discuss relate to each other (Dunne, 1998; Schmidt, 1998). Again, we wish to avoid this obligation. Even though some of the writers represented in this collection pick up themes from each other, we do not wish to present their work as a disciplinary narrative – in the period which this collection covers there was no discipline of international political theory whose history could be told. In short, while the expectation of historians of the discipline is that their work will be read as a history, in chronological order, and historians of thought expect and encourage their readers to use the categories they have developed, we have no such expectations. We anticipate that teachers and students will focus on certain authors, rearranging the order of presentation as they go, and, in line with our hope that we are allowing our authors to speak for themselves, we have organized the collection so that these reading strategies are possible. This has involved three main principles of selection and commentary.

First, the overall structure is pragmatically chronological, that is to say, we have departed from the chronology that underlies the selection when it makes sense to do so in terms of the work in question; thus, for example, it makes sense to treat Francisco de Vitoria as a writer of Christendom, and Machiavelli within the context of the European system of states, even though Vitoria wrote after Machiavelli. Similarly, it makes sense to bring together in one chapter the international lawyers from Grotius to Vattel, and in another the authors of the Enlightenment.

Second, we have tried to provide substantial extracts from the authors we have chosen, extracts of a length that would allow the reader to form a judgement on the work in question, as opposed to short, pre-digested, "sound-bites." Compromises here have been inevitable in order to contain the collection within one volume, but our hope is that even when we have been forced to cut writers to size, we have left enough for the reader to get their teeth into. Occasionally, to illustrate specific points, some short extracts have been included – Adam Smith on the international division of labor, for example – but mostly we present chapter-length extracts at a minimum, although, in many cases, we have edited out digressions, both to save space and to make the selections maximally accessible to the beginner.

Third, although we have provided quite extensive introductions to each of our eight main chapters, we have for the most part avoided using these introductions to present specific positions on the authors in question. Rather, the aim has been to provide the kind of background, contextual, commentary that will enable the reader to come to terms with the authors in question. Sometimes this commentary provides biographical material, sometimes it is a matter of summoning up the spirit of the age in which the work was written, but in any event the intention is not to form a judgement on behalf of the reader but to provide the information the reader needs to form his or her own judgement. Where we do take a stand, it is to provoke the reader's thinking and encourage especially careful reading of the relevant texts.

In addition to these three positive principles, there are certain limitations and parameters to this collection which deserve attention. It will not address post-1914–18 writings because this is the point at which the modern discipline of International Relations emerges and the nature of the discourse changes accordingly. Moreover, the sheer amount of material increases dramatically. While 1914–18 is the predetermined terminus for this collection, there is no such predetermined starting point, and the fact that the earliest texts extracted are from classical Greece represents a conscious choice on our part, and a choice with considerable implications. By starting this collection with the ancient Greeks we are, quite consciously, aligning the collection with the canon of Western political philosophy which commences at the same time and place. What this reflects is, on the one hand, a judgement that Greek thought is the first to address with real sophistication and at length the themes we have identified as central, and, on the other, the judgement that the way in which the Greeks addressed these themes can be connected to a sequence of thought which comes down to modern thinking about international relations in a way that possible alternative starting points – the thought of the period of the Warring States in China, for example – does not. The modern global international order developed out of the European states-system, which emerged in the sixteenth and seventeenth century CE from the wreckage of the medieval order which was constructed on the ruins of the Roman empire, in turn the product of the Roman republic and the inheritor of the thought of classical Greece.

It cannot, therefore, be denied that this collection privileges the Western experience. Islamic and Jewish thought does appear in the pages that follow, but only in terms of the legacy of late antiquity and in terms of its relationship to Western political thought. This is a collection that explicitly looks to and reflects the past, and it is the European past that is critical, though this does not deny the usefulness of, nor the need for, a similar kind of inquiry with a non-Western focus. As the present global order develops, that will probably cease to be the case and international political theory will be increasingly an amalgam of Western and non-Western thought, just as, for example, contemporary international relations theory is increasingly influenced by feminist writing.

The anthology is organized in eight, roughly equal chapters. The three authors accept collective responsibility for the whole, but primary responsibility for each chapter is noted below. Chapter 2 (NJR) examines writings from classical thought, with substantial extracts from Thucydides, but also from Aristotle, Cicero, Marcus Aurelius, and Plato. Picking up from Neoplatonism, chapter 3 (NJR) examines the period of late antiquity, with substantial extracts from Augustine and other Christian writers but also from al-Farabi, a Muslim scholar of the era. Chapter 4 (TN) covers debates on political authority in medieval Christendom, from John of Paris to Martin Luther, and the development of natural law and its early applications to international issues. Chapter 5 (TN) looks at the emergence of the modern European state and of the system of states, from Machiavelli through to Burke, Hamilton, and von Gentz. Chapter 6 (TN) covers the emergence of international law from Grotius and Hobbes to Wolff and Vattel. The international thought of the Enlightenment is examined in chapter 7 (NJR) with particular emphasis on Montesquieu, Rousseau, and Kant. The final chapters examine different features of post-Enlightenment, nineteenth-century thought, with chapter 8 (CJB) concentrating on nationalism and statism with Hegel, Mazzini, and Mill as key writers, and chapter 9 (CJB) examining the impact of industrial society on international thought, key writers extracted here being Cobden, List, and Hilferding. This introduction is more of a collective effort than the other chapters, but was keyed in by CJB.

FURTHER READING

There is a shortage of good overviews of classical international thought – those that cover specific periods are mostly noted below. Boucher (1998) is the most substantial overall history of international thought currently available. Williams (1992) is on a smaller scale but still valuable. Knutsen (1992) is more specifically a history of theory and has a more limited time span, as does Parkinson (1977), but is still useful. Forsyth *et al.* (1970) is a useful collection of texts but limited to the modern era. Williams *et al.* (1992) is not limited to the modern era, but has very little introductory material, and is highly selective.

2

Ancient thought
(500 BCE–312 CE)

It is a commonplace to allege that ancient thought, especially Greek thought, has little to offer the student of international relations. With the exception of Thucydides, the great political philosophers of the ancient world, it is usually argued, said little about relations between polities since they assumed that the feature that defined such relations – war – was a permanent and ever-present fixture in human affairs and that thus little could be done to change the characteristics of such relations. This view is common to many who otherwise differ profoundly: international relations scholars, historians of political thought, political theorists, philosophers, classicists, and, of course, many others (see, for example, Donelan, 1990; Knutsen, 1992, 2nd edn., 1996; Williams, 1992).

However, this is a misreading. On three issues in particular ancient thought offers a lot for the student of international relations: (1) the way in which the classical period established – and questioned – distinctions between insiders and outsiders; (2) the way in which this distinction is taken to generate, and limit, moral obligations between individuals; and (3) the ways in which this distinction is taken to generate, and limit, obligations between collectivities. In this section classical thought will be taken to consist of the thought of ancient Greece and Rome roughly between the political reforms of the Athenian statesman Cleisthenes in the fifth century BCE (which introduced democracy into Athens) and the coronation of Constantine as Roman emperor (after the battle of Milian Bridge in 312 CE). After this period, identifiably "classical" elements of thought become inextricably linked with debates over the character and future of Christianity and this moves into a different kind of problematic which will be discussed in the next chapter.

Background

To start with, however, it is necessary to say something about a writer who lies outside our chosen timeframe, but who is central to any understanding of Greek political thought: Homer. As T. A. Sinclair says, in one of the best general surveys of Greek political thought, most of the central figures of classical Greece, "had all been brought up on Homer ... they had learned to look to the *Iliad* and the *Odyssey*, not merely for historical facts but for ethical principles" (Sinclair, 1967: 9).

There are two aspects of Homer's thought worthy of special mention. The first is the centrality of Homer's epic poetry for the Greek language itself. The Greek language was a unity, although it had many different dialects, and the language of Homer, though not spoken as such at the times we are concerned with, was still a living language. It was the language of prose and dramatic poetry for the early classical period and it remained the language of epic verse for over a thousand years. This centrality has a number of implications. Most Greek political vocabulary we find first in Homer, for example, the key term *polis* itself. More significantly still, many central ethical terms are found first in Homer. Most significant of all, it is through the language of Homer that the Greeks experienced their strongest unity, but were also made aware, unambiguously and starkly, of their diversity and disunity.

The second significance of the Homeric epics, is, of course, that they deal very obviously with questions of "international relations" or at least with questions of war and peace. In the very heart of Greek culture, therefore, is to be found a presentation of the central dramas of politics as being wound around the differences of self and other, of individual loyalty versus communal obligation and of collectivities at odds with themselves and one another. And, one might add, of alliance politics, of betrayal, heroism, the perceptions and misperceptions of different regimes, and many other aspects of both domestic politics and international politics from Homer's day to our own.

It is useful to mention another issue here. Greek thought – and especially Platonic and Aristotelian thought – has often been held to be "communitarian" or "particularist" in orientation, in that it seeks to draw sharp distinctions between Greeks and non-Greeks and to use that distinction as a powerful designator of identity and thus as a central way of organizing politics both within and between political communities in the Greek world.

While there is some truth in this view, it is in tension with another aspect of Greek – especially Platonic/Aristotelian – reflections on the value of the *polis*. This political form is indeed special, but it is special in ways that are achievable by all – not just by Greeks. Here an instructive contrast is between Isocrates, an influential teacher of rhetoric, and his contemporary

Plato. Isocrates urged on his fellow Greeks a pan-Hellenism, built both on what we would today call "cultural" grounds and also pragmatic ones. Plato (and especially Aristotle) is usually held to have been broadly critical of such schemes, holding instead to the centrality of the *polis* and emphasizing the special characteristics of this political form as the form which allows (indeed encourages and enhances) the moral life, at least if it is properly arranged and organized. The real significance of this, in the current context, is that, to use contemporary language, most classical thought *combines* – though in different ways and to different degrees – "cosmopolitan" and "communitarian" aspects. The chief – though extremely important – exception to this view being that of the Sophists (a good discussion of this point, though put from a rather different standpoint, can be found in Pangle and Ahrensdorf, 1999, chs. 1 and 2).

For our purposes, there are five basic orientations discernible in classical thought. We will term these five orientations (a) the Sophistic; (b) the Thucydidean; (c) the Platonic (and Neoplatonic); (d) the Aristotelian; and (e) the Stoic. Added to this, however, should be the sensibilities of the great Greek tragedians and comic writers, whose influence on Greek political thought was so profound (M. Nussbaum, 1986; Euben, 1990). This chapter will focus on the last four, since Sophistic theory, though very important in general terms and powerful in terms of its influence on many Greek thinkers (to name but three: Thucydides, Plato, and Aristotle), had little to say directly about our concerns. However, a brief account would be helpful as an introduction.

The Sophists – the term literally means "wise men" – were a phenomenon which flowered in the changing atmosphere of the fifth century, especially in Athens (see Gomperz, 1912; Untersteiner, 1954; Kerferd, 1955; Barker, 1959, ch. 2; Coulter, 1964; Sinclair, 1967, ch. 4; Guthrie, 1969, vol. III). Especially significant for their development was the evolution of the notion of *Arete*, usually translated as "virtue." Once it became acceptable to think of "virtue" being "taught" and learned rather than being in some sense an innate characteristic (as, for example, Homer and Pindar had taught) and in so far as it was understood as the capacity *to do something really well*, then clearly there was likely to be a demand for those who could claim to teach it. In this context, the transition of Athens to democracy was especially significant since this created an enormous market for such teaching.

As Sinclair puts it, "the distinguishing marks of the ... Sophist were his claims (1) to expert knowledge (2) to ability to teach (3) for a fee for his teaching" (Sinclair, 1967: 47). What, however, was this knowledge that the Sophists claimed and for which they expected to be paid? Thus, in contrast to the general thrust of previous Greek thought, which in differing ways always subordinated *nomos* – convention – to something (*physis* – nature – in Heraclitus, the gods in Hesiod, for example), the Sophists proclaimed the centrality of *nomos*.

This was especially true in the political realm. Being able to be a man of true "virtue" would of course depend on the context in which you worked. *What* you were trying to do well was central. In politics, such knowledge depended upon knowing the details of the *nomoi* (laws, conventions) that dominated public life in any given city as well as the ability to manipulate such things to your own, or your cause's advantage. It was to acquire this knowledge, most of all, that the Sophists offered their services as teachers.

Thucydides

Alone among the writers of antiquity, Thucydides has earned himself a niche in conventional scholarship on International Relations, as an exemplar – some might say *the* exemplar – of a tradition called "realist" (Nardin and Mapel, 1992; Doyle, 1997). We know little about Thucydides himself. He was born around the mid point of the fifth century BCE and died at the end of the century or in the first few years of the fourth century BCE. He fought as an Athenian *strategos* (or general) in the war he was to chronicle and was exiled at one point for a military failure. His claim to fame is the book he wrote chronicling the war between the Athenians and the Spartans, or as we call it, the Peloponnesian War.

Thucydides wrote, he tells us, so that his book would be "a possession for all time" (Thucydides, *History:* 1, 22, 4), as Clifford Orwin has put it, "[for] students of political life of whatever time and place" (Orwin, 1994: 4). This, indeed, is what traditionally realists have claimed about realism – that it is "timeless wisdom" (Gilpin, 1984; Buzan, 1996) and by far the commonest portrayal of Thucydides in international relations is as a realist. However, some classical scholars, unhappy with this view, have claimed in contrast that Thucydides was a relatively conventional man of his time; conventionally pious, conventionally concerned with justice, but also conventionally accepting that the rules of politics are different among cities than among men. A man who, in other words, is responding to the challenges of the Sophists by re-asserting, albeit with some emendations, traditional moral views.

In contrast to both above positions, some other scholars have recently suggested that while it is certainly true to say that Thucydides is concerned with (for example) justice, his concern for it, and manner of portraying it, is anything but conventional (Grene, 1965; Strauss, 1968; Lloyd-Jones, 1983; Euben, 1990; Forde, 1992; Orwin, 1994; Donnelly, 2000). On this view, Thucydides is far from being a conventional man of his time but nor is he quite a conventional realist.

The details of these three interpretations cannot be examined here. Instead, the responses Thucydides might give to the three questions with which this chapter began are considered. On the question of "insiders and outsiders," Thucydides seems to take it as a given feature of political life that political communities engender the fiercest devotions and the greatest betrayals. In particular, the constant contrast, throughout the book, of the twin – and intertwined – problems of choice and necessity, suggests that human beings indeed live in communities which give them the greatest opportunities for nobility and glory, but that such communities themselves exist in a realm (or rather realms) of necessity. The tragedy is that all are locked into this cycle, the opportunity – Thucydides thinks – is that one can, therefore, learn from it.

As a number of recent commentators have eloquently demonstrated (Euben, 1990; Orwin, 1994), the artfulness of Thucydides in performing this task lies especially in the way he begins with seemingly opposed presentations, specifically the "Athenian thesis" proclaiming the realm of necessity abroad, if not always at home – the most famous example of this being the Melian dialogue (see pp. 53–60 below) – and the Spartans stressing the primacy of justice and piety in human affairs (think of the speech of the Spartan ambassadors at Athens, for example). Gradually, however, we are led to see the ambiguities and hesitations on both sides. The Athenians always insist that there are some things sheltered from necessity and justice perhaps appears less irrelevant than might at first be supposed; the Athenian envoys to Sparta, for example, claim that while Athens is compelled to rule, within the bounds of compulsion she rules justly (Thucydides, *History*, 1, 72–8: Orwin, 1994: 194). Perhaps the greatest ambiguity in the Athenian thesis is, however, revealed in the most celebrated exposition of it, that is to say Pericles' funeral oration (Thucydides, *History*, 2, 37–46 and pp. 36–42 below). Pericles presents the Athenian empire as what Orwin calls a "freely chosen project"; it is, indeed, precisely this aspect of choice necessity which makes Athenian imperialism so potentially glorious for the citizens of Athens. Yet in this, the rhetorical heart of "Athenianism", Pericles is almost endorsing the "Spartan" argument about the "freedom from necessity." Even the war, seen by Pericles as forced upon the Athenians, is cited as an opportunity for (freely chosen) nobility. At the same time, Thucydides shows us the ambiguities on the Spartan side also. For all its claim to justice and piety, we find the Spartans as deeply embedded in necessity as the Athenians, and far less willing to face up to the fact. As Orwin says "If, unlike Athens, Sparta never faces this issue, that is because necessity itself so shackles her that she lacks the freedom for such reflections. In practice the Spartans equate justice with the advantage of Sparta, that is to say, whatever is required to meet the necessities that anchor their regime" (Orwin, 1994: 194).

However, this debate is not one that stops at the "boundaries" of the "foreign." In domestic politics too, similar forces clash. One of the central characters in Thucydides' narrative, Alcibiades, sees domestic politics and foreign politics as the same, the city as simply an arena for citizen competition – an extrapolation, to be sure, but not perhaps a very great one, of Pericles' rhetoric in the funeral oration. But this leads to disaster, of course. As Euben, Forde, and Orwin all point out, Thucydides seems to be pointing up the fact that civic involvement, the creation of a common good, depends upon some sense of a common enemy and requires a degree of almost willful refusal of the "Athenian thesis" at the domestic level – Orwin and Forde go so far as to call it "hypocrisy."

Yet this view does not suggest that these features of politics are true only for Greeks. Quite the contrary. Thucydides plainly thinks that the war displays what we might call the "contours" of politics as such, which is why his account of it can be a "possession for all times." What, then, does this view imply for the second and third questions discussed above, to wit, what does Thucydides' view imply for the generation and limits of obligations among individuals and then, finally, among collectivities?

As Euben's discussion of Thucydides' account of the Corcyran revolution suggests (Euben, 1990), Thucydides was deeply aware of the perils and compromises, the errors and pettiness of political life, but he also seems convinced of the centrality for human beings of civic involvement. Perhaps the clearest example of this, and of what Thucydides thinks follows from this, is displayed in the contrasting speeches of Cleon and Diodotus in the Mytilenian debate (Thucydides, *History*, 3 and pp. 44–53 below). Orwin's view is that Diodotus' speech is the most careful reconsideration of the Athenian thesis offered in Thucydides. As he puts it,

The intention of Diodotus in propounding the [Athenian] thesis is formally the same as that of the others who do so. He seeks to extenuate alleged transgression as so deeply rooted in the character of the actor that indignation is an inappropriate response to it [essentially, of course, the argument also of the Athenian envoys at Melos]. This defence, however ... rests neither on individual pathology nor (as so often today) on allegations concerning environment. It accuses not the aberrations of this or that individual or society, but human nature itself ... Diodotus casts transgression not as an aberration but as the fundamental human fact and bids us reflect on the consequences. (Orwin, 1994: 156)

These consequences turn out to be not dissimilar either for individuals or for cities.

Individuals, like cities, seek the primacy of their own good. This is simply a fact and not a matter for outrage or indignation. However, it is not strictly speaking imposed by "necessity" (as the original formulation of the thesis suggested); rather it brings out the tendency of people (again both individually and collectively) to resist such necessity. Hence the ambiguities in both the Spartan thesis and in the original presentation of the Athenian thesis: perceptions of necessity and choice, concern for justice, and recognition of necessity "knowing no law." The chief obligation that emerges from a consideration of this claim is the obligation to be prudent and to avoid overreaching fragile, willful human capabilities either within cities (utopian plans for domestic politics, ideal cities, etc.) or between them. Diodotus, for example, stresses not the grandeur but the danger of the empire. The contrast between Athenian "overreaching" – and injustice – at Melos and the disaster of the Sicilian expedition points this up also.

On this understanding, then, neither conventional piety (which raises justice to the level of an ideal) nor strict necessity (the "logic of anarchy," as neorealists would today see it) is Thucydides' concern. Rather he tries to draw our attention to our political nature and its implications and in so doing shows us the role of "convention" as centrally subordinate to that "nature" – as Homer or Heraclitus also held, but for very different and potentially very radical reasons. This concern for our political nature as human beings unites us all in recognition of it even as it recognizes that we will be divided for all of the reasons that Thucydides' history so powerfully narrates and in this recognition lies our surest hope for real obligation and understanding.

Aristotle

Aristotle was born in Stagira, in northern Greece, in 384 BCE. His father, Nichomachus, was court physician to Amyntas III, king of Macedon, and thus Aristotle was brought up mainly in Macedonia. At seventeen, however, Aristotle was sent to Athens, the cultural centre of the Greek world, to pursue his education, where he became associated with Plato's Academy, and where he remained for more than twenty years. Plato was nearly sixty when Aristotle joined the Academy – and indeed when Aristotle actually arrived in Athens, Plato was in Syracuse taking part in the events described in the *Seventh Letter* to which we will return in a moment – yet he clearly recognized Aristotle's precocity and very soon Aristotle became a favored pupil. However, on Plato's death in 347 BCE Aristotle left Athens. It is often supposed he left Athens because Plato's nephew, Speusippus, was appointed Scholarch – head of the Academy – when he thought the position should have gone to him. However, as a metic – a non-Athenian-born resident of Athens – Aristotle could not own property in Athens and since the buildings and possessions of the Academy were transferred to Speusippus as well as the headship, it is unlikely that Aristotle had any expectations in that regard. By all accounts, he also got on well with Speusippus, at least personally. In any event, there were more personal reasons for leaving Athens. This was the time when Philip II of Macedon was gradually bringing all of Greece under the Macedonian sphere of influence and anyone with a strong Macedonian connection was likely to be suspect, especially in Athens. Thus for the next few years Aristotle traveled, becoming at one point tutor to a number of the sons of the Macedonian aristocracy, including Philip II's young son Alexander, later to be known simply as Alexander the Great! Eventually, however, Aristotle returned to Athens and established his own school, called the Lyceum – often called also the *peripatos*, because of Aristotle's habit of lecturing while striding up and down (and hence our term peripatetic) – and composed most of the *Corpus Aristotelicum* – the works of Aristotle – as we have it today. However, Aristotle clearly retained his links with Macedon – Antipater, Alexander's regent in Greece when he embarked on the Persian war, was a close friend – and when, in 323, Alexander died, there was a general anti-Macedonian uprising throughout Greece, and especially in Athens. Aristotle thus withdrew to the city of Calchis on the island of Euboa, remarking, in a reference to Athens' execution of Socrates, that he did not wish Athens to sin twice against philosophy. He died there the following year, at the age of sixty-two.

The above biography is important in a number of ways. First, it emphasizes the extent to which Aristotle was fully cognizant with the politics and indeed the international politics of his age and was a not insignificant actor in them. Second, it shows just how much he traveled and how much he must have encountered the breadth of cultures and characters active in the Greek world of his own time. Among the most controversial aspects of Aristotle's thought is the extent to which his views depend upon a distinction between Greeks and non-Greeks. Traditionally, it was widely believed that Aristotle insisted upon this distinction and on it he based a political theory and an ethics that was, as we might say today, radically communitarian in that it believed that the good life for humans was possible only in the *polis*, that the Greek *polis* was the highest form of political community. This is broadly the view one still finds in many good commentaries (Barker, 1959; Sinclair, 1967). However, some modern writers (Yack, 1993; M. Nussbaum, 1986) have begun to question it.

Of course, as is also well known, Aristotle's political and ethical views are predicated on a general conception of human – and indeed natural – life which structures and organizes his discussions more generally. Aristotle offers a broadly naturalistic account of human life, placing it in the context of a natural world in which conflict and cooperation, nobility and baseness are common, and, indeed, inevitable. Again, one can see overlaps with a Thucydidean temperament here, but dryer, more analytical, and more sensitive to the nuances of human sociality (see Kraut, 1989; Masters, 1990; Barnes, 1995).

For Aristotle, political community is a certain sort of community, not any sort of community. "Politics," "the political things" – *ta politika* – occurs when "a self sufficient group of free and relatively equal individuals ... have the opportunity to engage in regular and public discussion about which laws and policies should direct their activities and who take turns, according to regular and recognized rules, at ruling and being ruled" (Yack, 1993: 7). The point of this, of course, is that while Aristotle considers the Greek *polis* to be the only known example of such a community – though not always, or even often, a very good one – it is certainly not the only *possible* example. Another point is that for Aristotle, the *polis* is not itself natural, rather it flows from the naturalness of human beings. This has the powerful consequence that "the end of the *polis* is thus not to develop itself into a complete and perfected form but rather to contribute to the development and perfection of human beings into their complete and natural form. Aristotle makes this clear with his repeated claim that the *polis* exists for the sake of the good life" (Yack, 1993: 16). Thus, the *polis* exists for something other than itself (see pp. 62–8 below).

This conception of Aristotle's understanding of politics makes sense of the central role conflict plays in his account in the *Politics*; after all the core of the book, books 3–6, is concerned with conflict in politics. Yet many have seen in Aristotle, both in his own time and subsequently, an especial commitment to politics as an area free of conflict or, and perhaps particularly, for simply ignoring the necessary role of conflict in politics. In contrast, scholars like Yack and Nussbaum have emphasized that Aristotle is deeply aware of the fragility of the good life – another of the many ways in which Aristotle echoes Thucydides – and understands how inevitable conflict is in human social life generally and in politics – as he understands it – in particular. Aristotle's most famous phrase itself contains the seeds of this specific understanding of politics. Humans, he famously asserts, are political animals (*Zoon Politikon*). However, he also asserts, in the *Eudemian Ethics*, that human beings are *communal* animals. All polities are communities, of course, but not all communities are polities.

This understanding of community/political community has a number of more general implications. It first of all allows Aristotle to acknowledge the huge variety of communities of which humans are capable. All communities consist of individuals, sharing something (some good, some feature of their identity, or whatever); they engage in interaction related to what they share and, finally, they are bound to each other by some sense of friendship and some sense of justice (Yack, 1993: 29. See also Aristotle, *Nichomachean Ethics*, 1156a–1157b and 1159b27, *Politics*, 1252a1, 1261a–b). This latter point is perhaps the most important of all for as Aristotle says in the *Nichomachean Ethics*:

In every community there is thought to be some sense of justice and friendship too: ... men address as friends their fellow voyagers and fellow soldiers and so too those sharing with them in any other kind of community. And the extent of their community is the extent of their friendship, as it is the extent to which justice exists between them. (1159b27–31)

The term "friendship" here (the Greek term is *philia*) is clearly being used in a rather more general sense than we would today use the term. In fact it is one of the central categories of Aristotelian political thought. It effectively means a kind of "mutual sharing in ends and actions." A similar point is visible in Aristotle's understanding of justice. Just as there are different kinds of friendships, so there are different kinds of justice.

For Aristotle, then, humans are natural beings who necessarily live in communities. However, there is an enormously wide variety of possible communities: families, tribes, clans, empires, and, of course, polities, as he understands them. Indeed, we might say that for Aristotle, it is perfectly *possible* to talk of the community of all humankind, perhaps even – though this is much more speculative – of a cosmo-polis, a world political community. As we will see this aspect of Aristotle's thought is picked up by the Stoics and has been hugely influential in our own times as well. In the context of this variety, there are certain sorts of communities – political communities – wherein the human good is best served and within this notion of political community various kinds of possible regimes (Aristotle's famous six types of political regime found in the *Politics* – see pp. 69–77 below).

Thus, for Aristotle, the kinds of obligations generated among individuals in part depended upon the sort of community one was discussing. Political communities required certain kinds of relations and obligations and, Aristotle believed, these were the kinds of communities in which humans could aspire at least to the good life as such. However, humans were frail and fragile, and political communities, no less than other kinds, were inevitable victims of strife and dissension and even well-ordered cities, few and far between though they were, would not necessarily survive the winds of chance and irrationality. In non-political communities the obligations and relations would be of different kinds, but they would nonetheless be central to the workings of those communities.

As far as obligations between communities are concerned, the fact that the *polis* exists for the sake of the good life, not the other way around, implies at least a kind of cosmopolitanism, as Nussbaum and others have rightly asserted. Moreover, Aristotle is clear that although strife and conflict are always a feature of communal life (both intra- and inter-communal strife), the political community at least, whatever might be the case in other communities, has a responsibility to act in accordance with the welfare of other humans, not just other citizens. A notable example of this is given in Aristotle's discussion of

Sparta in the *Politics*, for example (1271b1, and see pp. 70–76 below). While in many respects favorably disposed towards Spartan virtue, Aristotle nonetheless condemns utterly the reason behind the cultivation of virtue, that is, military power. Moreover, to suppose that virtues exist for the sake of success in war is called by Aristotle "absolutely murderous" (*Nichomachean Ethics*, 1177b10. See also Swanson, 1992; Yack, 1993: 7). This, in fact, is a common tone throughout Aristotle's ethical and political thought. He is critical of the tendency of various communities – the Scythians, Persians, Thracians, and Celts are mentioned as well as the Spartans – to glorify war and to praise domination and conquest. It is not, Aristotle thinks, appropriate to conquer and rule other regimes since it is effectively a denial of their freedom and their status as fellow humans (see *Politics*, 1324b22, 1333b26–36). These views may, of course, partly account for the coolness that developed between both Aristotle personally and the Aristotelian school in general and Aristotle's most famous pupil, that is, Alexander the Great. As many have pointed out, Aristotle is widely reputed not to have been an admirer of Alexander's campaigns nor of his adoption of Persian manners and style. Some have supposed this was because Aristotle held that "Greekness" was somehow special and that Alexander was betraying it. There may well have been something in this. However, it seems more likely to have been a simple opposition to the practice of conquest, both for itself and for the likely effects it would have on those who practice it, and also that from being, in at least some sense, the ruler of a *political* community, Alexander had seemingly abandoned *political* community for empire, a very different, and for Aristotle, inferior kind.

Of course, Aristotle accepts that defensive war is perfectly permissible and even recommends the establishment of a citizen militia to help defend a city. Moreover, he thinks that offensive war is justified in two kinds of cases: when a free community is under attack and in need of help or outside intervention and when a community cannot rule itself. In both cases, "intervention," as we would today call it, benefits the humans of that community and, at least implicitly, the humans of the intervening community. Aristotle also speaks many times about the centrality of peace in the possibility of virtue in political communities: as Swanson puts it, for Aristotle "war must always serve peace and peace virtue" (Swanson, 1992: 117; see also *Politics*, 1325a5–7, 1333a30–b3, 1334a10).

Stoicism

It is traditional to refer to the period after Aristotle as the "Hellenistic" period of Greek thought (Sinclair, 1967, chs. 12–15; A. A. Long, 1986). The success of the great philosophical schools of Plato, Isocrates, and Aristotle led to a proliferation of schools and sects, with the Academy (for most of this period a shadow of its former self) and Aristotle's *peripatos* increasingly challenged by rivals.

Unquestionably, the dominant schools of the period, other than the above two, were the Cynics, Skeptics, Epicureans, and Stoics. Although all these schools had particular contributions to make to ethics and politics, it is the Stoics who are by far the most important for our current purposes. As A. A. Long says,

for more than four centuries [Stoicism] claimed the allegiance of a large number of educated men in the Graeco-Roman world [and, as Martha Nussbaum has recently shown, also some women (M. Nussbaum, 1996)], and its impact was not confined to Classical antiquity ... from the renaissance up to modern times the effect of stoic moral teaching on western culture has been pervasive ... (moreover) the influence of Stoicism has not been confined to ... philosophers. Cicero, Seneca and Marcus Aurelius were read and re-read by those who had time to read in the sixteenth, seventeenth and eighteenth centuries. (A. A. Long, 1986: 107)

While Stoicism began in Greece, and many of its most distinguished philosophical voices were Greek (most especially its founder, Zeno of Citium, who began teaching in the painted colonnade – or *stoa* – in Athens in about 300/301 BCE), its power partly depended on the influence it came to have in the new power in the classical world, Rome. Although over such a long period Stoic philosophy clearly evolved and changed, it is remarkable how consistent the basic Stoic orientation was.

Stoics were convinced that the universe was an ordered whole, amenable to rational explanation and proceeded so to explain it. The central human faculty, which allowed us to reason, think, and speak – the *logos* – is embodied in the universe. Humans and nature are thus one in the *logos*. If humans recognize this, they will act in ways wholly congruent with human rationality at its best. Of course, in order to do this humans must know how the universe is constructed and how you can reason. Hence the importance of natural philosophy and logic for Stoicism.

How did this cash out in terms of inside/outside? In principle, for the Stoics, no-one was "outside" the real community, the human community. Diogenes the Cynic, a powerful influence on the early stoa, is famous for having asserted, against all the customs and practices of the Greek views examined above, that he was a "citizen of the world." The Cynics were, of course, harshly critical of the customary attitude of the Greeks towards civic virtue – the attitude we have seen displayed in different ways in both Thucydides and Aristotle – and it is likely that, at least in part, Diogenes intended his saying as a deliberate provocation. However, the Stoics followed this lead and further developed the idea of the "world citizen" (*kosmou polites*), as Nussbaum and others have pointed out (M. Nussbaum, 1997: 7–9). She also gives a number of citations which show the extent of the Stoics' "cosmopolitanism." We live in two communities, Seneca tells us in *De Otio*, the local community of our birth and the wider city, that community which is "truly great and truly common, in which we look neither to this corner nor to that, but measure the boundaries of our nation by the sun." Or again, this time in Plutarch, we read that "we should see all human beings as our fellow citizens and neighbors" (M. Nussbaum, 1997: 7).

It is important to see, however, that the Stoics were not saying that actual political (in the non-Aristotelian sense) boundaries were unimportant or that they should be abolished. They were chiefly what Charles Beitz has called "moral" rather than "institutional" cosmopolitans (Beitz, 1994). Though it is worth pointing out that they were heavily involved with the Roman imperial project and much Stoic, and neo-Stoic, writing of this period often shaded into an institutional cosmopolitanism with the potentially universal institution being the empire. Lactantius' famous remark that Rome was "the city that sustains all things" (cited in Marcellinus' *History*) is an example. Their point was simply that our allegiance was, first and foremost, to the ethical community that is constituted by all human beings as such. This does not mean that local attachments are not themselves valuable. Seneca and Cicero were, in one sense, great spokesmen for the Roman idea of civic involvement and Marcus Aurelius, of course, as emperor, could hardly be indifferent to the presence or lack of civic activism in the empire (see the discussion in p. 89 below).

These views have, of course, clear implications for the question of our individual obligations. Stoics famously thought of humans as living in a series of concentric circles, first encircling the self, next the family, next the extended family and close personal friends, next neighbors and local groups, city dwellers, fellow countrymen, and outside all of these is the largest circle of all: humanity as a whole. As Martha Nussbaum puts it, citing the Stoic Hierocles, "our task as citizens of the world will be to draw the circles somehow towards the centre" (M. Nussbaum, 1997: 9. See also M. Nussbaum, 1996). Our obligations, in this context, consist in giving each of the circles their due weight and respect, and this requires education towards the capacity for Stoic virtue. As Marcus Aurelius puts it, "Accustom yourself not to be inattentive to what another person says, and as far as possible, enter into that other person's mind ... Generally, one must first learn many things before one can judge another's actions with understanding" (*Meditations*, VI, 53; see also A. A. Long, 1986: 179–209; M. Nussbaum, 1996; M. Nussbaum, 1997: 9).

This view has the implication that we need to restrain the passions that might otherwise get in the way of our being able to do this. It is this attempt that is the root of the popular sense of "stoical" as trying to rise above worldly hopes and fears. Stoics have often been criticized for trying to make human beings a bit "dry," lacking in color or ambition, even fatalists. None of this, however, is true. Rather, as for example Seneca shows brilliantly in *De Ira*, the Stoic concern is to rein in the passions, even virtuous ones, or ones that might be virtuous in a particular context (like anger), because such passions may distort how we behave to others. We will not be able, under the influence of this or that passion, to give each of the circles its due and weigh up our evaluations as they should be weighed.

Similar concerns, of course, structure Stoic thinking on the relations between communities. Indeed, in key respects there is simply no difference for Stoics on the obligations generated for individuals within society and those generated for particular societies, in their relations with one another – though, of course, humans should respect the rules and customs of individual communities in so far as these do not violate the rational order Stoics believed they saw in nature. The Stoics were not, of course, pacifists. They believed in the justice of defending the right. Marcus Aurelius spent many of his years as emperor on campaign; indeed the book we know as the *Meditations* was largely written on campaign and there are many passages in it that suggest that though the defense of the empire *is* just, it must be *done* justly as well, without the anger or rage that might unbalance the warrior and only in as far as the defense is actually necessary. There is a hint, too, of the Aristotelian distaste for war and conquest in Marcus and in the sense of his book as a set of "spiritual exercises" designed to ensure he develops as a rational soul (Hadot, 1995, ch. 6) (see pages 86–9 below).

Plato and Platonism

Anyone who knows anything about classical thought will realize that there is one major figure we have so far not discussed: Plato. But there is a reason. For all its centrality in ancient thought, there is a sense in which it is far more difficult to discuss the Platonic tradition in this context than the other traditions simply because its provenance is so difficult to determine. Plato wrote nothing that contains his own explicit views save a set of letters the authenticity of many of which is, at best, highly uncertain. Everything else in the Platonic corpus is written in the dialogue form and Plato virtually never appears in the dialogues (he is mentioned, though, in several) and never actually speaks in his own name. The central figure of virtually all the dialogues is Socrates and it has been conventional practice to assume that Socrates speaks for Plato, at least in the so-called middle and later dialogues, beginning roughly with the *Republic*. Of late, however, that assumption has been increasingly challenged from a variety of directions (Gadamer, 1980; Pangle, 1987; Griswold, 1988; Euben, 1990; Press, 1993). Various different schools of thought have emphasized the dramatic and dialogic character of the dialogues and challenged many of the received opinions about them as a result.

In the present context it is clearly not appropriate to engage in detailed discussion of this topic. Yet much more than simply interpretive differences are at stake in resolving it. A second point here is that rather than simply focusing on Plato himself, it is the role of the Platonic (and Neoplatonic) *tradition* as carriers of certain ideas which, while important in the classical period, become even more important later, in the late antique and early medieval periods – and in both the West and in Islam and Judaism – that it is important to look at here.

Thus, rather than offering detailed accounts of any of the Platonic dialogues, we shall say something about the only one of Plato's letters which most scholars accept as genuine – the seventh, which we will excerpt below (see below, pp. 91–3), and which says a good deal about topics that concern us here – before moving on to the legacy of Platonism in general.

So what does Plato do, in the *Seventh Letter*? In essence it is a public letter, explaining Plato's involvement in the political affairs of Syracuse, and in the process telling us almost everything we know about Plato's background and how he became involved in philosophy – perhaps its most important function. Plato had become involved in Syracusan politics at the invitation of Dion, the brother in law of Dionysius I, the tyrant of Syracuse. Dion admired Plato's ideas and wanted him to train the son of the tyrant in philosophy, to allow Plato to fulfill his conviction, of which Plato also talks in the letter, that the problems of politic he had observed in the Athens of the Peloponnesian war and, most especially, the revolution of the thirty tyrants and then the restoration of the democracy could only be met by the "unification" of philosophy and political power in the same person. Unfortunately, Dionysius II, as he became, proved a singularly inept pupil, and the politics of Syracuse went from bad to worse. Dion and the new Dionysius became increasingly estranged and Plato found himself caught in the middle. Eventually he left, only to return twice more; as the situation worsened still further, Dion was killed and Dionysius became increasingly unstable. At this point, Dionysius actually wrote a book expounding Plato's thought which Plato repudiates in the strongest possible terms, leading him to make one of the most curious remarks of his long career (Plato, *Seventh Letter*, 341), to the effect that there has never been, nor ever will be, an exposition of his doctrines, for the truth he seeks cannot be expressed in those terms.

Given Plato's many published works, it seems more than strange that he can say this. Yet, in this remark lies the paradox of Plato's thought and character. Clearly he intended his dialogues to mean something; to attract people perhaps to the study of philosophy, to venerate Socrates certainly. The question is, did he mean them to have wider implications? In the dialogues, Plato raises questions, introduces themes, charms possible recruits to his banner, develops ideas. In none of them, however, does he develop a "doctrine."

What does this mean for our subject here? In the first place, it suggests that we should rely not simply on what Plato wrote but on the practice of the Academy under his leadership (see Cherniss, 1945; Grayeff, 1974: 21–7; Kramer, 1990). The advice he gives to Dion's party in the *Seventh Letter* is echoed by many of the actions of the Academy while Plato lived and, indeed, for a while after his death, when his nephew Speusippus became head of the school. Broadly speaking, Plato, and the Academy, recommended the establishment of constitutional regimes, with complex systems of checks and balances, such as are outlined in Plato's own last work, the *Laws*, and similar to those we have already met in Aristotle.

As with Aristotle, Plato does not seem to be writing only with Greeks in mind. In a famous passage in the *Republic*, Socrates suggests that the "city built in speech" – the ideal city that it is the purpose of the *Republic* to sketch out – is "Greek" only contingently and incidentally. It can be populated, as it were, by those who live "in some Barbaric place beyond the reach of our vision" (*Republic*, 499c–d). However, in Plato's formulation of this there seems a touch of the mystical which is absent in Aristotle or Thucydides and which gives particular power to some of his most famous dialogues – for example, *The Phaedrus* and the *Timaeus*.

This is certainly the view which was taken by his most interesting disciples in the late Roman period, the so-called Neoplatonists. The Neoplatonists, most especially Plotinus, were hugely influential on early Christianity and, indeed, have been a powerful if sometimes submerged current of thought ever since. As they did not have discrete orientations towards political topics, however, they have usually been ignored in histories of political thought. However, in so far as they commented on Plato and Aristotle – and Porphyry, Plotinus' pupil and biographer, says that most of Plotinus' seminars began with a recent commentary on something of either Plato's or Aristotle's – then we can be sure political discussion was hardly absent. Rather than displaying political doctrines, they, like Plato, adapted doctrine to rhetorical and political circumstance and in this sense they retain the ghost of an echo of Plato's old opponents, the Sophists, saving only that they were as committed to the belief in virtue and reason as the latter were in opposing it. Plato's dialogues, whatever else they are, are among the supreme examples of philosophical turning of the tables in human history. The "experts" and the "teachers of rhetoric" were overcome by a more brilliant rhetorician than any of them, who used his genius not to "teach virtue" but to show how to habituate people to it.

FURTHER READING

As a general background to Greek thought, Sinclair (1967) is still unsurpassed. On Thucydides, Hornblower (1987) presents the best general interpretation, though it is very much a classicist's treatment, and Orwin (1994) is perhaps the best recent interpretation of Thucydides as political thinker. On Plato, a good general introduction to his political thought, though very wedded to the "traditional" interpretation, is Klosko (1986). An introduction to alternative ways of reading Plato can be found in Griswold (1988). Yack (1993) offers a thoughtful interpretation of Aristotle, which emphasizes issues of conflict in his political theory. Euben (1990) offers a splendid series of readings of Thucydides and Plato which foreground diversity and conflict. Wood (1988) is the best reading of Cicero's political thought in a long while, while A.A.Long (1986) offers an excellent interpretation of Stoicism in general. Alternative considerations of classical thought about International Relations to those offered here can be found in Boucher (1998) and Pangle and Ahrensdorf (1999).

SOURCES

Thucydides, from *History of the Peloponnesian War*, trans. and ed. Rex Warner (Harmondsworth: Penguin Books, 1954), Book 1, 21–3, pp. 47–9; Book 2, 34–46, pp. 143–51, and 50–4, pp. 150–6; Book 3, 36–49, pp. 212–23; Book 5, 84–116, pp. 400–8.

Aristotle, from *The Politics*, ed. Steven Everson (Cambridge: Cambridge University Press, 1988), Book 1, chs. 1–6 (pp. 1–9); Book 3, chs. 6–13 (pp. 59–73); Book 7, chs. 1–3 (pp. 156–61).

Cicero, from *On Duties*, ed. Miriam Griffin and Margaret Atkins (Cambridge: Cambridge University Press, 1988), sects. 53–60, pp. 22–5).

Marcus Aurelius, from *Meditations*, ed. and trans. C. R. Haines, Loeb Classical Library (London: Heinemann, 1930), Book 2, v. 17, pp. 41 and 43; Book 6, v. 36, pp. 149 and 151 and v. 44, pp. 155 and 157; Book 9, v. 1, pp. 231 and 233, and v. 9, p. 239; Book 12, v. 36, pp. 341 and 343.

Plato, from *Plato's Epistles*, trans. Glen R. Morrow, Library of Liberal Arts (New York: Bobbs-Merrill, 1962), 324–326b (pp. 215–17, and 330c–331d (pp. 223 and 224).

THUCYDIDES

THUCYDIDES, who simply refers to himself as "an Athenian," was born around the fifties of the fifth century BCE. He was possibly of royal Thracian descent – he also had political influence in Thrace and business interests there – and was certainly an aristocrat. We know little about his life with any certainty, save what he himself tells us in his *History*. He served as an Athenian military commander in 424 (and may have done so earlier) but was defeated by the great Spartan general Brasidas, and was sent into exile for a period as a result. The latter half of his life is largely unknown to us, although it is likely he died around the end of the century or possibly (according to some recent research) a little into the 390s. By his own account he began writing his *History* when the war between the Athenians and the Spartans began, convinced that it would be a unique event and that thus his record of it would be, as he suggests, "a possession for all times."

From *History of the Peloponnesian War*

Book 1, 21–3

Introduction

21 However, I do not think that one will be far wrong in accepting the conclusions I have reached from the evidence which I have put forward. It is better evidence than that of the poets, who exaggerate the importance of their themes, or of the prose chroniclers, who are less interested in telling the truth than in catching the attention of their public, whose authorities cannot be checked, and whose subject-matter, owing to the passage of time, is mostly lost in the unreliable streams of mythology. We may claim instead to have used only the plainest evidence and to have reached conclusions which are reasonably accurate, considering that we have been dealing with ancient history. As for this present war, even though people are apt to think that the war in which they are fighting is the greatest of all wars and, when it is over, to relapse again into their admiration of the past, nevertheless, if one looks at the facts themselves, one will see that this was the greatest war of all.

22   In this history I have made use of set speeches some of which were delivered just before and others during the war. I have found it difficult

to remember the precise words used in the speeches which I listened to myself and my various informants have experienced the same difficulty; so my method has been, while keeping as closely as possible to the general sense of the words that were actually used, to make the speakers say what, in my opinion, was called for by each situation.

And with regard to my factual reporting of the events of the war I have made it a principle not to write down the first story that came my way, and not even to be guided by my own general impressions; either I was present myself at the events which I have described or else I heard of them from eye-witnesses whose reports I have checked with as much thoroughness as possible. Not that even so the truth was easy to discover: different eye-witnesses give different accounts of the same events, speaking out of partiality for one side or the other or else from imperfect memories. And it may well be that my history will seem less easy to read because of the absence in it of a romantic element. It will be enough for me, however, if these words of mine are judged useful by those who want to understand clearly the events which happened in the past and which (human nature being what it is) will, at some time or other and in much the same ways, be repeated in the future. My work is not a piece of writing designed to meet the taste of an immediate public, but was done to last for ever.

The greatest war in the past was the Persian War; yet in this war the 23 decision was reached quickly as a result of two naval battles and two battles on land. The Peloponnesian War, on the other hand, not only lasted for a long time, but throughout its course brought with it unprecedented suffering for Hellas. Never before had so many cities been captured and then devastated, whether by foreign armies or by the Hellenic powers themselves (some of these cities, after capture, were resettled with new inhabitants); never had there been so many exiles; never such loss of life – both in the actual warfare and in internal revolutions. Old stories of past prodigies, which had not found much confirmation in recent experience, now became credible. Wide areas, for instance, were affected by violent earthquakes; there were more frequent eclipses of the sun than had ever been recorded before; in various parts of the country there were extensive droughts followed by famine; and there was the plague which did more harm and destroyed more life than almost any other single factor. All these calamities fell together upon the Hellenes after the outbreak of war.

War began when the Athenians and the Peloponnesians broke the Thirty Years Truce which had been made after the capture of Euboea. As to the reasons why they broke the truce, I propose first to give an account of the causes of complaint which they had against each other and of the specific instances where their interests clashed: this is in order that there should be no doubt in anyone's mind about what led to this great war falling upon the

Hellenes. But the real reason for the war is, in my opinion, most likely to be disguised by such an argument. What made war inevitable was the the growth of Athenian power and the fear which this caused in Sparta.

...

Book 2, 34–46, 50–4

Pericles' funeral oration

34   In the same winter the Athenians, following their annual custom, gave a public funeral for those who had been the first to die in the war. These funerals are held in the following way: two days before the ceremony the bones of the fallen are brought and put in a tent which has been erected, and people make whatever offerings they wish to their own dead. Then there is a funeral procession in which coffins of cypress wood are carried on wagons. There is one coffin for each tribe, which contains the bones of members of that tribe. One empty bier is decorated and carried in the procession: this is for the missing, whose bodies could not be recovered. Everyone who wishes to, both citizens and foreigners, can join in the procession, and the women who are related to the dead are there to make their laments at the tomb. The bones are laid in the public burial-place, which is in the most beautiful quarter outside the city walls. Here the Athenians always bury those who have fallen in war. The only exception is those who died at Marathon, who, because their achievement was considered absolutely outstanding, were buried on the battlefield itself.

When the bones have been laid in the earth, a man chosen by the city for his intellectual gifts and for his general reputation makes an appropriate speech in praise of the dead, and after the speech all depart. This is the procedure at these burials, and all through the war, when the time came to do so, the Athenians followed this ancient custom. Now, at the burial of those who were the first to fall in the war Pericles, the son of Xanthippus, was chosen to make the speech. When the moment arrived, he came forward from the tomb and, standing on a high platform, so that he might be heard by as many people as possible in the crowd, he spoke as follows:

35   'Many of those who have spoken here in the past have praised the institution of this speech at the close of our ceremony. It seemed to them a mark of honour to our soldiers who have fallen in war that a speech should be made over them. I do not agree. These men have shown themselves valiant in action, and it would be enough, I think, for their glories to be proclaimed in action, as you have just seen it done at this funeral organized by the state. Our belief in the courage and manliness of so many should not be hazarded on the goodness or badness of one man's speech.

Then it is not easy to speak with a proper sense of balance, when a man's listeners find it difficult to believe in the truth of what one is saying. The man who knows the facts and loves the dead may well think that an oration tells less than what he knows and what he would like to hear: others who do not know so much may feel envy for the dead, and think the orator over-praises them, when he speaks of exploits that are beyond their own capacities. Praise of other people is tolerable only up to a certain point, the point where one still believes that one could do oneself some of the things one is hearing about. Once you get beyond this point, you will find people becoming jealous and incredulous. However, the fact is that this institution was set up and approved by our forefathers, and it is my duty to follow the tradition and do my best to meet the wishes and the expectations of every one of you.

'I shall begin by speaking about our ancestors, since it is only right and proper on such an occasion to pay them the honour of recalling what they did. In this land of ours there have always been the same people living from generation to generation up till now, and they, by their courage and their virtues, have handed it on to us, a free country. They certainly deserve our praise. Even more so do our fathers deserve it. For to the inheritance they had received they added all the empire we have now, and it was not without blood and toil that they handed it down to us of the present generation. And then we ourselves, assembled here today, who are mostly in the prime of life, have, in most directions, added to the power of our empire and have organized our State in such a way that it is perfectly well able to look after itself both in peace and in war.

'I have no wish to make a long speech on subjects familiar to you all: so I shall say nothing about the warlike deeds by which we acquired our power or the battles in which we or our fathers gallantly resisted our enemies, Greek or foreign. What I want to do is, in the first place, to discuss the spirit in which we faced our trials and also our constitution and the way of life which has made us great. After that I shall speak in praise of the dead, believing that this kind of speech is not inappropriate to the present occasion, and that this whole assembly, of citizens and foreigners, may listen to it with advantage.

'Let me say that our system of government does not copy the institutions of our neighbours. It is more the case of our being a model to others, than of our imitating anyone else. Our constitution is called a democracy because power is in the hands not of a minority but of the whole people. When it is a question of settling private disputes, everyone is equal before the law; when it is a question of putting one person before another in positions of public responsibility, what counts is not membership of a particular class, but the actual ability which the man possesses. No one, so long as he has it in him to be of service to the state, is kept in political obscurity because of poverty.

And, just as our political life is free and open, so is our day-to-day life in our relations with each other. We do not get into a state with our next-door neighbour if he enjoys himself in his own way, nor do we give him the kind of black looks which, though they do no real harm, still do hurt people's feelings. We are free and tolerant in our private lives; but in public affairs we keep to the law. This is because it commands our deep respect.

'We give our obedience to those whom we put in positions of authority, and we obey the laws themselves, especially those which are for the protection of the oppressed, and those unwritten laws which it is an acknowledged shame to break.

38   'And here is another point. When our work is over, we are in a position to enjoy all kinds of recreation for our spirits. There are various kinds of contests and sacrifices regularly throughout the year; in our own homes we find a beauty and a good taste which delight us every day and which drive away our cares. Then the greatness of our city brings it about that all the good things from all over the world flow in to us, so that to us it seems just as natural to enjoy foreign goods as our own local products.

39   'Then there is a great difference between us and our opponents, in our attitude towards military security. Here are some examples: Our city is open to the world, and we have no periodical deportations in order to prevent people observing or finding out secrets which might be of military advantage to the enemy. This is because we rely, not on secret weapons, but in our own real courage and loyalty. There is a difference, too, in our educational systems. The Spartans, from their earliest boyhood, are submitted to the most laborious training in courage; we pass our lives without all these restrictions, and yet are just as ready to face the same dangers as they are. Here is a proof of this: When the Spartans invade our land, they do not come by themselves, but bring all their allies with them; whereas we, when we launch an attack abroad, do the job by ourselves, and, though fighting on foreign soil, do not often fail to defeat opponents who are fighting for their own hearths and homes. As a matter of fact none of our enemies has ever yet been confronted with our total strength, because we have to divide our attention between our navy and the many missions on which our troops are sent on land. Yet, if our enemies engage a detachment of our forces and defeat it, they give themselves credit for having thrown back our entire army; or, if they lose, they claim that they were beaten by us in full strength. There are certain advantages, I think, in our way of meeting danger voluntarily, with an easy mind, instead of with a laborious training, with natural rather than with state-induced courage. We do not have to spend our time practising to meet sufferings which are still in the future; and when they are actually upon us we show ourselves just as brave as these others who are always in strict training. This is one point in which, I think, our city deserves to be admired. There are also others:

'Our love of what is beautiful does not lead to extravagance; our love of   40
the things of the mind does not make us soft. We regard wealth as something
to be properly used, rather than as something to boast about. As for poverty,
no one need be ashamed to admit it: the real shame is in not taking practical
measures to escape from it. Here each individual is interested not only in his
own affairs but in the affairs of the state as well: even those who are mostly
occupied with their own business are extremely well-informed on general
politics – this is a peculiarity of ours: we do not say that a man who takes no
interest in politics is a man who minds his own business: we say that he has no
business here at all. We Athenians, in our own persons, take our decisions on
policy or submit them to proper discussions: for we do not think that there
is an incompatibility between words and deeds; the worst thing is to rush
into action before the consequences have been properly debated. And this is
another point where we differ from other people. We are capable at the same
time of taking risks and of estimating them beforehand. Others are brave out
of ignorance; and, when they stop to think, they begin to fear. But the man
who can most truly be accounted brave is he who best knows the meaning
of what is sweet in life and of what is terrible, and then goes out undeterred
to meet what is to come.

'Again, in questions of general good feeling there is a great contrast
between us and most other people. We make friends by doing good to others,
not by receiving good from them. This makes our friendship all the more
reliable, since we want to keep alive the gratitude of those who are in our
debt by showing continued good-will to them: whereas the feelings of one
who owes us something lack the same enthusiasm, since he knows that, when
he repays our kindness, it will be more like paying back a debt than giving
something spontaneously. We are unique in this. When we do kindnesses to
others, we do not do them out of any calculations of profit or loss: we do
them without afterthought, relying on our free liberality. Taking everything
together then, I declare that our city is an education to Greece, and I declare   41
that in my opinion each single one of our citizens, in all the manifold aspects
of life, is able to show himself the rightful lord and owner of his own person,
and do this, moreover, with exceptional grace and exceptional versatility.
And to show that this is no empty boasting for the present occasion, but real
tangible fact, you have only to consider the power which our city possesses
and which has been won by those very qualities which I have mentioned.
Athens, alone of the states we know, comes to her testing time in a greatness
that surpasses what was imagined of her. In her case, and in her case alone, no
invading enemy is ashamed at being defeated, and no subject can complain
of being governed by people unfit for their responsibilities. Mighty indeed
are the marks and monuments of our empire which we have left. Future ages
will wonder at us, as the present age wonders at us now. We do not need the

praises of a Homer, or of anyone else whose words may delight us for the moment, but whose estimation of facts will fall short of what is really true. For our adventurous spirit has forced an entry into every sea and into every land; and everywhere we have left behind us everlasting memorials of good done to our friends or suffering inflicted on our enemies.

42   'This, then, is the kind of city for which these men, who could not bear the thought of losing her, nobly fought and nobly died. It is only natural that every one of us who survive them should be willing to undergo hardships in her service. And it was for this reason that I have spoken at such length about our city, because I wanted to make it clear that for us there is more at stake than there is for others who lack our advantages; also I wanted my words of praise for the dead to be set in the bright light of evidence. And now the most important of these words has been spoken. I have sung the praises of our city; but it was the courage and gallantry of these men, and of people like them, which made her splendid. Nor would you find it true in the case of many of the Greeks, as it is true of them, that no words can do more than justice to their deeds.

'To me it seems that the consummation which has overtaken these men shows us the meaning of manliness in its first revelation and in its final proof. Some of them, no doubt, had their faults; but what we ought to remember first is their gallant conduct against the enemy in defence of their native land. They have blotted out evil with good, and done more service to the commonwealth than they ever did harm in their private lives. No one of these men weakened because he wanted to go on enjoying his wealth: no one put off the awful day in the hope that he might live to escape his poverty and grow rich. More to be desired than such things, they chose to check the enemy's pride. This, to them, was a risk most glorious, and they accepted it, willing to strike down the enemy and relinquish everything else. As for success or failure, they left that in the doubtful hands of Hope, and when the reality of battle was before their faces, they put their trust in their own selves. In the fighting, they thought it more honourable to stand their ground and suffer death than to give in and save their lives. So they fled from the reproaches of men, abiding with life and limb the brunt of battle; and, in a small moment of time, the climax of their lives, a culmination of glory, not of fear, were swept away from us.

43   'So and such they were, these men – worthy of their city. We who remain behind may hope to be spared their fate, but must resolve to keep the same daring spirit against the foe. It is not simply a question of estimating the advantages in theory. I could tell you a long story (and you know it as well as I do) about what is to be gained by beating the enemy back. What I would prefer is that you should fix your eyes every day on the greatness of Athens as she really is, and should fall in love with her. When you realize her greatness,

then reflect that what made her great was men with a spirit of adventure, men who knew their duty, men who were ashamed to fall below a certain standard. If they ever failed in an enterprise, they made up their minds that at any rate the city should not find their courage lacking to her, and they gave to her the best contribution that they could. They gave her their lives, to her and to all of us, and for their own selves they won praises that never grow old, the most splendid of sepulchres – not the sepulchre in which their bodies are laid, but where their glory remains eternal in men's minds, always there on the right occasion to stir others to speech or to action. For famous men have the whole earth as their memorial: it is not only the inscriptions on their graves in their own country that mark them out; no, in foreign lands also, not in any visible form but in people's hearts, their memory abides and grows. It is for you to try to be like them. Make up your minds that happiness depends on being free, and freedom depends on being courageous. Let there be no relaxation in face of the perils of the war. The people who have most excuse for despising death are not the wretched and unfortunate, who have no hope of doing well for themselves, but those who run the risk of a complete reversal in their lives, and who would feel the difference most intensely, if things went wrong for them. Any intelligent man would find a humiliation caused by his own slackness more painful to bear than death, when death comes to him unperceived, in battle, and in the confidence of his patriotism.

'For these reasons I shall not commiserate with those parents of the 44 dead, who are present here. Instead I shall try to comfort them. They are well aware that they have grown up in a world where there are many changes and chances. But this is good fortune – for men to end their lives with honour, as these have done, and for you honourably to lament them: their life was set to a measure where death and happiness went hand in hand. I know that it is difficult to convince you of this. When you see other people happy you will often be reminded of what used to make you happy too. One does not feel sad at not having some good thing which is outside one's experience: real grief is felt at the loss of something which one is used to. All the same, those of you who are of the right age must bear up and take comfort in the thought of having more children. In your own homes these new children will prevent you from brooding over those who are no more, and they will be a help to the city, too, both in filling the empty places, and in assuring her security. For it is impossible for a man to put forward fair and honest views about our affairs if he has not, like everyone else, children whose lives may be at stake. As for those of you who are now too old to have children, I would ask you to count as gain the greater part of your life, in which you have been happy, and remember that what remains is not long, and let your hearts be lifted up at the thought of the fair fame of the dead. One's sense of honour is the only thing that does not grow old, and the last pleasure, when one is worn

out with age, is not, as the poet said, making money, but having the respect
of one's fellow men.

45   'As for those of you here who are sons or brothers of the dead, I can
see a hard struggle in front of you. Everyone always speaks well of the dead,
and, even if you rise to the greatest heights of heroism, it will be a hard
thing for you to get the reputation of having come near, let alone equalled,
their standard. When one is alive, one is always liable to the jealousy of one's
competitors, but when one is out of the way, the honour one receives is
sincere and unchallenged.

46   'Perhaps I should say a word or two on the duties of women to those
among you who are now widowed. I can say all I have to say in a short word
of advice. Your great glory is not to be inferior to what God has made you,
and the greatest glory of a woman is to be least talked about by men, whether
they are praising you or criticizing you. I have now, as the law demanded, said
what I had to say. For the time being our offerings to the dead have been made,
and for the future their children will be supported at the public expense by
the city, until they come of age. This is the crown and prize which she offers,
both to the dead and to their children, for the ordeals which they have faced.
Where the rewards of valour are the greatest, there you will find also the best
and bravest spirits among the people. And now, when you have mourned for
your dear ones, you must depart'.

The plague

...

50   Words indeed fail one when one tries to give a general picture of this disease;
and as for the sufferings of individuals, they seemed almost beyond the capacity of human nature to endure. Here in particular is a point where this
plague showed itself to be something quite different from ordinary diseases:
though there were many dead bodies lying about unburied, the birds and
animals that eat human flesh either did not come near them or, if they did
taste the flesh, died of it afterwards. Evidence for this may be found in the
fact that there was a complete disappearance of all birds of prey: they were
not to be seen either round the bodies or anywhere else. But dogs, being
domestic animals, provided the best opportunity of observing this effect of
the plague.

51   These, then, were the general features of the disease, though I have omitted all kinds of peculiarities which occurred in various individual cases. Meanwhile, during all this time there was no serious outbreak of any of the usual
kinds of illness; if any such cases did occur, they ended in the plague. Some
died in neglect, some in spite of every possible care being taken of them. As

for a recognized method of treatment, it would be true to say that no such thing existed: what did good in some cases did harm in others. Those with naturally strong constitutions were no better able than the weak to resist the disease, which carried away all alike, even those who were treated and dieted with the greatest care. The most terrible thing of all was the despair into which people fell when they realized that they had caught the plague; for they would immediately adopt an attitude of utter hopelessness, and, by giving in in this way, would lose their powers of resistance. Terrible, too, was the sight of people dying like sheep through having caught the disease as a result of nursing others. This indeed caused more deaths than anything else. For when people were afraid to visit the sick, then they died with no one to look after them; indeed, there were many houses in which all the inhabitants perished through lack of any attention. When, on the other hand, they did visit the sick, they lost their own lives, and this was particularly true of those who made it a point of honour to act properly. Such people felt ashamed to think of their own safety and went into their friends' houses at times when even the members of the household were so overwhelmed by the weight of their calamities that they had actually given up the usual practice of making laments for the dead. Yet still the ones who felt most pity for the sick and the dying were those who had had the plague themselves and had recovered from it. They knew what it was like and at the same time felt themselves to be safe, for no one caught the disease twice, or, if he did, the second attack was never fatal. Such people were congratulated on all sides, and they themselves were so elated at the time of their recovery that they fondly imagined that they could never die of any other disease in the future.

A factor which made matters much worse than they were already was the 52 removal of people from the country into the city, and this particularly affected the incomers. There were no houses for them, and, living as they did during the hot season in badly ventilated huts, they died like flies. The bodies of the dying were heaped one on top of the other, and half-dead creatures could be seen staggering about in the streets or flocking around the fountains in their desire for water. The temples in which they took up their quarters were full of the dead bodies of people who had died inside them. For the catastrophe was so overwhelming that men, not knowing what would happen next to them, became indifferent to every rule of religion or of law. All the funeral ceremonies which used to be observed were now disorganized, and they buried the dead as best they could. Many people, lacking the necessary means of burial because so many deaths had already occurred in their households, adopted the most shameless methods. They would arrive first at a funeral pyre that had been made by others, put their own dead upon it and set it alight; or, finding another pyre burning, they would throw the corpse that they were carrying on top of the other one and go away.

53   In other respects also Athens owed to the plague the beginnings of a state of unprecedented lawlessness. Seeing how quick and abrupt were the changes of fortune which came to the rich who suddenly died and to those who had previously been penniless but now inherited their wealth, people now began openly to venture on acts of self-indulgence which before then they used to keep dark. Thus they resolved to spend their money quickly and to spend it on pleasure, since money and life alike seemed equally ephemeral. As for what is called honour, no one showed himself willing to abide by its laws, so doubtful was it whether one would survive to enjoy the name for it. It was generally agreed that what was both honourable and valuable was the pleasure of the moment and everything that might conceivably contribute to that pleasure. No fear of god or law of man had a restraining influence. As for the gods, it seemed to be the same thing whether one worshipped them or not, when one saw the good and the bad dying indiscriminately. As for offences against human law, no one expected to live long enough to be brought to trial and punished: instead everyone felt that already a far heavier sentence had been passed on him and was hanging over him, and that before the time for its execution arrived it was only natural to get some pleasure out of life.

54   This, then, was the calamity which fell upon Athens, and the times were hard indeed, with men dying inside the city and the land outside being laid waste.

...

Book 3, 36–49

The Mytilenian debate

36 When Salaethus and the other prisoners reached Athens, the Athenians immediately put Salaethus to death in spite of the fact that he undertook, among other things, to have the Peloponnesians withdrawn from Plataea, which was still being besieged. They then discussed what was to be done with the other prisoners and, in their angry mood, decided to put to death not only those now in their hands but also the entire adult male population of Mytilene, and to make slaves of the women and children. What they held against Mytilene was the fact that it had revolted even though it was not a subject state, like the others, and the bitterness of their feelings was considerably increased by the fact that the Peloponnesian fleet had actually dared to cross over to Ionia to support the revolt. This, it was thought, could never have happened unless the revolt had been long premeditated. So they sent a trireme to Paches to inform him of what had been decided, with orders to put the Mytilenians to death immediately.

Next day, however, there was a sudden change of feeling and people began to think how cruel and how unprecedented such a decision was – to destroy not only the guilty, but the entire population of a state. Observing this, the deputation from Mytilene which was in Athens and the Athenians who were supporting them approached the authorities with a view to having the question debated again. They won their point the more easily because the authorities themselves saw clearly that most of the citizens were wanting someone to give them a chance of reconsidering the matter. So an assembly was called at once. Various opinions were expressed on both sides, and Cleon, the son of Cleaenetus, spoke again. It was he who had been responsible for passing the original motion for putting the Mytilenians to death. He was remarkable among the Athenians for the violence of his character, and at this time he exercised far the greatest influence over the people. He spoke as follows:

'Personally I have had occasion often enough already to observe that 37 a democracy is incapable of governing others, and I am all the more convinced of this when I see how you are now changing your minds about the Mytilenians. Because fear and conspiracy play no part in your daily relations with each other, you imagine that the same thing is true of your allies, and you fail to see that when you allow them to persuade you to make a mistaken decision and when you give way to your own feelings of compassion you are being guilty of a kind of weakness which is dangerous to you and which will not make them love you any more. What you do not realize is that your empire is a tyranny exercised over subjects who do not like it and who are always plotting against you; you will not make them obey you by injuring your own interests in order to do them a favour; your leadership depends on superior strength and not on any goodwill of theirs. And this is the very worst thing – to pass measures and then not to abide by them. We should realize that a city is better off with bad laws, so long as they remain fixed, than with good laws that are constantly being altered, that lack of learning combined with sound common sense is more helpful than the kind of cleverness that gets out of hand, and that as a general rule states are better governed by the man in the street than by intellectuals. These are the sort of people who want to appear wiser than the laws, who want to get their own way in every general discussion, because they feel that they cannot show off their intelligence in matters of greater importance, and who, as a result, very often bring ruin on their country. But the other kind – the people who are not so confident in their own intelligence – are prepared to admit that the laws are wiser than they are and that they lack the ability to pull to pieces a speech made by a good speaker; they are unbiased judges, and not people taking part in some kind of a competition; so things usually go well when they are in control. We statesmen, too, should try to be like them, instead of being carried away by mere cleverness and a desire to show off our intelligence and so giving you, the people, advice which we do not really believe in ourselves.

38   'As for me, I have not altered my opinion, and I am amazed at those who have proposed a reconsideration of the question of Mytilene, thus causing a delay which is all to the advantage of the guilty party. After a lapse of time the injured party will lose the edge of his anger when he comes to act against those who have wronged him; whereas the best punishment and the one most fitted to the crime is when reprisals follow immediately. I shall be amazed, too, if anyone contradicts me and attempts to prove that the harm done to us by Mytilene is really a good thing for us, or that when we suffer ourselves we are somehow doing harm to our allies. It is obvious that anyone who is going to say this must either have such confidence in his powers as an orator that he will struggle to persuade you that what has been finally settled was, on the contrary, not decided at all, or else he must have been bribed to put together some elaborate speech with which he will try to lead you out of the right track. But in competitions of this sort the prizes go to others and the state takes all the danger for herself. The blame is yours, for stupidly instituting these competitive displays. You have become regular speech-goers, and as for action, you merely listen to accounts of it; if something is to be done in the future you estimate the possibilities by hearing a good speech on the subject, and as for the past you rely not so much on the facts which you have seen with your own eyes as on what you have heard about them in some clever piece of verbal criticism. Any novelty in an argument deceives you at once, but when the argument is tried and proved you become unwilling to follow it; you look with suspicion on what is normal and are the slaves of every paradox that comes your way. The chief wish of each one of you is to be able to make a speech himself, and, if you cannot do that, the next best thing is to compete with those who can make this sort of speech by not looking as though you were at all out of your depth while you listen to the views put forward, by applauding a good point even before it is made, and by being as quick at seeing how an argument is going to be developed as you are slow at understanding what in the end it will lead to. What you are looking for all the time is something that is, I should say, outside the range of ordinary experience, and yet you cannot even think straight about the facts of life that are before you. You are simply victims of your own pleasure in listening, and are more like an audience sitting at the feet of a professional lecturer than a parliament discussing matters of state.

39   'I am trying to stop you behaving like this, and I say that no single city has ever done you the harm that Mytilene has done. Personally I can make allowances for those who revolt because they find your rule intolerable or because they have been forced into it by enemy action. Here, however, we have the case of people living on an island, behind their own fortifications,

with nothing to fear from our enemies except an attack by sea against which they were adequately protected by their own force of triremes; they had their own independent government and they were treated by us with the greatest consideration. Now, to act as they acted is not what I should call a revolt (for people only revolt when they have been badly treated); it is a case of calculated aggression, of deliberately taking sides with our bitterest enemies in order to destroy us. And this is far worse than if they had made war against us simply to increase their own power. They learned nothing from the fate of those of their neighbours who had already revolted and been subdued; the prosperity which they enjoyed did not make them hesitate before running into danger; confident in the future, they declared war on us, with hopes that indeed extended beyond their means, though still fell short of their desires. They made up their minds to put might first and right second, choosing the moment when they thought they would win, and then making their unprovoked attack upon us.

'The fact is that when great prosperity comes suddenly and unexpectedly to a state, it usually breeds arrogance; in most cases it is safer for people to enjoy an average amount of success rather than something which is out of all proportion; and it is easier, I should say, to ward off hardship than to maintain happiness. What we should have done long ago with the Mytilenians was to treat them in exactly the same way as all the rest; then they would never have grown so arrogant; for it is a general rule of human nature that people despise those who treat them well and look up to those who make no concessions. Let them now therefore have the punishment which their crime deserves. Do not put the blame on the aristocracy and say that the people were innocent. The fact is that the whole lot of them attacked you together, although the people might have come over to us and, if they had, would now be back again in control of their city. Yet, instead, of doing this, they thought it safer to share the dangers, and join in the revolt of the aristocracy.

'Now think of your allies. If you are going to give the same punishment to those who are forced to revolt by your enemies and those who do so of their own accord, can you not see that they will all revolt upon the slightest pretext, when success means freedom and failure brings no very dreadful consequences? Meanwhile we shall have to spend our money and risk our lives against state after state; if our efforts are successful, we shall recover a city that is in ruins, and so lose the future revenue from it, on which our strength is based; and if we fail to subdue it, we shall have more enemies to deal with in addition to those we have already, and we shall spend the time which ought to be used in resisting our present foes in making war on our own allies.

'Let there be no hope, therefore, held out to the Mytilenians that we, 40 either as a result of a good speech or a large bribe, are likely to forgive them on the grounds that it is only human to make mistakes. There was nothing involuntary about the harm they did us; they knew what they were about and they planned it all beforehand; and one only forgives actions that were not deliberate. As for me, just as I was at first, so I am now, and I shall continue to impress on you the importance of not altering your previous decisions. To feel pity, to be carried away by the pleasure of hearing a clever argument, to listen to the claims of decency are three things that are entirely against the interests of an imperial power. Do not be guilty of them. As for compassion, it is proper to feel it in the case of people who are like ourselves and who will pity us in their turn, not in the case of those who, so far from having the same feelings towards us, must always and inevitably be our enemies. As for the speech-makers who give such pleasure by their arguments, they should hold their competitions on subjects which are less important, and not on a question where the state may have to pay a heavy penalty for its light pleasure, while the speakers themselves will no doubt be enjoying splendid rewards for their splendid arguments. And a sense of decency is only felt towards those who are going to be our friends in future, not towards those who remain just as they were and as much our enemies as they ever have been.

'Let me sum the whole thing up. I say that, if you follow my advice, you will be doing the right thing as far as Mytilene is concerned and at the same time will be acting in your own interests; if you decide differently, you will not win them over, but you will be passing judgement on yourselves. For if they were justified in revolting, you must be wrong in holding power. If, however, whatever the rights or wrongs of it may be, you propose to hold power all the same, then your interest demands that these too, rightly or wrongly, must be punished. The only alternative is to surrender your empire, so that you can afford to go in for philanthropy. Make up your minds, therefore, to pay them back in their own coins, and do not make it look as though you who escaped their machinations are less quick to react than they who started them. Remember how they would have been likely to have treated you, if they had won, especially as they were the aggressors. Those who do wrong to a neighbour when there is no reason to do so are the ones who persevere to the point of destroying him, since they see the danger involved in allowing their enemy to survive. For he who has suffered for no good reason is a more dangerous enemy, if he escapes, than the one who has both done and suffered injury.

'I urge you, therefore, not to be traitors to your own selves. Place yourselves in imagination at the moment when you first suffered and remember how then you would have given anything to have them in your power. Now pay them back for it, and do not grow soft just at this present moment, forgetting meanwhile the danger that hung over your heads then. Punish them as they deserve, and make an example of them to your other allies, plainly showing that revolt will be punished by death. Once they realize this, you will not have so often to neglect the war with your enemies because you are fighting with your own allies.'

So Cleon spoke. After him Diodotus, the son of Eucrates, who in the previous assembly also had vigorously opposed the motion to put the Mytilenians to death, came forward again on this occasion and spoke as follows: 41

'I do not blame those who have proposed a new debate on the subject of Mytilene, and I do not share the view which we have heard expressed, that it is a bad thing to have frequent discussions on matters of importance. Haste and anger are, to my mind, the two greatest obstacles to wise counsel – haste, that usually goes with folly, anger, that is the mark of primitive and narrow minds. And anyone who maintains that words cannot be a guide to action must be either a fool or one with some personal interest at stake; he is a fool, if he imagines that it is possible to deal with the uncertainties of the future by any other medium, and he is personally interested if his aim is to persuade you into some disgraceful action, and, knowing that he cannot make a good speech in a bad cause, he tries to frighten his opponents and his hearers by some good-sized pieces of misrepresentation. Then still more intolerable are those who go further and accuse a speaker of making a kind of exhibition of himself, because he is paid for it. If it was only ignorance with which he was being charged, a speaker who failed to win his case could retire from the debate and still be thought an honest man, if not a very intelligent one. But when corruption is imputed, he will be suspect if he wins his case, and if he loses it, will be regarded as dishonest and stupid at the same time. This sort of thing does the city no good; her counsellors will be afraid to speak and she will be deprived of their services. Though certainly it would be the best possible thing for the city if these gentlemen whom I have been describing lacked the power to express themselves; we should not then be persuaded into making so many mistakes. 42

'The good citizen, instead of trying to terrify the opposition, ought to prove his case in fair argument; and a wise state, without giving special honours to its best counsellors, will certainly not deprive them of the honour they already enjoy; and when a man's advice is not taken, he should not even be disgraced, far less penalized. In this way successful speakers will be less likely to pursue further honours by speaking against their own convictions in order to make themselves popular, and unsuccessful speakers, too, will not struggle to win over the people by the same acts of flattery. What we do here, however, is exactly the opposite. Then, too, if a man gives the best possible advice but is under the slightest suspicion of being influenced by his own private profit, we are so embittered by the idea (a wholly unproved one) of this profit of his, that we do not allow the state to receive the certain benefit of his good advice. So a state of affairs has been reached where a good proposal 43 honestly put forward is just as suspect as something thoroughly bad, and the result is that just as the speaker who advocates some monstrous measure has to win over the people by deceiving them, so also a man with good advice to give has to tell lies if he expects to be believed. And because of this refinement in intellectuality, the state is put into a unique position; it is only she to whom no one can ever do a good turn openly and without deception. For if one openly performs a patriotic action, the reward for one's pains is to be thought to have made something oneself on the side. Yet in spite of all this we are discussing matters of the greatest importance, and we who give you our advice ought to be resolved to look rather further into things than you whose attention is occupied only with the surface – especially as we can be held to account for the advice we give, while you are not accountable for the way in which you receive it. For indeed you would take rather more care over your decisions, if the proposer of a motion and those who voted for it were all subject to the same penalties. As it is, on the occasions when some emotional impulse on your part has led you into disaster, you turn upon the one man who make the original proposal and you let yourself off, in spite of the fact that you are many and in spite of the fact that you were just as wrong as he was.

44   'However, I have not come forward to speak about Mytilene in any spirit of contradiction or with any wish to accuse anyone. If we are sensible people, we shall see that the question is not so much whether they are guilty as whether we are making the right decision for ourselves. I might prove that they are the most guilty people in the world, but it does not follow that I shall propose the death penalty, unless that is in your interests; I might argue that they deserve to be forgiven, but should not recommend forgiveness unless that seemed to me the best thing for the state.

        'In my view our discussion concerns the future rather than the present. One of Cleon's chief points is that to inflict the death penalty will be useful to us in the future as a means for deterring other cities from revolt; but I, who am just as concerned as he is with the future, am quite convinced that this is not so. And I ask you not to reject what is useful in my speech for the sake of what is specious in his. You may well find his speech attractive, because it fits in better with your present angry feelings about the Mytilenians; but this is not a law-court, where we have to consider what is fit and just; it is a political assembly, and the question is how Mytilene can be most useful to Athens.

45   'Now, in human societies the death penalty has been laid down for many offences less serious than this one. Yet people still take risks when they feel sufficiently confident. No one has ever yet risked committing a crime which he thought he could not carry out successfully. The same is true of states. None has ever yet rebelled in the belief that it had insufficient resources, either in

itself or from its allies, to make the attempt. Cities and individuals alike, all are by nature disposed to do wrong, and there is no law that will prevent it, as is shown by the fact that men have tried every kind of punishment, constantly adding to the list, in the attempt to find greater security from criminals. It is likely that in early times the punishments even for the greatest crimes were not as severe as they are now, but the laws were still broken, and in the course of time the death penalty became generally introduced. Yet even with this, the laws are still broken. Either, therefore, we must discover some fear more potent than the fear of death, or we must admit that here certainly we have not got an adequate deterrent. So long as poverty forces men to be bold, so long as the insolence and pride of wealth nourish their ambitions, and in the other accidents of life they are continually dominated by some incurable master passion or another, so long will their impulses continue to drive them into danger. Hope and desire persist throughout and cause the greatest calamities – one leading and the other following, one conceiving the enterprise, and the other suggesting that it will be successful – invisible factors, but more powerful than the terrors that are obvious to our eyes. Then too, the idea that fortune will be on one's side plays as big a part as anything else in creating a mood of over-confidence; for sometimes she does come unexpectedly to one's aid, and so she tempts men to run risks for which they are inadequately prepared. And this is particularly true in the case of whole peoples, because they are playing for the highest stakes – either for their own freedom or for the power to control others – and each individual, when acting as part of a community, has the irrational opinion that his own powers are greater than in fact they are. In a word it is impossible (and only the most simple-minded will deny this) for human nature, when once seriously set upon a certain course, to be prevented from following that course by the force of law or by any other means of intimidation whatever.

'We must not, therefore, come to the wrong conclusions through having 46
too much confidence in the effectiveness of capital punishment, and we must not make the condition of rebels desperate by depriving them of the possibility of repentance and of a chance of atoning as quickly as they can for what they did. Consider this now: at the moment, if a city has revolted and realizes that the revolt cannot succeed, it will come to terms while it is still capable of paying an indemnity and continuing to pay tribute afterwards. But if Cleon's method is adopted, can you not see that every city will not only make much more careful preparations for revolt, but will also hold out against siege to the very end, since to surrender early or late means just the same thing? This is, unquestionably, against our interests – to spend money on a siege because of the impossibility of coming to terms, and, if we capture the place, to take over a city that is in ruins so that we lose the future revenue from it. And it is just on this revenue that our strength in war depends.

'Our business, therefore, is not to injure ourselves by acting like a judge who strictly examines a criminal; instead we should be looking for a method by which, employing moderation in our punishments, we can in future secure for ourselves the full use of those cities which bring us important contributions. And we should recognize that the proper basis of our security is in good administration rather than in the fear of legal penalties. As it is, we do just the opposite: when we subdue a free city, which was held down by force and has, as we might have expected, tried to assert its independence by revolting, we think that we ought to punish it with the utmost severity. But the right way to deal with free people is this – not to inflict tremendous punishments on them after they have revolted, but to take tremendous care of them before this point is reached, to prevent them even contemplating the idea of revolt, and, if we do have to use force with them, to hold as few as possible of them responsible for this.

47   'Consider what a mistake you would be making on this very point, if you took Cleon's advice. As things are now, in all the cities the democracy is friendly to you; either it does not join in with the oligarchies in revolting, or, if it is forced to do so, it remains all the time hostile to the rebels, so that when you go to war with them, you have the people on your side. But if you destroy the democratic party at Mytilene, who never took any hand in the revolt and who, as soon as they got arms, voluntarily gave the city up to you, you will first of all be guilty of killing those who have helped you, and, secondly, you will be doing exactly what the reactionary classes want most. For now, when they start a revolt, they will have the people on their side from the beginning, because you have already made it clear that the same punishment is laid down both for the guilty and the innocent. In fact, however, even if they were guilty, you should pretend that they were not, in order to keep on your side the one element that is still not opposed to you. It is far more useful to us, I think, in preserving our empire, that we should voluntarily put up with injustice than that we should justly put to death the wrong people. As for Cleon's point – that in this act of vengeance both justice and self-interest are combined – this is not a case where such a combination is at all possible.

48   'I call upon you, therefore, to accept my proposal as the better one. Do not be swayed too much by pity or by ordinary decent feelings. I, no more than Cleon, wish you to be influenced by such emotions. It is simply on the basis of the argument which you have heard that I ask you to be guided by me, to try at your leisure the men whom Paches has considered guilty and sent to Athens, and to allow the rest to live in their own city. In following this course you will be acting wisely for the future and will be doing something which will make your enemies fear you now. For those who make wise decisions are more formidable to their enemies than those who rush madly into strong action.'

This was the speech of Diodotus. And now, when these two motions, 49
each so opposed to each, had been put forward, the Athenians, in spite of
the recent change of feeling, still held conflicting opinions, and at the show
of hands the votes were nearly equal. However, the motion of Diodotus was
passed.

Immediately another trireme was sent out in all haste, since they feared
that, unless it overtook the first trireme, they would find on their arrival that
the city had been destroyed. The first trireme had a start of about twenty-
four hours. The ambassadors from Mytilene provided wine and barley for the
crew and promised great rewards if they arrived in time, and so the men made
such speed on the voyage that they kept on rowing while they took their food
(which was barley mixed with oil and wine) and rowed continually, taking it
in turn to sleep. Luckily they had no wind against them, and as the first ship
was not hurrying on its distasteful mission, while they were pressing on with
such speed, what happened was that the first ship arrived so little ahead of
them that Paches had just had time to read the decree and to prepare to put
it into force, when the second ship put in to the harbour and prevented the
massacre. So narrow had been the escape of Mytilene.

...

Book 5, 84–116

The Melian dialogue

Next summer Alcibiades sailed to Argos with twenty ships and seized 300 84
Argive citizens who were still suspected of being pro-Spartan. These were
put by the Athenians into the nearby islands under Athenian control.

The Athenians also made an expedition against the island of Melos.
They had thirty of their own ships, six from Chios, and two from Lesbos;
1,200 hoplites, 300 archers, and twenty mounted archers, all from Athens; and
about 1,500 hoplites from the allies and the islanders.

The Melians are a colony from Sparta. They had refused to join the
Athenian empire like the other islanders, and at first had remained neutral
without helping either side; but afterwards, when the Athenians had brought
force to bear on them by laying waste their land, they had become open
enemies of Athens.

Now the generals Cleomedes, the son of Lycomedes, and Tisias, the son
of Tisimachus, encamped with the above force in Melian territory and, before
doing any harm to the land, first of all sent representatives to negotiate. The
Melians did not invite these representatives to speak before the people, but
asked them to make the statement for which they had come in front of the governing body and the few. The Athenian representatives then spoke as follows:

85   'So we are not to speak before the people, no doubt in case the mass of the
people should hear once and for all and without interruption an argument
from us which is both persuasive and incontrovertible, and should so be led
astray. This, we realize, is your motive in bringing us here to speak before the
few. Now suppose that you who sit here should make assurance doubly sure.
Suppose that you, too, should refrain from dealing with every point in detail
in a set speech, and should instead interrupt us whenever we say something
controversial and deal with that before going on to the next point? Tell us
first whether you approve of this suggestion of ours.'

86   The Council of the Melians replied as follows:
'No one can object to each of us putting forward our own views in a calm
atmosphere. That is perfectly reasonable. What is scarcely consistent with
such a proposal is the present threat, indeed the certainty, of your making war
on us. We see that you have come prepared to judge the argument yourselves,
and that the likely end of it all will be either war, if we prove that we are in
the right, and so refuse to surrender, or else slavery.'

87   *Athenians:* If you are going to spend the time in enumerating your suspi-
cions about the future, or if you have met here for any other reason except to
look the facts in the face and on the basis of these facts to consider how you
can save your city from destruction, there is no point in our going on with
this discussion. If, however, you will do as we suggest, then we will speak on.

88   *Melians:* It is natural and understandable that people who are placed as
we are should have recourse to all kinds of arguments and different points
of view. However, you are right in saying that we are met together here to
discuss the safety of our country and, if you will have it so, the discussion
shall proceed on the lines that you have laid down.

89   *Athenians:* Then we on our side will use no fine phrases saying, for example, that we have a right to our empire because we defeated the Persians,
or that we have come against you now because of the injuries you have done
us – a great mass of words that nobody would believe. And we ask you on
your side not to imagine that you will influence us by saying that you, though
a colony of Sparta, have not joined Sparta in the war, or that you have never
done us any harm. Instead we recommend that you should try to get what it
is possible for you to get, taking into consideration what we both really do
think; since you know as well as we do that, when these matters are discussed
by practical people, the standard of justice depends on the equality of power
to compel and that in fact the strong do what they have the power to do and
the weak accept what they have to accept.

90   *Melians:* Then in our view (since you force us to leave justice out of
account and to confine ourselves to self-interest) – in our view it is at any
rate useful that you should not destroy a principle that is to the general good
of all men – namely, that in the case of all who fall into danger there should

be such a thing as fair play and just dealing, and that such people should be allowed to use and to profit by arguments that fall short of a mathematical accuracy. And this is a principle which affects you as much as anybody, since your own fall would be visited by the most terrible vengeance and would be an example to the world.

Athenians: As for us, even assuming that our empire does come to an end, 91 we are not despondent about what would happen next. One is not so much frightened of being conquered by a power which rules over others, as Sparta does (not that we are concerned with Sparta now), as of what would happen if a ruling power is attacked and defeated by its own subjects. So far as this point is concerned, you can leave it to us to face the risks involved. What we shall do now is to show you that it is for the good of our own empire that we are here and that it is for the preservation of your city that we shall say what we are going to say. We do not want any trouble in bringing you into our empire, and we want you to be spared for the good both of yourselves and of ourselves.

Melians: And how could it be just as good for us to be the slaves as for 92 you to be the masters?

Athenians: You, by giving in, would save yourselves from disaster; we, by 93 not destroying you, would be able to profit from you.

Melians: So you would not agree to our being neutral, friends instead of 94 enemies, but allies of neither side?

Athenians: No, because it is not so much your hostility that injures us; it 95 is rather the case that, if we were on friendly terms with you, our subjects would regard that as a sign of weakness in us, whereas your hatred is evidence of our power.

Melians: Is that your subjects' idea of fair play – that no distinction should 96 be made between people who are quite unconnected with you and people who are mostly your own colonists or else rebels whom you have conquered?

Athenians: So far as right and wrong are concerned they think that there 97 is no difference between the two, that those who still preserve their independence do so because they are strong, and that if we fail to attack them it is because we are afraid. So that by conquering you we shall increase not only the size but the security of our empire. We rule the sea and you are islanders, and weaker islanders too than the others; it is therefore particularly important that you should not escape.

Melians: But do you think there is no security for you in what we suggest? 98 For here again, since you will not let us mention justice, but tell us to give in to your interests, we, too, must tell you what our interests are and, if yours and ours happen to coincide, we must try to persuade you of the fact. Is it not certain that you will make enemies of all states who are at present neutral, when they see what is happening here and naturally conclude that in course of time you will attack them too? Does not this mean that you are strengthening the enemies you have already and are forcing others to become your enemies even against their intentions and their inclinations?

99   *Athenians:* As a matter of fact we are not so much frightened of states on the continent. They have their liberty, and this means that it will be a long time before they begin to take precautions against us. We are more concerned about islanders like yourselves, who are still unsubdued, or subjects who have already become embittered by the constraint which our empire imposes on them. These are the people who are most likely to act in a reckless manner and to bring themselves and us, too, into the most obvious danger.

100   *Melians:* Then surely, if such hazards are taken by you to keep your empire and by your subjects to escape from it, we who are still free would show ourselves great cowards and weaklings if we failed to face everything that comes rather than submit to slavery.

101   *Athenians:* No, not if you are sensible. This is no fair fight, with honour on one side and shame on the other. It is rather a question of saving your lives and not resisting those who are far too strong for you.

102   *Melians:* Yet we know that in war fortune sometimes makes the odds more level than could be expected from the difference in numbers of the two sides. And if we surrender, then all our hope is lost at once, whereas, so long as we remain in action, there is still a hope that we may yet stand upright.

103   *Athenians:* Hope, that comforter in danger! If one already has solid advantages to fall back upon, one can indulge in hope. It may do harm, but will not destroy one. But hope is by nature an expensive commodity, and those who are risking their all on one cast find out what it means only when they are already ruined; it never fails them in the period when such a knowledge would enable them to take precautions. Do not let this happen to you, you who are weak and whose fate depends on a single movement of the scale. And do not be like those people who, as so commonly happens, miss the chance of saving themselves in a human and practical way, and, when every clear and distinct hope has left them in their adversity, turn to what is blind and vague, to prophecies and oracles and such things which by encouraging hope lead men to ruin.

104   *Melians:* It is difficult, and you may be sure that we know it, for us to oppose your power and fortune, unless the terms be equal. Nevertheless we trust that the gods will give us fortune as good as yours, because we are standing for what is right against what is wrong; and as for what we lack in power, we trust that it will be made up for by our alliance with the Spartans, who are bound, if for no other reason, then for honour's sake, and because we are their kinsmen, to come to our help. Our confidence, therefore, is not so entirely irrational as you think.

105   *Athenians:* So far as the favour of the gods is concerned, we think we have as much right to that as you have. Our aims and our actions are perfectly

consistent with the beliefs men hold about the gods and with the principles which govern their own conduct. Our opinion of the gods and our knowledge of men lead us to conclude that it is a general and necessary law of nature to rule wherever one can. This not a law that we made ourselves, nor were we the first to act upon it when it was made. We found it already in existence, and we shall leave it to exist for ever among those who come after us. We are merely acting in accordance with it, and we know that you or anybody else with the same power as ours would be acting in precisely the same way. And therefore, so far as the gods are concerned, we see no good reason why we should fear to be at a disadvantage. But with regard to your views about Sparta and your confidence that she, out of a sense of honour, will come to your aid, we must say that we congratulate you on your simplicity but do not envy you your folly. In matters that concern themselves or their own constitution the Spartans are quite remarkably good; as for their relations with others, that is a long story, but it can be expressed shortly and clearly by saying that of all people we know the Spartans are most conspicuous for believing that what they like doing is honourable and what suits their interests is just. And this kind of attitude is not going to be of much help to you in your absurd quest for safety at the moment.

Melians: But this is the very point where we can feel most sure. Their   106 own self-interest will make them refuse to betray their own colonists, the Melians, for that would mean losing the confidence of their friends among the Hellenes and doing good to their enemies.

Athenians: You seem to forget that if one follows one's self-interest one   107 wants to be safe, whereas the path of justice and honour involves one in danger. And, where danger is concerned, the Spartans are not, as a rule, very venturesome.

Melians: But we think that they would even endanger themselves for our   108 sake and count the risk more worth taking than in the case of others, because we are so close to the Peloponnese that they could operate more easily, and because they can depend on us more than on others, since we are of the same race and share the same feelings.

Athenians: Good will shown by the party that is asking for help does   109 not mean security for the prospective ally. What is looked for is a positive preponderance of power in action. And the Spartans pay attention to this point even more than others do. Certainly they distrust their own native resources so much that when they attack a neighbour they bring a great army of allies with them. It is hardly likely therefore that, while we are in control of the sea, they will cross over to an island.

Melians: But they still might send others. The Cretan sea is a wide one,   110 and it is harder for those who control it to intercept others than for those who want to slip through to do so safely. And even if they were to fail in

this, they would turn against your own land and against those of your allies
left unvisited by Brasidas. So, instead of troubling about a country which
has nothing to do with you, you will find trouble nearer home, among your
allies, and in your own country.

111   *Athenians:* It is a possibility, something that has in fact happened before.
It may happen in your case, but you are well aware that the Athenians have
never yet relinquished a single siege operation through fear of others. But
we are somewhat shocked to find that, though you announced your intention of discussing how you could preserve yourselves, in all this talk you
have said absolutely nothing which could justify a man in thinking that
he could be preserved. Your chief points are concerned with what you hope
may happen in the future, while your actual resources are too scanty to give
you a chance of survival against the forces that are opposed to you at this
moment. You will therefore be showing an extraordinary lack of common
sense if, after you have asked us to retire from this meeting, you still fail to
reach a conclusion wiser than anything you have mentioned so far. Do not
be led astray by a false sense of honour – a thing which often brings men
to ruin when they are faced with an obvious danger that somehow affects
their pride. For in many cases men have still been able to see the dangers
ahead of them, but this thing called dishonour, this word, by its own force
of seduction, has drawn them into a state where they have surrendered to
an idea, while in fact they have fallen voluntarily into irrevocable disaster, in
dishonour that is all the more dishonourable because it has come to them
from their own folly rather than their misfortune. You, if you take the right
view, will be careful to avoid this. You will see that there is nothing disgraceful in giving way to the greatest city in Hellas when she is offering you such
reasonable terms – alliance on a tribute-paying basis and liberty to enjoy your
own property. And, when you are allowed to choose between war and safety,
you will not be so insensitively arrogant as to make the wrong choice. This
is the safe rule – to stand up to one's equals, to behave with deference towards one's superiors, and to treat one's inferiors with moderation. Think it
over again, then, when we have withdrawn from the meeting, and let this
be a point that constantly recurs to your minds – that you are discussing
the fate of your country, that you have only one country, and that its future
for good or ill depends on this one single decision which you are going to
make.

112   The Athenians then withdrew from the discussion. The Melians, left
to themselves, reached a conclusion which was much the same as they had
indicated in their previous replies. Their answer was as follows:

'Our decision, Athenians, is just the same as it was at first. We are not
prepared to give up in a short moment the liberty which our city has enjoyed from its foundation for 700 years. We put our trust in the fortune that

the gods will send and which has saved us up to now, and in the help of men – that is, of the Spartans; and so we shall try to save ourselves. But we invite you to allow us to be friends of yours and enemies to neither side, to make a treaty which shall be agreeable to both you and us, and so to leave our country.'

The Melians made this reply, and the Athenians, just as they were break- 113
ing off the discussion, said:

'Well, at any rate, judging from this decision of yours, you seem to us quite unique in your ability to consider the future as something more certain than what is before your eyes, and to see uncertainties as realities, simply because you would like them to be so. As you have staked most on and trusted most in Spartans, luck, and hopes, so in all these you will find yourselves most completely deluded.'

The Athenian representatives then went back to the army, and the 114
Athenian generals, finding that the Melians would not submit, immediately commenced hostilities and built a wall completely round the city of Melos, dividing the work out among the various states. Later they left behind a garrison of some of their own and some allied troops to blockade the place by land and sea, and with the greater part of their army returned home. The force left behind stayed on and continued with the siege.

About the same time the Argives invaded Phliasia and were ambushed 115
by the Phliasians and the exiles from Argos, losing about eighty men.

Then, too, the Athenians at Pylos captured a great quantity of plunder from Spartan territory. Not even after this did the Spartans renounce the treaty and make war, but they issued a proclamation saying that any of their people who wished to do so were free to make raids on the Athenians. The Corinthians also made some attacks on the Athenians because of private quarrels of their own, but the rest of the Peloponnesians stayed quiet.

Meanwhile the Melians made a night attack and captured the part of the Athenian lines opposite the market-place. They killed some of the troops, and then, after bringing in corn and everything else useful that they could lay their hands on, retired again and made no further move, while the Athenians took measures to make their blockade more efficient in future. So the summer came to an end.

In the following winter the Spartans planned to invade the territory 116
of Argos, but when the sacrifices for crossing the frontier turned out unfavourably, they gave up the expedition. The fact that they had intended to invade made the Argives suspect certain people in their city, some of whom they arrested, though others succeeded in escaping.

About this same time the Melians again captured another part of the Athenian lines where there were only a few of the garrison on guard. As a result of this, another force came out afterwards from Athens under the command of Philocrates, the son of Demeas. Siege operations were now carried on vigorously and, as there was also some treachery from inside, the Melians surrendered unconditionally to the Athenians, who put to death all the men of military age whom they took, and sold the women and children as slaves. Melos itself they took over for themselves, sending out later a colony of 500 men.

ARISTOTLE

ARISTOTLE was born in Stagira, in northern Greece, in 384 BCE. His father, Nichomachus, was court physician to Amyntas III, king of Macedon, and thus Aristotle was brought up mainly in Macedonia. At seventeen, however, Aristotle was sent to Athens, the cultural centre of the Greek world, to pursue his education. Very quickly he became primarily associated with Plato's Academy, where he remained for more than twenty years. Plato himself was nearly sixty when Aristotle joined the Academy yet he clearly recognized the young man's precocity and very soon Aristotle became a favored pupil – and leading disciple. However, on Plato's death in 347 BCE Aristotle left Athens. It is often supposed he left Athens because Plato's nephew, Speusippus, was appointed *Scholarch* – head of the Academy – when he thought the position should have gone to him. However, as a metic – a non-Athenian-born resident of Athens – Aristotle could not own property in Athens and since the buildings and possessions of the Academy were transferred to Speusippus as well as the headship, it is unlikely that Aristotle had any expectations in that regard. By all accounts, he also got on well with Speussipus, at least personally. In any event, there were more personal reasons for leaving Athens. This was the time when Philip II of Macedon was gradually bringing all of Greece under the Macedonian sphere of influence and anyone with a strong Macedonian connection was likely to be suspect, especially in Athens. Thus, for the next few years Aristotle traveled, becoming at one point tutor to a number of the sons of the Macedonian aristocracy, including Philip II's young son Alexander, later to be known simply as Alexander the Great! There is also some evidence that Aristotle acted, on occasion, as emissary for the Macedonian court, thus gaining first-hand knowledge of the politics and international affairs of his own day. Eventually, however, Aristotle returned to Athens and established his own school, called the Lyceum – often called also the *peripatos*, because of Aristotle's habit of lecturing while striding up and down (and hence our term peripatetic) – and composed most of the *Corpus Aristotelicum* (the works of Aristotle) as we have it today, including those most to do with politics and international affairs: the *Nichomachean Ethics* (so called because they were dedicated to Aristotle's son, called Nichomachus after Aristotle's father), *The Politics*, and the *Rhetoric*. However, Aristotle clearly retained his links with Macedon – Antipater, Alexander's regent in Greece when he embarked on the Persian war, was a close friend – and when, in 323, Alexander died, there was a general anti-Macedonian uprising throughout

Greece, and especially in Athens, Aristotle prudently withdrew to the city of
Calchis on the island of Euboa, remarking, in a reference to Athens' execution
of Socrates, that he did not wish Athens to sin twice against philosophy. He
died there the following year, at the age of sixty-two.

From *The Politics*

Book 1, chs. 1–6

1 . Every state is a community of some kind, and every community is established with a view to some good; for everyone always acts in order to obtain
that which they think good. But, if all communities aim at some good, the
state or political community, which is the highest of all, and which embraces
all the rest, aims at good in a greater degree than any other, and at the highest
good.

Some people think that the qualifications of a statesman, king, house-
holder, and master are the same, and that they differ, not in kind, but only
in the number of their subjects. For example, the ruler over a few is called a
master; over more, the manager of a household; over a still larger number, a
statesman or king, as if there were no difference between a great household
and a small state. The distinction which is made between the king and the
statesman is as follows: When the government is personal, the ruler is a king;
when, according to the rules of the political science, the citizens rule and are
ruled in turn, then he is called a statesman.

But all this is a mistake, as will be evident to any one who considers
the matter according to the method which has hitherto guided us. As in
other departments of science, so in politics, the compound should always
be resolved into the simple elements or least parts of the whole. We must
therefore look at the elements of which the state is composed, in order that
we may see in what the different kinds of rule differ from one another, and
whether any scientific result can be attained about each one of them.

2 . He who thus considers things in their first growth and origin, whether a
state or anything else, will obtain the clearest view of them. In the first place
there must be a union of those who cannot exist without each other; namely,
of male and female, that the race may continue (and this is a union which
is formed, not of choice, but because, in common with other animals and
with plants, mankind have a natural desire to leave behind them an image of
themselves), and of natural ruler and subject, that both may be preserved. For
that which can foresee by the exercise of mind is by nature lord and master,

1252^{a}1

5

10

15

20

25

30

and that which can with its body give effect to such foresight is a subject, and by nature a slave; hence master and slave have the same interest. Now nature has distinguished between the female and slave. For she is not niggardly, like the smith who fashions the Delphian knife for many uses; she makes each thing for a single use, and every instrument is best made when intended for one and not for many uses. But among barbarians no distinction is made 5 between women and slaves, because there is no natural ruler among them: they are a community of slaves, male and female. That is why the poets say, –

It is meet that Hellenes should rule over barbarians;

as if they thought that the barbarian and the slave were by nature one.

Out of these two relationships the first thing to arise is the family, and 10 Hesiod is right when he says, –

First house and wife and an ox for the plough,

for the ox is the poor man's slave. The family is the association established by nature for the supply of men's everyday wants, and the members of it are called by Charondas, 'companions of the cup-board', and by Epimenides the 15 Cretan, 'companions of the manager'. But when several families are united, and the association aims at something more than the supply of daily needs, the first society to be formed is the village. And the most natural form of the village appears to be that of a colony from the family, composed of the children and grandchildren, who are said to be 'suckled with the same milk'. And this is the reason why Hellenic states were originally governed by kings; because the Hellenes were under royal rule before they came together, as the 20 barbarians still are. Every family is ruled by the eldest, and therefore in the colonies of the family the kingly form of government prevailed because they were of the same blood. As Homer says:

Each one gives law to his children and to his wives.

For they lived dispersedly, as was the manner in ancient times. That is why men say that the Gods have a king, because they themselves either are or were 25 in ancient times under the rule of a king. For they imagine not only the forms of the Gods but their ways of life to be like their own.

When several villages are united in a single complete community, large enough to be nearly or quite self-sufficing, the state comes into existence, originating in the bare needs of life, and continuing in existence for the sake 30 of a good life. And therefore, if the earlier forms of society are natural, so is the state, for it is the end of them, and the nature of a thing is its end. For what each thing is when fully developed, we call its nature, whether we are speaking of a man, a horse, or a family. Besides, the final cause and end of a thing is the best, and to be self-sufficing is the end and the best. $1253^{a}1$

Hence it is evident that the state is a creation of nature, and that man is by nature a political animal. And he who by nature and not by mere accident is without a state, is either a bad man or above humanity; he is like the

Tribeless, lawless, heartless one,

5   whom Homer denounces – the natural outcast is forthwith a lover of war; he may be compared to an isolated piece at draughts.

Now, that man is more of a political animal than bees or any other gregarious animals is evident. Nature, as we often say, makes nothing in vain,
10   and man is the only animal who has the gift of speech. And whereas mere voice is but an indication of pleasure or pain, and is therefore found in other animals (for their nature attains to the perception of pleasure and pain and the intimation of them to one another, and no further), the power of speech is
15   intended to set forth the expedient and inexpedient, and therefore likewise the just and the unjust. And it is a characteristic of man that he alone has any sense of good and evil, of just and unjust, and the like, and the association of living beings who have this sense makes a family and a state.

Further, the state is by nature clearly prior to the family and to the
20   individual, since the whole is of necessity prior to the part; for example, if the whole body be destroyed, there will be no foot or hand, except homonymously, as we might speak of a stone hand; for when destroyed the hand will be no better than that. But things are defined by their function and power; and we ought not to say that they are the same when they no longer have their proper quality, but only that they are homonymous. The
25   proof that the state is a creation of nature and prior to the individual is that the individual, when isolated, is not self-sufficing; and therefore he is like a part in relation to the whole. But he who is unable to live in society, or who has no need because he is sufficient for himself, must be either a
30   beast or a god: he is no part of a state. A social instinct is implanted in all men by nature, and yet he who first founded the state was the greatest of benefactors. For man, when perfected, is the best of animals, but, when separated from law and justice, he is the worst of all; since armed injustice is the more dangerous, and he is equipped at birth with arms, meant to
35   be used by intelligence and excellence, which he may use for the worst ends. That is why, if he has not excellence, he is the most unholy and the most savage of animals, and the most full of lust and gluttony. But justice is the bond of men in states; for the administration of justice, which is the determination of what is just, is the principle of order in political society.

1253^{b}1   3 . Seeing then that the state is made up of households, before speaking of the state we must speak of the management of the household. The parts of household management correspond to the persons who compose the

household, and a complete household consists of slaves and freemen. Now 5
we should begin by examining everything in its fewest possible elements; and
the first and fewest possible parts of a family are master and slave, husband
and wife, father and children. We have therefore to consider what each of
these three relations is and ought to be: – I mean the relation of master and
servant, the marriage relation (the conjunction of man and wife has no name
of its own), and thirdly, the paternal relation (this also has no proper name). 10
And there is another element of a household, the so-called art of getting
wealth, which, according to some, is identical with household management,
according to others, a principal part of it; the nature of this art will also have
to be considered by us.

Let us first speak of master and slave, looking to our needs of practical 15
life and also seeking to attain some better theory of their relation than exists
at present. For some are of the opinion that the rule of a master is a science,
and that the management of a household, and the mastership of slaves, and
the political and royal rule, as I was saying at the outset, are all the same.
Others affirm that the rule of a master over slaves is contrary to nature, and 20
that the distinction between slave and freeman exists by convention only,
and not by nature; and being an interference with nature is therefore unjust.

4 . Property is a part of the household, and the art of acquiring property
is a part of the art of managing the household; for no man can live well,
or indeed live at all, unless he is provided with necessaries. And as in the 25
arts which have a definite sphere the workers must have their own proper
instruments for the accomplishment of their work, so it is in the management
of a household. Now instruments are of various sorts; some are living, others
lifeless; in the rudder, the pilot of a ship has a lifeless, in the look-out man, a
living instrument; for in the arts the servant is a kind of instrument. Thus, too, a 30
possession is an instrument for maintaining life. And so, in the arrangement
of the family, a slave is a living possession, and property a number of such
instruments; and the servant is himself an instrument for instruments. For
if every instrument could accomplish its own work, obeying or anticipating 35
the will of others, like the statues of Daedalus, or the tripods of Hephaestus,
which, says the poet,

of their own accord entered the assembly of the Gods;

if, in like manner, the shuttle would weave and the plectrum touch the
lyre, chief workmen would not want servants, nor masters slaves. Now the 1254ª1
instruments commonly so called are instruments of production, whilst a
possession is an instrument of action. From a shuttle we get something else
besides the use of it, whereas of a garment or of a bed there is only the use.
Further, as production and action are different in kind, and both require 5

instruments, the instruments which they employ must likewise differ in kind. But life is action and not production, and therefore the slave is the minister of action. Again, a possession is spoken of as a part is spoken of; for the part is not only a part of something else, but wholly belongs to it; and this is also true of a possession. The master is only the master of the slave; he does not belong to him, whereas the slave is not only the slave of his master, but wholly belongs to him. Hence we see what is the nature and office of a slave; he who is by nature not his own but another's man, is by nature a slave; and he may be said to be another's man who, being a slave, is also a possession. And a possession may be defined as an instrument of action, separable from the possessor.

5 . But is there any one thus intended by nature to be a slave, and for whom such a condition is expedient and right, or rather is not all slavery a violation of nature?

There is no difficulty in answering this question, on grounds both of reason and of fact. For that some should rule and others be ruled is a thing not only necessary, but expedient; from the hour of their birth, some are marked out for subjection, others for rule.

And there are many kinds both of rulers and subjects (and that rule is the better which is exercised over better subjects – for example, to rule over men is better than to rule over wild beasts; for the work is better which is executed by better workmen, and where one man rules and another is ruled, they may be said to have a work); for in all things which form a composite whole and which are made up of parts, whether continuous or discrete, a distinction between the ruling and the subject element comes to light. Such a duality exists in living creatures, originating from nature as a whole; even in things which have no life there is a ruling principle, as in a musical mode. But perhaps this is matter for a more popular investigation. A living creature consists in the first place of soul and body, and of these two, the one is by nature the ruler and the other the subject. But then we must look for the intentions of nature in things which retain their nature, and not in things which are corrupted. And therefore we must study the man who is in the most perfect state both of body and soul, for in him we shall see the true relation of the two: although in bad or corrupted natures the body will often appear to rule over the soul, because they are in an evil and unnatural condition. At all events we may firstly observe in living creatures both a despotical and a constitutional rule; for the soul rules the body with a despotical rule, whereas the intellect rules the appetites with a constitutional and royal rule. And it is clear that the rule of the soul over the body, and of the mind and the rational element over the passionate, is natural and expedient; whereas the equality of the two or the rule of the inferior is

always hurtful. The same holds good of animals in relation to men; for tame 10
animals have a better nature than wild and all tame animals are better off
when they are ruled by man; for then they are preserved. Again, the male is
by nature superior, and the female inferior; and the one rules, and the other is
ruled; this principle, of necessity, extends to all mankind. Where then there 15
is such a difference as that between soul and body, or between men and animals (as in the case of those whose business is to use their body, and who
can do nothing better), the lower sort are by nature slaves, and it is better 20
for them as for all inferiors that they should be under the rule of a master.
For he who can be, and therefore is, another's, and he who participates in
reason enough to apprehend, but not to have, is a slave by nature. Whereas
the lower animals cannot even apprehend reason, they obey their passions.
And indeed the use made of slaves and of tame animals is not very different;
for both with their bodies minister to the needs of life. Nature would like 25
to distinguish between the bodies of freemen and slaves, making the one
strong for servile labour, the other upright, and although useless for such
services, useful for political life in the arts both of war and peace. But the 30
opposite often happens – that some have the souls and others have the bodies
of freemen. And doubtless if men differed from one another in the mere
forms of their bodies as much as the statues of the Gods do from men, all 35
would acknowledge that the inferior class should be slaves of the superior.
And if this is true of the body, how much more just that a similar distinction
should exist in the soul? But the beauty of the body is seen, whereas the
beauty of the soul is not seen. It is clear, then, that some men are by nature 1255^a1
free, and others slaves, and that for these latter slavery is both expedient
and right.

6 . But that those who take the opposite view have in a certain way right on
their side, may be easily seen. For the words slavery and slave are used in two
senses. There is a slave or slavery by convention as well as by nature. The con- 5
vention is a sort of agreement – the convention by which whatever is taken in
war is supposed to belong to the victors. But this right many jurists impeach,
as they would an orator who brought forward an unconstitutional measure:
they detest the notion that, because one man has the power of doing violence and is superior in brute strength, another shall be his slave and subject. 10
Even among philosophers there is a difference of opinion. The origin of the
dispute, and what makes the views invade each other's territory, is as follows: in
some sense excellence, when furnished with means, has actually the greatest
power of exercising force: and as superior power is only found where there is 15
superior excellence of some kind, power seems to imply excellence, and the
dispute to be simply one about justice (for it is due to one party identifying
justice with goodwill, while the other identifies it with the mere rule of the

20   stronger). If these views are thus set out separately, the other views have no
      force or plausibility against the view that the superior in excellence ought
      to rule, or be master. Others, clinging, as they think, simply to a principle of
      justice (for convention is a sort of justice), assume that slavery in accordance
      with the custom of war is just, but at the same moment they deny this. For
25   what if the cause of the war be unjust? And again, no one would ever say that
      he is a slave who is unworthy to be a slave. Were this the case, men of the
      highest rank would be slaves and the children of slaves if they or their parents
      chanced to have been taken captive and sold. That is why people do not like
      to call themselves slaves, but confine the term to foreigners. Yet, in using this
30   language, they really mean the natural slave of whom we spoke at first; for it
      must be admitted that some are slaves everywhere, others nowhere. The same
      principle applies to nobility. People regard themselves as noble everywhere,
      and not only in their own country, but they deem foreigners noble only when
35   at home, thereby implying that there are two sorts of nobility and freedom,
      the one absolute, the other relative. The Helen of Theodectes says:

Who would presume to call me servant who am on both sides sprung from the stem
of the Gods?

      What does this mean but that they distinguish freedom and slavery, noble
1255^b1 and humble birth, by the two principles of good and evil? They think that
      as men and animals beget men and animals, so from good men a good man
      springs. Nature intends to do this often but cannot.
          We see then that there is some foundation for this difference of opinion,
5   and that all are not either slaves by nature or freemen by nature, and also that
      there is in some cases a marked distinction between the two classes, rendering
      it expedient and right for the one to be slaves and the others to be masters:
      the one practising obedience, the other exercising the authority and lordship
      which nature intended them to have. The abuse of this authority is injurious
10   to both: for the interests of part and whole, of body and soul, are the same,
      and the slave is a part of the master, a living but separated part of his bodily
      frame. Hence, where the relation of master and slave between them is natural
      they are friends and have a common interest, but where it rests merely on
15   convention and force the reverse is true.

                                        ...

                              Book 3, chs. 6–12

6 . Having determined these questions, we have next to consider whether
there is only one form of government or many, and if many, what they are,
and how many, and what are the differences between them.

A constitution is the arrangement of magistracies in a state, especially of the highest of all. The government is everywhere sovereign in the state, and the constitution is in fact the government. For example, in democracies the people are supreme, but in oligarchies, the few; and, therefore, we say that these two constitutions also are different: and so in other cases.

First, let us consider what is the purpose of a state, and how many forms of rule there are by which human society is regulated. We have already said, in the first part of this treatise, when discussing household management and the rule of a master, that man is by nature a political animal. And therefore, men, even when they do not require one another's help, desire to live together; not but that they are also brought together by their common interests in so far as they each attain to any measure of well-being. This is certainly the chief end, both of individuals and of states. And mankind meet together and maintain the political community also for the sake of mere life (in which there is possibly some noble element so long as the evils of existence do not greatly overbalance the good). And we all see that men cling to life even at the cost of enduring great misfortune, seeming to find in life a natural sweetness and happiness.

There is no difficulty in distinguishing the various kinds of rule; they have been often defined already in our popular discussions. The rule of a master, although the slave by nature and the master by nature have in reality the same interests, is nevertheless exercised primarily with a view to the interest of the master, but accidentally considers the slave, since, if the slave perish, the rule of the master perishes with him. On the other hand, the government of a wife and children and of a household, which we have called household management, is exercised in the first instance for the good of the governed or for the common good of both parties, but essentially for the good of the governed, as we see to be the case in medicine, gymnastic, and the arts in general, which are only accidentally concerned with the good of the artists themselves. For there is no reason why the trainer may not sometimes practise gymnastics, and the helmsman is always one of the crew. The trainer or the helmsman considers the good of those committed to his care. But, when he is one of the persons taken care of, he accidentally participates in the advantage, for the helmsman is also a sailor, and the trainer becomes one of those in training. And so in politics: when the state is framed upon the principle of equality and likeness, the citizens think that they ought to hold office by turns. Formerly, as is natural, everyone would take his turn of service; and then again, somebody else would look after his interest, just as he, while in office, had looked after theirs. But nowadays, for the sake of the advantage which is to be gained from the public revenues and from office, men want to be always in office. One might imagine that the rulers, being sickly, were only kept in health while they continued in office;

10

15

20

25

30

35

40

$1279^{a}1$

5

10

15

in that case we may be sure that they would be hunting after places. The conclusion is evident: that governments which have a regard to the common interest are constituted in accordance with strict principles of justice, and
20   are therefore true forms; but those which regard only the interest of the rulers are all defective and perverted forms, for they are despotic, whereas a state is a community of freemen.

7 . Having determined these points, we have next to consider how many forms of government there are, and what they are; and in the first place what are the true forms, for when they are determined the perversions of them
25   will at once be apparent. The words constitution and government have the same meaning, and the government, which is the supreme authority in states, must be in the hands of one, or of a few, or of the many. The true forms of
30   government, therefore, are those in which the one, or the few, or the many, govern with a view to the common interest; but governments which rule with a view to the private interest, whether of the one, or of the few, or of the many, are perversions. For the members of a state, if they are truly citizens, ought to participate in its advantages. Of forms of government in which one rules, we call that which regards the common interest, kingship; that in which more
35   than one, but not many, rule, aristocracy; and it is so called, either because the rulers are the best men, or because they have at heart the best interests of the state and of the citizens. But when the many administer the state for the common interest, the government is called by the generic name –
40   a constitution. And there is a reason for this use of language. One man or a
1279^{b}1   few may excel in excellence; but as the number increases it becomes more difficult for them to attain perfection in every kind of excellence, though they may in military excellence, for this is found in the masses. Hence in a constitutional government the fighting-men have the supreme power, and those who possess arms are the citizens.

    Of the above-mentioned forms, the perversions are as follows: – of
5   kingship, tyranny; of aristocracy, oligarchy; of constitutional government, democracy. For tyranny is a kind of monarchy which has in view the interest of the monarch only; oligarchy has in view the interest of the wealthy;
10   democracy, of the needy: none of them the common good of all.

8 . But there are difficulties about these forms of government, and it will therefore be necessary to state a little more at length the nature of each of them. For he who would make a philosophical study of the various sciences, and is not only concerned with practice, ought not to overlook or omit
15   anything, but to set forth the truth in every particular. Tyranny, as I was saying, is monarchy exercising the rule of a master over the political society; oligarchy is when men of property have the government in their hands; democracy, the

opposite, when the indigent, and not the men of property, are the rulers. And here arises the first of our difficulties, and it relates to the distinction just drawn. For democracy is said to be the government of the many. But what if the many are men of property and have the power in their hands? In like manner oligarchy is said to be the government of the few; but what if the poor are fewer than the rich, and have the power in their hands because they are stronger? In these cases the distinction which we have drawn between these different forms of government would no longer hold good.

Suppose, once more, that we add wealth to the few and poverty to the many, and name the governments accordingly – an oligarchy is said to be that in which the few and the wealthy, and a democracy that in which the many and the poor are the rulers – there will still be a difficulty. For, if the only forms of government are the ones already mentioned, how shall we describe those other governments also just mentioned by us, in which the rich are the more numerous and the poor are the fewer, and both govern in their respective states?

The argument seems to show that, whether in oligarchies or in democracies, the number of the governing body, whether the greater number, as in a democracy, or the smaller number, as in an oligarchy, is an accident due to the fact that the rich everywhere are few, and the poor numerous. But if so, there is a misapprehension of the causes of the difference between them. For the real difference between democracy and oligarchy is poverty and wealth. Wherever men rule by reason of their wealth, whether they be few or many, that is an oligarchy, and where the poor rule, that is a democracy. But in fact the rich are few and the poor many; for few are well-to-do, whereas freedom is enjoyed by all, and wealth and freedom are the grounds on which the two parties claim power in the state.

9 . Let us begin by considering the common definitions of oligarchy and democracy, and what is oligarchical and democratic justice. For all men cling to justice of some kind, but their conceptions are imperfect and they do not express the whole idea. For example, justice is thought by them to be, and is, equality – not, however, for all, but only for equals. And inequality is thought to be, and is, justice; neither is this for all, but only for unequals. When the persons are omitted, then men judge erroneously. The reason is that they are passing judgement on themselves, and most people are bad judges in their own case. And whereas justice implies a relation to persons as well as to things, and a just distribution, as I have already said in the *Ethics*, implies the same ratio between the persons and between the things, they agree about the equality of the things, but dispute about the equality of the persons, chiefly for the reason which I have just given – because they are bad judges in their own affairs; and secondly, because both the parties to the

argument are speaking of a limited and partial justice, but imagine themselves
to be speaking of absolute justice. For the one party, if they are unequal in
one respect, for example wealth, consider themselves to be unequal in all;
25   and the other party, if they are equal in one respect, for example free birth,
consider themselves to be equal in all. But they leave out the capital point.
For if men met and associated out of regard to wealth only, their share in the
state would be proportioned to their property, and the oligarchical doctrine
30   would then seem to carry the day. It would not be just that he who paid
one mina should have the same share of a hundred minae, whether of the
principal or of the profits, as he who paid the remaining ninety-nine. But
a state exists for the sake of a good life, and not for the sake of life only:
if life only were the object, slaves and brute animals might form a state,
but they cannot, for they have no share in happiness or in a life based on
35   choice. Nor does a state exist for the sake of alliance and security from injustice, nor yet for the sake of exchange and mutual intercourse; for then the
Tyrrhenians and the Carthaginians, and all who have commercial treaties with
one another, would be the citizens of one state. True, they have agreements
40   about imports, and engagements that they will do no wrong to one another,
1280^{b}1   and written articles of alliance. But there are no magistracies common to
the contracting parties; different states have each their own magistracies.
Nor does one state take care that the citizens of the other are such as they
ought to be, nor see that those who come under the terms of the treaty do
no wrong or wickedness at all, but only that they do no injustice to one
5   another. Whereas, those who care for good government take into consideration political excellence and defect. Whence it may be further inferred
that excellence must be the care of a state which is truly so called, and not
merely enjoys the name: for without this end the community becomes a mere
10   alliance which differs only in place from alliances of which the members
live apart; and law is only a convention, 'a surety to one another of justice',
as the sophist Lycophron says, and has no real power to make the citizens
good and just.

  This is obvious; for suppose distinct places, such as Corinth and Megara,
15   to be brought together so that their walls touched, still they would not be
one city, not even if the citizens had the right to intermarry, which is one of
the rights peculiarly characteristic of states. Again, if men dwelt at a distance
from one another, but not so far off as to have no intercourse, and there were
laws among them that they should not wrong each other in their exchanges,
20   neither would this be a state. Let us suppose that one man is a carpenter,
another a farmer, another a shoemaker, and so on, and that their number is
ten thousand: nevertheless if they have nothing in common but exchange,
alliance, and the like, that would not constitute a state. Why is this? Surely
not because they are at a distance from one another; for even supposing that

such a community were to meet in one place, but that each man had a house 25
of his own, which was in a manner his state, and that they made alliance with
one another, but only against evil-doers; still an accurate thinker would not
deem this to be a state, if their intercourse with one another was of the same
character after as before their union. It is clear then that a state is not a mere 30
society, having a common place, established for the prevention of mutual
crime and for the sake of exchange. These are conditions without which a
state cannot exist; but all of them together do not constitute a state, which
is a community of families and aggregations of families in well-being, for
the sake of a perfect and self-sufficing life. Such a community can only be 35
established among those who live in the same place and intermarry. Hence
there arise in cities family connexions, brotherhoods, common sacrifices,
amusements which draw men together. But these are created by friendship,
for to choose to live together is friendship. The end of the state is the good
life, and these are the means towards it. And the state is the union of families 40
and villages in a perfect and self-sufficing life, by which we mean a happy and 1281ª1
honourable life.

Our conclusion, then, is that political society exists for the sake of noble
actions, and not of living together. Hence they who contribute most to such
a society have a greater share in it than those who have the same or a greater 5
freedom or nobility of birth but are inferior to them in political excellence;
or than those who exceed them in wealth but are surpassed by them in
excellence.

From what has been said it will be clearly seen that all the partisans of
different forms of government speak of a part of justice only. 10

10 . There is also a doubt as to what is to be the supreme power in the state: –
Is it the multitude? Or the wealthy? Or the good? Or the one best man? Or a
tyrant? Any of these alternatives seems to involve disagreeable consequences.
If the poor, for example, because they are more in number, divide among
themselves the property of the rich – is not this unjust? No, by heaven (will be 15
the reply), for the supreme authority justly willed it. But if this is not extreme
injustice, what is? Again, when in the first division all has been taken, and the
majority divide anew the property of the minority, is it not evident, if this goes
on, that they will ruin the state? Yet surely, excellence is not the ruin of those 20
who possess it, nor is justice destructive of a state; and therefore this law of
confiscation clearly cannot be just. If it were, all the acts of a tyrant must of
necessity be just; for he only coerces other men by superior power, just as
the multitude coerce the rich. But is it just then that the few and the wealthy 25
should be the rulers? And what if they, in like manner, rob and plunder the
people – is this just? If so, the other case will likewise be just. But there can
be no doubt that all these things are wrong and unjust.

Then ought the good to rule and have supreme power? But in that case
30   everybody else, being excluded from power, will be dishonoured. For the
offices of a state are posts of honour; and if one set of men always hold them,
the rest must be deprived of them. Then will it be well that the one best man
should rule? That is still more oligarchical, for the number of those who
35   are dishonoured is thereby increased. Someone may say that it is bad in any
case for a man, subject as he is to all the accidents of human passion, to
have the supreme power, rather than the law. But what if the law itself be
democratic or oligarchical, how will that help us out of our difficulties? Not
at all; the same consequences will follow.

11 . Most of these questions may be reserved for another occasion. The prin-
40   ciple that the multitude ought to be in power rather than the few best might
seem to be solved and to contain some difficulty and perhaps even truth.
For the many, of whom each individual is not a good man, when they meet
$1281^b 1$ together may be better than the few good, if regarded not individually but
collectively, just as a feast to which many contribute is better than a dinner
provided out of a single purse. For each individual among the many has a
5   share of excellence and practical wisdom, and when they meet together, just
as they become in a manner one man, who has many feet, and hands, and
senses, so too with regard to their character and thought. Hence the many
are better judges than a single man of music and poetry; for some understand
one part, and some another, and among them they understand the whole.
10   There is a similar combination of qualities in good men, who differ from any
individual of the many, as the beautiful are said to differ from those who are
not beautiful, and works of art from realities, because in them the scattered
elements are combined, although, if taken separately, the eye of one person
or some other feature in another person would be fairer than in the pic-
15   ture. Whether this principle can apply to every democracy, and to all bodies
of men, is not clear. Or rather, by heaven, in some cases it is impossible to
apply; for the argument would equally hold about brutes; and wherein, it
20   will be asked, do some men differ from brutes? But there may be bodies of
men about whom our statement is nevertheless true. And if so, the difficulty
which has been already raised, and also another which is akin to it – viz. what
25   power should be assigned to the mass of freemen and citizens, who are not
rich and have no personal merit – are both solved. There is still a danger in
allowing them to share the great offices of state, for their folly will lead them
into error, and their dishonesty into crime. But there is a danger also in not
30   letting them share, for a state in which many poor men are excluded from
office will necessarily be full of enemies. The only way of escape is to assign
to them some deliberative and judicial functions. For this reason Solon and
certain other legislators give them the power of electing to offices, and of

calling the magistrates to account, but they do not allow them to hold office singly. When they meet together their perceptions are quite good enough, 35 and combined with the better class they are useful to the state (just as impure food when mixed with what is pure sometimes makes the entire mass more wholesome than a small quantity of the pure would be), but each individual, left to himself, forms an imperfect judgement. On the other hand the popular form of government involves certain difficulties. In the first place, it might be objected that he who can judge of the healing of a sick man would be one who 40 could himself heal his disease, and make him whole – that is, in other words, the physician; and so in all professions and arts. As, then, the physician ought 1282ª1 to be called to account by physicians, so ought men in general to be called to account by their peers. But physicians are of three kinds: – there is the ordinary practitioner, and there is the master physician, and thirdly the man educated in the art: in all arts there is such a class; and we attribute the power of judging 5 to them quite as much as to professors of the art. Secondly, does not the same principle apply to elections? For a right election can only be made by those who have knowledge; those who know geometry, for example, will choose a geometrician rightly, and those who know how to steer, a pilot; and, even 10 if there be some occupations and arts in which private persons share in the ability to choose, they certainly cannot choose better than those who know. So that, according to this argument, neither the election of magistrates, nor the calling of them to account, should be entrusted to the many. Yet possibly these objections are to a great extent met by our old answer, that if the people 15 are not utterly degraded, although individually they may be worse judges than those who have special knowledge, as a body they are as good or better. Moreover, there are some arts whose products are not judged of solely, or best, by the artists themselves, namely those arts whose products are recognized even by those who do not possess the art; for example, the knowledge of the house is not limited to the builder only; the user, or, in other words, the 20 master, of the house will actually be a better judge than the builder, just as the pilot will judge better of a rudder than the carpenter, and the guest will judge better of a feast than the cook.

This difficulty seems now to be sufficiently answered, but there is another akin to it. That inferior persons should have authority in greater matters 25 than the good would appear to be a strange thing, yet the election and calling to account of the magistrates is the greatest of all. And these, as I was saying, are functions which in some states are assigned to the people, for the assembly is supreme in all such matters. Yet persons of any age, and having but a small property qualification, sit in the assembly and deliberate and judge, 30 although for the great officers of state, such as treasurers and generals, a high qualification is required. This difficulty may be solved in the same manner as the preceding, and the present practice of democracies may be really

defensible. For the power does not reside in the juryman, or counsellor, or
35   member of the assembly, but in the court, and the council, and the assembly,
of which the aforesaid individuals – counsellor, assemblyman, juryman – are
only parts or members. And for this reason the many may claim to have a
higher authority than the few; for the people, and the council, and the courts
40   consist of many persons, and their property collectively is greater than the
property of one or of a few individuals holding great offices. But enough of
this.

1282^{b}1   The discussion of the first question shows nothing so clearly as that
laws, when good, should be supreme; and that the magistrate or magistrates
should regulate those matters only on which the laws are unable to speak
5   with precision owing to the difficulty of any general principle embracing
all particulars. But what are good laws has not yet been clearly explained;
the old difficulty remains. The goodness or badness, justice or injustice,
of laws varies of necessity with the constitutions of states. This, however,
10   is clear, that the laws must be adapted to the constitutions. But, if so, true
forms of government will of necessity have just laws, and perverted forms of
government will have unjust laws.

15   12 . In all sciences and arts the end is a good, and the greatest good and in the
highest degree a good in the most authoritative of all – this is the political
science of which the good is justice, in other words, the common interest. All
men think justice to be a sort of equality; and to a certain extent they agree
20   with what we have said in our philosophical works about ethics. For they say
that what is just is just *for* someone and that it should be equal for equals.
But there still remains a question: equality or inequality of what? Here is a
difficulty which calls for political speculation. For very likely some persons
will say that offices of state ought to be unequally distributed according to
superior excellence, in whatever respect, of the citizen, although there is
25   no other difference between him and the rest of the community; for those
who differ in any one respect have different rights and claims. But, surely, if
this is true, the complexion or height of a man, or any other advantage, will
30   be a reason for his obtaining a greater share of political rights. The error here
lies upon the surface, and may be illustrated from the other arts and sciences.
When a number of flute-players are equal in their art, there is no reason why
those of them who are better born should have better flutes given to them;
for they will not play any better on the flute, and the superior instrument
should be reserved for him who is the superior artist. If what I am saying is
35   still obscure, it will be made clearer as we proceed. For if there were a superior
flute-player who was far inferior in birth and beauty, although either of these
40   may be a greater good than the art of flute-playing and may excel flute-
playing in a greater ratio than he excels the others in his art, still he ought to

have the best flutes given to him, unless the advantages of wealth and birth   1283ᵃ1
contribute to excellence in flute-playing, which they do not. Moreover, upon
this principle any good may be compared with any other. For if a given height
may be measured against wealth and against freedom, height in general may   5
be so measured. Thus if A excels in height more than B in excellence, even if
excellence in general excels height still more, all goods will be comparable;
for if a certain amount is better than some other, it is clear that some other
will be equal. But since no such comparison can be made, it is evident that
there is good reason why in politics men do not ground their claim to office   10
on every sort of inequality. For if some be slow, and others swift, that is no
reason why the one should have little and the others much; it is in gymnastic
contests that such excellence is rewarded. Whereas the rival claims of candidates for office can only be based on the possession of elements which enter   15
into the composition of a state. And therefore the well-born, or free-born,
or rich, may with good reason claim office; for holders of offices must be
freemen and tax-payers: a state can be no more composed entirely of poor
men than entirely of slaves. But if wealth and freedom are necessary ele-   20
ments, justice and valour are equally so; for without the former qualities a
state cannot exist at all, without the latter not well.

...

Book 7, chs. 1–3

1 . He who would duly inquire about the best form of a state ought first to
determine which is the most eligible life; while this remains uncertain the   15
best form of the state must also be uncertain; for, in the natural order of
things, those men may be expected to lead the best life who are governed
in the best manner of which their circumstances admit. We ought therefore
to ascertain, first of all, which is the most generally eligible life, and then   20
whether the same life is or is not best for the state and for individuals.

Assuming that enough has been already said in discussions outside the
school concerning the best life, we will now only repeat what is contained
in them. Certainly no one will dispute the propriety of that partition of
goods which separates them into three classes, viz. external goods, goods   25
of the body, and goods of the soul, or deny that the happy man must have
all three. For no one would maintain that he is happy who has not in him
a particle of courage or temperance or justice or practical wisdom, who is
afraid of every insect which flutters past him, and will commit any crime,   30
however great, in order to gratify his lust for meat or drink, who will sacrifice
his dearest friend for the sake of half a farthing, and is as feeble and false
in mind as a child or a madman. These propositions are almost universally

35   acknowledged as soon as they are uttered, but men differ about the degree
     or relative superiority of this or that good. Some think that a very moderate
     amount of excellence is enough, but set no limit to their desires for wealth,
     property, power, reputation, and the like. To them we shall reply by an appeal
40   to facts, which easily prove that mankind does not acquire or preserve the
1323^{b}1 excellences by the help of external goods, but external goods by the help of the
     excellences, and that happiness, whether consisting in pleasure or excellence,
     or both, is more often found with those who are most highly cultivated in
     their mind and in their character, and have only a moderate share of external
5   goods, than among those who possess external goods to a useless extent but
     are deficient in higher qualities; and this is not only a matter of experience,
     but, if reflected upon, will easily appear to be in accordance with reason. For,
     whereas external goods have a limit, like any other instrument, and all things
     useful are useful for a purpose, and where there is too much of them they
10   must either do harm, or at any rate be of no use, to their possessors, every
     good of the soul, the greater it is, is also of greater use, if the epithet useful
     as well as noble is appropriate to such subjects. No proof is required to show
     that the best state of one thing in relation to another corresponds in degree
15   of excellence to the interval between the natures of which we say that these
     very states are states: so that, if the soul is more noble than our possessions
     or our bodies, both absolutely and in relation to us, it must be admitted that
     the best state of either has a similar ratio to the other. Again, it is for the sake
     of the soul that goods external and goods of the body are desirable at all, and
20   all wise men ought to choose them for the sake of the soul, and not the soul
     for the sake of them.
         Let us acknowledge then that each one has just so much of happiness
     as he has of excellence and wisdom, and of excellent and wise action. The
     gods are a witness to us of this truth, for they are happy and blessed, not
     by reason of any external good, but in themselves and by reason of their
25   own nature. And herein of necessity lies the difference between good for-
     tune and happiness; for external goods come of themselves, and chance is
     the author of them, but no one is just or temperate by or through chance.
30   In like manner, and by a similar train of argument, the happy state may be
     shown to be that which is best and which acts rightly; and it cannot act
     rightly without doing right actions, and neither individual nor state can
     do right actions without excellence and wisdom. Thus, the courage, jus-
35   tice, and wisdom of a state have the same form and nature as the qualities
     which give the individual who possesses them the name of just, wise or
     temperate.
         Thus much may suffice by way of preface: for I could not avoid touching
     upon these questions, neither could I go through all the arguments affecting
     them; these are the business of another science.

Let us assume then that the best life, both for individuals and states, is the life of excellence, when excellence has external goods enough for the performance of good actions. If there are any who dispute our assertion, we will in this treatise pass them over, and consider their objections hereafter.

2 . There remains to be discussed the question, whether the happiness of the individual is the same as that of the state, or different. Here again there can be no doubt – no one denies that they are the same. For those who hold that the well-being of the individual consists in his wealth, also think that riches make the happiness of the whole state, and those who value most highly the life of a tyrant deem that city the happiest which rules over the greatest number; while they who approve an individual for his excellence say that the more excellent a city is, the happier it is. Two points here present themselves for consideration: first, which is the more desirable life, that of a citizen who is a member of a state, or that of an alien who has no political ties; and again, which is the best form of constitution or the best condition of a state, either on the supposition that political privileges are desirable for all, or for a majority only? Since the good of the state and not of the individual is the proper subject of political thought and speculation, and we are engaged in a political discussion, while the first of these two points has a secondary interest for us, the latter will be the main subject of our inquiry.

Now it is evident that that form of government is best in which every man, whoever he is, can act best and live happily. But even those who agree in thinking that the life of excellence is the most desirable raise a question, whether the life of business and politics is or is not more desirable than one which is wholly independent of external goods, I mean than a contemplative life, which by some is maintained to be the only one worthy of a philosopher. For these two lives – the life of the philosopher and the life of the statesman – appear to have been preferred by those who have been most keen in the pursuit of excellence, both in our own and in other ages. Which is the better is a question of no small amount; for the wise man, like the wise state, will necessarily regulate his life according to the best end. There are some who think that while a despotic rule over others is the greatest injustice, to exercise a constitutional rule over them, even though not unjust, is a great impediment to a man's individual well-being. Others take an opposite view; they maintain that the true life of man is the practical and political, and that every excellence admits of being practised, quite as much by statesmen and rulers as by private individuals. Others, again, are of the opinion that arbitrary and tyrannical rule alone makes for happiness; indeed, in some states the entire aim both of the laws and of the constitution is to give men despotic power over their neighbours. And, therefore, although in most cities the laws may be said generally to be in a chaotic state,

40
1324ª1

5

10

15

20

25

30

35

40
1324ᵇ1

5

still, if they aim at anything, they aim at the maintenance of power: thus in
Lacedaemon and Crete the system of education and the greater part of the
10   laws are framed with a view to war. And in all nations which are able to gratify their ambition military power is held in esteem, for example among the
Scythians and Persians and Thracians and Celts. In some nations there are even
laws tending to stimulate the warlike virtues, as at Carthage, where we are
told that men obtain the honour of wearing as many armlets as they have
15   served campaigns. There was once a law in Macedonia that he who had not
killed an enemy should wear a halter, and among the Scythians no one who
had not slain his man was allowed to drink out of the cup which was handed
round at a certain feast. Among the Iberians, a warlike nation, the number
20   of enemies whom a man has slain is indicated by the number of obelisks
which are fixed in the earth round his tomb; and there are numerous practices among other nations of a like kind, some of them established by law and
others by custom. Yet to a reflecting mind it must appear very strange that
the statesman should be always considering how he can dominate and
25   tyrannize over others, whether they are willing or not. How can that which is
not even lawful be the business of the statesman or the legislator? Unlawful
it certainly is to rule without regard to justice, for there may be might where
there is no right. The other arts and sciences offer no parallel; a physician is
30   not expected to persuade or coerce his patients, nor a pilot the passengers in
his ship. Yet most men appear to think that the art of despotic government
is statesmanship, and what men affirm to be unjust and inexpedient in their
own case they are not ashamed of practising towards others; they demand
35   just rule for themselves, but where other men are concerned they care
nothing about it. Such behaviour is irrational; unless the one party is, and
the other is not, born to serve, in which case men have a right to command,
not indeed all their fellows, but only those who are intended to be subjects;
40   just as we ought not to hunt men, whether for food or sacrifice, but only
those animals which may be hunted for food or sacrifice, that is to say, such
1325ᵃ1   wild animals as are eatable. And surely there may be a city happy in isolation,
which we will assume to be well-governed (for it is quite possible that a city
thus isolated might be well-administered and have good laws); but such
a city would not be constituted with any view to war or the conquest of
5   enemies – all that sort of thing must be excluded. Hence we see very plainly
that warlike pursuits, although generally to be deemed honourable, are not
the supreme end of all things, but only means. And the good lawgiver should
10   inquire how states and races of men and communities may participate in a
good life, and in the happiness which is attainable by them. His enactments
will not be always the same; and where there are neighbours he will have
to see what sort of studies should be practised in relation to their several
characters, or how the measures appropriate in relation to each are to be

adopted. The end at which the best form of government should aim may be
properly made a matter of future consideration.   15

3 . Let us now address those who, while they agree that the life of excellence
is the most desirable, differ about the manner of practising it. For some
renounce political power, and think that the life of the freeman is different
from the life of the statesman and the best of all; but others think the life of   20
the statesman best. The argument of the latter is that he who does nothing
cannot do well, and that acting well is identical with happiness. To both we
say: 'you are partly right and partly wrong'. The first class are right in affirming
that the life of the freeman is better than the life of the despot; for there is   25
nothing noble in having the use of a slave, in so far as he is a slave; or in
issuing commands about necessary things. But it is an error to suppose that
every sort of rule is despotic like that of a master over slaves, for there is as
great a difference between rule over freemen and rule over slaves as there is
between slavery by nature and freedom by nature, about which I have said   30
enough at the commencement of this treatise. And it is equally a mistake to
place inactivity above action, for happiness is activity, and the actions of the
just and wise are the realization of much that is noble.

But perhaps someone, accepting these premises, may still maintain that
supreme power is the best of all things, because the possessors of it are   35
able to perform the greatest number of noble actions. If so, the man who
is able to rule, instead of giving up anything to his neighbour, ought rather to
take away his power; and the father should care nothing for his son, nor the
son for his father, nor friend for friend; they should not bestow a thought on
one another in comparison with this higher object, for the best is the most   40
desirable and 'acting well' is the best. There might be some truth in such a
view if we assume that robbers and plunderers attain the chief good. But this $1325^{b}1$
can never be; their hypothesis is false. For the actions of a ruler cannot really
be honourable, unless he is as much superior to other men as a man is to a
woman, or a father to his children, or a master to his slaves. And therefore he   5
who violates the law can never recover by any success, however great, what
he has already lost in departing from excellence. For equals the honourable
and the just consist in sharing alike, as is just and equal. But that the unequal
should be given to equals, and the unlike to those who are like, is contrary to
nature, and nothing which is contrary to nature is good. If, therefore, there   10
is anyone superior in excellence and in the power of performing the best
actions, he is the man we ought to follow and obey, but he must have the
capacity for action as well as excellence.

If we are right in our view, and happiness is assumed to be acting well, the   15
active life will be the best, both for every city collectively, and for individuals.
Not that a life of action must necessarily have relation to others, as some

persons think, nor are those ideas only to be regarded as practical which are pursued for the sake of practical results, but much more the thoughts and
20 contemplations which are independent and complete in themselves; since acting well, and therefore a certain kind of action, is an end, and even in the case of external actions the directing mind is most truly said to act. Neither, again, is it necessary that states which are cut off from others and choose to
25 live alone should be inactive; for activity, as well as other things, may take place by sections; there are many ways in which the sections of a state act upon one another. The same thing is equally true of every individual. If this were otherwise, the gods and the universe, who have no external actions over
30 and above their own energies, would be far enough from perfection. Hence it is evident that the same life is best for each individual, and for states and for mankind collectively.

CICERO

MARCUS TULLIUS CICERO was born on 3 January 106 BCE into a
wealthy family in Arpinum. As a young man he went to Rome to study
and by the year 70 BCE had established himself as the leading advocate in Rome.
At the same time he launched himself on a political career, being elected
praetor for 66, and finally – the highest honor the Roman republic could
bestow – consul for 63. He was, both at the time and since, recognized as the
most brilliant orator of his day and his forensic attack on the Senate rebel
Cataline remains a masterpiece of political invective. He was unusually principled for a Roman politician of the time, a key weakness in the struggles
that saw the younger, equally brilliant but much more ruthless Gaius Julius
Caesar eventually defeat Cicero's friend and ally Pompey and overthrow the
republic, creating what would become the Roman empire. Always a man
with intellectual interests, in the last few years of his life he wrote a number
of treatises of moral and political topics (most especially *On Duties*, excerpted
here) as well as publishing his speeches, all of which show the range of his classical learning and the range of influences upon him. He also left a collection
of 900 letters which were published after his death, which means we know
more about him that about almost any other comparable figure in antiquity.
In his final years he sought to prevent the decline of the republic and the rise
of what he saw as tyranny, opposing especially the second triumvirate, dominated by Caesar. The attempt was as brave as it was useless. On 7 December
42 BCE, on the orders of Caesar, Cicero was killed.

From *On Duties*

Book 1, 53–60

(53) There are indeed several degrees of fellowship among men. To move from
the one that is unlimited, next there is a closer one of the same race, tribe and
tongue, through which men are bound strongly to one another. More intimate
still is that of the same city, as citizens have many things that are shared
with one another: the forum, temples, porticoes and roads, laws and legal
rights, law-courts and political elections; and besides these acquaintances
and companionship, and those business and commercial transactions that

many of them make with many others. A tie narrower still is that of the fellowship between relations: moving from that vast fellowship of the human race we end up with a confined and limited one.

(54) For since it is by nature common to all animals that they have a drive to procreate, the first fellowship exists within marriage itself, and the next with one's children. Then, there is the one house in which everything is shared. Indeed that is the principle of a city and the seed-bed, as it were, of a political community. Next there follow bonds between brothers, and then between first cousins and second cousins, who cannot be contained in one house and go out to other houses, as if to colonies. Finally there follow marriages and those connections of marriage from which even more relations arise. In such propagation and increase political communities have their origin. Moreover, the bonding of blood holds men together by good-will and by love; (55) for it is a great thing to have the same ancestral memorials, to practise the same religious rites, and to share common ancestral tombs.

Of all fellowships, however, none is more important, and none stronger, than when good men of similar conduct are bound by familiarity. For honourableness – the thing that I so often mention – moves us, even if we see it in someone else, and makes us friends of him in whom it seems to reside. (56) (All virtue indeed lures us to itself and leads us to love those in whom it seems to reside, but justice and liberality do so the most.) Moreover, nothing is more lovable and nothing more tightly binding than similarity in conduct that is good. For when men have similar pursuits and inclinations, it comes about that each one is as much delighted with the other as he is with himself; the result is what Pythagoras wanted in friendship, that several be united into one. Important also are the common bonds that are created by kindnesses reciprocally given and received, which, provided that they are mutual and gratefully received, bind together those concerned in an unshakeable fellowship.

(57) But when you have surveyed everything with reason and spirit, of all fellowships none is more serious, and none dearer, than that of each of us with the republic. Parents are dear, and children, relatives and acquaintances are dear, but our country has on its own embraced all the affections of all of us. What good man would hesitate to face death on her behalf, if it would do her a service? How much more detestable, then, is the monstrousness of those who have savaged their country with all manner of crime and who have been, and are still, engaged in destroying her utterly?

(58) Now were there a comparison, or competition, as to who ought most to receive our dutiful services, our country and our parents would be foremost; for we are obliged to them for the greatest kindnesses. Next would be our children and our whole household, which looks to us alone and can have no other refuge. Then our relations, who are congenial to us and with whom even our fortunes are generally shared. Therefore whatever is

necessary to support life is most owed to those whom I have just mentioned; on the other hand a shared life and a shared living, counsel and conversation, encouragement, comfort, and sometimes even reproofs, flourish most of all in friendships; and friendship is most pleasing when it is cemented by similarity of conduct.

(59) But, one ought when bestowing all these dutiful services to look at what each person most greatly needs, and what each would or would not be able to secure without our help. Thus the degrees of ties of relationship will not be the same as those of circumstance. Some duties are owed to one group of people rather than to another. You should, for example, assist your neighbour sooner than your brother or companion in gathering his harvest; but you should in a suit in the lawcourts defend a relative or friend rather than your neighbour.

In every case of duty, therefore, considerations such as these ought to be examined, and we should adopt this habit and should practise so that we can become good calculators of our duties, and can see by adding and subtracting what is the sum that remains; from this you can understand how much is owed to each person. (60) But neither doctors nor generals nor orators are able, however much they have taken to heart advice about their art, to achieve anything very worthy of praise without experience and practice. Similarly, advice on observing duty certainly has been handed down, as I myself am now handing it down, but a matter of such importance also demands experience and practice. And now I have said enough on the question of how honourableness, upon which duty hangs, is derived from those things that constitute the justice of human fellowship.

MARCUS AURELIUS

MARCUS AURELIUS ANTONINUS was born in 121 CE, born into a family which had ruled Rome for generations. As a young man he became fascinated by philosophy and rhetoric, being tutored by a range of Greek and Roman thinkers, before coming under the spell of the most influential philosophy of the day, Stoicism. On becoming emperor in 161, at the age of forty, Marcus realized that the empire was besieged from both within and without. Much of his time as emperor was spent on campaign against barbarian threats to the empire and it was during these campaigns that he began what amounted to a philosophical diary "to myself" as he called it: a collection of philosophical maxims, judgements, and reflections written in Greek and ranging across an astonishingly wide range of concerns. Marcus was a remarkably honest man, both in his writings (which were not intended for publication) and in his dealings as emperor. He has been seen, since the publication of his "meditations," as his reflections have become known, as the very paradigm of the Stoic sage, yet he was also an extremely skilled warrior and diplomat with a true vision for his empire that was largely in tune with the Stoic philosophy he had developed. He never, however, had the chance to develop it. On campaign as usual in 180 CE he fell ill and was dead within days.

From *Meditations*

Book 2, 17

17 . Of the life of man the duration is but a point, its substance streaming away, its perception dim, the fabric of the entire body prone to decay, and the soul a vortex, and fortune incalculable, and fame uncertain. In a word all the things of the body are as a river, and the things of the soul as a dream and a vapour; and life is a warfare and a pilgrim's sojourn, and fame after death is only forgetfulness. What then is it that can help us on our way? One thing and one alone – Philosophy; and this consists in keeping the divine 'genius' within pure and unwronged, lord of all pleasures and pains, doing nothing aimlessly or with deliberate falsehood and hypocrisy, independent of another's action or

inaction; and furthermore welcoming what happens and is allotted, as issuing from the same source, whatever it be, from which the man himself has issued; and above all waiting for death with a good grace as being but a setting free of the elements of which every thing living is made up. But if there be nothing terrible in each thing being continuously changed into another thing, why should a man look askance at the change and dissolution of all things? For it is in the way of Nature, and in the way of Nature there can be no evil.

...

Book 6, 36 and 44

36 . Asia, Europe, corners of the Universe: the whole Ocean a drop in the Universe: Athos but a little clod therein: all the present a point in Eternity:— everything on a tiny scale, so easily changed, so quickly vanished.

All things come from that one source, from that ruling Reason of the Universe, either under a primary impulse from it or by way of consequence. And therefore the gape of the lion's jaws and poison and all noxious things, such as thorns and mire, are but after-results of the grand and the beautiful. Look not then on these as alien to that which thou dost reverence, but turn thy thoughts to the one source of all things.

...

44 . If the Gods have taken counsel about me and the things to befall me, doubtless they have taken good counsel. For it is not easy even to imagine a God without wisdom. And what motive could they have impelling them to do me evil? For what advantage could thereby accrue to them or to the Universe which is their special care? But if the Gods have taken no counsel for me individually, yet they have in any case done so for the interests of the Universe, and I am bound to welcome and make the best of those things also that befall as a necessary corollary to those interests. But if so be they take counsel about nothing at all – an impious belief – in good sooth let us have no more of sacrifices and prayers and oaths, nor do any other of these things every one of which is a recognition of the Gods as if they were at our side and dwelling amongst us – but if so be, I say, they do not take counsel about any of our concerns, it is still in my power to take counsel about myself, and it is for me to consider my own interest. And that is to every man's interest which is agreeable to his own constitution and nature. But my nature is rational and civic; my city and country, as Antoninus, is Rome; as a man, the world. The things then that are of advantage to these communities, these, and no other, are good for me.

...

Book 9, 1 and 9

1 . Injustice is impiety. For in that the Nature of the Universe has fashioned rational creatures for the sake of one another with a view to mutual benefit based upon worth, but by no means for harm, the transgressor of her will acts with obvious impiety against the most venerable of Deities.

And the liar too acts impiously with respect to the same Goddess. For the Nature of the Universe is the Nature of the things that are. And the things that are have an intimate connexion with all the things that have ever been. Moreover this Nature is named Truth, and is the primary cause of all that is true. The willing liar then is impious in so far as his deceit is a wrong-doing; and the unwilling liar too, for he is out of tune with the Nature of the Whole, and an element of disorder by being in conflict with the Nature of an orderly Universe; for he is in conflict who allows himself, as far as his conduct goes, to be carried into opposition to what is true. And whereas he had previously been endowed by nature with the means of distinguishing false from true, by neglecting to use them he has lost the power.

Again he acts impiously who seeks after pleasure as a good thing and eschews pain as an evil. For such a man must inevitably find frequent fault with the Universal Nature as unfair in its apportionments to the worthless and the worthy, since the worthless are often lapped in pleasures and possess the things that make for pleasure, while the worthy meet with pain and the things that make for pain. Moreover he that dreads pain will some day be in dread of something that must be in the world. And there we have impiety at once. And he that hunts after pleasures will not hold his hand from injustice. And this is palpable impiety.

But those, who are of one mind with Nature and would walk in her ways, must hold a neutral attitude towards those things towards which the Universal Nature is neutral – for she would not be the Maker of both were she not neutral towards both. So he clearly acts with impiety who is not himself neutral towards pain and pleasure, death and life, good report and ill report, things which the Nature of the Universe treats with neutrality. And by the Universal Nature treating these with neutrality I mean that all things happen neutrally in a chain of sequence to things that come into being and to their after products by some primeval impulse of Providence, in accordance with which She was impelled by some primal impulse to this making of an ordered Universe, when She had conceived certain principles for all that was to be, and allocated the powers generative of substances and changes and successions such as we see.

···

9 . All that share in a common element have an affinity for their own kind. The trend of all that is earthy is to earth; fluids all run together; it is the same

with the aerial; so that only interposing obstacles and force can keep them apart. Fire indeed has a tendency to rise by reason of the elemental fire, but is so quick to be kindled in sympathy with all fire here below that every sort of matter, a whit drier than usual, is easily kindled owing to its having fewer constituents calculated to offer resistance to its kindling. So then all that shares in the Universal Intelligent Nature has as strong an affinity towards what is akin, aye even a stronger. For the measure of its superiority to all other things is the measure of its readiness to blend and coalesce with that which is akin to it.

At any rate to begin with among irrational creatures we find swarms and herds and bird-colonies and, as it were, love-associations. For already at that stage there are souls, and the bond of affinity shews itself in the higher form to a degree of intensity not found in plants or stones or timber. But among rational creatures are found political communities and friendships and households and gatherings, and in wars treaties and armistices. But in things still higher a sort of unity in separation even exists, as in the stars. Thus the ascent to the higher form is able to effect a sympathetic connexion even among things which are separate.

...

Book 12, 36

36 . Man, thou hast been a citizen in this World-City, what matters it to thee if for five years or a hundred? For under its laws equal treatment is meted out to all. What hardship then is there in being banished from the city, not by a tyrant or an unjust judge but by Nature who settled thee in it? So might a praetor who commissions a comic actor, dismiss him from the stage. *But I have not played my five acts, but only three.* Very possibly, but in life three acts count as a full play. For he, that is responsible for thy composition originally and thy dissolution now, decides when it is complete. But thou art responsible for neither. Depart then with a good grace, for he also that dismisses thee is gracious.

PLATO

PLATO was born around the year 428 BCE, the scion of a distinguished and Aristocratic Athenian family with known and pronounced anti-democratic sympathies and was expected eventually to play a part in oligarchic politics himself. However, as he himself tells it (in his *Seventh Letter*, reprinted here), his meeting with Socrates changed his life. Socrates, an artisan by birth, was an enormously charismatic figure, and quite clearly a teacher of genius, gathering around him some of the most brilliant men of his day. Plato became one of his most ardent admirers. The circle around Socrates was characterized by a dedication to the development of true knowledge (as they understood it) and this often took a broadly anti-democratic form: Socrates himself was a man who often criticized the Athenian democracy for its espousal of "mere" opinion over knowledge. It is therefore unsurprising that when Socrates was charged with worshipping false gods and corrupting Athenian youth by the democracy and then sentenced to death by means of ingesting hemlock, Plato should have developed a distaste for Greek democracy that emerges in most of his writings from his early middle age until his death. However, it is worth bearing in mind also that Socrates equally disputed the oligarchs (for example, refusing a direct order of Plato's relative Critias when the latter was one of the so-called "thirty tyrants" who briefly seized power in Athens in 404). Socrates was a prickly pear for *any* established political view, a point worth remembering when considering the claims that Plato was an anti-democrat. He was also an anti-oligarch! Almost all Plato's writings until his extreme old age feature Socrates as the protagonist and clearly one of his intentions in writing as he did was to vindicate his master's memory and methods (though there is much scholarly debate about how much of his own "doctrine," if any, Plato puts into the mouth of his Socrates). After Socrates' death, Plato abandoned any idea of "going into politics" as his family had expected and instead set up a school – we would call it a university – called the Academy which rapidly became the most famous in the Greek world. While head of the Academy, Plato published his "dialogues," his philosophical writings, which included a number directly concerned with politics, most especially the *Republic* (widely considered his masterpiece), the *Statesman*, and the *Laws*. In keeping with his philosophic precepts he (and the Academy) also acted in politics, usually working to sustain or establish "constitutional" regimes. Most famously, he intervened twice in the tangled politics and international relations of the city of Syracuse, an intervention from which he barely escaped with his life, and of which he writes an account in the *Seventh Letter*. Still head of the Academy, still writing and thinking, he died in about 347 at the age of eighty-one.

From *The Epistles*

Seventh Letter, 324–326b

Plato to the friends and followers of Dion,

…

When I was a young man I had the same ambition as many others: I thought of entering public life as soon as I came of age. And certain happenings in public affairs favored me, as follows. The constitution we then had, being anathema   c to many, was overthrown; and a new government was set up consisting of fifty-one men, two groups – one of eleven and another of ten – to police the market place and perform other necessary duties in the city and the Piraeus respectively, and above them thirty other officers with absolute powers. Some   d of these men happened to be relatives and acquaintances of mine, and they invited me to join them at once in what seemed to be a proper undertaking. My attitude toward them is not surprising, because I was young. I thought that they were going to lead the city out of the unjust life she had been living and establish her in the path of justice, so that I watched them eagerly to see what they would do. But as I watched them they showed in a short time that the preceding constitution had been a precious thing. Among their other deeds   e they named Socrates, an older friend of mine whom I should not hesitate to call the wisest and justest man of that time, as one of a group sent to arrest a certain citizen who was to be put to death illegally, planning thereby to make   325 Socrates willy-nilly a party to their actions. But he refused, risking the utmost danger rather than be an associate in their impious deeds. When I saw all this and other like things of no little consequence, I was appalled and drew back from that reign of injustice. Not long afterwards the rule of the Thirty was overthrown and with it the entire constitution; and once more I felt the desire, though this time less strongly, to take part in public and political affairs.   b Now many deplorable things occurred during those troubled days, and it is not surprising that under cover of the revolution too many old enmities were avenged; but in general those who returned from exile acted with great restraint. By some chance, however, certain powerful persons brought into court this same friend Socrates, preferring against him a most shameless   c accusation, and one which he, of all men, least deserved. For the prosecutors charged him with impiety, and the jury condemned and put to death the very man who, at the time when his accusers were themselves in misfortune and exile, had refused to have a part in the unjust arrest of one of their friends.

The more I reflected upon what was happening, upon what kind of men were active in politics, and upon the state of our laws and customs, and the older I grew, the more I realized how difficult it is to manage a city's affairs rightly. For I saw it was impossible to do anything without friends and loyal followers; and to find such men ready to hand would be a piece of sheer good luck, since our city was no longer guided by the customs and practices of our fathers, while to train up new ones was anything but easy. And the corruption of our written laws and our customs was proceeding at such amazing speed that whereas at first I had been full of zeal for public life, when I noted these changes and saw how unstable everything was, I became in the end quite dizzy; and though I did not cease to reflect how an improvement could be brought about in our laws and in the whole constitution, yet I refrained from action, waiting for the proper time. At last I came to the conclusion that all existing states are badly governed and the condition of their laws practically incurable, without some miraculous remedy and the assistance of fortune; and I was forced to say, in praise of true philosophy, that from her height alone was it possible to discern what the nature of justice is, either in the state or in the individual, and that the ills of the human race would never end until either those who are sincerely and truly lovers of wisdom come into political power, or the rulers of our cities, by the grace of God, learn true philosophy.

...

Seventh Letter, 330c–331d

I will first advise what is to be done in the present circumstances. This, then, is what I have to say.

When one is advising a sick man who is living in a way injurious to his health, must one not first of all tell him to change his way of life and give him further counsel only if he is willing to obey? If he is not, I think any manly and self-respecting physician would break off counseling such a man, whereas anyone who would put up with him is without spirit or skill. So too with respect to a city: whether it be governed by one man or many, if its constitution is properly ordered and rightly directed, it would be sensible to give advice to its citizens concerning what would be to the city's advantage. But if it is a people who have wandered completely away from right government and resolutely refuse to come back upon its track and instruct their counselor to leave the constitution strictly alone, threatening him with death if he changes it, and order him instead to serve their interests and desires and show them how they can henceforth satisfy them in the quickest and easiest way – any man, I think, who would accept such a role as adviser is without spirit, and he who refuses is the true man. These are my principles; and whenever anyone consults me on a question of importance in his life, such as the making of money, or the care of his body or soul, if it appears to me that he follows some plan in his daily life or is willing to listen to reason on the matters he lays before me, I advise him gladly and don't stop with merely discharging my duty. But a man who does not consult me at all, or makes it clear that he will not follow advice that is given him – to such a man I do not take it upon myself to offer counsel; nor would I use constraint upon him, not even if he were my own son. Upon a slave I might force my advice, compelling him to follow it against his will; but to use compulsion upon a father or mother is to me an impious act, unless their judgment has been impaired by disease. If they are fixed in a way of life that pleases them, though it may not please me, I should not antagonize them by useless admonitions, nor yet by flattery and complaisance encourage them in the satisfaction of desires that I would die rather than embrace. This is the principle which a wise man must follow in his relations towards his own city. Let him warn her, if he thinks her constitution is corrupt and there is a prospect that his words will be listened to and not put him in danger of his life; but let him not use violence upon his fatherland to bring about a change of constitution. If what he thinks is best can only be accomplished by the exile and slaughter of men, let him keep his peace and pray for the welfare of himself and his city.

3

Late antiquity and the early middle ages
(312–1000)

With the coming of Christianity to Rome, the character of Graeco-Roman political thought began to change. Christianity introduced a whole series of questions which were largely alien to classical thought, most obviously for our purposes here the whole question of the justice of the use of force as such. At the same time, the political collapse of the Western half of the Roman empire in the second half of the fifth century CE, together with the political and military longevity of the East – which was to survive as a vibrant political force at least until at least the shattering Byzantine defeat at the battle of Manzikert in 1071 and to survive as a presence until 1453, when Constantinople was captured by the Ottoman Turks – led to ever-increasing plurality in political thought and practice. This was coupled, of course, with the rise and spread of new political and religious movements such as Islam (after the seventh century) which provided a very different context for political thought than the mix of Greek, Roman, and Christian ideas dominant in Western and Eastern Europe. However, classical – especially Greek – thought remained influential on all the major traditions – Christian, Jewish, and Islamic – of Europe and Asia Minor during this period (Lerner and Mahdi, 1963; Burns, 1988).

This chapter will principally focus on the Christian and Islamic worlds, for the interpenetrating and intellectual crossover at this time was very strong and because these two faiths were dominant – though by no means, of course, monolithic – and we shall also refer to Judaic thinking from time to time (an excerpt from Maimonides' *Logic* is included to show how Judaic political thinking was classified at the time – see pp. 174–5 below). To do this, the material has been broken down into five sections. The first examines the background to Christian thinking and its significance for political and international thought, and focuses on certain key texts of the early Christian period (an example, the so-called *Didache*, is excerpted – see pp. 111–14 below). The second then looks at the first influential tradition of Christian (Roman) statecraft – the Eusebian/Constantinian tradition (see pp. 115–18 below) – and traces its influence in that part of the Roman empire where it remained dominant until well into the high middle ages and in some ways even beyond, i.e. Byzantium.[1] Most especially we look at the practical political thought which emerged from this tradition, which, in *De Administrando Imperio* of the Emperor Constantine VII "Porphyrogenitus" (the nickname means literally "born to the purple"), offers us a particularly clear view of one of the ways in which our central concerns were addressed by one of the central traditions of the period (see pp. 136–47 below). The third section then looks at the evolution of international political thought in the Latin West after the collapse of Rome, concentrating on the most important political thinker of late antiquity in the West, Augustine of Hippo (354–430 AD) (see pp. 119–35 below). The fourth section then examines the legacy of Augustine and the emerging political thought of the Latin West up until the turn of the millennium. The fifth section then looks back to the origin and development of Islamic political thought and, specifically, to the related but different problems Islamic and Judaic thinkers had when incorporating classical thought (see pp. 148–73 below).

The rise of Christianity

The story of early Christian attitudes to politics in general and to the relationship between differing polities and communities in particular is a complex one. It is particularly complicated, of course, by the fact that until the late third century more or less serious persecutions of Christians were a familiar phenomenon from at least Nero's time, during which Christians were blamed for the great fire in 64 CE. As Henry Chadwick has said, "the experience of persecution produced a kind of schizophrenia in Christian attitudes to government which may be seen as a highly acute version of the common human sense of ambivalence towards all governmental authority ... moreover the Christians had from the start a strong sense of radical dualism between the people of God and 'the world', *kosmos* or *saeculum*, whose essential business consists in power, honor, sex and wealth" (Chadwick, 1988: 11–12).

---

1 Nomenclature here can be a problem. The city of Byzantium, already of considerable antiquity when Constantine made it his capital and after which it was renamed Constantinopolis, has traditionally given its name to that part of the empire that survived the crises of the fifth century and which remained an active power in European and Eurasian politics until finally being overwhelmed by the Ottoman empire in 1453. The members of the empire themselves always referred to themselves as "Romans" and were often called by their Latin fellows "Greeks." Here we follow tradition. After the fall of the Western empire, we refer to this political unit as the Byzantine empire.

The ambivalence was increased by the fact that, despite this dualism, from St. Paul onwards Christianity was clear that "the powers that be are ordained of God" (Romans 6.13) and thus, in perhaps the most famous biblical political remark, Christians should "render unto Caesar the things that are Caesar's" and "to God the things that are God's." This view was reinforced by a number of the Latin "fathers" of the church – as many of the early and immediately post-Apostolic church leaders are usually called (Irenaeus of Lyon, for example) – and perhaps especially by the radical otherworldliness of some, perhaps most influentially Tertullian.

In the early days of Christianity, the ambivalence was perhaps not too hard to bear, for most Christians did not expect the world to be around long enough for it to become a real problem. Perhaps the clearest example of the view early Christians at this time took is provided in a document known now simply as the "*Didache,*" or "the teaching" (the full title is *The Teaching of the Lord to the Gentiles through the Twelve Apostles*). This text is widely referred to by the Apostolic fathers and indeed by later writers (Eusebius, for example, refers to it) and although we do not know who wrote it, it seems to have originated from the area around Alexandria and been composed over a period of time – and probably by several hands – in the early Christian era. The document clearly shows the inward-looking character of the church at this time and, in the final passage, the expectation of the soon-to-arrive second coming of Christ, the "last things," which Christians call eschatology (see p. 114).

However, as time went on and the second coming did not arrive, and the church spread and became more organized, political questions became more and more unavoidable. The initial Christian response was that one could "render unto" Caesar without "acknowledging" Caesar; but increasingly questions that bordered on the political became part and parcel of Christian debate for example, the use of wealth or the gross disparity between rich and poor. Indeed, this aspect of Christian thought became a permanent feature of the Christian critique of Roman society, indeed of the *saeculum* – the secular, temporal world – generally and it was discussed by many of the fathers. Another area where Christianity became increasingly entwined in political questions was in their dealings with women and slaves. Without actively seeking a change in the legal status of either, Christian attitudes were at odds with those of Roman society (and indeed most ancient societies) in that slaves and women, along with men, were treated as children of God.

But nowhere were the early Christians more at odds with the prevailing mores of ancient societies than in their attitudes towards the use of military force. Of course, as was seen in chapter 2 above, it was far from the case

that ancient writers wholly approved of war or thought that it could not
be fought in more or less just ways. Virtually no ancient writer, however,
considered it, by definition, *wrong* to use lethal force in politics. Many early
Christians thought just this. By the second and third centuries, when the
practice of Christians joining the imperial army was not uncommon, leaders
of Christian communities faced the full ambivalence of their position in
this context. Origen, one of the most influential of the Apostolic fathers,
for example, believed that Christians could not take up arms and fight and
yet offered prayers for those engaged in the just defense of the empire and
the Basil, the Christian bishop of Caesarea, as late as the 370s, argues for
the possibility of a just war but says that a Christian soldier who fights in
it is excommunicate and subject to penance (Chadwick, 1988: 17–18; see also
Carlyle and Carlyle, 1903–36).

However, the central political event in changing early Christian attitudes
to politics is what followed Constantine's victory at Milvan bridge in 312 and
his subsequent rule as Roman emperor, so it is to this that we now turn.

"Constantinianism" and Byzantine thought

As we saw in chapter 2 above, one central them in classical reflection was
the unity of the world and the cosmos. "World order," in this context, was
often seen as the reflection of the unity of the natural world. Natural and
"human" order were in that sense perfectly at one. Equally, as we have just
seen, in early Christian thought this strand of classical thought was often
strongly emphasized, with creation and divine providence being substituted
for the eternal natural order (Chadwick, 1959; Momigliano, 1963a; Beranger,
1973). However, as the tensions within Christian thought became more acute,
this view became much less easy to sustain.

Constantine's victory offered a way of resolving these tensions and this
way was developed by his chief apologist, and the first historian of the church,
Eusebius Pamphili, bishop of Caesarea (263–339). Eusebius' synthesis of Greek
and Roman monarchical theory with Christian theology, contained chiefly
in his *Triakontaeterikos*, or *Tricennial Orations*, was hugely influential in the early
church, both in the East and in the West (Winkleman, 1975), but especially in
the East, where, for the thousand or so years until the Byzantine tradition
was finally scattered after the capture of the city by the Ottomans in 1453,
the Eusebian tradition, albeit somewhat modified and reinterpreted, remained central. In Eusebius' view, the emperor was seen as an "incarnate law"
(*lex animata, Nomos Empsuchos*) sent by God and thus beyond question or
reproach. Constantine's victory and reign was thus a unique sign of divine

providence and his empire is but an earthly reflection of the Kingdom of Heaven (see pp. 115–18 below).

For Eusebius, the victory of Constantine and then his conversion were clear signs of God's handiwork in history, and after Eusebius the Byzantine empire did not really produce political theory in the sense of a new approach to questions such as political authority, obligation, and so on. Of course, alternative currents did exist, particularly after the crisis of the eleventh century which followed the crushing defeat of Byzantine forces at the battle of Manzikert in 1071, but they were largely insignificant. What Byzantium did produce in abundance, however, was a welter of literature on the *exercise* of political power. Much of this was not dissimilar in kind from what became known in the West, at a later time, as "mirror for Princes" literature of which the most famous, if heterodox, example, is Machiavelli's *Prince*.

In this case, however, perhaps the most revealing treatise in Byzantine political thought for the purpose of the working conception of politics – which also is centrally concerned with questions of what we would today call international relations – is the *De Administrando Imperio* of Constantine Porphyrogenitus (see pp. 136–47 below). This private manual of statecraft, written by the Emperor (Constantine VII) for his son and heir (later Romanus II) is quite unlike the usual public-advice books for monarchs. It is written in plain language, rather than the rhetorical style favored by imperial apologists like Eusebius, and it is particularly revealing about how the empire should conduct foreign policy, and on how the empire should view both itself and others. *What* it reveals is a conception of political order based on a greatly exaggerated Eusebian tradition, not dissimilar in tone to the way much ancient Chinese writing tends to view "barbarians" (Ostrogorsky, 1968 [1940]; Barker, 1956; Toynbee, 1973). As D. M. Nicol has said, "The nations beyond the bounds of the Empire, insatiate in their greed, were to be dazzled and intimidated by the divinity of the successors of Constantine, by their sacred vestments and diadems and by the religious ceremonials of the court" (Nicol, 1988: 57). It is, as Ostrogorsky has called it, a work of "unique importance" for our understanding of Byzantine political thought (Ostrogorsky, 1968 [1940]: 214).

Constantine Porphyrogenitus was, by all accounts, a man of great scholarship, unremitting devotion to duty, and unimpeachable moral integrity. He overcame considerable obstacles, including an even more complex than usual series of courtly intrigues, in order to rule, and he ruled well, though in truth his actual rulership was of less importance than his scholarly activity. His main achievements as emperor were in the field of diplomacy and, internally, the elevation of culture and education. He wrote many works in a variety of genres, but *De Administrando Imperio* (in the later Latin name given to it) was the most significant of all. The book is a sometimes brilliant treatise on the rituals of Byzantine statecraft, a statement of practical wisdom that would have warmed the heart of an Aristotle or a Cicero – and a discussion of the ins and outs of politics, war, and diplomacy that would have impressed a Thucydides. Compiled between the years 948 and 952 (Moravscik, 1949), it aims, as Moravscik has said, to be avowedly practical, "teaching [Romanus] to be a wise sovereign, first by a knowledge of past and present affairs and secondly by giving him a summary of the experience of others in circumstances analogous to those likely to surround himself" (Moravscik, 1949: 10).

Constantine's preface divides the book into four parts, the first a key to foreign policy, the second a lesson in diplomacy, the third an historical and geographical survey of the regions of most relevance to the empire, and the fourth an internal history of the politics and organization of the empire. Unquestionably it was a secret document, and through it we get a powerful glimpse of how one of the central powers of the day viewed the three questions that are of central concern to us in this book. Its maxims remained at the heart of Byzantine diplomacy, foreign policy, and conception of its being and purpose well into the final phases of the decline of the empire. It may therefore stand as the most mature work of political thought produced by the empire and it is significant that it is, primarily, a work on "international" politics.

Augustine

The Eusebian tradition was initially equally strong in the West. The emperor was seen as God's representative throughout Constantine's reign and that of his son. By the late 380s, however, the Eusebian tradition was coming under attack – or at least revision – from a variety of sources. Among the most important was the work – and indeed the life – of the most impressive and influential Christian bishop of the day, Ambrose, bishop of Milan (334–397). As Peter Brown has said, Ambrose was "the most striking representative of the Roman Governing class of his age ... that is of men whose position depended less on their patrician birth, than on their ability to grasp and hold power in a ruthless society" (P. Brown, 1967: 81). He was also, in many ways, representative of the views of such men towards major political questions. Ambrose had two very different sides to his character. One was the politician and man of action, the bishop who humbled the emperor and his mother; the other a passionate churchman and scholar, a brilliant orchestrator of church ceremonial and powerful giver of sermons.

Ambrose tended to equate "Roman" and "Christian," in the manner that Eusebius does, and, as R. A. Markus says, he does it "almost instinctively." However, he does move away from the Eusebian view of the empire. While

Roman and Christian may be functionally equivalent, the church and the empire are seen as *partners*, with the church as very much the senior partner. The emperor, for Ambrose, was a "son of the Church," very different from the Constantinian and Byzantine model, and thus subject, at least potentially, to censure (Ambrose himself censured three emperors!). This view gradually paved the way for the most famous medieval compromise between church and state, Pope Gelasius I celebrated doctrine of the "two swords," the temporal and spiritual powers equally necessary for a Christian commonwealth.

The one thinker who challenges the effective equivalence of Roman and Christian, and certainly the most influential thinker of this period in the West for our purposes (and indeed many others) is Augustine of Hippo (354–430). Born in Thagaste in North Africa, Augustine was the offspring of a determined and strongly religious mother, Monica, and a kindly but non-Christian father (though he was baptized just before his death), but he drifted away from her Catholic faith after completing his early studies in Carthage. Initially, Augustine became a "Manichee" – a heretical sub-Christian sect which believed in the radical (and material) opposition of Good and Evil; all evil had to be purged from the heart and body of anyone who wished to be good. He also moved from North Africa to Italy where he taught rhetoric in Milan and, by his own account, lived a full (pagan) life which included a long-standing, but not legal, relationship with an unnamed woman which produced a son, Adeodatus, to whom by all accounts Augustine was devoted, though he died young, certainly before Augustine became a bishop. Later, Augustine abandoned this relationship to try and make an ambitious marriage. In other words, and this is in part the story we have from Augustine himself in his *Confessions*, he was a young man on the make and in a hurry.

However, in Milan, Augustine encountered Ambrose. Though it was Ambrose the churchman, rather than Ambrose the politician, who first influenced Augustine, the power of Ambrose's example cannot be doubted. Through this influence, he began to drift back towards faith. Not initially to Christianity, to be sure. Augustine's return to religion was marked initially by a passionate attachment to Platonism and philosophy – he even for a time sought to live the life of an ancient sage, retired from the world, in Cassiciacum (P. Brown, 1967: 115–27). Gradually, under Ambrose's influence, the persistent influence of Monica, and the relentless prodding of his own desires and intellect, Augustine returned to Catholicism. By 391 he was ordained a priest and by 395 he was consecrated as bishop of Hippo, the position he would hold for the rest of his life, and beginning to write the books that would shape the destiny of the Christian West and would make him famous. As a bishop, Augustine was an important local official and as his fame spread he also developed a huge and voluminous correspondence. He wrote and published on a huge variety of subjects, developing both his own ideas and criticisms of many of the heresies and schismatic movements prevalent in the church of his day. At his death his confirmed literary output ran to 113 books and treatises, more than two hundred letters, and over five hundred sermons (Dyson, 1998: xi).

Augustine's attitudes to politics in general obviously evolved considerably in the course of a writing career that spanned forty years of enormous political, social, and religious upheaval. R. A. Markus has suggested that Augustine's political thought can be divided up into five distinct areas: (1) the Roman empire and its place in the divine plan and relationship to Christianity, (2) human nature and relationships in society, (3) the church and its relations with the secular world, (4) religious coercion, and (5) the just war (Markus, 1988: 103).

The central distinction in Augustine's mature political thinking is, as is well known, between the "two cities," the earthly city and the city of God. In coming to this view, he rejected much of his own earlier thinking on politics which largely accepted the "Constantinian" and Eusebian assumptions discussed above, which were dominant amongst his contemporaries. The fullest statement of his political ideas is found in the book generally reckoned as his masterpiece, *The City of God Against the Pagans*. Beginning work on it in the year 413 and finally publishing it whole – portions had been previously published – in 426, Augustine himself tells us that the occasion for its composition was the "sack of Rome" by the Goths in 410, which had led many to "blaspheme against the true God more ferociously and bitterly than before" (Dyson, 1998: xi, quoting Augustine, *Retractiones* (Retractions) 2, 43, 2). He also, however, developed many of its key themes in lectures and sermons from about 405 onwards.

He first of all insists that "Rome" is not to be confused with the "city of God." As Markus puts it, "The Roman Empire (and by implication any earthly society) is of itself neither holy nor diabolical. Like all human work, its ultimate value is determined by the ultimate allegiances of its creators: their piety or impiety" (Markus, 1988: 105). The two cities, for Augustine, are mutually exclusive and everybody on earth belongs to one or the other; but all existing societies have "citizens" of both in them, including, significantly, even the church itself. Just as the secular power is not the image of the earthly city, so the spiritual power is not just the image of the city of God, although he is equally clear, particularly in his writings against the so-called "Donatist" heretics in his native Africa, that the church is, in a very special sense, the carrier of the idea of the heavenly city. "In this world," Augustine says, "the two cities are inextricably interwoven and mingled with each other, until they shall be separated in the last judgment" (*City of God*, 1.35). Thus all societies are ambiguous and riven, because the conflict between the two cities is at their heart (see pp. 119–35 below).

However, Augustine's analysis of the relations of the two cities in existing societies is extremely subtle (see pp. 125–35). Book 19 of the *City of God* is largely concerned with it. For Augustine, the "ultimate orientation" of people's "loves" – i.e. their wills – is directed towards one, and only one, of the two cities. However, lesser orientations, what are called their "intermediate loves," can be directed in other directions and thus can establish some commonality between citizens of both cities. For example, citizens of both cities value what Augustine calls "earthly peace," satisfaction of material needs, security from violence, and civil peace. The political realm is the realm, Augustine thinks, of these "intermediate" areas of human life.

It is obvious, of course, that there are tensions in this view. As many have observed, Augustine's view of the church, which feeds into his justification of religious coercion under some circumstances, makes it look at times suspiciously like a state and was certainly influential on much political thought in the early middle ages (Markus, 1970; C. Brown, 1995). However, it is clear that Augustine did not really see this point at the time he was writing.

A similar tension is visible in his discussion of the use of force more generally. Augustine saw war and conflict as inevitable features of the "fallen" human condition, and as such he believed that in some circumstances it might be justifiable and that it might be a Christian's duty to be involved. However, he is also far less sanguine about the use of force and far more skeptical about the likely virtue of political authority than many other fourth-century Christians. By the time he wrote the *City of God*, as we have seen, Augustine was a pronounced critic of the Eusebian / Constantinian way of seeing politics and he certainly refused to endorse the "Christian empire" as something that, by definition, deserved defence. As Jean Elshtain has recently pointed out (Elshtain, 1995), Augustine is savage in his condemnation of the pretenses of both war and peace in the Roman empire and in parts of the *City of God* engages in a critique of the follies of human militarism that would make many pacifists blush.

Yet there can be – sometimes even must be – for Augustine a just resort to force, though it is clear that such wars would be, to put it mildly, few and far between. They would have to be defensive or fight to remedy some grave injustice, and they would have to be fought by properly constituted public authorities and prosecuted within some bounds of human decency (Markus, 1988: 115). Yet even when admitting this, Augustine is clear that even when they are just, they are still terrible: "the wise man they say, will wage just wars. Surely, if he remembers he is a human being, he will rather lament the fact, that he is faced with the necessity of waging just wars; for if they were not just, he would not have to engage in them, and consequently there would be no wars for a wise man" (Augustine, *City of God*, quoted in Elshtain, 1995: 108).

The Latin West after Augustine

The period from the death of Augustine in 430 until the Aristotelian renaissance of the twelfth century saw many changes in the political shape of Western Europe. The barbarian kingdoms which had emerged out of the ruins of the Western empire were eventually replaced by the empire of Charlemagne, first proclaimed in 800. Yet the unity of his empire did not last long. It was divided at his death in 843 (though a member of his family carried the imperial title until 924) and the ninth and tenth centuries experienced many dislocations and tribulations, with many political forms remaining quite fluid until well into the new millennium.

For many, therefore, for example those great historians of medieval political thought R. W. and A. J. Carlyle, this period is really one of the "formation" of political thought. As they remarked, in this period, human beings had

in the writings of the Christian fathers a great body of theories and principles which had a constant influence upon them, while their habit of life and feeling was grounded in the traditions of the new teutonic societies, but in neither of these had they any ordered and articulated system of political thought, but rather a body of principles, significant indeed and profound, but not always easily to be reconciled with each other. (Carlyle and Carlyle, 1903–36: vol. III, 115)

Perhaps the central assumption in their political thought relevant to our concerns here, however, was the recurring notion of empire. This period saw the gradual emergence of the term that was to remain central for many centuries to European ideas of international politics: Latin Christendom, and the idea that fed into it most strongly was the idea of empire, inherited to be sure from Rome and even from some of the early Christian writings (the echoes of the old Eusebian tradition can surely be heard in it), but also predicated upon the rise of the Frankish and Carolingian empires in the eighth century. As Janet Nelson has said, the Carolingian imperial revival "brought to the spokesman of Latin Christendom a new sense of separateness from the world of the Greeks, Byzantium" (Nelson, 1988: 233). And thus, to quote another celebrated authority on the period, Geoffrey Barraclough, "the Christian *idea* of Empire ... was a powerful force ... influential in the minds and actions of many ... but we shall simply pile up confusion if we attempt to identify it with the historical empire in the west or indeed with any other empire of this world" (Barraclough, 1950: 26; editor's italics).

It is still, however, unquestionably Augustine who is the most important symbolic influence on the development of Western political thought, though it is perhaps the overarching framework erected most clearly in *The City of God*, rather than specific ideas, that is his greatest legacy. Although many other thinkers and ideas are of course significant – for example, the political thinking of Pope Gregory I, called "the Great" (540–604) – the model of the two cities is central. It remained what we might call the ideological "center of gravity" of the West until the Aristotelian revolution of the thirteenth century.

Islamic and Judaic thought

Christianity, of course, was not the only major world religion to make its growing impact on the world in this period. Islam, too, very quickly became a force to be reckoned with. As Albert Hourani has said,

By the early seventh century, there existed a combination of a settled world which had lost something of its strength and another world on its frontiers which was in closer contact with its Northern neighbors and opening itself to their cultures. The decisive meeting between them took place in the middle years of that century. A new political order was created which included the whole of the Arabian peninsula, the whole of the Sassanian lands [the old Sassanid empire] and the Syrian and Egyptian provinces of the Byzantine empire ... in this new order, the ruling group was formed ... by Arabs from Western Arabia, and to a great extent from Mecca. Before the end of the seventh century this Arab ruling group was identifying its new order with a revelation given by God to Mohammed, a citizen of Mecca, in the form of a holy book, the Qur'an: a revelation which completed those given to earlier prophets or messengers of God and created a new religion, Islam. (Hourani, 1991: 14–15; see also the discussion in Enayat, 1982: 1–17)

Following Mohammed's death, his successors (*Khalifa*, hence caliph) found the "new world order" very precarious. By a combination of luck and skill, however, in the space of a few years they had established a powerful military machine which began to sweep all before it until, by the eighth and ninth centuries, the caliphate (now named the 'Abbasid caliphate, after the ruling family) stretched from the Indus in the East to modern Tunisia in the West, and many other Muslim-dominated Arab societies existed in other parts of Africa and in modern Spain.

The basic political orientation of Islamic thought at this period was organized around the notion of the division of the world into Islamic and non-Islamic spheres, though there were differences in how this was articulated, especially between Sunni and Shia branches of Islam. In general "Muslims lived within an elaborated system of ritual, doctrine and law clearly different from those of non-Muslims" (Hourani, 1991: 47). Other faiths – Judaism, Christianity, and Zoroastrianism, for example – were recognized, though regarded as inferior. They were seen as "people of the book," however, and were not forced to convert – though, given the range of prescriptions that was visited upon them, a powerful incentive to convert was clearly present. Muslims also saw themselves as part of a greater whole, the "community of believers" (the *umma*), as well as members of their particular communities, communities symbolized by the unity of the Arab language and expressed in legal and religious terms by the "men of religious learning," the *'ulama* – those who led prayers in the mosque, or preached the Friday sermon, and who were the guardians of shared beliefs, values, and practices (Hourani, 1991: 115).

The status of political authority in Islam had been raised over the whole question of the successor to the Prophet. As Hourani has said,

Gradually there took place a crystallization of different attitudes to such problems. The attitude of those who at a certain point came to be called sunnis was that it was important for all Muslims to live together in peace and unity ... they came to accept all four of the first caliphs as legitimate and as virtuous and rightly guided (*rashidun*); later caliphs might not always have acted justly but they should be accepted as legitimate so long as they did not go against the basic commandments of God ... the shi' movements did not accept the claims of the first three caliphs but believed that 'Ali ibn Abi Talib [the fourth caliph] had been the sole legitimate and appointed successor as *imam*. (Hourani, 1991: 60–1)

Of course there were variations in each of these views. Many Shi'ites, for example, believed that the imamate was handed on only by the designation of the imam of the time. The most celebrated version of this thesis was so-called "twelver" shi'ism which argued that the succession had passed on to the twelfth in line in the ninth century. However, since they also believed that the world could not exist without an imam, it was assumed to be the case that the imam was living still in hiding, communicating with the faithful through intermediaries.

Each of these different views led to differing political theories, of course, which in turn were influenced, as political theories always are, by the ups and downs of politics in the world. In the aftermath of the threats to the 'Abbasid caliphate in the tenth and eleventh centuries, for example, considerable political thought focused on shoring up the power of the caliphate (the best-known writer of this kind being Al Marwardi, who died in 1058).

In addition to these aspects of Islamic thought, however, attempts were made, as in the West, to bring the wisdom of the ancient Greeks to bear on the problems of Islamic societies. However, as Lerner and Mahdi have said, "In Islam and Judaism ... the penetration of classical political philosophy led to the posing of a quite different question [than in the west. In Islam] the primary issue was whether these new and alien sciences are permitted or prohibited by religious law. This was a juridical, rather than a theological, question" (Lerner and Mahdi, 1963: 13). Thus the question became one for *legal* – as opposed, that is, to theological – dispute with Islamic and Judaic communities. They add that, of course, the extant texts in the Islamic world were largely different from those in the Latin West. For the Islamic world, copies of Plato's texts (especially the *Republic* and the *Laws*) were available (as they were not in the West until the Renaissance), but the influence of Aristotle was much weaker. And, obviously, the whole Latin tradition (for example Cicero and even Marcus Aurelius, despite the fact he wrote in Greek) was alien to them.

The most influential thinker to seek to reintroduce Greek learning was the philosopher al-Farabi (870–950), whose work is amongst the most important writings of this period of Islamic culture. As Muhsin Mahdi has said, "the central theme of al-Farabi's political writings is the virtuous regime, the political order whose guiding principle is the realization of human excellence or virtue" (Mahdi, 1963: 163). The Aristotelian provenance of this view is obvious. The virtuous regime is thus the regime in which people come together in order to be virtuous and happy. Given this understanding of the virtuous regime, al-Farabi is then able to sketch out, again after the manner of Aristotle, the characteristics of other regimes (see pp. 148–69 below). He divides them into three broad categories: *ignorant* regimes, whose citizens know nothing of divine and natural beings and of the attainment of happiness and virtue; *wicked* or *immoral* regimes, whose citizens possess such knowledge but choose not to act on it, and *erring* regimes, whose citizens believe they have true opinions about divinity, happiness, and virtue but who in truth – and for a variety of possible reasons – do not.

In each case, al-Farabi believed that since the citizens do not have the true knowledge of the virtuous regime, their character is formed with a view to attaining one or more lower ends. There are six of these and each of the above regimes can be classified in turn according to the end which dominates it. These are thus: the regime of *necessity*, where the end is the attainment of the bare necessities of life; the *vile* regime, where the end is wealth and property (an oligarchy in Aristotelian terms); the *base* regime, where the end is pleasure; the regime of *honor* where the end is praise and glory; the regime of *domination*, clearly modeled on the Greek tyranny, where the end is the domination of others; and the regime of *corporate association*, where the end is the freedom to do as you wish, which is equivalent to Aristotle's discussion of democracy.

Al-Farabi also discusses the character of political authority and amends Plato's famous doctrine of the philosopher ruler to contemporary Islamic circumstances. As Hourani puts it, for al-Farabi "the best of states is that which is ruled by one who is both a philosopher and a prophet ... in the absence of such a ruler the state can be virtuous if it is ruled by a combination of those who collectively possess the necessary characteristics, or by rulers who maintain and interpret laws given by a founder (such would have been the early caliphate)" (Hourani, 1991: 145).

Of course, the relationship of the various Muslim dynasties and communities to the world outside, the "world of war" (*Dar al harb*, as opposed to the world of Islam, *Dar al islam*) depended in part on local conditions and circumstances. However, this was also something to which scholars and thinkers like al-Farabi gave considerable thought. To begin with, al-Farabi clearly believes in a "just war," but there is little here of Augustine's hostility to military prowess as such. For al-Farabi, a war conducted by a ruler of a virtuous regime is by definition a just war and he is equally clear that amongst the qualities of the virtuous ruler is daring and warlike virtue. There are, however, he believes, two extreme views of war, one that it is the natural state of humankind and the second that peace is the natural state and war is necessarily wrong. These are views he associates with the ignorant and erring cities respectively and they give rise to two types of regimes, tyrannies (or regimes of domination) and peace-loving regimes. The latter are clearly regarded by al-Farabi as unusual and certainly not threatening. However, tyrannies where war is an end in itself have succumbed to the supreme vice.

The character of war is also shaped, however, by the reality of the world. For al-Farabi, there are in principle three "perfect" human associations; the largest is simply the association of all human beings in the inhabited world, the second is the association of a nation, and the third, the association of a city. However, he notes the obvious fact that the association of all human beings is divided up into nations and "nations are distinguished from each other by two things – natural make up and natural character – and by something that is composite (it is conventional but has a basis in natural things), namely language" (al-Farabi, *The Political Regime*, quoted in Mahdi, 1963: 176). Equally, he emphasizes constantly that "a virtuous nation is not a group of cities ruled by a virtuous or perfect city," but the nation, "all of whose cities cooperate regarding the things by which happiness is attained" and the association of all men in the entire inhabited world is virtuous "only when the nations in it cooperate to achieve happiness" (al-Farabi, *The Virtuous City*, quoted in Mahdi, 1963: 176–7). Thus, for all that war*like* virtue is expected of the ruler of virtuous cities, it would appear – for al-Farabi, as for Augustine – that the occasions for the virtuous exercise of that virtue would be few and far between.

Of course, Islamic political practice, both in this period and beyond, was influenced by a good deal more than the thinking and writings of '*ulama* or philosophers like al-Farabi. As with the other cultures we have looked at, a flourishing genre of "mirror for princes"-type books emerges in the tenth and eleventh centuries, perhaps the best example being the *Book of Government* of Nizam al-Mulk (1018–92), the chief minister of the first Seljuk sultan to rule in Baghdad, which offers practical advice on such things as how to choose officials, use intelligence, keep your armies loyal, and so on.

Later Islamic writers, such as Avicenna (980–1037), developed the work of al-Farabi whom, in eastern Islam at least, he replaced as the most influential writer. Perhaps his most important book was *The Healing* (sometimes called the "Sufficiency" by Latin writers). Divided into four sections, it treats political science in the third section, called metaphysics, and in the tenth book especially he illustrates the manner in which he has developed al-Farabi's general approach (see pp. 170–3 below).

One final point here is to emphasize the extent to which Judaic thinking in this period overlapped with Christian, but especially with Islamic thought. Of course Jewish "political" thinking was of a rather different character than either and was often principally concerned with specifically Jewish questions. However, many of the most important Jewish thinkers offered considerable insight into the range of questions which concern us here. Perhaps the most important Jewish thinker of the period is Moses Maimonides (1135–1204) who followed a medical career, serving at one point as court physician to the Islamic leader Saladin. However, he also wrote widely on many issues and was an influential Jewish communal leader (Lerner and Mahdi, 1963: 188). The excerpt we include here shows how he classified political science, and included within it "the governance of the nations" (see pp. 174–6).

Conclusion

This brings to a close this brief survey of the major evolution of international political thought in that period which we might, with R. W. Southern, call the "making of the Middle Ages" (Southern, 1953). By the end of the period, the major ideological and theoretical forces which will dominate the development of international political thought in Eurasia for the next five hundred years are present. The great interactions, political, military, and ideological, are still to come, but the players have taken the field; the game is about to commence.

FURTHER READING

The best general discussion of early medieval political thought as a whole is in Burns (1988). The relevant chapters of Carlyle and Carlyle (1903–36) are also still worth consulting, despite its age. On early Christian and Byzantine thought, Barker (1955) is indispensable. On Augustine, P. Brown (1967) is justly celebrated as one of the major biographies of the last forty years, and is superb on Augustine's political thought and experience, and Markus (1970), though controversial, is still essential. A wonderful modern reading, very good on Augustine's international thought, is Elshtain (1995). Toynbee (1973) is amongst the most evocative recreations of Byzantium available and is superb on *De Administrando Imperio*. On the evolution of post-Augustinian Christian thought, see especially Ullman (1975). On Islamic and Judiac political thought of the period, Lerner and Mahdi (1963) is still central.

SOURCES

Anonymous, *The Didache*, from *Early Christian Writings*, ed. and trans. Maxwell Staniforth (Harmondsworth: Penguin Books 1968), pp. 227–30 and 235.

Eusebius, from *Tricennial Orations*, ed. and trans. H. A. Drake (Berkeley: University of California Press, 1976), Part I, "In Praise of Constantine," IX, 8–19, pp. 99–101.

Augustine of Hippo, from *The City of God against the Pagans*, ed. and trans. Robert W. Dyson (Cambridge: Cambridge University Press, 1998) Book 4, chs. 1–5 (pp. 143–9) and Book 19, chs. 11–14 and 17 (pp. 932–47).

Constantine Porphyrogenitus, from *De Administrando Imperio* (Dumbarton Oaks edition, 1967, ed. G. Moravscik and R. J. H. Jenkins), proem and sects. 1–8, 13 and 14, pp. 46–55, 65–77).

Al-Farabi, *The Political Regime*, from *Medieval Political Philosophy*, ed. Ralph Lerner and Muhsin Mahdi (Ithaca: Cornell University Press, 1963), pp. 32–56.

Avicenna, *The Healing*, from *Medieval Political Philosophy* (as above), pp. 107–10.

Moses Maimonides, *Logic*, from *Medieval Political Philosophy* (as above), pp. 189–90.

ANONYMOUS

From *The Teaching of the Lord to the Gentiles through the Twelve Apostles* or *The Didache*

Part i. The two ways

THE WAY OF LIFE

1 . There are two Ways: a Way of Life and a Way of Death, and the difference between these two Ways is great.

The Way of Life is this: *Thou shalt love first the Lord thy Creator, and secondly thy neighbour as thyself; and thou shalt do nothing to any man that thou wouldst not wish to be done to thyself.*

What you may learn from those words is to bless them that curse you, to pray for your enemies, and to fast for your persecutors. For where is the merit in loving only those who return your love? Even the heathens do as much as that. But if you love those who hate you, you will have nobody to be your enemy.

Beware of the carnal appetites of the body. If someone strikes you on the right cheek, turn the other one to him as well, and perfection will be yours. Should anyone compel you to go a mile, go another one with him. If someone takes away your coat, let him have your shirt too. If someone seizes anything belonging to you, do not ask for it back again (you could not get it, anyway). Give to everyone that asks, without looking for any repayment, for it is the Father's pleasure that we should share His gracious bounty with all men. A giver who gives freely, as the commandment directs, is blessed; no fault can be found with him. But woe to the taker; for though he cannot be blamed for taking if he was in need, yet if he was not, an account will be required of him as to why he took it, and for what purpose, and he will be taken into custody and examined about his action, and he will not get out until he has paid the last penny. The old saying is in point here: 'Let your alms grow damp with sweat in your hand, until you know who it is you are giving them to.'

2 . The second commandment in the Teaching means: Commit no murder, adultery, sodomy, fornication, or theft. Practice no magic, sorcery, abortion, or infanticide. See that you do not covert anything your neighbour possesses, and

never be guilty of perjury, false witness, slander, or malice. Do not equivocate in thought or speech, for a double tongue is a deadly snare; the words you speak should not be false or empty phrases, but fraught with purposeful action. You are not to be avaricious or extortionate, and you must resist any temptation to hypocrisy, spitefulness, or superiority. You are to have no malicious designs on a neighbour. You are to cherish no feelings of hatred for anybody; some you are to reprove, some to pray for, and some again to love more than your own life.

3 . Keep away from every bad man, my son, and from all his kind. Never give way to anger, for anger leads to homicide. Likewise refrain from fanaticism, quarrelling, and hot-temperedness, for these too can breed homicide.

Beware of lust, my son, for lust leads to fornication. Likewise refrain from unclean talk and the roving eye, for these too can breed adultery.

Do not be always looking for omens, my son, for this leads to idolatry. Likewise have nothing to do with witchcraft, astrology, or magic; do not even consent to be a witness of such practices, for they too can all breed idolatry.

Tell no lies, my son, for lying leads to theft. Likewise do not be over-anxious to be rich or to be admired, for these too can breed thievishness.

Do not be a grumbler, my son, for this leads to blasphemy. Likewise do not be too opinionated, and do not harbour thought of wickedness, for these too can breed blasphemy.

Learn to be meek, for the meek are to inherit the earth. School yourself to forbearance, compassion, guilelessness, calmness, and goodness; and never forget to respect the teaching you have had.

Do not parade your own merits, or allow yourself to behave presumptuously, and do not make a point of associating with persons of eminence, but choose the companionship of honest and humble folk.

Accept as good whatever experience comes your way, in the knowledge that nothing can happen without God.

4 . By day and by night, my son, remember him who speaks the word of God to you. Give him the honour you would give the Lord; for wherever the Lord's attributes are the subject of discourse, there the Lord is present. Frequent the company of the saints daily, so as to be edified by their conversation. Never encourage dissensions, but try to make peace between those who are at variance. Judge with justice, reprove without fear or favour, and never be in two minds about your decisions.

Do not be like those who reach out to take, but draw back when the time comes for giving. If the labour of your hands has been productive, make an offering as a ransom for your sins. Give without hesitating and without grumbling, and you will see Whose generosity will requite you. Never turn away the needy; share all your possessions with your brother, and do not claim that anything is your own. If you and he are joint participators in things immortal, how much more so in things that are mortal?

You are not to withhold your hand from your son or daughter, but to bring them up in the fear of God from their childhood.

Never speak sharply when giving orders to male or female domestics whose trust is in the same God as yours; otherwise they may cease to fear Him who is over you both. He has not come to call men according to their rank, but those who have been already prepared by the Spirit. And you, servants, obey your masters with respectfulness and fear, as the representatives of God. See that you do not neglect the commandments of the Lord, but keep them just as you received them, without any additions or subtractions of your own.

In church, make confession of your faults, and do not come to your prayers with a bad conscience.

That is the Way of Life.

THE WAY OF DEATH

5 . The way of Death is this. To begin with, it is evil, and in every way fraught with damnation. In it are murders, adulteries, lusts, fornications, thefts, idolatries, witchcraft, sorceries, robberies, perjuries, hypocrisies, duplicities, deceit, pride, malice, self-will, avarice, foul language, jealousy, insolence, arrogance, and boastfulness. Here are those who persecute good men, hold truth in abhorrence, and love falsehood; who do not know of the rewards of righteousness, nor adhere to what is good, nor to just judgement; who lie awake planning wickedness rather than well-doing. Gentleness and patience are beyond their conception; they care for nothing good or useful, and are bent only on their own advantage, without pity for the poor or feeling for the distressed. Knowledge of their Creator is not in them; they make away with their infants and deface God's image; they turn away the needy and oppress the afflicted; they aid and abet the rich but arbitrarily condemn the poor; they are utterly and altogether sunk in iniquity.

CONCLUSION

6 . Take care that nobody tempts you away from the path of this Teaching, for such a man's tuition can have nothing to do with God. If you can shoulder the Lord's yoke in its entirety, then you will be perfect; but if that is too much for you, do as much as you can.

As regards diet, keep the rules so far as you are able; only be careful to refuse anything that has been offered to an idol, for that is the worship of dead gods.

...

ESCHATOLOGY

16 . Be watchful over your life; never let your lamps go out or your loins be ungirt, but keep yourselves always in readiness, for you can never be sure of the hour when our Lord may be coming. Come often together for spiritual improvement; because all the past years of your faith will be no good to you at the end, unless you have made yourselves perfect. In the last days of the world false prophets and deceivers will abound, sheep will be perverted and turn into wolves, and love will change to hate, for with the growth of lawlessness men will begin to hate their fellows and persecute them and betray them. Then the Deceiver of the World will show himself, pretending to be a Son of God and doing signs and wonders, and the earth will be delivered into his hands, and he will work such wickedness as there has never been since the beginning. After that, all humankind will come up for their fiery trial; multitudes of them will stumble and perish, but such as remain steadfast in the faith will be saved by the Curse. And then the signs of the truth will appear: first the sign of the opening heavens, next the sign of the trumpet's voice, and thirdly the rising of the dead – not of all the dead, but, as it says, *the Lord will come, and with him all his holy ones.* And then the whole world will see the Lord as He comes riding on the clouds of heaven.

EUSEBIUS

EUSEBIUS PAMPHILI, as he is sometimes known because of his association with the theologian and scholar Pamphilus, was born in 263 CE. At the age of about thirty, while still a lay disciple of Pamphilus, he met the future emperor of Rome, Constantine, while the latter was travelling through Caesarea. Eusebius, later to write a life of Constantine, was deeply impressed. Some years later, after he had become bishop of Caesarea and Constantine had become emperor, Eusebius became the chief apologist and expounder of Constantinian theories of kingship and a force in many of the key theological controversies of his day, being present for example at the Council of Nicaea held between 20 May and 19 June 325 CE, the central Christian conference of the time. His key political work was the so-called *Tricennial Orations*, orations delivered to celebrate the thirteenth year of Constantine's reign and which were to shape the political thought of the Byzantine empire (as the eastern Roman empire is usually called) for nearly a thousand years. His chief importance was the adaptation of the Greek theory of kingship and government to the very changed circumstances of Constantine's Rome and of early Christianity. Eusebius died in 339, two years after his beloved emperor.

From *Tricennial Orations*

Part I

"In Praise of Constantine"

(8) Where the column of God-defying giants and the hissing of serpents, who with sharpened tongues loosed godless voices against the Ruler of All?

Those who waged war against the Universal Sovereign, encouraged by the members of their gods, attacked with great strength in military forces, advancing behind phantoms of the strengthless dead. But he, fortified with the armor of piety, arrayed against the multitude of his foes the Saving and Life-Giving Sign like some safeguard and shield against evils, and gained a victory over his enemies and the spirits alike. Then with a well-founded conclusion rendering a thanksgiving prayer to the cause of the victory, by loud voice and by commemorative inscriptions he proclaimed to all men the Victory-Bringing Sign and erected in the midst of the ruling city this great trophy against all enemies, this explicit and indestructible salutary Sign of the Roman Empire and safeguard of the Universal Kingdom. (9) This he taught all men to acknowledge, above all the military, who surely most of all need to know not to pin one's hopes on spears and panoplies, nor on strength of body, but to recognize the God over all, the Giver of every good, and of victory itself. (10) Thus indeed did the sovereign himself – incredible as it sounds – become the teacher of rules of worship to his army, and he transmitted pious prayers in accordance with divine ordinances – to raise their outstretched hands above toward heaven while fixing the eyes of the mind on the highest point, the Heavenly Sovereign, and then to invoke Him in their prayers as Giver of Victory, Savior, Guardian, and Rescuer. In fact, he even ordained one especial day of prayer, the one which is truly supreme and first, belonging to the Lord and to salvation, the day, indeed, both of light and of life, named for immortality and every good. (11) He himself practices what he preaches, and celebrates his Savior in his royal chambers. Thus through his prayers he fulfills the divine ordinances, while through the hearing of holy accounts he has thoroughly educated his mind. His ministers and servants, dedicated to God, men distinguished by the most reverent and virtuous of lives, were made guardians of his entire estate, and his faithful lifeguards, bodyguards armored in the ways of a benevolent valor, acknowledged the sovereign as their teacher of a God-fearing life. (12) The sovereign cherished the Victory-Bearing Standard after he learned by trial in action of the divinity in it: to this have multitudes of a hostile army yielded, by this has the bombast of the God-defying ones been suppressed, by this have the tongues of the blasphemous and impious been silenced. By this were the barbarian races brought under control, the powers of the invisible spirits driven off, the follies of superstitious fraud refuted. To this, the sovereign, as if paying back some debt, dedicated as the crowning good of all triumphal monuments in every land, exhorting all with a bounteous and regal hand to form temples, precincts, and sacred oratories. (13) And at once in the very middle of the provinces and cities great works were raised on a royal scale, so that in a brief time these shone forth among every people, evidence of the refutation of godless tyranny. For those who had but lately been driven by madness of soul to war against God, raving like dogs yet powerless against God Himself, had vented their spleen on inanimate buildings. They tore down the oratories from top to bottom, digging up their very foundations, and so created the impression of a city captured by its enemies. And thus they displayed their villainy; but as soon as they assaulted the Divinity, they received immediate proof of their insanity. Not even a brief time passed for them, but with one blast of a heaven-sent squall He eradicated them, so that neither family, nor offspring, nor any relic of their memory was left behind among mankind, but in a brief time the whole lot, although widely separated, were utterly extinguished, punished by the scourge of God.

(14) Yes, those mad enough to oppose God met such an end. But he who triumphed under the Saving Trophy, one man all by himself (though not really alone because allied to and cooperating with him was The One) made new structures much stronger than those that a short while earlier had been condemned, second ones far more valuable than the first. Not only did he embellish the city named after him with distinguished houses of God and honor the capital of Bithynia with one of the greatest and most beautiful, but he also adorned the capital cities of the remaining provinces with their equals. (15) Two locations in the East he singled out from all others – one in the Palestinian nation, inasmuch as in that place as from a fount gushed forth the life-bearing stream to all, the other in the Eastern metropolis which glorifies the name of Antiochus which it bears. In the latter, since it is the capital of the whole region, he dedicated a certain structure marvelous and unique for its size and beauty. On the outside surrounding the whole temple with long walls, inside he raised the sanctuary to an extraordinary height and diversified it with an eight-walled plan. Encircling this with numerous aisles and niches, he crowned it with a variety of decorations. (16) Such things he accomplished in this place. In the Palestinian nation, in the heart of the Hebrew kingdom, on the very site of the evidence for salvation, he outfitted with many and abundant distinctions an enormous house of prayer and temple sacred to the Saving Sign, and he honored a memorial full of eternal significance and the Great Savior's own trophies over death with ornaments beyond all description. (17) In this same region, he recovered three sites revered for three mystical caves, and enhanced them with opulent structures. On the cave of the first theophany he conferred appropriate marks of honor; at the one where the ultimate ascension occurred he consecrated a memorial on the mountain ridge; between these, at the scene of the great struggle, signs of salvation and victory. To be sure, all these the sovereign adorned in order to herald the Saving Sign to all; (18) the Sign that, in turn, gives him compensation for his piety, augments his entire house and line, and strengthens the throne of his kingdom for long cycles of years, dispensing the fruits of virtue to his good sons, his family, and their descendants. (19) And surely this is the greatest proof of the power of the One he honors, that He has handled the scales of justice so impartially and has awarded to each party its due. On the heels of those who beleaguered the houses of prayer followed the wages of their sin, and straightway they became rootless and homeless, lost to hearth

and lost to sight. But he who honors his Master with every expression of
piety – at one time erecting imperial palaces for Him, at another making
Him known to his subjects by votive offerings everywhere on earth – has
found in Him the Savior and Guardian of his house, his kingdom, and his
line. Thus have the deeds of God become clear through the divine efficacy
of the Saving Sign.

AUGUSTINE OF HIPPO

AUGUSTINE was born into a lower middle class family at Thagaste in North Africa in 354 CE, the son of a pagan father and a Christian mother. Brought up as a Christian, he was educated locally and then at the age of sixteen went to the great North African metropolis of Carthage to complete his education, where he gradually lost his traditional Christian faith, becoming instead a Manichee (a follower of the heretic Mani). On completion of his studies, Augustine decided upon a teaching career and moved to Rome. In 383 he founded his own school of rhetoric at Rome and shortly thereafter he moved to teach rhetoric at Milan. By this point he had a mistress (whose name we do not know) who had borne him a son, Adeodatus, to whom Augustine was devoted. However, Adeodatus died young and Augustine and his mistress separated. Then, in 386, Augustine came under the spell of the powerful and charismatic Christian bishop of Milan, Ambrose, as well as intellectually becoming part of the Neoplatonic group in Milan. This swiftly undermined his Manicheanism and led him to become a Platonist. However, his mind and spirit gradually pulled him back to the church and he was baptized as a Christian in 387. He returned to Africa, where his mother, overjoyed at his return to the faith, finally died in 388. He was ordained as a priest in 391 and lived in a religious community until 395 when he was consecrated bishop of Hippo. He remained there till his death. In the course of the next thirty-six years, he not only ran the affairs of a large and complex episcopate but was increasingly involved in secular politics and foreign policy as this was the time when Roman rule in Africa was beginning to dissolve and the church and the secular power were, of necessity, thrown together. At the same time he was involved in nearly endless series of theological and philosophical disputes against various heretic groups (most famously Manichees, Donatists, and Pelagians), in the course of which he outlined a series of theological and philosophical positions which dominated the Western church until the high middle ages and in some respects beyond. His major political work, *The City of God*, written in part to account for the sack of Rome by the Goths in 410 which had shaken the faith of many, took thirteen years to write and became one of the most influential books in Christendom. Augustine finally died in 430 CE, amidst the ruins of his life's work – the Vandals were besieging his beloved Hippo and Roman Africa was collapsing everywhere – but with his hopes and his faith intact.

From *The City of God against the Pagans*

Book 4, chs. 1–5

1 *Of the matters discussed in the first book*

When I began to speak of the City of God, I thought it necessary first of all to answer its enemies, who pursue earthly joys and long only for fleeting things. They rail against the Christian religion, which is the one saving and true religion, for whatever sorrows they suffer in respect of these things. And they do this even though they suffer rather through the mercy of God in admonishing them than from His severity in punishing.

Among those enemies there are many ignorant men whose hatred of us is all the more grievously inflamed by the authority of the learned. For the former believe that the extraordinary events which have occurred in their own day did not occur at all in times gone by; and they are supported in this belief even by those who know it to be false, but who conceal their knowledge in order to seem to have just cause for murmuring against us. It was necessary, therefore, to demonstrate from the books in which their own authors have recorded and published the history of times gone by, that matters are far other than the ignorant suppose. At the same time, it was necessary to teach that the false gods whom once they worshipped openly, and still worship in secret, are most vile spirits and malignant and deceitful demons: so much so that they take delight in crimes which, whether real or fictitious, are nonetheless their own, and which they have desired to have celebrated for them at their own festivals. For human infirmity cannot be restrained from the perpetration of damnable deeds for as long as a seemingly divine authority is given to the imitation of such deeds.

In showing these things, I have not relied upon mere conjecture. I have drawn partly upon my own recent memory – for I have myself witnessed such spectacles as are exhibited to these deities – and partly upon the writings of those who have left accounts of these matters to posterity, not as a reproach to their gods, but in their honour. Varro, who is esteemed among our adversaries as a most learned man and the weightiest of authorities, is a case in point. He compiled separate books concerning things human and things divine, assigning some books to the human and some to the divine, according to the dignity of each. And he placed theatrical displays not among things human, but among the divine (although, if there had been none but good and honourable men in the city, theatrical displays could have had no rightful place even among things human). In doing this, he did not rely merely on his own authority. Rather, being born and educated in Rome, he found such displays already established among things divine.

At the end of the first book, I briefly set down the matters which were to be discussed next. Then, in the two books which followed, I discussed some of them. I see, therefore, that I must now pay the remainder of my debt, to satisfy the expectations of my readers.

2 *Of those things which are contained in the second and third books*

I undertook to say something against those who attribute to our religion the disasters lately sustained by the Roman commonwealth. I promised also that I should recall the evils – as many of them and as great as I could remember, or as might seem sufficient – which the city of Rome, or the provinces belonging to her empire, suffered even before it was forbidden to sacrifice to demons. For the Romans would no doubt have attributed all such evils to us if our religion had by then shone upon them or had already prohibited the sacrilegious reign of the demons.

These things, I think, I have disposed of satisfactorily in the second and third books. In the second, I dealt with moral evils, which are to be regarded either as the only evils or as the greatest evils. In the third, I dealt with those evils which only fools dread to suffer: namely, those of the body and of external things, to which good men also are commonly subject. But our adversaries accept moral evils – evils by which they are themselves made evil – not only patiently, but even with pleasure.

Yet how few of the incidents in the history of that one city and her empire have I mentioned! – not even all of them down to the time of Augustus Caesar. What if I had resolved to recall and enlarge upon not those evils which men do to one another, but those which befall the earth from the elements of the universe itself! Apuleius briefly touches upon these things in one part of the book which he wrote called *De mundo*, saying that all earthly things are subject to change, overthrow and destruction. For indeed, to use his own words,

by violent tremors of the earth the ground has opened and swallowed up cities with their peoples; whole regions have been washed away by sudden deluges; those also which had formerly been continents have been made into islands by the coming of strange floods; and others have been made accessible on foot by the withdrawing of the sea. Cities have been overthrown by wind and storm; fires have erupted from the clouds, by which regions of the east have been consumed and have perished; and on western coasts the same devastations have been wrought by the bursting forth of waters and floods. So also, rivers of fire kindled by the gods once flowed from the craters on Etna's summit and poured down the slopes like a torrent.

If I had wished to collect historical examples of this kind from wherever I could, when would I have finished? Yet all these things came to pass in the times before the name of Christ had suppressed those rites of the Romans: those rites which are so vain and inimical to true salvation.

I promised also that I would show what the morals of the Romans were, and for what reason the true God, in Whose power are all kingdoms, deigned to help them increase their empire. I promised to show how little help they received from those whom they esteemed as gods, and how much harm those gods did instead, by their deceit and falsehood. I see, then, that I must now speak of these things, and especially of the growth of the Roman empire. For I have already said much, especially in the second book, of the poisonous deceit of the demons whom the Romans worshipped as gods, and of the great damage that those demons did to their morals.

In all three of the books now completed, however, I have also shown, whenever opportunity arose, how much solace God has granted to good and evil men alike, even in the midst of the evils of war, through the name of Christ, to which the barbarians paid such great honour beyond the custom of war. In this way, 'He maketh His sun to rise on the good and the evil, and giveth rain to the just and to the unjust.'

3 *Whether so broad an empire, when acquired only by warfare, should be counted among the good things of the wise or happy*

Let us now see, therefore, how it is that our adversaries venture to attribute the great breadth and duration of the Roman empire to the gods: to those gods whom they claim to have worshipped with honour even when their service consisted of vile games and the ministry of vile men.

First, however, I should like to devote a little time to the following question. Is it wise or prudent to wish to glory in the breadth and magnitude of an empire when you cannot show that the men whose empire it is are happy? For the Romans always lived in dark fear and cruel lust, surrounded by the disasters of war and the shedding of blood which, whether that of fellow citizens or enemies, was human nonetheless. The joy of such men may be compared to the fragile splendour of glass: they are horribly afraid lest it be suddenly shattered.

That this may be understood more clearly, let us not allow ourselves to be swayed by idle bombast. Let us not allow the edge of our attention to be dulled by the splendid names of things when we hear of 'peoples', 'kingdoms' and 'provinces.' Instead, let us imagine two men (for each individual man, like one letter in a text, is, as it were, an element of the city or kingdom, no matter how extensive it is in its occupation of the earth). Let us suppose one of these men to be poor, or at any rate of moderate means, and the other to be very wealthy. The wealthy man, however, is troubled by fears; he pines with grief; he burns with greed. He is never secure; he is always unquiet and panting from endless confrontations with his enemies. To be sure, he adds to his patrimony in immense measure by these miseries; but alongside these additions he also heaps up the most bitter cares. By contrast, the man of moderate means is self-sufficient on his small and circumscribed estate. He is beloved of his own family, and rejoices in the most sweet peace with kindred, neighbours and friends. He is devoutly religious, well disposed in mind, healthy in body, frugal in life, chaste in morals, untroubled in conscience. I do not know if anyone could be such a fool as to dare to doubt which to prefer. As, therefore, in the case of these two men, so in two families, two peoples, two kingdoms, the same principle of tranquillity applies; and if we use this principle vigilantly, to guide our search, we shall very easily see where vanity dwells, and where happiness lies.

It is beneficial, then, that good men should rule far and wide and long, worshipping the true God and serving Him with true rites and good morals. Nor is this so much beneficial to them as to those over whom they rule. For as far as they themselves are concerned, their godliness and probity, which are great gifts of God, suffice to bring them the true felicity through which this life may be well spent and eternal life received hereafter. In this world, therefore, the rule of good men is of profit not so much to themselves as to human affairs. The reign of the wicked, however, does injury only to those who rule. For they lay waste their own souls by their greater licence in wickedness, whereas those who are placed under them in servitude are not harmed except by their own iniquity. For whatever evils are inflicted upon just men by unjust masters are not the punishment of crime, but the test of virtue. Therefore the good man is free even if he is a slave, whereas the bad man is a slave even if he reigns: a slave, not to one man, but, what is worse, to as many masters as he has vices. When Divine Scripture speaks of these vices, it says, 'For of whom any man is overcome, to the same he is also the bond-slave.'

4 How like kingdoms without justice are to bands of robbers

Justice removed, then, what are kingdoms but great bands of robbers? What are bands of robbers themselves but little kingdoms? The band itself is made up of men; it is governed by the authority of a ruler; it is bound together by a pact of association; and the loot is divided according to an agreed law. If, by the constant addition of desperate men, this scourge grows to such a size that it acquires territory, establishes a seat of government, occupies cities and subjugates peoples, it assumes the name of kingdom more openly. For this name is now manifestly conferred upon it not by the removal of greed, but by the addition of impunity. It was a pertinent and true answer which was made to Alexander the Great by a pirate whom he had seized. When the king asked him what he meant by infesting the sea, the pirate defiantly replied: 'The same as you do when you infest the whole world; but because I do it with a little ship I am called a robber, and because you do it with a great fleet, you are an emperor.'

5 Of the revolt of the gladiators, whose power came to resemble the dignity of kings

I here refrain from asking what sort of men they were that Romulus gathered together. For great care was taken in their case to ensure that, when they were removed from the life that they had led and received into the fellowship of the city, they should cease to dwell on the punishments due to them. Henceforth, therefore, they became more peaceful participants in human affairs. For it was the fear of such punishments which had driven them to ever greater crimes.

I say this, however: that the Roman empire itself, which had already grown great by subjugating many peoples, and which was an object of terror to the rest, was itself bitterly injured, gravely alarmed, and with no small effort avoided a disastrous reversal, when a very small number of gladiators, fleeing from the games in Campania, assembled a large army, appointed three generals, and laid waste the whole breadth of Italy with the utmost cruelty. Let our adversaries tell us what gods helped those men to rise from a small and inconsiderable band of robbers to a kingdom that the Romans, for all their great forces and fortresses, were obliged to fear. Or will they deny that the gladiators received divine assistance because they did not remain in power for long?

As if, however, the life of any man were long. According to that reasoning, the gods help no one to rule; for every man dies in a little while, nor is that to be deemed a benefit which vanishes like a mist in a moment of time for every man, and so for all men one by one. After all, what does it matter to those who worshipped the gods under Romulus and are now long dead that the Roman empire increased so greatly after their death? They are now pleading their causes before the gods of the underworld. (Whether those causes are good or bad is not pertinent to our present argument.) This remark applies even to those who, in the few days of their life, have passed swiftly and with haste through the imperial office itself, bearing with them the heavy burdens of their own deeds (although the office itself has endured throughout long ages of time, as one generation of mortals has died and been succeeded by another).

If, however, even those benefits which endure only for the shortest time are to be attributed to the gods, then those gladiators must have received considerable help. They burst the bonds of their servile condition: they fled; they escaped. They assembled a great and most powerful army, obedient to the counsel and commands of their kings and much feared by the proud might of Rome. Remaining unsubdued by several Roman generals, they seized much plunder, gained many victories, enjoyed whatever pleasures they wished, and did what their lust suggested. Until they were finally conquered – a feat achieved only with the greatest difficulty – they lived sublime and enthroned. Let us, however, come to weightier matters.

...

Book 19, chs. 11–14, 17

11 *Of the happiness of eternal peace, which is the end or true perfection of the saints*

We may say of peace, then, what we have already said of eternal life: that it is our Final Good. This is especially true in the light of what is said in the holy psalm concerning the subject of this laborious discourse, the City of God: 'Praise the Lord, O Jerusalem; praise thy God, O Sion. For He hath strengthened the bars of thy gates; He hath blessed thy children within thee, Who hath made thy borders peace.' For when the bars of her gates shall be strengthened, none shall enter her or go out from her. Thus, we should understand the peace of her borders to be a reference to that final peace which we here wish to demonstrate. The name of the City itself, that is, Jerusalem, has a mystic significance; for, as I have said already, it means 'Vision of Peace'.

The word 'peace', however, is frequently used in connexion with merely mortal affairs, where there is certainly no eternal life; and so I have preferred to use the expression 'eternal life' rather than 'peace' in depicting the end of this City, where its Supreme Good will be found. Of this end the apostle says, 'But now, being freed from sin, and become servants to God, ye have your fruit unto holiness, and the end life eternal.' On the other hand, those who have no familiarity with Holy Scripture may suppose that the life of the wicked also is eternal life. They may think this because, even according to some of their own philosophers, the soul is immortal. Or they may think it because of our own faith in the endless punishment of the ungodly, believing that these surely could not be tortured for ever unless they lived for ever. Thus, in order that everyone may more easily understand what we mean, let us say that the end of this City, in which it will possess its Supreme Good, is to be called either 'peace in life eternal' or 'life eternal in peace'. For peace is so great a good that, even in the sphere of earthly and mortal affairs, we hear no word more thankfully, and nothing is desired with greater longing: in short, it is not possible to find anything better. If I wish to speak at somewhat greater length on the subject, therefore, this will not, I think, be a burden to my readers. They will attend both for the sake of understanding the end of the City which is the subject of this discourse, and also for the sake of the sweetness of peace, which all men love.

12 *That even the ferocity of war and all the discords of men have, as their end, the peace which every nature desires*

Whoever who joins me in an examination, however cursory, of human affairs and our common human nature will acknowledge that, just as there is no one who does not wish to be joyful, so there is no one who does not wish to have peace. Indeed, even when men choose to wage war, they desire nothing but victory. By means of war, therefore, they desire to achieve peace with glory; for what else is victory but the subjugation of those who oppose us? And when this is achieved, there will be peace. Wars themselves, then, are conducted with the intention of peace, even when they are conducted by those who are concerned to exercise their martial prowess in command and battle. Hence it is clear that peace is the desired end of war. For every man seeks peace, even in making war; but no one seeks war by making peace. Indeed, even those who wish to disrupt an existing state of peace do so not because they hate peace, but because they desire the present peace to be exchanged for one of their own choosing. Their desire, therefore, is not that there should be no peace, but that it should be the kind of peace that they wish for. And even when they have separated themselves from others by sedition, they cannot bring about what they intend unless they maintain at least some kind of peace with their co-conspirators or confederates. Indeed, even robbers wish to have peace with their fellows, if only in order to invade the peace of others with greater force and safety. One robber may, of course, be so unsurpassed in strength, and so suspicious of others, that he does not trust any accomplice, but plots his crimes and commits his robberies and murders on his own. Even he, however, maintains some shadow of peace, at least with those whom he cannot kill, and from whom he wishes to conceal his deeds. Also, he is at pains to ensure peace in his own household, with his wife and children and whomever else he has there. Without doubt he takes delight in their obedience to his nod, and, if this does not happen, he is angry. He rebukes and punishes; and, if necessary, he employs harsh measures to impose upon his household a peace which, he believes, cannot exist unless all the other members of the same domestic society are subject to one head; and this head, in his own house, is himself. Thus, if he were offered the servitude of a larger number – of a city, or of a nation – who would serve him in just the same way as he had required his household to serve him, then he would no longer lurk like a robber in his lair; he would raise himself up as a king for all to see. But the same greed and malice would remain in him. All men, then, desire to have peace with their own people, whom they wish to see living according to their will. For they wish to make even those against whom they wage wars their own if they can, and to subdue them by imposing upon them the laws of their own peace.

Let us, however, consider a creature depicted in poetry and fable: a creature so unsociable and wild that people have preferred to call him a semi-man rather than a man. His kingdom was the solitude of an awful cavern, and he was so singular in his wickedness that a name was found for him reflecting that fact – for he was called Cacus, and *kakos* is the Greek word for 'wicked'. He had no wife with whom to give and receive caresses; no children to play with when little or to instruct when a little bigger; and no friends with whom to enjoy converse, not even his father Vulcan. He was happier than his father only in not having begotten another such monster as himself. He gave nothing to anyone; rather, he took what he wanted from anyone he could and whenever he could. Despite all this, however, in the solitude of his own cave, the floor of which, as Virgil describes it, ever reeked with the blood of recent butchery, he wished for nothing other than a peace in which no one should molest him, and a rest which no man's violence, or the fear of it, should disturb. Also, he desired to be at peace with his own body; and in so far as he had such peace, all was well with him. For he governed his members, and they obeyed him. His mortal nature rebelled against him when it needed anything, and stirred up the sedition of hunger, which threatened to banish and exclude the soul from the body; and so he made haste to pacify that nature as far as possible: he hunted, slew and devoured. Thus, for all his monstrous and wild savagery, his aim was peace; for he sought, by these monstrous and ferocious means, only to preserve the peace of his own life. Thus, had he been willing to make with other men the peace which he was ready enough to make in his own cave and with himself, he would not have been called wicked, nor a monster, nor a semi-man. Or if it was the appearance of his body and his vomiting of smoke and flames that frightened away human companions, perhaps it was not the desire to do harm that made him so ferocious, but the necessity of preserving his own life. Or perhaps he never existed after all, or, more probably, was not as the poets have in their vanity described him as being. For if Cacus had not been excessively blamed, Hercules would have been less fulsomely praised for slaying him. As in the case of many such poetic fictions, therefore, the existence of such a man–or rather, as I have said, semi-man – is not to be believed in.

Even the most savage beasts, then, from whom Cacus derived the ferocious part of his nature (for he is also called a semi-beast) protect their own kind by a kind of peace. They mate, they beget and bear young, and they rear and nourish them. They do this even when, as in most cases, they are unsocial and solitary: when they are not, that is, like sheep, deer, doves, starlings, and bees, but like lions, wolves, foxes, eagles and owls. What tigress does not purr softly over her cubs and lay her fierceness aside while she caresses them? What kite, solitary as he is while hovers over his prey, does not take a mate, make a nest, help to hatch the eggs, rear the chicks, and preserve with the mother of his family, as it were, a domestic society which is as peaceful as he can make it? How much more strongly, then, is a man drawn by the laws of his nature, so to speak, to enter into a similarly peaceful association with his fellow men, so far as it lies within his power to do so? For even the wicked wage war only to maintain the peace of their own people. They wish to make all men their own people, if they can, so that all men and all things might serve one master; but how could that happen, unless they should consent to be at peace with him, either through love or fear?

Thus, pride is a perverted imitation of God. For pride hates a fellowship of equality under God, and wishes to impose its own dominion upon its equals, in place of God's rule. Therefore, it hates the just peace of God, and it loves its own unjust peace; but it cannot help loving peace of some kind or other. For no vice is so entirely contrary to nature as to destroy even the last vestiges of nature.

Thus, he who has learnt to prefer right to wrong and the rightly ordered to the perverse, sees that, in comparison with the peace of the just, the peace of the unjust is not worthy to be called peace at all. Even that which is perverse, however, must of necessity be in, or derived from, or associated with, and to that extent at peace with, some part of the order of things among which it has its being or of which it consists. Otherwise, it would not exist at all. For example, if someone were to hang upside-down, this position of the body and disposition of the limbs would certainly be a perverted one. For what nature places above would be beneath, and what nature intends to be beneath would be above. This perversity disturbs the peace of the flesh, and therefore causes distress. Nonetheless, the spirit is at peace with its body and strives to secure its health: it is precisely for that reason that there is pain. And even if the spirit is driven out of the body by the latter's distresses, still, as long as the disposition of the body's members remains intact, what is left is not without a kind of peace: which is why there is still something to hang there. And if the earthly body presses down towards the ground, and strains against the bond by which it is suspended, it fends towards the position of its own peace, and by the voice of its own weight, so to speak, entreats a place where it may rest. And so even when lifeless and without any sensation, it does not depart from the peace of its natural position, either while occupying that position or tending towards it. Again, if remedies and preservatives are applied to prevent the dissolution and decomposition of the corpse in its present form, a kind of peace still joins one part to another and maintains the whole mass in an earthly condition which is suitable, and in that sense peaceable. If, on the other hand, no such treatment is applied, and the body is abandoned to the usual course of nature, there is for a while a kind of tumult of exhalations which are disagreeable and offensive to our senses (that is, the stench of decay of which we are aware). This persists until the body unites with the elements of the world and, little by little, particle by particle, passes away into their peace.

In all this, however, nothing is in any way removed from the sway of the laws made by the supreme Creator and Ordainer Who directs the peace of the universe. For although minute animals are produced in the carcase of a larger animal, all those little bodies, by the same law of their Creator, serve their little spirits in the peace that preserves their lives. Even when the flesh of dead animals is devoured by other animals, it still finds itself subject to the same laws: to the laws which are distributed throughout the universe for the preservation of every kind of mortal creature, and which give peace by bringing suitable things suitably together. This is true no matter where it is taken, no matter with what substances it is joined, and no matter what substances it is converted and changed into.

13 *Of the universal peace which the law of nature preserves through all disturbances, and by which, through God's ordinance, everyone comes to his just desert*

The peace of the body, therefore, lies in the balanced ordering of its parts; the peace of the irrational soul lies in the rightly ordered disposition of the appetites; the peace of the rational soul lies in the rightly ordered relationship of cognition and action; the peace of body and soul lies in the rightly ordered life and health of a living creature; peace between mortal man and God is an ordered obedience, in faith, under an eternal law; and peace between men is an ordered agreement of mind with mind. The peace of a household is an ordered concord, with respect to command and obedience, of those who dwell together; the peace of a city is an ordered concord, with respect to command and obedience, of the citizens; and the peace of the Heavenly City is a perfectly ordered and perfectly harmonious fellowship in the enjoyment of God, and of one another in God. The peace of all things lies in the tranquillity of order; and order is the disposition of equal and unequal things in such a way as to give to each its proper place.

The wretched, however, insofar as they are wretched, are clearly not in a condition of peace. Therefore, they lack that tranquillity of order in which there is no disturbance. Precisely because of their misery, however, even they cannot be said to lie beyond the sphere of order; for they are miserable deservedly and justly. They are not, indeed, united with the blessed; yet it is by the law of order that they are severed from them. And when they become accustomed to the condition in which they are, with at any rate some degree of harmony, they are then without disturbance of mind. Thus, they have among them some tranquillity of order, and therefore some peace. But they are still wretched, simply because, although they are to some extent serene and free from pain, they are not in that place where they would be wholly serene and free from pain. They would, however, be all the more wretched if they were not at peace with that law according to which the natural order is organised. For when they suffer, their peace is disturbed in the part where they suffer, yet there is still peace in that part which does not feel the pain of burning, and in so far as their nature is not dissolved. Just as there can be life without pain, therefore, but no pain without life, so there can be peace without any war, but no war without some degree of peace. This is not because of the nature of war itself, but because war can only be waged by or within persons who are in some sense natural beings: beings who could not exist at all if peace of some kind did not exist within them.

There exists, then, a nature in which there is no evil, and in which evil cannot exist at all. But there cannot exist a nature in which there is no good. Hence, in so far as it is a nature, not even the nature of the devil himself is evil. It is perversion that makes it evil. Thus, the devil did not abide in the truth, but he did not escape the judgment of the Truth. He did not remain in the tranquillity of order, but he did not thereby avoid the power of the Ordainer. The good imparted by God, which the devil has in his nature, does not remove him from God's justice, by which his punishment is ordained; nor does God punish the good which He has created, but the evil which the devil has committed. Moreover, God does not take away everything that He gave to that nature. He removes something, yet He leaves something also, so that there may be something left to feel pain at what has been taken away. And this pain itself testifies to both the good that was taken away and the good that is left; for, if there had been no good left, there could be no grief for the good which was taken away. He who sins is in a worse condition still if he rejoices in the loss of righteousness; but the sinner who suffers grief, even though he acquires no good thereby, is at least grieving at the loss of salvation. For righteousness and salvation are both goods, and the loss of any good is a matter for grief rather than rejoicing: if, that is, the loss is not counteracted by the gain of a greater good; for instance, righteousness of soul is a greater good than health of body. It is more fitting, therefore, for an unrighteous man to grieve over his punishment than to rejoice in his fault. Hence, just as the delight in forsaking good which a man takes when he sins is evidence of a bad will, so the grief which he feels at the loss of good when he is punished is evidence of a good nature. For when a man grieves over the loss of his nature's peace, his grief arises from some remnants of that peace, whereby his nature befriends itself. Moreover, it is right that, in the final punishment, the wicked and ungodly should in their torments lament the loss of their natural goods, knowing that they have been most justly deprived of those goods by the God Whom they despised when He most graciously bestowed them.

God, therefore, is the most wise Creator and just Ordainer of all natures, Who has established the mortal human race as the greatest adornment of things earthly, and Who has given to men certain good things appropriate to this life. These are: temporal peace, in proportion to the short span of a mortal life, consisting in bodily health and soundness, and the society of one's own kind; and all things necessary for the preservation and recovery of this peace. These latter include those things which are appropriate and accessible to our senses, such as light, speech, breathable air, drinkable water, and whatever the body requires to feed, clothe, shelter, heal or adorn it. And these things are given under a most fair condition: that every mortal who makes right use of these goods suited to the peace of mortal men shall receive ampler and better goods, namely, the peace of immortality and the glory and honour appropriate to it, in an eternal life made fit for the enjoyment of God and of one's neighbour in God. He who uses temporal goods ill, however, shall lose them, and shall not receive eternal goods either.

14 Of the order and law which hold sway in heaven and on earth, according to which it comes to pass that human society is served by those who rule it

In the earthly city, then, the whole use of temporal things is directed towards the enjoyment of earthly peace. In the Heavenly City, however, such use is directed towards the enjoyment of eternal peace. Thus, if we were irrational animals, we should desire nothing beyond the proper arrangement of the body's parts and the satisfaction of our appetites. We should, that is, desire only fleshly comfort and an abundant supply of pleasures, so that the body's peace might produce peace of soul. For if bodily peace is lacking, the peace of the irrational soul is also impeded, because it cannot achieve the satisfaction of its appetites. The two kinds of peace together, however, produce that mutual relation of body and soul which gives rise to an ordered harmony of life and health. For all living creatures show their love of bodily peace when they shun pain, and of peace of soul when they seek pleasure in order to satisfy the demands of their appetites. In the same way, they show clearly enough by shunning death how greatly they delight in that peace which consists in an harmonious relation of soul and body.

But because there is in man a rational soul, he subordinates all that he has in common with the beasts to the peace of that rational soul. He does this so that his mind may engage to some degree in contemplation, and so that he may in some degree act according to such contemplation, thereby displaying that ordered agreement of thought and action which, as we have said, constitutes the peace of the rational soul. And, for this purpose, he should wish to be neither distressed by pain, nor disturbed by desire, nor extinguished by death, so that he may arrive at some useful knowledge and regulate his life and morals according to that knowledge. But he has need of divine guidance, which he may obey with confidence, and of divine aid, so that he may obey it freely. Otherwise, in his zeal for knowledge, he may fall into some deadly error because of the infirmity of the human mind. Also, for as long as he is in this mortal body, he is a pilgrim, far from the Lord; and so he walks by faith, not by sight. That is why he refers all peace, whether of body or of soul, or of both, to that peace which mortal man has with the immortal God, so that he may exhibit an ordered obedience, in faith, to the eternal Law.

Now God, our Master, teaches two chief precepts: that is, love of God and love of neighbour. In these precepts, a man finds three things which he is to love: God, himself, and his neighbour; for a man who loves God does not err in loving himself. It follows, therefore, that he will take care to ensure that his neighbour also loves God, since he is commanded to love his neighbour as himself. Also, as far as he can, he will do the same for his wife, his children, his servants, and all other men. And, to the same end, he will wish his neighbour to do the same for him, if he should have need of such help. In this way, he will be at peace with all men as far as in him lies: there will be that peace among men which consists in well-ordered concord. And the order of this concord is, first, that a man should harm no one, and, second, that he should do good to all, so far as he can. In the first place, therefore, he must care for his own household; for the order of nature and of human society itself gives him readier access to them, and greater opportunity of caring for them. Hence, the apostle says, 'But if any provide not for his own, and specially for those of his own house, he hath denied the faith, and is worse than an infidel.' In this care lies the foundation of domestic peace: that is, of an ordered concord with respect to command and obedience among those who dwell together. For commands are given by those who care for the rest – by husband to wife, parents to children, and masters to servants. And those who are cared for obey: women obey their husbands, children their parents, and servants their masters. In the household of the just man, however, who 'lives by faith' and who is still a pilgrim on his way to that Heavenly City, even those who command are the servants of those whom they seem to command. For it is not out of any desire for mastery that they command; rather, they do so from a dutiful concern for others: not out of pride in ruling, but because they love mercy.

...

17 *What produces peace, and what discord, between the Heavenly City and the earthly*

But a household of men who do not live by faith strives to find an earthly peace in the goods and advantages which belong to this temporal life. By contrast, a household of men who live by faith looks forward to the blessings which are promised as eternal in the life to come; and such men make use of earthly and temporal things like pilgrims: they are not captivated by them, nor are they deflected by them from their progress towards God. They are, of course, sustained by them, so that they may more easily bear the burdens of the corruptible body which presses down the soul; but they do not in the least allow these things to increase such burdens.

Thus both kinds of men and both kinds of household make common use of those things which are necessary to this mortal life; but each has its own very different end in using them. So also, the earthly city, which does not live by faith, desires an earthly peace, and it establishes an ordered concord of civic obedience and rule in order to secure a kind of co-operation of men's wills for the sake of attaining the things which belong to this mortal life. But the Heavenly City – or, rather, that part of it which is a pilgrim in this condition of mortality, and which lives by faith – must of necessity make use of this peace also, until this mortal state, for which such peace is necessary, shall have passed away. Thus, it lives like a captive and a pilgrim, even though it has already received the promise of redemption, and the gift of the Spirit as a kind of pledge of it. But, for as long as it does so, it does not hesitate to obey the laws of the earthly city, whereby the things necessary for the support of this mortal life are administered. In this way, then, since this mortal condition is common to both cities, a harmony is preserved between them with respect to the things which belong to this condition.

But the earthly city has had among its members certain wise men whose doctrines are rejected by the divine teaching. Deceived either by their own speculations or by demons, these philosophers believed that there are many gods who must be induced to take an interest in human affairs. They believed also that these gods have, as it were, different spheres of influence with different offices attached to them. Thus the body is the responsibility of one god, the mind that of another; and, within the body, one god has charge of the head, another of the neck, and so on with each of the parts in turn. Similarly, within the mind, one god is responsible for intelligence, another for learning, another for anger, another for desire. And so too with all the things which touch our lives: there is a god who has charge of cattle, of corn, of wine, of oil, of woodlands, of money, of navigation, of war and victory, of marriage, of birth, of fertility, and so on. But the Heavenly City knows only one God Who is to be worshipped, and it decrees, with faithful piety, that to Him alone is to be given that service which the Greeks call *latreia*, and which is due only to God. Because of this difference, it has not been possible for the Heavenly City to have laws of religion in common with the earthly city. It has been necessary for her to dissent from the earthly city in this regard, and to become a burden to those who think differently. Thus, she has had to bear the brunt of the anger and hatred and persecutions of her adversaries, except insofar as their minds have sometimes been struck by the multitude of the Christians and by the divine aid always extended to them.

Therefore, for as long as this Heavenly City is a pilgrim on earth, she summons citizens of all nations and every tongue, and brings together a society of pilgrims in which no attention is paid to any differences in the customs, laws, and institutions by which earthly peace is achieved or maintained. She does not rescind or destroy these things, however. For whatever differences there are among the various nations, these all tend towards the same end of earthly peace. Thus, she preserves and follows them, provided only that they do not impede the religion by which we are taught that the one supreme and true God is to be worshipped. And so even the Heavenly City makes use of earthly peace during her pilgrimage, and desires and maintains the co-operation of men's wills in attaining those things which belong to the mortal nature of man, in so far as this may be allowed without prejudice to true godliness and religion. Indeed, she directs that earthly peace towards heavenly peace: towards the peace which is so truly such that – at least so far as rational creatures are concerned – only it can really be held to be peace and called such. For this peace is a perfectly ordered and perfectly harmonious fellowship in the enjoyment of God, and of one another in God. When we have reached that peace, our life will no longer be a mortal one; rather, we shall then be fully and certainly alive. There will be no animal body to press down the soul by its corruption, but a spiritual body standing in need of nothing: a body subject in every part to the will. This peace the Heavenly City possesses in faith while on its pilgrimage, and by this faith it lives righteously, directing towards the attainment of that peace every good act which it performs either for God, or – since the city's life is inevitably a social one – for neighbour.

CONSTANTINE PORPHYROGENITUS

CONSTANTINE was born in September 905 CE, the son of the Byzantine emperor, Leo, and his mistress (later wife), Zoe. Since there was no other son, an accommodation was reached with the church and the baby was proclaimed a prince on 6 January 906, though his position was not secure for some time. However, he soon became known as "born to the purple" (hence the Greek nickname Porphyrogenitus). Technically, Constantine became emperor in 912 at the age of seven, following the deaths of his father and uncle. His early life was surrounded by the internecine court intrigues for which Byzantium had already become famous and he was lucky to survive. Eventually, however, in 945 he became full and unchallenged emperor. He had himself always been primarily a scholar and his period as emperor – largely uneventful in terms of wars or major crises – was noted for its dedication to the arts and to scholarship in all fields. Constantine himself wrote three major works; the first an encyclopedia of Byzantine ritual (*De Ceremoniis Aulae Byzantinae*), the second a geographical and historical description of the Imperial provinces (*De Thematibus*), and the third, excerpted here, the political treatise known to us as *De Administrando Imperio*. In fact, Constantine himself simply entitled this "Constantine to his son Romanus" and clearly intended it as a kind of practical textbook of statecraft. He died in 959, his twenty-year-old son Romanus becoming emperor after him.

From *De Administrando Imperio*

In Christ the eternal emperor of the Romans to his son Romanus the emperor crowned of God and born in the purple

Proem

A wise son maketh glad a father, and an affectionate father taketh delight in a prudent son. For the Lord giveth wit to speak in season, and addeth thereto an ear to hear; with Him is the treasure of wisdom, and from him cometh every perfect gift; He setteth kings upon the throne and giveth unto them the lordship over all. Now therefore hearken unto me, my son, and being adept in this my teaching thou shalt be wise among the prudent, and be accounted prudent among the wise; the peoples shall bless thee, and the multitudes of the nations shall call thee blessed. Be instructed in what it behoves thee before all else to know, and lay hold skilfully upon the helm of the rule. Study the things that are now, and be instructed concerning the things that are to be, so that thou mayst amass experience with sound judgment, and thou shalt be most competent in thine affairs. Lo, I set a doctrine before thee, so that being sharpened thereby in experience and knowledge, thou shalt not stumble concerning the best counsels and the common good: first, in what each nation has power to advantage the Romans, and in what to hurt, and how and by what other nation each severally may be encountered in arms and subdued; then, concerning their ravenous and insatiate temper and the gifts they demand inordinately; next, concerning also the difference between other nations, *their* origins and customs and manner of life, and the position and climate of the land they dwell in, its geographical description and measurement, and moreover concerning events which have occurred at various times between the Romans and different nations; and thereafter, what reforms have been introduced from time to time in our state, and also throughout the Roman empire. These things have I discovered of my own wisdom, and have decreed that they shall be made known unto thee, my beloved son, in order that thou mayst know the difference between each of these *nations*, and how either to treat with and conciliate them, or to make war upon and oppose. For so shall they quake before thee as one mighty in wisdom, and as from fire shall they flee from thee; their lips shall be bridled, and as darts shall thy words wound them unto death. Thou shalt appear terrible unto them, and at thy face shall trembling take hold upon them. And the Almighty shall cover thee with his shield, and thy Creator shall endue thee with understanding: He shall direct thy steps, and shall establish thee upon a sure foundation. Thy throne shall be as the sun before Him, and His eyes shall be looking towards thee, and naught of harm shall touch thee, for He hath chosen thee and set thee apart from thy mother's womb, and hath given unto thee His rule as unto one excellent above all men, and hath set thee as a refuge upon a hill and as a statue of gold upon an high place, and as a city upon a mountain hath He raised thee up, that the nations may bring to thee their gifts and thou mayst be adored of them that dwell upon the earth. But Thou, O Lord my God, whose rule abideth unharmed for ever, prosper him in his ways who through Thee was begotten of me, and may the visitation of Thy face be toward him, and Thine ear be inclined to his supplications. May Thy hand cover him, and may he rule because of truth, and may Thy right hand guide him; may his ways be directed before Thee to keep thy statutes. May foes fall before his face, and his enemies lick the dust. May the stem of his race be shady with leaves of many offspring, and the shadow of his fruit cover the kingly mountains; for by Thee do kings rule, glorifying Thee for ever and ever.

1. Of the Pechenegs, and how many advantages accrue from their being at peace with the emperor of the Romans

Hear now, my son, those things of which I think you *should* not be ignorant, and be wise that you may attain to government. For I maintain that while learning is a good thing for all the rest as well, who are subjects, yet it is especially so for you, who are bound to take thought for the safety of all, and to steer and guide the laden ship of the world. And if in setting out my subject I have followed the plain and beaten track of speech and, so to say, idly running and simple prose, do not wonder at that, my son. For I have not been studious to make a display of fine writing or of an Atticizing style, swollen with the sublime and lofty, but rather have been eager by means of every-day and conversational narrative to teach you those things of which I think you should not be ignorant, and which may without difficulty provide that intelligence and prudence which are the fruit of long experience.

I conceive, then, that it is always greatly to the advantage of the emperor of the Romans to be minded to keep the peace with the nation of the Pechenegs and to conclude conventions and treaties of friendship with them and to send every year to them from our side a diplomatic agent with presents befitting and suitable to that nation, and to take from their side sureties, that is, hostages and a diplomatic agent, who shall come, together with the competent minister, to this city protected of God, and shall enjoy all imperial benefits and gifts suitable for the emperor to bestow.

This nation of the Pechenegs is neighbour to the district of Cherson, and if they are not friendly disposed towards us, they may make excursions and plundering raids against Cherson, and may ravage Cherson itself and the so-called Regions.

2. Of the Pechenegs and the Russians

The Pechenegs are neighbours to and march with the Russians also, and often, when the two are not at peace with one another, raid Russia, and do her considerable harm and outrage.

The Russians also are much concerned to keep the peace with the Pechenegs. For they buy of them horned cattle and horses and sheep whereby they live more easily and comfortably, since none of the aforesaid animals is found in Russia. Moreover, the Russians are quite unable to set out for wars beyond their borders unless they are at peace with the Pechenegs, because while they are away from their homes, these may come upon them and destroy and outrage their property. And so the Russians both to avoid being harmed by them and because of the strength of that nation, are the more concerned always to be in alliance with them and to have them for support, so as both to be rid of their enmity and to enjoy the advantage of their assistance.

Nor can the Russians come at this imperial city of the Romans, either for war or for trade, unless they are at peace with the Pechenegs, because when the Russians come with their ships to the barrages of the river and cannot pass through unless they lift their ships off the river and carry them past by porting them on their shoulders, then the men of this nation of the Pechenegs set upon them, and, as they cannot do two things at once, they are easily routed and cut to pieces.

3. Of the Pechenegs and Turks

The tribe of the Turks, too, trembles greatly at and fears the said Pechenegs, because they have often been defeated by them and brought to the verge of complete annihilation. Therefore the Turks always look on the Pechenegs with dread, and are held in check by them.

4. Of the Pechenegs and Russians and Turks

So long as the emperor of the Romans is at peace with the Pechenegs, neither Russians nor Turks can come upon the Roman dominions by force of arms, nor can they exact from the Romans large and inflated sums in money and goods as the price of peace, for they fear the strength of this nation which the emperor can turn against them while they are campaigning against the Romans. For the Pechenegs, if they are leagued in friendship with the emperor and won over by him through letters and gifts, can easily come upon the country both of the Russians and of the Turks, and enslave their women and children and ravage their country.

5. Of the Pechenegs and the Bulgarians

To the Bulgarians also the emperor of the Romans will appear more formidable, and can impose on them the need for tranquillity, if he is at peace with the Pechenegs, because the said Pechenegs are neighbours to these Bulgarians also, and when they wish, either for private gain or to do a favour to the emperor of the Romans, they can easily march against Bulgaria, and with their preponderating multitude and their strength overwhelm and defeat them. And so the Bulgarians also continually struggle and strive to maintain peace and harmony with the Pechenegs. For from having frequently been crushingly defeated and plundered by them, they have learned by experience the value and advantage of being always at peace with them.

6. Of the Pechenegs and Chersonites

Yet another folk of these Pechenegs lies over against the district of Cherson; they trade with the Chersonites, and perform services for them and for the emperor in Russia and Chazaria and Zichia and all the parts beyond: that is to say, they receive from the Chersonites a prearranged remuneration in respect of this service proportionate to their labour and trouble, in the form of pieces of purple cloth, ribbons, silks, gold brocade, pepper, scarlet or 'Parthian' leather, and other commodities which they require, according to a contract which each Chersonite may make or agree to with an individual Pecheneg. For these Pechenegs are free men and, so to say, independent, and never perform any service without remuneration.

7. Of the dispatch of imperial agents from Cherson to Patzinacia

When an imperial agent goes over to Cherson on this service, he must at once send to Patzinacia and demand hostages and an escort, and on their arrival he must leave the hostages under guard in the city of Cherson, and himself go off with the escort to Patzinacia and carry out his instructions. Now these Pechenegs, who are ravenous and keenly covetous of articles rare among them, are shameless in their demands for generous gifts, the hostages demanding this for themselves and that for their wives, and the escort something for their own trouble and some more for the wear and tear of their cattle. Then, when the imperial agent enters their country, they first ask for the emperor's gifts, and then again, when these have glutted the menfolk, they ask for the presents for their wives and parents. Also, all who come with him to escort him on his way back to Cherson demand payment from him for their trouble and the wear and tear of their cattle.

8. Of the dispatch of imperial agents with ships of war from the city protected of God to Patzinacia along the Danube and Dnieper and Dniester rivers

In the region of Bulgaria also is settled a folk of the Pechenegs, toward the region of the Dnieper and the Dniester and the other rivers of those parts. And when an imperial agent is dispatched from here with ships of war, he may, without going to Cherson, shortly and swiftly find these same Pechenegs here; and when he has found them, the imperial agent sends a message to them by his man, himself remaining on board the ships of war, carrying along with him and guarding in the ships of war the imperial goods. And they come down to him, and when they come down, the imperial agent gives them hostages of his men, and himself takes other hostages of these Pechenegs, and holds them in the ships of war, and then he makes agreement with them; and when the Pechenegs have taken their oaths to the imperial agent according to their 'zakana', he presents them with the imperial gifts, and takes from among them as many 'friends' as he sees fit, and returns. Agreement must be made with them on this condition, that wherever the emperor calls upon them, they are to serve him, whether against the Russians, or against the Bulgarians, or again against the Turks. For they are able to make war upon all these, and as they have often come against them, are now regarded by them with dread. And this is clear from what follows. For once when the cleric Gabriel was dispatched by imperial mandate to the Turks and said to them, 'The emperor declares that you are to go and expel the Pechenegs from their place and settle yourselves there (for in former days you used to be settled there yourselves) so that you may be near to my imperial majesty, and when I wish, I may send and find you speedily', then all the chief men of the Turks cried aloud with one voice, 'We are not putting ourselves on the track of the Pechenegs; for we cannot fight them, because their country is great and their people numerous and they are the devil's brats; and do not say this to us again; for we do not like it!'

When spring is over, the Pechenegs cross to the far side of the Dnieper river, and always pass the summer there.

...

13. *Of the nations that are neighbours to the Turks*

These nations are adjacent to the Turks: on their western side Francia; on their northern the Pechenegs; and on the south side great Moravia, the country of Sphendoplokos, which has now been totally devastated by these Turks, and occupied by them. On the side of the mountains the Croats are adjacent to the Turks.

The Pechenegs too can attack the Turks, and plunder and harm them greatly, as has been said above in the chapter on the Pechenegs.

Fix, my son, your mind's eye upon my words, and learn those things which I command you, and you will be able in due season as from ancestral treasures to bring forth the wealth of wisdom, and to display the sap of a sharp wit. Know therefore that all the tribes of the north have, as it were implanted in them by nature, a ravening greed of money, never satiated, and so they demand everything and hanker after everything and have desires that know no limit or circumscription, but are always eager for more, and desirous to acquire great profits in exchange for a small service. And so these importunate demands and brazenly submitted claims must be turned back and rebutted by plausible speeches and prudent and clever excuses, which, in so far as our experience has enabled us to arrive at them, will, to speak summarily, run more or less as follows:

Should they ever require and demand, whether they be Chazars, or Turks, or again Russians, or any other nation of the northerners and Scythians, as frequently happens, that some of the imperial vesture or diadems or state robes should be sent to them in return for some service or office performed by them, then thus you shall excuse yourself: 'These robes of state and the diadems, which you call "kamelaukia", were not fashioned by men, nor by human arts devised or elaborated, but, as we find it written in secret stories of old history, when God made emperor that famous Constantine the great, who was the first Christian emperor, He sent him these robes of state by the hand of His angel, and the diadems which you call "kamelaukia", and charged him to lay them in the great and holy church of God, which, after the name of that very wisdom which is the property of God, is called St. Sophia; and not to clothe himself in them every day, but *only* when it is a great public festival of the Lord. And so by God's command he laid them up, and they hang above the holy table in the sanctuary of this same church, and are for the ornament of the church. And the rest of the imperial vestments and cloaks lie spread out upon this holy table. And when a festival of our Lord and God Jesus Christ comes round, the patriarch takes up such of these robes of state and diadems as are suitable and appropriated to that occasion, and sends them to the emperor, and he wears them in the procession, and only in it, as the servant and minister of God, and after use returns them again to the church, and they are laid up in it. Moreover, there is a curse of the holy and great emperor Constantine engraved upon this holy table of the church of God, according as he was charged by God through the angel, that if an emperor for any use or occasion or unseasonable desire be minded to take of them and either himself misuse them or give them to others, he shall be anathematized as the foe and enemy of the commands of God, and shall be excommunicated from the church; moreover, if he himself be minded to make others like them, these too the church of God must take, with the freely expressed approval of all the archbishops and of the senate; and it shall not be in the authority either of the emperor, or of the patriarch, or of any other, to take these robes of state or the diadems from the holy church of God. And mighty dread hangs over them who are minded to transgress any of these divine ordinances. For one of the emperors, Leo by name, who also married a wife from Chazaria, out of his folly and rashness took up one of these diadems when no festival of the Lord was toward, and without the approval of the patriarch put it about his head. And straightway a carbuncle came forth upon his forehead so that in torment at the pains of it he evilly departed his evil life, and ran upon death untimely. And, this rash act being summarily avenged, thereafter a rule was made, that when he is about to be crowned the emperor must first swear and give surety that he will neither do nor conceive anything against what has been ordained and kept from ancient times, and then may he be crowned by the patriarch and perform and execute the rites appropriate to the established festival'.

Similar care and thought you shall take in the matter of the liquid fire which is discharged through tubes, so that if any shall ever venture to demand this too, as they have often made demands of us also, you may rebut and dismiss them in words like these: 'This too was revealed and taught by *God* through an angel to the great and holy Constantine, the first Christian emperor, and concerning this too he received great charges from the same angel, as we are assured by the faithful witness of our fathers and grandfathers, that it should be manufactured among the Christians only and in the city ruled by them, and nowhere else at all, nor should it be sent nor taught to any other nation whatsoever. And so, for the confirmation of this among those who should come after him, this great emperor caused curses to be inscribed on the holy table of the church of God, that he who should dare to give of this fire to another nation should neither be called a Christian, nor be held worthy of any rank or office; and if he should be the holder of any such, he should be expelled therefrom and be anathematized and made an example for ever and ever, whether he were emperor, or patriarch, or any other man whatever, either ruler or subject, who should seek to transgress this commandment. And he adjured all who had the zeal and fear of God to be prompt to make away with him who attempted to do this, as a common enemy and a transgressor of this great commandment, and to dismiss him to a death most hateful *and* cruel. And it happened once, as wickedness will still find room, that one of our military governors, who had been most heavily bribed by certain infidels, handed over some of this fire to them; and, since God could not endure to leave unavenged this transgression, as he was about to enter the holy church of God, fire came down out of heaven and devoured and consumed him utterly. And thereafter mighty dread and terror were implanted in the hearts of all men, and never since then has anyone, whether emperor, or noble, or private citizen, or military governor, or any man of any sort whatever, ventured to think of such a thing, far less to attempt to do it or bring it to pass.'

'But come, now, turn', and to meet another sort of demand, monstrous and unseemly, seemly and appropriate words discover and seek out.

For if any of these shifty and dishonourable tribes of the north shall ever demand a marriage alliance with the emperor of the Romans, and either to take his daughter to wife, or to give a daughter of their own to be wife to the emperor or to the emperor's son, this monstrous demand of theirs also you shall rebut with these words, saying: 'Concerning this matter also a dread and authentic charge and ordinance of the great and holy Constantine is engraved upon the sacred table of the catholic church of the Christians, St. Sophia, that never shall an emperor of the Romans ally himself in marriage with a nation of customs differing from and alien to those of the Roman order, especially with one that is infidel and unbaptized, unless it be with the Franks alone; for they alone were excepted by that great man, the holy Constantine, because he himself drew his origin from those parts; for there is much relationship and converse between Franks and Romans. And why did he order that with them alone the emperors of the Romans should intermarry? Because of the traditional fame of those lands and the nobility of those tribes. But with any other nation whatsoever it was not to be in their power to do this, and he who dared to do it was to be condemned as an alien from the ranks of the Christians and subject to the anthema, as a transgressor of ancestral laws and imperial ordinances. And that emperor Leo aforesaid, who also, as has been described above, unlawfully and rashly, without the consent of him who was then patriarch, took from the church the diadem and put it about his head and was summarily punished in full for his wicked attempt, dared to make light of and to disregard this commandment also of that holy emperor, which, as has already been made clear, is engraved on the holy table; and as he had once put himself outside the fear of God and His commandments, so also he contracted an alliance in marriage with the chagan of Chazaria, and received his daughter to be his wife, and thereby attached great shame to the empire of the Romans and to himself, because he annulled and disregarded the ancestral injunctions; yet he, however, was not even an orthodox Christian, but an heretic and a destroyer of images. And so for these his unlawful impieties he is continually excommunicated and anthematized in the church of God, as a transgressor and perverter of the ordinance of God and of the holy and great emperor Constantine. For how can it be admissable that Christians should form marriage associations and ally themselves by marriage with infidels, when the canon forbids it and the whole church regards it as alien to and outside the Christian order? Or which of the illustrious or noble or wise emperors of the Romans has admitted it?' But if they reply: 'How then did the lord Romanus, the emperor, ally himself in marriage with the Bulgarians, and give his grand-daughter to the lord Peter the Bulgarian?', this must be the defence: 'The lord Romanus, the emperor, was a common, illiterate fellow, and not from among those who have been bred up in the palace, and have followed the Roman national customs from the beginning; nor was he of imperial and noble stock, and for this reason in most of his actions he was too arrogant and despotic, and in this instance he neither heeded the prohibition of the church, nor followed the commandment and ordinance of the great Constantine, but out of a temper arrogant and self-willed and untaught in virtue and refusing to follow what was right and good, or to submit to the ordinances handed down by our forefathers, he dared to do this thing; offering, that is, this alone by way of specious excuse, that by this action so many Christian prisoners were ransomed, and that the Bulgarians too are Christians *and* of like faith with us, and that in any case she who was given in marriage was not daughter of the monarch and lawful emperor, but of the third and most junior, who was still subordinate and had no share of authority in matters of government; but this was no different from giving any other of the ladies of the imperial family, whether more distantly or closely related to the imperial nobility, nor did it make any difference that she was given for some service to the commonweal, or was daughter of the most junior, who had no authority to speak of. And because he did this thing contrary to the canon and to ecclesiastical tradition and the ordinance and commandment of the great and holy emperor Constantine, the aforesaid lord Romanus was in his lifetime much abused, and was slandered and hated by the senatorial council and all the commons and the church herself, so that their hatred became abundantly clear in the end to which he came; and after his death he is in the same way vilified and slandered and condemned inasmuch as he too introduced an unworthy and unseemly innovation into the noble polity of the Romans.' For each nation has different customs and divergent laws and institutions, and should consolidate those things that are proper to it, and should form and develop out of the same nation the associations for the fusion of its life. For just as each animal mates with its own tribe, so it is right that each nation also should marry and cohabit not with those of other race and tongue but of the same tribe and speech. For hence arise naturally harmony of thought and intercourse among one another and friendly converse and living together; but alien customs and divergent laws are likely on the contrary to engender enmities and quarrels and hatreds and broils, which tend to beget not friendship and association but spite and division. Mark, too, that it is not for those who wish to govern lawfully to copy and emulate what has been ill done by some out of ignorance or arrogance, but rather to have the glorious deeds of those who have ruled lawfully and righteously as noble pictures set up for an example to be copied, and after their pattern to strive himself also to direct all that he does; since the end which came upon him, I mean, the lord Romanus, through these his headstrong acts is a sufficient warning to restrain anyone who is minded to emulate his evil deeds.

But now, with the rest, you must know also what follows, my well-loved son, since knowledge of it may greatly advantage you and render you the object of greater admiration. That is, once again, knowledge 'of the difference between other nations, their origins and customs and manner of life, and the position and climate of the land they dwell in, and its geographical description and measurement', as they are more widely expounded hereafter.

14. *Of the genealogy of Mahomet*

The blasphemous and obscene Mahomet, whom the Saracens claim for their prophet, traces his genealogy by descent from the most widespread race of Ishmael, son of Abraham. For *Nizaros*, the descendant of Ishmael, is proclaimed the father of them all. Now he begat two sons, Moundaros and Rabias, and Moundaros begat Kousaros and Kaïsos and Themimes and Asandos and various others whose names are unknown, who were allotted the Madianite desert and reared their flocks, dwelling in tents. And there are others further off in the interior who are not of the same tribe, but of Iektan, the so-called Homerites, that is, Amanites. And the story is published abroad thus. This Mahomet, being destitute and an orphan, thought fit to hire himself out to a certain wealthy woman, his relative, Chadiga by name, to tend her camels and to trade for her in Egypt among the foreigners and in Palestine. Thereafter by little and little he grew more free in converse and ingratiated himself with the woman, who was a widow, and took her to wife. Now, during his visits to Palestine and intercourse with Jews and Christians he used to follow up certain of their doctrines and interpretations of scripture. But as he had the disease of epilepsy, his wife, a noble and wealthy lady, was greatly cast down at being united to this man, who was not only destitute but an epileptic into the bargain, and so he deceived her by alleging: 'I behold a dreadful vision of an angel called Gabriel, and being unable to endure his sight, I faint and fall'; and he was believed because a certain Arian, who pretended to be a monk, testified falsely in his support for love of gain. The woman being in this manner imposed on and proclaiming to other women of her tribe that he was a prophet, the lying fraud reached also the ears of a head-man whose name was Boubachar. Well, the woman died and left her husband behind to succeed her and to be heir of her estate, and he became a notable and very wealthy man, and his wicked imposture and heresy took hold on the district of Ethribos. And the crazy and deluded fellow taught those who believed on him, that he who slays an enemy or is slain by an enemy enters into paradise, and all the rest of his nonsense. And they pray, moreover, to the star of Aphrodite, which they call Koubar, and in their supplication cry out: 'Alla wa Koubar', that is, 'God and Aphrodite'. For they call God 'Alla', and 'wa' they use for the conjunction 'and', and they call the star 'Koubar', and so they say 'Alla wa Koubar'.

AL-FARABI

ABU NASR MUHAMMAD AL-FARABI was born in Transoxania around the year 870 CE. Although we do not know much for certain about his life, we do know that as a young man he studied in Khorsan and Baghdad, two major centers of learning in the Islamic world and it was in the latter city that he established his reputation as a writer. Although based there for much of his life, he traveled widely to other major centers of Islamic civilization, for example, Aleppo and Damascus in Syria and also Egypt. He was versatile in many areas of study and although the claim that he could speak seventy languages is hardly likely there is no reason to doubt the breadth and range of his learning. His most famous political works are usually called *The Political Regime* and *The Virtuous City*, though he also wrote many influential commentaries on ancient texts such as Plato's *Laws*. He was the first major Islamic thinker to found a "school" and was a major source of the manner in which Islamic civilization absorbed and adapted Greek thought. He died, at the age of eighty, in Damascus, loaded with honors.

From *The Political Regime*

Man belongs to the species that cannot accomplish their necessary affairs or achieve their best state, except through the association of many groups of them in a single dwelling-place. Some human societies are large, others are of a medium size, still others are small. The large societies consist of many nations that associate and cooperate with one another; the medium ones consist of a nation; the small are the ones embraced by the city. These three are the perfect societies. Hence the city represents the first degree of perfection. Associations in villages, quarters, streets, and households, on the other hand, are the imperfect associations. Of these the least perfect is the household association, which is a part of the association in the street, the latter being a part of the association in the quarter, and this in turn a part of the political association. Associations in quarters and villages are both for the sake of the city; they differ, however, in that the quarters are parts of the city while the villages only serve it. [40] The political [or civic] society is a part of the nation, and the nation is divided into cities. The absolutely perfect human societies are divided into nations. A nation is differentiated from another by two natural things – natural make-up and natural character – and by something that is composite (it is conventional but has a basis in natural things), which is language – I mean the idiom through which men express themselves. As a result some nations are large and others are small.

The primary natural cause of the differences between nations in these matters consists of a variety of things. One of them is the difference in the parts of the celestial bodies that face them, namely, the first [that is, the outermost] sphere and the sphere of the fixed stars, then the difference in the positions of the inclined spheres from the various parts of the earth and the variation in their proximity and remoteness. From this follows the difference between the parts of the earth that are the nations' dwelling-places; for from the outset, this difference results from the difference in the parts of the first sphere that face them, from the difference in the fixed stars that face them, and from the difference in the positions of the inclined spheres with respect to them. From the difference between the parts of the earth follows the difference in the vapors rising from the earth; since each vapor rises from a certain soil, it is akin to that soil. From the difference in the vapors follows the difference in the air and water, inasmuch as the water of each country is generated from its underground vapors, and the air of each country is mixed with the vapors that work their way up to it from the soil. In the same manner, the difference in the air and water [of each country] follows from the difference [in the parts] of the fixed stars and of the first sphere that face it, and from the difference in the positions of the inclined spheres. From all these differences, in turn, follows the difference in the plants and in the species of irrational animals, [41] as a result of which nations have different diets. From the difference in their diets follows the difference in the materials and crops that go into the composition of the individuals who succeed the ones who die. From this, in turn, follows the difference in the natural make-up and natural character. Moreover, the difference in the parts of the heaven that face them causes further differences in their make-up and character, in a different manner from the one mentioned above. The difference in the air, too, causes differences in make-up and character in a different manner from the one mentioned above. Furthermore, out of the cooperation and combination of these differences there develop different mixtures that contribute to differences in the make-up and character of the nations. It is in this manner and direction that natural things fit together, are connected with each other, and occupy their respective ranks; and this is the extent to which the celestial bodies contribute to their perfection. The remaining perfections are not given by the celestial bodies but by the Active Intellect; and the Active Intellect gives the remaining perfections to no other species but man.

In giving [these perfections] to man, the Active Intellect follows a course similar to that followed by the celestial bodies. First, it gives him a faculty and a principle with which, of his own accord, he seeks, or is able to seek, the remaining perfections. That principle consists of the primary knowledge and the first intelligibles present in the rational part of the soul; but it gives him this kind of knowledge and those intelligibles only after man (*a*) first develops the sensitive part of the soul and the appetitive part, which gives rise to the desire and aversion that adhere to the sensitive part. [42] (The instruments of the last two faculties develop from the parts of the body.) They, in turn, give rise to the will. For, at first, the will is nothing but a desire that follows from a sensation; and desire takes place through the appetitive part of the soul, and sensation through the sensitive. (*b*) Next, there has to develop the imaginative part of the soul and the desire that adheres to it. Hence a second will develops after the first. This will is a desire that follows from [an act of the] imagination. After these two wills develop, it becomes possible for the primary knowledge that emanates from the Active Intellect to the rational part to take place. At this point a third kind of will develops in man – the desire that follows from intellecting – which is specifically called "choice." This choice pertains specifically to man, exclusive of all other animals. By virtue of it, man is able to do either what is commendable or blamable, noble or base; and because of it there is reward and punishment. (The first two wills, on the other hand, can exist in the irrational animals too.) When this will develops in man, with it he is able to seek or not to seek happiness, and to do what is good or evil, noble or base, in so far as this lies in his power.

Happiness is the good without qualification. Everything useful for the achievement of happiness or by which it is attained, is good too, not for its own sake, however, but because it is useful with respect to happiness; and everything that obstructs the way to happiness in any fashion is unqualified evil. The good that is useful for the achievement of happiness may be something that exists by nature or that comes into being by the will, and the evil that obstructs the way to happiness may be something that exists by nature or that comes into being by the will. That of it which is by nature is given by the celestial bodies, but not because they intend to assist the Active Intellect toward its purpose or [43] to hamper it. For when the celestial bodies give something that contributes to the purpose of the Active Intellect, they do not do so with the intention of assisting the Active Intellect; neither are the natural things that obstruct the way to its purpose intended by the celestial bodies to hamper the Active Intellect. Rather, it is inherent in the substance of the celestial bodies to give all that it is in the nature of matter to receive, without concerning themselves with whether it contributes to, or harms, the purpose of the Active Intellect. Therefore it is possible that the sum total of what is produced by the celestial bodies should comprise at times things that are favorable, and at other times things that are unfavorable, to the purpose of the Active Intellect.

As to voluntary good and evil, which are the noble and the base respectively, they have their origin specifically in man. Now there is only one way in which the voluntary good can come into being. That is because the faculties of the human soul are five: the theoretical-rational, the practical-rational, the appetitive, the imaginative, and the sensitive. Happiness, which only man can know and perceive, is known by the theoretical-rational faculty and by none of the remaining faculties. Man knows it when he makes use of the first principles and the primary knowledge given to him by the Active Intellect. When he knows happiness, desires it by the appetitive faculty, deliberates by the practical-rational faculty upon what he ought to do in order to attain it, uses the instruments of the appetitive faculty to do the actions he has discovered by deliberation, and his imaginative and sensitive faculties assist and obey the rational and aid it in arousing man to do the actions with which he attains happiness, then everything that originates from man will be good. It is only in this way that the voluntary good comes into being. As to voluntary evil it originates in the manner that I shall state. Neither the imaginative nor the appetitive faculty perceives [44] happiness. Not even the rational faculty perceives happiness under all conditions. The rational faculty perceives happiness only when it strives to apprehend it. Now there are many things that man can imagine that they ought to be the aim and end of life, such as the pleasant and the useful, honor, and the like. Whenever man neglects to perfect his theoretical-rational part, fails to perceive happiness and hasten toward it, holds something other than happiness – what is useful, what is pleasant, domination, what is honorable, and the like – as an end toward which he aims in his life, desires it with the appetitive faculty, uses the practical-rational faculty to deliberate in the discovery of what enables him to attain this end, uses the instruments of the appetitive faculty to do the things he has discovered, and is assisted in this by the imaginative and the sensitive faculties, then everything that originates from him is evil. Similarly, when man apprehends and knows happiness but does not make it the aim and the end of his life, has no desire or has only a feeble desire for it, makes something other than happiness the end that he desires in his life, and uses all his faculties to attain that end, then everything that originates from him is evil.

Since what is intended by man's existence is that he attain happiness, which is the ultimate perfection that remains to be given to the possible beings capable of receiving it, it is necessary to state the manner in which man can reach this happiness. Man can reach happiness only when the Active Intellect first gives the first intelligibles, which constitute the primary knowledge. However, not every man is equipped by natural disposition to receive the first intelligibles, because individual human beings are made by nature with unequal powers and different preparations. Some of them are not prepared by nature to receive any of [45] the first intelligibles; others – for instance, the

insane – receive them, but not as they really are; and still others receive them
as they really are. The last are the ones with sound human natural dispositions;
only these, and not the others, are capable of attaining happiness.

...

Since what is intended by man's existence is that he attain supreme happiness,
he – [48] in order to achieve it – needs to know what happiness is, make it his
end, and hold it before his eyes. Then, after that, he needs to know the things
he ought to do in order to attain happiness, and then do these actions.

...

When the activities of the citizens of a city are not directed toward happiness,
they lead them to acquired [53] bad states of the soul – just as when the activities of [the art of] writing are badly performed, they produce bad writing,
and similarly, when the activities of any art are badly performed, they produce in the soul bad states, corresponding to the [badly performed] art. As a
result their souls become sick. Therefore they take pleasure in the states that
they acquire through their activities. Just as because of their corrupt sense
[of taste]. Those with bodily sickness – for example, the ones affected by
fever – take pleasure in bitter things and find them sweet, and suffer pain
from sweet things, which seem bitter to their palates; similarly, because of
their corrupt imagination, those who are sick in their souls take pleasure in
the bad states [of the soul]. And just as there are among the sick those who
do not feel their malady and those who even think that they are healthy, and
such sick men do not at all listen to the advice of a physician; similarly, the
sick in their souls who do not feel their sickness and even think that they are
virtuous and have sound souls, do not listen at all to the words of a guide, a
teacher, or a reformer. The souls of such individuals remain chained to matter
and do not reach that perfection by which they can separate from matter, so
that when the matter ceases to exist they too will cease to exist.

The ranks of order among the citizens of the city, as regards ruling
and serving, vary in excellence according to their natural dispositions and
according to the habits of character they have formed. The supreme ruler is
the one who orders the various groups and every individual in each group,
in the place they merit – that is, gives each a subservient or a ruling rank of
order. Therefore, there will be certain ranks of order that are close to his own,
others slightly further away, and still others that are far away from it. Such will
be the ruling ranks of order: beginning with the highest ruling rank of order,
they will descend gradually until they become subservient ranks of order
devoid of any element of ruling and below which there is no other rank of
order. After having ordered these ranks, if the supreme ruler wishes to issue
a command about a certain matter that [54] he wishes to enjoin the citizens
of the city or a certain group among them to do, and to arouse them toward
it, he intimates this to the ranks closest to him, these will hand it on to their

subordinates, and so forth, until it reaches down to those assigned to execute that matter. The parts of the city will thus be linked and fitted together, and ordered by giving precedence to some over the others. Thus the city becomes similar to the natural beings; the ranks of order in it similar to the ranks of order of the beings, which begin with the First and terminate in prime matter and the elements; and the way they are linked and fitted together will be similar to the way the beings are linked and fitted together. The prince of the city will be like the First Cause, which is the cause for the existence of all the other beings. Then the ranks of order of the beings gradually keep descending, each one of them being both ruler and ruled, until they reach down to those possible beings – that is, prime matter and the elements – that possess no ruling element whatever, but are subservient and always exist for the sake of others.

The achievement of happiness takes place only through the disappearance of evils – not only the voluntary but also the natural ones – from the cities and nations, and when these acquire all the goods, both the natural and the voluntary. The function of the city's governor – that is, the prince – is to manage the cities in such a way that all the city's parts become linked and fitted together, and so ordered to enable the citizens to cooperate to eliminate the evils and acquire the goods. He should inquire into everything given by the celestial bodies. Those of them that are in any way helpful and suitable, or in any way useful, in the achievement of happiness, he should maintain and emphasize; [55] those of them that are harmful he should try to turn into useful things; and those of them that cannot be turned into useful things he should destroy or reduce in power. In general, he should seek to destroy all the evils and bring into existence all the goods.

Each one of the citizens of the virtuous city is required to know the highest principles of the beings and their ranks of order, happiness, the supreme rulership of the virtuous city, and the ruling ranks of order in it; then, after that, the specified actions that, when performed, lead to the attainment of happiness. These actions are not merely to be known; they should be done and the citizens of the city should be directed to do them.

The principles of the beings, their ranks of order, happiness, and the rulership of the virtuous cities, are either cognized and intellected by man, or he imagines them. To cognize them is to have their essences, as they really are, imprinted in man's soul. To imagine them is to have imprinted in man's soul their images, representations of them, or matters that are imitations of them. This is analogous to what takes place with regard to visible objects, for instance, man. We see him himself, we see a representation of him, we see his image reflected in water and other reflecting substances, and we see the image of a representation of him reflected in water and in other reflecting substances. Our seeing him himself is like the intellect's

cognition of the principles of the beings, of happiness, and so forth; while
our seeing the reflection of man in water and our seeing a representation
of him is like imagination, for our seeing a representation of him or our
seeing his reflection in a mirror is seeing that which is an imitation of
him. Similarly, when we imagine those things, we are in fact having a cognition of matters that are imitations of them rather than a cognition of them
themselves.

Most men, either by nature or by habit, are unable to comprehend and
cognize those things; these are the men for whom one ought to represent the
manner in which the principles of the beings, their ranks of order, the Active
Intellect, and the supreme rulership, exist through things that are imitations
of them. Now while the meanings and essences [56] of those things are one
and immutable, the matters by which they are imitated are many and varied.
Some imitate them more closely, while others do so only remotely – just as
is the case with visible objects: for the image of man that is seen reflected
in water is closer to the true man than the image of a representation of
man that is seen reflected in water. Therefore, it is possible to imitate these
things for each group and each nation, using matters that are different in
each case. Consequently, there may be a number of virtuous nations and
virtuous cities whose religions are different, even though they all pursue the
very same kind of happiness. For religion is but the impressions of these
things or the impressions of their images, imprinted in the soul. Because it
is difficult for the multitude to comprehend these things themselves as they
are, the attempt was made to teach them these things in other ways, which
are the ways of imitation. Hence these things are imitated for each group
or nation through the matters that are best known to them; and it may very
well be that what is best known to the one may not be the best known to the
other.

Most men who strive for happiness, follow after an imagined, not a
cognized, form of happiness. Similarly, most men accept such principles as
are accepted and followed, and are magnified and considered majestic, in the
form of images, not of cognitions. Now the ones who follow after happiness
as they cognize it and accept the principles as they cognize them, are the
wise men. And the ones in whose souls these things are found in the form of
images, and who accept them and follow after them as such, are the believers.

The imitations of those things differ in excellence: some of them are
better and more perfect imaginative representations, while others are less
perfect; some are closer to, others are more removed from, the truth. In some
the points of contention are few or unnoticeable, or it is difficult to contend
against them, while in others the points [57] of contention are many or easy
to detect, or it is easy to contend against them and to refute them. It is also
possible that those things be presented to the imagination of men by means

of various matters, but that, despite their variety, these matters bear a certain relation to each other: that is, there are certain matters that are the imitations of those things, a second set that are the imitations of these matters, and a third set that are the imitations of the second. Finally, the various matters that are the imitations of those things – that is, of the principles of the beings and of happiness – may be on the same level as imitations. Now if they are of equal excellence as regards imitation, or with respect to having only a few or unnoticeable points of contention, then one can use all or any one of them indifferently. But if they are not of equal excellence, one should choose the ones that are the most perfect imitations and that either are completely free of points of contention or in which the points of contention are few or unnoticeable; next, those that are closer to the truth; and discard all other imitations.

The virtuous city is the opposite of (A) the ignorant city, (B) the immoral city, and (C) the erring city. (D) Then there are the Weeds in the virtuous city. (The position of the Weeds in the cities is like that of the darnel among the wheat, the thorns growing among the crop, or the other grass that is useless or even harmful to the crop or plants.) Finally, there are the men who are bestial by nature. But the bestial by nature are neither political beings nor could they ever form a political association. Instead, some of them are like gregarious beasts and others are like wild beasts, and of the latter some are like ravenous beasts. Therefore some of them live isolated in the wilderness, others live there together in depravity like wild beasts, and still others live near the cities. Some eat only raw meats, others graze on wild vegetation, and still others prey on their victims like [58] wild beasts. These are to be found in the extremities of the inhabited earth, either in the far north or in the far south. They must be treated like animals. Those of them that are gregarious and are in some way useful to the cities, should be spared, enslaved, and employed like beasts of burden. Those of them from whom no use can be derived or who are harmful, should be treated as one treats all other harmful animals. The same applies to those children of the citizens of the cities who turn out to have a bestial nature.

A. The ignorant cities

As for the citizens of the ignorant cities, they are political beings. Their cities and their political associations are of many kinds, which comprise (i) indispensable associations, (ii) the association of vile men in the vile cities, (iii) the association of base men in the base cities, (iv) timocratic association in the timocratic city, (v) despotic association in the despotic cities, (vi) free association in the democratic city and the city of the free.

i. *The indispensable city*

The indispensable city or the indispensable association is that which leads to cooperation to acquire the bare necessities for the subsistence and the safeguarding of the body. There are many ways to acquire these things, such as husbandry, grazing, hunting, robbery, and so forth. Both hunting and robbery are practiced either by stealth or openly. There are certain indispensable cities that possess all the arts that lead to the acquisition of the bare necessities. In others the bare necessities are obtained through one art only, such as husbandry alone or any other art. The citizens of this city regard the best man to be the one who is most excellent in skill, management, and accomplishment in obtaining the bare necessities through the ways of acquisition that they employ. Their ruler is he who can govern well and is skillful in [59] employing them to acquire the indispensable things, who can govern them well so as to preserve these things for them, or who generously provides them with these things from his own possessions.

ii. *The vile city*

The vile city or the association of the vile citizens is that whose members (*a*) cooperate to acquire wealth and prosperity, the excessive possession of indispensable things or their equivalent in coin and in money, and their accumulation beyond the need for them and for no other reason than the love and covetousness of wealth; and (*b*) avoid spending any of it except on what is necessary for bodily subsistence. This they do either by pursuing all the modes of acquisition or else such modes as are available in that country. They regard the best men to be the wealthiest and the most skillful in the acquisition of wealth. Their ruler is the man who is able to manage them well in what leads them to acquire wealth and always to remain wealthy. Wealth is obtained through all the methods employed to obtain the bare necessities, that is, husbandry, grazing, hunting, and robbery; and also through voluntary transactions like commerce, lease, and so forth.

iii. *The base city*

The base city or the base association is that in which the citizens cooperate to enjoy sensual pleasures or imaginary pleasures (play and amusement) or both. They enjoy the pleasures of food, drink, and copulation, and strive after what is most pleasant of these, in the pursuit of pleasure alone, rather than what sustains, or is in any way useful to, the body; and they do the same as regards play and amusement. This city is the one regarded by the citizens of the ignorant city as the happy and admirable city; for they can attain the goal of this city only after having acquired the bare necessities and acquired wealth, and only by means of much expenditure. They regard whoever possesses more resources for play and the pleasures as the best, the happiest, and the most enviable man.

iv. *The timocratic city*

The timocratic city or the timocratic association is that in which the citizens cooperate with a view to be [60] honored in speech and deed: that is, to be honored either by the citizens of other cities or by one another. Their honoring of one another consists in the exchange of either equal or unequal honors. The exchange of equal honors takes place through someone bestowing on someone else a certain kind of honor at a certain time so that the latter may at another time return the same kind of honor or another kind of honor that, in their eyes, is of equal worth. The exchange of unequal honors takes place through someone bestowing a certain kind of honor on someone else, with the latter bestowing on the former another kind of honor of greater worth than the first. In every case, moreover, this [exchange of unequal honors] among them takes place on the basis of merit (one of two men merits an honor of a certain worth, while the other merits a greater one), depending on what they consider merit to be. In the eyes of the citizens of the ignorant city, merits are not based on virtue, but (a) on wealth, or (b) on possessing the means of pleasure and play and on obtaining the most of both, or (c) on obtaining most of the necessities of life (when man is served and is well provided with all the necessities he needs), or (d) on man's being useful, that is, doing good to others with respect to these three things. (e) There is one more thing that is well liked by most of the citizens of the ignorant cities, that is, domination. For whoever achieves it is envied by most of them. Therefore this, too, must be regarded as one of the merits in the ignorant cities. For, in their eyes, the highest matter for which a man must be honored is his fame in achieving domination [that is, superiority] in one, two, or many things; not being dominated, because he himself is strong, because his supporters are either numerous or strong, [61] or because of both; and that he be immune to being harmed by others, while able to harm others at will. For, in their eyes, this is a state of felicity for which a man merits honor; hence the better he is in this respect, the more he is honored. Or the man [whom they honor] possesses, in their eyes, distinguished ancestors. But ancestors are distinguished because of the things mentioned above: namely, one's fathers and grandfathers were either wealthy, abundantly favored with pleasure and the means to it, had domination [that is, were superior] in a number of things, were useful to others – be they a group or the citizens of a city – with respect to these things, or were favored with the instruments of these things, such as nobility, endurance, or the contempt of death, all of which are instruments of domination. Honors of equal worth, on the other hand, are sometimes merited by virtue of an external possession, and sometimes honor itself is the reason for the merit, so that the one who begins and honors someone else merits thereby to be honored by the other, as is the case in market transactions.

Thus, in their eyes, the one who merits more honor rules over the one who merits less of it. This inequality continues on an ascending scale terminating in the one who merits more honors than anyone else in the city. This, therefore, will be the ruler and the prince of the city. By virtue of this office, he ought to be of greater merit than all the rest. Now we have already enumerated what they consider to be the bases of merit. Accordingly, if honor, according to them, is based on distinguished ancestry alone, the ruler ought to have a more distinguished ancestry than the others; and similarly if honor, according to them, is based on wealth alone. Next, men are distinguished and given ranks of order according to their wealth and ancestry; [62] and whoever lacks both wealth and a distinguished ancestry will have no claim to any rulership or honor. Such, then, is the case when merits are based on matters that are good to their possessor alone; and these are the lowest among timocratic rulers. When, on the other hand, the ruler is honored because of his usefulness to the citizens of the city in their pursuits and wishes, it is then because he benefits them with regard to wealth or pleasure; or because he brings others to honor the citizens of the city or to provide them with the other things desired by them; or because he supplies them with these things from his own or he enables them to obtain and preserve them through his good governance. Of such rulers, they consider the best to be the one who provides the citizens of the city with these things without seeking anything for himself except honor: for instance, the one who provides them with wealth or the pleasures without desiring any for himself, but rather seeks only honor (praise, respect, and exaltation in speech and deed), to become famous for it among all nations in his own lifetime and after, and to be remembered for a long time. This is the one who, in their eyes, merits honor. Often, such a man requires money and wealth to spend it on what enables the citizens of the city to fulfil their desires for wealth or pleasure or both, and on what helps them to preserve these things. The more he does in this respect, the greater his wealth must be. His wealth becomes a reserve for the citizens of the city. This is the reason why some of these rulers seek wealth and regard their expenditures as an act of generosity and liberality. They collect this money from the city in the form of taxes, or they conquer another group – other, that is, than the citizens of the city – for its money, which they bring to their treasury. They keep it as a reserve [63] out of which they disburse great expenditures in the city in order to obtain greater honor. The one who covets honor by whatever means, may also claim distinguished ancestry for himself and his offspring after him; and so that his fame survive through his offspring, he designates his immediate offspring or members of his family as his successors. Furthermore, he may appropriate a certain amount of wealth for himself to be honored for it, even though it is of no benefit to others. Also, he honors a certain group so that they may honor him in return. He thus possesses all the things for which men may honor him, reserving for himself alone the things regarded by them as manifesting splendor, embellishment, eminence, and magnificence – such as buildings, costumes, and medals, and, finally, inaccessibility to people. Further, he lays down the laws concerning honors. Once he assumes a certain office and people are accustomed to the fact that he and his family will be their princes, he then orders the people into ranks in such a way as to obtain honor and majesty. To each kind of rank, he assigns (a) a kind of honor and (b) things by virtue of which one merits honor, such as wealth, building, costume, medal, carriage, and so forth, and which contribute to his majesty; and he arranges all this in a definite order. Furthermore, he will show special preference for those men who honor him more or contribute more to the enhancement of his majesty, and he confers honor and distributes favor accordingly. The citizens of his city who covet honor keep honoring him until he acknowledges what they have done and confers honors on them, because of which they will be honored by their inferiors and superiors.

For all these reasons, this city can be likened to the virtuous city, especially when the honors, and men's ranks of order with respect to honors, are conferred because of other, more useful things: for example, wealth, pleasures, or anything else that is desired by whoever seeks after useful things. This city is the best among the ignorant cities; unlike those of the others, its citizens are [more properly] called "ignorant" [64] and so forth. However, when their love of honor becomes excessive, it becomes a city of tyrants, and it is more likely to change into a despotic city.

v. *The despotic city*

The despotic city or the despotic association is that in which the members cooperate to achieve domination. This happens when they are all seized by the love of domination, provided that it is in different degrees, and that they seek different kinds of domination and different things for the sake of which to dominate other men; for instance, some like to dominate another man in order to spill his blood, others, to take his property, still others, to possess him so that they may enslave him. People occupy different ranks of order in this city depending on the extent of one's love of domination. Its citizens love to dominate others in order to spill their blood and kill them, to possess them so that they may enslave them, or in order to take their property. In all this, what they love and aim at is to dominate, subdue, and humiliate others, and that the subdued should have no control whatever over himself or any of the things because of which he has been dominated, but should do as the subduer commands and wishes. (Indeed when the lover of domination and subjugation – who is inclined to, or desires, a certain thing – obtains it without having to subdue someone else, he does not take it and pays no attention to it.) Some of them choose to dominate through wiliness, others, through open combat alone, and still others, through both wiliness and open combat. Therefore many of those who subjugate others in order to spill their blood, do not kill a man when asleep and do not seize his property until they first wake him up; they prefer to engage him in combat and to be faced with some resistance in order to subdue him and harm him. Since every one of them loves to dominate the others, each one loves to dominate everyone else, [65] whether a fellow citizen or not. They refrain from dominating one another as regards the spilling of blood or the taking of property, only because they need one another so as to survive, cooperate in dominating others, and defend themselves against outside domination.

Their ruler is he who shows greater strength in governing well with a view to employing them to dominate others; who is the wiliest of them; and who has the soundest judgment about what they ought to do in order to continue to dominate forever and never be dominated by others. Such is their ruler and prince. They are the enemies of all other men.

All their laws and usages are such that, when followed, they enable them better to dominate others. Their rivalries and contentions center on how many times they dominate others or on the extent of their domination, or else on the abundant possession of the equipment and instruments of domination. (The equipment and instruments of domination exist either in man's mind, in his body, or in what is external to his body: in his body, like endurance; external to his body, like arms; and in his mind, like sound judgment regarding that which enables him to dominate others.) At times, such men become rude, cruel, irascible, extravagant, and excessively gluttonous; they consume great quantities of food and drink, overindulge in copulation, and fight each other for all the goods, which they obtain through subjugating and humiliating those who possess them. They think that they should dominate everything and everybody.

(1) Sometimes this is true of the entire city, whose citizens will then choose to dominate those outside the city for no other reason than the citizens' need for association [and hence for a common cause that would promote it]. (2) Sometimes the vanquished and the subjugators live side by side in a single city. [66] The subjugators then either (a) love to subjugate and dominate others to the same degree and hence have the same rank of order in the city, or (b) they occupy various ranks of order, each one of them having a certain kind of domination over their vanquished neighbors, which is lesser or greater than that of the other. In this way, and depending on the power and judgment through which they achieve domination, they occupy their respective places next to a prince who rules them and manages the subjugators' affairs as regards the instruments they use for subjugation. (3) And sometimes there is but a single subjugator, with a group of men as his instruments for subjugating all other men. The group in question does not seek to enable him to dominate and seize something for someone else's sake, but so that he dominate something that would belong to him alone. The single subjugator, in turn, is satisfied with what maintains his life and strength; he gives [the rest] to the others and dominates for the sake of the others, like dogs and falcons do. The rest of the citizens of the city, too, are slaves to that one, serving his every wish; they are submissive and humiliated, possessing nothing whatever of their own. Some of them cultivate the soil, others trade, for him. In all this, he has no other purpose beyond seeing a certain group subjugated and dominated and submissive to him alone, even though he derives no benefit or pleasure from them except that of seeing them humiliated and dominated. This (3), then, is the city whose prince alone is despotic, while the rest of its citizens are not despotic. In the one that preceded it (2), half of the city is despotic. In the first (1), all the citizens are despotic.

The despotic city may thus have such a character that it employs one of these methods in the pursuit of domination alone and the enjoyment of it. But if domination is loved only as a means for the acquisition of bare necessities, prosperity, the enjoyment of pleasures, honors, or all of these together, then this is a despotic city of a different sort; and its citizens belong to the other cities mentioned above. [67] Most people call such cities despotic; but this name applies more properly to the one among them that seeks all of these (three?) things by means of subjugation. There are three sorts of such cities: that is, (3) one of the citizens, (2) half of them, or (1) all of them are despotic. But they [that is, the citizens of these cities], too, do not pursue subjugation and maltreatment for their own sake; rather they pursue, and aim at, something else.

There are, further, other cities that aim at something else and at domination as well. The first of these cities, which aims at domination however and for whatever it may be, may include someone who inflicts harm on others without any benefit to himself, such as to murder for no other reason than the pleasure of subjugation alone; its citizens fight for the sake of base things, as it is told about some of the Arabs. In the second, the citizens love domination for the sake of certain things that they regard as praiseworthy and lofty, not lowly; and when they attain these things without subjugating others, they do not resort to it. The third city does not harm or murder, unless it knows that this enhances one of its noble qualities. Hence when one [of its citizens] gets to the things he wants, without having to dominate and subjugate others – for instance, when the thing exists in abundance, when someone else takes care of seizing it for him, or when someone else gives him the thing voluntarily – he will not harm others, remains indifferent to the thing in question, and does not take it from others. Such individuals are also called high-minded and manly. The citizens of the first city confine themselves to such subjugation as is indispensable for the achievement of domination. Sometimes they strive and struggle very hard to possess a certain property or human soul that is denied to them, and they persist until they get it and are able to do with it whatever they please; but at this point they turn away and do not seize it. Such men may also be praised, honored, and respected for what they do; also, [68] those who seek honor do most of these things so that they may be honored for them. Despotic cities are more often tyrannical than timocratic.

Sometimes the citizens of the [vile or] plutocratic city and the citizens of the [base] city that is dedicated to play and amusement imagine that they are the ones who are lucky, happy, and successful, and that they are more excellent than the citizens of all other cities. These delusions about themselves sometimes lead them to become contemptuous of the citizens of other cities and to suppose that others have no worth, and to love to be honored for whatever caused their happiness. Consequently, they develop traits of arrogance, extravagance, boastfulness, and the love of praise, and suppose that others cannot attain what they themselves have attained, and that the others are therefore too stupid to achieve these two kinds of happiness [which result from wealth, and play and amusement, respectively]. They create for themselves titles with which they embellish their ways of life, such as that they are the talented and the elegant, and that the others are the rude. Therefore they are supposed to be men of pride, magnanimity, and authority. Sometimes they are even called high-minded.

When the lovers of wealth and the lovers of pleasure and play do not happen to possess any of the arts by which wealth is obtained except the power to dominate, and they achieve wealth and play by subjugation and domination, then they become extremely arrogant and join the ranks of tyrants (in contrast, the former group are simply idiots). Similarly, it is possible to find among the lovers of honor some who love it, not for its own sake, but for the sake of wealth. For many of them seek to be honored by others in order to obtain wealth, either from those others or from someone else. They seek to rule, and to be obeyed by, the citizens of the city in order to obtain wealth alone. Many of these seek wealth for the sake of play and pleasure. Thus they seek to rule and to be obeyed in order to obtain wealth to make use of it in play; and they think that the greater and the more complete their authority and the obedience of others to them, the greater their share of these things. Hence they desire to be the sole rulers over the citizens of the city in order to possess majesty, by which to achieve great and incomparable wealth [69] in order to make use of it in obtaining a measure of play and pleasures (food, drink, sex) that no one else can obtain both as regards its quantity and quality.

vi. *The democratic city*

The democratic city is the one in which each one of the citizens is given free rein and left alone to do whatever he likes. Its citizens are equal and their laws say that no man is in any way at all better than any other man. Its citizens are free to do whatever they like; and no one, be he one of them or an outsider, has any claim to authority unless he works to enhance their freedom. Consequently, they develop many kinds of morals, inclinations, and desires, and they take pleasure in countless things. Its citizens consist of countless similar and dissimilar groups. This city brings together the groups – both the base and the noble – that existed separately in all the other cities; and positions of authority are obtained here by means of any one of the things we have mentioned. Those from among the multitude of this city, who possess whatever the rulers possess, have the upper hand over those who are called their rulers. Those who rule them do so by the will of the ruled, and the rulers follow the wishes of the ruled. Close investigation of their situation would reveal that, in truth, there is no distinction between ruler and ruled among them. However, they praise and honor those who lead the citizens of the city to freedom and to whatever the citizens like and desire, and who safeguard the citizens' freedom and their varied and different desires against [infringement] by one another and by outside enemies; and who limit their [70] own desires to bare necessities. Such, then, is the one who is honored, regarded as the best, and is obeyed among them. As to any other ruler, he is either (a) their equal or (b) their inferior. (a) He is their equal when it happens that, when he provides them with the good things that they want and desire, they reciprocate with comparable honors and wealth. In this case they do not consider him to be superior to them. (b) They are his superiors when they accord him honors and allot him a share of their possessions, without receiving any benefit from him in return. For it is quite possible to find in this city a ruler in this situation: he happens to be magnified in the eyes of the citizens either because they take a fancy to him or because his ancestors ruled them well and they let him rule in gratitude for what his ancestors did. In this case, the multitude would have the upper hand over the rulers.

All the endeavors and purposes of the ignorant cities are present in this city in a most perfect manner; of all of them, this is the most admirable and happy city. On the surface, it looks like an embroidered garment full of colored figures and dyes. Everybody loves it and loves to reside in it, because there is no human wish or desire that this city does not satisfy. The nations emigrate to it and reside there, and it grows beyond measure. People of every race multiply in it, and this by all kinds of copulation and marriages, resulting in children of extremely varied dispositions, with extremely varied education and upbringing. Consequently, this city develops into many cities, distinct yet intertwined, with the parts of each scattered throughout the parts of the others. Strangers cannot be distinguished from the residents. All kinds of wishes and ways of life are to be found in it. Consequently, it is quite possible that, with the passage of time, virtuous men will grow up in it. Thus it may include [71] philosophers, rhetoricians, and poets, dealing with all kinds of things. It is also possible to glean from it certain [men who form] parts of the virtuous city; this is the best thing that takes place in this city. Therefore, this city possesses both good and evil to a greater degree than the rest of the ignorant cities. The bigger, the more civilized, the more populated, the more productive, and the more perfect it is, the more prevalent and the greater are the good and the evil it possesses.

There are as many aims pursued by the ignorant rulerships as there are ignorant cities. Every ignorant rulership aims at having its fill of bare necessities; wealth; delight in the pleasures; honor, reputation, and praise; domination; or freedom. Therefore, such rulerships are actually bought for a price, especially the positions of authority in the democratic city; for here no one has a better claim than anyone else to a position of authority. Therefore, when someone finally holds a position of authority, it is either because the citizens have favored him with it, or else because they have received from him money or something else in return. In their eyes the virtuous ruler is he who has the ability to judge well and to contrive well what enables them to attain their diverse and variegated desires and wishes, safeguards them against their enemies, and takes nothing of their property, but confines himself to the bare necessities of life. As for the truly virtuous man – namely the man who, if he were to rule them, would determine and direct their actions toward happiness – they do not make him a ruler. If by chance he comes to rule them, he will soon find himself either deposed or killed or in an unstable and challenged position. And so are all the other ignorant cities; each one of them only wants the ruler who facilitates the attainment of its wishes [72] and desires, and paves the way for their acquisition and preservation. Therefore, they refuse the rule of virtuous men and resent it. Nevertheless, the construction of virtuous cities and the establishment of the rule of virtuous men are more effective and much easier out of the indispensable and democratic cities than out of any other ignorant city.

Bare necessity, wealth, the enjoyment of the pleasures and of play, and honors may be attained by subjugation and domination, or they may be attained by other means. Hence the four cities [the indispensable, vile, base, and timocratic] can be subdivided accordingly. Similarly, the rule that aims at these four things, or any one of them, pursues the achievement of its aim by domination and subjugation, or else pursues it by other means. Those who acquire these things by domination and subjugation, and safeguard what they have acquired by force and compulsion, need to be strong and powerful in body, and to be fierce, rough, rude, and contemptuous of death in moral traits, and not to prefer life to these pursuits; they need skill in the use of arms, and good judgment as regards the means of subjugating others: all this applies to all of them.

But as to the pleasure seekers [that is, the citizens of the base city], they develop, in addition, gluttony and lust for food, drink, and sex. Some of them are dominated by softness and luxury, weakening their irascible faculty to the extent that none or very little of it remains. Others are dominated by anger and its psychical and bodily instruments, and by the appetite and its psychical and bodily instruments, which strengthens and intensifies these two faculties, and facilitates the performance of their functions. Their judgment will be equally devoted to the actions of these two faculties, and their souls equally subservient to them. Of these, the final objective of some are the actions of the appetite. Thus they turn their irascible faculties and actions into instruments by which to achieve the appetitive actions, thus subordinating lofty and higher faculties to the lower; that is, they subordinate their rational faculty to [73] the irascible and appetitive, and further, the irascible faculty to the appetitive. For they devote their judgment to the discovery of what fulfils the irascible and appetitive actions, and devote the actions and instruments of their irascible faculties to what enables them to attain the enjoyment of the pleasures of food, drink, and sex, and all that enables them to seize and safeguard them for themselves, such as you see in the notables of the dwellers of the steppes from among the Arabs and the Turks. For the dwellers of the steppes generally love domination, and have insatiable lust for food, drink, and sex. Consequently, women are of great importance to them, and many of them approve of licentiousness, not considering it as being a degeneration and vileness since their souls are subservient to their appetites. You also see that many of them try to please women in everything they do, in order to gain importance in the eyes of women, considering disgraceful whatever women consider to be disgraceful, fair what women consider to be fair. In everything they do, they follow the desires of their women. In many cases, their women have the upper hand over them and control the affairs of their households. For this reason many of them accustom their women to luxury by shielding them from hard work and keeping them instead in luxury and comfort, while they themselves undertake to do everything that requires toil and labor and the endurance of pain and hardship.

B. The immoral cities

Immoral cities are the ones whose citizens once believed in, and cognized, the principles [of beings]; imagined, and believed in, what happiness is; and were guided toward, knew, and believed in, the actions by which to attain happiness. Nevertheless, they did not adhere to any of those actions, but came to desire and will one or another of the aims of the citizens of the ignorant cities – such as honor, domination, and so forth – and directed all their actions and faculties toward them. There are as many kinds [74] of these [immoral] cities as there are ignorant cities, inasmuch as all their actions and morals are identical with those of the ignorant cities. They differ from the citizens of the ignorant cities only in the opinions in which they believe. Not one of the citizens of these cities can attain happiness at all.

C. The erring cities

Erring cities are those whose citizens are given imitations of other matters than the ones we mentioned – that is, the principles that are established for, and imitated to, them are other than the ones we mentioned; a kind of happiness that is not true happiness is established for, and represented to, them; and actions and opinions are prescribed for them by none of which true happiness can be attained.

D. The Weeds in virtuous cities

The Weeds within the virtuous cities are of many classes. (i) [Members of] one class adhere to the actions conducive to the attainment of happiness; however, they do not do such actions in the pursuit of happiness, but rather of other things that man can attain by means of virtue, such as honor, rulership, wealth, and so forth. Such individuals are called opportunists. Some of them have an inclination to one of the ends of the citizens of the ignorant cities and they are prevented by the Laws and the religion of the city from pursuing such ends. Therefore they resort to the expressions of the lawgiver and the statements that embody his precepts, and interpret them as they wish, by which interpretation they make the thing they are after appear good. Such men are called the misinterpreters. Others among them do not deliberately misinterpret but, because they do not rightly understand the lawgiver and because of their misconception of his statements, they understand the Laws of the city in a different way than the one intended by the lawgiver. Their actions will therefore not conform to the intention of the supreme ruler. Hence they err without realizing it. These men are the apostates.

(ii) [Members of] another class do imagine the things we mentioned, yet they are not convinced of what they have imagined of them. Hence they use arguments to falsify them for themselves and for others. [75] In so doing, they are not contending against the virtuous city; rather they are looking for the right path and seeking the truth. He who belongs to this class, should have the level of his imagination raised to things that cannot be falsified by the arguments he has put forward. If he is satisfied with the level to which he has been raised, he should be left alone. But if he is again not satisfied, and discovers here certain places susceptible to contention, then he should be raised to a higher level. This process should continue until he becomes satisfied with one of these levels. And if it happens that he is not satisfied with any one of these levels of imagination, he should be raised to the level of the truth and be made to comprehend those things as they are, at which point his mind will come to rest.

(iii) [Members of] another class falsify whatever they imagine. Whenever they are raised to a higher level, they falsify it, even when they are conducted to the level of the truth – all this in the pursuit of domination alone, or in the pursuit of ennobling another of the aims of the ignorant cities that is desired by them. They falsify them in every way they can; they do not like to listen to anything that may establish happiness and truth firmly in the soul, or any argument that may ennoble and imprint them in the soul, but meet them with such sham arguments as they think will discredit happiness. Many of them do that with the intention of appearing as having a pretext for turning to one of the aims of the ignorant cities.

(iv) [Members of] another class imagine happiness and the principles [of beings], but their minds are totally lacking in the power to cognize them, or it is beyond the power of their minds to cognize them adequately. Consequently, they falsify the things they imagine and come upon the places of contention in them, and whenever they are raised to a level of imagination that is closer to the truth, they find it to be false. Nor is it possible to raise them to the level of the truth because their minds lack the power to comprehend it. And many of them may find most of what they imagine to be false, not because what they imagine truly contains places of contention, [76] but because they have a defective imagination, and they find these things false because of their defective minds, not because these things contain a place of contention. Many of them – when unable to imagine something sufficiently or discover the real points of contention and in the places where they are to be found, or are unable to comprehend the truth – think that the man who has apprehended the truth and who says that he has apprehended it, is a deliberate liar who is seeking honor or domination, or else think that he is a deluded man. So they try hard to falsify the truth also, and abase the man who has apprehended it. This leads many of them to think that all men are deluded in everything they claim to have apprehended. It leads (1) some of them to a state of perplexity in all things, and (2) others to think that no apprehension whatever is true, and that whenever someone thinks that he has apprehended something that he is lying about it and that he is not sure or certain of what he thinks. These individuals occupy the position of ignorant simpletons in the eyes of reasonable men and in relation to the philosophers. (For this reason it is the duty of the ruler of the virtuous city to look for the Weeds, keep them occupied, and treat each class of them in the particular manner that will cure them: by expelling them from the city, punishing them, jailing them, or forcing them to perform a certain function even though they may not be fond of it.) (3) Others among them think that the truth consists of whatever appears to each individual and what each man thinks it to be at one time or another, and that the truth of everything is what someone thinks it is. (4) Others among them exert themselves to create the illusion that everything that is thought to have been apprehended up to this time is completely false, and that, although a certain truth or reality does exist, it has not as yet been apprehended. (5) Others among them imagine – as if in a dream or as if a thing is seen from a distance – that there is a truth, and it occurs to them that the ones who claim to have apprehended it may have done so, or perhaps that one of them may have apprehended it. They feel that they themselves have missed it, either because they require a long time, and have to toil and exert themselves, in order to apprehend it, when they no longer have sufficient time or the power to toil and persevere; or because they are occupied by certain pleasures and so forth to which they have been accustomed and from which they find it very difficult to free themselves; or because they feel that they cannot apprehend it even if they had access to all the means to it. Consequently, they regret and grieve over what they think others may have attained. Hence, out of jealousy for those who may have apprehended the truth, they think it wise to endeavor, using sham argument, to create the illusion that whoever claims to have apprehended the truth is either deluded or else a liar who is seeking honor, wealth, or some other desirable thing, from the claim he makes. Now many of these perceive their own ignorance and perplexity; they feel sad and suffer pain because of what they perceive to be their condition, they are overcome by anxiety, and it torments them; and they find no way to free themselves of this by means of a science leading them to the truth whose apprehension would give them pleasure. Hence they choose to find rest from all this by turning to the various ends of the ignorant cities, and to find their solace in amusements and games until death comes to relieve them of their burden. Some of these – I mean the ones who seek rest from the torment of ignorance and perplexity – may create the illusion that the [true] ends are those that they themselves choose and desire, that happiness consists of these, and that the rest of men are deluded in what they believe in. They exert themselves to adorn the ends of the ignorant cities and the happiness [that they pursue]. They create the illusion that they have come to prefer some of these ends after a thorough examination of all that the others claim to have apprehended, that they have rejected the latter only after finding out that they are inconclusive, and that their position was arrived at on the basis of personal knowledge – therefore, theirs are the ends, not the ones claimed by the others.

These, then, are the classes of the Weeds growing among the citizens of the city. With such opinions, they constitute neither a city nor a large multitude; rather they are submerged by the citizen body as a whole.

AVICENNA

ABU ALI AL HUSAYN IBN SINA, to give him his proper name, was born in Afshana near Bukhara (in modern Uzbekistan) where his father was the Saminid governor, in the year 980 CE. Avicenna was trained there initially, chiefly as a physician, and was enrolled in the service of the Sultan Nuh Ibn Mansur. After the collapse of the Saminid kingdom of Persia in 999, the young Avicenna traveled throughout the warring principalities of Persia serving first one then another. Eventually, in the early to mid 1020s, he settled in the city of Isfahan where he befriended the prince and became his advisor and wrote the treatises for which he became famous. In eastern Islam, Avicenna replaced al-Farabi as the leading thinker, though al-Farabi's influence remained central in the West. Avicenna died in Isfahan in 1037.

From *The Healing*

Chapter 5
Concerning the caliph and the imam: the necessity of obeying them.
Remarks on politics, transactions, and morals

Next, the legislator must impose as a duty obedience to whosoever succeeds him. He must also prescribe that designation of the successor can only be made by himself or by the consensus of the elders. The latter should verify openly to the public that the man of their choice can hold sole political authority, that he is of independent judgment, that he is endowed with the noble qualities of courage, temperance, and good governance, and that he knows the law to a degree unsurpassed by anyone else. Such a verification must be openly proclaimed and must find unanimous agreement by the entire public. The legislator must lay down in the law that should they disagree and quarrel, succumbing to passion and whim, or should they agree to designate someone [452] other than the virtuous and deserving individual, then they would have committed an act of unbelief. Designation of the caliph through appointment by testament is best: it will not lead to partisanship, quarrels, and dissensions.

The legislator must then decree in his law that if someone secedes and lays claim to the caliphate by virtue of power or wealth, then it becomes the duty of every citizen to fight and kill him. If the citizens are capable of so doing but refrain from doing so, then they disobey God and commit an act of unbelief. The blood of anyone who can fight but refrains becomes free for the spilling after this fact is established in the assembly of all. The legislator must lay down in the law that, next to belief in the prophet, nothing brings one closer to God than the killing of such a usurper.

If the seceder, however, verifies that the one holding the caliphate is not fit for it, that he is afflicted with an imperfection, and that this imperfection is not found in the seceder, then it is best that the citizens accept the latter. The determining factor here is superiority of practical judgment and excellence in political management. The one whose attainment in the rest of the virtues [including knowledge] is moderate – although he must not be ignorant of them nor act contrary to them – but excels in these two is more fit than the one who excels in the other virtues but is not foremost in these two. Thus the one who has more knowledge must join and support the one who has better practical judgment. The latter, in turn, must accept the former's support and seek his advice, as was done by 'Umar and 'Alī.

He must then prescribe certain acts of worship that can be performed only in the caliph's presence, in order to extol his importance and make them serve his glorification. These are the congregational affairs, such as festivals. He must prescribe such public gatherings; for these entail the call for solidarity, the use of the instruments of courage, and competition. It is by competition that virtues are achieved. Through congregations, supplications are answered and blessings are received in the manner discussed in our statements.

Likewise, there must be certain transactions in which the imam participates. These are the transactions that lead to the building of the city's foundation, such as marriage and communal activities. He must also prescribe, in the transactions involving exchange, laws that prevent treachery and injustices. He must forbid unsound transactions where the objects of exchange change before being actually received or paid, as with moneychanging, [453] postponement in the payment of debt, and the like.

He must also legislate that people must help and protect others, their properties, and lives, without this, however, entailing that the contributor should penalize himself as a result of his contribution.

As for enemies and those who oppose his law, the legislator must decree waging war against them and destroying them, after calling on them to accept the truth. Their property and women must be declared free for the spoil. For when such property and women are not administered according to the constitution of the virtuous city, they will not bring about the good for which property and women are sought. Rather, these would contribute to corruption and evil. Since some men have to serve others, such people must be forced to serve the people of the just city. The same applies to people not very capable of acquiring virtue. For these are slaves by nature as, for example, the Turks and the Zinjis and in general all those who do not grow up in noble [that is, moderate] climes where the conditions for the most part are such that nations of good temperament, innate intelligence and sound minds thrive. If a city other than his has praiseworthy laws, the legislator must not interfere with it unless the times are such that they require the declaration that no law is valid save the revealed law. For when nations and cities go astray and laws are prescribed for them, adherence to the law must be assured. If the adherence to the law becomes incumbent, it might very well be the case that to ensure this adherence requires the acceptance of the law by the whole world. If the people of that [other] city, which has a good way of life, find that this [new] law, too, is good and praiseworthy and that the adoption of the new law means restoring the conditions of corrupted cities to virtue, and yet proceed to proclaim that this law ought not to be accepted and reject as false the legislator's claim that this law has come to all cities, then a great weakness will afflict the law. Those opposing it could then use as argument for their rejecting it that the people of that [other] city have rejected it. In this case these latter must also be punished and war waged on them; but this war must not be pursued with the same severity as against the people utterly in error. Or else an indemnity must be imposed on them in lieu of their preference. In any case, it must be enunciated as a truth that they are negators [of the true law]. For how are they not negators, when they refuse to accept the divine Law, which God, the Exalted, has sent down? Should they perish, they would have met what they deserve. For their death, though it means the end of some, results in a permanent good, particularly when the new law is more complete and better. [454] It should also be legislated with regard to these, that if clemency on condition that they pay ransom and tax is desired, this can be done. In general, they must not be placed in the same category as the other nonbelievers.

The legislator must also impose punishments, penalties, and prohibitions to prevent disobedience to the divine Law. For not everyone is restrained from violating the law because of what he fears of the afterlife. Most of these [penalties and so forth] must pertain to acts contrary to law that are conducive to the corruption of the city's order; for example, adultery, theft, complicity with the enemies of the city, and the like. As for the acts that harm the individual himself, the law should contain helpful advice and warning, and not go beyond this to the prescription of obligatory duties. The law concerning acts of worship, marriage, and prohibitions should be moderate, neither severe nor lenient. The legislator must relegate many questions, particularly those pertaining to transactions, to the exercise of the individual judgment of the jurists. For different times and circumstances call for decisions that cannot be pre-determined. As for the further control of the city involving knowledge of the organization of guardians, income and expenditure, manufacture of armaments, legal rights, border fortifications, and the like, it must be placed in the hands of the ruler in his capacity as caliph. The legislator must not impose specific prescriptions concerning these. Such an imposition would be defective since conditions change with time. Moreover, it is impossible to make universal judgments that cover every contingency in these matters. He must leave this to the body of counsellors.

It is necessary that the legislator should also prescribe laws regarding morals and customs that advocate justice, which is the mean. The mean in morals and customs is sought for two things. The one, involving the breaking of the dominance of the passions, is for the soul's purification and for enabling it to acquire the power of self-mastery so that it can liberate itself from the body untarnished. [455] The other, involving the use of these passions, is for worldly interests. As for the use of pleasures, these serve to conserve the body and procreation. As for courage, it is for the city's survival. The vices of excess are to be avoided for the harm they inflict in human interests, while the vices of deficiency are to be avoided for the harm they cause the city. By wisdom as a virtue, which is the third of a triad comprising in addition temperance and courage, is not meant theoretical wisdom – for the mean is not demanded in the latter at all – but, rather, practical wisdom pertaining to worldly actions and behavior. For it is deception to concentrate on the knowledge of this wisdom, carefully guarding the ingenious ways whereby one can attain through it every benefit and avoid every harm, to the extent that this would result in bringing upon one's associates the opposite of what one seeks for oneself and result in distracting oneself from the attainment of other virtues. To cause the hand to be thus fettered to the neck, means the loss of a man's soul, his whole life, the instrument of his well-being, and his survival to that moment at which he attains perfection. Since the motivating powers are three – the appetitive, the irascible, and the practical – the virtues consist of three things: (a) moderation in such appetites as the pleasures of sex, food, clothing, comfort, and other pleasures of sense and imagination; (b) moderation in all the irascible passions such as fear, anger, depression, pride, hate, jealousy, and the like; (c) moderation in practical matters. At the head of these virtues stand temperance, practical wisdom, and courage; their sum is justice, which, however, is extraneous to theoretical virtue. But whoever combines theoretical wisdom with justice, is indeed the happy man. And whoever, in addition to this, wins the prophetic qualities, becomes almost a human god. Worship of him, after the worship of God, becomes almost allowed. He is indeed the world's earthly king and God's deputy in it.

MOSES MAIMONIDES

M OSES MAIMONIDES – or to give him his Jewish name, Moshe ben Maimon – was born in Cordoba in Spain in 1135 CE. His father, himself a Jewish scholar of considerable repute, educated him to begin with, though he also studied philosophy and the natural sciences with local Muslim scholars. After having to flee Cordoba in 1148, the family settled in Fez in 1160 where Maimonides continued his studies. However, persecution forced them to flee again in 1165. Eventually settling in Old Cairo, Maimonides embarked upon a career as a physician, while continuing to write in various fields, finally serving as court physician to the great Muslim leader Saladin. He was also, however, a leading member of the Jewish community and much of his time was taken up in responding to questions from the wider Jewish Diaspora. Maimonides published in many areas of thought, although perhaps his most celebrated text is the *Guide to the Perplexed*, an attempt to address the challenge posed by Greek thought to Jewish faith. He also wrote a small treatise on *Logic* (excerpted here) which gives a clear statement of how he saw the character of the political and international realms. He died in Cairo in 1204.

From *Logic*

Chapter 14
Political science

Political science falls into four parts: first, the individual man's governance of himself; second, the governance of the household; third, the governance of the city; and fourth, the governance of the large nation or of the nations.

Man's governance of his self consists in his making it acquire the virtuous moral habits and removing from it the vile moral habits if these are already present. Moral habits are the settled states that form in the soul until they become habitual dispositions from which the actions originate. The philosophers characterize moral habit as being a virtue or a vice; they call the noble moral habits, moral virtues, and they call the base moral habits, moral vices. The actions stemming from the virtuous moral habits, they call good; and the actions stemming from the base moral habits, they call evil. Similarly, they characterize intellecting, too – that is, conceiving the intelligibles – as being a virtue or a vice. Thus they speak of intellectual virtues and of intellectual vices. The philosophers have many books on morals. They call every governance by which a man governs another, a regime.

The governance of the household consists in knowing how they [that is, the members of the household] help each other, and what is sufficient for them, so that their conditions may be well ordered, as far as this is possible in view of the requisites of that particular time and place.

The governance of the city is a science that imparts to its citizens knowledge of true happiness and imparts to them the [way of] striving to achieve it; and knowledge of true misery, imparting to them the [way of] striving to guard against it, and training their moral habits to abandon what are only presumed to be happiness so that they not take pleasure in them and doggedly pursue them. It explains to them what are only presumed to be miseries so that they not suffer pain over them and dread them. Moreover, it prescribes for them rules of justice that order their associations properly. The learned men of past religious communities used to formulate, each of them according to his perfection, regimens and rules through which their princes governed the subjects; they called them nomoi; and the nations used to be governed by those nomoi. On all these things, the philosophers have many books that have been translated into Arabic, and the ones that have not been translated are perhaps even more numerous. In these times, all this – I mean the regimes and the nomoi – has been dispensed with, and men are being governed by divine commands.

4

International relations in Christendom

The classical distinction between civilization and barbarism is replaced in medieval Europe by a religious dichotomy dividing Christians from non-Christians. The distinctions are cultural, but where the cultures they privilege are spatially bounded these distinctions can be interpreted geographically. The earliest Christians were scattered and oppressed, their faith divorced from the temporal world and therefore from its rulers and their territories. But as Christians grew more numerous and rulers were converted, Christianity came to be understood not only as a faith but as a realm of Christians and their lands. The church itself was organized into territorially defined bishoprics and Christian kingdoms distinguished collectively from the outer wilderness of paganism. With the expansion of Islam in the seventh, eight, and ninth centuries, Christian communities in Asia Minor, Persia, and Africa were destroyed or (as in the case of the Ethiopian church) cut off from European Christianity. The threat posed by Islam to Christian communities everywhere probably reinforced the developing sense of Christian unity (Hay, 1968: 24). By the high middle ages there had emerged the idea of a concrete Christian society: the spiritually defined, ecclesiastically organized, and geographically delimited Christendom.

One concern of medieval Christian thinkers is to articulate the laws governing this society, a problem made difficult by the diversity of kinds of law recognized within it. In treating what we have come to call international relations, these thinkers articulate principles to guide Christian princes in their relations with one another and, occasionally, with non-Christians. The texts assembled in this chapter consider three aspects of this intramural Christian debate. First, which laws – and which lawmakers – rightly govern Christendom? Second, what obligations did these laws prescribe in the conduct of relations between Christians? How, in particular, should one regard the vexing question of war between Christians? And, third, what did these laws prescribe in relations with non-Christians, especially the barbarians of the New World? These questions illustrate two of the main themes that Chris Brown identifies in his introduction to this book: whether conduct is to be judged according to local practices or general principles ("particularism/universalism") and how to apply the appropriate standards to relations between as well as within communities ("inside/outside").

Until the rediscovery of Aristotle's *Ethics* and *Politics* in the thirteenth century, Christian theology had understood human action, law, and government in Augustinian terms, that is, in terms of original sin, divine providence, and salvation. Neither of these works referred to the Christian story of humanity's creation, fall, and redemption by Christ. Instead of regarding politics, as Augustine did, as an expedient made necessary by original sin, Aristotle articulated a view of politics as a way of life particularly suited to human beings, and a conception of the common good of a community as an authentic and permanent good. *The Politics* introduced the idea of the city-state (*polis*) – the autonomous political community – into medieval thought about human affairs. For Aristotle, the *polis*, unlike the household or village, is "self-sufficient" because it possesses the resources needed to exist on its own. It is the only "complete" or "perfect" political community. This is one source of the idea of the independent European state, which would eventually dissolve the notional unity of Christendom. Because of Aristotle's stature as the authority on logic, philosophy, physics, and biology, what he had to say about politics could not simply be dismissed; it had to be reconciled with the received, Augustinian, understanding.

Aquinas attacked this task of reconciliation, articulating a view of the created order as both natural and divine. Insofar as the world is a natural order, it is governed by natural laws. He understands these laws not as the observed regularities of Galilean science, but as Aristotelian teleological principles according to which all things, behaving according to their inherent natures, pursue their own intrinsic ends. Human beings are a part of this natural world. It is their nature to think and act, their characteristic potential to do so rationally, and they are most likely to realize this potential within a political community. Aristotle had argued that political life is the condition of the good life. As Aquinas interprets the Aristotelian argument, the civil order provides laws under which human beings can live together and pursue their ends, and rulers are needed to make and apply these laws. But the world is also a spiritual order. Human beings not only live an earthly existence but have eternal souls that belong to this timeless spiritual realm, whose earthly manifestation is the church. The authority of this church comes directly from God. The civil community, with its human laws, and the ecclesiastical community, with its canon laws, are separate legal orders, even though the spritual arm depended on the temporal for physical protection and the enforcement of its laws. This dualism permeates political and international thought throughout the medieval and early modern periods.

The government of Christendom

Though distinct legal orders, church and state derive equally from God's rule over human beings. Both secular and ecclesiastical rulers receive their authority from God. How, then, should this authority be divided between them? The story of medieval church/state relations, as the powers of the church and various secular governments waxed and waned, is long and complicated. The twelfth-century dispute over whether the authority to "invest" (appoint) bishops in a realm belonged to the pope or to the king of that realm provides one illustrative episode. Another is the subsequent controversy over whether the pope could depose a secular ruler. The Holy Roman Emperor was by tradition crowned by the pope: if the pope had this power, might he not have the power to depose a sinful or unjust emperor? The pope could excommunicate a secular ruler, but that was not the same thing as taking away the power to govern. The tension between church and state, however it manifested itself, was always about where to draw the line between ecclesiastical and secular authority.

According to one view, the pope is the supreme ruler of Christendom, possessing ultimate authority over both church and state. All authority is hierarchical, and there can be only one supreme authority – the pope. Kings have secular power, but they must use that power in ways consistent with God's law, and the church is the ultimate judge of what is or is not consistent with God's law. It follows that kings exercise secular power under the authority and guidance of the church. Boniface VIII expressed this view in 1302 when he decreed that "both [the material and the spiritual swords] are in the power of the church ... One sword ought to be under the other and the temporal authority subject to the spiritual" (Black, 1993: 48). Fourteenth-century theologians and canon lawyers often drew upon Aristotle's idea of the *polis* as a self-sufficient or "perfect" community to argue that the *church* is the "highest and most perfect" society (Black, 1993: 52).

Others challenged this hierarchical understanding of church and state. Civil rulers and their defenders saw church and state as equal powers. That is, they rejected the claim of papal supremacy. After Boniface issued his decree, the French king, Philip IV, responded that the pope was a heretic and should be tried by a council of the church. And when Boniface excommunicated Philip, Philip retaliated by ordering his arrest. Philip's supporters argued that the pope and kings have their own proper spheres of authority. On this secular, dualist, view, the church has authority in spiritual affairs (and this includes the actual governance of the church), but everything else falls under the authority of secular rulers. Kings should obey the pope on spiritual matters, but on temporal matters kings are supreme and the pope may not interfere. In practice, as one might expect, this neat division of authority broke down in disputes over whether a particular issue (like taxing the clergy) was spiritual or temporal.

John of Paris (c. 1250–1306), a Dominican and perhaps a student of St. Thomas Aquinas, defends the secular position, that is, a dualist rather than hierarchical view of church and state. *On Royal and Papal Power*, written around 1302, may be read as a contribution to the debate between the pope and Philip IV over the latter's right to tax and otherwise regulate the French church. Like his papalist adversaries, John draws upon Aristotelian ideas, defining a kingdom as "perfected [i.e. self-sufficient] government ... by one person ... for the common good" (p. 191). For John, as for Aristotle, a human being is a creature whose defining quality, rationality, can only be realized by living with other human beings in a rational way, that is, according to laws rather than by brute force, and this means living in a civil order. And a civil order requires a ruler to make its laws: community means living in peace and concord, which means living under one law and one ruler. There can be only one ruler in any realm, and that ruler is its king.

By arguing that royal authority is not derived from the authority of the church, John can conclude that secular authorities are superior to the pope with respect to temporal matters. John's argument for secular power is therefore in effect an argument for a *multiplicity* of powers against the unified, hierarchical power of the church. And although the argument might be used in defending the idea of a universal secular monarchy, in the manner of Dante, John himself does not offer such a defense. He argues only that there should be one rather than many rulers in a political community. This is an argument for kingship over oligarchy within a realm, not an argument that the entire world should be governed by a single king. It therefore presumes the pluralist ordering of secular authority that eventually developed into the European international system.

John's arguments, then, can be seen as undermining the medieval ideals of unity and hierarchy inherited from Rome: one church, one empire. But the organization of medieval Christendom was in fact not a unified hierarchy. Following the division of the Roman empire into a Western empire centered on the city of Rome and an Eastern empire centered on Byzantium, the universal church split into western (Roman) and eastern (Orthodox) branches. By the late middle ages, the Holy Roman Empire, successor to the Western empire, was little more than a kingdom centered in what is today Germany, with territories in northern Italy: as Voltaire put it, "neither holy, nor Roman, nor an empire." The emperor, a figurehead elected by the various German princes and cities, had no authority outside this realm and little inside it. And, of course, the emperor was often at loggerheads with the pope: instead of unity, there was endless war between the "universal state" and the universal church.

Of those who wished to revive the empire, some argued that it was needed to preserve the Christian faith and to convert unbelievers, others that it was, or could be, a means of upholding peace and justice in the world. Writing around 1320, a couple of decades after John, the poet Dante (1265–1321) defends the idea of a single secular authority for the entire world. His *Monarchy* is sometimes seen as anticipating modern ideas about world government, but it is probably more accurate to read it as a work that looks back, nostalgically, to the never-realized ideal of a united Christendom.

By "monarchy" Dante does not mean the kingship of a realm but "empire" – "a single sovereign authority set over all others" in the temporal world (p. 198). What could justify such an authority? Dante proceeds deductively, in the manner of the scholastic philosophers, though he abandons the dialectic of objections and answers one finds in some of their works. His conclusion is that the highest human purposes can be fulfilled only by humanity acting under the direction of a single ruler.

Is there, Dante asks, some purpose for which God made human beings which can be achieved only by humanity as a whole, and not by a single person, household, city, or kingdom? Human beings exist to fulfill their highest capacities, which are intellectual. But intellect cannot be realized fully in any single individual, household, or kingdom, only in the world as a whole. Furthermore, the use of the mind – the activity of thinking – is best pursued in peace and tranquillity. Therefore universal peace is the condition that is most conducive to the flourishing of intellect in humanity as a whole. But *do* we think best in tranquillity? It might be argued that we use our minds best when challenged, like a writer trying to articulate a complicated idea or a trial lawyer arguing a difficult case. Dante may believe that such thinking, limited by the immediate situation, is not truly objective: we think more deeply and more universally not in acting but when we recollect past actions in tranquillity.

If the well-being of the world depends on the fulfillment of humanity's highest capacity, which is to achieve truth by thinking critically and reflectively, how can that well-being be achieved? Here, like John of Paris and Aquinas before him, Dante looks back to Aristotle: if people are to cooperate for a common purpose, someone must guide or direct them. Just as the mind directs our other faculties, so one paterfamilias guides the family, one government a city, one king a kingdom. Peace, which is required for the human race to reach its potential as a thinking species, depends on a unity of wills. But a single will cannot prevail unless everyone is ruled by one ruler. Therefore, one person – a "monarch" or "emperor" – must guide and direct humanity as a whole.

The views of those who defended imperial monarchy might be described as nostalgic because they focus on reviving a set of long-moribund institutions. But the same can be said about efforts to defend the papacy, for the fourteenth-century church, though still a political community with its own laws, rulers, subjects, and property, was disintegrating. And the Renaissance popes who came to preside over this community were also princes ruling Italian territories in thoroughly Machiavellian ways. This not only temporal but "worldly" church found itself vulnerable to the challenge of Lutheranism.

Martin Luther (1483–1546) began not as a revolutionary but as a scholar whose attacks on abuses within the church merely continued a medieval tradition of theological debate. But the church's alarmed reaction invited him both to articulate his theology and to resist efforts to suppress it. Salvation, Luther argued, depends solely on faith. It is bestowed by an omnipotent God as an act of grace and cannot be earned, as the church had taught, by participating in the sacraments. It follows that there is no need for priests, whose function is to perform these sacraments, or for the church itself as an organized priesthood. Luther did not conclude that the priesthood must disappear, but he did deprive the organized church of an important theological rationale. The true church is a community composed not of priests but of true believers in the teachings of Christ. Unlike the existing Catholic church, this true church "is not of this world" (John 18.36). What makes his theology so radical is that in restating the Augustinian dichotomy between the spiritual and temporal, Luther locates papal authority in the temporal realm.

Because he condemns the church for its worldliness, one might expect Luther to be equally hostile to secular governments. But he is not. In *On Secular Authority* (1523), Luther acknowledges the failings of secular government, condemning princes as criminals or fools. But he does not dismiss it out of hand. Unlike the existing church, the state has a function: it exists to govern the many who, because they are not true Christians, need laws and rulers to guide their conduct, settle their disputes, and punish their crimes. The Christians whom the gospel teaches to live by faith alone and who do not need governing – the true Christians – are not the majority of those who call themselves Christians. If all the world were truly Christian there would be no need for government. But only a few are true Christians. The rest require and are deservedly subject to secular authority. If there were no authority, such people, lacking guidance and restraint, would destroy one another. No matter what their defects, then, secular rulers are necessary, their authority divinely ordained: "These are God's jailers and hangmen ... The world is too wicked to deserve princes much wiser and more just than this" (Luther, 1991: 30). Luther often refers to the state as "the sword," a conventional metaphor but one that he uses quite deliberately to emphasize that civil order requires the executioner as well as the lawmaker and the judge (Höpfl, in Luther, 1991: xvi).

The government of the world resides, then, neither in an empire that is manifestly defunct nor a church that has no proper function to perform, spiritually or temporally. It resides, rather, with the separate princes who, simply because they exist, are the only instruments available for governing the great mass of sinning humanity. Like the argument of John of Paris two centuries before, Luther's defense of secular authority suggests that a multiplicity of secular realms is the necessary and legitimate order of the world.

Just and unjust wars

In defending the divinely ordained right of secular princes to pacify the wicked, Luther joins a long tradition of debate on the lawfulness of killing and war in Christian communities. St. Thomas Aquinas (c. 1225–74), who discusses the conditions under which war can be waged "without sin" in his *Summary of Theology* (1265–73) and other writings, is the most influential but by no means the only theologian to discuss this question (see Russell, 1975; Barnes, 1982).

Aquinas inherited Augustine's understanding of war as a consequence of sin. But against the view that all war is sinful, Aquinas argues that war can be justified if it punishes aggression or other injury. To overcome theological doubts that killing in war could ever be licit, Aquinas draws on Aristotle's argument that rulers are responsible for the common good of the community, and that they must often use deadly force to fulfill this responsibility. War, in other words, is not only a sin; it is also a way of combating sin and, more generally, of preserving the common good. But because force can be used for evil ends as well as for good, choices that result in war and killing must be carefully examined. And because not all uses of force are consistent with moral law, the circumstances under which war and killing are justified must be carefully specified. We call the continuing elaboration of these circumstances by theologians, lawyers, philosophers, and moralists "just-war theory" or "the just-war tradition."

A war is morally permissible when three conditions are met. First, it must be waged on the authority of a ruler, not of private individuals. Aquinas does not discuss the question, often contentious, of how public authorities are to be distinguished from private persons. Nor does he explicitly confront the objection that wars declared by public officials are often unjust, though a response to this objection is implicit in his second condition, that to be permissible a war must be waged for a "just cause." For Aquinas, this expression means that the enemy must be guilty of doing wrong: "Those who are attacked should be attacked because they deserve it on account of some fault" (p. 214). Aquinas cites Augustine: a licit war is "one that avenges wrongs" – for example, when a government is punished "for refusing to make amends for the wrongs inflicted by its subjects or to restore what it has seized unjustly" (p. 214). Today, we are inclined to identify just cause with self-defense: a country is right to go to war to defend itself from attack. We worry about the idea of attacking to punish wrongdoing by other countries. But Aquinas does not mention self-defense as a just cause; his concern is to identify the conditions under which rulers may use force to avenge injustices committed against them.

Aquinas does, however, discuss self-defense in relation to killing by individuals. One can kill in self-defense without sin, provided that one intends only to save one's own life and not, as such, to kill the attacker. One is not guilty of murder if the attacker's death is the unavoidable consequence of efforts to resist attack. This is the principle of double effect. The main application of the principle, by later just-war moralists, is not to the issue of when it is permissible to go to war, but to the question of what actions by soldiers are permissible once a war is under way. Such moralists use the principle of double effect to distinguish between the direct and indirect killing of innocents in war. There is a distinction between killing innocent bystanders by accident, in the course of fighting an enemy, and killing them on purpose. When the Allies bombed German cities during the Second World War, they intended the deaths of civilians as a means of undermining Germany's will to fight. When they bombed railway lines in France before the Normandy invasion, they killed civilians living near those lines – but not as their end or a means to their end. According to recent just-war moralists, then, the Allies acted wrongly in the first case, but not in the second (Walzer, 1977: 151–9). For Aquinas, however, those who kill under public authority are exempt from this constraint on intentions: they *can* intend the deaths of attackers, provided they do so for the common good and not from evil motives.

This brings us to the third of Aquinas' conditions for a morally justified war: those who wage war must have "a rightful intention." They must "intend the advancement of good or the avoidance of evil" (p. 214). The issue here is *motive*: the spirit in which one acts, the emotions that move one to action. If one is moved to wage war by hatred or cruelty, then the war one chooses is morally wrong, even if the other conditions (lawful authority and just cause) are met. This has always been the part of his just-war theory that is hardest for our own secular and legalistic culture to assimilate. Unlike Aquinas, we usually think of public morality ("justice") as a matter of external conduct, not internal motives. Motives may be relevant to judging character, but for the most part (and especially in law) it is enough if we can get people to obey rules governing their outward conduct.

All three conditions – authority, just cause, right intention – are controversial. As Russell (1975: 269) suggests, Aquinas is here trying to simplify earlier and far more complex lists of conditions linked to the specific conditions of medieval feudalism. By making his arguments in the language of theology and natural law, rather than feudal custom and canon law, Aquinas articulated a theory of the just war that could be applied in other times and places, which may be one reason for its subsequent influence. For example, because it makes being declared by proper authority a criterion of just war but fails to specify who holds such authority, the theory could be adapted to efforts to distinguish sovereigns from other nobles or officials on the grounds that only the former is entitled to initiate a war. Among those seeking to limit the right of war were advocates for papal or imperial authority, who claimed that only the pope (or the emperor) could authorize the use of force. Others insisted that the right of war belonged only to princes without temporal superiors. The feudal right of war was gradually suppressed and by the early seventeenth century "private war" was generally regarded not merely as illegal but as treason. But disagreement about who is "sovereign" continued into the modern period, and has indeed never entirely disappeared.

A quite different strand in Christian thought about war is illustrated in the writings of Desiderius Erasmus (1466–1536). Erasmus was born in Holland, the illegitimate son of a priest. After himself receiving a clerical education he went on to study theology at Paris. There he learned Greek and was drawn into the circle of Renaissance humanists, soon developing a preference for ancient literature over scholastic theology. Taking up biblical scholarship, Erasmus published a scholarly Greek version of the New Testament and worked to revive interest in the early church fathers. Like other Christian humanists, he hoped to purify Christian religion by turning away from medieval scholastics like Aquinas, seeking guidance from the Bible and early Christianity. As a religious reformer, Erasmus belonged to the movement that produced Martin Luther, though he eventually broke with the reformers in an effort to reconcile the emerging Protestant movement with the church in Rome. He hoped to preserve the unity of Christianity by avoiding the rigid positions that would make compromise impossible.

Erasmus' *Adages*, begun in 1500, comments on thousands of proverbs from the works of classical authors. His essay on the adage *dulce bellum inexpertis*, "war is sweet to those who have not tried it" (1515) expresses his understanding of Christianity and his belief in the values of moderation and peace. Though the intra-Christian religious wars of the sixteenth and seventeenth centuries were still in the future, war was endemic in Erasmus' day. The Turks were expanding into Europe, conquering Serbia and Bosnia and approaching Venice. Russia was expanding from Moscow. The Spaniards by 1492 had driven the Moors out of Spain in a bloody reconquest. Western Europe was peppered with small wars and revolts, and the French were engaged in repeated attempts to conquer the Italian states. Wars, then, were taken for granted not only as inevitable but as the proper court of appeal in disputes between rulers over matters of inheritance (Hale, 1994: 92). Erasmus was one of the few who condemned war on humanist grounds, arguing that the doctrine of the just war had no effect except to provide pretexts for war and for rulers to receive the blessing of their church.

Erasmus' style is rhetorical, not logical. Instead of refuting the syllogisms of medieval scholasticism, he dismisses them with ridicule. Truth, he suggests, springs not from argument and disputation but from piety, experience, and imagination. Christianity is learned by living a Christian life, not by formal study. The piety of the early church has been undermined by learning and eloquence. The teachings of Christ are simple; you don't have to be "crammed up to the ears with nonsense out of Aristotle" to be a good Christian. Worst of all, Christianity has borrowed from Roman law the idea that force may be met with force, even though Christ teaches us to turn the other cheek. The result is the doctrine of the just war, according to which "'just' is defined as what has been ordered by the prince, even if he be a child or a fool." This, though unfair as a restatement of Aquinas, captures the way in which just-war criteria are often used stupidly or disingenuously. Against the just-war ethic, Erasmus advocates a pacifism based on the gospel, reinvigorating a tradition of Christian pacifism that remains influential to this day.

The encounter with America

The question of whether the standards governing relations with infidels differ from those for relations among Christians became urgent in the wake of the European discovery of America. Unlike the Turks, who inhabited their own lands, the natives of the New World inhabited the territory of a European empire and their status as subjects and their rights against Christians could not be ignored.

Francisco de Vitoria (1486–1546) was a child when Columbus sailed in search of the Indies. By the time of his death the Spaniards had conquered the kingdoms of the Aztecs in Mexico and the Incas in Peru and were acquiring a vast empire in the Americas. This conquest, which resulted in the deaths of untold numbers of native Americans and the seizure of their lands and property, generated a vigorous debate between those who sought to justify it and those who were appalled by the behavior of the conquerors. Vitoria's lectures on the conquest, delivered at the University of Salamanca in the late

1530s, were not a mere exercise in scholastic theology, for the moral, legal, and theological issues at stake were directly relevant to the policies of the Spanish (imperial) crown. These issues were contested for the rest of the century, most famously in the public exchanges between Juan Ginés de Sepúlveda, a scholar and official in the government of Emperor Charles V, and Bartolomé de las Casas, a Dominican friar and advocate for the Indians (Hanke, 1949 and 1959; Pagden, 1987).

Europeans found the people of the New World as strange as its plants and animals, persistently viewing them through categories developed in a very different context. They saw most non-Europeans as "barbarians," a term the ancient Greeks had used for those who were not speakers of Greek. Because the Greeks lived in city-states and regarded city life as the life most suited to human beings as rational and free creatures, the term "barbarian" came to connote natural and moral inferiority. Barbarians are savage, cruel, even bestial: they have not learned to control their animal nature (Pagden, 1986: 18). They have failed to fulfill their potential as rational beings. They are, to use adjectives common in European discourse down to this century, not only different but "backward" or "primitive": inferior versions of what Europeans thought themselves to be.

Among the practices that were believed to distinguish barbarians from civilized peoples were the eating of human flesh and the sacrifice of human victims. The sacrifices practiced in Mexico by the Aztecs horrified the Spaniards and were often invoked to justify the Spanish conquest. Vitoria, however, was equally disgusted by the bloody massacres and plunder perpetrated by the Spaniards.

In one of his lectures, "On Dietary Laws, or Self-Restraint," Vitoria discusses whether cannibalism and human sacrifice among the Indians could justify conquest and expropriation. Although these practices are forbidden by divine and natural law, this in itself does not justify war against them: adultery, sodomy, perjury, and theft also violate divine and natural law yet do not justify war against communities in which these violations occur. But if the barbarians eat or sacrifice innocent people, their victims can be defended from harm. Such a war, which defends the innocent, resembles what would later be called "humanitarian intervention," and, like the latter, is strictly limited in its ends and means. Specifically, Vitoria argues, if the Spaniards wage war against the barbarians on these grounds, that is, to rectify an injustice, they cannot lawfully continue it once that goal is accomplished, and they are certainly barred from seizing Indian property. A lawful intervention cannot, without additional justification, become a lawful conquest. Furthermore, a Christian prince who comes, for whatever reason, to rule the Indians is morally obligated to rule them for their own good. This follows from the principle that in ruling a particular community a prince must be guided by the interests of that community.

Vitoria develops these principles in "On the American Indians." In this lecture, he asks "by what right were the barbarians [the Indians of the New World] subjected to Spanish rule?" Some attempted to justify the conquest by arguing that the Indians, being barbarians, were incapable of being true "masters" – rulers of kingdoms or owners of property. They used the Aristotelian idea of natural slavery to support the claim that Indians lacked government or ownership before the Spanish conquest. Natural slaves, for Aristotle, are human beings who possess only limited reason, creatures who can follow commands but not make choices of their own or command others. If the Indians are slaves by nature, they cannot own things or govern themselves, and, as slaves without masters, they may be owned and ruled by anyone and therefore by the Spaniards.

Vitoria is unimpressed by these arguments, arguing that what Aristotle calls natural slavery is unrelated to slavery as a practice (commonly rationalized on the grounds that those defeated in battle owed their lives to the victors, who might choose to exercise their acquired right by enslaving the conquered). By natural slavery, Aristotle means only that some human beings are insufficiently rational to be considered responsible for their own decisions. He does not mean that such persons cannot own things or that they can become the property of others. Slavery of the latter kind "is a civil and legal condition, to which no man can belong by nature" (p. 234). Those who are intellectually deficient may need to be governed by others, as parents govern their children. Like children, natural slaves have rights. If the Indians are natural slaves, in Aristotle's sense, this fact justifies nothing beyond ruling them for their own good. It cannot justify expropriation, legal slavery, or massacre. But, Vitoria argues, the Indians are, in any case, not natural slaves. They are neither stupid nor mad: that they have cities, laws, magistrates, and commerce proves that they possess judgement, like other human beings.

But if the Indians did own property and rule themselves before the Spanish conquest, on what grounds can that conquest be defended? One cannot argue that the Americans belong to the emperor (the Spanish king) because the emperor rules the entire world, or that Spain rules America on behalf of the pope. Nor can the Spaniards claim title to the Indies on the grounds that they discovered them – this argument, says Vitoria, offers no more support for the Spanish conquest than it would if the Indians had discovered Spain. But even though these and many other false arguments ("unjust titles") can be refuted, it does not follow that the Spaniards have no right to rule over the Indians. There are several legitimate grounds ("just titles") on which Spanish dominion in the New World might be defended.

Vitoria assumes that Spaniards are entitled to travel, settle, engage in trade, and appropriate common resources in the Americas, so long as they do not invade the rights of the indigenous inhabitants. But if they are attacked, they may defend themselves and also seek redress for the violation of their rights. And if the Indians continue to interfere with the Spaniards in the exercise of their legitimate rights, they can be treated as "treacherous foes against whom all rights of war can be exercised, including plunder, enslavement, deposition of their former masters, and the institution of new ones." Vitoria does say that whatever is done "must be done in moderation, in proportion to the actual offence." But can one really plunder, enslave, and conquer "in moderation"?

Christians have the right to preach Christianity among the barbarians and they may defend this right by force, if necessary. Those Indians who convert to Christianity may be protected from efforts to reverse their conversion. And if there are many converts, the pope may even depose "their infidel masters" and give them a Christian prince. Clearly, these precepts clear the way for Spanish rule. But not without doubts and resistance: critics ridiculed the characterization of Spaniards in America as "travelers," and one of the few books totally suppressed in Spain during the second half of the sixteenth century as morally objectionable was one in which Sepúlveda defended his view that the Indians were natural slaves (B. Hamilton, 1963: 10; Pagden, 1987: 89). Although by the end of the century the debate over the Indies had lost its practical importance because of a catastrophic decline in the Indian population and the waning of missionary fervor, the arguments it generated would echo in foreign policy debates until the collapse of the last European empires.

FURTHER READING

Black (1993) provides a good introduction to medieval political thought and to most of the authors and themes explored in this chapter. For additional discussion and bibliography, see Burns (1988) or Canning (1996). On Aquinas, Pieper (1962) is one place to start; Finnis (1998) is more difficult but also more up to date. Medieval just-war theory is ably surveyed by Barnes (1982) and, in more detail, by Russell (1975). To follow just-war thinking into modern times, see Johnson (1975), Walzer (1977), and Finnis (1996). On Erasmus and his context, Adams (1962) is helpful. B. Hamilton (1963) and Fernández-Santamaría (1977) discuss Vitoria's lecture on the American conquest in the context of Spanish neo-scholasticism. For more on the conquest itself, see Todorov (1999).

SOURCES

John of Paris, from *On Royal and Papal Power* (c .1302), in *Medieval Political Theory – A Reader*, ed. Cary J. Nederman and Kate Langdon Forhan (London: Routledge, 1993), chs. 1, 5, and 7, pp. 161–3 and 164–7.

Dante Alighieri, from *Monarchy* (*c*. 1320), ed. Prue Shaw (Cambridge: Cambridge University Press, 1996), Book 1, sections 2, 3, 5, 10, and 16, pp. 4–8, 9–11, 14–15, and 28–9. Most of the editor's notes have been omitted.

Martin Luther, from *On Secular Authority* (1523), in *Luther and Calvin on Secular Authority*, ed. and trans. Harro Höpfl (Cambridge: Cambridge University Press, 1996), Book 1, pp. 6–12, 13–14, 15, 17, 20–2. Most of the editor's notes have been omitted.

Thomas Aquinas, from *Summa Theologiae* (*c*. 1270), in St. Thomas Aquinas, *On Law, Morality, and Politics*, ed. William P. Baumgarth and Richard J. Regan, SJ (Indianapolis: Hackett, 1988), II–II, Q. 40, a. 1 and Q. 64, a. 6–8, pp. 220–8. The editors' notes have been omitted.

Desiderius Erasmus, from "Dulce Bellum Inexpertis" (1515, with additions from later editions), in *The "Adages" of Erasmus: A Study with Translations*, by Margaret Mann Phillips (Cambridge: Cambridge University Press, 1964), pp. 308–10, 317–22, 330–2, 338–44. Most of the editor's notes have been omitted.

Francisco de Vitoria, from "On the American Indians" (1539), in Francisco de Vitoria, *Political Writings*, ed. Anthony Pagden and Jeremy Lawrance (Cambridge: Cambridge University Press, 1991), pp. 233, 239–40, 249–51, 277–8, 279–80, 281–4, 285–6, 287–8, and 290–2. Translator's interpolations are in square brackets; most of the editor's notes have been omitted.

JOHN OF PARIS

JOHN of Paris (*c*. 1250–1306), an independent-minded theologian, philosopher, and priest in the Dominican order. John's promising career as a teacher of philosophy at the University of Paris was derailed when he was denounced to the authorities for defending the then unorthodox views of Thomas Aquinas. Restored to his position in 1300, he was again embroiled in controversy when he defended the claims the French crown in its conflict with the papacy over the king's right to regulate the church in France. Arguing that royal authority is not derived from that of the church, John concluded that the king was superior to the pope in temporal matters within the realm. His arguments for monarchical authority against the claims of the church strengthened the position of all monarchs against both pope and emperor.

From *On Royal and Papal Power*

Chapter 1:
What royal government is and whence it had its origins

In the first place, it is to be understood that a kingdom can be defined thus: a kingdom is the perfected government of a multitude by one person for the sake of the common good.

In connection with this definition, 'government' is taken to be the genus, while 'multitude' is added in order to differentiate it from government in which each person governs himself, whether by natural instinct (in the manner of brute animals) or by one's own reason (in the case of those who lead a solitary life). It is called 'perfected' in order to differentiate the multitude from the family, which is not perfected because it is not self-sufficient, except for a short time, and is not adequate for a full life in the manner of the civil community, according to the Philosopher in Book 1 of the *Politics*. 'Arranged for the good of the multitude' is mentioned in order to differentiate it from tyranny, oligarchy and democracy, in which the governing party attends only to its own good, especially in the case of tyranny. 'By one person' differentiates a kingdom from an aristocracy, that is, the rule of the better or the best, wherein a few hold sway on account of their virtue, which certain people call government according to the advice of the prudent or the expertise of the senate, and differentiates it from *polycratia*, in which the people hold sway by means of popular decrees. For the king is no one but he who holds sway alone, as is said by the Lord through Ezekiel [34:23]: 'My servant David will be king over everyone and he will be the sole pastor over them all.'

Such government is derived from natural law and from the law of nations. For since a human is naturally a political or civil animal, as is stated in *Politics* Book 1 (which is demonstrated, according to the Philosopher, by the cases of food, clothing and defence, in which one person alone is inadequate, as well as by speech, which is directed towards others – all factors which are uniquely intrinsic to human beings), it is necessary that human beings live in a multitude and in such a multitude as suffices for life itself, which is not the household or the village community, but the city or kingdom, for in a single house or village, one does not find everything in respect of food and clothing and defence necessary for a full life, as one does find in a city or kingdom. A multitude in which everyone strives only for what is one's own will disperse and divide into diverse parts unless it is ordered towards the common good by some one person, just as the human body would pass away unless there were some common force within the body which directed it towards the common good of all the members. On account of this, Solomon says in Proverbs 11:14: 'Where there is no governor, the people will disperse.' For this is necessarily the case, insofar as what is individual and what is common are not the same. Everyone differs in regard to individual matters, yet they are united in regard to common matters. Moreover, diverse things have diverse causes, for which reason it is necessary that everyone should incline towards what is for the common good of the many as well as inclining towards what is for one's individual good.

Furthermore, the governance of a multitude by one person who is preeminent on account of virtue is more expedient than by many or a few virtuous people, as is evident not only in regard to potency, since virtue is more united and therefore stronger in one ruler than in many different ones, but also in regard to the unity and peace which ought to be the aim of the government of a multitude. For many rulers do not preserve the peace of a multitude unless they are united and harmonious. Therefore, if on account of these factors a single ruler in accordance with virtue can better serve the peace, and the peace of the citizens cannot be as easily disturbed, then also the single ruler aiming at the common good has more of an eye on common affairs than if many people were to hold sway in accordance with virtue, because when more people are removed from the community, there is less that remains in common, and when fewer people are removed, there is more remaining in common. On account of this, the Philosopher says that among all of the forms of government aiming at their own advantage, the tyrant is the worst because he aims more greatly at his own advantage and more greatly despises common affairs. Besides, in the natural order, we observe that everything is reduced to a single order, so that in a body composed of mixed elements a single part holds sway: in the heterogeneous human body there is one principal member, namely, the soul, which restrains all the elements throughout the whole body; likewise, gregarious animals such as bees and cranes, for whom it is natural to live in society, naturally submit to one ruler.

From what has been said above, it is evident that it is necessary and expedient for human beings to live in a multitude and particularly a multitude which can meet the needs of a full life, such as a city or territory, and most especially under one person ruling by reference to the common good, who is called a king. And it is also evident that this government is derived from natural law, namely, by reason that a human is in large measure naturally a civil or political and social animal, since before Belus and Ninus, who for the first time exercised rulership, human beings lived neither naturally nor even in human fashion, but instead they lived in the manner of beasts without rulership, as is reported by certain people mentioned by Orosius in his *Against the Pagans*. And Tully [Cicero] says quite the same thing at the beginning of the *Old Rhetoric* [*De inventione*] and the Philosopher says of such creatures in the *Politics* that they do not live as human beings but as gods or beasts.

And since such human beings could not be recalled from the life of beasts to the communal life to which they are naturally suited solely through their common speech, those human beings who were more experienced in reason struggled by means of persuasive reasoning to recall their erring companions to a common life ordered under some one person, as Tully says; and so recalled, they were bound by fixed laws to the communal way of life; these laws can indeed be called the laws of nations. And thus it is evident that such rulership is derived from both natural law and the law of nations.

...

Chapter 5: Which is prior in dignity, kingship or priesthood?

From the preceding, it should be evident whether kingship or priesthood is prior in dignity, for what is later in time is routinely held to be prior in dignity, as in the case of what is imperfect in relation to what is perfect or a means in relation to an end. And therefore we say that priestly power is greater than royal power and surpasses it in dignity, because we always perceive that whatever pertains to the ultimate end is more perfect and better, and it directs whatever pertains to an inferior end. Now kingship is ordained in order that the assembled multitude may live in accordance with virtue, as has been stated, and it is furthermore ordained for the sake of a higher end, which is the enjoyment of God, whose guiding trusteeship is entrusted to Christ whose ministers and vicars are priests. And therefore priestly power is of greater dignity than secular power, and this is commonly conceded: 'As lead is not as precious as gold, so the priestly order is higher than royal power' [*Decretum* 96.10]; and the decretal *Solitae* says that spiritual ends are to be preferred to temporal goods just as the sun is preferred to the moon [*Decretals* 1.33.6]; and Hugh of St Victor says: 'To the extent that the spiritual life is of greater dignity than the earthly, and the soul than the body, so spiritual power surpasses the honour and dignity of secular or earthly power' [*On the Sacraments* 2.2.4]; and Bernard writes to Pope Eugenius: 'Does it seem to you that dignity or power rests with the forgiveness of sins or rather with the allotment of property? But there is no comparison', as if to say, 'Spiritual power is greater, therefore it is surpassing in dignity' [*On Deliberation* 1.6].

And yet, if the dignity of the priest is ultimately greater than that of the ruler, it is not necessary that it is greater in all ways. For the lesser, secular realm does not hold its power from the greater, spiritual realm in such a manner that the former originates in or was derived from the latter, as in the case of the power which a proconsul holds from the emperor who is greater in all matters, since the proconsul's power is derived from him; but secular power is held in the manner of the head of the household in relation to that of the commander of an army, since one is not derived from the other, but both are given from some superior power. And therefore secular power is in certain matters superior to spiritual power, namely, in respect of temporal affairs, regarding which it is not subject to the spiritual realm since it does not originate in that source, but instead both have immediate origins in a single supreme power, namely, the divine one, on account of which the inferior is not subject to the superior in all matters but only in regard to those in which the supreme power has placed it beneath the greater realm. For who would claim that, because a learned teacher of letters or a moral educator arranges all the affairs of a household towards a more noble end, namely, knowledge of the truth, he should therefore also subject the physician, who is concerned with an inferior end, namely, knowledge of the body, in regard to the administration of his medications? Surely this is not reasonable, since the head of the household, who brought them both into the house, would not have placed a greater authority over the physician in this way. Therefore, the priest is greater than the ruler in spiritual matters and conversely the ruler is greater in temporalities, although ultimately the priest is greater inasmuch as the spiritual is greater than the temporal.

This is also demonstrated by examples from the authorities cited previously, for although gold may be more precious than lead, still lead is not formed out of gold. This is expressly stated in *Decretum* 27.4.1. Yet it ought to be observed that what is said here we must understand in regard to the true priesthood of Christ. For the priesthood of the Gentiles and all veneration of deities existed by means of temporalities arranged for the common good of the multitude whose care fell under the king. Thus, the priests of the Gentiles were set under the kings, and kingship was greater than priesthood in just the same way as that power which concentrates upon the common good is greater than that which concentrates solely upon some particular good. Similarly, in the Old Law the only goods which the priesthood promised explicitly were temporal ones, although these were conferred upon the people not by demons but by the true God. Thus, in the Old Law the power of the priesthood was of less dignity than royal power, and the former was subjected to the latter, because the king was not directed by the priesthood towards anything other than the good of the multitude whose care fell upon him. And the converse is true of the New Law.

Also, it ought to be observed how, through the miraculous exercise of divine providence, there gradually grew up in the City of Rome, which God had prepared as the future principal seat of His priesthood, the practice among the leaders of the city of voluntarily subjecting themselves to priests more readily than in other places, although this was done not out of an obligation of justice, since they were greater in absolute terms than priests, but as a sign of the excellence of the future priesthood, to whom fuller reverence would be owed. In the words of Valerius:

Our city always regards everything to be less important than religion, even in regard to matters in which those of the greatest distinction wish to display their own prestige, on account of which leaders do not hesitate to serve sacred causes, thus discerning that one will control human beings if the divine powers are properly and steadily served. (Valerius Maximus, *Memorable Words and Deeds* 1.1.9)

Moreover, since it would later be the case that the priesthood of the Christian religion would thrive best in France, it was divinely provided among the Gauls that Gentile priests (who have been named druids) were especially central throughout the whole of Gaul, as Julius Caesar writes in his book, *On the Gallic War*. Therefore, the power of the priesthood of Christ is of greater dignity than royal power.

...

Chapter 7: In what way the supreme pontiff is related to the goods of the laity

The preceding makes evident the way in which the pope relates to the goods of the laity, because as little as he has lordship over the external goods of the laity, even less is he steward over them, except perhaps in instances of extreme necessity, in which case he is not really a steward, but a proclaimer of right. In regard to what has been stated, it ought to be observed that the external goods of the laity are not bestowed upon the community as are ecclesiastical goods, but they are acquired by the personal art, labour or industry of individual people, and individuals, inasmuch as they are individuals, have right and power and true lordship over their goods, and each can ordain, dispose, administer, preserve and alienate his own goods according to his will without injury to anyone else, since he is lord. And thus such goods do not have an order or connection either between them or in relation to a single common head that may have them to dispose or administer, since each person is to be arranger of his own property according to his own will. Thus, neither the ruler nor the pope has lordship or stewardship over such things.

Yet because it sometimes occurs that the communal peace is disturbed on account of such external goods, insofar as a certain person usurps what belongs to another, and also because sometimes human beings who are too fond of their own goods do not share them in cases of necessity nor release them for the utility of the country, so a ruler, who takes charge of such matters, is appointed by the people with the result that there is a judge discerning between justice and injustice and an avenger of injuries and a fair measure in the acquisition of goods from individuals in accordance with just proportion for the necessity or utility of the community. Because the pope is a type of supreme head not only over the clergy but generally over all the faithful inasmuch as they are believers, in the manner of a general instructor of faith and morals, he has the power, in the case of a great threat to faith and morals (in which instance all the goods of the faithful, even the chalices of the churches, are communal, that is, are to be shared), to administer the external goods of the faithful and to discern how these are to be put to use in proportion to what the community contributes towards the needs of the faith, which might otherwise be subverted by the invasion of pagans or something of the sort; and such danger can be so dire and so clear-cut that the pope can extract tenths or fixed payments from individual believers for the sake of alleviating the threat to the common faith, although in accordance with due proportion lest someone is unjustifiably burdened more greatly than the others. And such a decree by the pope is nothing other than the proclamation of right. Moreover, he can compel resisters and opponents by means of ecclesiastical censure. In the same way also, the pope can ordain that the faithful contribute additional amounts from their goods up to what is adequate to meet the debts of their parish, if in some parish there were a multiplication of new believers to such an extent that traditional revenues could not suffice for the care of parishioners because it would be necessary to retain new priests to perform services; in this case, such a papal decree would be the proclamation of right. Yet except for such cases of necessity on behalf of the spiritual community, the pope does not have stewardship over the goods of the laity, but each disposes of his own goods just as he wills, and the ruler administers them in special cases for the good of the temporal community. In instances where there is no necessity, but where there is some spiritual utility, or where it is not agreed that the external goods of the laity are to be granted on account of such utility or necessity, the pope may not compel anyone, but the pope can give indulgences to the faithful for the performance of services and, I think, nothing else is granted to him.

DANTE ALIGHIERI

D ANTE ALIGHIERI (1265–1321), Italian poet and author of the *Divine Comedy*. Dante served his native city, Florence, as a councilor and ambassador until he ended up on the wrong side in the turbulent civil conflicts of the period. Exiled from Florence, he abandoned politics for poetry, supported by patrons in Verona, Ravenna, and other Italian cities. In his *Monarchy* (*c*. 1320), Dante defends the medieval ideal of a single authority for the entire world. Only such an authority, he argues, can guarantee the universal peace and liberty that is required if human beings are to fulfill their potential.

From *Monarchy*

Book one

ii

Firstly therefore we must see what is meant by 'temporal monarchy', in broad terms and as it is generally understood. Temporal monarchy, then, which men call 'empire', is a single sovereign authority set over all others in time, that is to say over all authorities which operate in those things and over those things which are measured by time. Now there are three main points of inquiry which have given rise to perplexity on this subject: first, is it necessary to the well-being of the world? second, did the Roman people take on the office of the monarch by right? and third, does the monarch's authority derive directly from God or from someone else (his minister or vicar)?

Now since every truth which is not itself a first principle must be demonstrated with reference to the truth of some first principle, it is necessary in any inquiry to know the first principle to which we refer back in the course of strict deductive argument in order to ascertain the truth of all the propositions which are advanced later. And since this present treatise is a kind of inquiry, we must at the outset investigate the principle whose truth provides a firm foundation for later propositions. For it must be noted that there are certain things (such as mathematics, the sciences and divinity) which are outside human control, and about which we can only theorize, but which we cannot affect by our actions; and then there are certain things which are within our control, where we can not only theorize but also act, and in these action is not for the sake of theory, but theorizing is for the sake of taking action, since in these the objective is to take action. Now since our present subject is political, indeed is the source and starting-point of just forms of government, and everything in the political sphere comes under human control, it is clear that the present subject is not directed primarily towards theoretical understanding but towards action. Again, since in actions it is the final objective which sets in motion and causes everything – for that is what first moves a person who acts – it follows that the whole basis of the means for attaining an end is derived from the end itself. For there will be one way of cutting wood to build a house, and another to build a ship. Therefore whatever constitutes the purpose of the whole of human society (if there is such a purpose) will be here the first principle, in terms of which all subsequent propositions to be proved will be demonstrated with sufficient rigour; for it would be foolish to suppose that there is one purpose for this society and another for that, and not a common purpose for all of them.

iii

We must therefore now see what is the purpose of human society as a whole; when we have seen this, more than half our work will be done, as Aristotle says in the *Ethics*. And to throw light on the matter we are inquiring into, it should be borne in mind that, just as there is a particular purpose for which nature produces the thumb, and a different one for which she produces the whole hand, and again a purpose different from both of these for which she produces the arm, and a purpose different from all of these for which she produces the whole person; in the same way there is one purpose for which the individual person is designed, another for the household, another for the small community, yet another for the city, and another for the kingdom; and finally the best purpose of all is the one for which God Everlasting with his art, which is nature, brings into being the whole of mankind. And it is this purpose we are seeking here as the guiding principle in our inquiry. Consequently the first point to bear in mind is that God and nature do nothing in vain; on the contrary whatever they bring into being is designed for a purpose. For in the intention of its creator *qua* creator the essential nature of any created being is not an ultimate end in itself; the end is rather the activity which is proper to that nature; and so it is that the activity does not exist for the sake of the essential nature, but the essential nature for the sake of that activity. There is therefore some activity specific to humanity as a whole, for which the whole human race in all its vast number of individual human beings is designed; and no single

person, or household, or small community, or city, or individual kingdom
can fully achieve it. Now what this activity is will become clear when once
we clarify what is the highest potentiality of the whole of mankind. I say
therefore that no faculty shared by many different species is the highest
potentiality of any one of them; because, since it is precisely that highest
potentiality which is the defining characteristic of the species, it would
follow that one and the same essential nature was specific to several species;
and this is impossible. So the highest faculty in a human being is not simply
to exist, because the elements too share in the simple fact of existence;
nor is it to exist in compound form, for that is found in minerals; nor is
it to exist as a living thing, for plants too share in that; nor is it to exist
as a creature with sense perception, for that is also shared by the lower
animals; but it is to exist as a creature who apprehends by means of the
potential intellect: this mode of existence belongs to no creature (whether
higher or lower) other than human beings. For while there are indeed
other beings [i.e. the celestial intelligences or angels, who are pure dis-
embodied intellect] who like us are endowed with intellect, nonetheless
their intellect is not 'potential' in the way that man's is, since such beings
exist only as intelligences and nothing else, and their very being is simply
the act of understanding that their own nature exists; and they are engaged
in this ceaselessly, otherwise they would not be eternal. It is thus clear that
the highest potentiality of mankind is his intellectual potentiality or faculty. And since that potentiality cannot be fully actualized all at once in
any one individual or in any one of the particular social groupings enumerated above, there must needs be a vast number of individual people in the
human race, through whom the whole of this potentiality can be actualized;
just as there must be a great variety of things which can be generated
so that the whole potentiality of prime matter can continuously be actualized; otherwise one would be postulating a potentiality existing separately from actualization, which is impossible. And Averroes is in agreement
with this opinion in his commentary on the *De anima*. Now the intellectual
potentiality of which I am speaking is not only concerned with universal
ideas or classes, but also (by extension as it were) with particulars; and so
it is often said that the theoretical intellect by extension becomes practical, its goal then being *doing* and *making*. I am referring to actions, which
are regulated by political judgment, and to products, which are shaped by
practical skill; all of these are subordinate to thinking as the best activity for
which the Primal Goodness brought mankind into existence. This sheds light
on that statement in the *Politics* that 'men of vigorous intellect naturally rule
over others'.

...

v

Returning then to the point made at the beginning, there are three main points of inquiry concerning temporal monarchy (or 'empire' as it is more commonly called) which have given rise to and continue to give rise to perplexity; and as we have already said, it is our intention to investigate these questions in the order in which we set them out and taking the principle we have just established as our starting-point. So the first question is this: is temporal monarchy necessary for the well-being of the world? That it *is* necessary can be shown with powerful and persuasive arguments, and neither reason nor authority provides any strong counter-argument. The first of these arguments may be taken from the authority of Aristotle in his *Politics*. Now this revered authority states in that work that when a number of things are ordered to a single end, one of them must guide or direct, and the others be guided or directed; and it is not only the author's illustrious name which requires us to believe this, but inductive reasoning as well. For if we consider a single person, we shall see that what happens in the individual is this: while all the faculties are directed towards happiness, it is the intellectual faculty which guides and directs all the others; otherwise happiness is unattainable. If we consider a household, whose purpose is to prepare its members to live the good life, there must be one person who guides and directs, who is called the 'pater familias' or his representative, in line with Aristotle's observation that 'Every household is governed by the eldest'; and his role, as Homer says, is to guide everyone and impose rules on the others. Hence the proverbial curse: 'May you have an equal in your house.' If we consider a small community, whose purpose is neighbourly support in relation both to people and to goods, there must be one person who guides the others, either appointed by someone from outside or emerging as leader from among their number with the agreement of the others; otherwise not only will they fail to achieve that neighbourly collaboration, but sometimes, if a number of people contest the leadership, the whole community is destroyed. If we consider a city, whose purpose is to be self-sufficient in living the good life, there must be one ruling body, and this is so not only in just government, but in perverted forms of government as well; if this should not be the case, not only is the purpose of social life thwarted, but the city itself ceases to be what it was. Lastly, if we consider an individual kingdom – and the purpose of a kingdom is the same as that of a city, but with greater confidence that peace can be maintained – there must be one king who rules and governs; otherwise not only do those who live in the kingdom not achieve that purpose, but the kingdom itself falls to ruin, in accordance with those words of the infallible Truth: 'Every kingdom divided against itself shall be laid waste.' If this holds true in these cases and in individuals who are ordered to one particular goal, then the proposition advanced above is true; now it is agreed that the whole of mankind is ordered to one goal, as has already been demonstrated: there must therefore be one person who directs and rules mankind, and he is properly called 'Monarch' or 'Emperor'. And thus it is apparent that the well-being of the world requires that there be a monarchy or empire.

...

x

Now wherever there can be conflict there must be judgment to resolve it, otherwise there would be an imperfection without its proper corrective; and this is impossible, since God and nature never fail in their provision of what is necessary. There is always the possibility of conflict between two rulers where one is not subject to the other's control; such conflict may come about either through their own fault or the fault of their subjects (the point is self-evident); therefore there must be judgment between them. And since neither can judge the other (since neither is under the other's control, and an equal has no power over an equal) there must be a third party of wider jurisdiction who rules over both of them by right. And this person will either be the monarch or not. If he is, then our point is proved; if he is not, he in his turn will have an equal who is outside the sphere of *his* jurisdiction, and then it will once again be necessary to have recourse to a third party. And so either this procedure will continue *ad infinitum*, which is not possible, or else we must come to a first and supreme judge, whose judgment resolves all disputes either directly or indirectly; and this man will be the monarch or emperor. Thus monarchy is necessary to the world. And Aristotle saw the force of this argument when he said: 'Things do not wish to be badly ordered; a plurality of reigns is bad; therefore let there be one ruler.'

...

xvi

All the arguments advanced so far are confirmed by a remarkable historical fact: namely the state of humanity which the Son of God either awaited, or himself chose to bring about, when he was on the point of becoming man for the salvation of mankind. For if we review the ages and the dispositions of men from the fall of our first parents (which was the turning-point at which we went astray), we shall not find that there ever was peace throughout the world except under the immortal Augustus, when a perfect monarchy existed. That mankind was then happy in the calm of universal peace is attested by all historians and by famous poets; even the chronicler of Christ's gentleness deigned to bear witness to it; and finally Paul called that most happy state 'the fullness of time'. Truly that time was 'full', as were all temporal things, for no ministry to our happiness lacked its minister. What the state of the world has been since that seamless garment [the unity of the empire] was first rent by the talon of cupidity we can read about – would that we might not witness it.

O human race, how many storms and misfortunes and shipwrecks must toss you about while, transformed into a many-headed beast, you strive after conflicting things. You are sick in your intellects [theoretical and practical], and in your affections; you do not nurture your higher intellect with inviolable principles, nor your lower intellect with the lessons of experience, nor your affections with the sweetness of divine counsel, when it is breathed into you by the trumpet of the holy spirit: 'Behold how good and how pleasant it is for brethren to dwell together in unity.'

MARTIN LUTHER

M ARTIN LUTHER (1483–1546), German priest and theologian whose defiance of the church in the matter of the sale of indulgences is taken as the beginning of the Protestant Reformation. Defending the idea of the church as a community of believers, rather than a hierarchy of priests, Luther relegated the existing church to what he saw as the corrupt realm of temporal affairs, radically undercutting its claims to provide spiritual guidance to the faithful. In *On Secular Authority* (1523), he argues that secular rule is necessary to control the behavior of the majority of human beings who are not true Christians. Luther's defense of secular authority suggests that a multiplicity of secular realms is the necessary and legitimate order of the temporal world.

From *On Secular Authority*

Square brackets indicate words needed to complete the sense in the translation which are not in the original text. They are also used in Luther's scriptural references where, as not infrequently, they are inaccurate or Luther did not supply them, and to give verse references.

1 . Our first task is [to find] a firm grounding for secular law and the Sword, in order to remove any possible doubt about their being in the world as a result of God's will and ordinance. The passages [of Scripture] which provide that foundation are these: Romans, 12 [in fact 13.1–2]: 'Let every soul be subject to power and superiority. For there is no power but from God and the power that exists everywhere is ordained by God. And whoever resists the power, resists God's ordinance. But whosoever resists God's ordinance shall receive condemnation on himself.' And again 1 Peter 2[13–14]: 'Be subject to every kind of human order, whether it be to the king as the foremost, or governors as sent by him, as a vengeance on the wicked and a reward to the just.'

The Sword and its law have existed from the beginning of the world. When Cain beat his brother Abel to death, he was terrified that he would be killed in turn. But God imposed a special prohibition, suspending [punishment by] the sword for Cain's sake: no one was to kill him. The only possible reason why Cain should have been afraid is that he had seen and heard from Adam that murderers should be killed. Furthermore, God re-instituted and confirmed [this command] in express words after the Flood when he says in Genesis 9[6]: 'Whosoever sheds man's blood, by man let his blood be shed.' This cannot be interpreted as a reference to God [himself] inflicting suffering and punishment on murderers, since many of them, either because they repent or by favour, remain alive and die [naturally] without the sword. No: it refers to the right of the Sword: a murderer forfeits his life, and it is right that he should be killed by the sword. And if something prevents the law being enforced, or if the sword is dilatory and the murderer dies a natural death, that does not prove Scripture wrong. What Scripture says is that whosoever sheds man's blood, that person's blood ought to be shed by men. It is the fault of men if God's law is not carried out, just as other commandments of God are not obeyed either.

The Law of Moses afterwards confirmed this [command]: 'If a man should kill his neighbour out of malice, him shall you drag from my altar, to kill him' (Exodus 21[14]). And again: 'A life for a life, an eye for an eye, a tooth for a tooth, a foot for a foot, a hand for a hand, a wound for a wound, a bruise for a bruise.' And what is more, Christ too confirms it when he said to Peter in the garden [of Gethsemane, Matt. 26.52]: 'Whoever takes up the sword shall perish by the sword', which is to be understood in the same sense as Genesis 9[6]: 'Whoever sheds man's blood etc.'; there is no doubt that Christ is here invoking those words, and wishes to have this commandment introduced and confirmed [in the New Covenant]. John the Baptist teaches the same [Luke 3.14]. When the soldiers asked him what they were to do, he told them: 'Do no violence or injustice to anyone and be content with your pay.' If the Sword were not an occupation approved by God, John ought to have commanded them to cease to be soldiers, all the more since [his vocation] was to make the people perfect and to teach them in a true Christian manner. How the secular Sword and law are to be employed according to God's will is thus clear and certain enough: to punish the wicked and protect the just.

2 . But what Christ says in Matthew 5[38–9] sounds as if it were emphatically opposed to this: 'You have heard what was said to your ancestors: an eye for an eye, a tooth for a tooth. But I say to you: resist no evil. Rather, if anyone strikes you on the right cheek, turn him the other cheek. And if someone will dispute with you at law, to take your coat, let him have your cloak also. And if a man should compel you to go with him one mile, go two miles etc.' To the same effect, Paul in Romans 12[19]: 'Dearly beloved, do not defend yourselves, but rather give place unto the wrath of God. For it is written: Vengeance is mine; I will repay, says the Lord.' And again, Matthew 5[44]: 'Love your enemies. Do good unto them that hate you.' And 1 Peter 2[error for 3.9]: 'No one shall render evil for evil, or insults for insults etc.' These and others of the same

sort are hard sayings, and sound as if Christians in the New Covenant were to have no secular Sword.

This is why the sophists say that Christ has abolished the Law of Moses, and why they make [mere] 'counsels of perfection' out of such commands. They then divide up Christian doctrine and the Christian estate into two parts. The one part they call 'those who are perfect,' and to this they allot the 'counsels'; the other part they term 'the imperfect' and to them they allot the commands. But this is pure effrontery and wilfulness, without any warrant from Scripture. They fail to notice that in that very place Christ imposes his teachings so emphatically, that he will not have the slightest thing removed from it, and condemns to hell those who do not love their enemies [Matt. 5.22ff]. We must therefore interpret him in another way, so that his words continue to apply to all, be they 'perfect' or 'imperfect'. For perfection and imperfection do not inhere in works, and do not establish any distinction in outward condition or status between Christians; rather, they inhere in the heart, in faith, in love, so that whoever believes more [firmly] and loves more, that person is perfect, irrespective of whether it be a man or a woman, a prince or a peasant, monk or layman. For love and faith create no factions and no outward distinctions.

3 . Here we must divide Adam's children, all mankind, into two parts: the first belong to the kingdom of God, the second to the kingdom of the world. All those who truly believe in Christ belong to God's kingdom, for Christ is king and lord in God's kingdom, as the second Psalm [v. 6] and the whole of Scripture proclaims. And Christ came in order to begin the kingdom of God and to establish it in the world. This is why he said before Pilate [John 18.36ff]: 'My kingdom is not of this world, but whoever belongs to the truth hears my voice,' and why throughout the Gospel he announces the kingdom of God, saying [Matt. 3.2]: 'Repent, for the kingdom of God is at hand'; and again [Matt. 6.33]: 'Seek first the kingdom of God and its righteousness.' And indeed he calls the Gospel a gospel of the kingdom of God, in that it teaches, governs and preserves the kingdom of God.

Now: these people need neither secular (*weltlich*) Sword nor law. And if all the world (*Welt*) were true Christians, that is, if everyone truly believed, there would be neither need nor use for princes, kings, lords, the Sword or law. What would there be for them to do? Seeing that [true Christians] have the Holy Spirit in their hearts, which teaches and moves them to love everyone, wrong no one, and suffer wrongs gladly, even unto death. Where all wrongs are endured willingly and what is right is done freely, there is no place for quarrelling, disputes, courts, punishments, laws or the Sword. And therefore laws and the secular Sword cannot possibly find any work to do among Christians, especially since they of themselves do much more than any laws or teachings might demand. As Paul says in 1 Tim. 1[9]: 'Laws are not given to the just, but to the unjust.'

Why should this be? It is because the just man (*der Gerechte*) of his own accord does all and more than any law (*Recht*) demands. But the unjust (*Ungerechten*) do nothing that is right (*recht*), and therefore they need the law to teach, compel and urge them to act rightly. A good tree needs no teaching and no law in order for it to bear good fruit; it is its nature to do so without teaching or law. A man would have to be an idiot to write a book of laws for an apple-tree telling it to bear apples and not thorns, seeing that the apple-tree will do it naturally and far better than any laws or teaching can prescribe. In the same way, because of the spirit and faith, the nature of all Christians is such that they act well and rightly, better than any laws can teach them, and therefore they have no need of any laws for themselves.

You will reply: 'Why then has God given all mankind so many laws and why has Christ in the Gospel taught so much about what we ought to do?' I have written at length about this in my 'Postil' [i.e. *Sermons on the Church's Year*] and elsewhere and therefore I shall state the matter very briefly. St Paul says that the law is given for the sake of the unjust. In other words, those who are not Christians are constrained by laws to refrain outwardly from wicked deeds, as we shall see below. But since no man is by nature a Christian or just, but all are sinners and evil, God hinders them all, by means of the law, from doing as they please and expressing their wickedness outwardly in actions. And St Paul assigns another task to the law in Romans 7[7], and Galatians 2 [in fact 3.19 and 24]: it teaches how sin may be recognized, so as to humble man into a willingness to accept grace and faith in Christ. Christ teaches the same in Matthew 5[39]: evil is not to be resisted. Here he is explaining the law and is teaching us the nature of a true Christian, as we shall hear below.

4 . All those who are not Christians [in the above sense] belong to the kingdom of the world or [in other words] are under the law. There are few who believe, and even fewer who behave like Christians and refrain from doing evil [themselves], let alone not resisting evil [done to them]. And for the rest God has established another government, outside the Christian estate and the kingdom of God, and has cast them into subjection to the Sword. So that, however much they would like to do evil, they are unable to act in accordance with their inclinations, or, if they do they cannot do so without fear, or enjoy peace and good fortune. In the same way, a wicked, fierce animal is chained and bound so that it cannot bite or tear, as its nature would prompt it to do, however much it wants to; whereas a tame, gentle animal needs nothing like chains or bonds and is harmless even without them.

If there were [no law and government], then seeing that all the world is evil and that scarcely one human being in a thousand is a true Christian,

people would devour each other and no one would be able to support his
wife and children, feed himself and serve God. The world (*Welt*) would become a desert. And so God has ordained the two governments, the spiritual
[government] which fashions true Christians and just persons through the
Holy Spirit under Christ, and the secular (*weltlich*) government which holds
the Unchristian and wicked in check and forces them to keep the peace outwardly and be still, like it or not. It is in this way that St Paul interprets the
secular Sword when he says in Romans 13[3]: 'It [the Sword] is not a terror
to good works, but to the wicked.' And Peter says [1 Pet. 2.14]: 'It is given as a
punishment on the wicked.'

If someone wanted to have the world ruled according to the Gospel, and
to abolish all secular law and the Sword, on the ground that all are baptized
and Christians and that the Gospel will have no law or sword used among
Christians, who have no need of them [in any case], what do you imagine the
effect would be? He would let loose the wild animals from their bonds and
chains, and let them maul and tear everyone to pieces, saying all the while
that really they are just fine, tame, gentle, little things. But my wounds would
tell me different. And so the wicked under cover of the name of Christians,
would misuse the freedom of the Gospel, would work their wickedness and
would claim that they are Christians and [therefore] subject to no law and no
Sword. Some of them are raving like this already.

Such a person must be told that it is of course true that Christians are
subject to neither the law nor the Sword for their own sake, and do not need
them. But before you rule the world in the Christian and Gospel manner,
be sure to fill it with true Christians. And that you will never do, because
the world and the many are unchristian and will remain so, whether they
are made up of baptized and nominal Christians or not. But Christians, as
the saying goes, are few and far between, and the world will not tolerate a
Christian government ruling over one land or a great multitude, let alone
over the whole world. There are always many more of the wicked than there
are of the just. And so to try to rule a whole country or the world by means
of the Gospel is like herding together wolves, lions, eagles and sheep in the
same pen, letting them mix freely, and saying to them: feed, and be just and
peaceable; the stable isn't locked, there's plenty of pasture, and you have no
dogs or cudgels to be afraid of. The sheep would certainly keep the peace
and let themselves be governed and pastured peaceably, but they would not
live long.

Therefore care must be taken to keep these two governments distinct,
and both must be allowed to continue [their work], the one to make [people]
just, the other to create outward peace and prevent evildoing. Neither is
enough for the world without the other. Without the spiritual government of
Christ, no one can be made just in the sight of God by the secular government

[alone]. However, Christ's spiritual government does not extend to everyone; on the contrary, Christians are at all times the fewest in number and live in the midst of the Unchristian. Conversely, where the secular government or law rules on its own, pure hypocrisy must prevail, even if it were God's own commandments [that were being enforced]. For no one becomes truly just without the Holy Spirit in his heart, however good his works. And equally where the spiritual government rules over a country and its people unaided, every sort of wickedness is let loose and every sort of knavery has free play. For the world in general is incapable of accepting it or understanding it [i.e. the spiritual government].

...

5. You will object here: seeing that Christians need neither the secular Sword nor law, why does Paul in Romans 13[1] say to all Christians: 'Let every soul be subject to power and superiority'? And St Peter [1 Pet. 2.13]: 'Be subject to every human ordinance etc.', as cited above? My answer is: I have already said that Christians among themselves and for themselves need no law and no Sword, for they have no use for them. But because a true Christian, while he is on the earth, lives for and serves his neighbour and not himself, he does things that are of no benefit to himself, but of which his neighbour stands in need. Such is the nature of the Christian's spirit. Now the Sword is indispensable for the whole world, to preserve peace, punish sin, and restrain the wicked. And therefore Christians readily submit themselves to be governed by the Sword, they pay taxes, honour those in authority, serve and help them, and do what they can to uphold their power, so that they may continue their work, and that honour and fear of authority may be maintained. [All this] even though Christians do not need it for themselves, but they attend to what others need, as Paul teaches in Ephesians 5[21].

In the same way, the Christian performs every other work of love that he does not require for himself. He visits the sick, but not in order to become well himself. He does not feed others because he needs food for himself. And neither does he serve authority because he himself stands in need of it, but because others do, in order that they might enjoy protection, and so that the wicked might not grow even worse.

...

6. You ask whether a Christian can even wield the secular Sword and punish the wicked [himself], seeing that Christ's words 'Do not resist evil' seem so peremptory and clear that the sophists have to water them down into a mere 'counsel'. Answer, you have now heard two [conflicting] things. One is that there can be no Sword amongst Christians. And therefore you cannot bear the Sword over or among Christians. So the question is irrelevant in that context and must instead be asked in connection with the other group [the Unchristian]: can a Christian use be made of it with regard to them? This

is where the second part [of what I have said] applies, the one that says that you owe the Sword your service and support, by whatever means are available to you, be it with your body, goods, honour or soul. For this is a work of which you yourself have no need, but your neighbour and the whole world most certainly do. And therefore if you see that there is a lack of hangmen, court officials, judges, lords or princes, and you find that you have the necessary skills, then you should offer your services and seek office, so that authority, which is so greatly needed, will never come to be held in contempt, become powerless, or perish. The world cannot get by without it.

. . .

But to prove my point from the New Testament as well, we can rely on John the Baptist (Luke 3[15]), whose duty was without a doubt to witness to, show forth, and teach Christ; that is, his doctrine was to be evangelical, the pure New Testament, and he was to lead a perfect people to Christ. John confirms the office of soldier, saying that they are to be content with their pay. If it were unchristian to bear the sword, he should have punished them and told them to throw away both their swords and their pay; otherwise he would not have been teaching them what is fitting for Christians. And when St Peter in Acts 10[34ff] was teaching Cornelius about Christ, he did not tell him to abandon his office, as he should have done if it had been a hindrance to Cornelius' [attaining] the status of a Christian. Furthermore, before [Cornelius] was baptized [Acts 10.44], the Holy Spirit descended on him. And St Luke praised him as a just man [Acts 10.2] before Peter taught him, and did not find fault with him for being a commander of soldiers and a captain of the pagan Emperor. What it was right for the Holy Spirit to leave unchanged and unpunished in Cornelius is equally right for us.

. . .

You can see here that Christ did not abolish the Law when he said: 'You have heard how it was said to your ancestors: an eye for an eye. But I say to you: you shall not resist evil etc.' [Matthew 5.38f]. Rather, he is interpreting the meaning of the Law and telling us how it ought to be understood, as if to say: you Jews think that it is right and proper in the sight of God for you to recover what is yours by [recourse to] the law, and you rely on Moses saying 'an eye for an eye etc.' But I say to you that Moses gave this law on account of the wicked, who do not belong to God's kingdom, to prevent them from taking revenge themselves or doing worse. By such externally imposed law they would be compelled to desist from evil, and would be hedged about by outward law and government, and subjected to authority. But you are so to conduct yourselves that you neither need nor seek such law. For although secular authority must have such laws, to judge the unbelieving, and even though you yourselves may make use of it to judge others, all the same for yourselves and in your own

affairs you are neither to resort to it nor to use it, for you have the kingdom
of heaven and you should leave the earthly kingdom (*Erdreich*) to those who
take it from you.

You see, then, that Christ did not interpret his [own] words as abolishing
the Law of Moses or as prohibiting secular authority. Rather he withdraws
those who are his own from it, so that they will make no use of it for themselves,
but leave it for the unbelievers, whom they may indeed serve with such laws,
since the Unchristian do exist, and no one can be made a true Christian by
compulsion. But it becomes clear that Christ's words are directed to his alone
when he says somewhat later that they are to love their enemies and to be
perfect, as their heavenly father is perfect [Matt. 5.44, 48]. But a man who is
perfect and loves his enemy, leaves the law behind; he does not need it to exact
an eye for an eye. But neither does he hinder the Unchristian who do not love
their enemy and who do want to employ the law; on the contrary, he helps
the law to catch the wicked, to prevent them doing still more wickedness.

This, in my view, is how the words of Christ are reconciled with those
texts that institute the Sword. What they mean is that Christians are neither
to employ nor to call on the Sword for themselves and in their own concerns.
But they may and should use it and call on it for the sake of others, so that
evil may be prevented and justice upheld. In just the same way the Lord says
in the same place that Christians shall not take oaths, but that their speech is
to be yea, yea and nay, nay [Matt. 5.34ff]. In other words, they are not to take
oaths on their own behalf or of their own will and inclination. But when the
necessity, benefit and salvation [of others] or the honour of God demands
it, they should take oaths. They make use of the [otherwise] forbidden oath
to help others, in precisely the same way that they use the prohibited sword.
Indeed Christ and Paul themselves often swear on oath, in order to make their
teaching and witness beneficial and credible to mankind, as people do, and
are allowed to do, in those treaties and compacts of which the 62nd Psalm [in
fact 63 v. 12] speaks. 'They are praised, who swear by his name.'

A further question that arises is whether beadles, hangmen, lawyers,
advocates and all the rest of their sort can be Christians and in a state of
grace? The answer is that if government (*die Gewalt*) and the Sword serve God,
as has been shown above, then everything that government needs in order
to bear the Sword, is equally a service to God. There has to be someone to
catch the wicked, to accuse them, and execute them, and to protect, acquit,
defend and save the good. And therefore if the intention of those who carry
out these tasks is not that of looking to their own advantage, but only of
helping to uphold the laws and authorities, in order to repress the wicked,
then there is no danger in it for them, and they can do it like any other job,
and get their living by it. As has already been said, love of one's neighbour
has no regard for self, neither does it consider whether what is to be done is

important or trivial, so long as it is for the good of one's neighbour or the community.

Finally, you might ask: can't I use the Sword for myself and my own concerns, provided I am not out for my own good, but merely intend that evil should be punished? My answer is that such a miracle is not impossible, but very unusual and dangerous. It may happen where the Spirit is present in great fulness. We do indeed read in Judges 15[11] that Samson said: 'I have done unto them as they did unto me.' But against this is Proverbs 24[29]: 'Do not say: I will do unto him, as he has done unto me.' And Proverbs 20[22]: 'Do not say: I will repay his wickedness.' Samson was required by God to plague the Philistines and save the children of Israel. And even though he used his private concerns as a pretext for declaring war against them, he nevertheless did not do it to avenge himself or to seek his own advantage, but to help [the Israelites] and punish the Philistines. But no one can follow this precedent unless he be a true Christian, filled with the [Holy] Spirit. Where [ordinary human] reason wants to do likewise, it no doubt pretends that it is not seeking its own advantage, but the claim will be false from top to bottom. The thing is impossible without grace. So if you want to act like Samson, then first become like Samson.

THOMAS AQUINAS

ST. THOMAS AQUINAS (*c*. 1225–74), the greatest theologian of the medieval, and perhaps of any, era. His efforts to reconcile Christian and Aristotelian understandings of humanity's place in the world yielded a powerful synthesis that continues to inspire moral and political theorizing. Aquinas rejects the view, powerfully articulated by Augustine in antiquity and reiterated in modern times by Luther, that human nature is inherently corrupt. Like Aristotle, he regards human beings as capable of self-control and self-government. One of the tasks of theology, then, is to articulate principles to guide human conduct. Because these moral principles apply in every sphere of life, their authority extends even to war.

From *Summa Theologiae*

II–II, Question 40, Of War

First Article: Is it Always Sinful to Wage War?

We proceed thus to the First Article:

Objection 1. It would seem that it is always sinful to wage war, because punishment is not inflicted except for sin. Now, those who wage war are threatened by Our Lord with punishment, according to Mt. 26:52: "All that take up the sword shall perish by the sword." Therefore, all wars are unlawful.

Obj. 2. Further, whatever is contrary to a divine precept is a sin. But war is contrary to a divine precept, for it is written: "But I say to you not to resist evil," and "Do not defend yourselves, my dearly beloved, but yield to [God's] wrath." Therefore, war is always sinful.

Obj. 3. Further, nothing except sin is contrary to an act of virtue. But war is contrary to peace. Therefore, war is always a sin.

Obj. 4. Further, the exercise of a lawful thing is itself lawful, as is evident in scientific exercises. But the warlike exercises which take place in tournaments are forbidden by the Church, since those who are slain in these trials are deprived of ecclesiastical burial. Therefore, it seems that war is a sin in itself.

On the contrary, Augustine says in a sermon on the servant of the centurion, "If Christian discipline forbad war altogether, those who sought salutary counsel in the Gospel would have been advised to cast aside their arms and to give up soldiering altogether. On the contrary, they were told: 'Do violence to no man, ... and be content with your pay.' If He commanded them to be content with their pay, He did not forbid soldiering."

I answer that, In order for a war to be just, three things are necessary. First, the authority of the ruler, by whose command the war is to be waged; it is not the business of a private individual to declare war, because he can seek redress of his rights from the tribunal of his superior. Similarly, it is not the business of a private individual to summon together the people, something which has to be done in wars. But since the care of the common weal is committed to those who are in authority, it is their business to watch over the common weal of the city, kingdom, or province subject to them. And just as it is lawful for them to have recourse to the sword in defending that common weal against internal disturbances, when they punish evil-doers, according to the words of the Apostle: "He bears not the sword without cause, for he is God's minister, an avenger to execute wrath upon him that does evil," so too it is their business to have recourse to the sword of war in defending the common weal against external enemies. Hence it is said to those who are in authority: "Rescue the poor and deliver the needy out of the hand of the sinner," and for this reason Augustine says, "The natural order conducive to peace among mortals demands that the power to declare and counsel war should be in the hands of those who hold the supreme authority."

Secondly, a just cause is required, namely, that those who are attacked, should be attacked because they deserve it on account of some fault. Wherefore, Augustine says, "A just war is wont to be described as one that avenges wrongs, when a nation or state has to be punished for refusing to make amends for the wrongs inflicted by its subjects or to restore what it has seized unjustly."

Thirdly, it is necessary that the belligerents should have a rightful intention, so that they intend the advancement of good or the avoidance of evil. Hence Augustine says, "True religion looks upon as peaceful those wars that are waged not for motives of aggrandizement or cruelty but with the object of securing peace, of punishing evil-doers, and of uplifting the good." For it may happen that, even if war be declared by legitimate authority and for a just cause, it is nonetheless rendered unlawful through a wicked intention. Hence Augustine says, "The passion for inflicting harm, the cruel thirst to vengeance, an unpacific and relentless spirit, the fever of revolt, the lust of power, and such like things, all these are rightly condemned in war."

Reply Obj. 1. As Augustine says, "To take up the sword is to arm oneself in order to take the life of someone without the command or permission of superior or lawful authority." On the other hand, to have recourse to the sword (as a private person) by the authority of the ruler or judge or (as a public person) through zeal for justice and by the authority, so to speak, of God, is not to "take up the sword" but to use it as commissioned by another; wherefore it does not deserve punishment. And yet even those who make sinful use of the sword are not always slain by the sword, yet they always perish by their own sword, because, unless they repent, they are punished eternally for their sinful use of the sword.

Reply Obj. 2. Such like precepts, as Augustine observes, should always be borne in readiness of mind, so that we be ready to obey them and, if necessary, to refrain from resistance or self-defense. Nevertheless, it is necessary sometimes for a man to act otherwise for the common good or for the good of those with whom he is fighting. Hence Augustine says, "Those whom we have to punish with a kindly severity it is necessary to handle in many ways against their will. For when we are stripping a man of the lawlessness of sin, it is good for him to be vanquished, since nothing is more hopeless than the happiness of sinners, whence arises a guilty impunity and an evil will, like an internal enemy."

Reply Obj. 3. Those who wage war justly aim at peace, and so they are not opposed to peace, except to the evil peace which Our Lord "came not to send upon earth." Hence Augustine says, "We do not seek peace in order to be at war, but we go to war that we may have peace. Be peaceful therefore, in warring, so that you may vanquish those whom you war against and bring them to the prosperity of peace."

Reply Obj. 4. Not all exercises by men in warlike feats of arms are forbidden but those which are inordinate and perilous and end in slaying or plundering. In older times, warlike exercises presented no such danger, and hence they were called "exercises of arms" or "bloodless wars," as Jerome states in an epistle.

...

II–II, Question 64, Of Killing

Sixth Article: Is it Ever Lawful to Kill the Innocent?

We proceed thus to the Sixth Article:

Obj. 1. It would seem that in some cases it is lawful to kill the innocent. The fear of God is never manifested by sin, since, on the contrary, "the fear of the Lord drives out sin." Now, Abraham was commended in that he feared the Lord, since he was willing to slay his innocent son. Therefore, one may without sin kill an innocent person.

Obj. 2. Further, among those sins that are committed against one's neighbor, the more grievous seem to be those whereby a more grievous injury is inflicted on the person sinned against. Now, to be killed is a greater injury to a sinful than to an innocent person, because the latter, by death, passes forthwith from the unhappiness of this life to the glory of heaven. Since, then, it is lawful in certain cases to kill a sinful man, much more is it lawful to slay an innocent or a righteous person.

Obj. 3. Further, what is done in keeping with the order of justice is not a sin. But sometimes a man is forced, according to the order of justice, to slay an innocent person, for instance, when a judge, who is bound to judge according to the evidence, condemns to death a man whom he knows to be innocent, but who is convicted by false witnesses, and likewise the executioner, who in obedience to the judge puts to death the man who has been unjustly sentenced.

On the contrary, It is written: "The innocent and just person you shall not put to death."

I answer that An individual man may be considered in two ways: first, in himself; secondly, in relation to something else. If we consider a man in himself, it is unlawful to kill any man, since in every man, though he be sinful, we ought to love the nature which God has made and which is destroyed by slaying him. Nevertheless, as stated above, the slaying of a sinner becomes lawful in relation to the common good, which is corrupted by sin. On the other hand, the life of righteous men preserves and forwards the common good, since they are the chief part of the community. Therefore, it is in no way lawful to slay the innocent.

Reply Obj. 1. God is Lord of death and life, for by His decree both the sinful and the righteous die. Hence, he who at God's command kills an innocent man does not sin, as neither does God, at Whose behest he executes; indeed, his obedience to God's commands is a proof that he fears God.

Reply Obj. 2. In weighing the gravity of a sin, we must consider the essential rather than the accidental. Wherefore, he who kills a just man sins more grievously than he who slays a sinful man: first, because he injures one whom he should love more and so acts more in opposition to charity; secondly, because he inflicts an injury on a man who is less deserving of one and so acts more in opposition to justice; thirdly, because he deprives the community of a greater good; fourthly, because he despises God more, according to Luke 10:16, "He that despises you despises Me." On the other hand, it is accidental to the slaying that the just man whose life is taken be received by God into glory.

Reply Obj. 3. If the judge knows that a man who has been convicted by false witnesses is innocent, he must, like Daniel, examine the witnesses with great care, so as to find an occasion for acquitting the innocent. But if he cannot do this, he should remit him for judgment by a higher tribunal. If even this is impossible, he does not sin if he pronounce sentence in accordance with the evidence, for it is not he that puts the innocent man to death but they who stated him to be guilty. He who is assigned to carry out the sentence of the judge who has condemned an innocent man, if the sentence contains an intolerable error, should not obey, else they would be excused who executed the martyrs. If, however, it contain no manifest injustice, he does not sin by carrying out the sentence, because he has no right to discuss the judgment of his superior, nor is it he who slays the innocent man but the judge whose minister he is.

Seventh Article, Is it Lawful to Kill a Man in Self-Defense?

We proceed thus to the Seventh Article:

Obj. 1. It would seem that nobody may lawfully kill a man in self-defense. For Augustine says to Publicola, "I do not agree with the opinion that one may kill a man lest one be killed by him, unless one be a soldier or hold a public office, so that one does it not for oneself but for others, having the legitimate power to do so, provided it be fitted to the person." Now, he who kills a man in self-defense kills him lest he be killed by him. Therefore, this would seem to be unlawful.

Obj. 2. Further, Augustine says, "How are they free from sin in sight of divine Providence who are guilty of taking a man's life for the sake of these contemptible things?" Now, among contemptible things he reckons "those which men can lose unwillingly," as appears from the context, and the chief of these is the life of the body. Therefore, it is unlawful for any man to take another's life for the sake of the life of his own body.

Obj. 3. Further, Pope Nicolas says, and we have in the *Decretum*, "Concerning the clerics about whom you have consulted us, those, namely, who have killed a pagan in self-defense, as to whether, after making amends by repenting, they may return to their former state or rise to a higher degree, know that in no case is it lawful for them to kill any man under any circumstances whatever." Now, clerics and laymen are alike bound to observe the moral precepts. Therefore, neither is it lawful for laymen to kill anyone in self-defense.

Obj. 4. Further, murder is a more grievous sin than fornication or adultery. Now, nobody may lawfully commit simple fornication or adultery or any other mortal sin in order to save his own life, since the spiritual life is to be preferred to the life of the body. Therefore, no man may lawfully take another's life in self-defense in order to save his own life.

Obj. 5. Further, if the tree be evil, so is the fruit, according to Mt. 7:17. Now, self-defense itself seems to be unlawful, according to Rom. 12:19: "Do not defend yourselves, my dearly beloved." Therefore, its result, which is the slaying of a man, is also unlawful.

On the contrary, It is written: "If a thief be found breaking into a house or undermining it and be wounded so as to die, he that slew him shall not be guilty of blood." Now, it is much more lawful to defend one's life than one's house. Therefore, neither is a man guilty of murder if he kill another in defense of his own life.

I answer that Nothing hinders one act from having two effects, only one of which is intended, while the other is beside the intention. Now, moral acts take their species according to what is intended and not according to what is beside the intention, since this is accidental, as explained above. Accordingly, the act of self-defense may have two effects: one, the saving of one's life; the other, the slaying of the aggressor. Therefore, this act, since one's intention is to save one's own life, is not unlawful, seeing that it is natural to everything to keep itself in being as far as possible. And yet, though proceeding from a good intention, an act may be rendered unlawful if it be out of proportion to the end. Wherefore, if a man in self-defense uses more than necessary violence, it will be unlawful, whereas, if he repel force with moderation, his defense will be lawful, because according to the jurists, "It is lawful to repel force by force, provided one does not exceed the limits of a blameless defense." Nor is it necessary for salvation that a man omit an act of moderate self-defense in order to avoid killing the other man, since one is bound to take more care of one's own life than of another's. But as it is unlawful to take a man's life, except by public authority acting for the common good, as stated above, it is not lawful for a man to intend killing a man in self-defense, except by such as have public authority, who, while intending to kill a man in self-defense, refer this to the public good, as in the case of a soldier fighting against the foe or a judge's servant struggling with robbers, although even these sin if they be moved by private animosity.

Reply Obj. 1. The words quoted from Augustine refer to the case when one man intends to kill another to save himself from death. The passage quoted in the *Second Objection* is to be understood in the same sense. Hence he says pointedly, "for the sake of these things," whereby he indicates the intention. This suffices for the *Reply* to the *Second Objection.*

Reply Obj. 3. Irregularity results from the act, though sinless, of taking a man's life, as appears in the case of a judge who justly condemns a man to death. For this reason, a cleric, though he kill a man in self-defense, is irregular, albeit he intends not to kill him but to defend himself.

Reply Obj. 4. The act of fornication or adultery is not necessarily directed to the preservation of one's own life, as is the act whence sometimes results the taking of a man's life.

Reply Obj. 5. The defense forbidden in this passage is that which is maliciously vengeful. Hence a gloss says, "Do not defend yourselves, that is, do not strike your enemy in return."

Eighth Article, Is One Guilty of Murder through Killing Someone by Chance?

We proceed thus to the Eighth Article:

Obj. 1. It would seem that one is guilty of murder through killing someone by chance. For we read that Lamech slew a man in mistake for a wild beast, and that he was accounted guilty of murder. Therefore, one incurs the guilt of murder through killing a man by chance.

Obj. 2. Further, it is written: "If ... one strike a woman with child, and causes a miscarriage ... if her death ensue thereupon, he shall render life for life." Yet this may happen without any intention of causing her death. Therefore, one is guilty of murder through killing someone by chance.

Obj. 3. Further, the *Decretum* contains several canons prescribing penalties for unintentional homicide. Now, penalty is not due save for guilt. Therefore, he who kills a man by chance incurs the guilt of murder.

On the contrary, Augustine says to Publicola, "When we do a thing for a good and lawful purpose, if thereby we unintentionally cause harm to anyone, it should by no means be imputed to us." Now, it sometimes happens by chance that a person is killed as a result of something done for a good purpose. Therefore, the person who did it is not accounted guilty.

I answer that, According to the Philosopher, "chance is a cause that acts beside one's intention." Hence chance happenings, strictly speaking, are neither intended nor voluntary. And, since every sin is voluntary, according to Augustine, it follows that chance happenings, as such, are not sins.

Nevertheless, it happens that what is not actually and directly voluntary and intended is accidentally voluntary and intended, and so that which removes an obstacle is called an accidental cause. Wherefore, he who does not remove something whence homicide results, whereas he ought to remove it, is in a sense guilty of voluntary homicide. This happens in two ways: first, when a man causes another's death through occupying himself with unlawful things which he ought to avoid; secondly, when he does not take sufficient care. Hence, according to jurists, if a man pursue a lawful occupation and take due care, the result being that a person loses his life, he is not guilty of that person's death, whereas, if he be occupied with something unlawful or even with something lawful but without due care, he does not escape being guilty of murder if his action results in someone's death.

Reply Obj. 1. Lamech did not take sufficient care to avoid taking a man's life, and so he was not excused from being guilty of homicide.

Reply Obj. 2. He that strikes a woman with child does something unlawful; wherefore, if there results the death either of the woman or of the ensouled fetus, he will not be excused from murder, especially seeing that death is the natural result of such a blow.

Reply Obj. 3. According to the canons, a penalty is inflicted on those who cause death unintentionally through doing something unlawful or failing to take sufficient care.

DESIDERIUS ERASMUS

D ESIDERIUS ERASMUS (1466–1536), Dutch humanist, theologian, and religious reformer. Like other Christian humanists, Erasmus aspired to recapture the spirit of early Christianity by placing the teachings of scripture and of the early church fathers above those of Aquinas and the medieval scholastic tradition. Unlike Luther, however, Erasmus sought to preserve the unity of Christianity by reconciling Protestant ideas with those of the Roman church. His essay on the adage *dulce bellum inexpertis*, "war is sweet to those who have not tried it," may be read as a defense of pacifism against the Thomistic doctrine of just war.

From "Dulce Bellum Inexpertis"

Among the choicest proverbs, and widely used in literature, is the adage 'war is sweet to those who have not tried it.' Vegetius uses it thus, in his book on the Art of War, III, chapter xiv, 'Do not be too confident, if a new recruit hankers after war, for it is to the inexperienced that fighting is sweet.' There is a quotation from Pindar: 'War is sweet to those who have not tried it, but anyone who knows what it is is horrified beyond measure if he should meet it.'

There are some things in the affairs of men, fraught with dangers and evils of which one can have no idea until one has put them to the test.

> How sweet, untried, the favour of the great!
> But he who knows it, fears it.

It seems a fine and splendid thing to walk among the nobles at court, to be occupied with the business of kings, but old men who know all about the matter from experience are glad enough to deny themselves this pleasure. It seems delightful to be in love with girls, but only to those who have not yet felt what bitter there is in the sweet. In the same way this idea can be applied to any enterprise carrying with it great risks and many evils, such as no one would undertake unless he were young and without experience. Indeed Aristotle in his *Rhetoric* says this is the reason why youth tends to be bold and age to be diffident, because the former is given confidence by inexperience, and the latter acquires diffidence and hesitancy from familiar knowledge of many ills. If there is anything in mortal affairs which should be approached with hesitancy, or rather which ought to be avoided in every possible way, guarded against and shunned, that thing is war; there is nothing more wicked, more disastrous, more widely destructive, more deeply tenacious, more loathsome, in a word more unworthy of man, not to say of a Christian. Yet strange to say, everywhere at the present time war is being entered upon lightly, for any kind of reason, and waged with cruelty and barbarousness, not only by the heathen but by Christians, not only by lay people but by priests and bishops, not only by the young and inexperienced, but by the old who know it well; not so much by the common people and the naturally fickle mob, but rather by princes, whose function should be to restrain with wisdom and reason the rash impulses of the foolish rabble. Nor are there lacking lawyers and theologians who add fuel to the fire of these misdeeds and, as they say, sprinkle them with cold water. [Erasmus connects this saying with racehorses who were sprinkled with water to make them fiery, or with water used in forges.] And the result of all this is, that war is now such an accepted thing that people are astonished to find anyone who does not like it; and such a respectable thing that it is wicked (I nearly said heretical) to disapprove of the thing of all things which is most criminal and most lamentable. How much more reasonable it would be to turn one's astonishment to wondering what evil genius, what a plague, what madness, what Fury first put into the mind of man a thing which had been hitherto reserved for beasts – that a peaceful creature, whom nature made for peace and loving-kindness (the only one, indeed, whom she intended for the safety of all), should rush with such savage insanity, with such mad commotion, to mutual slaughter. This is a thing which will supply even more food for wonder to anyone who has turned his mind away from accepted opinions to discern the real meaning and nature of things, and who considers for a little with the eye of the philosopher, on the one hand the image of man, on the other the picture of war.

…

No one falls all at once to depths of shame as the satiric poet says. The greatest evils have always found their way into the life of men under the semblance of good. Long ago, then, when rude primitive men lived in the woods, naked, without ramparts, roofless, it sometimes happened that they were attacked by wild beasts. And so it was on them that man first made war, and the one who had defended the human race from the onslaught of the wild animals was held to be a man of mettle, and taken for leader. Indeed it seemed entirely right that the stabbers should be stabbed, the butchers butchered, especially when they were attacking us without provocation. Since these exploits won high praise – for that was how Hercules was made a god – spirited youth began to hunt the animals far and wide, and to show off their skins as a trophy. Then, not content with having killed them, the hunters wrapped themselves in their skins against the winter's cold. These were the first murders

and the first spoils. After this they went further and dared to do a thing
which Pythagoras deemed thoroughly wicked, and which might seem monstrous to us, were it not for custom, which has such power everywhere that
among some races it was considered dutiful to throw an aged parent into
a pit after battering him to death, and so take away life from the one who
gave it; or it was thought pious to feed on the flesh of one's intimate friends,
and fine to prostitute a virgin in the temple of Venus; and many other things
more absurd than these, which would appear shocking to everyone if they
were described. So true it is that nothing is too wicked or too cruel to win
approval, if it has the sanction of habit. What then was the deed they dared
to do? They were not afraid to feed on the carcasses of slain animals, to tear
with their teeth the dead flesh, to drink the blood and suck the juices, and as
Ovid says, 'to stuff their entrails with other entrails.' That deed, horrible as it
might seem to more gentle minds, was sanctioned by use and convenience.
'The very look of the carcasses became a pleasure. The flesh was buried in
coffers, and preserved with spices; an epitaph was written, "Here lies a boar,
here is a bear's grave." Cadaverous pleasures!' They went still further. From the
harmful beasts they proceeded to the harmless ones. They made a general
attack on sheep, 'beast without trickery or guile', they attacked the hare, who
had committed no other crime than to be eatable. They did not hold their
hands from the domestic ox, which had kept the ungrateful family for so long
by its labours; they spared no species of bird or fish, and the rule of gluttony
reached such a point that no animal was ever safe from the cruelty of man.
Habit made it possible for them not to see the savagery of this treatment of
all forms of life, as long as there was no slaughter of man.

But vice is like the sea: we have the power to shut it out altogether, but
once we have let it in, there are few of us who can impose a limit; both are
forces which roll on by their own impulsion and are not controlled by our
will. Once these beginnings had given them practice in killing, men were
incited by anger to turn their attacks on men, either with sticks and stones
or fisticuffs. So far they fought with arms like these, I imagine, and they had
already learnt from the slaughter of flocks and herds that man too could be
killed with very little trouble. But this kind of barbarity was confined for a
long time to single combat. The war was brought to an end by the defeat of
one antagonist; sometimes both fell, but then both were unfit to live. One
may add that there was often some semblance of right in withstanding an
enemy; it began to be a matter of praise to have destroyed some violent and
dangerous man, such as they say Cacus and Busiris were and to have rid the
world of such monsters. Exploits of this kind are among Hercules' titles to
praise. Then people began to band themselves together, according to kinship,
neighbourhood, or friendly alliance. And what is now called brigandage was
then called war. It was waged with stones and burnt stakes. A stream in the way,

or a rock, or some similar obstruction put an end to the battle. But meanwhile, as ferocity increases by being exercised, anger rises, ambition grows hotter, ingenuity provides weapons for the use of fury. They invent arms to defend themselves with, and they invent missiles to destroy the enemy. Now it was everywhere, and in greater numbers, and under arms, that they began to make war on each other. This was clearly madness, but it was not without honour. They called it 'bellum', and decided it was valour if anyone risked his own life to defend his children, his wife, his flocks, his dwelling from the attacks of the enemy. And so little by little, military science developed with civilisation, and city began to declare war on city, region on region, kingdom on kingdom. Yet there still remained, in a thing so cruel in itself, a few traces of the humanity of earlier times; they sent priests to demand satisfaction, they called the gods to witness, they skirmished with words before coming to blows. The battle was fought with ordinary weapons, and with courage, not trickery. It was a sin to attack before the signal was given; fighting must cease when the general had sounded the retreat. In short, it was more a contest of bravery and honour than a lust for killing. Nor did they take up arms except against foreigners, whom they called for this reason 'hostile' (*hostes*, the enemy, as it were *hospites*, strangers). So empires were built, and never did any nation achieve empire without great shedding of human blood. From then onwards there have been continual changes and chances of war, as one thrusts the other from the seat of empire and seizes it himself. After all this, as the supreme power had come into the hands of the worst rogues, anybody and everybody was attacked at will, and it began to be not the evildoers but the wealthy who were in most danger from the perils of war; the whole aim of fighting was not glory now but base profit, or something even more discreditable than that. I have no doubt that Pythagoras, wisest of men, foresaw all this when he made his philosophical observation urging the inexperienced multitude to abstain from slaughtering the flocks. He saw what would happen – that those who accustomed themselves to shed the innocent blood of an animal which had done them no harm, would not hesitate to abolish a man, when they were moved by anger or provoked by injury. What is war, indeed, but murder shared by many, and brigandage, all the more immoral from being wider spread? But this view is jeered at, and called scholastic ravings, by the thick-headed lords of our day, who seem to themselves to be gods, though they are not even human except in appearance.

From these beginnings, however, such a point of lunacy has been reached, as we see, that it fills the whole of life. We are continually at war, race against race, kingdom against kingdom, city against city, prince against prince, people against people, and (the heathen themselves admit this to be wicked) relation against relation, kinsman against kinsman, brother against brother, son against father; finally, a thing which in my opinion is worse than these, Christians fight against men; reluctantly I must add, and this is the very worst of all, Christians fight Christians. And, O blindness of the human mind! no one is astonished, no one is horrified. There are those who applaud this thing, greet it with cheers and call it holy when it is worse than hellish, and urge on the princes already crazed with fury, adding as they say 'oil to the flames.' One, from the sacred pulpit, promises pardon for all the sins committed by those who fight under the banners of his prince. Another cries: 'Your invincible highness, only remain in your present favourable state of mind towards religion and God will fight on your side.' Another promises certain victory, perverting the words of the prophets by applying them to wickedness, quoting such things as: 'Thou shalt not be afraid of any terror by night, nor for the arrow that flieth by day, nor for the demon of noon,' and, 'A thousand shall fall beside thee, and ten thousand at thy right hand,' and, 'Thou shalt go upon the asp and the basilisk, the lion and the dragon shalt thou tread under thy feet.' In short, the whole of this mystical psalm was twisted to apply to profane things, to this or that prince. There was no lack of prophets like these on both sides, and no lack of people to applaud such prophets. We heard warlike sermons of this sort from monks, theologians, bishops. All go to war, the decrepit, the priest, the monk, and we mix up Christ with a thing so diabolical! Two armies march against each other each carrying the standard of the Cross, which in itself might teach them how Christians should conquer. Under that heavenly banner, symbolising the perfect and ineffable union of all Christians, there is a rush to butcher each other, and we make Christ the witness and authority for so criminal a thing!

...

Where did it come from, this plague that creeps through the people of Christ? Probably it was little by little that this evil, like most others, found acceptance with the heedless. Every bad thing either finds its way into human life by imperceptible degrees, or else insinuates itself under the pretext of good. What crept in first was erudition, the ideal instrument, apparently, for confuting the heretics, armed as they were with the writings of the philosophers, poets, and orators. At the beginning these things were not learnt by Christians, but any who had made their acquaintance before having knowledge of Christ turned what he already possessed to pious uses. Eloquence too, at first disguised rather than spurned, was finally openly approved. Then, on the pretext of combating heresy, a conceited taste for controversy crept in, which was the cause of no little evil to the Church. Finally, things came to the point where the whole of Aristotle was accepted as an integral part of theology, and accepted in such a way that his authority was almost as sacred as that of Christ. For if Christ has said anything which is not easily fitted to our way of life, it is permitted to interpret it differently; but anyone who dares to oppose the oracular pronouncements of Aristotle is immediately hooted off the stage.

From him we have learnt that human felicity cannot be complete without worldly goods – physical or financial. From him we have learnt that a state cannot flourish where all things are held in common. We try to combine all his doctrines with the teaching of Christ, which is like mixing water and fire.

We have also taken over some things from Roman law, for the sake of its evident justice, and to make everything fit together we have twisted the Gospel teaching to it, as much as possible. But this code of laws permits us to meet force with force, to strive each for his own rights; it sanctions bargaining, allows usury – within limits; it regards war as praiseworthy, if it is just. 'Just' is defined as what has been ordered by the prince, even if he be a child or a fool. In fact the whole of Christ's teaching has been so contaminated by the writings of the dialecticians, sophists, mathematicians, orators, poets, philosophers and lawyers of the pagan world that a great part of one's life must be spent before one can turn to reading the Scriptures, and the result is that when one does get to them one is so corrupted by all these worldly ideas that the precepts of Christ either seem thoroughly shocking, or are distorted in accordance with the doctrines of these other authorities. And there is so little disapproval of this state of things, that it is regarded as sacrilege for anyone to speak about Christian scriptures without having crammed himself 'up to the ears' as they say with nonsense out of Aristotle, or rather out of the sophists. As if the teaching of Christ were not truly something that could be shared by all, or had any kind of connection with the wisdom of the philosophers.

…

They say, however, 'the law of nature dictates it, it has legal sanction, it is accepted by custom, that we should repel force by force, and each defend our own life, and our money too, when it is "the breath of our body" as Hesiod says.' Very well. But grace, the grace of the Gospel, is more efficacious than all this, and lays down that we must not curse those who curse us, but repay evil with good, that if someone takes away part of our possessions we must give him the whole, that we must also pray for those who seek to kill us. 'All that applies to the Apostles', they say; but it applies still more to the whole people of Christ, to the body, as we said before, which must be a complete whole, even if one member excels another in endowments. The people to whom the teaching of Christ may not apply are those who do not hope to reach their reward with Christ. Let those struggle for money and lands and sovereignty who mock at Christ's words 'Blessed are the poor in spirit', but these are the truly rich who wish for nothing in this world in the way of wealth or honours. Those who place the greatest happiness in riches fight to save their own life, but without understanding that this is death rather than life, and that immortality is prepared for the faithful.

They raise the objection that some Popes have both instigated and abetted war. They produce writings of the fathers in which war is apparently mentioned with approval. There are certainly some of these, but they date from the later times, when the fervour of the Gospel was weakening, and they are very few, while there are innumerable writings of authors of unquestioned sanctity which argue against war. Why should these few come into our minds rather than all the rest? Why do we turn our eyes away from Christ to men, and prefer to follow doubtful examples rather than the infallible authority? The Popes were men, first of all. And then it might well be that they were badly advised, or not attentive enough, or lacking in prudence or piety. However even these, you will find, did not approve of the kind of war which we are constantly waging. I could prove this by the clearest arguments, if I did not want to avoid being held up by this digression. St Bernard praised warriors, but in such terms as to condemn all our soldiering. However, why should I be more impressed by the writings of Bernard or the arguments of Thomas than by the teaching of Christ, which forbids us entirely to resist evil, at any rate by the popular methods?

'But,' they say, 'it is permissible to sentence a criminal to punishment; therefore it is permissible to take vengeance on a state by war.' What is there to say in answer to this? So much, that one can hardly begin. I will only point out the difference between the two cases; that the felon has been convicted in the courts before he is punished by the law, but in war each side is prosecuting the other; in the first case the suffering falls only on the person who did wrong, and the example is before everyone, but in the second case the greatest part of the suffering falls on those who have least deserved it, namely on the peasants, old people, wives, orphans, young girls. Moreover, if there is any advantage to be gained from this worst of all experiences, it is entirely drawn off by a few thieving scoundrels – it goes to pay the mercenaries, the out-and-out profiteers, perhaps a few leaders by whose instigation the war was stirred up (for this very reason) and who are never so well off as when the state is on the rocks. In the case of the felon, the reason for not sparing one is that all should be the safer; but in war, it is for the sake of taking vengeance on a few, or perhaps even one person, that we inflict such cruel suffering on so many thousands of innocent people. It would be better for the fault of a few to go unpunished than to demand an uncertain retribution from one or another, and meanwhile throw both our own people and those whom we call our enemies – our neighbours, who have done us no harm – into certain danger. Better leave the wound alone, if no surgery can be done without grave harm to the whole body. If anyone cries that it is unjust that the sinner should go unpunished, I answer that it is much more unjust to bring desperate calamity on so many thousands of innocent people who have not deserved it.

However, in these days we notice that almost every war arises from some claim or other, and from the selfish treaties of princes; for the sake of asserting the right of dominion over one small town, they gravely imperil their whole realm. And then they either sell or give away the very thing they have laid claim to with so much bloodshed. Someone may say, 'Do you want princes not to assert their rights?' I know it is not for such as myself to argue boldly about the affairs of princes, and even if it were safe to do so, it would take longer than we have time for here. I will only say this: if a claim to possession is to be reckoned sufficient reason for going to war, then in such a disturbed state of human affairs, so full of change, there is no one who does not possess such a claim. What people has not, at one time or another, been driven out of its lands or driven others out? How many migrations have there been from one place to another? How often has there been a transfer of sovereignty, either by chance or by treaty? I suppose the Paduans might try to recover the site of Troy, because Antenor was a Trojan of old; or the Romans expect to own Africa and Spain, because these were once provinces of Rome. In addition we call rule what is really administration. No one can have the same rights over men, free by nature, as over herds of cattle. This very right which you hold, was given you by popular consent. Unless I am mistaken, the hand which gave can take it away. And look what petty affairs are in question: the matter under debate is not whether this or that state is to obey a good prince or be enslaved by a tyrant, but whether it is to be counted as belonging to Ferdinand or Sigismund, or pay tax to Philip or Louis. This is that important right for which the whole world is to be entangled with war and slaughter.

But let us suppose that this 'right' is really worth something, that there is really no difference between a privately owned field and a state, nor between cattle bought with your money and men, not only free men but Christians – still it would be only acting like a prudent man to consider whether it is worth so much that you should pursue it to the immense detriment of your own people. If you cannot show that you have the mind of a prince, at least act like a man of business. For him, expense is not to be considered, if he sees that the only way of avoiding it would cost much more, and he takes it as a gain, if what he chances to lose he loses without much loss. In the state's emergency, you might follow an example from private life about which they tell a rather amusing story. There was a disagreement between two kinsmen about an inheritance. As neither would give in to the other, it looked as though the affair would have to go to court and the quarrel be ended by the decision of the judge. Counsel had been approached, the action was prepared, the affair was in the hands of the lawyers. When the judges had been addressed and the case formally opened, pleading began – in fact, war was declared. At this point one of the contestants came to his senses just in time. He went to see his opponent privately and spoke to him as follows: 'To start with, it is really not very decent that those whom nature has joined by blood should be parted by money. And then, the workings of the law are always uncertain in their results, no less so than war. It is in our power to begin this, but not to end it. The whole case is about a matter of a hundred gold pieces. We shall spend twice that, if we go to law, on clerks, investigators, barristers, solicitors, judges, and the judges' friends. We shall have to be polite to them, flatter them, and make them presents; not to speak of the worry of canvassing, the trouble of running here and there. Even if I win hands down, it seems to me more loss than gain. Why don't we have an understanding between ourselves, not with these knaves, and share out between us what we should have to pay out uselessly to them? You give up half yours, and I will give up half mine. In this way we shall be the richer for our friendship, which we were going otherwise to lose, and we shall escape a great deal of trouble. If you refuse to give up anything, I will leave the whole business for you to arrange. I would rather this money went to a friend than to those insatiable blood-suckers. It will be a great gain to me to have preserved my fair fame, kept a friend, and avoided such a mass of troubles.' His adversary was convinced by the truth of this and by his relative's sense of humour. They settled the thing between them, to the wrath of lawyers and judges, those crows whose gaping beaks they had foiled. Take a lesson from their good sense, when you are dealing with a much more dangerous thing. Do not think only of what you wish to gain, but think too of what you will lose to gain it – the sacrifice of so much that is good, the danger and disasters you will incur. If you find, by balancing one set of advantages and disadvantages with another, that an unjust peace is far preferable to a just war, why do you want to try the fortune of Mars? Who except a lunatic would fish with a golden hook? If it is clear that the cost would far exceed the gain, even if everything were to go well for you, would it not be better to give up a little of your rights, rather than buy a small advantage with such innumerable ills? I would rather anyone had the title to possession, rather than have it proved mine by the shedding of so much Christian blood. There is one man, whoever he may be, who has been in possession for many years, has got used to the reins of government, is acknowledged by his subjects, and fulfils the duties of a prince, and then another is to arise who rakes up a claim out of chronicles or faded charters and turns a well-established state of affairs upside down? Especially when we see that in human affairs nothing stays the same for long, but ebbs and flows like the tide, at the whim of fortune. What is the use of asserting one's claim so noisily to something which will soon, by chance or another, belong to someone else anyway?

Finally, if Christians cannot bring themselves to despise these trivialities, what need is there to fly to arms at once? The world has so many earnest and learned bishops, so many venerable abbots, so many aged peers with the wisdom of long experience, so many councils, so many conclaves set up by our ancestors, not without reason. Why do we not use their arbitration to settle these childish disputes between princes? But there is more credit given to those who bring forward the pretext of the defence of the Church, as if the people were not really the Church, or as if the whole dignity of the Church rested on the wealth of the clergy, or as if the Church had originated, grown and established itself by war and carnage, instead of by those who shed their own blood, and lived in tolerance and forgetfulness of their own life!

FRANCISCO DE VITORIA

FRANCISCO DE VITORIA (1486–1546), a Spanish Dominican, was one of the founders of the revival of scholastic philosophy during the sixteenth and seventeenth centuries. Vitoria's ideas are preserved in notes on his lectures at the University of Salamanca, where he held the most prestigious chair of theology in late medieval Spain. Vitoria argued that the rights of sovereigns are derived from the universal laws governing the human community, and that the conduct of sovereigns must be judged by those laws. In his lecture "On the American Indians" (1539), Vitoria considers claims made on behalf of the Spanish conquest from the standpoint of this universal law.

From "On the American Indians"

Relection of the Very Reverend Father Friar Francisco de Vitoria, Master of Theology and Most Worthy Prime Professsor at the University of Salamanca, Delivered in the Said University, A.D. 1539

The text to be re-read is 'Go ye therefore, and teach all nations, baptizing them in the name of the Father, and of the Son, and of the Holy Ghost' (Matt. 28: 19). This raises the following problem: *whether it is lawful to baptize the children of unbelievers against the wishes of their parents?* The problem is discussed by the doctors on Lombard's *Sentences* IV. 4. 9, and by Aquinas in *ST* [*Summa Theologiae*] II–II. 10. 12 and III. 68. 10.

This whole dispute and relection has arisen again because of these barbarians in the New World, commonly called Indians, who came under the power of the Spaniards some forty years ago, having been previously unknown to our world.

My present discussion of these people will be divided into three parts: first, by what right (*ius*) were the barbarians subjected to Spanish rule? Second, what powers has the Spanish monarchy over the Indians in temporal and civil matters? And third, what powers has either the monarchy or the Church with regard to the Indians in spiritual and religious matters? The conclusion to the last question will thus lead back to a solution of the question posed at the outset.

...

Question 1, Article 1: Whether these barbarians, before the arrival of the
Spaniards, had true dominion, public and private?

That is to say, whether they were true masters of their private chattels and
possessions, and whether there existed among them any men who were true
princes and masters of the others. It may seem in the first place that they have
no right of ownership (*dominium rerum*):

1. 'A slave cannot own anything as his own' (*Institutions* II.9.3 *Item vobis; Digest*
XXIX. 2. 79 *Placet*). Hence everything a slave acquires belongs to his master
(*Institutions* I. 8. 1 *Nam apud omnes*). But these barbarians are slaves by nature.
This last point is proved by Aristotle, who says with elegant precision: 'the
lower sort are by nature slaves, and it is better for them as inferiors that
they should be under the rule of a master' (*Politics* 1254^{b}20). By 'lower sort'
he meant men who are insufficiently rational to govern themselves, but are
rational enough to take orders; their strength resides more in their bodies
than in their minds (1252^{a}32). And if indeed it is true that there are such men,
then none fit the bill better than these barbarians, who in fact appear to be
little different from brute animals and are completely unfitted for government. It is undoubtedly better for them to be governed by others, than to
govern themselves. Since Aristotle states that it is a natural law that such
men should be slaves, they cannot be true masters. Furthermore, it is no
objection to argue that before the Spaniards arrived the barbarians had no
other masters; it is not impossible that a slave may be a slave even without a master, as stated by the *Glossa* on the law *Si usum fructum* (*Digest* XL.
12. 23); indeed, the law concerned expressly says so, and there is an actual
case adduced in the law *Quid seruum* (*Digest* XLV. 3. 36 *pr.*) on the unclaimed
slave abandoned by his master, which shows that such a slave may be appropriated by anyone. Therefore, if the barbarians were slaves, the Spaniards could
appropriate them.

But on the other hand it may be argued that they were in undisputed
possession of their property, both publicly and privately. Therefore, failing
proofs to the contrary, they must be held to be true masters, and may not be
dispossessed without due cause.

I reply that if the barbarians were not true masters before the arrival
of the Spaniards, it can only have been on four possible grounds. To avoid
wasting time, I omit any recapitulation here of the many writings of the
theologians on the definition and distinctions of dominion (*dominium*),
which I have quoted at length elsewhere (see my discussion of restitution in
my lectures on Lombard's *Sentences* IV. 15 and *ST* II–II. 62). These four grounds
are that they were either sinners (*peccatores*), unbelievers (*infideles*), madmen
(*amentes*), or insensate (*insensati*).

...

Question 1, Article 6: Whether madmen can be true masters

But what of madmen (I mean the incurably mad, who can neither have nor expect ever to have the use of reason)?

Let us answer with this third proposition:

3. *These madmen too may be true masters.* For a madman too can be the victim of an injustice (*iniuria*); therefore he can have legal rights. I leave it to the experts on Roman law to decide whether madmen can have civil rights of ownership (*dominium ciuile*).

Whatever the answer to that, I conclude with this final proposition:

4. *The barbarians are not prevented by this, or by the argument of the previous article, from being true masters.* The proof of this is that they are not in point of fact madmen, but have judgment like other men. This is self-evident, because they have some order (*ordo*) in their affairs: they have properly organized cities, proper marriages, magistrates and overlords (*domini*), laws, industries, and commerce, all of which require the use of reason. They likewise have a form (*species*) of religion, and they correctly apprehend things which are evident to other men, which indicates the use of reason. Furthermore, 'God and nature never fail in the things necessary' for the majority of the species, and the chief attribute of man is reason; but the potential (*potentia*) which is incapable of being realized in the act (*actus*) is in vain (*frustra*).

Nor could it be their fault if they were for so many thousands of years outside the state of salvation, since they were born in sin but did not have the use of reason to prompt them to seek baptism or the things necessary for salvation.

Thus if they seem to us insensate and slow-witted, I put it down mainly to their evil and barbarous education. Even amongst ourselves we see many peasants (*rustici*) who are little different from brute animals.

[Question 1, Conclusion]

The conclusion of all that has been said is that the barbarians undoubtedly possessed as true dominion, both public and private, as any Christians. That is to say, they could not be robbed of their property, either as private citizens or as princes, on the grounds that they were not true masters (*ueri domini*). It would be harsh to deny to them, who have never done us any wrong, the rights we concede to Saracens and Jews, who have been continual enemies of the Christian religion. Yet we do not deny the right of ownership (*dominium rerum*) of the latter, unless it be in the case of Christian lands which they have conquered.

To the original objection one may therefore say, as concerns the argument that *these barbarians are insufficiently rational to govern themselves* and so on (1.1 ad 2):

1. Aristotle certainly did not mean to say that such men thereby belong by nature to others and have no rights of ownership over their own bodies and possessions (*dominium sui et rerum*). Such slavery is a civil and legal condition, to which no man can belong by nature.

2. Nor did Aristotle mean that it is lawful to seize the goods and lands, and enslave and sell the persons, of those who are by nature less intelligent. What he meant to say was that such men have a natural deficiency, because of which they need others to govern and direct them. It is good that such men should be subordinate to others, like children to their parents until they reach adulthood, and like a wife to her husband. That this was Aristotle's true intention is apparent from his parallel statement that some men are 'natural masters' by virtue of their superior intelligence. He certainly did not mean by this that such men had a legal right to arrogate power to themselves over others on the grounds of their superior intelligence, but merely that they are fitted by nature to be princes and guides.

Hence, granting that these barbarians are as foolish and slow-witted as people say they are, it is still wrong to use this as grounds to deny their true dominion (*dominium*); nor can they be counted among the slaves. It may be, as I shall show, that these arguments can provide legal grounds for subjecting the Indians, but that is a different matter.

For the moment, the clear conclusion to the first question is therefore *that before arrival of the Spaniards these barbarians possessed true dominion, both in public and private affairs.*

…

Question 3: The just titles by which the barbarians of the New World passed under the rule of the Spaniards

I shall now discuss the legitimate and relevant titles by which the barbarians could have come under the control of the Spaniards.

Question 3, Article 1: First just title, of natural partnership and communication

My first conclusion on this point will be that *the Spaniards have the right to travel and dwell in those countries, so long as they do no harm to the barbarians, and cannot be prevented by them from doing so.*

The first proof comes from the law of nations (*ius gentium*), which either is or derives from natural law, as defined by the jurist: 'What natural reason has established among all nations is called the law of nations' (*Institutions* 1.2.1). Amongst all nations it is considered inhuman to treat strangers and travellers badly without some special cause, humane and dutiful to behave hospitably to strangers. This would not be the case if travellers were doing something evil by visiting foreign nations. Second, in the beginning of the world, when all things were held in common, everyone was allowed to visit and travel through any land he wished. This right was clearly not taken away by the division of property (*diuisio rerum*); it was never the intention of nations to prevent men's free mutual intercourse with one another by this division. Certainly it would have been thought inhuman to do so in the time of Noah. Third, all things which are not prohibited or otherwise to the harm and detriment of others are lawful. Since these travels of the Spaniards are (as we may for the moment assume) neither harmful nor detrimental to the barbarians, they are lawful.

···

My second proposition is that *the Spaniards may lawfully trade among the barbarians, so long as they do no harm to their homeland*. In other words, they may import the commodities which they lack, and export the gold, silver, or other things which they have in abundance; and their princes cannot prevent their subjects from trading with the Spaniards, nor can the princes of Spain prohibit commerce with the barbarians.

The proof follows from the first proposition. In the first place, the law of nations (*ius gentium*) is clearly that travellers may carry on trade so long as they do no harm to the citizens; and second, in the same way it can be proved that this is lawful in divine law. Therefore any human enactment (*lex*) which prohibited such trade would indubitably be unreasonable. Third, their princes are obliged by natural law to love the Spaniards, and therefore cannot prohibit them without due cause from furthering their own interests, so long as this can be done without harm to the barbarians. Fourth, to do so would appear to fly in the face of the old proverb, 'do as you would be done by'.

In sum, it is certain that the barbarians can no more prohibit Spaniards from carrying on trade with them, than Christians can prohibit other Christians from doing the same. It is clear that if the Spaniards were to prohibit the French from trading with the Spanish kingdoms, not for the good of Spain but to prevent the French from sharing in any profits, this would be an unjust enactment, and contrary to Christian charity. But if this prohibition cannot justly be proscribed in law, neither can it be justly carried out in practice, since an unjust law becomes inequitable precisely when it is carried into execution. And 'nature has decreed a certain kinship between all men' (*Digest* 1.1.3), so that it is against natural law for one man to turn against another without due cause; man is not a 'wolf to his fellow man', as Ovid says, but a fellow.

···

My fifth proposition is that if the barbarians attempt to deny the Spaniards in these matters which I have described as belonging to the law of nations (*ius gentium*), that is to say from trading and the rest, the Spaniards ought first to remove any cause of provocation by reasoning and persuasion, and demonstrate with every argument at their disposal that they have not come to do harm, but wish to dwell in peace and travel without any inconvenience to the barbarians. And they should demonstrate this not merely in words, but with proof. As the saying goes, 'in every endeavour, the seemly course for wise men is to try persuasion first' (Terence, *Eunuchus* 789). But if reasoning fails to win the acquiescence of the barbarians, and they insist on replying with violence, the Spaniards may defend themselves, and do everything needful for their own safety. It is lawful to meet force with force. And not only in this eventuality, but also if there is no other means of remaining safe, they may build forts and defences; and if they have suffered an offence, they may on the authority of their prince seek redress for it in war, and exercise the other rights of war. The proof is that the cause of the just war is to redress and avenge an offence, as said above in the passage quoted from St Thomas (*ST* II–II.40.1; see above, 2.4 §11). But if the barbarians deny the Spaniards what is theirs by the law of nations, they commit an offence against them. Hence, if war is necessary to obtain their rights (*ius suum*), they may lawfully go to war.

But I should remark that these barbarians are by nature cowardly, foolish, and ignorant besides. However much the Spaniards may wish to reassure them and convince them of their peaceful intentions, therefore, the barbarians may still be understandably fearful of men whose customs seem so strange, and who they can see are armed and much stronger than themselves. If this fear moves them to mount an attack to drive the Spaniards away or kill them, it would indeed be lawful for the Spaniards to defend themselves, within the bounds of blameless self-defence; but once victory has been won and safety secured, they may not exercise the other rights of war against the barbarians such as putting them to death or looting and occupying their communities, since in this case what we may suppose were understandable fears made them innocent. So the Spaniards must take care for their own safety, but do so with as little harm to the barbarians as possible since this is a merely defensive war. It is not incompatible with reason, indeed, when there is right on one side and ignorance on the other, that a war may be just on both. For instance, the French hold Burgundy in the mistaken but colourable belief that it belongs to them. Now our emperor Charles V has a certain right to that province and may seek to recover it by war; but the French may defend it. The same may be true of the barbarians. This is a consideration which must be given great weight. The laws of war against really harmful and offensive enemies are quite different from those against innocent or ignorant ones. The provocations of the Pharisees are to be met with quite a different response from the one appropriate to weak and childish foes.

My sixth proposition is that if all other measures to secure safety from the barbarians besides conquering their communities and subjecting them have been exhausted, the Spaniards may even take this measure. The proof is that the aim of war is peace and security, as St Augustine says in his letter to Boniface (*Epistles* 189.6). Therefore, once it has become lawful for the Spaniards to take up war or even to declare it themselves for the reasons stated above, it becomes lawful for them to do everything necessary to the aim of war, namely to secure peace and safety.

My seventh proposition goes further: once the Spaniards have demonstrated diligently both in word and deed that for their own part they have every intention of letting the barbarians carry on in peaceful and undisturbed enjoyment of their property, if the barbarians nevertheless persist in their wickedness and strive to destroy the Spaniards, they may then treat them no longer as innocent enemies, but as treacherous foes against whom all rights of war can be exercised, including plunder, enslavement, deposition of their former masters, and the institution of new ones. All this must be done with moderation, in proportion to the actual offence. The conclusion is evident enough: if it is lawful to declare war on them, then it is lawful to exercise to the full the rights of war. And is confirmed by the fact that all things are lawful against Christians if they ever fight an unjust war; the barbarians should receive no preferential treatment because they are unbelievers, and therefore can be proceeded against in the same way. It is the general law of nations (*ius gentium*) that everything captured in war belongs to the victor, as stated in the laws *De captiuis* and *Si quid in bello* (*Digest* XLIX. 15. 28 and 24), in the canon *Ius gentium* (*Decretum* D. 1. 9), and more expressly still in the law *Item ea quae ab hostibus* (*Institutions* II. 1. 17), which reads: 'in the law of nations, anything taken from the enemy immediately becomes ours, even to the extent that their people become our slaves'. Furthermore, as the doctors explain in their discussions of war, the prince who wages a just war becomes *ipso jure* the judge of the enemy, and may punish them judicially and sentence them according to their offence.

The foregoing is confirmed by the fact that ambassadors are inviolable in the law of nations (*ius gentium*). The Spaniards are the ambassadors of Christendom, and hence the barbarians are obliged at least to give them a fair hearing and not expel them.

This, then, is the first title by which the Spaniards could have seized the lands and rule of the barbarians, so long as it was done without trickery or fraud and without inventing excuses to make war on them. But on these grounds, if the barbarians allowed the Spaniards to carry on their business in peace among them, the Spaniards could make out no more just a case for seizing their goods than they could for seizing those of other Christians.

Question 3, Article 2: Second possible title, for the spreading of the Christian religion

My first proposition in support of this is that *Christians have the right to preach and announce the Gospel in the lands of the barbarians*. This conclusion is clear from the passage 'Go ye into all the world and preach the gospel to every creature' (Mark 16: 15); and 'the word of God is not bound' (2 Tim. 2: 9). Second, it is clear from the preceding article, since if they have the right to travel and trade among them, then they must be able to teach them the truth if they are willing to listen, especially about matters to do with salvation and beatitude, much more so than about anything to do with any other human subject. Third, if it were not lawful for Christians to visit them to announce the Gospel, the barbarians would exist in a state beyond any salvation. Fourth, brotherly correction is as much part of natural law as brotherly love; and since all those peoples are not merely in a state of sin, but presently in a state beyond salvation, it is the business of Christians to correct and direct them. Indeed, they are clearly obliged to do so. Fifth and finally, they are our neighbours, as I have said above (3. 1 §2 *ad fin.*), 'and God gave them commandment, each man concerning his neighbour' (Ecclus, 17: 14). Therefore it is the business of Christians to instruct them in the holy things of which they are ignorant.

...

My fourth conclusion is that if the barbarians, either in the person of their masters or as a multitude, obstruct the Spaniards in their free propagation of the Gospel, the Spaniards, after first reasoning with them to remove any cause of provocation, *may preach and work for the conversion of that people even against their will*, and may if necessary take up arms and declare war on them, insofar as this provides the safety and opportunity needed to preach the Gospel. And the same holds true if they permit the Spaniards to preach, but do not allow conversions, either by killing or punishing the converts to Christ, or by deterring them by threats or other means. This is obvious, because such actions would constitute a wrong committed by the barbarians against the Spaniards, as I have explained, and the latter therefore have just cause for war. Second, it would be against the interests of the barbarians themselves, which their own princes may not justly harm; so the Spaniards could wage war on behalf of their subjects for the oppression and wrong which they were suffering, especially in such important matters.

From this conclusion it follows that on this count too, if the business of religion cannot otherwise be forwarded, that the Spaniards may lawfully conquer the territories of these people, deposing their old masters and setting up new ones and carrying out all the things which are lawfully permitted in other just wars by the law of war, so long as they always observe reasonable limits and do not go further than necessary. They must always be prepared to forego some part of their rights rather than risk trespassing on some unlawful thing, and always direct all their plans to the benefit of the barbarians rather than their own profit, bearing constantly in mind the saying of St Paul: 'all things are lawful unto me, but all things are not expedient' (1 Cor. 6: 12). Everything that has been said so far is to be understood as valid in itself; but it may happen that the resulting war, with its massacres and pillage, obstructs the conversion of the barbarians instead of encouraging it. The most important consideration is to avoid placing obstructions in the way of the Gospel. If such is the result, this method of evangelization must be abandoned and some other sought. All that I have demonstrated is that this method is lawful *per se*. I myself have no doubt that force and arms were necessary for the Spaniards to continue in those parts; my fear is that the affair may have gone beyond the permissible bounds of justice and religion.

This, then, is the second possible legitimate title by which the barbarians may have fallen under the control of the Spaniards. But we must always keep steadfastly before us what I have just said, lest what is in substance lawful becomes by accident evil. Good comes from a single wholly good cause, whereas evil can come from many circumstances, according to Aristotle (*Nicomachean Ethics* 1106^{b}35) and Dionysius the Pseudo-Areopagite (*Divine Names* 4.30).

...

Question 3, Article 5: *Fifth just title, in defence of the innocent against tyranny*

The next title could be either on account of the personal tyranny of the barbarians' masters towards their subjects, or because of their tyrannical and oppressive laws against the innocent, such as human sacrifice practised on innocent men or the killing of condemned criminals for cannibalism. I assert that *in lawful defence of the innocent from unjust death, even without the pope's authority, the Spaniards may prohibit the barbarians from practising any nefarious custom or rite*. The proof is that God gave commandment to each man concerning his neighbour (Ecclus. 17: 14). The barbarians are all our neighbours, and therefore anyone, and especially princes, may defend them from such tyranny and oppression. A further proof is the saying: 'deliver them that are drawn unto death, and forbear not to deliver those that are ready to be slain' (Prov. 24: 11). This applies not only to the actual moment when they are being dragged to death; they may also force the barbarians to give up such rites altogether. If they refuse to do so, war may be declared upon them, and the laws of war enforced upon them; and if there is no other means of putting an end to these sacrilegious rites, their masters may be changed and new princes set up. In this case, there is truth in the opinion held by Innocent IV and Antonino of Florence, that sinners against nature may be punished. It makes no difference that all the barbarians consent to these kinds of rites and sacrifices, or that they refuse to accept the Spaniards as their liberators in the matter. This could therefore be the fifth legitimate title.

...

Question 3, Article 8: An eighth possible title, the mental incapacity of the barbarians

There is one further title which may be mentioned for the sake of the argument, though certainly not asserted with confidence; it may strike some as legitimate, though I myself do not dare either to affirm or condemn it out of hand. It is this: These barbarians, though not totally mad, as explained before, are nevertheless so close to being mad, that *they are unsuited to setting up or administering a commonwealth both legitimate and ordered in human and civil terms*. Hence they have neither appropriate laws nor magistrates fitted to the task. Indeed, they are unsuited even to governing their own households (*res familiaris*); hence their lack of letters, of arts and crafts (not merely liberal, but even mechanical), of systematic agriculture, of manufacture, and of many other things useful, or rather indispensable, for human use. It might therefore be argued that for their own benefit the princes of Spain might take over their administration, and set up urban officers and governors on their behalf, or even give them new masters, so long as this could be proved to be in their interest.

As I have said, this argument would be persuasive if the barbarians were in fact all mad; in that case, it is beyond doubt that such a course would be not merely lawful, but wholly appropriate, and princes would be bound to take charge of them as if they were simply children. In this respect, there is scant difference between the barbarians and madmen; they are little or no more capable of governing themselves than madmen, or indeed than wild beasts. They feed on food no more civilized and little better than that of beasts. On these grounds, they might be handed over to wiser men to govern. And an apparent confirmation of this argument is if some mischance were to carry off all the adult barbarians, leaving alive only the children and adolescents enjoying to some degree the use of reason but still in the age of boyhood and puberty, it is clear that princes could certainly take them into their care and govern them for as long as they remained children. But if this is admitted, it seems impossible to deny that the same can be done with their barbarian parents, given the supposed stupidity which those who have lived among them report of them, and which they say is much greater than that of children and madmen among other nations. Such an argument could be supported by the requirements of charity, since the barbarians are our neighbours and we are obliged to take care of their goods.

But I say all this, as I have already made clear, merely for the sake of argument; and even then, with the limitation that only applies if everything is done *for the benefit and good of the barbarians, and not merely for the profit of the Spaniards*. But it is in this latter restriction that the whole pitfall to souls and salvation is found to lie.

In this connexion, what was said earlier about some men being natural slaves might be relevant. All these barbarians appear to fall under this heading, and they might be governed partly as slaves.

Conclusion

The conclusion of this whole dispute appears to be this: that if all these titles were inapplicable, that is to say if the barbarians gave no just cause for war and did not wish to have Spaniards as princes and so on, *the whole Indian expedition and trade would cease*, to the great loss of the Spaniards. And this in turn would mean a huge loss to the royal exchequer, which would be intolerable.

1. My first reply is that *trade would not have to cease*. As I have already explained, the barbarians have a surplus of many things which the Spaniards might exchange for things which they lack. Likewise, they have many possessions which they regard as uninhabited, which are open to anyone who wishes to occupy. Look at the Portuguese, who carry on a great and profitable trade with similar sorts of peoples without conquering them.

2. My second reply is that *royal revenues would not necessarily be diminished*. A tax might just as fairly be imposed on the gold and silver brought back from the barbarian lands, say of a fifth part of the value or more, according to the merchandise. This would be perfectly justifiable, since the sea passage was discovered by our prince, and our merchants would be protected by his writ.

3. My third reply is that it is clear that once a large number of barbarians have been converted, it would be neither expedient nor lawful for our prince to abandon altogether the administration of those territories.

5

The modern European state
and system of states

By the middle of the seventeenth century monarchs had consolidated their powers at the expense of other princes and the church. The modern territorial state was on its way to displacing the complicated feudal, urban, and ecclesiastical arrangements of medieval Europe. Advances in military technology and administrative machinery provided territorial sovereigns with instruments of power to reinforce their claims to authority, and the resulting concentration of power and authority generated an identifiable system of states ordered by its own imperatives and practices. These changes invited efforts to define the rights of sovereigns in their dealings with one another and to articulate principles of statecraft, prudential as well as moral, appropriate to the new international system.

In this chapter, we focus on the theories of sovereignty and reason of state that accompanied the emergence of the modern European state from its medieval antecedents, and on the new conceptions of diplomacy and statecraft to which these theories gave rise. The former are best illustrated in the sixteenth-century writings of Machiavelli and Bodin; the latter in writings of the statesmen and scholars who theorized the new, decentralized, system of states during its "classical" period, the eighteenth century. We leave to chapters 6 and 7 the writings of more philosophical writers, like Hobbes, Rousseau, and Kant, who, in criticizing the presuppositions of this system, pointed the way toward its transformation.

Acquiring and maintaining power

Early modern thought about the emerging entities called states, though springing from debates between would-be rulers, is not limited to considering claims to legal authority. Rulers had long been accumulating power as well as authority at the expense of lesser nobles, and a literature concerned with the proper use of this power gradually emerged. But around 1500 this literature took a marked turn: instead of preaching the virtuous use of power, it purported to offer practical advice regarding the effective use of power. This change occurred first in Italy.

The Italian cities, which revived and flourished long before the Renaissance, provided opportunities for an increasing diversity of human activities. A new interest in temporal affairs displaced religious concerns. And there emerged a new ideal of individuality, based on the idea that human beings, being inherently free to make their own choices, ought to cultivate that freedom. In politics these changes are expressed in the movement we call civic humanism – "civic" because it translated the humanist ideal of individual expression and self-development from the realm of literature and art to that of government. Taking ancient Athens and the Roman republic as models, the humanists saw politics as an arena for asserting individuality, enacting virtue, and winning glory. Civic humanism strengthened the liberties of citizens by nurturing a politics of "popular" (as opposed to monarchical) government.

Civic humanism also strengthened the freedom of the Italian cities from outside rule. In alliance with the papacy, the cities gradually made themselves independent of the German emperors (the medieval Holy Roman Empire, though centered in Germany, included the Italian north). Then, as the empire in Italy declined, the larger cities were able to free themselves from papal rule. While asserting their own autonomy, Florence, Venice, Genoa, and Milan expanded at the expense of their lesser neighbors. By the fifteenth century power in northern and central Italy had been consolidated in a dozen or so independent city-states comprising a miniature international system.

New practices of international relations emerged within this Italian system. One of these was what a later age called the balance of power, the continual making and remaking of alliances to resist the dominant power of the day, thereby preventing weak states from being conquered by the powerful. Another was the practice of exchanging resident ambassadors authorized to negotiate on behalf of their governments and, equally important, instructed to provide the intelligence their governments needed. And there were certain "rules of the game" that constrained the diplomacy, the alliances, and the wars of these states in their struggle for power. Such rules provided the germ of an emerging system of international law. Although the Italian system disappeared in the French conquests of the early sixteenth century, its practices were adopted by the rest of Europe and eventually by all the world.

Most of the Italian city-states were either republics or, more often, principalities ruled by nobles, like the Medicis in Florence, who could pretend no convincing title to rule and who relied on arts of coercion like those investigated by Machiavelli in *The Prince* to stay in power. The absence of legitimate authority in these states, as elsewhere in Europe, made their governments insecure. Their rulers were constantly alert to internal and external threats and often engaged in adventures designed to unite their restive subjects against a common enemy. As a result, the Italian cities were perpetually at war with one another, the stronger expanding their territories at the expense of the weaker. Enterprising rulers recruited professional soldiers from other parts of Italy and beyond (the Vatican's Swiss guards are a vestige of this practice), turning war into an expensive, though not especially bloody, game fought by mercenaries. This continual warfare militarized the Italian states and corrupted their internal politics.

Of the contributors to the literature of practical statecraft that flourished in this environment, Niccolò Machiavelli (1469–1527) is undoubtedly the most influential. But he is also a curiously opaque thinker: playful, ironic, multifaceted, and seemingly inconsistent. On a host of contested issues, his works have invited diverse interpretations. At one extreme, Machiavelli is a teacher of evil, the originator of "Machiavellism," an ethic of unscrupulous egoism in individual conduct. At the other, he is a moralist who satirizes this ethic from an essentially Christian standpoint. Between these extremes we find readings of Machiavelli as a theorist of the principles of practical wisdom required to establish, maintain, and strengthen a state. It is this last Machiavelli whose writings inspired both the tradition of reason of state connected with the rise of absolutism in Italy, France, and Germany (Meinecke, 1957) and the anti-absolutist civic republican tradition in England and America (Pocock, 1975). It is also this Machiavelli who, along with Hobbes, helped to generate the tradition of political realism in foreign policy. According to the realists, because each state must defend its own interests, there can be no moral limits on the competition of states for power. Reason of state, here, means that international relations is a realm in which the rules of civil society do not apply: rules guiding personal conduct or domestic politics are irrelevant to foreign policy.

Although Machiavelli is often seen as an advocate for reason of state, the expression does not appear in his writings. One must therefore be careful to avoid anachronism in reading later understandings of the concept back into his work. Nevertheless, something like reason of state as a prudential ethic of the common good is present in *The Discourses*, if not in *The Prince*, which considers how a ruler can increase his personal power.

Machiavelli does not analyze the moral and legal concepts he uses in articulating this ethic, perhaps because he does not find them problematic. He is concerned with the practical means by which a desirable or justifiable order can be established and maintained. To understand the conditions for successful princely rule, or for preserving or expanding republics, requires a new method of political argument, one that is historical and prudential rather than philosophical or moral. One learns how to succeed in ruling, Machiavelli argues, not from precept but from experience. But this can include the vicarious experience made available by historians. And because they were the most gloriously successful, one can learn most of all from the ancient Romans. Machiavelli presents his *Discourses on the First Ten Books of Titus Livy* (to give the book its full title) as his reflections on that historian's account of the founding of Rome. Through Livy we can learn to imitate the early Romans, who succeeded, as none of Machiavelli's contemporaries have been able to do, in establishing a great and lasting republic.

Rome was founded, the story goes, when Romulus killed his brother and made himself sole ruler of the city. Machiavelli defends this crime, arguing that undivided authority is indispensable in a state, and that good effects excuse reprehensible actions. Implicit in Machiavelli's discussion of the origins of Rome is a distinction between ruling and founding: acts that would be unlawful under an existing constitution may be necessary to establish a new one. But "founding" is not limited to starting a new community where there was none before; it usually means establishing a new regime to replace the old. And the chief method by which a new regime is established – revolution – is, by definition, unlawful. Machiavelli is not, however, an uncritical partisan of revolutionary change. Only the founders of a republic or a well-governed principality, like Romulus, deserve praise; those, like Caesar, who institute a tyranny must be condemned. In these and many other passages throughout his works, Machiavelli invokes moral standards in a way that undercuts the effort to read him as a consistent immoralist.

Machiavelli insists, then, that extraordinary measures, praiseworthy or not, are sometimes necessary to establish and preserve a regime. Actual or would-be rulers may have no alternative but to override the laws, even the laws of morality, to restore good government or ensure stability. Such methods are especially useful to the new ruler of a state, who, to secure his rule, should

organize everything in that state afresh ... as did David when he became king, "who filled the hungry with good things and the rich sent empty away"; as well as to build new cities, to destroy those already built, and to move the inhabitants from one place to another far distant from it; in short, to leave nothing of that province intact, and nothing in it, neither rank, nor institution, nor form of government, nor wealth, except as it be held by such as recognize that it comes from you.

He should imitate Philip of Macedon, the father of Alexander the Great, who "moved men from province to province as shepherds move their sheep" (p. 268). As Mansfield points out, this passage contains the only quotation from the New Testament in Machiavelli's writings, and in the original it is said of God, not of David. Machiavelli seems to imply here that "the new prince must imitate God rather than obey him" (Mansfield, 1979: 99). If you are squeamish about taking and holding power, you should live as a private citizen and not seek to rule. In Discourse 41 of Book 3, Machiavelli tells the story of how the general, Lucius Lentulus, advised a Roman army that had been defeated by the Samnites, to "pass under the yoke," thereby symbolically acknowledging their subservience – good advice, since the army survived to fight again. Where the security of one's country is at stake, one should set aside all considerations of honor, justice, and humanity, and do whatever is expedient.

Such arguments can be found in many Roman writers. Cicero and Tacitus, for example, argue that the laws may be violated if the public welfare requires it. In the middle ages, the label *ratio status*, which might be translated as "reason of state," was applied to the argument that the laws could be set aside for the good of a realm (Gilbert, 1973: 116–26). But the medieval argument differs in at least one significant respect from that offered by Machiavelli and his successors. In the medieval version, human laws can be set aside to protect the civil order, but only because that order is necessary for peace and justice. Human laws are instruments of, and therefore subordinate to, natural and divine law, and can be set aside only in obedience to that higher law. Machiavelli helped to convert this medieval idea into the modern realist doctrine that, in pursuing the national interest, governments are excused from the obligations of morality as well as those of positive law.

Sovereignty

Machiavelli uses the word "state" in *The Prince* to mean the status and power of a ruler. A prince must concern himself with maintaining his estate, his position, his possessions – just as we maintain our jobs, homes, bank accounts, and reputations, which are the sources of our status and power in the world. The modern idea of the state is quite different. The ruler of a modern state is neither the proprietor of a landed estate nor the master of its inhabitants. A modern state is a legal person distinct from the natural person of its ruler or rulers: "an apparatus of power whose existence remains independent of those who may happen to control it at any given time" (Skinner, 1989: 102).

Long before Machiavelli, royal authority was being slowly depersonalized in the habit of distinguishing between the royal office, "the crown," and the person holding that office and wearing the crown (Black, 1993: 190). But this distinction, important as it was in distinguishing rulers of a realm from lords of a manor, could not solve the problem of how conflicting claims to ruling authority should be reconciled. The idea of sovereignty emerged as a way of solving this problem.

The idea of sovereignty is implicit in the thirteenth-century French formula, "the king is emperor in his own realm" – in other words, that the law of the king of France overrides that of any other lord, baron, or noble in France. It is a way of saying that a king is superior in authority to all other lords within the same realm. The idea of sovereignty, which is based on the principle of Roman law that the emperor has supreme authority, came to play a key role in the debate over the power of kings. But the effort to articulate the idea of supreme or sovereign power is more than a stage in the emergence of the idea of royal absolutism in early modern Europe. It is also a stage in the emergence of the idea of a modern state.

In the sixteenth century, the question of where authority in a community is to be located gained urgency in the face of intractable religious disagreements. In the states of early modern Europe, racked by religious disputes and civil wars, the only plausible basis for peace was shared recognition within each state of the authority of its ruler. But who, among the various competitors, truly possessed the authority to rule? Where there are competing authorities, some criterion by which to delimit their respective claims is required. The ruling authority in a state must possess some identifying characteristic by which it can be distinguished from competitors. In early modern Europe the distinguishing characteristic of this ruling authority was its "sovereignty," that is, its superiority to any other title or office within the state. A state is a territorial association of subjects ruled by a single sovereign.

These ideas are illustrated in Bodin's *Six Books of the Commonwealth* (1576). Jean Bodin (1530–96) was educated as a humanist and civil lawyer and worked as a barrister and administrator, but he was above all a scholar. Bodin's interest in the idea of sovereignty was in part a response to the wars of late sixteenth-century France, in which religious differences fueled competing claims to authority. Civil order and peace could not be established, Bodin thought, until these disputes over authority were settled. And to settle them requires a criterion for distinguishing the authority of a prince from other kinds of authority. For Bodin, it is the possession of "sovereignty" that distinguishes the ruler of a state from other authorities both inside and outside the state.

Unlike many of his contemporaries, Bodin is concerned with the criteria of sovereignty in general, not in one particular state. His inquiry therefore transcends the parochial concern to defend the claims of this or that claimant to power and becomes a philosophical analysis of the concept of sovereignty.

Sovereign authority (Bodin often says "power") is "absolute," that is, "not limited either in power, or in function, or in length of time" (Bodin, 1992: 3). This definition implies that the authority to rule is perpetual. A person given such authority for a determinate period is not the sovereign; sovereignty remains with those who conferred the authority, while those that hold it temporarily are merely its trustees or custodians. The definition of sovereignty as absolute authority also implies that those who hold sovereign authority are not subject to the commands of any person. A sovereign prince is not bound by the laws of his predecessors, for he can alter these laws. Nor is a sovereign bound by his own laws because he can rescind any law that he prescribes. But he *is* bound by his treaties with other sovereigns, because he cannot unilaterally terminate an agreement. A prince is as much bound by his contracts and promises as any private individual. Finally, a sovereign is bound by divine and natural laws because he also cannot alter these laws: "Even Dionysius, the tyrant of Sicily, told his mother that he could readily exempt her from the laws and customs of Syracuse, but not from the laws of nature" (Bodin, 1992: 32).

The sovereign, then, is the person (individual or collective) who gives laws to others. Furthermore, only a sovereign can make and repeal laws. The right to enact laws is, therefore, one of the defining "marks" of supreme or sovereign authority, one of the criteria by which it can be distinguished from other kinds of authority. Working out a more detailed typology of such marks, Bodin suggests that only a sovereign has the authority to appoint lower officials, to define their duties, to enact and repeal laws, to declare war, to decide judicial appeals, and to pardon persons who have been condemned to death. Bodin articulates a formula which was to become famous in legal theory when he says that law is "nothing but the command of a sovereign" (Bodin, 1992: 38).

Sovereignty, as Bodin understands it, is more clearly defined in a monarchy than in a mixed regime – one in which authority is shared between, say, a prince and a legislature. For Bodin, in other words, the difficulty with a mixed constitution is conceptual and not merely practical. He cannot imagine that authority could be shared or distributed between different branches of government. Therefore, he concludes, erroneously, that the sovereign authority in a state cannot be divided (Bodin, 1992: xvii). It is true that in any single legal system there must ultimately be one and only one way of settling legal disputes. There must be a single ultimate criterion by which the question "what is the law?" is decided. But it does not follow that the authority to enact and apply laws cannot be shared among different branches of government.

Bodin's confusion on this point is not the only one to which the word "sovereignty" has given rise. Sovereign or supreme authority is often confused with unlimited authority. But there is, in fact, no such thing: because the authority to govern is always conferred by laws, it is necessarily limited by law. And just as authority (which is the right to govern) is often confused with power (the ability to govern effectively), sovereignty is easily confused with unlimited power. But there is no such thing as unlimited power, either: because its effective use always depends on circumstances, power can never be total. "Totalitarian" regimes may seek unlimited power, but they cannot achieve it. Defining sovereignty as a kind of power suggests, moreover, that a government's right to rule is dependent on its power. But just as the authority of a law is independent of a government's ability to enforce it effectively, so a government's ability to enforce its laws, though one of the conditions of its existence, is not the criterion of its authority. It took several centuries for theorists to unravel the tangle of confusions spun by careless use of the word "sovereignty."

The state as a territorial association ruled by a single sovereign must deny authority to external as well as internal competitors. Like internal sovereignty, external sovereignty – the notion that a state is independent of the legal authority of any other state – has deep roots in medieval thought and practice. The thirteenth-century metaphor of a king as emperor in his own realm implies, for example, that a king is independent of any ruler outside the realm, including even the Holy See. The assertion of the independence of kings from imperial authority received papal support early in the fourteenth century when the pope intervened in a dispute between the emperor and his vassal, the king of Sicily. The dispute raised the question of whether a king could be summoned to appear in the court of the emperor. The pope's decision that one king could not be made to appear before another, even if the summoning king were the emperor, strengthened the idea of territorial sovereignty by denying that a king had authority outside his own realm. And by denying that imperial rule was universal, it demoted the emperor to the status of king with jurisdiction over a limited territory (Ullmann, 1975: 198). More than three hundred years later, the Peace of Westphalia recognized the right of the princes, bishops, and cities of the empire to conduct their foreign affairs as independent states, thereby reinforcing the principle of sovereignty as the cornerstone of the international order. By the seventeenth century, the idea that the world was divided among a number of independent states whose sovereigns held supreme authority within their own territories but no authority in the realms of other sovereigns was firmly entrenched in European political thought and practice.

Diplomacy and the balance of power

It is hard to distinguish between the international and the internal in medieval Europe because of the way authority was divided and shared. Instead of clearly demarcated territorial communities, we find "a tangle of overlapping feudal jurisdictions, plural allegiances and asymmetrical suzerainties" (Holzgrefe, 1989: 11). Not only kings, lords, vassals, and church officials but also towns, parliaments, guilds, and universities exchanged diplomatic missions, settled their disputes by negotiation and arbitration, and concluded formal treaties. As Garrett Mattingly observes, "kings made treaties with their own vassals and with the vassals of their neighbors. They received embassies from their own subjects and from the subjects of other princes ... Subject cities negotiated with one another without reference to their respective sovereigns" (1955: 26). In modern international society, by contrast, only states are "international legal persons" capable of sending and receiving ambassadors, signing treaties, or appearing before international tribunals.

The idea of exclusive territorial sovereignty implies a new basis for the ancient practice of diplomatic immunity, which excludes an ambassador from the jurisdiction of all laws except those of his own country. Because no sovereign is under the authority of any other, and because an ambassador is no mere envoy but a permanent representative of one sovereign residing in the territory of another, ambassadors are subject only to the laws of their own state. The lengths to which a theorist of territorial sovereignty might go to preserve its assumptions is illustrated in the fiction of extraterritoriality, according to which the citizens of one state located in another, but immune from the application of its laws, are imagined to remain in the territory of their own state.

The practice of treaty-making also illustrates the differences between medieval and modern international relations. Medieval "treaties" were more like private contracts than like modern international agreements, in part because they were made under the law common to all peoples (*ius gentium*), not under a distinct body of international law. Medieval practice did not always distinguish between a public office and the person occupying that office. This blurred the distinction between personal agreements binding rulers and official agreements binding the communities they ruled. Often, a treaty made by a prince had to be reaffirmed by his successor to remain in force. This is an echo of the feudal relationship between vassal and lord: the vassal's oath to serve the lord is personal and therefore not binding on his heirs. But with the decline of feudalism, the law began to distinguish between the office of the prince and the person, between the crown and the person wearing it. Once this distinction was in place, treaties could be understood as contracts between states rather than between persons, and therefore as imposing obligations on successive princes or governments. Grotius observes that a feudal oath binds the person, but a treaty binds the heir as well (Grotius, 1925: 419). Only sovereign states can be party to treaties, understood as agreements between rulers on behalf of their respective communities.

The early modern literature of diplomacy mixes discussion of the maxims of effective diplomacy with discussion of the rights and duties of diplomats. A practicing diplomat like François de Callières (1645–1717) emphasized the pragmatic requirements of skillful diplomacy, a lawyer like Cornelius van Bynkershoek (1673–1743) the "right of legation" in civil and international law. Both, however, describe a complicated practice in which matters of expediency and principle are intertwined. And both contrast existing practices with the ideal standards those practices intimate and yet rarely meet.

Callières wrote *De la manière de négocier avec les Souverains*, a handbook whose title might be freely translated as "How to Deal with Foreign Governments," in 1716 for the regent of the infant king of France, Louis XV. In it, he summarizes the fruits of his long experience as an ambassador (and secret agent) in the regime of Louis XIV. He discusses the aims and value of diplomacy, praising the contributions of Cardinal Richelieu, who established in the court of Louis XIII a centralized foreign office and professional diplomatic corps. He examines the education, knowledge, and personal qualities needed for successful diplomacy. And he discusses the rules governing the practice of diplomacy, including those defining the different ranks of diplomatic office and the scope of diplomatic immunity.

Bynkershoek, a lawyer who served as a member and eventually as president of the Supreme Court of Holland, is perhaps best known for his treatise on the law of the sea, a topic of particular concern to the Dutch of the seventeenth and eighteenth centuries. But he wrote on many other branches of law. His *Quaestionum Juris Publici* (1737) contains several chapters concerned with diplomacy and one concerning the fundamental principle of the law of treaties: the obligation to respect treaties in good faith. Although Bynkershoek rejects the arguments commonly used to justify the unilateral abrogation of treaties, he acknowledges that a state cannot be required to perform a promised act if circumstances have made its performance impossible.

The tension between realism and good faith underlying Bynkershoek's discussion of treaties is dramatically illustrated in the debates provoked by French foreign policy after the revolution of 1789. The revolution unsettled European politics as its democratic and egalitarian principles spread beyond France and anti-revolutionary emigrés worked to turn Austria and Prussia into enemies of the new regime. By 1793, France was at war with most of her neighbors, to whom she posed an ideological as well as a military threat.

One of these debates concerned the American policy of neutrality adopted during the first years of independence. At this time, the United States was not only a new nation but a weak one. Alexander Hamilton (1757–1804), like many other Americans, feared that Britain would soon try to regain its American possessions. These fears are evident in the controversy over whether the United States should provide assistance to revolutionary France after she went to war with Britain in February 1793. American public opinion favored France, reflecting a sympathy based on shared republican ideals as well as on residual hostility to Britain. In April 1793 President Washington, in an extremely unpopular act, declared the country neutral in the war between Britain and France.

In *Letters of Pacificus*, Hamilton (whose own sympathies were with Britain) defends Washington's policy of neutrality. He argues that there is no way the United States can assist France. Furthermore, France has no navy capable of protecting its overseas trade. Were the United States to side with France, Britain would simply destroy the American trade as well. Siding with France would therefore cost the United States a great deal while doing little for France. Worse, the country would expose itself to invasion by Britain and her ally Spain, another formidable power. Gratitude toward France for her help in the war of independence and sympathy for the French cause are minor considerations in view of the dangers the United States would run in siding with France. Hamilton generalizes this argument in the "Farewell Address" which he drafted for President Washington: the United States must avoid the "entangling alliances" through which the country would be drawn into the dangerous game of European power politics. This policy, which became part of a myth of national virtue, was in fact a prudent isolationism adopted by a weak state for its own security.

While the neutrality debate was going on in America, Britain was debating its own policy toward France. Britain's Tory prime minister, William Pitt, advocated intervention to protect the Dutch, from whose ports the French might launch an invasion of Britain. He argued that by invading its neighbors and installing revolutionary regimes, France was creating a new empire. Britain must therefore prepare to fight France on the Continent to preserve the states system of Europe and even Britain herself. Charles James Fox, leader of the opposition Whigs, challenged this policy, arguing that the decrees of the French government offering aid to any nation choosing to overthrow its monarch were mere propaganda and that Britain should avoid associating herself with the cause of counterrevolution. For Fox, the question is one to be settled according to the principles of popular sovereignty and nonintervention, not those of power politics.

Though a Whig, Edmund Burke (1729–97) supported Pitt's policy of intervention, but he did so on different grounds. For Burke, the threat to Britain comes not from France but from Jacobinism, the egalitarian, antimonarchical ideology of the French revolution. If the revolutionaries in France are permitted to get away with overturning property rights and the rights of monarchs, England too will succumb to revolution. Britain must defeat the French to teach its own citizens that revolution does not pay. Burke develops these arguments, which he formulated as early as 1789, in his *Letters on a Regicide Peace* (1796–7). The revolutionary regime, he argues here, has turned France into an outlaw state. The French have repudiated not only their treaty obligations but "the law of nations," not only international law but the laws and traditions of Christian Europe. By executing their king, encouraging children to spy on their parents, and establishing a new "Cult of Reason" to replace the Christian faith, they violate and destroy civilized morality. Citing reports of ceremonies in which revolutionaries would drink the blood of their executed captives, Burke even accuses them of cannibalism.

Europe, for Burke, is not a mere system of states; it is a commonwealth resting on a foundation of shared beliefs and practices: "virtually one great state having the same basis of general law, with some diversity of provincial customs and local establishments" (p. 297). International cooperation depends not only on formal treaties but on similarities of culture and custom. One of the basic principles of European society is the "law of neighborhood" or "civil vicinity," which prescribes that no member of this society may innovate in ways that offend its neighbors. When it does, those neighbors are free to judge whether the innovation is tolerable. And if they deem it dangerous, they can act to suppress it, by force if necessary.

In pressing for British intervention in French affairs, Burke invokes law, custom, and moral principle, as does Fox in opposing it. Pitt, in contrast, rests his case for action against France on the necessity of preserving equilibrium within the European system by resisting the dominant power of the day. This policy of balance derives from the idea of reason of state, according to which a government, as the custodian of the public welfare, the *salus populi*, must be allowed to do whatever is necessary to protect that welfare. And because a state's independence is the presupposition of its welfare, the first imperative of foreign policy is to maintain that independence. The idea underlying the balance of power is that each state can maintain its own independence by combining with others to prevent the concentration of overwhelming power in the hands of any state seeking to dominate its neighbors. All may act to preserve the multiplicity of states in the face of hegemonic threats, as the states of the day did against the Habsburgs in the sixteenth century and against France under Louis XIV and again under Napoleon.

Many writers helped to articulate the balance of power as the central organizing idea of European foreign policy. One of the earliest is François de Salignac de la Mothe Fénelon (1651–1715), an archbishop during the reign of Louis XIV, when France was the dominant power in Europe. Fénelon's essay on the balance of power, written about 1700, illustrates how easy it is to run prudential and moral considerations together in discussing foreign policy. Starting from the Hobbesian premise that states are engaged in a constant struggle for power, Fénelon argues that each must be continually alert to changes in the power of the others and prepared to resist any augmentation of a neighbor's power that threatens its own. Given the nature of power, states will seek to dominate if they can, and those that cannot will be driven to combine to resist being dominated. But Europe (which Fénelon calls "Christendom") is not a mere aggregate of competing states; it is also a society, "a sort of general republic" defined by common concerns and principles. Its members not only have an interest in combining against any state that threatens to grow too powerful but a duty to combine.

Fénelon is attempting to reconcile the balance of power with natural law: what is conducive to the interests of the European community as a whole must also be morally obligatory. The view that any policy that is truly expedient or useful must be morally right goes back to Cicero and is part of the Stoic or Ciceronian vocabulary of early modern political thought. Later on this identification of the useful and the right turns into the doctrine of utility: the utilitarians *define* moral right as that which is useful (for those whose interests are being considered). It may be contrasted with the Tacitean or realist language of Machiavelli and others who emphasize the distinction between expediency and morality.

Friedrich von Gentz (1764–1832), a Prussian diplomat in the period of the Napoleonic wars, provides a statement of the balance-of-power concept that more clearly distinguishes utility and rights. Though not a matter of right and wrong, the balance of power serves to protect the rights as well as the interests of states. The essential right of a state is to exist as the equal of other states, regardless of differences in power. Europe is an international society (whose members have rights) as well as an international system (whose members affect one another's interests). This idea that states are equal members of international society has come to be known as "the equality of states."

If the European system is a kind of great republic, its members must be formal equals with equal rights under international law, regardless of discrepancies in wealth and power. There can be no privileges (literally, "private laws") for rich and powerful states – or else the system is not a true republic. These principles are, in effect, the constitution of international society. "The true character of an international community (such as is being formed in modern Europe) ... will be that a certain number of states at very different levels of power and wealth, under the protection of a common bond, shall each remain unassailed within its own secure borders" (p.308). The balance of power, for Gentz, preserves this common bond under which states have their rights as members of international society. It is the mechanism that enforces international law, a kind of "approximation" to the judicial and executive power within a state.

FURTHER READING

Standard general works on early modern political thought include Skinner (1978) and Burns with Goldie (1991). From the vast literature on Machiavelli, the student of international relations might begin with Skinner (1981) and Hulliung (1983). Among many works dealing with classical European diplomacy and the balance of power, one might single out Mattingly (1955),

Gulick (1955), Wright (1975), and, for the nineteenth century, Holbraad (1970). Winston Churchill provides a classic statement of the balance of power as British foreign policy in chapter 12 of Churchill (1948). For Burke, see Welsh (1995).

SOURCES

Niccolò Machiavelli, from *The Prince* (1532), ed. Quentin Skinner and Russell Price (Cambridge: Cambridge University Press, 1988), chs. 1, 2, 3 (parts), and 15, pp. 5–10 and 54–5. The editors' notes have been omitted.

Niccolò Machiavelli, from *The Discourses*, translated Leslie J. Walker (London: Routledge, 1950), Book 1, Chapters 6, 9, 26 and Book 3, Chapter 41 [reprinted in *The Discourses*, ed. Bernard Crick, with revisions by Brian Richardson (Harmondsworth: Penguin, 1970) pp. 118–24, 131–4, 176–7 and 514–15]. Reprinted by permission of Routledge.

Jean Bodin, from *Six Books of the Commonwealth* (1576), in Jean Bodin, *On Sovereignty*, ed. Julian H. Franklin (Cambridge: Cambridge University Press, 1992), Book 1, ch. 8 (parts), pp. 1–2, 4–5, 7–8, 11, 13–14, and 15. Most of the editor's notes have been omitted.

Fr. François de Callières, from *On the Manner of Negotiating with Princes* (1716), trans. A. F. Whyte (Notre Dame, IN: University of Notre Dame Press, 1963), pp. 11–19.

Cornelius van Bynkershoek, from *On Questions of Public Law* (1737), trans. Tenney Frank (Oxford: Clarendon Press, 1930), Book 2, ch. 10 (parts), pp. 190–4.

Alexander Hamilton, from *Letters of Pacificus* (1793), in *Letters of Pacificus and Helvidius* (Washington, DC: Gideon, 1845), Letters 3 and 4, pp. 24–32.

Edmund Burke, from *Letters on a Regicide Peace* (1796), in Burke, *Works*, vol. v (London: Bell, 1906), pp. 152–3, 206–9, 213–19, and 223. Author's footnotes omitted.

François de Salignac de la Mothe Fénelon, from "Examen de conscience sur les devoirs de la royauté" (1700), in *Oeuvres complètes de Fénelon*, vol. vii (Paris, 1850), pp. 98–101. Translated for this anthology by Susan Rosa.

Friedrich von Gentz, "The True Concept of a Balance of Power" (1806), trans. Patricia M. Sherwood, in *Theory and Practice of the Balance of Power*, ed. Moorhead Wright (London: Dent, 1975), pp. 94–8.

NICCOLÒ MACHIAVELLI

NICCOLÒ MACHIAVELLI (1469–1527), a minor Florentine official and diplomat, posthumously infamous for the advice to tyrants on how to seize or maintain power contained in his little book *The Prince* (1532). Machiavelli's political career came to an end in 1512 when he was imprisoned and tortured by the recently restored Medici regime, after which he retired to his farm near San Casciano outside Florence to study the works of the ancient Romans, whose wisdom he revered. Neither *The Prince* nor his longer and, arguably, more substantial *Discourses on the First Ten Books of Livy* (1531) was published during his lifetime. Rightly or wrongly, both books have been read as articulating a doctrine of reason of state, and for that reason are considered classics of political realism.

From *The Prince*

Chapter 1

The different kinds of principality and how they are acquired

All the states, all the dominions that have held sway over men, have been either republics or principalities. Principalities are either hereditary (their rulers having been for a long time from the same family) or they are new. The new ones are either completely new (as was Milan to Francesco Sforza) or they are like limbs joined to the hereditary state of the ruler who annexes them (as is the Kingdom of Naples to the King of Spain). States thus acquired are either used to living under a prince or used to being free; and they are acquired either with the arms of others or with one's own, either through luck or favour or else through ability.

Chapter 2

Hereditary principalities

I shall not discuss republics, because I have previously treated them at length. I shall consider only principalities, and shall weave together the warps mentioned above, examining how principalities can be governed and maintained.

I say, then, that states which are hereditary, and accustomed to the rule of those belonging to the present ruler's family, are very much less difficult to hold than new states, because it is sufficient not to change the established order, and to deal with any untoward events that may occur; so that, if such a ruler is no more than ordinarily diligent and competent, his government will always be secure, unless some unusually strong force should remove him. And even if that happens, whenever the conqueror encounters difficulties, the former ruler can re-establish himself.

...

Chapter 3

Mixed principalities

However, it is in new principalities that there are real difficulties. First, if the principality is not completely new but is like a limb that is joined to another principality (which taken together may almost be called a mixed principality), its mutability arises first from a very natural problem, which is to be found in all new principalities. This is that men are very ready to change their ruler when they believe that they can better their condition, and this belief leads them to take up arms against him. But they are mistaken, because they later realise through hard experience that they have made their condition worse. This arises from another natural and normal constraint, which is that anyone who becomes a new ruler is always forced to injure his new subjects, both through his troops and countless other injuries that are involved in conquering a state. The outcome is that you make enemies of all those whom you have injured in annexing a principality, yet you cannot retain the friendship of those who have helped you to become ruler, because you cannot satisfy them in the ways that they expect. Nor can you use strong medicine against them, since you have obligations to them. For even if one possesses very strong armies, the goodwill of the inhabitants is always necessary in the early stages of annexing a country.

These were the reasons why Louis XII of France quickly annexed Milan, and just as quickly lost it; and Ludovico's own troops were sufficiently powerful to deprive him of it the first time. For when the people who had opened the gates to Louis found that they did not receive the benefits they had expected, they could not endure the oppressive rule of the new master.

It is certainly true that, after a country that has rebelled has been reconquered a second time, it is less likely to be lost, since the ruler, because of the rebellion, will be more ruthless in consolidating his power, in punishing the guilty, unmasking suspects, and remedying weaknesses in his government. Thus, a Duke Ludovico creating a disturbance on the borders was enough to cause the King of France to lose Milan the first time. But to lose it a second time, it was necessary to have all the powers acting against him, and for his armies to be defeated or driven out of Italy. This happened for the reasons mentioned above.

Nevertheless, he did lose Milan twice. The general reasons for the first loss have been discussed; it remains now to discuss the reasons for the second, and to consider what solutions were available to him, and what someone in his position might do, in order to maintain better than the King of France did the territory annexed.

I say, then, that the territories a conqueror annexes and joins to his own well-established state are either in the same country, with the same language, or they are not. If they are, it is extremely easy to hold them, especially if they are not used to governing themselves. To hold them securely, it is enough to wipe out the family of the ruler who held sway over them, because as far as other things are concerned, the inhabitants will continue to live quietly, provided their old way of life is maintained and there is no difference in customs. This has happened with Burgundy, Brittany, Gascony and Normandy, which have been joined to France for a long time. Although there are some linguistic differences, nevertheless their way of life is similar, so no difficulties have arisen. Anyone who annexes such countries, and is determined to hold them, must follow two policies: the first is to wipe out their old ruling families; the second is not to change their laws or impose new taxes. Then the old principality and the new territory will very soon become a single body politic.

But considerable problems arise if territories are annexed in a country that differs in language, customs and institutions, and great good luck and great ability are needed to hold them. One of the best and most effective solutions is for the conqueror to go and live there. This makes the possession more secure and more permanent. This is what the Turks did in Greece: all the other measures taken by them to hold that country would not have sufficed, if they had not instituted direct rule. For if one does do that, troubles can be detected when they are just beginning and effective measures can be taken quickly. But if one does not, the troubles are encountered when they have grown, and nothing can be done about them. Moreover, under direct rule, the country will not be exploited by your officials; the subjects will be content if they have direct access to the ruler. Consequently, they will have more reason to be devoted to him if they intend to behave well, and to fear him if they do not. Any foreigners with designs on that state will proceed very carefully. Hence, if the state is ruled directly, it is very unlikely indeed to be lost.

The other very good solution is to establish colonies in a few places, which become, as it were, offshoots of the conquering state. If this is not done, it will be necessary to hold it by means of large military forces. Colonies involve little expense; and so at little or no cost, one establishes and maintains them. The only people injured are those who lose their fields and homes, which are given to the new settlers; but only a few inhabitants are affected in this way. Moreover, those whom he injures can never harm him, because they are poor and scattered. All the other inhabitants remain unharmed, and should therefore be reassured, and will be afraid of causing trouble, for fear that they will be dispossessed, like the others. I conclude that these colonies are not expensive, are more loyal, and harm fewer people; and those that are harmed cannot injure you because, as I said, they are scattered and poor.

It should be observed here that men should either be caressed or crushed; because they can avenge slight injuries, but not those that are very severe. Hence, any injury done to a man must be such that there is no need to fear his revenge.

However, if military forces are sent instead of colonists, this is much more expensive, because all the revenue of the region will be consumed for its security. The outcome is that the territory gained results in loss to him; and it is much more injurious, because it harms the whole of that region when his troops move round the country. Everyone suffers this nuisance, and becomes hostile to the ruler. And they are dangerous enemies because, although defeated, they remain in their own homes. From every point of view, then, this military solution is misguided, whereas establishing colonies is extremely effective.

Again, as I have said, anyone who rules a foreign country should take the initiative in becoming a protector of the neighbouring minor powers and contrive to weaken those who are powerful within the country itself. He should also take precautions against the possibility that some foreign ruler as powerful as himself may seek to invade the country when circumstances are favourable. Such invaders are always helped by malcontents within the country, who are moved either by their own overweening ambition or by fear, as happened in Greece, where the Aetolians were responsible for the invasion by the Romans. And in every country that the Romans attacked, some of the inhabitants aided their invasion. What usually happens is that, as soon as a strong invader attacks a country, all the less powerful men rally to him, because they are enviously hostile to the ruler who has held sway over them. The invader has no trouble in winning over these less powerful men, since they will all be disposed to support the new power he has acquired. He needs only to be careful that they do not acquire too much military power and influence. And using his own forces, and with their consent, he can easily put down those who are powerful, thus gaining complete control of that country. A ruler who does not act in this way will soon lose what he has gained and, even while he does hold it, he will be beset by countless difficulties and troubles.

...

Chapter 15

The things for which men, and especially rulers, are praised or blamed

It remains now to consider in what ways a ruler should act with regard to his subjects and allies. And since I am well aware that many people have written about this subject I fear that I may be thought presumptuous, for what I have to say differs from the precepts offered by others, especially on this matter. But because I want to write what will be useful to anyone who understands, it seems to me better to concentrate on what really happens rather than on theories or speculations. For many have imagined republics and principalities that have never been seen or known to exist. However, how men live is so different from how they should live that a ruler who does not do what is generally done, but persists in doing what ought to be done, will undermine his power rather than maintain it. If a ruler who wants always to act honourably is surrounded by many unscrupulous men his downfall is inevitable. Therefore, a ruler who wishes to maintain his power must be prepared to act immorally when this becomes necessary.

I shall set aside fantasies about rulers, then, and consider what happens in fact. I say that whenever men are discussed, and especially rulers (because they occupy more exalted positions), they are praised or blamed for possessing some of the following qualities. Thus, one man is considered generous, another miserly (I use this Tuscan term because *avaro* in our tongue also signifies someone who is rapacious, whereas we call *misero* someone who is very reluctant to use his own possessions); one is considered a free giver, another rapacious; one cruel, another merciful; one treacherous, another loyal; one effeminate and weak, another indomitable and spirited; one affable, another haughty; one lascivious, another moderate; one upright, another cunning; one inflexible, another easy-going; one serious, another frivolous; one devout, another unbelieving, and so on.

I know that everyone will acknowledge that it would be most praiseworthy for a ruler to have all the above-mentioned qualities that are held to be good. But because it is not possible to have all of them, and because circumstances do not permit living a completely virtuous life, one must be sufficiently prudent to know how to avoid becoming notorious for those vices that would destroy one's power and seek to avoid those vices that are not politically dangerous; but if one cannot bring oneself to do this, they can be indulged in with fewer misgivings. Yet one should not be troubled about becoming notorious for those vices without which it is difficult to preserve one's power, because if one considers everything carefully, doing some things that seem virtuous may result in one's ruin, whereas doing other things that seem vicious may strengthen one's position and cause one to flourish.

From *The Discourses*

Book 1

6. *Whether in Rome such a Form of Government could have been set up as would have removed the Hostility between the Populace and the Senate*

We have just been discussing the effects produced by the controversies between the populace and the senate. Now, since these controversies went on until the time of the Gracchi when they became the causes which led to the destruction of liberty, it may occur to some to ask whether Rome could have done the great things she did without the existence of such animosities. Hence it seems to me worth while to inquire whether it would have been possible to set up in Rome a form of government which would have prevented these controversies. In order to discuss this question it is necessary to consider those republics which have been free from such animosities and tumults and yet have enjoyed a long spell of liberty, to look at their govern-ments, and to ask whether they could have been introduced into Rome.

Among ancient states Sparta is a case in point, and among modern states Venice, as I have already pointed out. Sparta set up a king and a small senate to govern it. Venice did not distinguish by different names those who took part in its government, but all who were eligible for administrative posts were classed under one head and called gentry. This was due to chance rather than to the prudence of its legislators; for many people having retired to those sandbanks on which the city now stands and taken up their abode there for the reasons already assigned, when their numbers grew to such an extent that it became necessary for them to make laws if they were to live together, they devised a form of government. They had frequently met together to discuss the city's affairs, so, when it seemed to them that the population was sufficient to form a body politic, they decided that all newcomers who meant to reside there, should not take part in the government. Then, when in course of time they found that there were quite a number of inhabitants in the place who were disbarred from government, with an eye to the reputation of those who governed they called them gentlefolk and the rest commoners.

Such a form of government could arise and be maintained without tumult because, when it came into being, whoever then dwelt in Venice was admitted to the government, so that no one could complain. Nor had those who came to dwell there later on and found the form of government firmly established, either cause or opportunity to make a commotion. They had no cause because they had been deprived of nothing. They had no opportunity because the government had the whip-hand and did not employ them in matters which would enable them to acquire authority. Besides, there were not many who came later to dwell in Venice, nor were they so numerous as to upset the balance between rulers and ruled; for the number of gentlefolk was either equal to, or greater than, that of the newcomers. These, then, were the causes which enabled Venice to set up this form of government and to maintain it without disruption.

Sparta, as I have said, was governed by a king and by a small senate. It was able to maintain itself in this way for a long time, because in Sparta there were few inhabitants and access to outsiders desirous of coming to dwell there was forbidden. Moreover, it had adopted the laws of Lycurgus and shared in his repute, and, as these laws were observed, they removed all occasion for tumult, so that the Spartans were able to live united for a long time. The reason was that the laws of Lycurgus prescribed equality of property and insisted less on equality of rank. Poverty was shared by all alike, and the plebeians had less ambition, since offices in the city were open but to few citizens and from them the plebs were kept out; nor did it desire to have them since the nobles never ill-treated the plebs. This was due to the position assigned to the Spartan kings, for, since in this principality they were surrounded by nobles, the best way of maintaining their position was to protect the plebs from injustice. It thus came about that the plebs neither feared authority nor desired to have it, and, since they neither feared it nor desired it, there was no chance of rivalry between them and the nobility, nor any ground for disturbances, and they could live united for a long time. It was, however, mainly two things which brought this union about: (i) the smallness of Sparta's population, which made it possible for a few to rule, and (ii) the exclusion of foreigners from the state, which gave it no chance either to become corrupt or to become so unwieldy that it could no longer be managed by the few who governed it.

All things considered, therefore, it is clear that it was necessary for Rome's legislators to do one of two things if Rome was to remain tranquil like the aforesaid states: either to emulate the Venetians and not employ its plebs in wars, or, like the Spartans, not to admit foreigners. Rome did both these things, and, by doing so, gave to its plebs alike strength, increase and endless opportunities for commotion. On the other hand, had the government of Rome been such as to bring greater tranquillity, there would have ensued this inconvenience, that it would have been weaker, owing to its having cut off the source of supply which enabled it to acquire the greatness at which it arrived, so that, in seeking to remove the causes of tumults, Rome would have removed also the causes of expansion.

So in all human affairs one notices, if one examines them closely, that it is impossible to remove one inconvenience without another emerging. If, then, you want to have a large population and to provide it with arms so as to establish a great empire, you will have made your population such that you cannot now handle it as you please. While, if you keep it either small or unarmed so as to be able to manage it, and then acquire dominions, either you will lose your hold on it or it will become so debased that you will be at the mercy of anyone who attacks you. Hence in all discussions one should consider which alternative involves fewer inconveniences and should adopt this as the better course; for one never finds any issue that is clear cut and not open to question. Rome might indeed have emulated Sparta, have appointed a prince for life, and have made its senate small; but it would not in that case have been able to avoid increasing its population with a view to establishing a great empire; nor would the appointment of a king for life and of a small number of senators have been of much help in the matter of unity.

Should, then, anyone be about to set up a republic, he should first inquire whether it is to expand, as Rome did, both in dominion and in power, or is to be confined to narrow limits. In the first case it is essential to constitute it as Rome was constituted and to expect commotions and disputes of all kinds which must be dealt with as best they can, because without a large population, and this well armed, such a republic will never be able to grow, or to hold its own should it grow. In the second case it might be constituted as Sparta and Venice were, but, since expansion is poison to republics of this type, it should use every endeavour to prevent it from expanding, for expansion, when based on a weak republic, simply means ruin. This happened both in Sparta's case and in that of Venice. For of these republics the first, after having subjugated almost the whole of Greece, revealed, on an occasion of slight importance in itself, how weak its foundation was, since, when Thebes revolted at the instigation of Pelopidas and other cities followed suit, this republic entirely collapsed. In like manner Venice, having occupied a large part of Italy, most of it not by dint of arms, but of money and astute diplomacy, when its strength was put to the test, lost everything in a single battle.

I am firmly convinced, therefore, that to set up a republic which is to last a long time, the way to set about it is to constitute it as Sparta and Venice were constituted; to place it in a strong position, and so to fortify it that no one will dream of taking it by a sudden assault; and, on the other hand, not to make it so large as to appear formidable to its neighbours. It should in this way be able to enjoy its form of government for a long time. For war is made on a commonwealth for two reasons: (i) to subjugate it, and (ii) for fear of being subjugated by it. Both these reasons are almost entirely removed by the aforesaid precautions; for, if it be difficult to take by assault owing to its being well organized for defence, as I am presupposing, rarely or never will it occur to anyone to seize it. And, if it be content with its own territory, and it becomes clear by experience that it has no ambitions, it will never occur that someone may make war through fear for himself, especially if by its constitution or by its laws expansion is prohibited. Nor have I the least doubt that, if this balance could be maintained, there would be genuine political life and real tranquillity in such a city.

Since, however, all human affairs are ever in a state of flux and cannot stand still, either there will be improvement or decline, and necessity will lead you to do many things which reason does not recommend. Hence if a commonwealth be constituted with a view to its maintaining the *status quo*, but not with a view to expansion, and by necessity it be led to expand, its basic principles will be subverted and it will soon be faced with ruin. So, too, should heaven, on the other hand, be so kind to it that it has no need to go to war, it will then come about that idleness will either render it effeminate or give rise to factions; and these two things, either in conjunction or separately, will bring about its downfall.

Wherefore, since it is impossible, so I hold, to adjust the balance so nicely as to keep things exactly to this middle course, one ought, in constituting a republic, to consider the possibility of its playing a more honourable role, and so to constitute it that, should necessity actually force it to expand, it may be able to retain possession of what it has acquired. Coming back, then, to the first point we raised, I am convinced that the Roman type of constitution should be adopted, not that of any other republic, for to find a middle way between the two extremes I do not think possible. Squabbles between the populace and the senate should, therefore, be looked upon as an inconvenience which it is necessary to put up with in order to arrive at the greatness of Rome. For, besides the reasons already adduced to show that the authority of the tribunes was essential to the preservation of liberty, it is easy to see what benefit a republic derives when there is an authority that can bring charges in court, which was among the powers vested in the tribunes, as will be shown in the following chapter.

...

9. That it is necessary to be the Sole Authority if one would constitute a Republic afresh or would reform it thoroughly regardless of its Ancient Institutions

To some it will appear strange that I have got so far in my discussion of Roman history without having made any mention of the founders of that republic or of either its religious or its military institutions. Hence, that I may not keep the minds of those who are anxious to hear about such things any longer in suspense, let me say that many perchance will think it a bad precedent that the founder of a civic state, such as Romulus, should first have killed his brother, and then have acquiesced in the death of Titus Tatius, the Sabine, whom he had chosen as his colleague in the kingdom. They will urge that, if such actions be justifiable, ambitious citizens who are eager to govern, will follow the example of their prince and use violence against those who are opposed to *their* authority. A view that will hold good provided we leave out of consideration the end which Romulus had in committing these murders.

One should take it as a general rule that rarely, if ever, does it happen that a state, whether it be a republic or a kingdom, is either well-ordered at the outset or radically transformed *vis-à-vis* its old institutions unless this be done by one person. It is likewise essential that there should be but one person upon whose mind and method depends any similar process of organization. Wherefore the prudent organizer of a state whose intention it is to govern not in his own interests but for the common good, and not in the interest of his successors but for the sake of that fatherland which is common to all, should contrive to be alone in his authority. Nor will any reasonable man blame him for taking any action, however extraordinary, which may be of service in the organizing of a kingdom or the constituting of a republic. It is a sound maxim that reprehensible actions may be justified by their effects, and that when the effect is good, as it was in the case of Romulus, it always justifies the action. For it is the man who uses violence to spoil things, not the man who uses it to mend them, that is blameworthy.

The organizer of a state ought further to have sufficient prudence and virtue not to bequeath the authority he has assumed to any other person, for, seeing that men are more prone to evil than to good, his successor might well make ambitious use of that which he had used virtuously. Furthermore, though but one person suffices for the purpose of organization, what he has organized will not last long if it continues to rest on the shoulders of one man, but may well last if many remain in charge and many look to its maintenance. Because, though the many are incompetent to draw up a constitution since diversity of opinion will prevent them from discovering how best to do it, yet when they realize it has been done, they will not agree to abandon it.

That Romulus was a man of this character, that for the death of his brother and of his colleague he deserves to be excused, and that what he did was done for the common good and not to satisfy his personal ambition, is shown by his having at once instituted a senate with which he consulted and with whose views his decisions were in accord. Also, a careful consideration of the authority which Romulus reserved to himself will show that all he reserved to himself was the command of the army in time of war and the convoking of the senate. It is clear, too, that when the Tarquins were expelled and Rome became free, none of its ancient institutions were changed, save that in lieu of a permanent king there were appointed each year two consuls. This shows that the original institutions of this city as a whole were more in conformity with a political and self-governing state than with absolutism or tyranny.

I might adduce in support of what I have just said numberless examples, for example Moses, Lycurgus, Solon and other founders of kingdoms and republics who assumed authority that they might formulate laws to the common good; but this I propose to omit since it is well known. I shall adduce but one further example, not so celebrated but worth considering by those who are contemplating the drawing up of good laws. It is this. Agis, King of Sparta, was considering how to confine the activities of the Spartans to the limits originally set for them by the laws of Lycurgus, because it seemed to him that it was owing to their having deviated from them in part that this city had lost a good deal of its ancient virtue, and, in consequence, a good deal of its power and of its empire. He was, however, while his project was still in the initial stage, killed by the Spartan ephors, who took him to be a man who was out to set up a tyranny. But Cleomenes, his successor in that kingdom, having learned from some records and writings of Agis which he had discovered, what was the latter's true mind and intention, determined to pursue the same plan. He realized, however, that he could not do this for the good of his country unless he became the sole authority there, and, since it seemed to him impossible owing to man's ambition to help the many against the will of the few, he took a suitable opportunity and had all the ephors killed and anybody else who might obstruct him. He then renewed in their entirety the laws of Lycurgus. By so doing he gave fresh life to Sparta, and his reputation might thereby have become as great as that of Lycurgus if it had not been for the power of the Macedonians and the weakness of other Greek republics. For, after Sparta had thus been reorganized, it was attacked by the Macedonians, and, since its forces proved to be inferior and it could get no outside help, it was defeated, with the result that Cleomenes' plans, however just and praiseworthy, were never brought to completion.

All things considered, therefore, I conclude that it is necessary to be the sole authority if one is to organize a state, and that Romulus' action in regard to the death of Remus and Titus Tatius is excusable, not blameworthy.

...

26. In a City or Province which he has seized, a New Prince should make Everything New

Should anyone become the ruler either of a city or of a state, especially if he has no sure footing in it and it is suited neither for the civic life characteristic of a monarchy nor yet that of a republic, the best thing he can do in order to retain such a principality, given that he be a new prince, is to organize everything in that state afresh; e.g. in its cities to appoint new governors, with new titles and a new authority, the governors themselves being new men; to make the rich poor and the poor rich; as did David when he became king, '*who filled the hungry with good things and the rich sent empty away*'; as well as to build new cities, to destroy those already built, and to move the inhabitants from one place to another far distant from it; in short, to leave nothing of that province intact, and nothing in it, neither rank, nor institution, nor form of government, nor wealth, except it be held by such as recognize that it comes from you.

His aim should be to emulate Philip of Macedon, the father of Alexander, who, starting as a little king, by these methods made himself prince of Greece. Of him a writer says that he moved men from province to province as shepherds move their sheep.

Such methods are exceedingly cruel, and are repugnant to any community, not only to a Christian one, but to any composed of men. It behoves, therefore, every man to shun them, and to prefer rather to live as a private citizen than as a king with such ruination of men to his score. None the less, for the sort of man who is unwilling to take up this first course of well doing, it is expedient, should he wish to hold what he has, to enter on the path of wrong doing. Actually, however, most men prefer to steer a middle course, which is very harmful; for they know not how to be wholly good nor yet wholly bad, as in the next chapter will be shown by means of an example.

...

Book 3

41. *That one's Country should be defended whether it entail Ignominy or Glory, and that it is Good to defend it in any way whatsoever*

The consul and the Roman army were surrounded by the Samnites, as has just been said. The Samnites had imposed on the Romans ignominious conditions. They were to pass under the yoke and to be sent back to Rome without their arms and equipment. At this the consuls being astonished and the whole army being in despair, Lucius Lentulus, the Roman legate, told them that it did not seem to him that they should reject any alternative in order to save their country; for, since the survival of Rome depended on the survival of this very army, it should be saved in any way that offered; and that it is good to defend one's country in whatever way it be done, whether it entail ignominy or glory; for, if this army was saved, Rome might in time wipe out the ignominy; but that, if it were not saved and even if it should die gloriously, Rome and its freedom would be lost. So Lentulus's advice was followed.

This counsel merits the attention of, and ought to be observed by, every citizen who has to give advice to his country. For when the safety of one's country wholly depends on the decision to be taken, no attention should be paid either to justice or injustice, to kindness or cruelty, or to its being praiseworthy or ignominious. On the contrary, every other consideration being set aside, that alternative should be whole-heartedly adopted which will save the life and preserve the freedom of one's country.

This is the course the French adopt – both in what they say and what they do – in order to defend the majesty of their king or the power of their kingdom; for no voice is heard with greater impatience than one that should say: 'Such an alternative it would be ignominious for the king to adopt.' No decision the king makes can be shameful, they say, whether it leads to good or to adverse fortune, for, whether he wins or loses is entirely his business, they claim.

JEAN BODIN

JEAN BODIN (1530–96), French humanist, lawyer, administrator, and scholar. Bodin was one of the first to attribute rising prices in sixteenth-century Europe to the influx of gold from America and he also wrote a book on the detection and punishment of witches. He is one of several thinkers of the period who were concerned to explore the question of how competing claims to rule within the emerging territorial states of Europe might be resolved. For Bodin, it is the possession of "sovereignty" that distinguishes the ruler of a state from other authorities. Despite his erroneous conclusion that sovereign authority cannot be divided between different branches of government, his discussion of the concept constitutes an innovative and enduring contribution to the legal theory, one with momentous consequences for international relations.

From *Six Books of the Commonwealth*

Book 1, chapter 8

On sovereignty

Sovereignty is the absolute and perpetual power of a commonwealth, which the Latins call *maiestas*; the Greeks *akra exousia, kurion arche,* and *kurion politeuma*; and the Italians *segnioria*, a word they use for private persons as well as for those who have full control of the state, while the Hebrews call it *tomech shévet* – that is, the highest power of command. We must now formulate a definition of sovereignty because no jurist or political philosopher has defined it, even though it is the chief point, and the one that needs most to be explained, in a treatise on the commonwealth. Inasmuch as we have said that a commonwealth is a just government, with sovereign power, of several households and of that which they have in common, we need to clarify the meaning of sovereign power.

I have said that this power is perpetual, because it can happen that one or more people have absolute power given to them for some certain period of time, upon the expiration of which they are no more than private subjects. And even while they are in power, they cannot call themselves sovereign princes. They are but trustees and custodians of that power until such time as it pleases the people or the prince to take it back, for the latter always remains in lawful possession (*qui en demeure tousiours saisi*). For just as those who lend someone else their goods always remain its owners and possessors, so also those who give power and authority to judge or to command, either for some limited and definite period of time or for as much and as long a time as it shall please them. They still remain lawfully possessed of power and jurisdiction, which the others exercise in the manner of a loan or grant on sufferance (*précaire*). That is why the [Roman civil] law holds that the governor of a region, or the lieutenant of a prince, being a trustee and guardian of someone else's power, returns it when his term has expired. And in this respect, it makes no difference whether the officer is high or petty.

If it were otherwise, and the absolute power conceded to a lieutenant of the prince were called sovereignty, he would be able to use it against his prince, who would then be no more than a cipher, and the subject would then command his lord, and the servant his master, which would be absurd. The person of the sovereign, according to the law, is always excepted no matter how much power and authority he grants to someone else; and he never gives so much that he does not hold back even more. He is never prevented from commanding, or from assuming cognizance – by substitution, concurrence, removal, or any way he pleases – of any cause that he left to the jurisdiction of a subject. Nor does it matter whether the subject is a commissioner or an officer. In either case the sovereign can take away the power with which he was endowed by virtue of the commission or the statute of his office, or he can retain him on sufferance in so far and for as long as it pleases him.

...

But let us suppose that a people chooses one or several citizens, to whom it gives absolute power to manage the state and to govern freely, without having to submit to vetoes or appeals of any sort, and that this measure is reenacted every year. Shall we not say that they have sovereignty? For he is absolutely sovereign who recognizes nothing, after God, that is greater than himself. I say, however, that they do not have sovereignty, since they are nothing but trustees of a power that was confided to them for a definite period of time. Hence the people did not divest itself of sovereignty when it established one or more lieutenants with absolute power for a definite time, even though that is more generous than if the power was subject to recall at the people's pleasure without a pre-established time limit. In either case the lieutenant has nothing of his own and remains answerable for his charge to the person of whom he holds the power to command, unlike a sovereign prince who is answerable only to God.

But what would we say if absolute power were conceded for nine or ten years, as it was in the early days of Athens when the people made one of the citizens sovereign and called him archon? I still maintain that he was not a prince and did not have sovereignty, but was rather a sovereign magistrate who was accountable to the people for his actions after his time in office had expired. One might still object that absolute power can be given to a citizen as I have indicated, yet without requiring him to answer to the people. Thus the Cnidians annually chose sixty citizens whom they called "amnemones" – that is to say, beyond reproach – and granted them sovereign power with no appeal from them, either during their term in office or after it, for anything that they had done. Yet I say that they did not have sovereignty in view of the fact that, as custodians, they were obliged to give it back when their year was up. Sovereignty thus remained in the people, and only its exercise was in the amnemones, whom one could call sovereign magistrates, but not sovereigns pure and simple. For the first is a prince, the other is a subject; the first is a lord, the other is a servant; the first is a proprietor and in lawful possession of the sovereignty (*et saisi de la souveraineté*), the other is neither its owner nor possessor, but merely holds in trust.

The same applies to regents established during the absence or minority of sovereign princes, no matter whether edicts, orders, and letters patent are signed and sealed with the regents' signature and seal and are issued in their name, which was the practice in this kingdom prior to the ordinance of King Charles V of France, or whether it is all done in the king's name and orders are sealed with his seal. For in either case it is quite clear that, according to the law, the master is taken to have done whatever a deputy (*procureur*) did on his authority. But the regent is properly the deputy of the king and the kingdom, so that the good Count Thibaut called himself *procurator regni Francorum* (deputy of the French kingdom). Hence when the prince, either present or absent, gives absolute power to a regent or perhaps to the senate, to govern in his name, it is always the king who speaks and who commands even if the title of regent is used on edicts and letters of command.

...

So whether it is by commission, nomination to office, or delegation that one exercises someone else's power, and whether it is for a definite time or in perpetuity, he who exercises this power is not sovereign even if he is not described as an agent or lieutenant in his letters patent. This applies even if the power is conferred by the law of the land, which is an even stronger basis than appointment (*election*). The ancient law of Scotland thus gave the entire government of the kingdom to the closest relative of a king who was in tutelage or under age, with the requirement that all business be carried on in the king's name. But the rule was suppressed because of the inconveniences that went with it.

We now turn to the other part of our definition and to what is meant by the words "absolute power." For the people or the aristocracy (*seigneurs*) of a commonwealth can purely and simply give someone absolute and perpetual power to dispose of all possessions, persons, and the entire state at his pleasure, and then to leave it to anyone he pleases, just as a proprietor can make a pure and simple gift of his goods for no other reason than his generosity. This is a true gift because it carries no further conditions, being complete and accomplished all at once, whereas gifts that carry obligations and conditions are not authentic gifts. And so sovereignty given to a prince subject to obligations and conditions is properly not sovereignty or absolute power.

This does not apply if the conditions attached at the creation of a prince are of the law of God or nature (*la loy de Dieu ou de nature*), as was done after the death of a Great King of Tartary. The prince and the people, to whom the right of election belongs, choose any relative of the deceased they please, provided that he is a son or nephew, and after seating him on a golden throne, they pronounce these words, "We beg you, and also wish and bid you, to reign over us." The king then says, "If that is what you want of me, you must be ready to do as I command, and whom I order killed must be killed forthwith and without delay, and the whole kingdom must be entrusted to me and put into my hands." The people answers, "So be it." Then the king, continuing, says, "The word that I speak shall be my sword," and all the people applaud him. After that he is taken hold of, removed from his throne, and set on the ground seated on a bench, and *the prince*s address him in these words: "Look up and acknowledge God, and then look at this lowly bench on which you sit. If you govern well, you will have your every wish; otherwise you will be put down so low and so completely stripped, that even this bench on which you sit will not be left to you." This said, he is lifted on high, and acclaimed king of the Tartars. This power is absolute and sovereign, for it has no other condition than what is commanded by the law of God and of nature.

...

[A] subject who is exempted from the force of the laws always remains in subjection and obedience to those who have the sovereignty. But persons who are sovereign must not be subject in any way to the commands of someone else and must be able to give the law to subjects, and to suppress or repeal disadvantageous laws and replace them with others – which cannot be done by someone who is subject to the laws or to persons having power of command over him.

This is why the law says that the prince is not subject to the law; and in fact the very word "law" in Latin implies the command of him who has the sovereignty.

...

But as for divine and natural laws, every prince on earth is subject to them, and it is not in their power to contravene them unless they wish to be guilty of treason against God, and to war against Him beneath whose grandeur all the monarchs of this world should bear the yoke and bow the head in abject fear and reverence. The absolute power of princes and of other sovereign lordships (*seigneuries souverains*), therefore, does not in any way extend to the laws of God and of nature. Indeed he (Innocent IV) who best understood what absolute power is, and made [Christian] kings and emperors bow to him, said that it is nothing but the power of overriding ordinary law. He did not say the laws of God and of nature.

But is the prince not subject to those laws of the land that he has sworn to keep? Here we must distinguish. If the prince swears to himself that he will keep his own law, he is not bound by that law any more than by an oath made to himself. For even subjects are in no way bound by the oath they take in making contracts of a sort that the law permits them to ignore even when the terms are honest and reasonable. And if a sovereign prince promises another prince to keep laws that he or his predecessors have made, he is obligated to keep them if the prince to whom he gave his word has an interest in his so doing – and even if he did not take an oath. But if the prince to whom the promise was made does not have an interest, neither the promise nor the oath can obligate the prince who made the promise. The same may be said of a promise given to a subject by the prince either when he is sovereign or before he is elected, for in this [latter] respect his status makes no difference, despite what many think.

It is not that the prince is bound by his own or his predecessors' laws, but rather by the just contracts and promises that he has made, whether with or without an oath, as is any private individual. And just as a private individual can be relieved of a promise that is unjust or unreasonable, or burdens him too much, or was put upon him to his substantial loss through trickery, fraud, error, force, or reasonable fear, so for the same reasons can a prince, if he is sovereign, be relieved of anything that involves a diminution of his majesty. And so our maxim stands. The prince is not subject to his own laws or to the laws of his predecessors, but only to his just and reasonable contracts in the observation of which his subjects in general or particular subjects have an interest.

Here many commentators mistakenly confuse the prince's laws with his contracts, which they call laws, and mistaken also is he [Pedro Belluga] who takes what are called compacted laws (*loix pactionees*) in the Estates of Aragon to be contracts of the prince. When the king makes an ordinance at the request of the Estates and receives money for it, or a subsidy, they say that the king is bound by it, and as for other laws that he is not bound. Nevertheless they admit that the prince can override it if the reason for the law should cease. This is true enough, and well founded in reason and authority. But there is no need for money and an oath to oblige a sovereign ruler if the subjects to whom he has given his promise have an interest in the law being kept. For the word of the prince should be like an oracle, and his dignity suffers when one has so low an opinion of him that he is not believed unless he swears, or is not [expected to be] faithful to his promises unless one gives him money. Nevertheless the force of the legal maxim still remains. A sovereign prince can override a law that he has promised and sworn to keep if it ceases to be just without the consent of his subjects, although it is true that in this case a general derogation does not suffice unless a special derogation goes along with it. But if there is no just cause to set aside a law that he has promised to maintain, the prince ought not and cannot [justly] contravene it.

...

It is essential, therefore, not to confuse a law and a contract. Law depends on him who has the sovereignty and he can obligate all his subjects by a law but cannot obligate himself. A contract between a prince and his subjects is mutual; it obligates the two parties reciprocally and one party cannot contravene it to the prejudice of the other and without the other's consent. In this case the prince has no advantage over the subject except that, if the justice of a law that he has sworn to keep ceases, he is no longer bound by his promise, as we have said, which is a liberty that subjects cannot exercise with respect to each other unless they are relieved [of their obligations] by the prince.

FRANÇOIS DE CALLIÈRES

FRANÇOIS DE CALLIÈRES (1645–1717), ambassador and spy during the reign of Louis XIV. His *On the Manner of Negotiating with Princes* (1716) was written for Philip, duke of Orleans, regent during the minority of Louis XV. Neither the first nor the last of innumerable handbooks of good diplomacy, it ably records the diplomatic ideals of a period in which imperial arrogance had been temporarily replaced by a concern for the principled conduct of foreign affairs.

From *On the Manner of Negotiating with Princes*

The usefulness of negotiation

To understand the permanent use of diplomacy and the necessity for continual negotiations, we must think of the states of which Europe is composed as being joined together by all kinds of necessary commerce, in such a way that they may be regarded as members of one Republic and that no considerable change can take place in any one of them without affecting the condition, or disturbing the peace, of all the others. The blunder of the smallest of sovereigns may indeed cast an apple of discord among all the greatest Powers, because there is no state so great which does not find it useful to have relations with the lesser states and to seek friends among the different parties of which even the smallest state is composed. History teems with the results of these conflicts which often have their beginnings in small events, easy to control or suppress at their birth, but which when grown in magnitude became the causes of long and bloody wars which have ravaged the principal states of Christendom. Now these actions and reactions between one state and another oblige the sagacious monarch and his ministers to maintain a continual process of diplomacy in all such states for the purpose of recording events as they occur and of reading their true meaning with diligence and exactitude. One may say that knowledge of this kind is one of the most important and necessary features of good government, because indeed the domestic peace of the state depends largely upon appropriate measures taken in its foreign service to make friends among well-disposed states, and by timely action to resist those who cherish hostile designs. There is indeed no prince so powerful that he can afford to neglect the assistance offered by a good alliance, in resisting the forces of hostile powers which are prompted by jealousy of his property to unite in a hostile coalition.

The diplomat: an agent of high policy

Now, the enlightened and assiduous negotiator serves not only to discover all projects and cabals by which coalitions may arise against his prince in the country where he is sent to negotiate, but also to dissipate their very beginnings by giving timely advice. It is easy to destroy even the greatest enterprises at their birth; and as they often require several springs to give them motion, it can hardly be possible for a hostile intrigue to ripen without knowledge of it coming to the ears of an attentive negotiator living in the place where it is being hatched. The able negotiator will know how to profit by the various dispositions and changes which arise in the country where he lives, not merely in order to frustrate designs hostile to the interests of his master, but also for the positive and fruitful purpose of bringing to an apt result those other designs which may work to his advantage. By his industry and application he may himself produce changes of opinion favourable to the office which he has to discharge; indeed, if he do but once in an apt moment catch the tide at the flood he may confer a benefit on his prince a hundredfold greater than any expense in treasure or personal effort which he may have put forth. Now if a monarch should wait, before sending his envoys to countries near and far, until important events occur – as for instance, until it is a question of hindering the conclusion of some treaty which confers advantage on an enemy Power, or a declaration of war against an ally which would deprive the monarch himself of the assistance of that very ally for other purposes – it will be found that the negotiators, sent thus at the eleventh hour on urgent occasions, have no time to explore the terrain or to study the habits of mind of the foreign court or to create the necessary liaisons or to change the course of events already in full flood, unless indeed they bring with them enormous sums whose disbursement must weigh heavily on the treasury of their master, and which run the risk, in truth, of being paid too late.

Cardinal Richelieu

Cardinal Richelieu, whom I set before me as the model for all statesmen, to whom France owes a very great debt, maintained a system of unbroken diplomacy in all manner of countries, and beyond question he thus drew enormous advantage for his master. He bears witness to this truth in his own political testament, speaking thus: –

'The states of Europe enjoy all the advantages of continual negotiation in the measure in which they are conducted with prudence. No one could believe how great these advantages are who has not had experience of them. I confess that it was not till I had had five or six years' experience of the management of high affairs that I realised this truth, but I am now so firmly persuaded of it that I will boldly say that the service which a regular and unbroken system of diplomacy, conducted both in public and in secret in all countries, even where no immediate fruit can be gathered, is one of the first necessities for the health and welfare of the state. I can say with truth that in my time I have seen the face of affairs in France and in Christendom completely changed because under the authority of his Majesty I have been enabled to practise this principle which till my time had been absolutely neglected by the ministers of this kingdom.' The Cardinal says further: 'The light of nature teaches each of us in his private life to maintain relations with his neighbours because as their near presence enables them to injure so it also enables them to do us service, just as the surroundings of a city either hinder or facilitate the approach to it.' And he adds: 'The meaner sort of men confine their outlook within the cities where they were born. But those to whom God has given a greater light will neglect no means of improvement whether it come from near or from far.' The evidence of this great genius demands all the greater consideration because the high services which he rendered to his King by means of negotiation convincingly prove that he speaks the truth. No considerable event occurred in Europe during his ministry in which he did not play a great part, and he was often the principal agent in the great movements of his time. He it was who designed the revolution in Portugal in 1640, by which the legitimate heir to the Crown resumed the throne. He profited by the discontent of the Catalans who rose in revolt in that same year. He did not hesitate to encourage negotiations even with the African Moors. Previously he brought his labours to success in the north by persuading Gustavus Adolphus, King of Sweden, to invade Germany, and thus to deliver her from slavery to the House of Austria which then reigned despotically, dethroning her princes and disposing of their states and their titles to its own court minions. Rumour even attributes the revolution in Bohemia to the action of Cardinal Richelieu. He formed and maintained several leagues; he won for France many great allies who contributed to the success of his high designs, in which the abasement of the prodigious power of the House of Austria was always the chief; and throughout all these designs we can trace the unbroken thread of a well-maintained system of diplomacy, acting as the obedient and capable agent of the great minister himself, whose profound capacity and vast genius thus found a favourable field of action.

Value of diplomacy

It is not necessary to turn far back into the past in order to understand what can be achieved by negotiation. We see daily around us its definite effects in sudden revolutions favourable to this great design of state or that, in the use of sedition in fermenting the hatreds between nations, in causing jealous rivals to arm against one another so that the *tertius gaudens* may profit, in the formation of leagues and other treaties of various kinds between monarchs whose interests might otherwise clash, in the dissolution by crafty means of the closest unions between states: in a word, one may say that the art of negotiation, according as its conduct is good or evil, gives form to great affairs and may turn a host of lesser events into a useful influence upon the course of the greater. Indeed, we can see in diplomacy thus conducted a greater influence in many ways upon the conduct and fortunes of mankind than even in the laws which they themselves have designed, for the reason that, however scrupulous private man may be in obedience to the law, misunderstandings and conflicts of ambition easily arise between nations, and cannot be settled by a process of law but only by a convention between the contending parties. It is on the occasion of such conventions that diplomacy plays a decisive part.

It is thus easy to conclude that a small number of well-chosen negotiators posted in the different states in Europe may render to their sovereign and their state the greatest services; that a single word or act may do more than the invasion of whole armies because the crafty negotiator will know how to set in motion various forces native to the country in which he is negotiating, and thus may spare his master the vast expense of a campaign. Nothing can be more useful than a timely diversion thus set on foot.

It is also of high interest to all great princes that their negotiators should be of such character and standing as to act appropriately as mediators in the disputes between other sovereigns and to produce peace by the authority of their intervention. Nothing can contribute more to the reputation, the power, and the universal respect of a monarch, than to be served by those who themselves inspire respect and confidence. A powerful prince who maintains a constant system of diplomacy served by wise and instructed negotiators in the different states of Europe, and who thus cultivates well-chosen friendships and maintains useful sources of information, is in a position to influence the destiny of neighbouring foreign states, to maintain peace between all states, or to pursue war where it is favourable to his design. In all these concerns the prosperity of his plans and the greatness of his name depend first and last on the conduct and qualities of the negotiators to whom he entrusts his services. So now we examine in detail the qualities necessary for a good negotiator.

Personal qualities of the good negotiator

God having endowed men with diverse talents, the best advice that one can give is to take counsel with themselves before choosing their profession. Thus he who would enter the profession of diplomacy must examine himself to see whether he was born with the qualities necessary for success. These qualities are an observant mind, a spirit of application which refuses to be distracted by pleasures or frivolous amusements, a sound judgment which takes the measure of things as they are, and which goes straight to its goal by the shortest and most natural paths without wandering into useless refinements and subtleties which as a rule only succeed in repelling those with whom one is dealing. The negotiator must further possess that penetration which enables him to discover the thoughts of men and to know by the least movement of their countenances what passions are stirring within, for such movements are often betrayed even by the most practised negotiator. He must also have a mind so fertile in expedients as easily to smooth away the difficulties which he meets in the course of his duty; he must have presence of mind to find a quick and pregnant reply even to unforeseen surprises, and by such judicious replies he must be able to recover himself when his foot has slipped. An equable humour, a tranquil and patient nature, always ready to listen with attention to those whom he meets; an address always open, genial, civil, agreeable, with easy and ingratiating manners which assist largely in making a favourable impression upon those around him – these things are the indispensable adjuncts to the negotiator's profession.

CORNELIUS VAN BYNKERSHOEK

CORNELIUS VAN BYNKERSHOEK (1673–1743), Dutch jurist and author of many works on public and international law, including comprehensive treatises on Roman law, the law of the sea, and the rights and duties of ambassadors. Because he sometimes draws upon the practice of states to establish his conclusions, Bynkershoek is often, if misleadingly, considered a pioneer of international legal positivism, the theory that international law must be inferred from state practice rather than deduced from natural law; in fact, he draws upon both. The following extract from his *On Questions of Public Law* (1737), dealing with the law of treaties, illustrates how international lawyers handled the tensions between principle and expediency during the classical age of European diplomacy.

From *On Questions of Public Law*

Book 2, Chapter 10
*On the observance of public agreements and whether
there are any tacit exceptions*

Civil law guards the contracts of individuals, considerations of honour, those of princes. If you destroy good faith, you destroy all intercourse between princes, for intercourse depends expressly upon treaties; you even destroy international law, which has its origin in tacitly accepted and presupposed agreements founded upon reason and usage. That treaties must be kept in good faith lest you destroy all this is readily granted, even by those who have learned nothing but treachery and all but frustrate the rules of good faith by numberless exceptions. Whether, however, a public agreement is always and everywhere to be kept inviolate is a very difficult question. Justin says about the ancient Parthians: 'No reliance can be placed upon their words and promises unless these are advantageous to them', and Seneca makes the general statement about the human race: 'Hardly anywhere is good faith found when its observance is inexpedient.' The master of iniquity in his *Principe* teaches that treachery is lawful for princes, saying that any and every method of securing the safety of the state is honourable provided only it makes a pretence at being honourable. But that doctrine, long since exploded, has been superseded by another, somewhat more respectable but perhaps no more just. This latter doctrine holds that the saving clause, *rebus sic stantibus*, lies in every compact, and accordingly compacts can be broken: (1) if a new condition has arisen suitable for reopening discussion; (2) if circumstances have come to such a pass that one cannot take action; (3) if the reasons that promoted the alliance have ceased to exist; (4) if the needs of the state or expedience demand a different course. Christian Otho of Boekelen, who writes more learnedly and elegantly than you would expect of one so young, has published a *Diatribe* on these *Tacit exceptions in public compacts*. But though you employ all the restrictions with which Boekelen circumscribes these exceptions, you would hardly save yourself from Machiavelianism, if you would slink off to these dens of treachery with the itching soul of a prince.

Particularly that last exception which permits the breach of oath in case of the state's needs and advantages, what else is it but the thing they call *ratio status*, a monster of many heads which almost no prince resists? And what are the three former exceptions but cloaks of treachery? He who employs any one of them will presently conclude that he can break his treaties if the observance of them under changed conditions may do harm to the state, and he who thinks thus, is treading upon treacherous ashes that hide the fires beneath. If you once grant so much, there is no case whatsoever for which you may not break your pledge with impunity. But, you will say, I made the agreement for the very reason that under the conditions of the state the agreement was advantageous, while now when circumstances are altered the compact is inexpedient and so the reasons for making it have vanished, consequently it cannot be considered that I have given my consent. Furthermore, whatever a prince agrees to, he signs for the good of his state, and binds himself with this in view, but if disadvantage comes from it, he is not bound, because to that he has not actually consented and without consent there is no obligation.

This argument may be subtle, but it does not accord with facts, and in that manner you can rescind any act whatsoever, on whatever occasion you choose. There is no such thing as a compact without consent, or consent without reasons for consenting; there is no change of will without a reason that was not applied at the time when you chose differently. By your argument no promise binds unless the results are advantageous, and if war is profitable you will reject the peace you have made. In this way a man who buys goods will repudiate the purchase if the price of them should go down, since he would change his mind with the change of price. Thus the result would be that a pledge which is binding according to all law would have no value whatsoever either in public or in private affairs.

Between the several independent nations there is no legal compulsion since the laws do not apply to international affairs, and the sole source of compulsion lies in the law. But the dictates of good faith and expediency require that international agreements should be observed, and to these must be attributed as much force as to the strongest pledge. In fact no pledge has more force than one that rests wholly upon greatness of soul. This first of all personal qualities is a particular adornment in a prince, and if it be absent, his state must fall into confusion. What prince will make a compact with a prince whose word is notoriously worth no more than a Carthaginian pledge? What will be the value of his agreements about trade, and aid in war, and the exchange of prisoners? In general these agreements are valid even between enemies, but it will be a small matter to break your word given to an enemy, if you may even break the pledge given to a friend.

If you are so capricious, you will probably break every pledge in ordinary social intercourse, for if I say that in daily life one must observe one's pledge because the law commands it, you will presently ask why one must obey the law, and you will ask for a definite demonstration of this proposition. If I say that each man must be given his own, because he is the master and is so considered by the state, I suppose you will ask why he is so considered, and you will inquire into the origin of property. You say that nature did not give such and such a piece of land to *A* more than to *B*; and if *A* has taken possession of it you will insist that since he has taken possession of what was common property, he could not legally deprive *B* of his share without some action on *B*'s part. Finally, perhaps you would acknowledge that as long as *A* holds possession of the land conformably to natural laws, *B* has no right to take it, since *A* has as good standing before the law as *B*, and other things being equal, possession is itself a point in his favour, since also the existing status should not be disturbed, except for a better cause, and since, accordingly, the cause of the defendant and of the plaintiff being on a par, no alterations should be made. But if you do not even concede this point but demand a division, then surely there is hardly a fixed point left in any case of ownership, or obligation, or finally any case that rests upon considerations of justice.

We must therefore attack the question with blunter weapons. When law has prescribed certain methods of acquiring ownership, we must observe these since no state can subsist without laws, and very expediency, the mother, I might say, of justice and equity, commands us to observe the laws. Even expediency obliges the several princes to keep their word, even though there are no laws between them, for you cannot conceive of empires without sovereigns, nor of sovereigns without compacts, nor of compacts without good faith. One must promise because one approves of the terms, and one must observe the terms because one has promised. But you will say, the observance of the terms often entails detriment and even destruction for the state. Granted, even on these terms it will perhaps be profitable to keep one's word. The courage of the citizens and kind good fortune may possibly restore the fallen state, but honour is like the breath of life, when once it is gone, it never returns. In political as well as in civil cases the words of Cicero hold very true: 'Nothing is more effective in binding the state together than the sense of honour.' In my opinion, therefore, a promise must be kept even when its observance is not expedient to the state, nay even when it is dangerous. This is my opinion, and it is also that of Cyriacus Lentulus in *Augustus*, where he vigorously defends the view with arguments and especially with examples.

Yet I would not reject all tacit exceptions, for there are some which all nations approve of; as, for instance, if I promise aid to an ally in case he is attacked, I need not furnish the aid if the prince himself has unjustly provided cause for the attack ... I say I would not reject all exceptions, but neither would I admit all exceptions and qualifications of treaties that Grotius admits with captious concern, and from which Boekelen (in the above-cited *Diatribe*) draws most of his adornment of tacit exceptions. Nor would I adopt those of some other writers who though apparently more scrupulous are no less dishonourable. For while they hold that political agreements are inviolable, they admit that such can readily be frustrated by cleverness if they are harmful to the state. The author of the *Political Disquisitions* [Boxhorn] holds this opinion, but since he cannot support it by arguments, he does so only by instances of crimes.

I know that there are also other authorities in public law who tread the same path, but if we followed these leaders, all princes would soon understand how easy it is not only to deceive but also to be deceived. We must carefully beware lest this happen, and exclude all those excuses by which unprincipled rulers hide their perfidy. The ancient Romans knew well that there was a difference between the debtor 'who had wasted borrowed moneys in pleasures and in gambling and the one who had lost it with his own through fire or theft or some other misfortune'. Yet Seneca says: 'They recognize no exceptions, so that men may know that above all else good faith must be observed'; adding: 'for it was better that the just excuse of a few should not be recognized than that some exception should lie open for all to attempt'. In the case of state treaties also the situation is such that it would be better to recognize no exceptions than so to increase their number that men would all but destroy the rule which demands the observance of good faith.

What then shall we say? Perhaps one or two exceptions may be allowed. It would surely be just if the question of my keeping the promise were submitted to the prince to whom I gave the promise, as in the kind of case I just mentioned ... Perhaps, however, you will say that this is actually not an exception, but an interpretation of treaties common in all usage. I care little what you call it; if you call it an exception, I will add another, namely that a prince is not bound beyond his capacity to perform the act promised, and the question of his capacity should be referred to the decision of a third prince who is to be a man of principle. Just as we give the favour of considering the competence (as it is called) of the individual who 'has lost others' property with his own in some misfortune' – as Seneca says – so would we grant this the more readily to princes if they act in good faith. A prince who is unable through circumstances to keep his promise should not have to submit to force or compulsion, for since force cannot be applied to him except by warfare, what would it profit to attack a prince with an armed force in order to compel him to give what he cannot give? If, despite this fact, you use compulsion, you have undertaken a war in an unjust cause. But the question whether the prince can or cannot keep his agreement, or whether it is due to another prince that he cannot, I would not leave to the arbitrament of the two princes involved, since judges may not sit upon their own cases; but I would refer it to neutrals. In former days public matters were often referred to the arbitration of other nations, as you may find in the passage of Grotius which I cited above.

ALEXANDER HAMILTON

ALEXANDER HAMILTON (1757–1804), American statesman and first secretary of the treasury in the federal government established by the constitution of 1789. With James Madison and John Jay, Hamilton authored the series of articles, collectively known as *The Federalist* (1787–8), exploring and defending the republican principles underlying this constitution. When war broke out between Britain and France after the revolution in France in 1789, Hamilton argued that the new American nation should remain neutral. In *Letters of Pacificus* (1793), he disputes the popular view that the United States should side with France, arguing that the national interest must come before sympathy with the French as fellow revolutionaries against monarchical rule.

From *Letters of Pacificus*

No. 3

France, at the time of issuing the proclamation, was engaged in war with a considerable part of Europe, and likely to be embroiled with almost all the rest, without a single ally in that quarter of the globe.

In such a situation, it is evident, that however she may be able to defend herself at home, of which her factions and internal agitations furnish the only serious doubt, she cannot make external efforts in any degree proportioned to those which can be made against her.

This state of things alone discharges the United States from an obligation to embark in her quarrel.

It is known, that we are wholly destitute of naval force. France, with all the great maritime powers united against her, is unable to supply this deficiency. She cannot afford us that species of cooperation which is necessary to render our efforts useful to her, and to prevent our experiencing the destruction of our trade, and the most calamitous inconveniences in other respects.

Our guaranty does not look to France herself. It does not relate to her immediate defence, but to the defence and preservation of her American colonies; objects of which she might be deprived, and yet remain a great, a powerful, and a happy nation.

In the actual situation of this country, and in relation to a matter of only secondary importance to France, it may fairly be maintained, that an ability in her to supply, in a competent degree, our deficiency of naval force, is a condition of our obligation to perform the guaranty on our part.

Had the United States a powerful marine, or could they command one in time, this reasoning would not be solid; but circumstanced as they are, it is presumed to be well founded.

There would be no proportion between the mischiefs and perils to which the United States would expose themselves, by embarking in the war, and the benefit which the nature of their stipulation aims at securing to France, or that which it would be in their power actually to render her by becoming a party.

This disproportion would be a valid reason for not executing the guaranty. All contracts are to receive a reasonable construction. Self-preservation is the first duty of a nation; and though in the performance of stipulations relating to war, good faith requires that its ordinary hazards should be fairly met, because they are directly contemplated by such stipulations, yet it does not require that extra-ordinary and extreme hazards should be run; especially where the object to be gained or secured is only a partial or particular interest of the ally, for whom they are to be encountered.

As in the present instance, good faith does not require that the United States should put in jeopardy their essential interests, perhaps their very existence, in one of the most unequal contests in which a nation could be engaged, to secure to France – what? Her West India islands and other less important possessions in America. For it is always to be remembered, that the stipulations of the United States do, in no event, reach beyond this point. If they were, upon the strength of their guaranty, to engage in the war, and could make any arrangement with the belligerant powers, for securing to France those islands and those possessions, they would be at perfect liberty instantly to withdraw. They would not be bound to prosecute the war one moment longer.

They are under no obligation in any event, as far as the faith of treaties is concerned, to assist France in defence of her liberty; a topic on which so much has been said, so very little to the purpose, as it regards the present question.

The contest in which the United States would plunge themselves, were they to take part with France, would possibly be still more unequal than that in which France herself is engaged. With the possessions of Great Britain and Spain on both flanks, the numerous Indian tribes under the influence and direction of those powers, along our whole interior frontier, with a long extended seacoast, with no maritime force of our own, and with the maritime force of all Europe against us, with no fortifications whatever, and with a population not exceeding four millions: it is impossible to imagine a more unequal contest, than that in which we should be involved in the case supposed. From such a contest we are dissuaded by the most cogent motives of self-preservation, no less than of interest.

We may learn from Vatel, one of the best writers on the laws of nations, "that if a state which has promised succours, finds itself unable to furnish them, its very inability is its exemption; and if the furnishing the succours would expose it to an evident danger, this also is a lawful dispensation. The case would render the treaty pernicious to the state, and therefore not obligatory. But this applies to an imminent danger threatening the safety of the state: the case of such a danger is tacitly and necessarily reserved in every treaty."

If too, as no sensible and candid man will deny, the extent of the present combination against France, is in a degree to be ascribed to imprudences on her part; the exemption to the United States is still more manifest and complete. No country is bound to partake in hazards of the most critical kind, which may have been produced or promoted by the indiscretion and intemperance of another. This is an obvious dictate of reason, with which the common sense and common practice of mankind coincide.

To the foregoing considerations, it may perhaps be added with no small degree of force, that military stipulations in national treaties, contemplate only the ordinary case of foreign war, and are irrelative to the contests which grow out of revolutions of government; unless where they have express reference to a revolution begun, or where there is a guaranty of the existing constitution of a nation, or where there is a personal alliance for the defence of a prince and his family.

The revolution in France is the primitive source of the war in which she is engaged. The restoration of the monarchy is the avowed object of some of her enemies, and the implied one of all. That question then is essentially involved in the principle of the war; a question certainly never in the contemplation of the government with which our treaty was made, and it may thence be fairly inferred, never intended to be embraced by it.

The inference is, that the United States fulfilled the utmost that could be claimed by the nation of France, when they so far respected its decision as to recognise the newly constituted authorities; giving operation to the treaty of alliance for future occasions, but considering the present war as a tacit exception. Perhaps too, this exception is, in other respects, due to the circumstances under which the engagements between the two countries were contracted. It is impossible, prejudice apart, not to perceive a delicate embarrassment between the theory and fact of our political relations to France.

On these grounds, also, as well as that of the present war being offensive on the side of France, the United States have valid and honourable pleas to offer against the execution of the guaranty, if it should be claimed by France. And the president was in every view fully justified in pronouncing, that the duty and interest of the United States dictated a neutrality in the war.

No. 4

A third objection to the proclamation is, that it is inconsistent with the gratitude due to France, for the services rendered to us in our revolution.

Those who make this objection disavow, at the same time, all intention to maintain the position, that the United States ought to take part in the war. They profess to be friends to our remaining at peace. What then do they mean by the objection?

If it be no breach of gratitude to refrain from joining France in the war, how can it be a breach of gratitude to declare, that such is our disposition and intention?

The two positions are at variance with each other; and the true inference is, either that those who make the objection really wish to engage this country in the war, or that they seek a pretext for censuring the conduct of the chief magistrate, for some purpose very different from the public good.

They endeavour in vain to elude this inference by saying, that the proclamation places France upon an equal footing with her enemies; while our treaties require distinctions in her favour, and our relative situation would dictate kind offices to her, which ought not to be granted to her adversaries.

They are not ignorant, that the proclamation is reconcileable with both those objects, as far as they have any foundation in truth or propriety.

It has been shown, that the promise of "a friendly and impartial conduct" towards all the belligerent powers, is not incompatible with the performance of any stipulations in our treaties, which would not include our becoming an associate in the war; and it has been observed, that the conduct of the executive, in regard to the seventeenth and twenty-second articles of the treaty of commerce, is an unequivocal comment upon the terms. They were, indeed, naturally to be understood, with the exception of those matters of positive compact, which would not amount to taking part in the war; for a nation then observes a friendly and impartial conduct towards two contending powers, when it only performs to one of them what it is obliged to do by stipulations in antecedent treaties, which do not constitute a participation in the war.

Neither do those expressions imply, that the United States will not exercise their discretion in doing kind offices to some of the parties, without extending them to the others, so long as they have no relation to war: for kind offices of that description may, consistently with neutrality, be shown to one party and refused to another.

If the objectors mean, that the United States ought to favour France, in things relating to war, and where they are not bound to do it by treaty; they must in this case also abandon their pretension of being friends to peace. For such a conduct would be a violation of neutrality, which could not fail to produce war.

It follows then, that the proclamation is reconcileable with all that those who censure it contend for; taking them upon their own ground, that nothing is to be done incompatible with the preservation of peace.

But though this would be a sufficient answer to the objection under consideration; yet it may not be without use, to indulge some reflections on this very favourite topic of gratitude to France; since it is at this shrine that we are continually invited to sacrifice the true interests of the country; as if "all for love, and the world well lost," were a fundamental maxim in politics.

Faith and justice, between nations, are virtues of a nature the most necessary and sacred. They cannot be too strongly inculcated, nor too highly respected. Their obligations are absolute, their utility unquestionable; they relate to objects which, with probity and sincerity, generally admit of being brought within clear and intelligible rules.

But the same cannot be said of gratitude. It is not very often that between nations, it can be pronounced with certainty, that there exists a solid foundation for the sentiment; and how far it can justifiably be permitted to operate, is always a question of still greater difficulty.

The basis of gratitude is a benefit received or intended, which there was no right to claim, originating in a regard to the interest or advantage of the party on whom the benefit is, or is meant to be, conferred. If a service is rendered from views relative to the immediate interest of the party who performs it, and is productive of reciprocal advantages, there seems scarcely in such a case, to be an adequate basis for a sentiment like that of gratitude. The effect at least would be wholly disproportioned to the cause, if such a service ought to beget more than a disposition to render in turn a correspondent good office, founded on mutual interest and reciprocal advantage. But gratitude would require much more than this; it would exact to a certain extent, even a sacrifice of the interest of the party obliged to the service or benefit of the one by whom the obligation had been conferred.

Between individuals, occasion is not unfrequently given for the exercise of gratitude. Instances of conferring benefits from kind and benevolent dispositions or feelings towards the person benefited, without any other interest on the part of the person who renders the service, than the pleasure of doing a good action, occur every day among individuals. But among nations they perhaps never occur. It may be affirmed as a general principle, that the predominant motive of good offices from one nation to another, is the interest or advantage of the nation which performs them.

Indeed, the rule of morality in this respect is not precisely the same between nations, as between individuals. The duty of making its own welfare the guide of its actions, is much stronger upon the former, than upon the latter; in proportion to the greater magnitude and importance of national, compared with individual happiness, and to the greater permanency of the effects of national, than of individual conduct. Existing millions, and for the most part future generations, are concerned in the present measures of a government; while the consequences of the private actions of an individual ordinarily terminate with himself, or are circumscribed within a narrow compass:

Whence it follows, that an individual may, on numerous occasions, meritoriously indulge the emotions of generosity and benevolence, not only without an eye to, but even at the expense of, his own interest. But a government can rarely, if at all, be justifiable in pursuing a similar course; and, if it does so, ought to confine itself within much stricter bounds.[1] Good offices which are indifferent to the interest of a nation performing them, or which are compensated by the existence or expectation of some reasonable equivalent, or which produce an essential good to the nation to which they are rendered, without real detriment to the affairs of the benefactors, prescribe perhaps the limits of national generosity or benevolence.

It is not here meant to recommend a policy absolutely selfish or interested in nations; but to show, that a policy regulated by their own interest, as far as justice and good faith permit, is, and ought to be, their prevailing one; and that either to ascribe to them a different principle of action, or to deduce, from the supposition of it, arguments for a self-denying and self-sacrificing gratitude on the part of a nation, which may have received from another good offices, is to misrepresent or misconceive what usually are, and ought to be, the springs of national conduct.

These general reflections will be auxiliary to a just estimate of our real situation with regard to France; of which a closer view will be taken in a succeeding paper.

---

1 This conclusion derives confirmation from the reflection, that under every form of government, rulers are only trustees for the happiness and interest of their nation, and cannot, consistently with their trust, follow the suggestions of kindness or humanity towards others, to the prejudice of their constituents.

EDMUND BURKE

EDMUND BURKE (1729–97), British statesman and political thinker. After a brief career as an author of philosophical works on ethics and aesthetics, Burke gained prominence as a Whig pamphleteer and then as a Member of Parliament. He wrote brilliantly on the need to conciliate the American colonies, the evils of British rule in India, and – most famously – the dangers to Britain posed by the revolutionary regime in France. Burke presented his case against the French revolution in his *Reflections on the Revolution in France* (1790), then in *Thoughts on French Affairs* (1791), and again in four *Letters on a Regicide Peace* (1796–7). In the *Letters*, his last work, he argues that the revolution had placed France in the hands of a barbaric regime whose principles were a threat not only to Britain but to European civilization.

From *Letters on a Regicide Peace*

Letter 1

On the overtures of peace

My dear Sir,

Our last conversation, though not in the tone of absolute despondency, was far from cheerful. We could not easily account for some unpleasant appearances. They were represented to us as indicating the state of the popular mind; and they were not at all what we should have expected from our old ideas even of the faults and vices of the English character. The disastrous events, which have followed one upon another in a long, unbroken, funereal train, moving in a procession that seemed to have no end, – these were not the principal causes of our dejection. We feared more from what threatened to fail within, than what menaced to oppress us from abroad. To a people who have once been proud and great, and great because they were proud, a change in the national spirit is the most terrible of all revolutions.

I shall not live to behold the unravelling of the intricate plot, which saddens and perplexes the awful drama of Providence, now acting on the moral theatre of the world. Whether for thought or for action, I am at the end of my career. You are in the middle of yours. In what part of its orbit the nation, with which we are carried along, moves at this instant, it is not easy to conjecture. It may, perhaps, be far advanced in its aphelion. – But when to returns.

Not to lose ourselves in the infinite void of the conjectural world, our business is with what is likely to be affected, for the better or the worse, by the wisdom or weakness of our plans. In all speculations upon men and human affairs, it is of no small moment to distinguish things of accident from permanent causes, and from effects that cannot be altered. It is not every irregularity in our movement that is a total deviation from our course. I am not quite of the mind of those speculators, who seem assured, that necessarily, and by the constitution of things, all states have the same periods of infancy, manhood, and decrepitude, that are found in the individuals who compose them. Parallels of this sort rather furnish similitudes to illustrate or to adorn, than supply analogies from whence to reason. The objects which are attempted to be forced into an analogy are not found in the same classes of existence. Individuals are physical beings subject to laws universal and invariable. The immediate cause acting in these laws may be obscure; the general results are subjects of certain calculation. But commonwealths are not physical but moral essences. They are artificial combinations, and, in their proximate efficient cause, the arbitrary productions of the human mind. We are not yet acquainted with the laws which necessarily influence the stability of that kind of work made by that kind of agent. There is not in the physical order (with which they do not appear to hold any assignable connexion) a distinct cause by which any of those fabrics must necessarily grow, flourish, or decay; nor, in my opinion, does the moral world produce anything more determinate on that subject, than what may serve as an amusement (liberal indeed, and ingenious, but still only an amusement) for speculative men. I doubt whether the history of mankind is yet complete enough, if ever it can be so, to furnish grounds for a sure theory on the internal causes which necessarily affect the fortune of a state. I am far from denying the operation of such causes: but they are infinitely uncertain, and much more obscure, and much more difficult to trace, than the foreign causes that tend to raise, to depress, and sometimes to overwhelm a community.

...

A government of the nature of that set up at our very door has never been hitherto seen, or even imagined, in Europe. What our relation to it will be cannot be judged by other relations. It is a serious thing to have connexion with a people, who live only under positive, arbitrary, and changeable institutions; and those not perfected, nor supplied, nor explained, by any common acknowledged rule of moral science. I remember that in one of my last conversations with the late Lord Camden, we were struck much in the same manner with the abolition in France of the law, as a science of methodized and artificial equity. France, since her revolution, is under the sway of a sect, whose leaders have deliberately, at one stroke, demolished the whole body of that jurisprudence which France had pretty nearly in common with other civilized countries. In that jurisprudence were contained the elements and principles of the law of nations, the great ligament of mankind. With the law they have of course destroyed all seminaries in which jurisprudence was taught, as well as all the corporations established for its conservation. I have not heard of any country, whether in Europe or Asia, or even in Africa on this side of Mount Atlas, which is wholly without some such colleges and such corporations, except France. No man in a public or private concern, can divine by what rule or principle her judgments are to be directed; nor is there to be found a professor in any university, or a practitioner in any court, who will hazard an opinion of what is or is not law in France, in any case whatever. They have not only annulled all their old treaties, but they have renounced the law of nations, from whence treaties have their force. With a fixed design they have outlawed themselves, and to their power outlawed all other nations.

Instead of the religion and the law by which they were in a great politic communion with the Christian world, they have constructed their republic on three bases, all fundamentally opposite to those on which the communities of Europe are built. Its foundation is laid in regicide, in Jacobinism, and in atheism; and it has joined to those principles a body of systematic manners, which secures their operation.

If I am asked, how I would be understood in the use of these terms, regicide, Jacobinism, atheism, and a system of corresponding manners, and their establishment? I will tell you:

I call a commonwealth *regicide*, which lays it down as a fixed law of nature, and a fundamental right of man, that all government, not being a democracy, is an usurpation. That all kings, as such, are usurpers; and for being kings may and ought to be put to death, with their wives, families, and adherents. The commonwealth which acts uniformly upon those principles, and which, after abolishing every festival of religion, chooses the most flagrant act of a murderous regicide treason for a feast of eternal commemoration, and which forces all her people to observe it – this I call *regicide by establishment*.

Jacobinism is the revolt of the enterprising talents of a country against its property. When private men form themselves into associations for the purpose of destroying the pre-existing laws and institutions of their country; when they secure to themselves an army, by dividing amongst the people of no property the estates of the ancient and lawful proprietors; when a state recognises those acts; when it does not make confiscations for crimes, but makes crimes for confiscations; when it has its principal strength, and all its resources, in such a violation of property; when it stands chiefly upon such a violation; massacring by judgments, or otherwise, those who make any struggle for their old legal government, and their legal, hereditary, or acquired possessions – I call this *Jacobinism by establishment*.

I call it *atheism by establishment*, when any state, as such, shall not acknowledge the existence of God as a moral governor of the world; when it shall offer to him no religious or moral worship; – when it shall abolish the Christian religion by a regular decree; – when it shall persecute with a cold, unrelenting, steady cruelty, by every mode of confiscation, imprisonment, exile, and death, all its ministers; – when it shall generally shut up or pull down churches; when the few buildings which remain of this kind shall be opened only for the purpose of making a profane apotheosis of monsters, whose vices and crimes have no parallel amongst men, and whom all other men consider as objects of general detestation, and the severest animadversion of law. When, in the place of that religion of social benevolence, and of individual self-denial, in mockery of all religion, they institute impious, blasphemous, indecent theatric rites, in honour of their vitiated, perverted reason, and erect altars to the personification of their own corrupted and bloody republic; – when schools and seminaries are founded at the public expense to poison mankind, from generation to generation, with the horrible maxims of this impiety; – when wearied out with incessant martyrdom, and the cries of a people hungering and thirsting for religion, they permit it, only as a tolerated evil – I call this *atheism by establishment*.

When to these establishments of regicide, of Jacobinism, and of atheism, you add the *correspondent system of manners*, no doubt can be left on the mind of a thinking man concerning their determined hostility to the human race. Manners are of more importance than laws. Upon them, in a great measure, the laws depend. The law touches us but here and there, and now and then. Manners are what vex or soothe, corrupt or purify, exalt or debase, barbarize or refine us, by a constant, steady, uniform, insensible operation, like that of the air we breathe in. They give their whole form and colour to our lives. According to their quality, they aid morals, they supply them, or they totally destroy them. Of this the new French legislators were aware; therefore, with the same method, and under the same authority, they settled a system of manners, the most licentious, prostitute, and abandoned, that ever has been known, and at the same time the most coarse, rude, savage, and ferocious. Nothing in the Revolution, no, not to a phrase or a gesture, not to the fashion of a hat or a shoe, was left to accident. All has been the result of design; all has been matter of institution. No mechanical means could be devised in favour of this incredible system of wickedness and vice, that has not been employed. The noblest passions, the love of glory, the love of country, have been debauched into means of its preservation and its propagation. All sorts of shows and exhibitions, calculated to inflame and vitiate the imagination, and pervert the moral sense, have been contrived. They have sometimes brought forth five or six hundred drunken women, calling at the bar of the Assembly for the blood of their own children, as being royalists or constitutionalists. Sometimes they have got a body of wretches, calling themselves fathers, to demand the murder of their sons, boasting that Rome had but one Brutus, but that they could show five hundred. There were instances, in which they inverted, and retaliated the impiety, and produced sons, who called for the execution of their parents. The foundation of their republic is laid in moral paradoxes. Their patriotism is always prodigy. All those instances to be found in history, whether real or fabulous, of a doubtful public spirit at which morality is perplexed, reason is staggered, and from which affrighted nature recoils, are their chosen, and almost sole, examples for the instruction of their youth.

The whole drift of their institution is contrary to that of the wise legislators of all countries, who aimed at improving instincts into morals, and at grafting the virtues on the stock of the natural affections. They, on the contrary, have omitted no pains to eradicate every benevolent and noble propensity in the mind of men. In their culture it is a rule always to graft virtues on vices. They think everything unworthy of the name of public virtue, unless it indicates violence on the private. All their new institutions (and with them everything is new) strike at the root of our social nature. Other legislators, knowing that marriage is the origin of all relations, and consequently the first element of all duties, have endeavoured, by every art, to make it sacred.

...

The operation of dangerous and delusive first principles obliges us to have recourse to the true ones. In the intercourse between nations, we are apt to rely too much on the instrumental part. We lay too much weight upon the formality of treaties and compacts. We do not act much more wisely when we trust to the interests of men as guarantees of their engagements. The interests frequently tear to pieces the engagements; and the passions trample upon both. Entirely to trust to either, is to disregard our own safety, or not to know mankind. Men are not tied to one another by papers and seals. They are led to associate by resemblances, by conformities, by sympathies. It is with nations as with individuals. Nothing is so strong a tie of amity between nation and nation as correspondence in laws, customs, manners, and habits of life. They have more than the force of treaties in themselves. They are obligations written in the heart. They approximate men to men, without their knowledge, and sometimes against their intentions. The secret, unseen, but irrefragable bond of habitual intercourse holds them together, even when their perverse and litigious nature sets them to equivocate, scuffle, and fight, about the terms of their written obligations.

As to war, if it be the means of wrong and violence, it is the sole means of justice amongst nations. Nothing can banish it from the world. They who say otherwise, intending to impose upon us, do not impose upon themselves. But it is one of the greatest objects of human wisdom to mitigate those evils which we are unable to remove. The conformity and analogy of which I speak, incapable, like everything else, of preserving perfect trust and tranquillity among men, has a strong tendency to facilitate accommodation, and to produce a generous oblivion of the rancour of their quarrels. With this similitude, peace is more of peace, and war is less of war. I will go further. There have been periods of time in which communities, apparently in peace with each other, have been more perfectly separated than, in latter times, many nations in Europe have been in the course of long and bloody wars. The cause must be sought in the similitude throughout Europe of religion, laws, and manners. At bottom, these are all the same. The writers on public law have often called this *aggregate* of nations a commonwealth. They had reason. It is virtually one great state having the same basis of general law, with some diversity of provincial customs and local establishments. The nations of Europe have had the very same Christian religion, agreeing in the fundamental parts, varying a little in the ceremonies and in the subordinate doctrines. The whole of the polity and economy of every country in Europe has been derived from the same sources. It was drawn from the old Germanic or Gothic custumary, from the feudal institutions which must be considered as an emanation from that custumary; and the whole has been improved and digested into system and discipline by the Roman law. From hence arose the several orders, with or without a monarch, (which are called states,) in every European country; the strong traces of which, where monarchy predominated, were never wholly extinguished or merged in despotism. In the few places where monarchy was cast off, the spirit of European monarchy was still left. Those countries still continued countries of states; that is, of classes, orders, and distinctions such as had before subsisted, or nearly so. Indeed the force and form of the institution called states continued in greater perfection in those republican communities than under monarchies. From all those sources arose a system of manners and of education which was nearly similar in all this quarter of the globe; and which softened, blended, and harmonized the colours of the whole. There was little difference in the form of the universities for the education of their youth, whether with regard to faculties, to sciences, or to the more liberal and elegant kinds of erudition. From this resemblance in the modes of intercourse, and in the whole form and fashion of life, no citizen of Europe could be altogether an exile in any part of it. There was nothing more than a pleasing variety to recreate and instruct the mind, to enrich the imagination, and to meliorate the heart. When a man travelled or resided for health, pleasure, business, or necessity from his own country, he never felt himself quite abroad.

The whole body of this new scheme of manners, in support of the new scheme of politics, I consider as a strong and decisive proof of determined ambition and systematic hostility. I defy the most refining ingenuity to invent any other cause for the total departure of the Jacobin republic from every one of the ideas and usages, religious, legal, moral, or social, of this civilized world, and for her tearing herself from its communion with such studied violence, but from a formed resolution of keeping no terms with that world. It has not been, as has been falsely and insidiously represented, that these miscreants had only broke with their old government. They made a schism with the whole universe, and that schism extended to almost everything great and small. For one, I wish, since it is gone thus far, that the breach had been so complete, as to make all intercourse impracticable: but partly by accident, partly by design, partly from the resistance of the matter, enough is left to preserve intercourse, whilst amity is destroyed or corrupted in its principle.

This violent breach of the community of Europe we must conclude to have been made (even if they had not expressly declared it over and over again) either to force mankind into an adoption of their system, or to live in perpetual enmity with a community the most potent we have ever known. Can any person imagine, that, in offering to mankind this desperate alternative, there is no indication of a hostile mind, because men in possession of the ruling authority are supposed to have a right to act without coercion in their own territories? As to the right of men to act anywhere according to their pleasure, without any moral tie, no such right exists. Men are never in a state of *total* independence of each other. It is not the condition of our nature: nor is it conceivable how any man can pursue a considerable course of action without its having some effect upon others; or, of course, without producing some degree of responsibility for his conduct. The *situations* in which men relatively stand produce the rules and principles of that responsibility, and afford directions to prudence in exacting it.

Distance of place does not extinguish the duties or the rights of men: but it often renders their exercise impracticable. The same circumstance of distance renders the noxious effects of an evil system in any community less pernicious. But there are situations where this difficulty does not occur; and in which, therefore, these duties are obligatory, and these rights are to be asserted. It has ever been the method of public jurists to draw a great part of the analogies, on which they form the law of nations, from the principles of law which prevail in civil community. Civil laws are not all of them merely positive. Those, which are rather conclusions of legal reason than matters of statutable provision, belong to universal equity, and are universally applicable. Almost the whole prætorian law is such. There is a *Law of Neighbourhood* which does not leave a man perfectly master on his own ground. When a neighbour sees a *new erection*, in the nature of a nuisance, set up at his door, he has a right to represent it to the judge; who, on his part, has a right to order the work to be stayed; or, if established, to be removed. On this head the parent law is express and clear, and has made many wise provisions, which, without destroying, regulate and restrain the right of *ownership*, by the right of *vicinage*. No *innovation* is permitted that may redound, even secondarily, to the prejudice of a neighbour. The whole doctrine of that important head of prætorian law, "*De novi operis nunciatione*," is founded on the principle, that no *new* use should be made of a man's private liberty of operating upon his private property, from whence a detriment may be justly apprehended by his neighbour. This law of denunciation is prospective. It is to anticipate what is called *damnum infectum*, or *damnum nondum factum*, that is, a damage justly apprehended, but not actually done. Even before it is clearly known, whether the innovation be damageable or not, the judge is competent to issue a prohibition to innovate, until the point can be determined. This prompt interference is grounded on principles favourable to both parties. It is preventive of mischief difficult to be repaired, and of ill blood difficult to be softened. The rule of law, therefore, which comes before the evil, is amongst the very best parts of equity, and justifies the promptness of the remedy; because, as it is well observed, *Res damni infecti celeritatem desiderat, et periculosa est dilatio*. This right of denunciation does not hold, when things continue, however inconveniently to the neighbourhood, according to the *ancient* mode. For there is a sort of presumption against novelty, drawn out of a deep consideration of human nature and human affairs; and the maxim of jurisprudence is well laid down, *Vetustas pro lege semper habetur*.

Such is the law of civil vicinity. Now, where there is no constituted judge, as between independent states there is not, the vicinage itself is the natural judge. It is, preventively, the assessor of its own rights, or remedially, their avenger. Neighbours are presumed to take cognizance of each other's acts. "*Vicini vicinorum facta presumuntur scire*." This principle, which, like the rest, is as true of nations as of individual men, has bestowed on the grand vicinage of Europe a duty to know, and a right to prevent, any capital innovation which may amount to the erection of a dangerous nuisance. Of the importance of that innovation, and the mischief of that nuisance, they are, to be sure, bound to judge, not litigiously; but it is in their competence to judge. They have uniformly acted on this right. What in civil society is a ground of action, in politic society is a ground of war. But the exercise of that competent jurisdiction is a matter of moral prudence. As suits in civil society, so war in the political, must ever be a matter of great deliberation. It is not this or that particular proceeding, picked out here and there, as a subject of quarrel, that will do. There must be an aggregate of mischief. There must be marks of deliberation, there must be traces of design, there must be indications of malice, there must be tokens of ambition. There must be force in the body where they exist, there must be energy in the mind. When all these circumstances are combined, or the important parts of them, the duty of the vicinity calls for the exercise of its competence; and the rules of prudence do not restrain, but demand it.

...

I have therefore been decidedly of opinion, with our declaration at Whitehall, in the beginning of this war, that the vicinage of Europe had not only a right, but an indispensable duty, and an exigent interest, to denunciate this new work before it had produced the danger we have so sorely felt, and which we shall long feel. The example of what is done by France is too important not to have a vast and extensive influence; and that example, backed with its power, must bear with great force on those who are near it; especially on those who shall recognise the pretended republic on the principle upon which it now stands. It is not an old structure which you have found as it is, and are not to dispute of the original end and design with which it had been so fashioned. It is a recent wrong, and can plead no prescription. It violates the rights upon which not only the community of France, but those on which all communities are founded. The principles on which they proceed are *general* principles, and are as true in England as in any other country. They, who (though with the purest intentions) recognise the authority of these regicides and robbers upon principle, justify their acts and establish them as precedents. It is a question not between France and England. It is a question between property and force. The property claims; and its claim has been allowed. The property of the nation is the nation. They, who massacre, plunder, and expel the body of the proprietary, are murderers and robbers. The state, in its essence, must be moral and just: and it may be so, though a tyrant or usurper should be accidentally at the head of it. This is a thing to be lamented: but this notwithstanding, the body of the commonwealth may remain in all its integrity and be perfectly sound in its composition. The present case is different. It is not a revolution in government. It is not the victory of party over party. It is a destruction and decomposition of the whole society; which never can be made of right by any faction, however powerful, nor without terrible consequences to all about it, both in the act and in the example. This pretended republic is founded in crimes, and exists by wrong and robbery; and wrong and robbery, far from a title to anything, is war with mankind. To be at peace with robbery is to be an accomplice with it.

...

And is then example nothing? It is everything. Example is the school of mankind, and they will learn at no other. This war is a war against that example. It is not a war for Louis the Eighteenth, or even for the property, virtue, fidelity of France. It is a war for George the Third, for Francis the Second, and for the dignity, property, honour, virtue, and religion of England, of Germany, and of all nations.

FRANÇOIS DE SALIGNAC DE LA MOTHE FÉNELON

FRANÇOIS DE SALIGNAC DE LA MOTHE FÉNELON (1651–1715), French bishop and author of works of popular philosophy, rhetoric, and education. A passionate enemy of repression, Fénelon attacked the abuses of absolute monarchy, among them Louis XIV's recurrent wars of national aggrandizement, and may be counted as a feminist of sorts for his denunciation of the inferior education open to women in his day. For Fénelon, not only are kings subject to the moral law but there can be no real conflict between morality and policy. His brief "On the Necessity of Forming Alliances" (1700), which explains the true principles of the balance of power, was appended to an essay intended to instruct a future Louis XV on the duties of kingship. The translation, by Susan Rosa, appears for the first time in this volume.

"On the Necessity of Forming Alliances"

An Examination of Conscience on the Duties of
Kingship, composed for the instruction of Louis
de France, Duc de Bourgogne, supplement I: on
the necessity of forming alliances, both offensive
and defensive, against a foreign power that
manifestly aspires to universal monarchy

Neighboring states are obliged not only to treat one another according to the rules of justice and good faith, but must also, both for the sake of their own security and the common interest, create for themselves a kind of society and general republic.

It is inevitable that the greatest power will always prevail in the long run, and overthrow the others, if they do not unite so as to provide a counter-weight to it. Among men, it is not possible to hope that a superior power will contain itself within the bounds of an exact moderation, or that in a condition of strength it will be content with what it could have obtained in its greatest weakness. For even if a prince were excellent enough to make so admirable a use of his prosperity, such a marvel would end with the conclusion of his reign. The natural ambition of sovereigns, the flatteries of their advisors, and the prejudices of entire nations, all make it impossible to believe that a nation capable of subjugating others would abstain from doing so for centuries at a time. A reign distinguished by such extraordinary uprightness would be the ornament of history, and a wonder not to be met with more than once.

It is therefore necessary to be prepared for what we observe every day in fact, and that is that every nation will seek to prevail over all those in its vicinity. Every nation is thus obliged, for the sake of its own security, unceasingly to keep watch in order to prevent the excessive aggrandizement of each and every one of its neighbors. To prevent a neighbor from becoming too powerful is not at all to do harm; it is merely to protect oneself and one's other neighbors from enslavement; in a word, it is to cultivate liberty, tranquility, and the public good: for the aggrandizement of one nation beyond a certain limit transforms the relations among all those nations that have some connection with it. For example, all the successive changes that occurred in the House of Burgundy, and those that raised up the House of Austria, changed the entire face of Europe. All of Europe had reason to dread the prospect of universal monarchy under Charles V, especially after Francis I was defeated and taken prisoner at Pavia. It is beyond question that any nation – even one that did not have any quarrel with Spain – would still have been entitled for the sake of public liberty to thwart the rapid growth of a power that seemed ready to devour everything in its path.

Private persons, on the other hand, are not entitled to oppose the increasing prosperity of their neighbors in this manner, because greater wealth in the hands of others cannot be assumed to do them harm. There are written laws and magistrates to suppress injustice and violence among families unequal in possessions; but the case of states is different. Here, the too great extension of one can prove to be the ruin and enslavement of all its neighbors: here, there are neither written laws, nor established judges to prevent the incursions of the stronger. And it may always be assumed that in the long run the most powerful will prevail on account of its strength, when there is no force of equal weight to oppose it. Therefore, every prince has both the right and obligation to prevent on the part of his neighbor an increase in power that would endanger the liberty of his own people and that of his neighbors.

For example, after having conquered Portugal, Philip II, king of Spain, wanted to make himself master of England. I know very well that his claim to that throne was ill-founded, because he had none except through his wife, Queen Mary, who had died without offspring. [It is true that] Elizabeth, who was illegitimate, ought not to have assumed the crown because it belonged to Mary Stuart and to her son. But even supposing that the claim of Philip had been incontestable, all of Europe would nevertheless have been right to oppose his establishment in England; because that powerful kingdom, joined to his dominions of Spain, Italy, Flanders, and the east and west Indies, put him in the position to dictate, especially by virtue of his naval forces, to all the other powers of Christendom. Thus, *summum jus, summa injuria*. In this case, a particular right of succession or donation ought to have yielded to the natural law that enjoins the security of so many nations. In a word, anything that upsets the balance of power and strikes a decisive blow for universal monarchy cannot be just, even if it is based on the written laws of a particular country. The reason for this is that the written laws of a people cannot prevail over the natural law of liberty and common security that is engraved in the hearts of all other peoples on earth. When a power has become so great that all the neighboring powers together can no longer resist it, those powers are entitled to band together in order to prevent its growth, which if allowed to proceed unchecked, would make it impossible for them to defend their common liberty. But in order to make confederations restraining the growing power of a state legitimate, the danger must be real and pressing: the league must be defensive, or offensive only insofar as is required for a just and necessary defense; and those treaties that establish offensive leagues must set precise limits for them so that they do not destroy a power under the pretext of restraining it.

This care to maintain a kind of equality and balance among neighboring nations assures their common tranquility. In this respect, all nations that are neighbors and joined together by commerce compose a great body and a kind of community. For example, Christendom is a kind of general republic, one that has its interests, its fears, and its policies: all the members that compose this great body owe it to one another and to themselves, for the sake of the common good and the security of their own nation, to oppose the growth of any one member that would upset the balance and contribute to the inevitable ruin of all the other members of the same body. Whatever changes or alters this general system of Europe is extremely dangerous, and draws in its wake innumerable evils.

All neighboring nations are so closely bound to one another and to all of Europe on account of their interests that the least growth of any one can alter the general balance, which alone makes for the general security of the whole. Remove one stone from an arch, and the whole construction falls, because all the stones support one another even as they counteract each other.

Humanity therefore enjoins on neighboring nations a mutual duty to defend the common good against one that grows too powerful, just as fellow citizens must unite to defend the liberty of their country. If every citizen owes much to his country, every nation, with better reason, owes even more to the tranquility and health of the universal republic of which it is a member, and in which are included all the countries composed of private persons.

Defensive confederations are therefore just and necessary, especially when it is a case of preventing an overweening power from devouring them all. This superior power thus has no right to breach the peace with other less powerful states, precisely on account of their defensive association, which they had the right and obligation to establish.

The legitimacy of an offensive league depends on the circumstances; it must be based on some breach of the peace, or on the seizure of some lands of the allies, or on some similar foundation that has been established with certainty. Moreover, as I have already said, such agreements ought to be limited by certain conditions that will prevent what we see quite often: one nation's claiming the need to destroy another who aspires to universal tyranny only in order to succeed in the same design. Prudence, as well as justice and good faith, dictates that treaties of alliance be worded most precisely, that they avoid all ambiguities, and limit themselves to an immediate and identifiable goal. If you are not careful, the agreements that you make will turn against you by doing too much damage to your enemy and offering your ally an overweening advantage: in that case, you will have either to suffer what may be ruinous to you, or break your word; and of these it is hard to determine which is the more fatal.

Let us continue to reason about these principles, applying them to the specific example of Christendom, in which we are most interested.

There are only four conditions in which a state may find itself. The first is to be absolutely superior to all other powers, even when they are united: that was the condition of the Romans and of Charlemagne. The second is to be the power superior to all others in Christendom, who nevertheless together form a counterbalance. The third is to be a power inferior to another, but which nonetheless supports itself against the superior power by uniting with its neighbors. Finally, the fourth is to be a power more or less equal to another, but one which maintains peace by preserving a kind of balance in good faith and without regard to ambition.

The condition of the Romans and of Charlemagne is by no means one that you are permitted to aspire to: first, because in order to attain it, you would be forced to commit all manner of injustice and violence; you would have to seize what is not your own, and do so by resorting to wars abominable in their extent and continuance. Second, such a design is most dangerous: quite often states perish through this kind of wild-eyed ambition. Third, those vast empires, which rise to power by means of so much suffering, are soon the occasion of even greater evils when they fall. The first minority or weak reign weakens the over-extended body, and divides the peoples who as yet are not accustomed either to the yoke of subjection or to mutual union. And then, what divisions, what confusions, what irremediable anarchy! To understand this, we have only to remember the disasters caused in the West by the sudden downfall of Charlemagne's empire, and in the East by the overthrow of that of Alexander, whose captains wreaked greater havoc in dividing his spoils than did he himself in ravaging Asia. This then is the condition which is the most dazzling, the most deceptively flattering, and the most fatal even for those who are successful in achieving it.

The second condition is that of a power superior to all others, who nevertheless form a counterweight to it. This superior power has an advantage over the others in that it is thoroughly united, homogeneous, unthwarted in its commands, and sure in its strategies. But if it does not cease to unite against itself all the other powers by exciting their jealousy, it must succumb in the long run. It exhausts itself, and thus becomes subject to many unforeseen internal accidents, or to sudden external attacks that can result in its downfall. In addition, it exerts itself to no purpose and engages in destructive efforts to maintain a superiority that gains it nothing, and exposes it to all sorts of disgraces and dangers. This is certainly the most wretched condition for any state; inasmuch as even in its most astonishing prosperity it can only succeed in passing into the first condition, which we have already found to be unjust and pernicious.

The third condition is that of a power inferior to another, but united to the rest of Europe in such a manner that it creates a counter-weight to the superior power, and ensures the security of all the other lesser states. This condition has its annoyances and disadvantages; but it is less risky than the preceding one, because the inferior power is on the defensive; relying on allies, it exhausts itself less, and in its condition of inferiority is often less blinded by the foolish presumption that threatens more prosperous states. We almost always see that with the passage of time, the more dominant powers exhaust themselves and begin to decline. Provided that this inferior power acts with wisdom and moderation, remains firm in its alliances, takes care not to give offense, and to do nothing except in concert with its allies and in the common interest, it can contend successfully with the superior power and at length reduce it.

The fourth condition is that of a power more or less equal to another with which it maintains a balance for the sake of the public security. This condition, without any ambitious attempts to alter it, is the wisest and happiest of all. You are the common arbiter: all your neighbors are your friends; or at least, those who are not run the risk of being distrusted by the rest. You do nothing that does not appear to be done for the good of your neighbors as well as for that of your own people. You add daily to your strength, and if you succeed, as you will almost certainly do in the long run by governing wisely, in gaining more internal strength and concluding more external alliances than your opponent, then you must continue to follow the policy of wise moderation that directs you to maintain the balance and the common security. You must always be mindful of the evils that are wrought both inside and outside a state by great conquests: remember that they are fruitless, and be cognizant of the risks entailed by undertaking them; finally, recall the vanity, the uselessness, and the short duration of great empires, and the calamities that attend their fall.

But, since it is not possible to hope that a power superior to all others will maintain itself for long without abusing this superiority, a prince who is wise and just must never wish to leave to his successors, who in all likelihood will be less moderate than he, the continual and violent temptation of a too pronounced superiority. Thus, for the good of his successors and his people, he ought to confine himself to some equality with his neighbors. There are, it is true, two kinds of superiority: one external, which consists in the extent of territories, in fortified places, in access to the lands of one's neighbors etc. This kind of superiority only causes temptations that are equally fatal to the prince and to his neighbors, and excites against him hatred, jealousy, and hostile alliances. The other superiority is inward and substantial: it consists in a people more numerous, more disciplined, more devoted to agriculture and the necessary arts. Usually, this superiority is easy to acquire, secure, less exposed to envy and to the alliances of neighboring powers, and more suited than conquests and fortified places, to render a people invincible. Therefore, a state cannot be too diligent in seeking this second kind of superiority, nor in avoiding the first, which has only a false lustre.

FRIEDRICH VON GENTZ

F RIEDRICH VON GENTZ (1764–1832), Prussian diplomat and advocate for international cooperation to resist the French revolution and the Napoleonic expansion that followed it. Working closely with the Austrian chancellor, Metternich, Gentz played a prominent role in the Congress of Vienna, which brought the Napoleonic wars to an end. In his essay on the European balance of power (1806), Gentz anticipated the post-war system in which the balance operates to maintain the equal rights of states as members of an international society. By enforcing international law, the balance of power functions in international society in a way analogous to the judicial and executive power within a state.

From "The True Concept of a Balance of Power"

What is usually termed a *balance of power* is that constitution which exists among neighbouring states more or less connected with each other, by virtue of which none of them can violate the independence or the essential rights of another without effective resistance from some quarter and consequent danger to itself.

Many misconceptions have arisen as a result of the similarity with physical objects upon which the term was based. It has been supposed that those who saw in the *balance of power* the basis of an association of states were aiming at the most complete *equality*, or *equalization*, of power possible, and were demanding that the various states of an area which is politically united should be most precisely measured, weighed and rounded off, one against the other, in respect of size, population, wealth, resources, etc. This false assumption, upon being applied to state relations with either credulity or scepticism, has led to two opposite errors, one almost as damaging as the other. Those who fully accepted this imaginary principle were led to believe that in every case where one state became stronger, either through external growth or internal development, the others would offer resistance and would feel obliged to struggle until they had either matched this increase in strength or reduced the state to its former condition. But, on the other hand, others, in their quite correct conviction that such a system is impossible, have called the whole idea of a balance of power a chimera, invented by dreamers and skilfully manipulated by artful men so that there should be no lack of pretexts for dispute, injustice and violence. The former of these errors would banish peace from the earth; the latter would offer the most desirable prospects of absolute power to any state thirsting for conquest.

Both errors are based on the same confusion of ideas to which, in the field of internal state relations, we owe all the frivolous and airy theories of *civil equality* and all the unsuccessful practical attempts to carry them out. All the citizens in every well-ordered state, and all the states in every well-ordered community of nations, should be *equal in law* or *equal before the law*, but by no means *equal in rights*. True equality, the only kind attainable by legitimate means, consists in both cases only in this, that the smallest as well as the greatest is assured of his right, and cannot be compelled or harmed by unlawful authority.

The basis of a properly organized state and the triumph of its constitution is, namely, that a host of people, absolutely unequal in rights and power, in ability and its application, in inherited and acquired possessions, can exist alongside each other by means of common laws and government, that no-one can arbitrarily seize his neighbour's territory, and that the poorest man owns his cottage and his field as completely as the richest owns his palace and estates. Similarly, the true character of an international community (such as is being formed in modern Europe) and the triumph of its excellence will be that a certain number of states at very different levels of power and wealth, under the protection of a common bond, shall each remain unassailed within its own secure borders, and that he whose domain is bounded by a single town wall shall be held as inviolate by his neighbours as he whose possessions and authority extend over land and sea.

But as the best state constitution devised by man is never completely adequate for its purpose, and always leaves room for individual acts of violence, oppression and injustice, so the most perfect international constitution is never strong enough to prevent every attack of a stronger state on the rights of a weaker one. Furthermore, under otherwise identical conditions, an international association will always be less able to protect the independence and security of its members than a state will be to protect the legal equality and security of its citizens.

The security of the citizens of a state is based on the unity of its legislation and administration. The laws all emanate from the same central point; upholding them is the task of one and the same authority, which can dissuade those who would break the law by ordinary coercion at the outset, and bring those who have actually broken it to answer for it before a tribunal. The law binding states together lies only in their mutual treaties; and as these are open to endless variation in their essence, spirit and character because of the unlimited diversity of the relations from which they spring, so the nature of their origin excludes any higher, common sanction, in the strictest sense of the word. Among independent nations there is neither an executive nor a judicial power; to create the one, like the other, by means of external organizations has long been a fruitless pious wish and the vain endeavour of many a well-meaning man. But what the nature of the relation prevented from being achieved in its entirety was at least attained in approximation; and in the state system of modern Europe the problem was solved as happily as could be expected of men and the sensible application of human skill.

An extensive social union was formed among the states in this part of the world, of which the essential and characteristic aim was the preservation and mutual guarantee of the well-won rights of each of its members. From the time when this noble purpose was recognized in all its clarity there gradually developed also the vital and everlasting conditions on which its achievement depended. Men became aware that there were certain basic rules in the relationship between the strength of each individual part and the whole, without whose constant influence order could not be assured; and gradually the following maxims were established as a perpetual objective:

That if the state system of Europe is to exist and be maintained by common effort, no one of its members must ever become so powerful that the others cannot overcome it by joint action;

That if the system is not only to exist but also to be maintained without constant danger and violent concussions, then the other states must be capable of overcoming any individual who violates it, either by joint or majority action, if not by the action of a single state;

But that, in order to escape the alternative danger of an uninterrupted series of wars or arbitrary suppression of the weaker members in the short intervals of peace, the *fear* of common opposition or common vengeance by the others should normally be enough to keep each one in bounds; and

That if any European state attempted to attain power through unlawful activities, or had indeed attained it, so that it could defy the distant danger of an alliance between several of its neighbours, or the actual commencement of it, or even a federation of the whole, such a state should be treated as the common enemy of the whole community; if on the other hand such a power should appear somewhere on the stage through an accidental chain of events and through no illegal actions, no means of weakening it which the state has at its disposal should be left untried.

The essence of these maxims is the only generally understood theory of a balance of power in the political world.[1]

---

1 It could perhaps more safely have been called a theory of *counterpoise*. For even the highest of its results is not so much a perfect *balance* as a constant *oscillation*, which can, however, never stray beyond certain limits because it is controlled by counterweights.

The original inequality of the parties in this type of association is not to be seen as an accidental circumstance, even less as an accidental evil, but to a certain extent as the precondition and foundation of the whole system;[2] not *how much power* one or the other possesses; but only whether he possesses it in such a way and under such limitations that he cannot with impunity deprive one of the rest of its own power – this is the question which must be decided in order to pass judgment at any given moment on the relation between individual parts or on the general proficiency of the edifice. Hence even a subsequent increase in that original necessary inequality may in itself be blameless, provided it does not come from sources, nor introduce incongruities, which violate one of the basic maxims.

Only when one or another state wilfully, or supported by fictitious pretexts and contrived titles, undertakes such acts which immediately or as an unavoidable consequence cause, on the one hand, the subjugation of its weaker neighbours and, on the other hand, perpetual danger, gradual debilitation and the final downfall of its stronger neighbours, only then, according to sound conceptions of the interest of a union of states, is a breakdown of the balance effected; only then do several states combine to prevent by means of an opportune counterweight the predominance of an individual state.

2   If the world had been divided only into equal rectangles, large or small, no such union of states would ever have occurred, and the eternal war of each against the others would probably be the only world-event.

6

The emergence of international law

Although a society of states has been in the making in Europe since at least the fifteenth century, the idea of a distinct body of law springing from and regulating this society remained hazy throughout the early modern period. The term "international law" (and cognate expressions in other languages) did not come into general use until the nineteenth century. Even then, the rules governing international relations were sometimes referred to as the "public law of Europe." But most writers clung to the antiquated and equivocal term "law of nations" (*ius gentium*, *droit des gens*, *Völkerrecht*, etc.), struggling to describe new modes of diplomacy using a conceptual vocabulary inherited from ancient Rome and medieval Christendom.

The modern debate over whether a law-governed order is possible in a world of sovereign states reflects the growing importance of individualism. Theorists who base civil law on individual interests argue that the sole purpose of government is to protect the lives and property of its subjects. For some, this argument points toward constitutional government and the protection of individual rights. To others it suggests an instrumental conception of government in which laws are tools of rather than constraints on policy. Such a conception threatens individual rights by undermining the laws that define and protect them.

In its most extreme versions, individualism regards human beings as appetitive creatures, driven, in the absence of a superior earthly power, to be their own law in matters affecting their survival. In such a condition there is no authoritative superior law, only instrumental rules which freely choosing human beings devise for their own convenience. Natural law gives way to natural right – one's *de facto* liberty to use one's powers as best one can. The proposition that sovereign states are subject to a law prescribing limits on the pursuit of power, already undermined by radical conceptions of reason of state, had to be reasserted against this new theory of natural right. What we call international law is one of the outcomes of an intellectual effort to reconstruct the Stoic/Christian universal human community as a community of territorial states. Whether states really do constitute a community regulated by international law is, of course, a debate that has not yet run its course.

Natural law and natural rights

According to the Stoics, there is a divine and natural law governing everything in the universe, including human conduct. In the Christian version of this view, the law is divine in being promulgated by God and natural in being knowable by reason without the aid of revelation. Because human beings are free, rational beings, they can choose to disobey this law. And natural law, understood as a morality binding on all human beings, must be distinguished from the laws observed in particular communities. This conception of morality goes back through Aquinas to the Stoic view that all human beings are citizens not only of a particular polis with its own local laws but of an ideal universal community: a "cosmopolis" whose law is this rationally knowable natural law. There are, in other words, objective, universal, and eternal standards of right and wrong by which human laws as well as human conduct are to be judged.

The most significant natural law theorists of the sixteenth and early seventeenth centuries were Catholic theologians working in the tradition of medieval scholasticism. But by the middle of the seventeenth century, Protestant writers drawing directly on the Bible and the classics were at the center of natural law theorizing. Chief among them were Grotius and Hobbes.

Hugo Grotius (1583–1645) was, among other things, a humanist scholar, poet, historian, and self-taught theologian. Trained in Latin and Greek and then in law, he sometimes combined these interests in odd ways: one of his poems, for example, is a Latin verse paraphrase of the passages on *dominium* (property) from Justinian's *Institutes*, a manual of Roman law commissioned by the sixth-century emperor. Grotius held a series of offices under the patronage of the chief of the United Provinces of the Netherlands, Johan van Oldenbarnevelt. But his public career was abruptly terminated in 1619 when Oldenbarnevelt tangled with more powerful rivals and was executed for treason. Sentenced to prison for life, Grotius escaped to Paris, where he later served as the Swedish ambassador to France.

Grotius made his first significant contribution to international affairs in response to the Dutch rivalry with Portugal and Spain in the East Indies. In 1603 the Dutch East India Company captured a Portuguese vessel in the Straits of Malacca and brought it back to Holland, claiming ownership of the vessel and its cargo as "prize" (property seized lawfully in a war). Grotius, who at this time was a celebrated Latin author as well as a prominent lawyer, was a natural choice not only to defend the company's claim in court but to make a compelling public case for Dutch efforts to disrupt Portuguese trade in the East Indies (Roelofsen, 1990: 105). This assignment resulted in a manuscript known as *The Law of Prize*. Except for a chapter printed in 1609 as *Freedom of the Seas*, the work remained unpublished until 1864.

The Law of Prize is more than a legal brief on behalf of the Dutch East India Company or a moral defense of the Dutch challenge to Portuguese and Spanish imperial claims, for it offers an elaborate philosophical argument for the right of individual and collective self-preservation and for the lawfulness of war, private as well as public, as an instrument of self-preservation. Instead of devising a narrow legal argument that would be sufficient to win his case in a Dutch court, Grotius develops a general justification of the use of armed force based on principles that could be acknowledged in Portugal as well as in Holland, and by Catholics as well as Protestants.

Grotius is grappling with a significant problem: how can one establish the truth of moral principles if people adhere to different traditions of moral belief? There are three obvious ways of handling this problem, which we might call dogmatism, relativism, and consensus. First, one can ground morality on some premise that one believes to be beyond doubt. The difficulty with this solution is that those who reject the premise will remain unconvinced: the premise and the conclusions it supports may be true, but this won't make any practical difference. Second, one can reason from within one of the competing traditions of moral belief, leaving others to reason within their own traditions. But this solution is even less likely than the first to generate moral agreement because it offers no basis for choosing between traditions. Third, one can seek a foundation in principles common to all systems of belief. But this solution, too, is problematic, for a proposition might be generally accepted and yet be false. This, however, is the solution Grotius finds most compelling.

Grotius argues that one cannot establish the truth of a moral conclusion by invoking principles drawn from some particular, historically contingent moral system. He therefore rejects both civil law and Holy Scripture as a source of universal moral principles. The rules of civil law are binding only on the citizens of a particular state. Nor is Scripture a source of universal principles: the law revealed to the Hebrews is law only for them, and even Christian teaching has limited universal validity because it is mainly concerned with how to lead a more Christian life. Only natural law – which consists of moral principles correctly derived from universally valid premises – possesses the required generality.

But how, we might ask, do we know where to begin? How can we discover which moral premises are universally true? Why should we embrace the Stoic idea of a universal law of nature? Grotius reasons that what Stoicism and the other philosophical traditions of antiquity – which are, for him, the most authoritative systems of rational morality – agree upon must in fact be true. And all the ancient schools, including the "Academics" (Skeptics), agree on the primacy of self-preservation (Grotius, 1950: 10–11). Ancient Skepticism is not a purely epistemological view: it recommends suspending belief to achieve a state of mind in which one is free from anxiety. But because one must go on living to enjoy this state, Skepticism implicitly views self-preservation as the basic human motive. Grotius therefore concludes that the injunction to preserve oneself, which even the Skeptic acknowledges, is the indisputable foundation for morality (Tuck, 1987: 110–11).

Grotius establishes a moral right of self-preservation by reasoning that if the desire for self-preservation is inherent in human nature, no-one can be blamed for acting on this desire. And once we grant a right of self-preservation, we must grant other rights that are implied by it. Grotius uses the most important of these implied rights, self-defense and ownership, to formulate two fundamental principles of natural law: that it is permissible to defend one's life and to acquire things useful for life (Grotius, 1950: 10).

According to this theory, the basis of natural law, *ius naturae*, is natural rights. The word *ius*, Grotius writes, stands for what is "just" by nature and, by extension, for the "law" by which natural justice and injustice is measured. But there is another meaning of *ius* which is close to what we mean today by "a right." *Ius*, in this sense, means the moral quality by which a person can be said to justifiably perform an action or possess a thing. It includes moral powers which one has over oneself (freedom), others (mastery), and things (ownership), as well as contractual rights (Grotius, 1950: 35–6). This meaning of *ius* (plural *iure*) as a power owned by someone is not novel. Grotius' Spanish contemporary, Francisco Suárez, for example, distinguishes *ius* as "the moral right to acquire or retain something" from *ius* as "law, which is the rule of righteous conduct" (1944: 326), and there is evidence that the use of *ius* to mean a right goes back at least to canon lawyers of the twelfth century (Tierney, 1997). In using the idea of natural right, then, Grotius is reshuffling the elements of an inherited tradition. But in making rights the foundation of natural law, he gives the individualist element in that tradition an importance it did not have in medieval thought.

Because of the primacy of self-preservation, Grotius argues, human beings have a right to defend themselves against attack – a right they retain even in civil society. And because the justification of civil society is that it secures the right of self-preservation, individuals may use force to defend their lives and property when government fails to protect them or to resist a government that attempts to deprive them of these things. In this way Grotius maps out a line of thought that is central to political theory for the next two centuries: that civil society is an artificial entity constructed by individuals endowed with natural (pre-civil) rights, including the right of property. The idea that persons "have" rights, that civil law exists to protect their rights, and that government is illegitimate when it interferes with these rights, helped transform the Aristotelian/scholastic premises of medieval thought into the secular individualism we take for granted today.

Grotius does not, however, push his individualist premises to the limit. He argues that the natural kinship human beings feel for their fellows makes it reasonable to demand that they refrain from injuring one another. This demand generates two additional natural laws: that one may not physically harm others or seize their possessions (Grotius, 1950: 10). When Grotius says that "one's own good takes precedence over the good of another" (1950: 21), he does not mean that in pursuing one's own ends one can violate these two natural laws. A person is morally entitled to act in ways that injure the interests of other persons, but not their bodies or property.

The natural moral order implicit in these additional principles is nevertheless quite minimal. Natural law, as Grotius understands it, is a morality based on coexistence between self-regarding individuals, not on benevolence or on cooperation to secure shared social goods. Human beings may be inherently social, but the law of nature does not require that they assist one another, only that they leave one another alone, though there may be a duty to assist those who are the victims of violent injustice. Grotius' understanding of sociality is only superficially like that of Aristotle and Aquinas, for it attributes to human beings no more than a natural propensity to respect one another's interests. Founding natural law on natural rights undermines the Aristotelian assumption of natural human sociality and narrows the scope of natural law to mutual noninterference.

Grotius develops the implications of his theory of natural rights for international relations in *The Law of War and Peace* (1625). Like the earlier work, it is concerned with both private and public war. It is therefore not a treatise on international law, understood as a distinct body of law regulating international relations. Instead, it articulates a single theory of morality applicable to any person, individual or collective, whose natural rights are threatened by the actions of others. Civil societies are associations of persons cooperating to secure their lives and property, and one purpose of a government is to defend the rights of its citizens against injury by foreigners. Although individual human beings live in civil societies, these societies remain in a natural (pre- or non-civil) condition with respect to one another. Like the persons they protect, states have a right to self-preservation. The natural rights of states are analogous to the natural rights of individuals.

For Grotius, to defend one's own life and property is the most fundamental ground for using armed force – hence the title of the chapter (Book 2, chapter 1) in which Grotius opens his discussion of the circumstances under which war is justified: "The Causes of War: First, Defense of Life and Property." In defending one's rights by force one must, however, avoid violating the rights of others: "it is not ...contrary to the nature of society to look out for oneself and advance one's own interests, provided the rights of others are not infringed; and consequently the use of force which does not violate the rights of others is not unjust" (Grotius, 1925: 54). In the state of nature, one individual may punish another for violating the rights of any person, because such injuries set a bad example and are therefore the concern of all. The same is true of injuries inflicted on a state. Just as each person in the state of nature may fight to preserve the rights of all, so each state may fight to preserve the rights of all states. A state is therefore permitted to punish injuries to others as well as to itself. Any state, for example, may justly use force to suppress piracy or barbaric practices like cannibalism. But only the most serious crimes against nature can justify punitive war, which is always "under suspicion of being unjust, unless the crimes are very atrocious and very evident" (Grotius, 1925: 508).

If the cause for which a war is fought is unjust, then, Grotius argues, everything done in the course of waging it is unjust. He does not recognize the modern principle that would excuse soldiers in an unjust war from the charge of criminality on the grounds that the rights and wrongs of conduct in war are independent of the justice of the war's aims. Nor does he offer moral reasons (that is, reasons based on natural law) for refraining from atrocities; instead, he condemns atrocities as un-Christian and inexpedient. This failure to connect the laws of war with the natural rights of noncombatants suggests that Grotius did not grasp the full implications of his own moral system.

Perhaps no consistent system of moral precepts is possible, however, if the right of self-preservation is treated as foundational. For Thomas Hobbes (1588–1679), self-preservation erodes rather than supports natural law. Grotius deduces natural law principles from the right of self-preservation. But the human beings whose right he postulates are not the ruthless powerseekers imagined by Hobbes. What Hobbes calls "the right of nature" is the unrestricted liberty of appetitive creatures competing for life and power: isolated selves who are driven to use one another, each for its own purposes. Human beings are rational creatures, but their rationality is the ends/means prudence of creatures concerned with self-preservation. Because their only motive in refraining from harming one another is self-regarding, Hobbesian selves lack even the minimal sociality that Grotius ascribes to human beings in the natural condition. Hobbes' theory of natural rights is therefore more radically individualist than Grotius'.

For Grotius, the state of nature, the situation of persons outside civil society, is still a moral order, but for Hobbes it is a lawless war of all against all: there can be no moral life without authority to declare and enforce a common law. For Grotius, as for the Thomists, moral principles create obligations even in the absence of security. For Hobbes they do not: if others will not behave decently, you don't have to, either. In the absence of security, each person is free to do whatever, in his or her own judgement, is necessary for self-preservation. For Hobbes, outside civil society the laws of nature are in effect de-moralized: they become maxims of prudence for persons seeking self-preservation. If others are willing to cooperate, it will benefit you to cooperate as well, but you have no obligation to cooperate because in the state of nature there is no guarantee that others won't exploit your cooperation.

Hobbes uses these prudential maxims to generate civil society: rational persons, he argues, will put themselves under a system of authoritative and enforceable civil law. But the resulting states system is, paradoxically, still a state of nature. Whether sovereigns, too, might profit by establishing a world state depends on circumstances: for Hobbes, the costs of remaining in the state of nature are not as high for commonwealths as for individuals, so the motive for creating a super-state is weaker than that which brings individuals into civil society. But that is a contingent judgement; one can imagine circumstances in which the costs of remaining independent might motivate states to institute a world state (Airaksinen and Bertman, 1989).

Hobbes' view of international relations is, then, one we would call "realist" or Machiavellian. Within civil society, law rules; between civil societies "policy" (expediency) comes to the fore. The eighteenth-century theory of the balance of power illustrates how far international political theory can go on Hobbesian premises.

Seventeenth- and eighteenth-century theorists tried ingeniously to reconcile the new theory of natural rights articulated by Grotius and Hobbes with the older understanding of natural law. The most famous of these in his day was the German philosopher Samuel Pufendorf (1632–94). Pufendorf accepts Hobbes' argument that enforcement is essential to the idea of law. But instead of concluding that natural law is not enforceable and therefore not really law, he argues that it is authentic law because it is willed by God and backed by the threat of divine punishment. He also argues that Hobbes is mistaken in thinking that there can be rights without correlative duties. If there is a natural right of self-preservation, there must also be a natural duty to respect the lives and property of others. Finally, against Grotius, Pufendorf argues that our natural duties include a positive duty of benevolence:

Everyone should be useful to others, so far as he conveniently can ... It is not enough not to have harmed ... others. We must also ... share such things as will encourage mutual goodwill. (Pufendorf, 1934/1991: 64)

Underlying these duties is the fundamental principle of morality: that one should cultivate "sociality." This is Pufendorf's version of the Golden Rule, and it is fundamental in the sense that all the other precepts of morality derive from it. With these arguments, Pufendorf retreats from Hobbes' and even

Grotius' theory of natural right to a position less hostile to that of Thomistic natural law.

Pufendorf's *On the Duties of Man and Citizen* (1673) is a compact survey for students of the principles of natural law expounded in a massive treatise published the year before, *On the Law of Nature and of Nations* (1672). In these works, Pufendorf identifies natural law as a kind of moral knowledge. It is knowledge of one's duties as a human being, acquired by the use of reason, as distinguished from knowledge of one's duties as a citizen, as determined by the civil laws of one's country, or knowledge of one's duties as a Christian, based on divine revelation. In modern terms, we might say that Pufendorf distinguishes philosophical ethics from positive jurisprudence, on the one hand, and moral theology, on the other.

If natural law is really law, then international relations is governed by law. But it is of course moral, not positive, law. Morally speaking, a state has no unlimited right to wage war for its own security, only a right to defend itself against unjust attack or to rectify some other injury to itself. Like Grotius, Pufendorf relies on customary practice as well as natural law in discussing the moral limits that govern the conduct of war. He observes, for example, that international custom permits states at war to use all measures necessary for victory, though civilized nations may choose to forego such measures as the use of poison or the assassination of rulers. And although immovable property seized in war belongs to the conquering sovereign, custom entitles soldiers to keep movable property they have taken as booty. Pufendorf is reluctant to ascribe such principles, which reflect the state of civilized opinion regarding the conduct of war, to natural law.

From *ius gentium* to *ius inter gentes*

Much attention has been given since the middle of the nineteenth century to the origins of international law. While some have claimed the title of founder of international law for Grotius, others bestow the honor on Gentili, Vitoria, or Suárez (A. Nussbaum, 1954: 296–306; Haggenmacher, 1990). The dispute, fueled in part by national and religious rivalries, presupposes a naive conception of history. Modern international law is a complex practice, and the concept that corresponds to this practice was only slowly clarified. The main elements of this modern concept of international law – that there exists a body of rules specifically regulating the relations of independent territorial states, and that these rules have their source not in natural reason but in the customs and agreements of states – were articulated by theorists using a vocabulary ill-suited for the task.

The Romans distinguished *ius* (customary law) from *lex* (enacted law). Every *lex*, being enacted at a particular time, is law only after it has been enacted. And, because it has been enacted, it can be amended or repealed. Civil law, which governs relations between Roman citizens, is *lex* but the law governing relations between citizens and foreigners – that is, aliens living under Roman authority – was not the product of legislation; rather, it was originally case law emerging from the decisions of administrators and judges handling disputes between the two classes of persons. It is, therefore, a body of common or customary law. The Romans called this customary law governing relations between members of different *gentes* or peoples *ius gentium*. In late medieval and early modern Europe, *ius gentium* meant the customary law common to all or most civil societies. It is positive law in the sense of being a social practice, not in being *lex* declared by a sovereign (Haakonssen, 1996: 18–19).

In the legal and political theory of early modern Europe, *ius gentium* occupies an ambiguous place between natural and human law. Theorists devoted much thought to untangling the relationship between *ius gentium* and other kinds of law. Some, like Grotius, identified *ius gentium* with natural law on the grounds that any practice acknowledged as lawful among many peoples must be inherently reasonable. But even those who rejected this identification regarded *ius gentium* as closer to natural law than to the enactments of particular sovereigns. Yet because *ius gentium* is composed of generally recognized principles, it could be characterized as the "civil law" of a single human community. As Vitoria puts it:

The law of nations (*ius gentium*) does not have the force merely of pacts or agreements between men, but has the validity of a positive enactment (*lex*). The whole world, which is in a sense a commonwealth, has the power to enact laws which are just and convenient to all men; and these make up the law of nations. (Vitoria, 1991: 40)

The idea of enactment here is of course metaphorical. Bodin, too, is drawn toward identifying *ius gentium* as a kind of *lex* – he calls it *lex omnium gentium communis*, the law common to all peoples. For neither author, however, does *ius gentium* carry any suggestion of international law as an autonomous system of rules, based on treaties and customary state practice, binding independent territorial states in their relations with one another.

But as the selections from Grotius and Hobbes illustrate, as soon as sovereigns were seen as persons outside civil society – persons governed by natural law – theorists could begin to connect natural law with the practices governing sovereigns in exchanging ambassadors, regulating trade, making treaties and alliances, and waging war. For some, these practices were essentially a reflection of natural law applied to the relations of states. For others, they constituted a body of human law which, though similar in content to

natural law, was based on custom, not on reason. The existence of such practices also suggested a distinction between two kinds of *ius gentium*, one comprising norms common to the domestic laws of different states, the other
comprising norms observed by sovereigns in their dealings with one another –
a system of law springing from and regulating relations between states. In the
early modern period there is much confusion because a single expression,
the law of nations (*ius gentium*) is used for both kinds of law. International
law proper, sometimes identified by the label *ius inter gentes* ("law between
nations"), only gradually separated itself from the law of nations understood
as principles common to different systems of civil law.

Among the first to discuss the two meanings of *ius gentium* was the Spanish
Jesuit theologian Francisco Suárez. Writing in 1612, Suárez distinguishes "laws
which individual states or kingdoms observe within their own borders, but
which is called *ius gentium* because the said laws are similar and are commonly
accepted" from "the law which all the various peoples and nations ought to
observe in their relations with one another" (1944: 447). Only the latter is *ius
gentium* proper, Suárez argues; the former is really part of the civil law of each
state. Suárez continues, however, to presuppose a community of mankind:
each state, though a "perfect" (independent) community, is also a member
of the universal society comprising humanity as a whole. But this universal
society is not a society of states. It is an undifferentiated society of persons,
some of whom happen to be sovereigns.

Hobbes, writing several decades after Suárez, is perhaps the first to
restrict the expression *ius gentium* or "law of nations" to the law between
sovereigns: just as civil law is the law of nature applied to the citizens of a
commonwealth, the law of nations is natural law applied to sovereigns, who
are not members of any commonwealth, and for whom it serves not as binding law but as prudential good sense. And in a 1650 treatise, Richard Zouche,
an English lawyer, distinguishes "the law which is observed between princes
or peoples of different nations" from the civil laws common to all or most
nations (1650/1911: 1). Zouche calls the former *ius inter gentes* and identifies it
with the *ius feciale*, the law of the early Roman "college of fecials" or priests
whose office was to ascertain the lawfulness of Rome's wars and treaties.
Seventeenth-century writers often turned to the *ius feciale* to make sense of the
emerging practice of international law. Leibniz, for example, labels natural
law applied to the relations of sovereign states *iuris feciales inter gentes* (1988: 175).
Because it is confined to this body of law and includes a discussion of treaties,
Zouche's treatise is recognizably a work on international law as we now understand that subject.

The late seventeenth-century understanding of the law of nations as
a distinct body of international law is represented here by some passages
from "On the Law of Nations" (1676) by Samuel Rachel (1628–91). For Rachel,

who was a contemporary and critic of Pufendorf, the law of nations "properly so called" consists of positive laws springing not from the will of a superior but from the joint will of sovereigns as expressed in agreements between them. This international law, which we can conceive as being jointly enacted by the participating states, must be distinguished from the civil laws common to various states, on the one hand, and from natural law, on the other. But international law, which rests on agreement and good faith, is not enforced by any superior state. To remedy this implicit defect, Rachel proposes that states agree to establish a new "college of fecials" to decide disputes under international law (p. 355). For Rachel, the idea of international law implies the need for a world court.

During the course of the eighteenth century, legal theorists gradually distinguished international law from domestic public law, regarding it as an autonomous system rooted in international practice. A steadily increasing volume of treaties, the availability of records concerning state practice, and the increasing professionalization of law contributed to this development by inviting new ways of establishing international legal rules.

In his *The Law of Nations Treated According to a Scientific Method* (1748), Christian von Wolff (1679–1754), like Pufendorf a prominent figure in the German Enlightenment, defines the law of nations as "the *science* of that law which nations or peoples use in their relations with each other" (p. 356). This definition reveals an academic's rather than a practitioner's conception of the subject. Wolff, who had no legal training or experience, was interested in international law solely as a subject for philosophical analysis.

For Wolff, international law begins with natural law: because nations are "individual free persons living in a state of nature" (p. 356), the law of nations is natural law applied to nations. Wolff calls this law the "necessary law of nations" (p. 358) because the obligations it prescribes are unchanging and unchangeable: this kind of international law belongs to natural law (morality), and we can't change morality. But unlike Grotius, Pufendorf, and other natural law theorists, Wolff treats the principles of natural law that apply to states as a separate branch of natural law. Because states have qualities that distinguish them from individual persons, the natural law of nations is not merely an application of the natural law of individuals (Knight, 1925: 200).

Wolff develops a philosophical foundation for international law, so understood, in his theory of the universal or supreme state (*civitas maxima*). We must imagine that states comprise a society governed by natural law, and that this natural society of states constitutes a universal state. All states are united in this universal state and subject to its laws. In other words, all states, considered collectively, must be imagined to hold a kind of sovereignty over each state considered individually. And because its decisions are made by the agreement of its free and equal members, the "government" of the universal state is democratic. Here, as in other democracies, the majority rules: this is why customary international law is binding on all, even if some do not comply with it. But because the member states cannot assemble, we must deduce their agreement from what is reasonable. Finally, we must imagine a fictitious ruler of the universal state who wills the law of nations on the basis of right reason. The natural law of nations may be said to be "voluntary" in reflecting the will of an imagined world sovereign who represents the presumed rational will of the member states. But this voluntary law of nations, which rests on the presumed will and consent of nations, must be distinguished from the law that springs from the actual will and consent of nations and is embodied in the positive law of nations.

It is easy to scoff at this pyramid of definitions and fictions, but Wolff is in fact exploring, philosophically, the concept of international law as a body of rules governing the relations of independent states. A system of rules implies authoritative procedures for declaring and interpreting rules. If we cannot identify a real sovereign who performs these functions, we can try to grasp the logic of the system by attributing their performance to a postulated notional sovereign. This would seem to call for an organized union of states with institutions for securing the rule of law. Wolff does not, however, understand the *civitas maxima* as a proposal for such a union: it is, for him, a pure philosophical construct reflecting the internal logic of international law.

When Emmerich de Vattel (1714–67) decided to popularize Wolff's system, he dismissed Wolff's metaphysics and wrote a book designed to be useful to statesmen and diplomats. Trained in philosophy, Vattel pursued a brief and undistinguished diplomatic career in the service of several minor sovereigns. His *Law of Nations or the Principles of Natural Law Applied to the Conduct and Affairs of Nations and Sovereigns*, which appeared in dozens of editions in various languages, was widely used for more than a century after its publication in 1758. The American founders owed their knowledge of international law in part to Vattel.

As its title implies, Vattel's book treats international law as a branch of natural law. And it is concerned with internal as well as foreign affairs. In both respects, the book resembles the works of Grotius and Pufendorf more than it does a modern textbook of international law. Vattel's modernity, like that of Grotius, has been exaggerated by those seeking the origins of international law (Hurrell, 1996). But unlike his predecessors, Vattel pays attention to contemporary diplomatic practice and understands international law as an autonomous body of law.

The passages in which Vattel discusses the equality of states and the laws of war indicate the gulf that separates eighteenth-century international law from the laws of medieval Christendom. States have equal rights under international law, no matter how weak or powerful they may be: "A dwarf is as much a man as a giant is; a small republic is no less a sovereign state than the most powerful kingdom" (Vattel, 1916: 7). This equality provides the justification for the balance of power, which according to Vattel conditionally justifies preventive war against a would-be hegemonic state. And it means that the laws governing the conduct of war apply equally to all, regardless of whose cause is just: what is permitted to one side as a lawful means of war is also permitted to the other belligerents. The rationale for this equality is that it brings war within the bounds of law: if war cannot be forbidden, it should at least be regulated.

Vattel justifies retaining a link with natural law on the grounds that if consent were the only source of international law we could not condemn evil practices like the slave trade. Though much of international law rests on the consent of states expressed in treaties and customary practice, Vattel argues that this law is binding because it is consistent with natural law. It is the natural law principle *pacta sunt servanda* ("agreements must be honored"), for example, that requires states to keep their promises. But his is the last mainstream work in which international law is identified with natural law. From the late eighteenth century onwards, international law is usually understood to be positive, not natural law. It is positive not in being enacted by a superior but in being jointly willed by states, who bind themselves explicitly through treaties or implicitly through customary international law.

FURTHER READING

For Grotius, beginners are well served by Bull, Kingsbury, and Roberts (1990), more advanced students by Haggenmacher (1983) and Onuma (1993). For Hobbes, beginners might start with Tuck (1989) and then read the speculative essays on the international implications of Hobbes' political thought in Airaksinen and Bertman (1989). Schiffer (1954), Linklater (1990), and Boucher (1998) each devote a chapter to Pufendorf, on whom the standard work by Krieger (1965) may also be consulted. The standard history of international law, superficial, dated, but nevertheless useful in the absence of competitors, is A. Nussbaum (1954). The history of international law is considered from the standpoint of political theory by Nardin (1983).

SOURCES

Hugo Grotius, from *The Law of War and Peace* (1625), trans. Francis W. Kelsey (Oxford: Clarendon Press, 1925), Prolegomena, sections 1, 5–13, 15–23, 25, 28–9, 39–40, 48, 50, and Book 1, ch. 2, sections 1, 2, 4 (part), 5 (part), and 6 (part), pp. 1, 10–18, 20, 23–4, 26–7, 51–4. Author's and translator's notes omitted.

Thomas Hobbes, from *Leviathan* (1651), ed. Richard Tuck (Cambridge: Cambridge University Press, 1996), chs.13 and 14 (part), pp.86–92. Hobbes' spelling has been modernized and his marginal headings omitted.

Samuel Pufendorf, from *On the Duties of Man and Citizen* (1673), ed. James Tully (Cambridge: Cambridge University Press, 1991), Book 2, chs. 1 and 16, pp. 115–19 and 168–72.

Samuel Rachel, from "On the Law of Nations" (1676), in *Dissertations on the Law of Nature and Nations*, trans. John Pawley Bate (Washington, DC: Carnegie Institution, 1916), sections 1–3 (part), 11–12, 84–91, and 119, pp. 157–8, 164–5, 204–8, and 223.

Christian von Wolff, from *The Law of Nations Treated According to a Scientific Method* (1748), trans. Joseph H. Drake (Oxford: Clarendon Press, 1934), Prolegomena, pp. 9–19. The translator's notes have been omitted.

Emmerich de Vattel, from *The Law of Nations or Principles of Natural Law* (1758), trans. Charles G. Fenwick (Washington, DC: Carnegie Institution, 1916), Book 2, ch. 3, and Book 3, ch. 12, pp. 126–9 and 304–6. The author's notes, cross-references, and marginal headings have been omitted.

HUGO GROTIUS

HUGO GROTIUS (1583–1645), Dutch humanist, theologian, and jurist. Grotius achieved fame first as a poet and later for his efforts to reconcile Protestant and Catholic Christianity. He is known to students of international relations for his defense of the principle of freedom of the seas and, even more, as the author of *The Law of War and Peace* (1625), which he wrote while living as an exile in France. Despite its baroque style and almost complete neglect of contemporary international practice, Grotius' famous work continues to be read as a statement of the view that the jurisdiction of morality extends even to war (the law of war, for Grotius, is natural, not positive, law). Although the habit of regarding Grotius as the founder of international law both ignores the contributions of his predecessors and reads back into his work ideas that belong to a later period, his writings contain, in embryo, a powerful theory of international justice.

From *The Law of War and Peace*

Prolegomena

1 . The municipal law of Rome and of other states has been treated by many, who have undertaken to elucidate it by means of commentaries or to reduce it to a convenient digest. That body of law, however, which is concerned with the mutual relations among states or rulers of states, whether derived from nature, or established by divine ordinances, or having its origin in custom and tacit agreement, few have touched upon. Up to the present time no one has treated it in a comprehensive and systematic manner; yet the welfare of mankind demands that this task be accomplished.

...

5 . Since our discussion concerning law will have been undertaken in vain if there is no law, in order to open the way for a favourable reception of our work and at the same time to fortify it against attacks, this very serious error must be briefly refuted. In order that we may not be obliged to deal with a crowd of opponents, let us assign to them a pleader. And whom should we choose in preference to Carneades? For he had attained to so perfect a mastery of the peculiar tenet of his Academy that he was able to devote the

power of his eloquence to the service of falsehood not less readily than to that of truth.

Carneades, then, having undertaken to hold a brief against justice, in particular against that phase of justice with which we are concerned, was able to muster no argument stronger than this, that, for reasons of expediency, men imposed upon themselves laws, which vary according to customs, and among the same peoples often undergo changes as times change; moreover that there is no law of nature, because all creatures, men as well as animals, are impelled by nature toward ends advantageous to themselves; that, consequently, there is no justice, or, if such there be, it is supreme folly, since one does violence to his own interests if he consults the advantage of others.

6 . What the philosopher here says, and the poet reaffirms in verse,

And just from unjust Nature cannot know,

must not for one moment be admitted. Man is, to be sure, an animal, but an animal of a superior kind, much farther removed from all other animals than the different kinds of animals are from one another; evidence on this point may be found in the many traits peculiar to the human species. But among the traits characteristic of man is an impelling desire for society, that is, for the social life – not of any and every sort, but peaceful, and organized according to the measure of his intelligence, with those who are of his own kind; this social trend the Stoics called 'sociableness'. Stated as a universal truth, therefore, the assertion that every animal is impelled by nature to seek only its own good cannot be conceded.

7 . Some of the other animals, in fact, do in a way restrain the appetency for that which is good for themselves alone, to the advantage, now of their offspring, now of other animals of the same species. This aspect of their behaviour has its origin, we believe, in some extrinsic intelligent principle, because with regard to other actions, which involve no more difficulty than those referred to, a like degree of intelligence is not manifest in them. The same thing must be said of children. In children, even before their training has begun, some disposition to do good to others appears, as Plutarch sagely observed; thus sympathy for others comes out spontaneously at that age. The mature man in fact has knowledge which prompts him to similar actions under similar conditions, together with an impelling desire for society, for the gratification of which he alone among animals possesses a special instrument, speech. He has also been endowed with the faculty of knowing and of acting in accordance with general principles. Whatever accords with that faculty is not common to all animals, but peculiar to the nature of man.

8 . This maintenance of the social order, which we have roughly sketched, and which is consonant with human intelligence, is the source of law properly so called. To this sphere of law belong the abstaining from that which is

another's, the restoration to another of anything of his which we may have, together with any gain which we may have received from it; the obligation to fulfil promises, the making good of a loss incurred through our fault, and the inflicting of penalties upon men according to their deserts.

9 . From this signification of the word law there has flowed another and more extended meaning. Since over other animals man has the advantage of possessing not only a strong bent towards social life, of which we have spoken, but also a power of discrimination which enables him to decide what things are agreeable or harmful (as to both things present and things to come), and what can lead to either alternative: in such things it is meet for the nature of man, within the limitations of human intelligence, to follow the direction of a well-tempered judgement, being neither led astray by fear or the allurement of immediate pleasure, nor carried away by rash impulse. Whatever is clearly at variance with such judgement is understood to be contrary also to the law of nature, that is, to the nature of man.

10 . To this exercise of judgement belongs moreover the rational allotment to each man, or to each social group, of those things which are properly theirs, in such a way as to give the preference now to him who is more wise over the less wise, now to a kinsman rather than to a stranger, now to a poor man rather than to a man of means, as the conduct of each or the nature of the thing suggests. Long ago the view came to be held by many, that this discriminating allotment is a part of law, properly and strictly so called: nevertheless law, properly defined, has a far different nature, because its essence lies in leaving to another that which belongs to him, or in fulfilling our obligations to him.

11 . What we have been saying would have a degree of validity even if we should concede that which cannot be conceded without the utmost wickedness, that there is no God, or that the affairs of men are of no concern to Him. The very opposite of this view has been implanted in us partly by reason, partly by unbroken tradition, and confirmed by many proofs as well as by miracles attested by all ages. Hence it follows that we must without exception render obedience to God as our Creator, to Whom we owe all that we are and have; especially since, in manifold ways, He has shown Himself supremely good and supremely powerful, so that to those who obey Him He is able to give supremely great rewards, even rewards that are eternal, since He Himself is eternal. We ought, moreover, to believe that He has willed to give rewards, and all the more should we cherish such a belief if He has so promised in plain words; that He has done this, we Christians believe, convinced by the indubitable assurance of testimonies.

12 . Herein, then, is another source of law besides the source in nature, that is, the free will of God, to which beyond all cavil our reason tells us we must render obedience. But the law of nature of which we have spoken, comprising

alike that which relates to the social life of man and that which is so called in a larger sense, proceeding as it does from the essential traits implanted in man, can nevertheless rightly be attributed to God, because of His having willed that such traits exist in us. In this sense, too, Chrysippus and the Stoics used to say that the origin of law should be sought in no other source than Jupiter himself; and from the name Jupiter the Latin word for law (*ius*) was probably derived.

13 . There is an additional consideration in that, by means of the laws which He has given, God has made those fundamental traits more manifest, even to those who possess feebler reasoning powers; and He has forbidden us to yield to impulses drawing us in opposite directions – affecting now our own interest, now the interest of others – in an effort to control more effectively our more violent impulses and to restrain them within proper limits.

...

15 . Again, since it is a rule of the law of nature to abide by pacts (for it was necessary that among men there be some method of obligating themselves one to another, and no other natural method can be imagined), out of this source the bodies of municipal law have arisen. For those who had associated themselves with some group, or had subjected themselves to a man or to men, had either expressly promised, or from the nature of the transaction must be understood impliedly to have promised, that they would conform to that which should have been determined, in the one case by the majority, in the other by those upon whom authority had been conferred.

16 . What is said, therefore, in accordance with the view not only of Carneades but also of others, that

> Expediency is, as it were, the mother
> Of what is just and fair,

is not true, if we wish to speak accurately. For the very nature of man, which even if we had no lack of anything would lead us into the mutual relations of society, is the mother of the law of nature. But the mother of municipal law is that obligation which arises from mutual consent; and since this obligation derives its force from the law of nature, nature may be considered, so to say, the great-grandmother of municipal law.

The law of nature nevertheless has the reinforcement of expediency; for the Author of nature willed that as individuals we should be weak, and should lack many things needed in order to live properly, to the end that we might be the more constrained to cultivate the social life. But expediency afforded an opportunity also for municipal law, since that kind of association of which we have spoken, and subjection to authority, have their roots in expediency. From this it follows that those who prescribe laws for others in so doing are accustomed to have, or ought to have, some advantage in view.

17 . But just as the laws of each state have in view the advantage of that state, so by mutual consent it has become possible that certain laws should originate as between all states, or a great many states; and it is apparent that the laws thus originating had in view the advantage, not of particular states, but of the great society of states. And this is what is called the law of nations, whenever we distinguish that term from the law of nature.

This division of law Carneades passed over altogether. For he divided all law into the law of nature and the law of particular countries. Nevertheless if undertaking to treat of the body of law which is maintained between states – for he added a statement in regard to war and things acquired by means of war – he would surely have been obliged to make mention of this law.

18 . Wrongly, moreover, does Carneades ridicule justice as folly. For since, by his own admission, the national who in his own country obeys its laws is not foolish, even though, out of regard for that law, he may be obliged to forgo certain things advantageous for himself, so that nation is not foolish which does not press its own advantage to the point of disregarding the laws common to nations. The reason in either case is the same. For just as the national, who violates the law of his country in order to obtain an immediate advantage, breaks down that by which the advantages of himself and his posterity are for all future time assured, so the state which transgresses the laws of nature and of nations cuts away also the bulwarks which safeguard its own future peace. Even if no advantage were to be contemplated from the keeping of the law, it would be a mark of wisdom, not of folly, to allow ourselves to be drawn towards that to which we feel that our nature leads.

19 . Wherefore, in general, it is by no means true that

> You must confess that laws were framed
> From fear of the unjust,

a thought which in Plato some one explains thus, that laws were invented from fear of receiving injury, and that men are constrained by a kind of force to cultivate justice. For that relates only to the institutions and laws which have been devised to facilitate the enforcement of right; as when many persons in themselves weak, in order that they might not be overwhelmed by the more powerful, leagued themselves together to establish tribunals and by combined force to maintain these, that as a united whole they might prevail against those with whom as individuals they could not cope.

And in this sense we may readily admit also the truth of the saying that right is that which is acceptable to the stronger; so that we may understand that law fails of its outward effect unless it has a sanction behind it. In this way Solon accomplished very great results, as he himself used to declare,

> By joining force and law together,
> Under a like bond.

20 . Nevertheless law, even though without a sanction, is not entirely void of effect. For justice brings peace of conscience, while injustice causes torments and anguish, such as Plato describes, in the breast of tyrants. Justice is approved, and injustice condemned, by the common agreement of good men. But, most important of all; in God injustice finds an enemy, justice a protector. He reserves His judgements for the life after this, yet in such a way that He often causes their effects to become manifest even in this life, as history teaches by numerous examples.

21 . Many hold, in fact, that the standard of justice which they insist upon in the case of individuals within the state is inapplicable to a nation or the ruler of a nation. The reason for the error lies in this, first of all, that in respect to law they have in view nothing except the advantage which accrues from it, such advantage being apparent in the case of citizens who, taken singly, are powerless to protect themselves. But great states, since they seem to contain in themselves all things required for the adequate protection of life, seem not to have need of that virtue which looks toward the outside, and is called justice.

22 . But, not to repeat what I have said, that law is not founded on expediency alone, there is no state so powerful that it may not some time need the help of others outside itself, either for purposes of trade, or even to ward off the forces of many foreign nations united against it. In consequence we see that even the most powerful peoples and sovereigns seek alliances, which are quite devoid of significance according to the point of view of those who confine law within the boundaries of states. Most true is the saying, that all things are uncertain the moment men depart from law.

23 . If no association of men can be maintained without law, as Aristotle showed by his remarkable illustration drawn from brigands, surely also that association which binds together the human race, or binds many nations together, has need of law; this was perceived by him who said that shameful deeds ought not to be committed even for the sake of one's country. Aristotle takes sharply to task those who, while unwilling to allow any one to exercise authority over themselves except in accordance with law, yet are quite indifferent as to whether foreigners are treated according to law or not.

···

25 . Least of all should that be admitted which some people imagine, that in war all laws are in abeyance. On the contrary war ought not to be undertaken except for the enforcement of rights; when once undertaken, it should be carried on only within the bounds of law and good faith. Demosthenes well said that war is directed against those who cannot be held in check by judicial

processes. For judgements are efficacious against those who feel that they are too weak to resist; against those who are equally strong, or think that they are, wars are undertaken. But in order that wars may be justified, they must be carried on with not less scrupulousness than judicial processes are wont to be.

...

28 . Fully convinced, by the considerations which I have advanced, that there is a common law among nations, which is valid alike for war and in war, I have had many and weighty reasons for undertaking to write upon this subject. Throughout the Christian world I observed a lack of restraint in relation to war, such as even barbarous races should be ashamed of; I observed that men rush to arms for slight causes, or no cause at all, and that when arms have once been taken up there is no longer any respect for law, divine or human; it is as if, in accordance with a general decree, frenzy had openly been let loose for the committing of all crimes.

29 . Confronted with such utter ruthlessness many men, who are the very furthest from being bad men, have come to the point of forbidding all use of arms to the Christian, whose rule of conduct above everything else comprises the duty of loving all men. To this opinion sometimes John Ferus and my fellow-countryman Erasmus seem to incline, men who have the utmost devotion to peace in both Church and State; but their purpose, as I take it, is, when things have gone in one direction, to force them in the opposite direction, as we are accustomed to do, that they may come back to a true middle ground. But the very effort of pressing too hard in the opposite direction is often so far from being helpful that it does harm, because in such arguments the detection of what is extreme is easy, and results in weakening the influence of other statements which are well within the bounds of truth. For both extremes therefore a remedy must be found, that men may not believe either that nothing is allowable, or that everything is.

...

39 . ... I have made it my concern to refer the proofs of things touching the law of nature to certain fundamental conceptions which are beyond question, so that no one can deny them without doing violence to himself. For the principles of that law, if only you pay strict heed to them, are in themselves manifest and clear, almost as evident as are those things which we perceive by the external senses; and the senses do not err if the organs of perception are properly formed and if the other conditions requisite to perception are present. Thus in his *Phoenician Maidens* Euripides represents Polynices, whose cause he makes out to have been manifestly just, as speaking thus:

> Mother, these words, that I have uttered, are not
> Inwrapped with indirection, but, firmly based

> On rules of justice and of good, are plain
> Alike to simple and to wise.

The poet adds immediately a judgement of the chorus, made up of women, and barbarian women at that, approving these words.

40. In order to prove the existence of this law of nature, I have, furthermore, availed myself of the testimony of philosophers, historians, poets, finally also of orators. Not that confidence is to be reposed in them without discrimination; for they were accustomed to serve the interests of their sect, their subject, or their cause. But when many at different times, and in different places, affirm the same thing as certain, that ought to be referred to a universal cause; and this cause, in the lines of inquiry which we are following, must be either a correct conclusion drawn from the principles of nature, or common consent. The former points to the law of nature; the latter, to the law of nations.

The distinction between these kinds of law is not to be drawn from the testimonies themselves (for writers everywhere confuse the terms law of nature and law of nations), but from the character of the matter. For whatever cannot be deduced from certain principles by a sure process of reasoning, and yet is clearly observed everywhere, must have its origin in the free will of man.

...

48. I frequently appeal to the authority of the books which men inspired by God have either written or approved, nevertheless with a distinction between the Old Testament and the New. There are some who urge that the Old Testament sets forth the law of nature. Without doubt they are in error, for many of its rules come from the free will of God. And yet this is never in conflict with the true law of nature; and up to this point the Old Testament can be used as a source of the law of nature, provided we carefully distinguish between the law of God, which God sometimes executes through men, and the law of men in their relations with one another.

This error we have, so far as possible, avoided, and also another opposed to it, which supposes that after the coming of the New Testament the Old Testament in this respect was no longer of use. We believe the contrary, partly for the reasons which we have already given, partly because the character of the New Testament is such that in its teachings respecting the moral virtues it enjoins the same as the Old Testament or even enjoins greater precepts. In this way we see that the early Christian writers used the witnesses of the Old Testament.

...

50. The New Testament I use in order to explain – and this cannot be learned from any other source – what is permissible to Christians. This, however –

contrary to the practice of most men – I have distinguished from the law of nature, considering it as certain that in that most holy law a greater degree of moral perfection is enjoined upon us than the law of nature, alone and by itself, would require. And nevertheless I have not omitted to note the things that are recommended to us rather than enjoined, that we may know that, while the turning aside from what has been enjoined is wrong and involves the risk of punishment, a striving for the highest excellence implies a noble purpose and will not fail of its reward.

…

Book 1 chapter 2

Whether it is ever lawful to wage war

I. THAT WAR IS NOT IN CONFLICT WITH THE LAW OF NATURE IS PROVED BY SEVERAL CONSIDERATIONS

1 . Having seen what the sources of law are, let us come to the first and most general question, which is this: whether any war is lawful, or whether it is ever permissible to war. This question, as also the others which will follow, must first be taken up from the point of view of the law of nature.

Marcus Tullius Cicero, both in the third book of his treatise *On Ends* and in other places, following Stoic writings learnedly argues that there are certain first principles of nature – 'first according to nature', as the Greeks phrased it – and certain other principles which are later manifest but which are to have the preference over those first principles. He calls first principles of nature those in accordance with which every animal from the moment of its birth has regard for itself and is impelled to preserve itself, to have zealous consideration for its own condition and for those things which tend to preserve it, and also shrinks from destruction and things which appear likely to cause destruction. Hence also it happens, he says, that there is no one who, if the choice were presented to him, would not prefer to have all the parts of his body in proper order and whole rather than dwarfed or deformed; and that it is one's first duty to keep oneself in the condition which nature gave to him, then to hold to those things which are in conformity with nature and reject those things that are contrary thereto.

2 . But after these things have received due consideration (Cicero continues), there follows a notion of the conformity of things with reason, which is superior to the body. Now this conformity, in which moral goodness becomes the paramount object, ought to be accounted of higher import than the things to which alone instinct first directed itself, because the first principles of nature commend us to right reason, and right reason ought to be more dear

to us than those things through whose instrumentality we have been brought
to it.

Since this is true and without other demonstration would easily receive
the assent of all who are endowed with sound judgement, it follows that in
investigating the law of nature it is necessary first to see what is consistent
with those fundamental principles of nature, and then to come to that which,
though of later origin, is nevertheless more worthy – that which ought not
only to be grasped, if it appear, but to be sought out by every effort.

...

4 . In the first principles of nature there is nothing which is opposed to
war; rather, all points are in its favour. The end and aim of war being the
preservation of life and limb, and the keeping or acquiring of things useful to
life, war is in perfect accord with those first principles of nature. If in order
to achieve these ends it is necessary to use force, no inconsistency with the
first principles of nature is involved, since nature has given to each animal
strength sufficient for self-defence and self-assistance.

...

5 . Right reason, moreover, and the nature of society, which must be studied
in the second place and are of even greater importance, do not prohibit all
use of force, but only that use of force which is in conflict with society, that
is which attempts to take away the rights of another. For society has in view
this object, that through community of resource and effort each individual
be safeguarded in the possession of what belongs to him.

...

6 . It is not, then, contrary to the nature of society to look out for oneself and
advance one's own interests, provided the rights of others are not infringed;
and consequently the use of force which does not violate the rights of others
is not unjust.

THOMAS HOBBES

THOMAS HOBBES (1588–1679), English philosopher and author of *Leviathan* (1651), a work acknowledged to be a masterpiece of political theorizing even by those who abominate its conclusions. Central to its argument is a metaphor, the state of nature, to which Hobbes contrasts the civil state. Unlike the state of nature, the civil state is a condition in which human beings are associated on the basis of a common body of laws. Law, Hobbes argued, can only exist where there are agreed procedures for enacting rules and resolving disputes about their proper interpretation. Sovereigns, being outside civil society, must be regarded as being in a state of nature with respect to one another. And the state of nature is a state of war. It is not easy to refute this Skepticism regarding the claims of international law, and for that reason Hobbes' writings continue to provoke thought about the character and conditions of justice in international relations.

From *Leviathan*

Chapter 13

Of the natural condition of mankind, as concerning their felicity, and misery

Nature has made men so equal, in the faculties of body, and mind; as that though there be found one man sometimes manifestly stronger in body, or of quicker mind then another; yet when all is reckoned together, the difference between man, and man, is not so considerable, as that one man can thereupon claim to himself any benefit, to which another may not pretend, as well as he. For as to the strength of body, the weakest has strength enough to kill the strongest, either by secret machination, or by confederacy with others, that are in the same danger with himself.

And as to the faculties of the mind, (setting aside the arts grounded upon words, and especially that skill of proceeding upon general, and infallible rules, called science; which very few have, and but in few things; as being not a native faculty, born with us; nor attained, (as prudence,) while we look after somewhat else,) I find yet a greater equality amongst men, than that of strength. For prudence, is but experience; which equal time, equally bestows on all men, in those things they equally apply themselves unto. That which may perhaps make such equality incredible, is but a vain conceit of one's own wisdom, which almost all men think they have in a greater degree, than the vulgar; that is, than all men but themselves, and a few others, whom by fame, or for concurring with themselves, they approve. For such is the nature of men, that howsoever they may acknowledge many others to be more witty, or more eloquent, or more learned; yet they will hardly believe there be many so wise as themselves: for they see their own wit at hand, and other men's at a distance. But this proves rather that men are in that point equal, than unequal. For there is not ordinarily a greater sign of the equal distribution of any thing, than that every man is contented with his share.

From this equality of ability, arises equality of hope in the attaining of our ends. And therefore if any two men desire the same thing, which nevertheless they cannot both enjoy, they become enemies; and in the way to their end, (which is principally their own conservation, and sometimes their delectation only,) endeavor to destroy, or subdue one an other. And from hence it comes to pass, that where an invader has no more to fear, than another man's single power; if one plant, sow, build, or possess a convenient seat, others may probably be expected to come prepared with forces united, to dispossess, and deprive him, not only of the fruit of his labour, but also of his life, or liberty. And the invader again is in the like danger of another.

And from this diffidence of one another, there is no way for any man to secure himself, so reasonable, as anticipation; that is, by force, or wiles, to master the persons of all men he can, so long, till he see no other power great enough to endanger him: And this is no more than his own conservation requires, and is generally allowed. Also because there be some, that taking pleasure in contemplating their own power in the acts of conquest, which they pursue farther than their security requires; if others, that otherwise would be glad to be at ease within modest bounds, should not by invasion increase their power, they would not be able, long time, by standing only on their defence, to subsist. And by consequence, such augmentation of dominion over men, being necessary to a man's conservation, it ought to be allowed him.

Again, men have no pleasure, (but on the contrary a great deal of grief) in keeping company, where there is no power able to overawe them all. For every man looks that his companion should value him, at the same rate he sets upon himself: And upon all signs of contempt, or undervaluing, naturally endeavours, as far as he dares (which among them that have no common power to keep them in quiet, is far enough to make them destroy each other,) to extort a greater value from his condemners, by damage; and from others, by the example.

So that in the nature of man, we find three principal causes of quarrel. First, competition; secondly, diffidence; thirdly, glory.

The first, makes men invade for gain; the second, for safety; and the third, for reputation. The first use violence, to make themselves masters of other men's persons, wives, children, and cattle; the second, to defend them; the third, for trifles, as a word, a smile, a different opinion, and any other sign of undervalue, either direct in their persons, or by reflection in their kindred, their kriends, their nation, their profession, or their name.

Hereby it is manifest, that during the time men live without a common power to keep them all in awe, they are in that condition which is called war; and such a war, as is of every man, against every man. For WAR, consists not in battle only, or the act of fighting; but in a tract of time, wherein the will to contend by battle is sufficiently known: and therefore the notion of *time*, is to be considered in the nature of war; as it is in the nature of weather. For as the nature of foul weather, lies not in a shower or two of rain; but in an inclination thereto of many days together: So the nature of war, consists not in actual fighting; but in the known disposition thereto, during all the time there is no assurance to the contrary. All other time is PEACE.

Whatsoever therefore is consequent to a time of war, where every man is enemy to every man; the same is consequent to the time, wherein men live without other security, than what their own strength, and their own invention shall furnish them withal. In such condition, there is no place for industry; because the fruit thereof is uncertain: and consequently no culture of the earth; no navigation, nor use of the commodities that may be imported by sea; no commodious building; no instruments of moving, and removing such things as require much force; no knowledge of the face of the earth; no account of time; no arts; no letters; no society; and which is worst of all, continual fear, and danger of violent death; and the life of man, solitary, poor, nasty, brutish, and short.

It may seem strange to some man, that has not well weighed these things; that nature should thus dissociate, and render men apt to invade, and destroy one another: and he may therefore, not trusting to this inference, made from the passions, desire perhaps to have the same confirmed by experience. Let him therefore consider with himself, when taking a journey, he arms himselfe, and seeks to go well accompanied; when going to sleep, he locks his doors; when even in his house he locks his chests; and this when he knows there be laws, and public officers, armed, to revenge all injuries shall be done him; what opinion he has of his fellow subjects, when he rides armed; of his fellow citizens, when he locks his doors; and of his children, and servants, when he locks his chests. Does he not there as much accuse mankind by his actions, as I do by my words? But neither of us accuse man's nature in it. The desires, and other passions of man, are in themselves no sin. No more are the actions, that proceed from those passions, till they know a law that forbids them: which till laws be made they cannot know: nor can any law be made, till they have agreed upon the person that shall make it.

It may peradventure be thought, there was never such a time, nor condition of war as this; and I believe it was never generally so, over all the world: but there are many places, where they live so now. For the savage people in many places of *America*, except the government of small families, the concord whereof depends on natural lust, have no government at all; and live at this day in that brutish manner, as I said before. Howsoever, it may be perceived what manner of life there would be, where there were no common power to fear; by the manner of life, which men that have formerly lived under a peaceful government, use to degenerate into, in a civil war.

But though there had never been any time, wherein particular men were in a condition of war one against another; yet in all times, kings, and persons of sovereign authority, because of their independency, are in continual jealousies, and in the state and posture of gladiators; having their weapons pointing, and their eyes fixed on one another; that is, their forts, garrisons, and guns upon the frontiers of their kingdoms; and continual spies upon their neighbours, which is a posture of war. But because they uphold thereby, the industry of their subjects; there does not follow from it, that misery, which accompanies the liberty of particular men.

To this war of every man against every man, this also is consequent; that nothing can be unjust. The notions of right and wrong, justice and injustice have there no place. Where there is no common Power, there is no law: where no law, no injustice. Force, and fraud, are in war the two cardinal virtues. Justice, and injustice are none of the faculties neither of the body, nor mind. If they were, they might be in a man that were alone in the world, as well as his senses, and passions. They are qualities, that relate to men in society, not in solitude. It is consequent also to the same condition, that there be no propriety, no dominion, no *mine* and *thine* distinct; but only that to be every man's, that he can get; and for so long, as he can keep it. And thus much for the ill condition, which man by mere nature is actually placed in; though with a possibility to come out of it, consisting partly in the passions, partly in his reason.

The passions that incline men to peace, are fear of death; desire of such things as are necessary to commodious living; and a hope by their industry to obtain, them. And reason suggests convenient articles of peace, upon which men may be drawn to agreement. These articles, are they, which otherwise are called the Laws of Nature: whereof I shall speak more particularly, in the two following chapters. [*Only the first part of the first of these chapters is reprinted here.*]

Chapter 14

Of the first and second natural laws, and of contracts

The RIGHT OF NATURE, which Writers commonly call *jus naturale*, is the liberty each man hath, to use his own power, as he will himself, for the preservation of his own nature; that is to say, of his own life; and consequently, of doing any thing, which in his own judgement, and reason, he shall conceive to be the aptest means thereunto.

By LIBERTY, is understood, according to the proper signification of the word, the absence of external impediments: which impediments, may oft take away part of a man's power to do what he would; but cannot hinder him from using the power left him, according as his judgement, and reason shall dictate to him.

A LAW OF NATURE, *(lex naturalis)*, is a precept, or general rule, found out by reason, by which a man is forbidden to do, that, which is destructive of his life, or taketh away the means of preserving the same; and to omit, that, by which he thinks it may be best preserved. For though they that speak of this subject, use to confound *jus*, and *lex*, *right* and *law*; yet they ought to be distinguished; because RIGHT, consists in liberty to do, or to forbear; whereas LAW, determines, and binds to one of them: so that law, and right, differ as much, as obligation, and liberty; which in one and the same matter are inconsistent.

And because the condition of man, (as has been declared in the precedent chapter) is a condition of war of every one against every one; in which case every one is governed by his own reason; and there is nothing he can make use of, that may not be a help unto him, in preserving his life against his enemies; it follows, that in such a condition, every man has a right to every thing; even to one another's body. And therefore, as long as this natural right of every man to every thing endures, there can be no security to any man, (how strong or wise soever he be,) of living out the time, which nature ordinarily allows men to live. And consequently it is a precept, or general rule of reason, *That every man ought to endeavor peace, as far as he has hope of obtaining it; and when he cannot obtain it, that he may seek, and use, all helps, and advantages of war*. The first branch of which rule, contains the first, and fundamental law of nature; which is, *to seek peace, and follow it*. The second, the sum of the right of nature; which is, *By all means we can, to defend our selves*.

From this fundamental law of nature, by which men are commanded to endeavour peace, is derived this second law; *That a man be willing, when others are so too, as far forth, as for peace, and defence of himself he shall think it necessary, to lay down this right to all things; and be contented with so much liberty against other men, as he would allow other men against himself.* For as long as every man holds this right, of doing any thing he likes; so long are all men in the condition of war. But if other men will not lay down their right, as well as he; then there is no reason for any one, to divest himself of his: for that were to expose himself to prey, (which no man is bound to) rather than to dispose himself to peace. This is that law of the gospel; *Whatsoever you require that others should do to you, that do ye to them.* And that law of all men, *Quod tibi fieri non vis, alteri ne feceris* [What you would not have done unto you, do not do unto others].

SAMUEL PUFENDORF

S AMUEL PUFENDORF (1632–94), German philosopher and jurist, from 1662 professor of "the law of nature and of nations" at Heidelberg. Rejecting Hobbes' theory of natural law in favor of Grotius', Pufendorf built upon the latter a comprehensive system of private, public, and international law. He also wrote extensively on the public law of the German states, in the course of which he was forced to grapple with the distinction between a state and a system of states, making him a pioneer theorist of international relations as well as of international law. *On the Duties of Man and Citizen* (1673), a distillation of his system of natural law which he wrote for his students, is his most accessible work.

From *On the Duties of Man and Citizen*

Book 2

1. *On men's natural state*

1 . We must next inquire into the duties which fall to man to perform as a result of the different states in which we find him existing in social life. By 'state' (*status*) in general, we mean a condition in which men are understood to be set for the purpose of performing a certain class of actions. Each state also has its own distinctive laws (*jura*).

2 . Men's state is either natural or adventitious. Natural state may be considered, in the light of reason alone, in three ways: in relation to God the Creator; or in the relation of each individual man to himself; or in relation to other men.

3 . Considered from the first point of view, the natural state of man is the condition in which he was placed by his Creator with the intention that he be an animal excelling other animals. It follows from this state that man should recognize and worship his Creator, admire His works, and lead his life in a manner utterly different from that of the animals. Hence this state is in complete contrast with the life and condition of the animals.

4 . From the second point of view, we may consider the natural state of man, by an imaginative effort, as the condition man would have been in if he had been left to himself alone, without any support from other men, given the

condition of human nature as we now perceive it. It would have been, it seems, more miserable than that of any beast, if we reflect on the great weakness of man as he comes into this world, when he would straight away die without help from others, and on the primitive life he would lead if he had no other resources than he owes to his own strength and intelligence. One may put it more strongly: the fact that we have been able to grow out of such weakness, the fact that we now enjoy innumerable good things, the fact that we have cultivated our minds and bodies for our own and others' benefit – all this is the result of help from others. In this sense the natural state is opposed to life improved by human industry.

5 . From the third point of view, we consider the natural state of man in terms of the relationship which men are understood to have with each other on the basis of the simple common kinship which results from similarity of nature and is antecedent to any agreement or human action by which particular obligations of one to another have arisen. In this sense men are said to live in a natural state with each other when they have no common master, when no one is subject to another and when they have no experience either of benefit or of injury from each other. In this sense the natural state is opposed to the civil state.

6 . The character of the natural state, furthermore, may be considered either as it is represented by fiction or as it is in reality. It would be a fiction if we supposed that in the beginning there existed a multitude of men without any dependence on each other, as in the myth of the brothers of Cadmus,[1] or if we imagined that the whole human race was so widely scattered that every man governed himself separately, and the only bond between them was likeness of nature. But the natural state which actually exists shows each man joined with a number of other men in a particular association, though having nothing in common with all the rest except the quality of being human and having no duty to them on any other ground. This is the condition (*status*) that now exists between different states (*civitas*) and between citizens of different countries (*respublica*), and which formerly obtained between heads of separate families.

7 . Indeed it is obvious that the whole human race was never at one and the same time in the natural state. The children of our first parents, from whom the Holy Scriptures teach that all mortal men take their origin, were subject to the same paternal authority (*patria potestas*). Nevertheless, the natural state emerged among certain men later. For the earliest men sought to fill the empty world and to find more ample living space for themselves and their cattle, and so left the paternal home scattering in different directions; and individual males established their own families. Their descendants dispersed in the same way, and the special bond of kinship, and the affection that goes with it, gradually withered away leaving only that common element that results

---

1   Phoenix and Cilix, eponymous ancestors of, respectively, the Phoenicians and the Cilicians.

from similarity of nature. The human race then multiplied remarkably; men recognized the disadvantages of life apart; and gradually, those who lived close to each other drew together, at first in small states (*civitates*), then in larger states as the smaller coalesced, freely or by force. Among these states the natural state (*status*) still certainly exists; their only bond is their common humanity.

8 . The principal law of those who live in the natural state is to be subject only to God and answerable to none but Him. In that respect this state has the name of natural liberty. By natural liberty every man is understood to be in his own right and power and not subject to anyone's authority without a preceding human act. This is also the reason why every man is held to be equal to every other, where there is no relationship of subjection.

Since, moreover, men have the light of reason implanted in them to govern their actions by its illumination, it follows that someone living in natural liberty does not depend on anyone else to rule his actions, but has the authority to do anything that is consistent with sound reason by his own judgement and at his own discretion. And owing to the inclination which a man shares with all living things, he must infallibly and by all means strive to preserve his body and life and to repel all that threatens to destroy them, and take measures necessary to that end; and since in the natural state no one has a superior to whom he has subjected his will and judgement, everyone decides for himself whether the measures are apt to conduce to self-preservation or not. For no matter how attentively he listens to the advice of others, it is still up to him whether he will take it or not. It is, however, essential that he conduct his government of himself, if it is to go well, by the dictates of right reason and natural law.

9 . The state of nature may seem extraordinarily attractive in promising liberty and freedom from all subjection. But in fact before men submit to living in states, it is attended with a multitude of disadvantages, whether we imagine individuals existing in that state or consider the condition of separate heads of households. For if you picture to yourself a person (even an adult) left alone in this world without any of the aids and conveniences by which human ingenuity has relieved and enriched our lives, you will see a naked dumb animal, without resources, seeking to satisfy his hunger with roots and grasses and his thirst with whatever water he can find, to shelter himself from the inclemencies of the weather in caves, at the mercy of wild beasts, fearful of every chance encounter. Those who were members of scattered families may have enjoyed a somewhat more developed way of life but in no way comparable with civil life; and this not so much because of poverty, which the family (where desires are limited) seems capable of relieving, as because it can do little to ensure security. To put the matter in a few words, in the state of nature each is protected only by his own strength; in the state by the

strength of all. There no one may be sure of the fruit of his industry; here
all may be. There is the reign of the passions, there there is war, fear, poverty,
nastiness, solitude, barbarity, ignorance, savagery; here is the reign of reason,
here there is peace, security, wealth, splendour, society, taste, knowledge,
benevolence.

10 . In the natural state, if one does not do for another what is due by agreement, or does him wrong, or if a dispute arises in other ways, there is no one
who can by authority compel the offender to perform his part of the agreement or make restitution, as is possible in states, where one may implore the
aid of a common judge. But as nature does not allow one to plunge into war
on the slightest provocation, even when one is fully convinced of the justice
of his cause, an attempt must first be made to settle the matter by gentler
means, namely, by friendly discussion between the parties and an absolute
(not conditional) mutual promise or by appeal to the decision of arbitrators.

Such arbitrators must be fair to both sides and not show prejudice or
favour in giving their verdict; they must look only at the merits of the case.
For the same reason a man is not appointed as arbitrator in a case in which
he has greater expectation of benefit or glory from the victory of one of the
parties than from the other, and so has an interest in one party winning the
case no matter how. So there must be no agreement or promise between
the arbitrator and the parties, to oblige him to pronounce in favour of one
rather than the other.

If the arbitrator cannot ascertain the state of the facts either from the
common admissions of the parties or on the basis of reliable documents or
of arguments and evidence that admit no doubt, the facts will have to be
ascertained from statements by witnesses. Natural law, and in many cases the
sanctity of an oath, constrain witnesses to tell the truth; but it would be safest
not to accept as witnesses those who have such feelings about either of the
parties that their conscience must struggle so to speak with friendship, hatred,
vindictiveness or some other strong emotional impulse, or even with some
more intimate bond; not everybody has sufficient firmness to overcome these
feelings. Sometimes litigation may be avoided by the mediation of mutual
friends, which is rightly considered to be among the most sacred duties.
But in the natural state, the individual is responsible for execution of the
judgement, when one party will not voluntarily render what is due.

11 . Nature herself has willed that there should be a kind of kinship among
men, by force of which it is wrong to harm another man and indeed right
for everyone to work for the benefit of others. However, kinship usually has
a rather weak force among those who live in natural liberty with each other.
Consequently, we have to regard any man who is not our fellow-citizen, or
with whom we live in a state of nature, not indeed as our enemy, but as a friend
we cannot wholly rely on. The reason is that men not only can do each other

very great harm, but do very often wish to do so for various reasons. Some are driven to injure others by their wickedness of character, or by lust for power and superfluous wealth. Others, though men of moderation, take up arms to preserve themselves and not to be forestalled by others. Many find themselves in conflict because they are competing for the same object, others through rivalry of talents. Hence in the natural state there is a lively and all but perpetual play of suspicion, distrust, eagerness to subvert the strength of others, and desire to get ahead of them or to augment one's own strength by their ruin. Therefore as a good man should be content with his own and not trouble others or covet their goods, so a cautious man who loves his own security will believe all men his friends but liable at any time to become enemies; he will keep peace with all, knowing that it may soon be exchanged for war. This is the reason why that country is considered happy which even in peace contemplates war.

...

16. *On war and peace*

1. It is most agreeable to natural law that men should live in peace with each other by doing of their own accord what their duty requires; indeed peace itself is a state peculiar to man, insofar as he is distinct from the beasts. Nevertheless, for man too war is sometimes permitted, and occasionally necessary, namely when by the ill will of another we cannot preserve our property or obtain our right without the use of force. In this situation, however, good sense and humanity counsel us not to resort to arms when more evil than good is likely to overtake us and ours by the prosecution of our wrongs.

2. The just causes of engaging in war come down to the preservation and protection of our lives and property against unjust attack, or the collection of what is due to us from others but has been denied, or the procurement of reparations for wrong inflicted and of assurance for the future. Wars waged for the first of these causes are said to be defensive, for the other causes, offensive.

3. One should not have immediate recourse to arms as soon as one thinks oneself wronged, particularly so long as there remains some doubt about right or fact. One should explore the possibility of amicable settlement of the matter by various means, for example by initiating dialogue between the parties, by appealing to an arbitrator, or by submitting the question to lot. The claimant particularly is obliged to try this method, since there is in any case a predisposition to favour possession with some title.

4. Unjust causes of war are either openly such or have some plausible pretext, however weak. Open causes come down to two main types: avarice and

ambition, namely lust for wealth and lust for power. Those covered by pretexts are various: they include fear of the wealth and power of a neighbour,
unjustified aggrandizement, desire for better territory, refusal of something
which is simply and straight-forwardly owed, stupidity on the part of a possessor, a desire to extinguish another's legitimately acquired right which the
aggressor finds rather inconvenient, and others of this kind.

5 . The most proper forms of action in war are force and terror. But one
has equal right to use fraud and deceit against an enemy, provided one does
not violate one's pledged faith. Hence one may deceive an enemy by false
statements or fictitious stories, but never by promises or agreements.

6 . As for force used in war against an enemy and his property, one must
distinguish between what an enemy may suffer without wrong and what we
ourselves may inflict without loss of humanity. When a man has declared
himself my enemy, he has by that fact made known his intention to inflict
the last degree of suffering on me, and by that same fact he grants me, so
far as he can, an unlimited right against himself. Humanity however requires
that so far as the momentum of warfare permits, we should inflict no more
suffering on an enemy than defence or vindication of our right and its future
assurance requires.

7 . War is normally divided into two forms: declared and undeclared. There
are two necessary conditions of a declared war: first that it be waged by the
authority of the sovereigns on both sides, and secondly that it be preceded by a
declaration. Undeclared war is either war waged without formal declaration
or war against private citizens. Civil wars also are in this category.

8 . The right of initiating war in a state lies with the sovereign. It is beyond the
capacity of an official to exercise that right without the authority delegated
to him by the sovereign to do so, even in a situation in which he infers that
the sovereign, if consulted, would decide upon immediate war. However, all
who have charge of a province or fortified place with military forces under
their command are understood to be obliged by the nature of their office to
repel an invading enemy from the area entrusted to them by whatever means
they can. But they should not without grave cause move the war on to the
enemy's territory.

9 . Whereas one who lives in natural liberty may be pursued in war only for
wrongs he has committed himself, in civil society the ruler of a state or the
state as a whole is often attacked, even though he or it was not the source of the
wrong. But for this to be justified, it is essential that the wrong pass in some
way to the ruler. And in fact rulers of states do share in wrongs committed
by their long-settled citizens or by those who have recently taken refuge
with them, if the rulers allowed the commission of the wrongs or provide
refuge. For such allowance to be culpable, there must be a knowledge of the
crime and ability to prevent it. Rulers are presumed to be aware of the open

and habitual actions of their citizens, and there is always a presumption of their ability to prevent them, unless there is obvious evidence of its absence. However, the right to make war upon a ruler who accepts and protects a delinquent, who is seeking refuge with him solely to escape punishment, arises more from particular agreements between neighbours and allies than from any common obligation. This is not the case, however, if the refugee while with us is planning hostilities against the state he has left.

10 . It is also accepted among nations that the goods of private citizens may be held for a debt which is properly the state's or for something which the state confiscated without observing the requirements of justice, so that foreigners to whom the debt is due may impound any goods of citizens from the debtor state which they find on their own territories: In such cases, however, the citizens whose goods have been taken in this way should obtain restitution from the actual debtors. Such exactions are known as reprisals and are frequently preludes to war.

11 . One may wage war on another's behalf as well as for oneself. This is justified where the party for whom one is going to war has a just cause, and where the party coming to aid has a reasonable ground for conducting hostilities on his behalf against the third party.

The first among those for whom we not only may but should take up arms are our subjects both as a whole and as individuals, provided that the state would not evidently be involved in greater suffering as a result. Then come allies who have a treaty which includes this provision. However, they yield precedence to our own citizens, if the latter need our help at the same moment; and it is assumed that they have a just cause of war and that they are showing some prudence in undertaking it. Next in order are friends, even if no such specific promise has been given them. And finally, where no other ground exists, kinship alone may suffice for us to go to the defence of an oppressed party who makes a plea for assistance, so far as we conveniently may.

12 . The extent of licence in war is such that, however far one may have gone beyond the bounds of humanity in slaughter or in wasting and plundering property, the opinion of nations does not hold one in infamy nor as deserving of being shunned by honest men. However, the more civilized nations condemn certain ways of inflicting harm on an enemy: for instance, the use of poison or bribing the citizens or soldiers of other rulers to assassinate them.

13 . Movable property is considered to be captured from the moment that it is beyond enemy pursuit, immovable property when we hold it so effectively as to have the ability to keep the enemy off it. However, the condition of the absolute extinction of the former owner's right of recovery is his renunciation by subsequent agreement of all claim to it. Otherwise what is ours by force may be taken back by force.

As soldiers fight by the authority of the state, so what they take from the enemy is acquired for the state, not for themselves. However, it is a universal practice that movable property, especially if of no great value, is tacitly left to the soldiers who took it, either as a reward, or sometimes in lieu of pay, or to give incentive to men to put their lives on the line without compulsion.

When captured property is taken back from an enemy, immovable property returns to its former owners. So too should movable property, but among most peoples it is left to the soldiers as booty.

14 . Rule over conquered peoples as over individuals is also won by war. For it to be legitimate and binding upon the consciences of subjects, the conquered must swear loyalty to the conquerors and the conquerors give up their state of enmity and hostile intention towards the conquered.

15 . Acts of war are suspended by a truce, which is an agreement to refrain from acts of war for a period of time, without ending the state of war or settling the dispute from which the war started. When the period of the truce has expired, there is a return to a state of war without a new declaration, unless peace has been made in the meantime.

16 . Truces may be divided into those which are made with the armies remaining in the field and fighting readiness maintained on both sides (the period of such truces is fairly short), and truces in which fighting readiness is disbanded on both sides. The latter may be made for quite long periods of time and normally are; they have the appearance of complete peace, and sometimes are even termed peace with the specification of a fixed period of time. For otherwise every peace is assumed to be perpetual and to lay permanently to rest the disputes from which the war broke out. The arrangements normally called tacit truces impose no obligation; in such cases the parties remain quiet on both sides at their discretion and may resume acts of war whenever they so please.

17 . A war is definitively ended only when peace is ratified by the sovereigns on both sides. Both the parties to the agreement must define its terms and conditions, and have equally the obligation to put them into effect at the agreed time, and to observe them faithfully. To assure this, an oath is normally included and hostages given, and often other parties, particularly those who take part in the peace-making, accept the duty of ensuring compliance by promising aid to the party which is injured by the other contrary to the terms of the peace.

SAMUEL RACHEL

S AMUEL RACHEL (1628–91), German jurist, diplomat, and professor of moral philosophy. In contrast to Pufendorf, who, like Grotius, based international law (or "the law of nations," as it was then called) on natural law, Rachel argued that the law of nations consists of positive laws jointly enacted by sovereigns and expressed in treaties between them. This international law must be distinguished from natural as well as civil law. In rejecting natural law as a source of international law and emphasizing the importance of treaties, Rachel adopts a positivist view of international law as resting on state practice, anticipating mainstream international legal doctrine by more than a century.

From "On the Law of Nations"

I. Not only has Nature provided its own Law for men, whereby, as if by a world-wide chain, they are bound to one another in virtue of being men, but mankind has itself also laid down various positive laws for its own guidance, not merely those by which in every State the government binds its subjects to itself or by which these bind themselves to one another, but also those which the human race, divided up as it is into independent peoples and different States, employs as a common bond of obligation; and peoples of different forms of government and of different size lie under the control of these rules, which depend for their efficacy upon mutual good faith. "Custom and human necessity compelled the people of mankind to adopt certain Laws for themselves" (*Institutes* 1, 2, 1). Now these words are spoken of the Law of Nations properly so called, with which it is our purpose to deal here; and so the principle indicated, and the various examples there given under it, are ill adapted to Natural Law, as Bachov, in his *Commentaries*, has correctly observed, following Wesenbec.

II. Now the Law of Nations is founded on the agreement of Nations. For one State has no authority over another, nor one free people over another; nor is one of them under liability to another of them, and much less are several free peoples and States subordinate to some one power – but each of them has its own ... independence and self-rule. And so, if they are united to one another by any arbitrary Law, to which all those who are so associated must render obedience, that Law can not but be set up by Agreement. For, just as equal can have no right and power over equal, nor private person over private person, save such as may come from agreement, so also free peoples and races are joined together just as private persons are by agreements, and they are in no other way capable of a positive Law which shall operate between them with a common binding effect. (*Digest* 4, 8, 4.)

III. Two points deserve to be made and carefully noted. The first is that it is by Agreement after the manner of private individuals that the Law of Nations is set up by free peoples. The second is that by means of that Law they are formed into a Society and are bound to one another. For if there be any Law observed among many peoples, but no obligation springing therefrom obtains among them so that by its bond they are constrained into a Society and kept therein, that is no Law of Nations at all and ought not to be so called, but it is a Civil Law common to many peoples and belonging to them as individual peoples.

...

XI. When I say "Law of Nations," I am thinking of those nations each of which is marked off and distinguished from the rest by its own separate government, whether of one person or many or of the whole people. I do not propose any fixed number of such nations, nor define the number within which the obligation and observance of that Law extends. Least of all do I wish to suggest that all nations of the whole globe have entered by consent into any such common Arbitrary Law, with the intention of being mutually bound thereby. Consistently herewith, Grotius (*De jure belli ac pacis*, bk. 1, ch. 1, n. 14), after distinguishing the Law of Nations from Natural Law, goes on to say,

"Law in a wider sphere is the Law of Nations, that Law which has received an obligatory force from the will of all nations or of many. I add 'or many' because scarce any law, except Natural Law (which also is often called Law of Nations), is found common to all nations. Indeed, that is often Law of Nations in one part of the world, which is not so in another as we shall show when we come to speak of captivity and postliminy."

Now not all nations are known; so how can there be any manifestation of the consent, whether express or tacit, and intent of all of them about an arbitrary matter? Indeed, I do not think that even all known nations are under the obligation of this Law. And although there may be certain principles of a common Law of Nations which bind all the more cultured of known peoples, still I will not make any general assertion to that effect about any Law of Nations. (See Selden, *De jure nature et gentium juxta disciplinam Hebraorum*, bk. 1, ch. 6, p. 77, Strassburg edition, for the threefold meaning and interpretation of "all nations.")

XII. It is, then, enough for my purpose that "Nations," in the Law of Nations considered generally, means "many Nations," without any definite number being fixed, even if there be but two; for this justifies the use of the plural number. Conring supports me in this matter, saying (*Disputatio de legibus*, th. 24):

"The Law of Nations is that which many nations have instituted among themselves for their own use, not at random or by imitation [*sc.* adapted to individual needs] one of the other, but as if by agreement. I say 'many' in the same way in which grammarians oppose the plural to the singular number, and without any suggestion that that alone deserves the name of Law of Nations which operates between numerous States or the majority of States. Thus, there is at the present day a special arrangement between the Spanish and the Dutch that a prisoner of war may ransom himself from his captor with one month's pay. I do not see why this has less claim to be called Law of Nations than the old rule whereby prisoners of war became the slaves of their captors. Each of these is a law of Nations, albeit the former only of two nations and the latter of many."

This view has also the support of the English jurist Richard Zouche, who, in his book entitled *Jus inter gentes* (part i, § i), makes the Law of Nations twofold: one part he derives from a common assent; and of the other he says, "Furthermore, besides common customs, anything upon which single nations agree with other single nations, for example by compacts, conventions, and treaties, must also be deemed to be law between nations."

. . .

LXXXIV. The supreme task now awaits me of showing that there is a Law of Nations; for if none there be, I have lost all my time and trouble. Some babbler may say that I ought to have placed the discussion of this question at the beginning, and not at the end, of my treatise; for what is the use of enquiring into the contents and character of the Law of Nations before we are sure that there is a Law of Nations at all! I admit that there is some substance in this criticism, if you look at the natural order. But every branch of learning ought to be derived, not from what is in its nature better known, but from what is better known by us; and so I found it advisable to deal first with the matters referred to, in the hope that, if I removed all verbal ambiguities by classifying the species of the Law of Nations and by adopting a distinctive nomenclature therefore, and by explaining the more important heads of the Law, I should clear the way for a perspicuous presentment and understanding of the question Whether there be a Law of Nations at all, such as I have described and classified, and illustrated with various individual examples.

LXXXV. When I come to close quarters with the reasons why the whole Law of Nations is nowadays so much assailed, four chief ones present themselves, which have seduced many persons into this attitude of doubt. In the first place they think it unlikely that the Consent of all Nations ever established any Arbitrary Law among them. Next, that no sufficiently general

Custom or Usage of all Nations is apparent, wherefrom the consent or tacit agreement of these Nations to this Law can be deduced or presumed. Thirdly, that Nations and Princes repeatedly profess by their conduct that what is commonly passed off as a Law of Nations is no concern of theirs, but is a play that does not suit their stage. Lastly, that the topics which are usually referred to a Law of Nations are based in part on the Law of Nature, so that there is no need to feign an Arbitrary Law of Nations, and in part rest on no legal basis whatever. We will first weigh these arguments one by one; and when we have found how light they weigh, or naught, the truth will begin to be more and more clear.

LXXXVI. The theme of the first argument is that there is no Law of Nations, approved and established by all and every Nation. Now this I readily grant, and indeed have already granted (sections XI, XII and XXXVI), and have shown how the somewhat inaccurate modes of speech of that sort may be toned down and improved. But that there is a Peculiar Law of Nations, of the character described in sections XXIV and LXXIII, onwards, I think too clear to call for proof, and so I will not give any, lest I appear to accuse my critics of the sheer lust of dissent. For who but knows, or who doubts, that various Nations are bound to one another by the arbitrary bond of various Public Conventions? So the argument under examination simply amounts to this, that there is no Law of Nations of the type which we have called Common. But by how many rules in vogue among numerous Nations, the chief of which rules we have seen, is it made abundantly clear that, over and above the Peculiar Law of Nations, there is a Common Law, and that this is not only distinct from the Peculiar, but also, I shall have established this latter position more carefully, no one will continue an opposition to the Common Law of Nations, which is really no less an opposition to sense and experience.

LXXXVII. The second argument relates to the manner in which Nations have established the Law in question as a Common Law for themselves, and have come to an agreement about it. Of course, it is not suggested that all Nations met together in order to sanction that Law, but that it has been approved by the tacit consent of Nations and received by them all on grounds of a common expediency. (Vinnius, n. 2, on *Institutes* 1, 2, 1.) And just as one can seldom trace the beginnings of any law which owes its introduction to usage or custom, whether indigenous or borrowed (by inference from *Digest* 1, 3, 20), so, and much less, will any one show the origin and development of the Common Law of Nations, dependent, as they are, on usage spread over so long a period of time and handed on from Nation to Nation. That is enough for us which is manifest in other ways, namely, that certain rules of Nations do exist and are observed among Nations as Law, alike now and in times past, albeit we can only form a probable conjecture as to their origin and the way in which they first appeared. "That," says Cicero (*De inventione*, bk. 2), "is considered Customary

Law which its long duration has shown to be approved by all without any express enactment. Among usages there are some which are unmistakably Law because of their long duration." Compare section XV, onwards.

LXXXVIII. Nor does the third argument advance the cause, for there is nothing to be got out of the reasoning: The observance of Law is often neglected, and therefore there is no Law or else it has ceased to be. I will not deny that there are some topics of the Law of Nations which can be abrogated by desuetude, either because they are not firmly settled in the usage of free Nations, and so can be easily abrogated by a contrary intent, or because they have no inevitableness to commend them; but this is subject to the proviso that the Nations which may fairly be considered affected, and whose assent in times gone by gave a sanction to the rules in question, are at one as to their desuetude and abrogation. As regards those rules of the Law of Nations which are over-rigid, Natural Equity commends the abrogation, or at any rate the mitigation, of these; and in the case of any that are manifestly unjust, this treatment is ordered by the Law of Nature, and much more by Christian piety, despite any inequitable and impious dissent on the part of others. But those rules of the Law of Nations which are void of offense and inequity, and much more those which expediency or necessity has introduced, can not be wantonly changed or abrogated by any given Nations, especially if this would enure to the hurt of the other Nations. For it is a rule of Civil Law that a society or partnership can not be quitted in any way that savors of fraud (*Digest* 17, 2, 14); and the same rule holds even more in the society of Nations. Even if, then, any Princes or Nations, as the case may be, decline to be bound by the rules of the Law of Nations and will not have their conduct tested by that standard, that is no reason at all for depriving the Law of Nations of authority in the same way that it has been deprived of observance and its pacts deprived of good faith. For this is proof only of weakness in good faith, of an unjust cause, and of a headstrong masterfulness that insults both God and man. In cases like these, Divine Providence often interposes, to sap the strength, to place a bound to studied tyranny, and to curb the fierceness that will not suffer Law, and to visit it with punishment.

LXXXIX. The greatest force seems to remain in the fourth and last argument; namely, that there is no need of this imaginary Law of Nations, seeing that the Law of Nature alone is enough to regulate the conduct of free Nations and that some of the heads of this Law of Nations do not deserve to be dignified by the name of Law. I have already admitted that there are some rules of the Law of Nations of this sort, and I have insisted that such as are repugnant to Natural Law or Christian piety can and ought to be rejected, as being, indeed, incapable of ever acquiring any obligatory force, seeing that the supremely great authority of Natural or Divine Law prevents this. But the question whether Nations and States are bound by no other than the Law of

Nature, to the exclusion of all Voluntary Law between them, either Common or Peculiar, is one which claims our careful attention now. It will be useful to hear the words of some of those who have made this affirmation.

XC. Let Thomas Hobbes have precedence among them, for he seems to have drawn others into his way of thinking. In his book *Philosophical Rudiments concerning Government and Society* (ch. 14, §4), he says that "The Natural Law may be divided into that of Men, which alone hath obtained the title of the Law of Nature; and that of Cities, which may be called that of Nations, but vulgarly it is called the Right of Nations. The precepts of both are alike; but because Cities, once instituted, do put on the personal properties of men, that Law which, speaking of the duty of single men, we call Natural, being applied to whole Cities, and Nations, is called the Right of Nations." Samuel Puffendorf quotes this from Hobbes in his *De jure nature et gentium* (bk. 2, ch. 3, §22), and then adds, "To this opinion we entirely subscribe, thinking, moreover, that there is no other Law of Nations, Voluntary or Positive, which has the force of Law, properly so called, so as to bind Nations as if it issued from a superior." Robert Sharrock, who thought himself especially chosen for the refutation of his fellow-citizen Hobbes, nevertheless agrees with him in this matter, making profession as follows, in his *De officiis* (ch. 10, p. 129): "The Law of Nations does not seem to me to differ any whit from the Law of Nature, and I make bold to assert that no Prince will ever offend against the Law of Nations who conforms his conduct in all respects to the standard here set up by Nature." He than adds examples from treaties, embassages, and other matters of the Law of Nations, in which no one can be unjustly injured without the commission of a sin against Innocence, Good Faith, *philautia* or Self-love, and Charity, which are all precepts of Natural Law.

XCI. Two things in the above call for special note. Although I freely grant to Puffendorf that the Law of Nations does not issue in the form of laws of the sort that are decreed by a superior, yet the Law of Nations does not for that reason fall to the ground. Granted that, according to the received mode of speech, Law especially means a rule of human conduct imposed by a law-giver upon his subjects, still pacts are not on that account to be barred from all Law, and not even from Law properly so called. For law-givers are no more able than Nature is to lay down a fixed rule beforehand for every detail of business and for every case. Accordingly, the same liberty that Nature allowed law-givers of settling by a reference to the Law of Nature the matters that are not covered by their legislation, that same liberty private individuals receive from both alike, of legislating for themselves mutually by means of such pacts as are not opposed to the Law of Nature or the Civil Laws, and of binding themselves thereby. Bœcler, on Grotius' *De jure belli ac pacis*, bk. 2, ch. 4, n. 9, as cited by Puffendorf, is even more in my favor; for he there says clearly that there is a Law of Nations, established on considerations of its utility by the free consent of Nations; and hereby he obviously marks it off from the Law of Nature. Even if, then, one free Nation is not the superior of another, and one can not lay down Law specially so called for another, yet if they choose to bind themselves by pacts, they are reciprocally bound just as if by true Law; so that, should one of them break faith, it by that very fact makes the other or others its superior so far as that they can compel it to keep faith. Now if two subjects of the same State have bound themselves by an agreement and one commits a fraud on the agreement, the other can restrain him by judicial authority and obtain redress by action at Law; in just the same way, as there is no common tribunal for free Nations, one of them may, other things being equal, resort to war as a means of compelling another, who has proved perfidious, to carry out what has been agreed on. And although the issue of war is doubtful and uncertain, yet, if the Nation that has acted up to its agreements makes war on the perfidious one, it will be in its right in so doing and will have on its side not only the other Nations who are heedful of justice, but also God Himself, the supreme umpire and arbiter of good faith.

...

CXIX. As, then, all Nations with one mouth call for these and similar rules, and give assent to them, and individually acknowledge that they are bound by them, it is indeed rash to try to sever this bond as those would do who impugn this Law of Nations. The teaching of these persons is fraught with grave danger to public safety; and this throws out in relief the excellent zeal for the public safety, and the sound intelligence, of those who have before this date given to Nations, States and Princes the following advice and suggestion, namely: To erect of their own motion, by common agreement, a College of Fecials wherein, as a necessary first step, controversies which have arisen between States should be cognized and argued and decided, in such sort that nothing save necessity would open the way to war, it being undertaken only against those who have declined to obey a judgement rendered, or who in other ways have shown contumacy towards the authority and decrees of this College. To many men of sound intelligence this idea may seem a good one – yet, if you look at the times and at the tone of to-day, a matter for mockery. Now many philosophers and historians have shaped the ideal State or the ideal Prince after the idea in their own minds, and have found their imitators, up and down, who have borrowed their teachings for the use of their own State to its great profit; but the idea I have mentioned is not of the same brand as Plato's Communion of Property, though it may not impossible be considered to be such: and its utility would be unsurpassed.

CHRISTIAN VON WOLFF

C HRISTIAN VON WOLFF (1679–1754), German mathematician, philosopher, and, after 1740, professor of law at the University of Halle.
Inspired in part by Leibniz, Wolff gradually developed a comprehensive, and
thoroughly rationalist, philosophical system. In ethics, he held that moral
laws depend not on God's will but are part of the natural world and can therefore be known by natural reason. His ideas about international law, which are
imbued by this rationalist spirit, constitute but a tiny part of his philosophical
system.

From *The Law of Nations*
Treated According to a Scientific Method

Prolegomena
§ 1. *Definition of the Law of Nations*

By the Law of Nations we understand the science of that Law which nations
or peoples use in their relations with each other and of the obligations corresponding thereto.

We propose to show, of course, how nations as such ought to determine their actions,
and consequently to what each nation is bound, both to itself and to other nations,
and what laws of nations arise therefrom, both as to itself and as to other nations. For
laws arise from passive obligation, so that, if there were no obligation, neither would
there be any law.

§ 2. *How nations are to be regarded*

Nations are regarded as individual free persons living in a state of nature. For
they consist of a multitude of men united into a state. Therefore since states
are regarded as individual free persons living in a state of nature, nations also
must be regarded in relation to each other as individual free persons living
in a state of nature.

Here, of course, we are looking at nations as they are at their beginning, before one has bound itself to another by definite promises restricting the civil liberty which belongs to a people, or has been subjected, either by its own act or that of another, to some other nation. For that the liberty of nations, which originally belongs to them, can be taken away or diminished, will be evident from proof later.

§ 3. *Of what sort the law of nations is originally*

Since nations are regarded as individual persons living in a state of nature, moreover, as men in a state of nature use nothing except natural law, nations also originally used none other than natural law; therefore the law of nations is originally nothing except the law of nature applied to nations.

The only law given to men by nature is natural law. This then can be changed by the act of men voluntarily, by agreement between individuals, so far as concerns those things which belong to permissive law, and so far as concerns the performance of those things which belong to mankind; it can be changed in the state by force of the legislative power, as we have shown in our natural theory of the civil laws. In like manner the only law given to nations by nature is natural law, or the law of nature itself applied to nations. This then can be changed by the act of nations voluntarily, so far as concerns those things which belong to permissive law, and so far as concerns the performance of those things which belong to mankind, as we shall see in the following discussion. But far be it from you to think that therefore there is no need of our discussing in detail the law of nations. For the principles of the law of nature are one thing, but the application of them to nations another, and this produces a certain diversity in that which is inferred, in so far as the nature of a nation is not the same as human nature. For example, man is bound to preserve himself by nature, every nation by the agreement through which it is made a definite moral person. But there is one method of preservation required for a man, another for a nation. Likewise the right of defending one's self against the injuries of others belongs to man by nature, and the law of nature itself assigns it to a nation. But the method of one man's defence against another is not, of course, the same as the proper method of defence for nations. There will be no difficulty in this for those who have understood the force of the fundamental principle of reduction, which is of especial importance in the art of logic. And if any mists still obscure the minds of some, the following discussion will dispel them. Therefore we are not embarrassed by the objections of those who argue that the law of nations ought not to be distinguished from the law of nature, and that the law of nations ought to be presented as nothing other than the law of nature. So far as we are concerned, each may indulge his own belief. With none shall we start a dispute. For us it is sufficient to have explained those things which seem to be in harmony with the truth.

§ 4. *Definition of the necessary law of nations*

We call that the necessary law of nations which consists in the law of nature applied to nations. It is even called by Grotius and his successors, the internal law of nations, since it evidently binds nations in conscience. It is likewise called by some the natural law of nations.

Of course, the necessary law of nations contains those things which the law of nature prescribes to nations, which, just as it regulates all acts of men, so likewise controls the acts of nations as such.

§ 5. *Of the immutability of this law*

Since the necessary law of nations consists in the law of nature applied to nations, furthermore as the law of nature is immutable, the necessary law of nations also is absolutely immutable.

The immutability of the necessary law of nations arises from the very immutability of natural law, and is finally derived from the essence and nature of man as a source whence flows the very immutability of natural law. The law of nature therefore rules the acts of nations, because men coming together into a state and thereby becoming a nation, do not lay aside their human nature, consequently they remain subject to the law of nature, in as much as they have desired to combine their powers for the promotion of the common good.

§ 6. *The nature of the obligation which comes from the necessary law of nations*

In like manner since the necessary law of nations consists in the law of nature applied to nations, and consequently the obligation which arises from the necessary law of nations comes from the law of nature, furthermore, since this obligation itself, which comes from the law of nature, is necessary and immutable, the obligation also which comes from the law of nations is necessary and immutable; consequently neither can any nation free itself nor can one nation free another from it.

These things are to be well considered, lest some one may think, when he sees that a certain licence of action must be allowed among nations, that the necessary law of nations is of no value. For this would be just as if one should argue that the law of nature is of no value, because the abuse of their liberty must be allowed to men in a state of nature and the same is turned to licence of action, nor can this be prohibited except by positive law in a civil state, where they can be compelled by a superior force to do what they are unwilling to do of their own accord. The abuse of power remains illicit even among nations, even though it cannot be checked. Nor do good nations do all they can, but they have respect for conscience no less than every good man has, who does not gauge his right by might, but by the obligation that comes from the law of nature. A good nation differs from a bad in the same way that a good man differs from a bad, or, if you prefer, the virtuous from the vicious.

§ 7. *Of the society established by nature among nations*

Nature herself has established society among all nations and binds them to preserve society. For nature herself has established society among men and binds them to preserve it. Therefore, since this obligation, as coming from the law of nature, is necessary and immutable, it cannot be changed for the reason that nations have united into a state. Therefore society, which nature has established among individuals, still exists among nations and consequently, after states have been established in accordance with the law of nature and nations have arisen thereby, nature herself also must be said to have established society among all nations and bound them to preserve society.

If we should consider that great society, which nature herself has established among men, to be done away with by the particular societies, which men enter, when they unite into a state, states would be established contrary to the law of nature, in as much as the universal obligation of all toward all would be terminated; which assuredly is absurd. Just as in the human body individual organs do not cease to be organs of the whole human body, because certain ones taken together constitute one organ; so likewise individual men do not cease to be members of that great society which is made up of the whole human race, because several have formed together a certain particular society. And in so far as these act together as associates, just as if they were all of one mind and one will; even so are the members of that society united, which nature has established among men. After the human race was divided into nations, that society which before was between individuals continues between nations.

§ 8. *Of the purpose of that state*

Since nature herself has established society among all nations, in so far as she has established it among all men, as is evident from the demonstration of the preceding proposition, since, moreover, the purpose of natural society, and consequently of that society which nature herself has established among men, is to give mutual assistance in perfecting itself and its condition; the purpose of the society therefore, which nature has established among all nations, is to give mutual assistance in perfecting itself and its condition, consequently the promotion of the common good by its combined powers.

Just as one man alone is not sufficient unto himself, but needs the aid of another, in order that thereby the common good may be promoted by their combined powers; so also one nation alone is not sufficient for itself, but one needs the aid of the other, that thereby the common good may be promoted by their combined powers. Therefore since nature herself unites men together and compels them to preserve society, because the common good of all cannot be promoted except by their combined powers, so that nothing is more beneficial for a man than a man; the same nature likewise unites nations together and compels them to preserve society, because the common good of all cannot be promoted except by their combined powers, so that nothing can be said to be more beneficial for a nation than a nation. For although a nation can be thought of which is spread over a vast expanse, and does not seem to need the aid of other nations; nevertheless it cannot yet be said that it could not improve its condition still more by the aid of other nations, much less that other nations could not be aided by it, however much it could itself dispense with the aid of others. Just as man ought to aid man, so too ought nation to aid nation.

§ 9. *Of the state which is made up of all nations*

All nations are understood to have come together into a state, whose separate members are separate nations, or individual states. For nature herself has established society among all nations and compels them to preserve it, for the purpose of promoting the common good by their combined powers. Therefore since a society of men united for the purpose of promoting the common good by their combined powers, is a state, nature herself has combined nations into a state. Therefore since nations, which know the advantages arising therefrom, by a natural impulse are carried into this association, which binds the human race or all nations one to the other, since moreover it is assumed that others will unite in it, if they know their own interests; what can be said except that nations also have combined into society as if by agreement? So all nations are understood to have come together into a state, whose separate nations are separate members or individual states.

Reasoning throws a certain light upon the present proposition, by which we have proved that nature has established society among men and compels them to protect society. Nay, rather the state, into which nature herself orders nations to combine, in truth depends on that great society which she has established among all men, as is perfectly evident from the above reasoning. But that those things may not be doubtful which we have said concerning the quasi-agreement, by which that supreme state is understood to have been formed between nations; those things must be reconsidered which we have mentioned elsewhere. Furthermore, in establishing this quasi-agreement we have assumed nothing which is at variance with reason, or which may not be allowed in other quasi-agreements. For that nations are carried into that association by a certain natural impulse is apparent from their acts, as when they enter into treaties for the purpose of commerce or war, or even of peace, concerning which we shall speak below in their proper place. Therefore do not persuade yourself that there is any nation that is not known to unite to form the state, into which nature herself commands all to combine. But just as in tutelage it is rightly presumed that the pupil agrees, in so far as he ought to agree, nay, more, as he would be likely to agree, if he knew his own interest; so none the less nations which through lack of insight fail to see how great an advantage it is to be a member of that supreme state, are presumed to agree to this association. And since it is understood in a civil state that the tutor is compelled to act, if he should be unwilling to consent of his own accord, but that even when the agreement is extorted by a superior force that does not prevent the tutelage from resting upon a quasi-agreement; why, then, is it not allowable to attribute the same force to the natural obligation by which nations are compelled to enter into an alliance as is attributed to the civil obligation, that it is understood to force consent even as from one unwilling? But if these arguments seem more ingenious than true, and altogether too complicated; putting them aside, it is enough to recognize that nature herself has combined nations into a state, therefore whatever flows from the concept of a state, must be assumed as established by nature herself. We have aimed at nothing else.

§ 10. *What indeed may be called the supreme state*

The state, into which nations are understood to have combined, and of which they are members or citizens, is called the supreme state.

The size of a state is determined by the number of its citizens. Therefore a greater state cannot be conceived of than one whose members are all nations in general, inasmuch as they together include the whole human race. This concept of a supreme state was not unknown to Grotius, nor was he ignorant of the fact that the law of nations was based on it, but nevertheless he did not derive from it the law of nations which is called voluntary, as he could and ought to have done.

§ 11. *Of the laws of the supreme state*

Since the supreme state is a certain sort of state, consequently a society, moreover since every society ought to have its own laws and the right exists in it of promulgating laws with respect to those things which concern it, the supreme state also ought to have its own laws and the right exists in it of promulgating laws with respect to those things which concern it; and because civil laws, that is, those declared in a state, prescribe the means by which the good of a state is maintained, the laws of the supreme state likewise ought to prescribe the means by which its good is maintained.

It occasions very little difficulty that laws may be promulgated in the state by a superior such as nations do not have, and certainly do not recognize. For since the law of nature controls the will of the ruler in making laws, and since laws ought to prescribe the means by which the good of the state is maintained, by virtue of the present proposition, then, it is evident enough of what sort those laws ought to be that nations ought to agree to, consequently may be presumed to have agreed to. No difficulty will appear in establishing a law of nations which does not depart altogether from the necessary law of nations, nor in all respects observe it, as will appear in what follows.

§ 12. *How individual nations are bound to the whole and the whole to the individuals*

Inasmuch as nations are understood to have combined in a supreme state, the individual nations are understood to have bound themselves to the whole, because they wish to promote the common good, but the whole to the individuals, because it wishes to provide for the especial good of the individuals. For if a state is established, individuals bind themselves to the whole, because they wish to promote the common good, and the whole binds itself to the individuals, because it wishes to provide for adequate life, for peace and security, consequently for the especial good of the individuals. Inasmuch then as nations are understood to have combined in a supreme state, individual nations also are understood to have bound themselves to the whole, because they wish to promote the common good, and the whole to the individuals, because it wishes to provide for the especial good of the individuals.

Nature herself has brought nations together in the supreme state, and therefore has imposed upon them the obligation which the present proposition urges, that because they ought to agree, they may be presumed to have agreed, or it may rightly be assumed that they have agreed, just as something similar exists in patriarchal society, which we have said is valid as a nature quasi-agreement. But if all nations had been equipped with such power of discernment as to know how effort might be made for the advantage of themselves, and what losses might be avoided by them, if the individual nations performed the duty of a good citizen, and their leaders did not allow themselves to be led astray by some impulse of passion, certainly there would be no doubt that in general all would expressly agree to that to which nature leads them, which produces and maintains harmony even among the ignorant and unwilling. But this must be shown by us, how nature provides for the happiness of the human race in accordance with the human lot. For men ought not to be imagined to be what they are not, however much they ought to be so. And for this reason it will be plain from what follows, that laws which spring from the concept of the supreme state, depart from the necessary law of nations, since on account of the human factor in the supreme state things which are illicit in themselves have to be, not indeed allowed, but endured, because they cannot be changed by human power.

§ 13. *Of the law of nations as a whole in regard to individual nations*

In the supreme state the nations as a whole have a right to coerce the individual nations, if they should be unwilling to perform their obligation, or should show themselves negligent in it. For in a state the right belongs to the whole of coercing the individuals to perform their obligation, if they should either be unwilling to perform it or should show themselves negligent in it. Therefore since all nations are understood to have combined into a state, of which the individual nations are members, and inasmuch as they are understood to have combined in the supreme state, the individual members of this are understood to have bound themselves to the whole, because they wish to promote the common good, since moreover from the passive obligation of one party the right of the other arises; therefore the right belongs to the nations as a whole in the supreme state also of coercing the individual nations, if they are unwilling to perform their obligation or show themselves negligent in it.

This will seem paradoxical to those who do not discern the connexion of truths and who judge laws from facts. But it will be evident in what follows that we need the present proposition as a basis of demonstration of others which must be admitted without hesitation. And in general it must be observed that our question is one of law, for which men are fitted in their present state, and not at all of facts, by which the law is either defied or broken. For there would be no purpose in the supreme state, into which nature has united nations, unless from it some law should arise for the whole in regard to the individuals. Of what sort this is will be shown in what follows.

§ 14. *How this is to be measured*

The law of nations as a whole with reference to individual nations in the supreme state must be measured by the purpose of the supreme state. For the law of the whole with reference to individuals in a state must be measured by the purpose of that state. Therefore, since in the supreme state too a certain right belongs to nations as a whole with reference to the individual nations, this right also must be measured by the purpose of the supreme state.

Since in any state the right of the whole over the individuals must not be extended beyond the purpose of the state, so also the right of nations as a whole over individual nations cannot be extended beyond the purpose of the supreme state into which nature herself has combined them, so that forthwith individual nations may be known to have assigned a right of this sort to the whole.

§ 15. *Of what sort this is*

Some sovereignty over individual nations belongs to nations as a whole. For a certain sovereignty over individuals belongs to the whole in a state. Therefore, as is previously shown, some sovereignty over individual nations belongs also to nations as a whole.

That sovereignty will seem paradoxical to some. But these will be such as do not have a clear notion of the supreme state, nor recognize the benefit which nature provides, when she establishes a certain civil society among nations. Moreover, it will be evident in its own place that nothing at all results from this, except those things which all willingly recognize as in accordance with the law of nations, or what it is readily understood they ought to recognize. Nor is it less plain that this sovereignty has a certain resemblance to civil sovereignty.

§ 16. *Of the moral equality of nations*

By nature all nations are equal the one to the other. For nations are considered as individual free persons living in a state of nature. Therefore, since by nature all men are equal, all nations too are by nature equal the one to the other.

It is not the number of men coming together into a state that makes a nation, but the bond by which the individuals are united, and this is nothing else than the obligation by which they are bound to one another. The society which exists in the greater number of men united together, is the same as that which exists in the smaller number. Therefore just as the tallest man is no more a man than the dwarf, so also a nation, however small, is no less a nation than the greatest nation. Therefore, since the moral equality of men has no relation to the size of their bodies, the moral equality of nations also has no relation to the number of men of which they are composed.

§ 17. *In what it consists*

Since by nature all nations are equal, since moreover all men are equal in a moral sense whose rights and obligations are the same; the rights and obligations of all nations also are by nature the same.

Therefore a great and powerful nation can assume no right to itself against a small and weak nation such as does not belong to the weaker against the stronger, nor is a small and weak nation bound to a great and powerful one in any way in which the latter is not equally bound to it.

§ 18. *Whether by nature anything is lawful for one nation which is not lawful for another*

Since by nature the rights and obligations of all nations are the same, and since that is lawful which we have a right to do, and unlawful which we are obliged not to do or to omit; what is lawful by nature for one nation, that likewise is lawful for another, and what is not lawful for one, is not lawful for another.

Might gives to no nation a special privilege over another, just as force gives none to one man over another. Just as might is not the source of the law of nature, so that any one may do what he can to another, so neither is the might of nations the source of the law of nations, so that right is to be measured by might.

§ 19. *What form of government is adapted to the supreme state*

The supreme state is a kind of democratic form of government. For the supreme state is made up of the nations as a whole, which as individual nations are free and equal to each other. Therefore, since no nation by nature is subject to another nation, and since it is evident of itself that nations by common consent have not bestowed the sovereignty which belongs to the whole as against the individual nations, upon one or more particular nations, nay, that it cannot even be conceived under human conditions how this may happen, that sovereignty is understood to have been reserved for nations as a whole. Therefore, since the government is democratic, if the sovereignty rests with the whole, which in the present instance is the entire human race divided up into people or nations, the supreme state is a kind of democratic form of government.

The democratic form of government is the most natural form of a state, since it begins at the very beginning of the state itself and is only *de facto* changed into any other form, a thing which cannot even be conceived of in the supreme state. Therefore for the supreme state no form of government is suitable other than the democratic form.

§ 20. *What must be conceived of in the supreme state as the will of all the nations*

Since in a democratic state that must be considered the will of the whole people which shall have seemed best to the majority, since moreover the supreme state is a kind of democratic form of government, and is made up of all the nations, in the supreme state also that must be considered the will of all the nations which shall have seemed best to the majority. Nevertheless, since in a democratic state it is necessary that individuals assemble in a definite place and declare their will as to what ought to be done, since moreover all the nations scattered throughout the whole world cannot assemble together, as is self-evident, that must be taken to be the will of all nations which they are bound to agree upon, if following the leadership of nature they use right reason. Hence it is plain, because it has to be admitted, that what has been approved by the more civilized nations is the law of nations.

Grotius recognized that some law of nations must be admitted which departs from the law of nature, the inflexibility of which cannot possibly be observed among nations. Moreover, he does not think that this law is such that it can be proved otherwise than by precedents and decisions, and especially the agreements of the more civilized nations. We indeed shall enter upon a safer course if we point out that nations following reason ought to agree as to either this or that which has prevailed, or now prevails, among them as law – a thing which can be proved from the concept of the supreme state no less plainly than the necessary or natural law of nations can.

§ 21. *Of the ruler of the supreme state*

Since in the supreme state that is to be considered as the will of all nations, to which they ought to agree, if following the leadership of nature they use right reason, and since the superior in the state is he to whom belongs the right over the actions of the individuals, consequently he who exercises the sovereignty, therefore he can be considered the ruler of the supreme state who, following the leadership of nature, defines by the right use of reason what nations ought to consider as law among themselves, although it does not conform in all respects to the natural law of nations, nor altogether differ from it.

Fictions are advantageously allowed in every kind of science, for the purpose of eliciting truths as well as for proving them. For example, the astronomers, in order to calculate the movements of the planets, assume that a planet is carried by a regular motion in a circular orbit concentric with the sun and about it, and, in the reckoning of time, the sun is assumed to be carried by a regular motion around the equator. Nay, all moral persons and, too, the supreme state itself in the law of nature and nations have something fictitious in them. Those who disapprove of such things, abundantly show that they are only superficially acquainted with the sciences. Moreover the fictitious ruler of the supreme state is assumed, in order to adapt the natural or necessary law of nations to the purpose of the supreme state, as far as human conditions allow, using the right of making laws, which we have shown above belongs to the supreme state.

§ 22. *Definition of the voluntary law of nations and what it is*

With Grotius we speak of the voluntary law of nations, which is derived from the concept of the supreme state, therefore it is considered to have been laid down by its fictitious ruler and so to have proceeded from the will of nations. The voluntary law of nations is therefore equivalent to the civil law, consequently it is derived in the same manner from the necessary law of nations, as we have shown that the civil law must be derived from the natural law in the fifth chapter of the eighth part of 'The Law of Nature.'

And so we have a fixed and immovable foundation for the voluntary law of nations, and there are definite principles, by force of which that law can be derived from the concept of the supreme state, so that it is not necessary to rely by blind impulse on the deeds and customs and decisions of the more civilized nations, and from this there must be assumed as it were a certain universal consensus of all, just as Grotius seems to have perceived.

§ 23. *The stipulative law of nations*

There is a stipulative law of nations, which arises from stipulations entered into between different nations. Since stipulations are entered into between two or more nations, as is plain from the meaning of 'pact', since moreover no one can bind another to himself beyond his consent, therefore much less contrary to his consent, nor acquire from him a right which he does not wish to transfer to him; stipulations therefore bind only the nations between whom they are made. Therefore the law of nations, which arises from stipulations, or the stipulative, is not universal but particular.

The stipulative law of nations has its equivalent in the private law of citizens, because it has its origin in their agreements. Therefore just as the private law for citizens, derived from agreements entered into between themselves, is considered as having no value at all as civil law for a certain particular state, so also the law for nations derived from agreements entered into with other nations, it seems cannot be considered as the law of nations. Therefore it is plain that the stipulative law of nations is to be accepted only in a certain general sense, in so far as through stipulations nations can bind themselves to one another and acquire certain rights, and there is a certain proper subject-matter of these stipulations, so that therefore the stipulative law of nations has regard only to those things which must be observed concerning the stipulations of nations and their subject matter in general. For the particular stipulations and the rights and obligations arising therefrom as to the states stipulating, since they are simply factitious, do not belong to the science of the law of nations, but to the history of this law or of the nation, which it enjoys in respect of certain of other nations. The general theory of the stipulative law of nations could have been referred to the voluntary law of nations; whoever desires so to do, will not have the least objection from us.

§ 24. *Of the customary law of nations*

The customary law of nations is so called, because it has been brought in by long usage and observed as law. It is also frequently called simply custom, in the native idiom *das Herkommen* [usage]. Since certain nations use it one with the other, the customary law of nations rests upon the tacit consent of the nations, or, if you prefer, upon a tacit stipulation, and it is evident that it is not universal, but a particular law, just as was the stipulative law.

What we have just remarked about the stipulative law must likewise be maintained concerning the customary law.

§ 25. *Of the positive law of nations*

That is called the positive law of nations which takes its origin from the will of nations. Therefore since it is plainly evident that the voluntary, the stipulative, and the customary law of nations take their origin from the will of nations, all that law is the positive law of nations. And since furthermore it is plain that the voluntary law of nations rests on the presumed consent of nations, the stipulative upon the express consent, the customary upon the tacit consent, since moreover in no other way is it conceived that a certain law can spring from the will of nations, the positive law of nations is either voluntary or stipulative or customary.

Those who do not have a clear conception of the supreme state, and therefore do not derive from it the voluntary law of nations, which Grotius has mentioned, and even wholly reject it, or refer some part of it to the customs of certain nations, such recognize no other positive law of nations at all, aside from the stipulative or customary. But certainly it is wrong to refer to customs, what reason itself teaches is to be observed as law among all nations.

§ 26. *General observation*

We shall carefully distinguish the voluntary, the stipulative, and the customary law of nations from the natural or necessary law of nations, nevertheless
we shall not teach the former separately from the latter, but when we have
shown what things belong to the necessary law of nations, we shall straightway
add, where, why, and in what manner that must be changed to the voluntary,
and here and there, when we have carefully considered it, we shall add the
stipulative and the customary, which are by no means to be confused with
the voluntary, especially since they have not been distinguished from it with
sufficient care by Grotius. And the method which we have thus far used,
both in the law of nature and in the other parts of philosophy already taught
by us, and which we shall likewise use in the other parts, to be taught by us
in their own time and order, this too we use in the law of nations, although
the particular laws peculiar to some nations, which either come from stipulations or are due to customs, we do not consider, inasmuch as they are at
variance with our plan, with which only those things which belong to science
are in harmony. And why one must use such a method is plain from our proofs
and our notes in the Prolegomena to 'The Law of Nature.'

EMMERICH DE VATTEL

EMMERICH DE VATTEL (1714–67), Swiss jurist and diplomat. A disciple of Wolff, Vattel was inspired to restate the famous philosopher's theory of international law for a wider and more practically minded audience. The result of this effort, *The Law of Nations* (1758), became an instant classic. Though often called the first really modern work of international law, Vattel's book remains firmly in the tradition of natural law and for that reason might equally be seen as one of the last specimens of a moribund genre. Its fame rests not on its theoretical power but on Vattel's impressive practical grasp of international affairs and his skill in balancing moral and prudential considerations in a way suited to the prejudices of his day.

From *The Law of Nations or Principles of Natural Law*

Book 2, chapter 3
The Dignity and Equality of Nations. Titles and Other Marks of Honor

Every Nation, every sovereign and independent State, is deserving of honor and respect as having a recognized position in the great society of the human race, as being independent of any power on earth, and as possessing, by reason of its numbers, a greater importance than belongs to the individual. The sovereign represents the entire Nation of which he is head, and unites in his person the attributes which belong to the Nation. No individual, however free and independent, can stand in comparison with a sovereign; it would be as if a single man were to claim the same importance as belongs to a body of his equals. Nations and sovereigns have, therefore, both the obligation and the right to uphold their dignity and to cause it to be respected, as a thing of importance to their peace and their security.

We have already remarked that nature has established a perfect equality of rights among independent Nations. In consequence, no one of them may justly claim to be superior to the others. All the attributes which one possesses in virtue of its freedom and independence are possessed equally by the others.

Hence, since precedence or priority of rank is a mark of superority, no Nation or sovereign may claim a natural right to it. Why should Nations which are not subject to another Nation show deference to it against their will? However, as a large and powerful State has a much more important position in the universal society than that of a small State, it is reasonable that the latter should defer to the former on occasions where one must give place to the other, as in an assembly. The deference thus shown is a matter of mere ceremony, which takes away nothing from their essential equality and indicates only a priority of position, the first place among equals. The others will naturally give first place to the most powerful Nation, and it would be both useless and ridiculous for the weakest of them to attempt to contest it. The great age of a State will likewise be a consideration on such occasions; a new comer among States may not dispossess another of the honors it is enjoying, and very strong reasons are needed to obtain precedence in such a case.

The form of a Nation's government naturally does not affect the question of rank. The honor due to a Nation belongs fundamentally to the body of the people; and it is shown to the sovereign merely as the representative of the Nation. Is a State to be more or less worthy of honor according as it is governed by one man or by several? In these days kings claim superiority of rank over republics; but the claim has no other foundation than superiority of power. In former times the Roman Republic looked upon kings as far beneath it in rank; the monarchs of Europe came in contact with weak republics and refused to admit them on a basis of equality. Venice and the United Provinces have obtained, as republics, the honors of crowned heads; but their ambassadors yield precedence to those of kings.

Following the principles we have just laid down, if a Nation should happen to change its form of government it will not lose the rank and the honors of which it is in possession. When England drove out its Kings, Cromwell would suffer no diminution in the honors which had been shown to the crown or to the Nation; and he saw to it that the English ambassadors retained the rank they had always held.

If the relative rank of Nations has been fixed by treaty, or by long custom founded upon implied consent, the established rule must be conformed to. To deny the right of a prince to the rank he has thus acquired would be regarded as an injury, since it would be a mark of contempt or a violation of the agreement guaranteeing him his right. Thus when the partition was unfortunately made between the sons of Charlemagne, the Empire went to the eldest; and the younger son, who received the Kingdom of France, gave precedence to the elder all the more easily, as there still persisted at that time a memory of the supremacy of the true Roman Empire. Succeeding French Kings followed the rule thus established, and the other European Kings imitated them, so that the imperial crown is recognized as holding the first rank in Christendom. The majority of the other crowned heads are not in agreement of the question of rank.

Certain persons have tried to find in the Emperor's precedence something more than the first place among equals, and to attribute to him a superiority over all kings; in a word, to make him the temporal head of Christendom. And it seems in fact, that several emperors have been minded to make like claims, as if, in reviving the name of the Roman Empire, they could also revive its rights. The other States have been on their guard against such pretensions. Mezeray shows us the precautions taken by Charles V when the Emperor Charles IV came to France, "for fear," says the historian, "lest the courtesy shown to the Emperor, and to his son the King of the Romans, might be made the basis of a right of superiority." Bodin relates that the French took great offense because the Emperor Sigismund "sat in the royal seat in full Parliament, and knighted the Sénéchal de Beaucaire," adding that "to repair the grievous mistake of permitting it," they were unwilling to permit the same Emperor, when at Lyons, to make the Comte de Savoie a duke. In these days a King of France would doubtless think himself demeaned if he gave the slightest sign which might be taken as an indication of any authority held by another State over his Kingdom.

A Nation, having the right to confer upon its ruler the degree of authority and the rights which it thinks proper, is no less free with respect to the name, titles, and honors which it may choose to bestow upon him. But if it be wise, and look to the interests of its reputation, it will not depart too far from the general practice of civilized Nations in this respect. Moreover, prudence will lead a Nation to proportion the title and the honors of its ruler to the degree of power and authority which it wishes to confer upon him. It is true that titles and honors decide nothing; they are but empty names and idle ceremonies when they are not appropriate. But who can deny their influence upon men's minds? This is what makes them of more consequence than they would appear to be at first glance. A Nation should take care not to demean itself in the eyes of other Nations or to degrade its ruler by too humble a title; but it should be even more on its guard not to encourage pride by an empty name and immoderate honors, or to put it into his mind to seek to obtain a corresponding power, either by usurpation at home or conquest abroad. On the other hand, an exalted title may animate the ruler to maintain with greater firmness the dignity of the Nation. Circumstances will determine what it is prudent to do, and in every case due bounds should be observed. "The fact that it was a Kingdom," says a reputable author who can be believed on this subject, "delivered the House of Brandenburg from the yoke of servitude under which Austria at that time held all the German princes." It was an ambition which Frederic III put up before his successors, as if he said to them: "I have won a title for you; do you act up to it; I have laid the foundations of your greatness; it is for you to complete the edifice."

If the ruler of a State is possessed of sovereign power he has in his hands the rights and the authority of the body politic, and he may therefore determine for himself his title and the honors which must be shown him, unless they are prescribed in the fundamental law, or unless the limitations put upon his power are a clear check upon the position he seeks to assume. His subjects owe him obedience in this case, as in all others where he acts within his lawful authority. Thus the Czar Peter I, basing his claim upon the vast extent of his States, took for himself the title of Emperor.

But foreign Nations are not obliged to defer to the wishes of a sovereign who assumes a new title, or of a Nation which gives what title it pleases to its ruler.

However, if the title is not an unreasonable one, nor opposed to accepted custom, it is perfectly in keeping with the mutual duties which exist between Nations to give to the sovereign of a State or to a ruler of whatever character the same title which his people apply to him. But if this title be contrary to custom, if it indicates a position which the bearer does not hold, foreign Nations may refuse to accord it to him without his having any ground of complaint. The title of "Majesty" is consecrated by custom to the monarchs of great Nations. The Emperors of Germany for a long time claimed it for themselves, as belonging solely to the imperial crown. But the Kings claimed with good reason that there was no position on earth more venerable than their own, and they refused the title to him who had refused it to them; and to-day, with only a few exceptions founded on special reasons, the title of Majesty is peculiar to Kings.

As it would be ridiculous for a petty prince to assume the title of King and have himself addressed as "His Majesty," foreign Nations, in refusing to recognize him as such, would only be acting conformably to reason and their duty. However, if in other lands a sovereign should be in the habit of receiving from his neighbors the title of King, in spite of the small extent of his power, distant Nations desiring to trade with him may not refuse him the title. It is not for them to reform the customs of remote countries.

A sovereign who wishes to receive regularly certain titles and honors from other powers should secure them by treaty. Those who make agreements of this character are thereafter bound by them, and they may not act contrary to the treaty without doing an injury. Thus, in the cases we have just related, the Czar and the King of Prussia took care to negotiate in advance with friendly powers to secure their recognition under the new titles they wished to assume.

In former times it was the claim of Popes that it belonged to the tiara to create new crowns, and they relied upon the superstition of princes and peoples in their assertion of so sublime a right. But the claim ceased to be recognized at the period of the Renaissance, as phantoms disappear before the rising sun. The Emperors of Germany, who have made a similar claim, had at least before them the example of the ancient Romans; had they the same power they would have the same right.

In default of treaties, the generally received custom should be followed in the matter of titles and marks of honor in general. To seek to depart from it, when there is no special reason for not showing a Nation or sovereign the customary honors, would be a mark of contempt or of ill-will and contrary both to good policy and to the duties of one Nation to another.

The greatest monarch ought to respect in every ruler the sovereign character with which he is invested. The independence and equality of Nations and the mutual duties of humanity are reason for showing even to the ruler of a petty State the respect due to the office he holds. The weakest State, no less than the most powerful, is made up of men who, whether few or many in number, are the object of our respect.

But this precept of the natural law does not extend further than the respect which is due from one independent Nation to another; in a word, that respect which acknowledges a State or its ruler as truly sovereign and independent, and deserving therefore of all that is due to that character. On the other hand, since a great monarch has, as we have already remarked, a very important position in human society, it is but natural that, in all that is a mere matter of form and affects in no way the essential equality of Nations, certain honors be shown him to which a petty prince could not pretend; and the latter may not refuse to the monarch such deference as does not compromise his sovereignty and independence.

Nations and sovereigns should uphold their dignity by insisting that due honor be shown them, and above all by not permitting any offense against their honor. Hence, if certain titles and marks of respect belong to them by long custom, they may insist upon them, and they should do so whenever a case arises where national honor is involved.

But a careful distinction must be drawn between neglect, or the failure to do what received custom calls for, and positive acts of disrespect, or insults. Mere neglect may be a subject of complaint, and, if no apology be made, may be regarded as a mark of ill-will; whereas a Nation may demand, even by force of arms, the redress of an insult. The Czar Peter I, in his manifesto against Sweden, complained that no salute had been fired when he passed at Riga. He had reason to think it strange that this mark of respect had not been shown him, and he might complain of the omission; but to go to war about it would show a strange readiness to shed blood.

...

Book 3, chapter 12

The Voluntary Law of Nations with Respect to the Effects of the Regular War,
Independently of the Justice of the Cause

The doctrines laid down in the preceding chapter are a logical inference from
sound principles, from the eternal rules of justice; they are the provisions of
that sacred law which Nature, or the Divine Author of Nature, has imposed
upon Nations. He alone whose sword is drawn from necessity and in the
cause of justice has the right to make war; he alone has the right to attack
his enemy, to take away his life, and to deprive him of his property. Such is
the decree of the *necessary Law of Nations,* or of the natural law, as it must
be observed in all its strictness by Nations; it is the inviolable law binding
upon each of them in conscience. But how shall this law be made to prevail
in the quarrels of the Nations and sovereigns who live together in the state
of nature? They recognize no superior who shall decide between them and
define the rights and obligations of each, who shall say to this one, "You have
a right to take up arms, to attack your enemy and subdue him by force,"
and to that other, "Your hostilities are unwarranted, your victories are but
murder, your conquests are but the spoil of robbery and pillage." It belongs to
every free and sovereign State to decide in its own conscience what its duties
require of it, and what it may or may not do with justice. If others undertake
to judge of its conduct, they encroach upon its liberty and infringe upon its
most valuable rights. Moreover, since each Nation claims to have justice on
its side, it will arrogate to itself all the rights of war and claim that its enemy
has none, that his hostilities are but deeds of robbery, acts in violation of the
Law of Nations, and deserving of punishment by all Nations. The decision of
the rights at issue will not be advanced thereby, and the contest will become
more cruel, more disastrous in its effects, and more difficult of termination.
Further still, neutral Nations themselves will be drawn into the dispute and
implicated in the quarrel. If an unjust war can give rise to no legal rights, no
certain possession can be obtained of any property captured in war until a
recognized judge, and there is none such between Nations, shall have passed
definitely upon the justice of the war; and such property will always be subject
to a claim for recovery, as in the case of goods stolen by robbers.

Let us, therefore, leave to the conscience of sovereigns the observance
of the natural and necessary law in all its strictness; and indeed it is never
lawful for them to depart from it. But as regards the external operation of
that law in human society, we must necessarily have recourse to certain rules
of more certain and easy application, and this in the interest of the safety and
welfare of the great society of the human race. These rules are those of the
voluntary Law of Nations. The natural law which looks to the greatest good of

human society, which protects the liberty of each Nation, and which desires that the affairs of sovereigns be settled and their quarrels come to a speedy issue – the natural law, I say, recommends for the common advantage of Nations the observance of the voluntary Law of Nations, just as it approves of the changes which the civil law makes in the natural law for the purpose of adapting the latter to the conditions of civil society and of making its application easier and more certain. Let us, therefore, apply to the special subject of war the general statements which we made in the Introduction. When a sovereign, or a Nation, is deliberating upon the steps he must take to fulfill his duty, he must never lose sight of the *necessary* law, which is always binding in conscience; but when it is a question of determining what he can demand of other States, he must consider the *voluntary* Law of Nations, and restrict even his just claims within the bounds of a law whose principles are consecrated to the safety and welfare of the universal society of Nations. Let him make the *necessary* law the constant rule of his own conduct; he must allow others to take advantage of the voluntary Law of Nations.

The first rule of that law, with respect to the subject under consideration, is that *regular war, as regards its effects, must be accounted just on both sides*. This principle, as we have just shown, is absolutely necessary if any law or order is to be introduced into a method of redress as violent as that of war, if any bounds are to be set to the disasters it occasions, and if a door is to be left at all times open for the return of peace. Moreover, any other rule would be impracticable as between Nation and Nation, since they recognize no common judge.

Thus the rights founded upon the state of war, the legal nature of its effects, the validity of the acquisitions made in it, do not depend, externally and in the sight of men, upon the justice of the cause, but upon the legality of the means as such, that is to say, upon the presence of the elements constituting a regular war. If the enemy observes all the rules of formal warfare, we are not to be heard in complaint of him as a violator of the Law of Nations; he has the same right as we to assert a just cause; and our entire hope lies in victory or in a friendly settlement.

Second rule: Since two enemies are regarded as having an equally just cause, *whatever is permitted to one because of the state of war is also permitted to the other*. In fact, no Nation, on the ground of having justice on its side, ever complains of the hostilities of its enemy, so long as they remain within the bounds prescribed by the common laws of war. In the preceding chapters we have treated of what may lawfully be done in a just war. It is precisely that, and no more, which the voluntary law equally authorizes both parties in doing. That law makes the same acts lawful on both sides, but it allows neither party any act unlawful in itself, and can not approve of unbridled license. Consequently, if Nations overstep those limits, if they carry hostilities beyond what is in general permitted by the internal and necessary law for the support of a just cause, let us be careful not to ascribe these excesses to the voluntary Law of Nations; they are to be attributed solely to a moral degeneracy which has given rise to iniquitous and barbarous customs. Such are those excesses to which soldiers sometimes abandon themselves when a town is taken by assault.

Thirdly, it must never be forgotten that *this voluntary Law of Nations*, established from necessity and for the avoidance of greater evils, *does not confer upon him whose cause is unjust any true rights capable of justifying his conduct and appeasing his conscience, but merely makes his conduct legal in the sight of men, and exempts him from punishment*. This is sufficiently clear from the principles on which the voluntary Law of Nations is based. Consequently, the sovereign who has no just cause in authorization of his hostilities is not less unjust, or less guilty of violating the sacred Law of Nature, merely because that same natural law, in the effort not to increase the evils of human society while seeking to prevent them, requires that he be conceded the same legal rights as more justly belong to his enemy. Thus the civil law allows a debtor to refuse payment in a case of prescription; but the debtor nevertheless violates his moral duty; he takes advantage of a law enacted to prevent a multiplicity of lawsuits, but he acts without any true right.

From the fact that Nations actually concur in observing the rules which we assign to the voluntary Law of Nations, Grotius bases them upon a real consent upon the part of Nations, and refers them to the arbitrary Law of Nations. But apart from the difficulty of proving the existence of such an agreement, it would only be enforceable against those who had formally entered into it. If such an agreement existed, it would come under the conventional Law of Nations, which is a matter of historical proof, not of reasoning, and is based, not upon principles, but upon facts. In this work we are laying down the natural principles of the Law of Nations; we deduce them from nature itself; and what we call the voluntary Law of Nations consists in the rules of conduct, of external law, to which the natural law obliges Nations to consent; so that we rightly presume their consent, without seeking any record of it; for even if they had not given their consent, the Law of Nature supplies it, and gives it for them. Nations are not free in this matter to consent or not; the Nation which would refuse to consent would violate the common rights of all Nations.

The voluntary Law of Nations, thus substantiated, is of very wide application; it is by no means a fantasy, an arbitrary invention destitute of foundation. It is derived from the same source and based upon the same principles as the *natural* or *necessary* law. Why has nature appointed to men such and such rules of conduct, except because those rules are necessary to the welfare and happiness of the human race? Now, the principles of the necessary Law of Nations are founded directly upon the nature of things, and particularly upon the nature of man and of political society, while the voluntary Law of Nations supposes a further principle, namely, the nature of the great society of Nations and of the intercourse which they have with one another. The necessary law prescribes what is of absolute necessity for Nations and what tends naturally to their advancement and their common happiness; the voluntary law tolerates what it is impossible to forbid without causing greater evils.

7

The Enlightenment

International politics in the seventeenth and eighteenth centuries is usually seen as the high water mark of the "traditional" view of the European states-system. It is in this period, as seen in the previous chapter, that the notion of the "balance of power," so central to realist thinking, first emerges, self-consciously at least, and it is the writings of scholars such as Vattel (whose *The Law of Nations* was first published in 1758) that establish or cement the meanings of some of the central terms of modern international thought (such as sovereignty).

However, it is also in this period that some of the major challenges to conventional understanding of the states-system also emerged. Most specifically, in the thinking of some of the writers associated with what is usually called the "European Enlightenment," some of the basic assumptions underlying the emerging states-system were challenged, a challenge which has lasted until our own day and is still continuing.

What is the "Enlightenment"?

At its simplest, the "Enlightenment" is a phrase that represents the collective, overlapping (and not always congruent) views of a group of scholars, writers, activists, and campaigners in eighteenth-century Europe. Especially prominent in France, it had representatives in almost every major European country and, as the eighteenth century went on, it became increasingly important both intellectually and politically. Figures especially associated with it include David Hume and Immanuel Kant, Montesquieu and Jean-Jacques Rousseau, Edward Gibbon and Adam Smith, Voltaire and Denis Diderot. The legacy of these thinkers was to have an increasing power in the nineteenth and twentieth centuries. Just as they effectively created many of the contemporary social sciences – for example, political economy, sociology,

379

even anthropology – their legacy is a central site of contestation in many contemporary sciences, including Political Science and International Human Relations.

Perhaps the most important aspect of that legacy – and one of the central sites of contest today – was best expressed by Kant in a famous essay, *An Answer to the Question "What is Enlightenment?,"* first published in 1784. "Enlightenment," Kant wrote, "is man's emergence from his self-incurred immaturity. Immaturity is the inability to use one's own understanding without the guidance of another ... for Enlightenment ... all that is needed is freedom ... freedom to make public use of one's reason in all matters ... if it is asked whether we at present live in an enlightened age the answer is no, but we do live in an age of *Enlightenment*" (Reiss, 1970: 54–5, 58). This conception of Enlightenment echoes down the eighteenth century and is as central for Enlightenment conceptions of international relations as it is for other aspects of their concerns, as we shall see. Emphasizing emergence from "self-incurred immaturity" and the freedom to develop the "public use of reason" inevitably sets the Enlightenment on a collision course with tradition, with established ways of doing things in many different areas of life, though the extent and character of that collision differed from thinker to thinker.

This chapter, therefore, will seek to outline the thinking of some of the major figures of this movement, and specifically it will discuss the ideas of Montesquieu, Hume, Smith, Rousseau, and Kant, the most important luminaries of the eighteenth-century Enlightenment to discuss international relations. However, also included will be an extract from the first expression of an idea – the idea of perpetual peace – that exerted considerable influence on the way in which many Enlightenment thinkers saw international politics, especially Rousseau and Kant. This is the original "project on perpetual peace in Europe" penned by the Abbé de Saint-Pierre (pp. 394–8 below). At first, however, a general discussion of the Enlightenment's central political ideas is offered.

Enlightenment political thought:
Montesquieu and his legacy

"The philosophy of Enlightenment," writes Peter Gay, in perhaps the most exhaustive contemporary survey of Enlightenment thought, "insisted on man's essential autonomy: man is responsible to himself, to his own rational interests, to his self-development and *by an inescapable extension*, to the welfare of his fellow man" (Gay, 1970; editor's italics).

Gay is here referring explicitly to the alleged "universalism" of Enlightenment political theory, but the one thing that immediately strikes one about
this assertion is simply the fact that the political writings of *philosophes* are
remarkable not for their unity but for their apparent diversity: Voltaire
(1694–1778) is a relativist and a believer in enlightened autocracy; Rousseau
(1712–78) a democratic radical; Beccaria a legal (though humane) absolutist;
Hume (1711–76), a Whig constitutionalist. Can we make a unity out of
such diverse material? Or is the proclaimed unity a false creature created,
as Roy Porter has suggested, by "mingled academic imperialism and tidy-
mindedness"? (Porter and Teich, 1981.)

Diversity was indeed a hallmark of the Enlightenment. However, it
also had a unity in aim, though a diversity in method, and in its political
aspect this unity in aim follows directly from generally accepted values of the
Enlightenment: liberty, tolerance, progress, criticism. Almost all *philosophes*
would have agreed that these were the cardinal values. Within this broad
agreement on the general aspects of what politics should aim toward, there
was, however, one crucial and far-reaching difference both in method and
solution which divided the Enlightenment, best seen perhaps as a divsion
between a "mainstream" of Enlightenment political thought – rational,
critical, naturalistic, and modelled on the growing power and influence of
natural science – and a powerful, though muted, undercurrent, which is far
more skeptical about the "scientific" ambitions of the mainstream.

In most respects in this field (as in so many others) the true originator
is Charles, Baron de Montesquieu, and especially his *The Spirit of the Laws*
(1748), perhaps the master text of the mainstream Enlightenment. "I have not
drawn my principles from my prejudices," writes Montesquieu, announc-
ing his project in the preface, "but from the nature of things." As many have
pointed out, Montesquieu was by some way the most influential writer of the
eighteenth century, for the Enlightenment itself and even outside it (Cassirer,
1951; Hampson, 1968; Gay, 1970). Across Europe, from Scotland to France and
Italy – and indeed beyond Europe, in North America – *The Spirit of the Laws*
was hugely successful. Beccaria, the great Italian legal theorist, called its author the "immortal Montesquieu"; Alexander Hamilton, a signatory of the
US declaration of independence, referred to him as "that great man";
Montesquieu's chief Anglo-Saxon colleague, David Hume, corresponded
with him, seeking to translate *The Spirit of the Laws*; and even Catherine the
Great, the empress of Russia – not a woman noted for her commitment to
the cause of Enlightenment – found it at least politic to claim that she was
his devoted follower.

Montesquieu's great treatise is, of course, extraordinarily wide and frus-
tratingly resistant to easy summary. Essentially it seeks to ally reason, humanity, and liberality, putting them together as a form of social relativism uneasily

combined with a radical individualism, which together lead to the conclusion that there is no specific universal solution to everything, rather there are only types of solution. Most important for our concerns, the mainstream Enlightenment's basic approach to international relations is characteristically summed up by a passage from *The Spirit of the Laws*: "The right of nations is by nature founded on the principle that the various nations should do to one another in times of peace the most good possible and in times of war the least ill possible, without harming their true interests" (*The Spirit of the Laws*, 1, 3) (see p. 400 below).

This leads (in practical terms) to some of Montesquieu's most influential ideas about the way individuals should respond to one another and, indeed, how collectivities should conduct their relations – his criticism of slavery, his treatment of war as necessary but distasteful, his hostility to torture and the death penalty, his critique of existing European manners and morals (most effectively displayed in his *Persian Letters* [1721]), and especially his general relativism and contextualism, which emphasises a tolerant, flexible view of cultures and maners different from one's own (a point made much of in recent thought by Tzvetan Todorov [1999]).

Not all of these issues are central to International Relations, of course, even broadly conceived, but they set the tone for how the mainstream Enlightenment tends to see the international realm.

Hume and Smith

Two writers in particular elaborated this side of Enlightenment thinking about international politics, aside from Montesquieu himself: Hume and his friend and fellow Scot Adam Smith. Excerpts from both are included below (see pp. 407–15), and examined in turn.

Hume's political writings are divided into three main kinds. In the first place are the political sections of his major philosophical works, the *Treatise on Human Nature* (1740) and the *Enquiry Concerning the Principles of Morals* (1751), usually called the "second" *Enquiry*, to distinguish it from the "first" *Enquiry* (the *Enquiry Concerning Human Understanding* of 1748). The latter two works were, in fact, heavily revised and rewritten versions of the first, which Hume believed had fallen (as he put it) "dead born from the press," and therefore needed recasting. There is a huge scholarly literature about the similarities and differences between the two works but in large part the political aspects of Hume's thought remain relatively constant in them both, though neither deals directly with questions of international politics. The second type of writing is the essays Hume published on political topics, specifically those he published in 1752 as the *Political Discourses*. It is worth pointing out that these were Hume's most successful publications up to that point and were widely read among the literate public across Europe; they contained a number of essays on international politics, most famously those on the balance of power and on the balance of trade (see pp. 407–9 below). The third type of writing relevant for Hume's political thought is his mammoth *History of England*, begun the same year, 1752, though not finished until the 1760s, which contains many political asides and astute political judgements. It is also worth pointing out that Hume had practical experience of politics and diplomacy, having served in the 1760s as secretary to the British Ambassador to Paris and later as Under Secretary of State himself.

Hume follows Montesquieu's lead in being empirical and skeptical in his political thinking. His writings about international relations show a recognition of the realities of the European scene of his own day coupled with a sense (more powerfully developed by Smith) of the growing importance for European politics of economic questions such as trade and a sense also of how this might (though certainly also might not) change the characteristic way that international politics was conducted. He certainly sees Europe as bound by many indissoluble bonds, and in that sense is a thinker closer to the "international society" tradition than he is to realism as conventionally understood, yet his commitment to Enlightenment norms goes deep and he is always on the look-out for the possibilities of advance in "civilized politics," both within and outside the European international society.

Adam Smith, of course, is famous today as the author of *The Wealth of Nations* (1776). He was also unusual amongst Enlightenment thinkers in being, at one time, an academic (he held the chair of Moral Philosophy at Glasgow University). His masterpiece is, indeed, *An Inquiry into the Nature and Causes of the Wealth of Nations*, but much of what he says in it is prefigured in his essays and lectures of the previous twenty years and in his *The Theory of Moral Sentiments* of 1759. Well versed in the various traditions of political economy which had emerged in the eighteenth century, especially mercantilism – the theory that economics should be based on national interests – which he detested, and the Fench school called the "physiocrats," on whose ideas he partly drew, Smith's arguments extended the sort of reasoning about international politics we have seen displayed in Montesquieu and Hume to the increasingly important realm of the political economy. The humanity, empiricism, skepticism, and rationality which are the hallmarks of all mainstream Enlightenment political thought culminates for Smith in his vision of an economy which benefits from the freedom of trade – his famous "invisible hand" – but which also requires carefully calibrated statecraft to mitigate the free play of self-interest both within states and between them. The final sections of the book, excerpted here (pp. 410–15 below), demonstrate these qualities especially well.

The counter current: Jean-Jacques Rousseau

To say that there is a "mainstream" to Enlightenment thought is obviously to indicate that there is also a counter current, an opposition to the mainstream. This was, of course, Jean-Jacques Rousseau (1712–78). Rousseau was, perhaps along with Diderot, the most multi-faceted writer of the Enlightenment: composer, playwright, novelist (*La Nouvelle Héloïse*, 1761; *Emile*, 1762), and social thinker (*The Social Contract*, 1762). Yet he was the outcast of the philosophic family. His views were in many ways opposed to theirs, and his temperament and ever-increasing paranoia drove a firm wedge between him and all who were – at one time or another – his friends, for example, Diderot, Voltaire, and Hume, who all ended up estranged from him.

The main difference between Rousseau's political thought and the mainstream Enlightenment is predicated – as might be expected – on his view of humanity and its possibilities. In an essay which won first prize in the celebrated competition organized by the Dijon Academy, the "Discourse on the Arts and Sciences" (usually known as the first discourse), he proclaims the importance of the "science of man" in characteristically rhetorical (but firmly Enlightenment) terms. However, the conclusions Rousseau arrives at about the state of existing society – and the reasons for it – go far beyond anything his fellow *philosophes* had suggested. At the heart of these conclusions is his view that man was – by nature – pre-moral (neither bad nor good, but innocent), and that he was not civilized, but fatally corrupted by existing cultures and society. Rousseau's intense exhortations to virtue as a counter to this corruption only point it up the more, and his insistence many years later that "our spirits have been corrupted to the degree that our arts and sciences have advanced towards perfection" showed that however much he might have cause to qualify that early work, the idea central to it was still in the same place at the end of his career that it was at its beginning. His later works, in particular the three great works of the late 1750s and early 1760s, *La Nouvelle Héloïse*, *The Social Contract*, and *Emile*, all pose this problem again, in their different ways, and offer partial solutions to it.

However, Rousseau was not a simple opponent of civilization as such. He was, after all, very insistent that mere destruction of institutions would only serve to kill possible avenues of remedy, while leaving the vice and corruption extant. The view of man on which this was based was, therefore, not a simple case of primitivism, for all that Rousseau has often been pilloried as having recourse to the idea of the "noble savage." Rousseau's account of man, culled from *The Social Contract* and *Emile*, is an imaginative reconstruction of man's "nature, duties, and end." It is not an "historical" recreation of man's nature, for it is partly through the process of history itself that man's nature has become corrupted, but it uses that history to provide insight and illumination. In a powerful image, Rousseau describes just what an onslaught man's true nature faces: "Man's nature [he wrote in *Emile*] is like a young tree which has, by mischance, been born in the middle of a large highway ... how important it is to separate the new tree from the great highway, to protect it from the crushing force of social conventions."

In *Emile*, Rousseau seeks to isolate the "young tree," to "build a wall around the root." *The Social Contract* is the second half of that solution: to erect a society which can then allow the wall to be dismantled. Both halves of this solution are, Rousseau believes, necessary because of the interdependence he perceives between corrupt man and corrupt society. An uncorrupted man in present society would soon – and inevitably – become corrupt; equally, corrupt men would soon destroy a society based on the principles of *The Social Contract*. Thus, both moral men and a moral society are necessary and this means, of course, that both are, in their present state, corrupt. This is the centerpiece of the real point at issue between Rousseau and the mainstream Enlightenment. Those of the *philosophes* who reflected on it certainly believed that there were serious things wrong with their society. Yet there is a crucial difference between these critical attitudes and Rousseau's. For him, when man passes from the state of nature to civil society, Rousseau argues, justice is substituted for instinct and thus morality enters man's nature. It is this prospect which brings forth man's greatest opportunity but also (and at the same time) his greatest danger. It is this danger that Rousseau's account in *Emile* and *The Social Contract* are designed to counter. In *Emile* the Stoic tag "live according to nature" is wedded to human educational development, and in *The Social Contract* it is used to help set up a state that will permit the truly "educated" man to live a moral life. This transition is the centerpiece of Rousseau's moral theory and the arena of his greatest clash with the other *philosophes*. His political theory, somewhat relativistic like theirs as far as forms of government were concerned, was in one vital respect different. For Rousseau, the citizen must be "ruler and ruled," "law giver and subject" and the means of achieving this was, in perhaps Rousseau's most famous phrase, submission to the "general will." The "general will" has its source in Rousseau's view of alienation. For alienation to be avoided, the social structure must be such that all individuals rule themselves at the same time as they rule others for "the natural man exists entirely for himself. He is the numerical, the whole, he enters into relations only with himself or with men like him." The citizen is only the numerator of "a fraction whose value depends on the denominator, his value depends the whole," as he puts it in *The Social Contract*. The conversion of "natural men" into (non-corrupt) "citizens" is what the "general will" is designed to accomplish.

How then, does this analysis map onto the questions we are concerned with in this book? Rousseau's thinking about international politics flows naturally and directly from his political thought more generally. Indeed, he had sketched out in Venice in 1743 an outline for a complete and comprehensive treatment of all forms of politics, domestic and international, to be called the *Institutions Politiques*. Even though this was never written, his political works are all of a piece. Just as he believed that human societies in general were corrupt for the reasons just outlined, the corruption was naturally much greater when you look at the society of such societies, that is, *international* society. His account of the origin of this society (given predominantly in his 1755/6 essay, *The State of War* [see pp. 416–25 below] parallels his account in the better-known works of the late 1750s and early 1760s, though it is perhaps (if possible) darker still. In a famous phrase, he bemoans "unfortunate nations groaning under yokes of Iron, the human race crushed by a handful of oppressors, a starving crowd overwhelmed with pain and hunger, whose blood and tears the rich drink in peace and everywhere the strong armed against the weak with the formidable power of the law" (*The State of War*).

How optimistic was he that such a situation could be overcome? The general answer (see, for example, Hoffmann and Fidler, 1991) is that Rousseau is not optimistic and, indeed, if one examines works like his *Abstract and Judgement of Saint-Pierre's Project for Perpetual Peace* (1761) (see pp. 425–7) it is hard to see Rousseau as an optimist. Unlike his colleagues in the mainstream Enlightenment and in apparent opposition to the views discussed above, he seems to see international politics as an (admittedly complex) version of a Hobbesian war of all against all (see, for example, Waltz, 1959; Hinsley, 1963). Some have thus suggested that Rousseau might be seen as a realist, though certainly one interested in constitutional and more widely republican questions, hence Michael Doyle's suggestion that he be seen as the fountainhead of a "constitutional" realism (Doyle, 1997: 137–60; for another prominent treatment of Rousseau as a "realist" see Waltz, 1959, ch. 6).

This is clearly an arguable point, and we do not have time or space to argue it here. However, we suggest it might be better to argue that for Rousseau the *questions* of international political ethics and those of domestic political ethics are effectively identical for they spring from the same source: the character of human being within contemporary societies, which is a state of alienation. The *answer* in each case, however, is obviously different and it amounts to assuming that change in international relations is dependent on change of a certain sort in domestic polities which is itself dependent on a spiritual change in human beings, which is – as Rousseau certainly came to believe towards the end of his life – very unlikely.

On this reading, Rousseau is not so much a "realist" – constitutional, or otherwise – as an "anti-realist." He agrees with realism, for example, that war is a permanent feature of the contemporary international system as it is currently configured, and he agrees again – this time with the mainstream Enlightenment – that war is horrible and irrational. However, he recognizes too (as, say, Montesquieu and Hume do not) how *seductive* it is and how interwoven with our sense of identity, belonging, and membership. Few have written more powerfully about the follies of war than Rousseau, but he fears also that it has too great a hold over them for human beings to break, certainly unless they are educated as Emile was, and enveloped by a society like that envisaged in *The Social Contract*. Which, of course, they are not.

Thus Rousseau's pessimism about international politics, though real enough, is derived from very different sources than usual "realist" claims. Whereas realists would normally claim that the "natural" way to live is in conflict, that the international system magnifies this, and that thus conflict is an inevitable and inescapable feature of international politics, for Rousseau it is precisely because we have moved *away* from nature into civilization that this situation has arisen.

However, at least in the 1750s and 1760s Rousseau considered a number of mechanisms whereby conflict and hostility could be reduced. In his *Constitutional Project for Corsica* of 1765, and more especially in his *Considerations on the Government of Poland* (1772), he investigated the possibility of progressive institutional reform leading to a situation where (for example) civic sentiment could create insuperable obstacles for a would-be conqueror. Yet this possibility is also, in Rousseau's mind, tied to the sort of educational reform – though of a less radical kind – he championed in *Emile*. It is, perhaps, his growing doubts about the feasibility of this scheme in its entirety which might account for his growing pessimism about any of these possibilities towards the end of his life (for a discussion see Shklar, 1969).

Thus, Rousseau's international thought can be said to hover uneasily between a number of stools. Neither fully realist, nor confident after the manner of the mainstream Enlightenment that reform was on the march, it expresses in a very powerful way the tensions and ambiguities that thinking hard about the parlous state of international relations and what we might do to improve it, often leads to.

The synthesis? Kant

Immanuel Kant (1724–1804) is probably the most influential writer of the Enlightenment in the literature of political theory and international political theory today. Born in Königsberg, the son of a poor saddlemaker, Kant struggled for most of his early life and middle age as a poorly paid *privatdozent*, or private lecturer, at the university in Königsberg. It was not until he was fifty-seven that he published the *Critique of Pure Reason*, the book that established his philosophical reputation, but after this he published a range of works that reshaped the philosophical agenda of his day and remain hugely important in our own.

Like Rousseau, whom he greatly admired, Kant's thought on the topics that concern us here is impossible to understand without first looking at the general structure of his philosophy as a whole. Given that the literature on this is vast, however, we will attempt only the merest summary here (for good general discussions see Reiss, 1970, introduction; Williams, 1983; Beiner and Booth, 1993; Doyle, 1997).

First, we need to go back to the very beginning of critical philosophy – the philosophical edifice that Kant started to create with the publication of the *Critique of Pure Reason* in 1781 – and remind ourselves that even the "first Critique," as it is usually called, predominantly concerned as it is with the problems of speculative reason, has a practical purpose:

So far ... as our Critique limits speculative reason it is indeed negative; but since it thereby removes an obstacle which stands in the way of the employment of practical reason ... it has ... a positive and very important use immediately we are convinced that there is an absolutely necessary practical employment of pure reason – the moral – in which it inevitably goes beyond the limits of sensibility. (Kant, 1982: Bxxv, pp. 26–7)

Kant's whole moral philosophy rests on the distinction between the material world and the moral world (to use his own terminology, respectively between the *phenomenal* and *noumenal* worlds) for which the *Critique of Pure Reason* was intended to lay the most important conceptual foundations. For Kant, moral principles must be inviolable from empirical attack: "A law, if it is to hold morally (i.e., as a ground of obligation), must imply absolute necessity ... the ground of obligation ... must [therefore] not be sought in the nature of man or in the circumstances in which he is placed but sought a priori solely in the concepts of pure reason" (Beck, 1965: 5–6).

Kant intended his moral philosophy to be a guide for individual moral action and equally his political philosophy is a guide for political action. "A state," he says in *The Metaphysics of Morals* (1797),

is a union of an aggregate of men under rightful laws. In so far as these laws are necessary a priori and follow automatically from the concepts of external justice [the word Reiss and Nisbet use is 'Right'] in general ... the form of the state will be that of a state in the absolute sense, i.e. as the idea of what a state ought to be according to pure principles of justice. This idea can serve as an internal guide for every actual case where men unite to form a commonwealth. (Reiss, 1970: 138)

In his general political theory Kant distinguishes between a state of nature, which can include societies of sorts, and a state under rightful laws, which is out of the state of nature. What makes the difference is the organization of the three branches of government – sovereign, executive, and judicial – and Kant makes quite clear that the sovereign is, in fact, supreme. It is the sovereign, of course, who passes the laws which establish the framework of civil society. For Kant this means what he calls "Public Law," for he argues that there are two types of law: natural law (or Private Law) and civil law (or Public Law). This division is predicated upon the distinction he makes between a society within a state of nature and one beyond the state of nature. The transition from state of nature to civil society is made by means of the separation of powers and conceived through the idea of the original contract, a move strongly influenced by his reading of Rousseau.

Now Kant, of course, does not consider this to have been a necessary historical process (though approximations to it may have occurred in the past). It is a conceptual device, but a conceptual device of great practical importance, for in the way he develops it he displays the key for grasping the complexities of his mature political thought, especially his international thought.

It is worth bearing in mind here that Kant's major political works were all written after the principal books of the critical philosophy had been written. Thus, while they were often the products of an elderly, even tiring man, they were also composed when Kant's system was in its maturity. As Reiss comments, however, Kant had been thinking hard about political questions for many years before he published on them (Reiss, 1970: 15). There are notes and scattered fragments in the 1760s, some twenty years before the publication of the first critique. However the first writings explicitly concerned with politics are the essay *What is Enlightenment?* and the *Idea for a Universal History*, both published in 1784. His mature writings on politics and international politics, however, came much later: *Theory and Practice* in 1792 (see pp. 429–32 below), most famously of all *Perpetual Peace* in 1795 (pp. 432–50 below) and finally and most exhaustively the *Metaphysics of Morals* in 1797 (pp. 450–5 below).

The manner in which Kant combines both a normative theory about international ethics and an explanatory theory about the character (and possible future direction) of the international system is central to his international political thought. As we saw at the outset of this chapter, in his essay *An Answer to the Question "What is Enlightenment?"* Kant stated: "All that is needed is freedom ... freedom to make public use of one's reason on all matters" (Reiss, 1970: 55). In a paper published the same year (1784), the *Idea for A Universal History with A Cosmopolitan Purpose*, Kant enlarges upon this theme. He does so tentatively, with no great certainty, regarding the enterprise chiefly as what a "philosophical mind well acquainted with history" (Reiss, 1970: 53) might derive from its study but, nonetheless, believes that it can "give us some guidance in explaining the thoroughly confused interplay of human affairs" (Reiss, 1970: 52).

Kant develops his thesis by arguing first, that all natural capacities develop in conformity with some end; secondly, that, in man, such capacities as are associated with reason could be developed fully only in the species (not the individual) and thirdly, that nature intended man's happiness to be a product of his own instinct and reason. With these three observations made, Kant argues that the inevitable antagonism within society creates "law-governed social order and thus leads to the greatest problem for the human species ... that of attaining a civil society which can administer justice universally" (Reiss, 1970: 45). This state may never come into being, Kant thinks, but some approximation to it will. The crucial move for Kant is to reverse Rousseau's reasoning and to suggest that the route to this is through the emergence of a more stable and secure international order. A law-governed relationship between states will begin the process, in its turn brought about by the same antagonism that operates in the civil union, "Distress (of wars, etc.) ... force ... states ... to renounce brutish freedom and seek calm and security within a law-governed constitution" (Reiss, 1970: 48). Gradually, as nations become more and more interdependent, war will be seen as prohibitively expensive and internally too damaging to be considered and thus "after many revolutions ... a universal cosmopolitan existence will at last be realised as the matrix within which all the original capacities of the human race may develop ... The history of the human race ... can be regarded as the realisation of a hidden plan of nature to bring out an internally – and for this purpose also externally – perfect constitution as the only possible state within which all natural capacities of mankind can be developed completely" (Reiss, 1970: 51).

Kant's argument in the *Idea for a Universal History* is, be it noted, purely explanatory; it attempts to show how an end manifestly good in the context of Kant's general moral philosophy, can (or even will) be achieved. We might call it Kant's "phenomenal" teleology. Thus, in the different context of rebellion (for example), Kant can agree with, even approve of, the aims for which (say) the French Revolution was launched, and see it as a positive and progressive development without approving of the actual act of revolution.

It is this sense of the likely (if certainly not necessary) movement of history that makes Kant a much greater optimist than Rousseau and it affects his treatment of international relations perhaps more than any other aspect of his work. However, it also makes it as clear as it possibly could be that what we might call the problem of international politics as such is central to the tasks of philosophy as Kant conceived them. As Reiss puts it, for Kant, "Right cannot possibly prevail among men within a state if their freedom is threatened by the action of other states" (Reiss, 1970: 33). Thus we are obliged (ethically) to work for the establishment of a "cosmopolitan society" and, Kant thinks, there is evidence that history is moving in this general direction. However, such a society neither would nor should take the form of a world state. Kant is convinced that such a state would be far too prone to despotism. Rather, the cosmopolitan society would be a federation of pacific republican states, governed by cosmopolitan law. This aspect of Kant's international theory is that which has had the most impact upon recent international theory, in giving rise to what is usually called the "liberal (or democratic) peace thesis" (see Waltz, 1962; Doyle, 1983, 1997, ch. 8).

Of course, Kant is fully aware that such a development will be hard fought, hardly inevitable, and always fragile. Nonetheless, what distinguishes him from Rousseau, despite his acceptance of the difficulties, is his optimism about the possibilities. In this sense, perhaps more than any other, Kant represents a synthesis between the mainstream and Rousseau's Enlightenments. It is this fact which makes him such a central philosophical voice for contemporary thought and it is as true in international political theory as anywhere else. He is a source of inspiration and ideas for liberals and radicals, at least some traditional supporters of the states-system, and many of those who seek (however gently) to transcend it. Ernst Cassirer once said that Kant's philosophy represented the completion of the Enlightenment at the same time as, in some respects at least, it transcended it (Cassirer, 1951). Nowhere is this truer than in his international theory. It has allowed a wide range of contemporary international theorists to find in Kant a powerful source of inspiration both normatively and empirically. Thus writers such as Carl Freidrich, Fernando Teson, Andrew Hurrell, and Michael Doyle (see Freidrich, 1962; Doyle, 1983, 1997; Hurrell, 1990; Tesón, 1988 and 1998) deploy readings of Kant that emphasize his constitutional liberalism but also his commitment to the state as a political form (the pacific union is a union of republican *states*), whilst thinkers such as Pierre Laberge and, especially, Onora O'Neill and Andrew Linklater offer us readings of a Kant who, however concerned for republican government, is a statist only secondarily and whose thought, both noumenal and phenomenal, leads towards a universalist cosmopolitanism that would transcend the states-system, at least in anything like its present form (O'Neill, 1989 and 1996 and Linklater, 1990 and 1998).

The core text for Kant's international political thought is, of course, *Perpetual Peace* (1795). In this essay, his commitment to ethics and his "phenomenal teleology" come together to form a powerful argument about how the currently deplorable state of international society – on this he is in complete agreement with Rousseau – might be reformed. It is interesting, in fact, to read Kant and Rousseau's treatment of the Abbé de Saint Pierre's project side by side; it reveals a good deal about the philosophical assumptions of each (for this reason we not only include excerpts from each of their respective essays here, but also from the Abbé de St Pierre's original *Project for Perpetual Peace* itself). The arguments discussed in the *Idea for a Universal History* are revised and elaborated and Kant presents a remarkably sensitive and powerful account both of the ethics of international politics and of the character of international politics and how each relates to the other. It represents the most sustained attempt he ever made to outline the structure of his universalist, cosmopolitan account of how we should view the character and the possible future of world politics.

It is obviously important that all of Kant's arguments are read for themselves. However, in closing this chapter on the Enlightenment's contribution to international political theory, a brief summary and recapitulation will perhaps be helpful. In his international thought, Kant starts from the assumption, shared by realists and Rousseau alike, that states exist under international anarchy and that this is a situation that aggravates the likelihood of conflict and war. It is also a situation that supports the existing unjust arrangements within countries as well. Morally, noumenally as we might say, we recognize that it is an obligation to seek to work towards the establishment of a society governed by cosmopolitan law at all levels. Empirically, however, a world state would seem to be the logical corollary of this. Yet it is neither feasible (there are too many problems with establishing it) nor, in fact, especially desirable (the possibility of tyranny or despotism in a world state would be both very high and exceedingly unpleasant). However, Kant thinks that nature and history are working towards a different kind of solution. War will become more and more expensive. It is peoples, not governments who will bear the brunt of this, as they have always borne the brunt of the horrors of war. War, and all that is associated with it, will become decreasingly popular as a result. As peoples push ever more insistently for republican government, a small number of republican (effectively liberal) states will emerge. These will band together to form a "pacific union" to protect each other from the depredations of those sovereigns outside the union. As they do this they will change the manner of conducting international politics between themselves; they will settle disputes without war and on the basis of right (justice). As their success becomes more obvious – and as they become more prosperous – so this will encourage other peoples to establish republican governments and thus the pacific union will grow and the realm of traditional international politics (the balance of power, etc.) will shrink. This will in turn remove many of the obstacles that have stood in the way of domestic and even personal reform and that so haunted Rousseau. Thus, for Kant, as he says in the seventh proposition of the *Idea for a Universal History*, "the problem of establishing a perfect civil constitution is subordinate to the problem of a law-governed external relationship with other states, and cannot be solved unless the latter is also solved" (Reiss, 1970: 47). Kant's international political theory consists in showing how this might be solved and how, in the process, the noumenal and phenomenal worlds can reinforce each other.

FURTHER READING

The best general interpretation of the Enlightenment as a whole is still Peter Gay (1970). On Montesquieu, Pangle (1973) is excellent, though it should be read alongside Shklar (1987). On Hume, Mossner (1980) is the best introduction to Hume's life and work, though Forbes (1975) is the most detailed treatment of his political thought. The best book-length treatment of Smith's politics is Winch (1978). Shklar (1969) remains the best general study of Rousseau but the introductory essay in Hoffmann and Fidler (1991) is superb on Rousseau's international thought. Williams (1983) is the best single-volume account of Kant's political thought, emphasizing its international and historical aspects. Good treatments of Rousseau and Kant on international relations can also be found in Boucher (1998) and Doyle (1997).

SOURCES

The Abbé de Saint-Pierre, *Project on Perpetual Peace* (1712–13), from *Basic Texts in International Relations*, ed. Evan Luard (London: Macmillan, 1992), pp. 411–14.

Montesquieu, from *The Spirit of the Laws* (1741), trans. and ed. Anne M. Cohler, Basia Carolyn Miller, and Harold Samuel Stone, (Cambridge: Cambridge University Press, 1989), Part 1, Book 1, ch. 3 (pp. 7–9), Part 2, Book 10, chs. 1–3 (pp. 138–9), Part 5, Book 26, chs. 20–1 (pp. 514, 515).

David Hume, from *Of the Balance of Power* (1752), in *Hume: Political Essays*, ed. Charles W. Hendel (New York: Bobbs-Merrill, 1953), pp. 142–4.

Adam Smith, from *The Wealth of Nations* (1776) (London: Dent, 1910) Book 4, ch. 6, pp. 43–8.

Jean Jacques Rousseau, *Abstracts and Judgement of Saint-Pierre's Project of Peace*, taken from *A Lasting Peace through the Federation of Europe and the State of War*, trans. C. E. Vaughan. Reprinted with the permission of Constable & Robinson. Copyright © Constable & Co., London 1917. *The State of War*; extracts taken from Forsythe, Keens-Soper and Savigear, *The Theory of International Relations: Selected Texts from Gentili to Treitschke* (London: Unwin Hyman Limited, 1970). Both reprinted in *Rousseau on International Relations*, ed. Stanley Hoffman and David P. Fidler (Oxford: Clarendon Press, 1991).

Immanuel Kant, selections from *Essay on Theory and Practice* (1793), pp. 89–92, *Perpetual Peace* (1795), 93–109, 112–30 (removing all footnotes) and *The Metaphysical Elements of Right* (1797), from Hans Reiss, ed., *Kant's Political Writings* (Cambridge: Cambridge University Press, 1970), 164–5, 168–9, 172–5.

THE ABBÉ DE SAINT-PIERRE

CHARLES-IRENÉE CASTEL, ABBÉ DE SAINT-PIERRE, was born in 1658 into the minor aristocracy. He frequented the Parisian salons fashionable in the seventeenth and eighteenth centuries and gained his entrance to court through the patronage of the Duchess of Orleans. He was a member of the French delegation which negotiated the Treaty of Utrecht in 1713 and thus had diplomatic and political experience. He wrote on many aspects of French politics, but it was his *A Project for Settling an Everlasting Peace in Europe* (1713) for which he is chiefly remembered and which spurred thinkers much greater than he (Leibniz, Rousseau, and Kant to name but three) to consider his proposals and develop their own. He died in 1743.

A project for settling an everlasting peace in Europe

"First proposed by Henry IV of France, and approved of by Queen Elizabeth, and most of the then Princes of Europe, and now discussed at large and made practicable

Fundamental articles

"ARTICLE I

The Present Sovereigns, by their under-written Deputies, have agreed to the following articles: There shall be from this Day following a Society, a permanent and perpetual Union, between the Sovereigns subscribed, and if possible among all the Christian Sovereigns, in the Design to make the Peace unalterable in Europe; and in that view the Union shall make, if possible, with its neighbours the Mahometan Sovereigns, Treaties of Alliance, offensive and defensive, to keep each of them in Peace within the Bounds of his Territory, by taking of them and giving to them, all possible reciprocal Securities. The Sovereigns shall be perpetually represented by their Deputies, in a perpetual Congress or Senate, in a free City.

"ARTICLE II

The European Society shall not at all concern itself about the Government of any State, unless it be to preserve the Fundamental Form of it, and give speedy and sufficient Assistance to the Princes in Monarchies, and to the Magistrates in Republicks, against any that are Seditious and Rebellious. Thus it will be a Guarantee that the Hereditary Sovereignties shall remain hereditary according to the Manner and Custom of each Nation; that those that are elective shall remain elective in that Country where Election is usual; that among the Nations where there are Capitulations, and Conventions which are called *Pacta Conventa*, those sorts of Treaties shall be exactly observed, and that those who in Monarchies should have taken up Arms against the Prince, or in Republicks against some of the chief Magistrates shall be punished with Death and Confiscation of Goods.

"ARTICLE III

The Union shall employ its whole Strength and Care to hinder, during the Regencies, the Minorities, the weak Reigns of each State, any Prejudice from being done to the Sovereign, either in his Person, or in his Prerogatives, either by his Subjects, or by Strangers, and if any Sedition, Revolt, Conspiracy, Suspicion of Poison, or any other Violence should happen to the Prince, or to the Royal Family, the Union, as its Guardian and Protectress born, shall send Commissioners into that State, to look into the Truth of the Facts, and shall at the same time send Troops to punish the guilty according to the Rigour of the Laws.

"ARTICLE IV

Each Sovereign shall be contented, he and his Successors, with the Territory he actually possesses, or which he is to possess by the Treaty hereunto joyned. All the Sovereignties of Europe shall always remain in the condition they are in, and shall always have the same Limits that they have now. No Territory shall be dismembered from any Sovereignty, nor shall any be added to it by Succession, Agreement between different Houses, Election, Donation, Cession, Sale, Conquest, voluntary Submission of the Subjects or otherwise. No Sovereign, nor Member of a Sovereign Family, can be Sovereign of any State besides that or those which are actually in the possession of his Family ... No Sovereign shall assume the Title of Lord of any Country, of which he is not in actual Possession, or the Possession of which shall not be promised him by the Treaty hereunto joyned. The Sovereigns shall not be permitted to make an Exchange of any Territory, nor to sign any Treaty among themselves, but with the Consent and under the Guarantee of the Union by the three-fourths of the four and twenty Voices, and the Union shall remain Guarantee for the execution of reciprocal Promises.

"ARTICLE V

No Sovereign shall henceforth possess two Sovereignties, either Hereditary or Elective; however the Electors of the Empire may be elected Emperors, so long as there shall be Emperors. If by Right of Succession there should fall to a Sovereign a State more considerable than that which he possesses, he may leave that he possesses, and settle himself in that which is fallen to him.

...

"ARTICLE VIII

No Sovereign shall take up Arms or commit any Hostility, but against him who shall be declared an Enemy to the European Society. But if he has any cause to complain of any of the Members, or any Demand to make upon them, he shall order his Deputy to give a Memorial to the Senate in the City of Peace, and the Senate shall take care to reconcile the Differences by its mediating Commissioners; or if they cannot be reconciled, the Senate shall judge them by Arbitral Judgement by Plurality of Voices provisionally, and by the three-fourths of the Voices definitely. This Judgement shall not be given till each Senator shall have received the Instructions and Orders of his Master upon the Fact, and till he shall have communicated them to the Senate. The Sovereign who shall take up Arms before the Union has declared War, or who shall refuse to execute a Regulation of the Society, or a Judgement of the Senate, shall be declared an Enemy to the Society, and it shall make War upon him, 'Till he be disarmed, and 'Till the Judgement and Regulations be executed; and he shall even pay the Charges of the War, and the Country that shall be conquered from him at the time of the Suspension of Arms shall be for ever departed from his Dominions. If after the Society is formed to the number of fourteen Voices, a Sovereign shall refuse to enter into it, it shall declare him an enemy to the Repose of Europe, and shall make War upon him 'till he enter into it, or 'till he be entirely dispossessed.

"ARTICLE IX

There shall be in the Senate of Europe four and twenty Senators, or Deputies of the united Sovereigns, neither more nor less, namely, France, Spain, England, Holland, Savoy, Portugal, Bavaria and Associates, Venice, Genoa and Associates, Florence and Associates, Switzerland and Associates, Lorraine and Associates, Sweden, Denmark, Poland, the Pople, Muscovy, Austria, Courland and Associates, Prussia, Saxony, Palatine and Associates, Hanover and Associates, Ecclesiastical Electors and Associates. Each Deputy shall have but one Vote.

"ARTICLE X

The Members and Associates of the Union shall contribute to the Expenses of the Society, and to the Subsidies for its Security, each in Proportion to his Revenues, and to the Riches of his People, and every one's Quota shall at first be regulated provisionally by Plurality, and afterwards by the three-fourths of the Voices, when the Commissioners of the Union shall have taken, in each State, what Instructions and Informations shall be necessary thereupon; and if anyone is found to have paid too much provisionally, it shall afterwards be made up to him in Principal and Interest, by those who shall have paid too little. The less powerful Sovereigns and Associates in forming one Voice, shall alternately nominate their Deputy in Proportion to their Quota.

"ARTICLE XI

When the Senate shall deliberate upon any thing pressing and provisionable for the Security of the Society, either to prevent or quell Sedition, the Question may be decided by plurality of Voices provisionally, and before it is deliberated they shall begin by deciding, by plurality, whether the matter is provisionable.

"ARTICLE XII

None of the eleven fundamental Articles above named shall be in any point altered without the *unanimous* Consent of All the Members; but as for the other Articles, the Society may always, by the three-fourths of the Voices, add or diminish, for the common Good, whatever it shall think fit.

...

"The Language of the Senate shall be the Language most in use in Europe.

"The Revenue of the Union shall consist in the ordinary Quota each Sovereign shall pay.

"The Army shall be composed of an equal number of Troops from each State, but the Union can lend Money to the poorer and smaller States, through the most powerful Sovereigns. So the Quota of the international Army can be in Money or in Troops. In Peace, there shall be a reduction of Armaments to six thousand for each State.

"The Sovereigns, Princes, chief Officers, and Ministers shall renew their oaths Annually.

"If the Union enters upon a War it shall appoint a Generalissimo, who shall be elected by a majority of Voices, shall be revocable at pleasure of the Union, and shall not be a member of a Sovereign Family.

"The Union shall appoint Commissioners to settle Limits and Boundaries in America and elsewhere. Nothing in these remote Lands should be left to Sovereigns to seize at their pleasure. These Colonies cost more than they bring in: Colonies are opening a Door for the common People to desert the State. Commerce is not so good when Populations are dispersed, as when People are gathered in a small compass – as in Holland and Zeeland.

"The Union shall endeavour to procure a permanent Society in Asia, that Peace may be maintained there too. If the Union had been established two hundred years ago, Europe would now be four times richer than it is. It will cost very little to establish the Union – chiefly the restitution of unjust Conquests – and will cost almost nothing to maintain it, in comparison with the expense of War. Neither the Balance of Power nor Treaties are sufficient to maintain Peace; the only way is by a European Union."

MONTESQUIEU

C HARLES DE SECONDAT, BARON DE LA BREDE ET DE MONTESQUIEU, was born in 1689. His life and career were fairly normal for a French aristocrat of his time, save that he was, and remained, a staunch enthusiast for freedom and an equally staunch opponent of despotism. After a good education locally, Montesquieu went to the University of Bordeaux to study law, graduating after three years and then moving to Paris to continue his studies. In 1713, on his father's death, Montesquieu returned to Bordeaux to take up his duties on his estates and in 1716 he became, on his uncle's death, President of the Parlement of Bordeaux. He was thus a local nobleman of considerable consequence with wide commercial and landowning interests, including a special interest in his vineyards and the international trade in wine. His intellectual interests remained, however. On his return to Bordeaux, he had been elected to the Academy at Bordeaux and remained active in it for the rest of his life. His first major work, *Persian Letters*, was published anonymously in 1721 and was a biting satire on the political and ecclesiastical conditions in Europe in general and France in particular. It was a great success and afterwards Montesquieu began to move in French and European literary circles, becoming a regular in the salon of Madame Lambert and attending the Club de l'entresol, which featured detailed discussion of political and international affairs and amongst whose members was the Abbé de Saint-Pierre. He spent the years 1728 and 1729 in England and developed a profound admiration for aspects of the constitution of that country. This bore final fruit in his masterpiece, seventeen years in the making, published in 1748 as *The Spirit of the Laws*. The book became, and has remained, a major statement of the burgeoning European Enlightenment and Montesquieu one of its most important figures. He died seven years after its publication, in 1755.

From *The Spirit of The Laws*

Part 1, Book 1, chapter 3
On positive laws

As soon as men are in society, they lose their feeling of weakness; the equality that was among them ceases, and the state of war begins.

Each particular society comes to feel its strength, producing a state of war among nations. The individuals within each society begin to feel their strength; they seek to turn their favor the principal advantages of this society, which brings about a state of war among them.

These two sorts of states of war bring about the establishment of laws among men. Considered as inhabitants of a planet so large that different peoples are necessary, they have laws bearing on the relation that these peoples have with one another, and this is the RIGHT OF NATIONS.[1] Considered as living in a society that must be maintained, they have laws concerning the relation between those who govern and those who are governed, and this is the POLITICAL RIGHT.[2] Further, they have laws concerning the relation that all citizens have with one another, and this is the CIVIL RIGHT.

The *right of nations* is by nature founded on the principle that the various nations should do to one another in times of peace the most good possible, and in times of war the least ill possible, without harming their true interests.

The object of war is victory; of victory, conquest; of conquest, preservation. All the laws that form the *right of nations* should derive from this principle and the preceding one.

All nations have a right of nations; and even the Iroquois, who eat their prisoners, have one. They send and receive embassies; they know rights of war and peace: the trouble is that their right of nations is not founded on true principles.

In addition to the right of nations, which concerns all societies, there is a *political right* for each one. A society could not continue to exist without a government. "*The union of all individual strengths*," as Gravina aptly says, "forms what is called the POLITICAL STATE."[3]

The strength of the whole society may be put in the hands of *one alone* or in the hands of *many*.[4] Since nature has established paternal power, some have thought that government by one alone is most in conformity with nature. But the example of paternal power proves nothing. For, if the power of the father is related to government by one alone, then after the death of the father, the power of the brothers, or after the death of the brothers, the power of the first cousins, is related to government by many. Political power necessarily includes the union of many families.

---

1   *le droit des gens* is translated "right of nations"
    throughout.
2   We have translated *droit* as "right" and *loi* as
    "law." Although the French *droit* is usually
    closer to the meaning of "law" in English, we
    have kept Montesquieu's usage so that his
    distinction and his version of the changes in
    meaning would not be obscured.
3   Giovanni Vincenzo Gravina, *Origine Romani
    juris* (1739), bk. 2, chap. 18, p. 160.
4   The eighteenth-century meaning of *plusieurs*
    was "many." The opposition is between "one"
    and "many," as between monarchies or
    despotisms and republics in Book 2.

It is better to say that the government most in conformity with nature is the one whose particular arrangement best relates to the disposition of the people for whom it is established.[5]

Individual strengths cannot be united unless all wills are united. *The union of these wills,* as Gravina again aptly says, *is what is called the CIVIL STATE.*[6]

Law in general is human reason insofar as it governs all the peoples of the earth; and the political and civil laws of each nation should be only the particular cases to which human reason is applied.

Laws should be so appropriate to the people for whom they are made that it is very unlikely that the laws of one nation can suit another.

Laws must relate to the nature and the principle of the government that is established or that one wants to establish, whether those laws form it as do political laws, or maintain it, as do civil laws.

They should be related to the *physical aspect* of the country; to the climate, be it freezing, torrid, or temperate; to the properties of the terrain, its location and extent; to the way of life of the peoples, be they plowmen, hunters, or herdsmen; they should relate to the degree of liberty that the constitution can sustain, to the religion of the inhabitants, their inclinations, their wealth, their number, their commerce, their mores and their manners; finally, the laws are related to one another, to their origin, to the purpose of the legislator, and to the order of things on which they are established. They must be considered from all these points of view.

This is what I undertake to do in this work. I shall examine all these relations; together they form what is called THE SPIRIT OF THE LAWS.[7]

I have made no attempt to separate *political* from *civil* laws, for, as I do not treat laws but the spirit of the laws, and as this spirit consists in the various relations that laws may have with various things, I have had to follow the natural order of laws less than that of these relations and of these things.

I shall first examine the relations that laws have with the nature and the principle of each government, and, as this principle has a supreme influence on the laws, I shall apply myself to understanding it well; and if I can once establish it, the laws will be seen to flow from it as from their source. I shall then proceed to other relations that seem to be more particular.

...

---

5 *Il vaut mieux dire que le gouvernement le plus conforme à la nature est celui dont la disposition particulière se rapporte mieux à la disposition du peuple pour lequel il est établi.* No English word covers all the disparate topics Montesquieu joins with the word *disposition.*

6 Giovanni Vincenzo Gravina, *Origine Romani juris* (1739), bk. 3, chap. 7, footnote, p. 311.

7 L'ESPRIT DES LOIX. Whenver possible, we translate *esprit* as "spirit," but "mind" and "wit" also appear.

Part 2, Book 10 On laws in their relation with offensive force

Chapter 1

On offensive force

Offensive force is regulated by the right of nations, which is the political law of the nations considered in their relation with each other.

Chapter 2

On war

The life of states is like that of men. Men have the right to kill in the case of natural defense; states have the right to wage war for their own preservation.

In the case of natural defense, I have the right to kill, because my life is mine, as the life of the one who attacks me is his; likewise a state wages war because its preservation is just, as is any other preservation.

Among citizens, the right to natural defense does not carry with it a necessity to attack. Instead of attacking they have the recourse of the tribunals. Therefore, they can exercise that right of defense only in cases that occur so suddenly that one would be lost if one waited for the aid of the laws. But among societies, the right of natural defense sometimes carries with it a necessity to attack, when one people sees that a longer peace would put another people in a position to destroy it and that an attack at this moment is the only way to prevent such destruction.

Hence small societies more frequently have the right to wage wars than large ones, because they are more frequently in a position to fear being destroyed.

Therefore, the right of war derives from necessity and from a strict justice. If those who direct the conscience or the councils of princes do not hold to these, all is lost; and, when that right is based on arbitrary principles of glory, of propriety, of utility, tides of blood will inundate the earth.

Above all, let one not speak of the prince's glory; his glory is his arrogance; it is a passion and not a legitimate right.

It is true that his reputation for power could increase the forces of his state, but his reputation for justice would increase them in any case.

Chapter 3

On the right of conquest

From the right of war derives that of conquest, which is its consequence; therefore, it should follow the spirit of the former.

When a people is conquered, the right of the conqueror follows four sorts of laws: the law of nature, which makes everything tend toward the preservation of species; the law of natural enlightenment,[8] which wants us to do to others what we would want to have done to us; the law that forms political societies, which are such that nature has not limited their duration; lastly, the law drawn from the thing itself. Conquest is an acquisition; the spirit of acquisition carries with it the spirit of preservation and use, and not that of destruction.

One state that has conquered another treats it in one of these four ways: the state continues to govern its conquest according to its own laws and takes for itself only the exercise of the political and civil government; or it gives its conquest a new political and civil government; or it destroys the society and scatters it into others; or, finally, it exterminates all the citizens.

The first way conforms to the right of nations we follow at present; the fourth is more is conformity with the right of nations among the Romans; on this point, I leave others to judge how much better we have become. Here homage must be paid to our modern times, to contemporary reasoning, to the religion of the present day, to our philosophy, and to our mores.

When the authors of our public right, for whom ancient histories provided the foundation, have no longer followed cases strictly, they have fallen into great errors. They have moved toward the arbitrary; they have assumed among conquerors a right, I do not know which one, of killing; this has made them draw consequences as terrible as this principle and establish maxims that the conquerors themselves, when they had the slightest sense, never adopted. It is clear that, once the conquest is made, the conqueror no longer has the right to kill, because it is no longer for him a case of natural defense and of his own preservation.

What has made them think in this way is that they have believed the conqueror had the right to destroy the society; thus they have concluded that he had the right to destroy the men composing it, which is a consequence wrongly drawn from a wrong principle. For, from the annihilation of the society, it would not follow that the men forming that society should also be annihilated. The society is the union of men and not the men themselves; the citizen may perish and the man remain.

From the right to kill during conquest, political men have drawn the right to reduce to servitude, but the consequence is as ill founded as the principle.

One has the right to reduce a people to servitude only when it is necessary for the preservation of a conquest. The purpose of conquest is preservation; servitude is never the purpose of conquest, but it is sometimes a necessary means for achieving preservation.

---

8 Montesquieu uses *lumières*, which we translate as "enlightenment"; it also implies insight or illumination.

In this case, it is against the nature of the thing for this servitude to be eternal. It must be possible for the enslaved people to become subjects. Slavery is accidental to conquest. When, after a certain length of time, all the parts of the conquering state are bound to those of the conquered state by customs, marriage, laws, associations, and a certain conformity of spirit, servitude should cease. For the rights of the conqueror are founded only on the fact that these things do not exist and that there is a distance between the two nations, such that the one cannot trust the other.

Thus, the conqueror who reduces a people to servitude should always reserve for himself means (and these means are innumerable) for allowing them to leave it.

I am not saying vague things here. Our fathers who conquered the Roman Empire acted in this way. They softened the laws that they made in the heat, impetuosity, and arrogance of victory; their laws had been hard, they made them impartial. The Burgundians, the Goths, and the Lombards wanted the Romans to continue to be the vanquished people; the laws of Euric, of Gundobad, and of Rotharis made the barbarian and the Roman fellow citizens.

To subdue the Saxons, Charlemagne deprived them of their freeborn status and of the ownership of goods. Louis the Pious freed them; he did nothing better during his reign. Time and servitude had softened their mores; they were forever faithful to him.

Chapter 4

Some advantages for the conquered peoples

Instead of drawing such fatal consequences from the right of conquest, political men would have done better to speak of the advantages this right can sometimes confer on a vanquished people. They would have been more sensitive to these advantages if our right of nations were followed exactly and if it were established around the earth.

Ordinarily states that are conquered do not have the force they had at their institution: corruption has entered them; their laws have ceased to be executed; the government has become an oppressor. Who can doubt that there would be gain for such a state and that it would draw other advantages from the conquest itself, if the conquest were not destructive? What would the government lose by being recast, if it had reached the point of being unable to reform itself? A conqueror who comes to a people among whom the rich, by a thousand rushes and a thousand tricks, have imperceptibly practiced an infinite number of usurpations; where the unfortunate man who trembles as he watches what he believed to be abuses become laws is oppressed and believes himself wrong to feel so; a conqueror, I say, can change the course of everything, and muffled tyranny is the first thing which is liable to violence.

For example, one has seen states whose oppression by tax-collectors was relieved by the conqueror, who had neither the engagements nor the needs of the legitimate prince. Abuses were corrected even without the conqueror's correcting them.

The frugality of the conquering nation has sometimes put it in a position to leave the vanquished people the necessities that had been taken from them under the legitimate prince.

A conquest can destroy harmful prejudices, and, if I dare speak in this way, can put a nation under a better presiding genius.

What good could the Spanish not have done the Mexicans? They had a gentle religion to give them; they brought them a raging superstition. They could have set the slaves free, and they made freemen slaves. They could have made clear to them that human sacrifice was an abuse; instead they exterminated them. I would never finish if I wanted to tell all the good things they did not do, and all the evil ones they did.

It is for the conqueror to make amends for part of the evils he has done. I define the right of conquest thus: a necessary, legitimate, and unfortunate right, which always leaves an immense debt to be discharged if human nature is to be repaid.

...

Part 5, Book 26, chapter 20

That things that belong to the right of nations must not be decided by the principles of civil laws

Liberty consists principally in not being forced to do a thing that the law does not order, and one is in this state only because one is governed by civil laws; therefore, we are free because we live under civil laws.

It follows that princes, who do not live under civil laws among themselves, are not free; they are governed by force, and they can continually force or be forced. From this it follows that the treaties they have made by force are as obligatory as those they may have made willingly. When we, who live under civil laws, are constrained to make some contract not required by law, we can, with the favor of the law, recover from the violence; but a prince, who is always in this state of forcing or being forced, cannot complain of a treaty that violence has had him make. It is as if he complained of his natural state; it is as if he wanted to be a prince in regard to other princes and wanted the other princes to be citizens in regard to him; that is, as if he wanted to run counter to the nature of things.

Chapter 21

That things that belong to the right of nations must not be decided by political laws

Political laws require that every man be subject to the criminal and civil tribunals of the country in which he lives and to the animadversion of the sovereignty.

The right of nations has wanted princes to send ambassadors to each other, and reason, drawn from the nature of the thing, has not permitted these ambassadors to depend on the sovereign to whom they are sent or on his tribunals. They speak for the prince who sends them, and that speech should be free. No obstacle should prevent them from acting. They can often displease because they speak for an independent man. One might impute crimes to them, if they could be punished for crimes; one might assume they had debts, if they could be seized for debts. A prince who has a natural pride would speak through the mouth of a man who would have everything to fear. Therefore, with regard to ambassadors the reasons drawn from the right of nations must be followed, and not those derived from political right. For if they abuse their status as a representative, this is stopped by sending them home; one can even accuse them before their master, who becomes in this way their judge or their accomplice.

DAVID HUME

D AVID HUME was born at Edinburgh in Scotland in 1711. His family hoped he would follow a legal career, though Hume from quite a young age was obsessed with literature and philosophy. However, the family was not wealthy and so Hume could not initially follow this path. After a brief stint working in Bristol, Hume went to France determined to live as frugally as possible and to become a writer. In France he composed the first of his major works, his *Treatise on Human Nature*, which was published in three volumes (1738–40) but which met with little critical success (at the time). After returning from France in 1737 Hume lived with his family in Scotland and in 1741–2 he published *Essays, Moral and Political*, which was much more successful. After this, Hume rewrote much of the *Treatise* (which was later published as *An Enquiry Concerning Human Understanding* and *An Enquiry Concerning the Principles of Morals* in 1748 and 1751) and wrote a series of *Political Discourses* (1752), which became his most successful book to date. That same year he became Librarian to the Faculty of Advocates in Edinburgh and set up house with his sister in the city. Helped by his access to a magnificent library, he turned to writing a mammoth *History of England* (1756, 1759, 1761). In 1763 Hume traveled to France as secretary to the British Ambassador and while there he became a major figure among the French *philosophes* (becoming especially friendly with Diderot), returning to England in 1766, while trying (and failing) to help the increasingly paranoid Jean-Jacques Rousseau. For two years thereafter Hume held the post of Under-Secretary of State, but in 1769 he returned to Edinburgh and continued to write, with some of his major works (especially the *Dialogues Concerning Natural Religion*) appearing after his death. He died in 1776.

From *Of the Balance of Power*

It is a question whether the *idea* of the balance of power be owing entirely to modern policy, or whether the *phrase* only has been invented in these later ages? It is certain that Xenophon, in his *Institution of Cyrus*, represents the combination of the Asiatic powers to have arisen from a jealousy of the increasing force of the Medes and Persians; and though that elegant composition should be supposed altogether a romance, this sentiment, ascribed by the author to the Eastern princes, is at least a proof of the prevailing notion of ancient times.

...

In short, the maxim of preserving the balance of power is founded so much on common sense and obvious reasoning that it is impossible it could altogether have escaped antiquity, where we find in other particulars so many marks of deep penetration and discernment. If it was not so generally known and acknowledged as at present, it had at least an influence on all the wiser and more experienced princes and politicians. And indeed, even at present, however generally known and acknowledged among speculative reasoners, it has not in practice an authority much more extensive among those who govern the world.

After the fall of the Roman Empire, the form of government established by the northern conquerors incapacitated them, in a great measure, for further conquests and long maintained each state in its proper boundaries. But when vassalage and the feudal militia were abolished, mankind were anew alarmed by the danger of universal monarchy from the union of so many kingdoms and principalities in the person of the Emperor Charles. But the power of the house of Austria, founded on extensive but divided dominions, and their riches, derived chiefly from mines of gold and silver, were more likely to decay of themselves from internal defects than to overthrow all the bulwarks raised against them. In less than a century, the force of that violent and haughty race was shattered, their opulence dissipated, their splendor eclipsed. A new power succeeded more formidable to the liberties of Europe, possessing all the advantages of the former and laboring under none of its defects, except a share of that spirit of bigotry and persecution with which the house of Austria was so long, and still is, so much infatuated.

In the general wars maintained against this ambitious power, Great Britain has stood foremost, and she still maintains her station. Beside her advantages of riches and situation, her people are animated with such a national spirit and are so fully sensible of the blessings of their government that we may hope their vigor never will languish in so necessary and so just a cause. On the contrary, if we may judge by the past, their passionate ardor seems rather to require some moderation, and they have oftener erred from a laudable excess than from a blamable deficiency.

In the *first* place, we seem to have been more possessed with the ancient Greek spirit of jealous emulation than actuated by the prudent views of modern politics. Our wars with France have been begun with justice, and even perhaps from necessity, but have always been too far pushed, from obstinancy and passion. The same peace which was afterward made at Ryswick in 1697 was offered so early as the year ninety-two; that concluded at Utrecht in 1712 might have been finished on as good conditions at Gertruytenberg in the year eight; and we might have given at Frankfort in 1743 the same terms which we were glad to accept of at Aix-la-Chapelle in the year forty-eight. Here, then, we see that above half of our wars with France and all our public debts are owing more to our own imprudent vehemence than to the ambition of our neighbors.

In the *second* place, we are so declared in our opposition to French power and so alert in defense of our allies that they always reckon upon our forces as upon their own and, expecting to carry on war at our expense, refuse all reasonable terms of accommodation. *Habent subjectos tanquam suos; viles ut alienos.* All the world knows that the factious vote of the House of Commons in the beginning of the last Parliament, with the professed humor of the nation, made the Queen of Hungary inflexible in her terms and prevented that agreement with Prussia which would immediately have restored the general tranquillity of Europe.

In the *third* place, we are such true combatants that, when once engaged, we lose all concern for ourselves and our posterity and consider only how we may best annoy the enemy. To mortgage our revenues at so deep a rate in wars where we are only accessories was surely the most fatal delusion that a nation which had any pretension to politics and prudence has ever yet been guilty of. That remedy of funding, if it be a remedy and not rather a poison, ought, in all reason, to be reserved to the last extremity; and no evil but the greatest and most urgent should ever induce us to embrace so dangerous an expedient.

These excesses to which we have been carried are prejudicial and may perhaps in time become still more prejudicial another way, by begetting, as is usual, the opposite extreme and rendering us totally careless and supine with regard to the fate of Europe.

ADAM SMITH

A DAM SMITH was born at Kirkcaldy in Fife in 1723, the son of a government official. At the age of three he was stolen by gypsies but before long was returned to his parents and educated in Glasgow and from the age of seventeen at Oxford as an exhibitioner at Balliol College. He stayed in Oxford for six years, immersing himself in philosophy and literature. In 1748 he was appointed lecturer in literature at Edinburgh and then, in 1751, professor of literature at Glasgow. From 1752, he held the chair of Moral Philosophy at Glasgow. During the next ten years he worked on and eventually published his first major book, the *Theory of Moral Sentiments*, and lectured on a range of topics in moral philosophy (under which he included political economy). In 1763, he resigned his chair and became private tutor to the duke of Buccleuch and in that capacity spent some years travelling in Europe with the duke, during which time he got to know the major French school of economic thinkers (or physiocrats) well. He returned to Kirkcaldy in 1767, where he lived quietly writing the second of his major books, moving to London in 1773, and publishing *An Inquiry into the Nature and Causes of the Wealth of Nations* in 1776. He moved back to Scotland a couple of years later and accepted a post of Commissioner of Customs in Scotland, where he lived until his death in 1790.

From *The Wealth of Nations*

Book 4, chapter 6

Of treaties of commerce

When a nation binds itself by treaty either to permit the entry of certain goods from one foreign country which it prohibits from all others, or to exempt the goods of one country from duties to which it subjects those of all others, the country, or at least the merchants and manufacturers of the country, whose commerce is so favoured, must necessarily derive great advantage from the treaty. Those merchants and manufacturers enjoy a sort of monopoly in the country which is so indulgent to them. That country becomes a market both more extensive and more advantageous for their goods: more extensive, because the goods of other nations being either excluded or subjected to heavier duties, it takes off a greater quantity of theirs: more advantageous, because the merchants of the favoured country, enjoying a sort of monopoly there, will often sell their goods for a better price than if exposed to the free competition of all other nations.

Such treaties, however, though they may be advantageous to the merchants and manufacturers of the favoured, are necessarily disadvantageous to those of the favouring country. A monopoly is thus granted against them to a foreign nation; and they must frequently buy the foreign goods they have occasion for dearer than if the free competition of other nations was admitted. That part of its own produce with which such a nation purchases foreign goods must consequently be sold cheaper, because when two things are exchanged for one another, the cheapness of the one is a necessary consequence, or rather is the same thing with the dearness of the other. The exchangeable value of its annual produce, therefore, is likely to be diminished by every such treaty. This diminution, however, can scarce amount to any positive loss, but only to a lessening of the gain which it might otherwise make. Though it sells its goods cheaper than it otherwise might do, it will not probably sell them for less than they cost; nor, as in the case of bounties, for a price which will not replace the capital employed in bringing them to market, together with the ordinary profits of stock. The trade could not go on long if it did. Even the favouring country, therefore, may still gain by the trade, though less than if there was a free competition.

Some treaties of commerce, however, have been supposed advantageous upon principles very different from these; and a commercial country has sometimes granted a monopoly of this kind against itself to certain goods of a foreign nation, because it expected that in the whole commerce between them, it would annually sell more than it would buy, and that a balance in gold and silver would be annually returned to it. It is upon this principle that the treaty of commerce between England and Portugal, concluded in 1703 by Mr. Methuen, has been so much commended. The following is a literal translation of that treaty, which consists of three articles only.

Art. I

His sacred royal majesty of Portugal promises, both in his own name, and that of his successors, to admit, for ever hereafter, into Portugal, the woollen cloths, and the rest of the woollen manufactures of the British, as was accustomed, till they were prohibited by the law; nevertheless upon this condition:

Art. II

That is to say, that her sacred royal majesty of Great Britain shall, in her own name, and that of her successors, be obliged, for ever hereafter, to admit the wines of the growth of Portugal into Britain; so that at no time, whether there shall be peace or war between the kingdoms of Britain and France, anything more shall be demanded for these wines by the name of custom or duty, or by whatsoever other title, directly or indirectly, whether they shall be imported into Great Britain in pipes or hogsheads, or other casks, than what shall be demanded for the like quantity or measure of French wine, deducting or abating a third part of the custom or duty. But if at any time this deduction or abatement of customs, which is to be made as aforesaid, shall in any manner be attempted and prejudiced, it shall be just and lawful for his sacred royal majesty of Portugal, again to prohibit the woollen cloths, and the rest of the British woollen manufactures.

Art. III

The most excellent lords the plenipotentiaries promise and take upon themselves, that their above-named masters shall ratify this treaty; and within the space of two months the ratifications shall be exchanged.

By this treaty the crown of Portugal becomes bound to admit the English woollens upon the same footing as before the prohibition; that is, not to raise the duties which had been paid before that time. But it does not become bound to admit them upon any better terms than those of any other nation, of France or Holland for example. The crown of Great Britain, on the contrary, becomes bound to admit the wines of Portugal upon paying only two-thirds of the duty which is paid for those of France, the wines most likely to come into competition with them. So far this treaty, therefore, is evidently advantageous to Portugal, and disadvantageous to Great Britian.

It has been celebrated, however, as a msterpiece of the commercial policy of England. Portugal receives annually from the Brazils a greater quantity of gold than can be employed in its domestic commerce, whether in the shape of coin or of plate. The surplus is too valuable to be allowed to lie idle and locked up in coffers, and as it can find no advantageous market at home, it must, notwithstanding any prohibition, be sent abroad, and exchanged for something for which there is a more advantageous market at home. A large share of it comes annually to England, in return either for English goods, or for those of other European nations that receive their returns through England. Mr. Baretti was informed that the weekly packet-boat from Lisbon brings, one week with another, more than fifty thousand pounds in gold to England. The sum had probably been exaggerated. It would amount to more than two millions six hundred thousand pounds a year, which is more than the Brazils are supposed to afford.

Our merchants were some years ago out of humour with the crown of Portugal. Some privileges which had been granted them, not by treaty, but by the free grace of that crown, at the solicitation indeed, it is probable, and in return for much greater favours, defence and protection, from the crown of Great Britain had been either infringed or revoked. The people, therefore, usually most interested in celebrating the Portugal trade were then rather disposed to represent it as less advantageous than it had commonly been imagined. The far greater part, almost the whole, they pretended, of this annual importation of gold, was not on account of Great Britain, but of other European nations; the fruits and wines of Portugal annually imported into Great Britain nearly compensating the value of the British goods sent thither.

Let us suppose, however, that the whole was on account of Great Britain, and that it amounted to a still greater sum than Mr. Baretti seems to imagine; this trade would not, upon that account, be more advantageous than any other in which, for the same value sent out, we received an equal value of consumable goods in return.

It is but a very small part of this importation which, it can be supposed, is employed as an annual addition either to the plate or to the coin of the kingdom. The rest must all be sent abroad and exchanged for consumable goods of some kind or other. But if those consumable goods were purchased directly with the produce of English industry, it would be more for the advantage of England than first to purchase with that produce the gold of Portugal, and afterwards to purchase with that gold those consumable goods. A direct foreign trade of consumption is always more advantageous than a round-about one; and to bring the same value of foreign goods to the home market, requires a much smaller capital in the one way than in the other. If a smaller share of its industry, therefore, had been employed in producing goods fit for the Portugal market, and a greater in producing those fit for the other markets, where those consumable goods for which there is a demand in Great Britain are to be had, it would have been more for the advantage of England. To procure both the gold, which it wants for its own use, and the consumable goods, would, in this way, employ a much smaller capital than at present. There would be a spare capital, therefore, to be employed for other purposes, in exciting an additional quantity of industry, and in raising a greater annual produce.

Though Britain were entirely excluded from the Portugal trade, it could find very little difficulty in procuring all the annual supplies of gold which it wants, either for the purposes of plate, or of coin, or of foreign trade. Gold, like every other commodity, is always somewhere or another to be got for its value by those who have that value to give for it. The annual surplus of gold in Portugal, besides, would still be sent abroad, and though not carried away by Great Britain, would be carried away by some other nation, which would be glad to sell it again for its price, in the same manner as Great Britain does at present. In buying gold of Portugal, indeed, we buy it at the first hand;

whereas, in buying it of any other nation, except Spain, we should buy it at the second, and might pay somewhat dearer. This difference, however, would surely be too insignificant to deserve the public attention.

Almost, all our gold, it is said, comes from Portugal. With other nations the balance of trade is either against us, or not much in our favour. But we should remember that the more gold we import from one country, the less we must necessarily import from all others. The effectual demand for gold, like that for every other commodity, is in every country limited to a certain quantity. If nine-tenths of this quantity are imported from one country, there remains a tenth only to be imported from all others. The more gold besides that is annually imported from some particular countries, over and above what is requisite for plate and for coin, the more must necessarily be exported to some others; and the more that most insignificant object of modern policy, the balance of trade, appears to be in our favour with some particular countries, the more it must necessarily appear to be against us with many others.

It was upon this silly notion, however, that England could not subsist without the Portugal trade, that, towards the end of the late war, France and Spain, without pretending either offence or provocation, required the King of Portugal to exclude all British ships from his ports, and for the security of this exclusion, to receive into them French or Spanish garrisons. Had the king of Portugal submitted to those ignominious terms which his brother-in-law the king of Spain proposed to him, Britain would have been freed from a much greater inconveniency than the loss of the Portugal trade, the burden of supporting a very weak ally, so unprovided of everything for his own defence that the whole power of England, had it been directed to that single purpose, could scarce perhaps have defended him for another campaign. The loss of the Portugal trade would, no doubt, have occasioned a considerable embarrassment to the merchants at that time engaged in it, who might not, perhaps, have found out, for a year or two, any other equally advantageous method of employing their capitals; and in this would probably have consisted all the inconveniency which England could have suffered from this notable piece of commercial policy.

The great annual importation of gold and silver is neither for the purpose of plate nor of coin, but of foreign trade. A round-about foreign trade of consumption can be carried on more advantageously by means of these metals than of almost any other goods. As they are the universal instruments of commerce, they are more readily received in return for all commodities than any other goods; and on account of their small bulk and great value, it costs less to transport them backward and forward from one place to another than almost any other sort of merchandise, and they lose less of their value by being so transported. Of all the commodities, therefore, which are bought in one foreign country, for no other purpose but to be sold or exchanged again for some other goods in another, there are none so convenient as gold and silver. In facilitating all the different round-about foreign trades of consumption which are carried on in Great Britain consists the principal advantage of the Portugal trade; and though it is not a capital advantage, it is no doubt a considerable one.

That any annual addition which, it can reasonably be supposed, is made either to the plate or to the coin of the kingdom, could require but a very small annual importation of gold and silver, seems evident enough; and though we had no direct trade with Portugal, this small quantity could always, somewhere or another, be very easily got.

Though the goldsmiths' trade be very considerable in Great Britain, the far greater part of the new plate which they annually sell is made from other old plate melted down; so that the addition annually made to the whole plate of the kingdom cannot be very great, and could require but a very small annual importation.

JEAN-JACQUES ROUSSEAU

JEAN-JACQUES ROUSSEAU was born in Geneva in 1712. He was orphaned at the age of ten and left Geneva in 1728, embarking on a life-long career of wandering through Europe. In Turin he briefly converted to Catholicism and traveled through France and Switzerland as footman and servant, seminarist, music teacher, and private tutor. For eight years, between 1732 and 1740, he was (more or less) settled at Chambery, the country home of Madame de Warens, with whom Rousseau had an odd – though clearly sexual – liaison. In 1741 he moved to Paris where he was commissioned by Denis Diderot, editor-in-chief of the great "Encyclopedia," to write articles on music. He also embarked on a lifelong (and also very odd) relationship with Therese Levasseur, who bore him five children, all of whom were abandoned to foundling homes. His major works were written in the 1750s and 1760s and, as far as politics and international relations are concerned, these consisted principally of his *Abstract of the Abbé De St Pierre's Project for Perpetual Peace* (1761), the novel *Emile* and the treatise *The Social Contract* (both published in 1762), and then the *Considerations on the Government of Poland* (1772). Other essays (for example, the *Discourse on Political Economy*) are, of course, also important, especially an essay, *The State of War*, probably written in the 1750s but not published until 1896. Rousseau clearly saw all politics as being connected. In 1743, while working as the private secretary to the French Ambassador in Venice, Rousseau had composed an outline of a comprehensive treatment of politics as such (including international politics). The work, to be called *Institutions Politiques*, was never written as planned, but all of Rousseau's various political works can be seen as parts of a greater whole. From the mid 1760s onwards, however, Rousseau was in almost constant flight from opponents or enemies, real or imagined. Following the completion of his last major work, his *Confessions*, in 1770, most of his last years were spent (relatively serenely) in Paris where he died in 1778.

From *The State of War*

But even if it were true that this boundless and uncontrollable greed had developed in all men to the extent which our sophist imagines, it still would not produce that state of universal war between everyone which Hobbes dares to depict in all its repulsiveness. The frantic desire to possess every-thing is incompatible with the desire to destroy all one's fellow men; and the conqueror who had the misfortune to remain alone in the world, having killed everyone else, would not thereby enjoy anything for the very reason that he would possess all. What are the riches themselves good for if not to be imparted to others? What would be the use of possessing the whole universe, if he was its sole inhabitant? What! Would his stomach devour all the fruits of the earth? Who would gather the produce of the world's cli-mates for him? Who would witness his empire in the vast solitudes where he did not live? What would he do with his treasures? Who would eat his food? For whose eyes would he display his power? I see. Instead of mas-sacring everyone, he would put them all in irons, so that at least he would have slaves. This immediately changes the whole nature of the question; since it is no longer a question of destroying, the state of war is abolished. The reader here may suspend judgement. I shall not omit to discuss this point.

Man is naturally peaceful and timid; at the least danger, his first reaction is to flee; he only fights through the force of habit and experience. Honour, interest, prejudices, vengeance, all those passions which make him brave danger and death, are remote from him in the state of nature. It is only when he has entered into society with other men that he decides to attack another, and he only becomes a soldier after he has become a citizen. There are no strong natural dispositions to make war on all one's fellow men. But I am lingering too long over a system both revolting and absurd, which has already been refuted a hundred times.

There is then no general war between men; and the human species has not been created solely in order to engage in mutual destruction. It remains to consider war of an accidental and exceptional nature which can arise between two or more individuals.

If natural law were inscribed solely in human reason, it would scarcely be capable of guiding the bulk of our actions. But it is also indelibly engraved in the human heart; and it is there that it speaks to man more powerfully than all the precepts of philosophers; it is there that it tells him that he is not permitted to sacrifice the life of his fellow man except in order to preserve his own, and it is there that it gives him a horror of killing in cold blood, even when he is obliged to do so.

I can conceive that, in the unarbitrated quarrels which can arise in the state of nature, a man whose anger has been roused can sometimes kill another, either by open force or by surprise. But if a real war were to take place, imag-ine the strange position which this same man would have to be in if he could only preserve his life at the expense of that of another, and if an estab-lished relationship between them required that one died so that the other could live. War is a permanent state which presupposes constant relations; and these relations are a rare occurrence between men, for between individuals there is a continual flux which constantly changes relationships and interests. Thus a matter of dispute rises and disappears almost at the same moment; a quarrel begins and ends within a day; and one can have fights and murders, but never, or very rarely, long enmities and wars.

In the civil state, where the life of all the citizens is in the power of the sovereign and where no one has the right to dispose either of his own life or that of another person, the state of war can no longer take place between private individuals; as for duels, challenges, agreements or appeals to single combat, apart from the fact that they represent an illegal and barbarous abuse of a military settlement, they do not give rise to a true state of war, but only to a specific event, limited in time and space, which requires a new challenge if a second combat is to take place. An exception must be made for those private wars which were suspended by daily truces, called the peace of God, and which were sanctioned by the Institutions of St Louis. But this example is unique in history.

It may still be asked whether kings, who are in fact independent of all human power, can establish personal and private wars between themselves, separate from those of the state. This is surely a trifling question; for as one knows it is not the custom of princes to spare others in order to expose themselves personally. Moreover, this question depends on another which it is not incumbent upon me to decide; that is whether the prince is himself subject to the state's laws or not; for if he is subject to them, his person is bound and his life belongs to the state, like that of the lowest citizen. But if the prince is above the laws, he lives in the pure state of nature and is accountable neither to his subjects nor to anyone for any of his actions.

The social state

We now enter a new order of things. We are about to see men, united in artificial harmony, band together to cut each other's throats, and to see all the horrors of war arise from the very efforts which have been taken to prevent them. But first it is crucial to formulate a more exact idea of the essence of the body politic than has been done so far. The reader must realize that it is here less a question of history and facts than of right and justice, and that I wish to examine things according to their nature rather than according to our prejudices.

As soon as the first society is formed, the formation of all the others necessarily follows. One has either to join it or to unite to resist it; to imitate it or let oneself be swallowed up by it. Thus the whole face of the earth is changed; everywhere nature has disappeared; everywhere human artifice takes its place; independence and natural liberty give way to laws and slavery; free beings no longer exist; the philosopher searches for man and no longer finds him. But it is fruitless to expect the annihilation of nature; it springs to life again and reveals itself where one least expects it. The independence which is removed from men takes refuge in societies; and these great bodies, left to their own impulses, produce collisions which grow more terrible the more their weight takes precedence over that of individuals.

But how, it will be asked, is it possible that these bodies, each of which has so solid a foundation, should ever come to run up against one another? Ought not their very formation to keep perpetual peace between them? Are they obliged, like men, to look outside themselves for the satisfaction of their needs? Do they not possess in themselves all that is necessary for their preservation? Are competition and trade a source of inevitable discord? And have not people existed in all lands before commerce started, an irrefutable proof that they are able to survive without it?

I could content myself with replying to this question with facts, and I would fear no rejoinder. However, I have not forgotten that I am reasoning here about the nature of things and not about events, which can have a thousand particular causes, independent of the common principle. Let us consider closely the formation of political bodies, and we will find that, although each of them has, if need be, enough for its own preservation, their mutual relations are none the less far more intimate than those of individuals. For basically man has no necessary connection with his fellow men; he can maintain his full strength without their help; his need is not so much for men's care as for the earth's produce; and the earth produces more than enough to feed its inhabitants. Also the strength and size of man has a limit set by nature which he cannot go beyond. Whichever way he looks at himself, he finds all of his faculties are limited. His life is short, his years are numbered. His stomach does not grow with his riches; his passions increase in vain, his pleasures are bounded; his heart is confined, like all the rest; his capacity for enjoyment is always the same. He can rise up in his imagination, yet he always remains small.

The state on the other hand, being an artificial body, has no fixed measure; its proper size is undefined; it can always grow bigger; it feels weak so long as there are others stronger than itself. Its safety and preservation demand that it makes itself stronger than its neighbours. It cannot increase, foster, or exercise its strength except at their expense; and even if it has no need to seek for provisions beyond its borders, it searches ceaselessly for new members to give itself a more unshakeable position. For the inequality of men has its limits set by nature, but the inequality of societies can grow incessantly, until one of them absorbs all the others.

Thus the size of the body politic being purely relative, it is forced to compare itself in order to know itself; it depends on its whole environment and has to take an interest in all that happens. In vain it wishes to stay within its own bounds, neither gaining nor losing; it becomes big or small, strong or weak according to the extent that its neighbour expands or contracts, grows stronger or weaker. Finally its very consolidation, by making its relations more constant, gives greater sureness to all its actions and makes all its quarrels more dangerous.

It looks as if one has set out to turn every true idea of things upside down. Everything inclines natural man to peace; the sole needs he knows are eating and sleeping, and only hunger drags him from idleness. He is made into a savage continually ready to torment his fellow men because of passions of which he knows nothing. On the contrary, these passions, aroused in the bosom of society by everything that can inflame them, are considered not to exist there at all. A thousand writers have dared to say that the body politic is passionless, and that there is no other *raison d'état* than reason itself. As if no one saw that, on the contrary, the essence of society consists in the activity of its members, and that a state without movement would be nothing but a corpse. As if all the world's histories do not show us that the best-constituted societies are also the most active and that the continual action and reaction of all their members, whether within or without, bear witness to the vigour of the whole body.

The difference between human artifice and the work of nature is made evident in its effects. The citizens may well call themselves members of the state, but they are incapable of uniting themselves to it like real members of a body; it is impossible to prevent each one of them from having a separate and individual existence through which he can be self-sufficing; the nerves are less sensitive, the muscles have less strength, all the bonds are looser, the slightest accident can break everything asunder.

If one considers how inferior the public power is to the sum of particular powers within the totality of the body politic, and how much, so to speak, friction there is in the working of the whole machine, one will discover that the feeblest man has proportionately more power to preserve himself than the strongest state has to preserve itself.

For the state to survive then, it is necessary for the intensity of its passions to compensate for that of its movements and for its will to quicken as its power slackens. This is the law of preservation that nature herself establishes between the species, and which maintains them all, despite their inequality. It is also, one may note in passing, the reason why small states have proportionately more vigour than big ones. Public feeling does not grow with territory; the more the latter extends, the more the will relaxes and movements grow weaker, until finally the huge body, overloaded with its own weight, caves in, and falls into listlessness and decay.

These examples suffice to give an idea of the various methods whereby a state can be weakened, and of those which war seems to sanction in order to harm its enemy. As for treaties in which some of these means are incorporated, what basically is a peace of this sort except a war continued with all the more cruelty in that the enemy no longer has the right to defend himself? I will speak of this elsewhere.

Add to this the visible signs of ill will, which indicate the intention to do harm; such as refusing to accord a power the status due to it, or ignoring its rights, rejecting its claims, refusing its subjects freedom to trade, rousing enemies against it, or finally breaking international law towards it, under some pretext or other. These various ways of offending a body politic are neither equally practicable nor equally useful to the state that uses them, and those which result simultaneously in our own advantage and the enemy's disadvantage are naturally preferred. Land, money, men, all the booty that one can carry off thus become the principal object of reciprocal hostilities. As this base greed imperceptibly changes people's ideas about things, war finally degenerates into brigandage, and little by little enemies and warriors become tyrants and thieves.

From fear of thoughtlessly adopting this change of ideas ourselves, let us fix our own thoughts by a definition, and try to make it so simple that it cannot be abused.

I call then war between power and power the effect of a constant, overt, mutual disposition to destroy the enemy state, or at least to weaken it by all the means one can. When this disposition is transformed into action it is war properly called; in so far as it remains untransformed it is only the state of war.

I foresee an objection: since according to me the state of war is natural between powers, why does the disposition in which it results have to be overt? To this I reply that I have been speaking up to now of the natural state and that I am here speaking of the legitimate state, and that I shall show below how, in order to make it legitimate, war must be declared.

Fundamental distinctions

I beg readers not to forget that I am not searching for what makes war advantageous to him who wages it, but for what makes it legitimate. It almost always costs something to be just. Is one therefore exempted from being so?

If there has never been, and if it is impossible to have, a true war between individuals, between whom then does it take place, and who can really call themselves enemies? I reply that they are public persons. And what is a public person? I reply that it is the moral being which one calls sovereign, which has been brought into existence by the social pact, and whose will always carries the name of law. Let us apply here the distinctions made earlier; one can say that, in considering the effects of war, the sovereign inflicts the injury and the state receives it.

If war only takes place between moral beings, it is not intended to be between men, and one can conduct a war without depriving anyone of their life. But this requires an explanation.

If one looks at things solely and strictly in the light of the social pact, land, money, men, and everything contained within the boundary of the state, belongs unreservedly to it. But as the rights of society, founded on those of nature, cannot abolish the latter, all these objects must be considered in a double context: that is, the earth must be seen both as public land and as the patrimony of individuals; goods belong in one sense to the sovereign, and in another to their owners; people are both citizens and men. Basically the body politic, in so far as it is only a moral being, is merely a thing of reason. Remove the public convention and immediately the state is destroyed, without the least change in all that composes it; for all man's conventions are unable to change anything in the nature of things. What then does it mean to wage war on a sovereign? It means an attack on the public convention and all that results from it; for the essence of the state consists solely in that. If the social pact could be sundered with one blow, immediately there would be no more war; and by this one blow the state would be killed, without the death of one man. Aristotle states that in order to authorize the cruel treatment which the Helots were made to suffer in Sparta, the Ephors, when they took charge, solemnly declared war on them. This declaration was as superfluous as it was barbarous. A state of war existed of necessity between them from the very fact that the ones were masters and the others slaves. There can be no doubt that the Helots had the right to kill Lacedaemonians since the latter killed them.

I open books on law and ethics, and listen to the scholars and legal experts. Permeated with their persuasive talk, I lament the miseries of nature, admire the peace and justice established by the civil order, bless the wisdom of public institutions, and console myself for being a man by looking upon myself as a citizen. Well versed in my duties and happiness, I shut my book, leave the classroom, and look around me. I see unfortunate nations groaning under yokes of iron, the human race crushed by a handful of oppressors, a starving crowd overwhelmed with pain and hunger, whose blood and tears the rich drink in peace, and everywhere the strong armed against the weak with the formidable power of the law.

All this happens peacefully and without resistance. It is the tranquillity of Ulysses' comrades, shut in the cave of the Cyclops, waiting to be eaten. One must groan and keep silent. Let us draw a veil over these horrifying subjects. I raise my eyes and look into the distance. I see fires and flames, the countryside deserted, towns pillaged. Savages, where are you dragging those unfortunate people? I hear a terrible noise; what an uproar! I draw near; I see a scene of murder, ten thousand butchered men, the dead piled in heaps, the dying trampled under horses' hooves, everywhere the face of death and agony. So this is the fruit of these peaceful institutions! Pity and indignation rise from the bottom of my heart. Barbarous philosopher! Come and read us your book on the field of battle!

Whose stomach would not be turned by these sad subjects? But one is no longer allowed to be human and to plead the cause of humanity. Justice and truth must be bent to serve the most powerful: that is the rule. The people give neither pensions, nor employment, nor chairs, nor places at the Academies; why protect them? Magnanimous princes, I speak in the name of the literary body; oppress the people with a good conscience; it is from you alone that we expect everything; the people cannot do anything for us.

How can such a weak voice make itself heard above so much mercenary clamour? Alas! I must keep silent. But is the voice of my heart unable to pierce so sad a silence? No; without entering into odious details which would pass for satire solely because they are true, I will limit myself, as I always do, to examining institutions according to their principles, to correcting if possible the false ideas that have been given us by biased authors, and to ensuring that at least injustice and violence do not shamelessly masquerade as fairness and right.

The first thing I notice, in considering the condition of the human species, is an open contradiction in its constitution which causes it to vacillate incessantly. As individual men we live in a civil state subject to laws; as people we each enjoy a natural liberty; this makes our position fundamentally worse than if these distinctions were unknown. For living simultaneously in the social order and in the state of nature we are subjected to the inconveniences of both, without finding security in either. The perfection of the social order consists, it is true, in the conjunction of force and law. But this demands that law guides the use of force; whereas according to the ideas of absolute independence held by princes, force alone, speaking to citizens under the name of law and to foreigners under the name of *raison d'état*, removes from the latter the power, and from the former the will to resist, in such a way that everywhere the empty name of justice serves only as a safeguard for violence.

As for what is commonly called international law, because its laws lack any sanction, they are unquestionably mere illusions, even feebler than the law of nature. The latter at least speaks in the heart of individual men; whereas the decisions of international law, having no other guarantee than their usefulness to the person who submits to them, are only respected in so far as interest accords with them. In the mixed condition in which we find ourselves, whichever system we prefer, making too much or too little of it, we have achieved nothing, and are in the worst state of all. That, it seems to me, is the true origin of public disasters.

Let us contrast these ideas for a moment with Hobbes's horrible system, and we will find the very reverse of his absurd doctrine. Far from the state of war being natural to man, war springs from peace, or at least from the precautions that men have taken to ensure a lasting peace.

Who could have imagined without shuddering the insane system of a natural war of all against all? What could be stranger than a creature who thought his own welfare depended on the destruction of his whole species! And how could one conceive that such a species, so monstrous and detestable, would last only two generations? Yet that is where one of the finest geniuses who ever lived has been led by his desire, or rather frenzy, to establish despotism and passive obedience. So ferocious a principle was worthy of its object.

The social state which restrains all our natural inclinations cannot however extinguish them; in spite of our prejudices and in spite of ourselves, they still speak from the bottom of our hearts and often lead us back to the truth which we abandon for illusions. If this mutual and destructive hostility formed part of our make-up, it would still make itself felt, pushing us back, in spite of ourselves, across all social bonds. A terrible hatred of humanity would gnaw man's heart. He would grieve at the birth of his own children; he would rejoice at the death of his brothers; and if he discovered someone asleep his first reaction would be to kill him.

The goodwill which makes us share in the happiness of our fellow men, the compassion which identifies us with the sufferer and afflicts us with his sorrow, these would be unknown feelings directly contrary to nature. The sufferer would be a monster rather than a sensitive man worthy of pity; and we would be by nature the kind of person we have difficulty in becoming even in the midst of the depravity which pursues us.

In vain the sophist will say that this mutual enmity is not innate and immediate, but founded on the inevitable competition which arises from the right of each to everything. For the awareness of this supposed right is no more natural to man than the war which it produces.

I have already stated, and I cannot repeat it too often, that the error of Hobbes and the philosophers is to confuse natural man with the man before their eyes, and to transpose into one system a being who can only exist in another. Man desires his own well-being and all that can contribute towards it; that is incontestable. But his well-being is limited by nature to physical necessity; for what does a man lack in order to be happy according to his constitution if he has a healthy spirit and a body free from suffering? He who has nothing desires little; he who commands no one has little ambition. But abundance arouses greed; the more one gets the more one desires. He who has much wants to have it all; and the madness of universal monarchy only ever tormented the heart of a great king. Such is the march of nature, such is the development of the passions. A superficial philosopher observes souls that have been kneaded and worked a hundred times in the leaven of society, and thinks he has observed man. But in order to know him well, one must be able to disentangle the natural hierarchy of his feelings, and it is not amongst the inhabitants of a big town that one must look for the first sign of nature imprinted in the human heart.

Thus this analytic method only produces chasms and mysteries in which the wisest understands the least. Ask why morals become corrupted as minds become more enlightened. Unable to find a reason, they will have the audacity to deny the fact. Ask why savages brought amongst us do not share either our passions or our pleasures, and care nothing for the things we so ardently cherish. They will never explain, or explain only by my principles. They know only what they see and have never seen nature. A citizen of London or Paris they understand very well; but they can never understand man.

Abstract and Judgement of Saint-Pierre's Project for Perpetual Peace

...

We have thus seen that all the alleged evils of federation, when duly weighed, come to nothing. I now ask whether anyone in the world would dare to say as much of those which flow from the recognized method of settling disputes between one prince and another – the appeal to the sword: a method inseparable from the state of anarchy and war, which necessarily springs from the absolute independence conceded to all sovereigns under the imperfect conditions now prevailing in Europe. In order to put the reader in a better position to estimate these evils, I will give a short summary of them and leave him to judge of their significance.

(1) The existence of no solid right, except that of the stronger. (2) The perpetual and inevitable shifting of the balance from nation to nation, which makes it impossible for any one of them to keep in its grasp the power it holds at any moment. (3) The absence of complete security for any nation, so long as its neighbours are not subdued or annihilated. (4) The impossibility of annihilating them, in view of the fact that, directly one is conquered, another

springs up in its place. (5) The necessity of endless precautions and expenses to keep guard against possible enemies. (6) Weakness, and consequent exposure to attack, during minorities or revolts; for, when the state is divided, who can support one faction against the other? (7) The absence of any guarantee for international agreements. (8) The impossibility of obtaining justice from others without enormous cost and loss, which even so do not always obtain it, while the object in dispute is seldom worth the price. (9) The invariable risk of the prince's possessions, and sometimes of his life, in the quest of his rights. (10) The necessity of taking part against his will in the quarrels of his neighbours and of engaging in war at the moment when he would least have chosen it. (11) The stoppage of trade and revenue at the moment when they are most indispensable. (12) The perpetual dangers threatened by a powerful neighbour, if the prince is weak, and by an armed alliance, if he is strong. (13) Finally, the uselessness of prudence, when everything is left to chance; the perpetual impoverishment of nations; the enfeeblement of the state alike in victory and defeat; and the total inability of the prince ever to establish good government, ever to count upon his own possessions, ever to secure happiness either for himself or for his subjects.

...

Judgement of Saint-Pierre's project

The scheme of a lasting peace was of all others the most worthy to fascinate a man of high principle. Of all those which engaged the Abbé de Saint-Pierre, it was therefore that over which he brooded the longest and followed up with the greatest obstinacy. It is indeed hard to give any other name to the missionary zeal which never failed him in this enterprise in spite of the manifest impossibility of success, the ridicule which he brought upon himself day by day, and the rebuffs which he had continually to endure. It would seem that his well-balanced spirit, intent solely on the public good, led him to measure his devotion to a cause purely by its utility, never letting himself be daunted by difficulties, never thinking of his own personal interest.

If ever moral truth were demonstrated, I should say it is the utility, national no less than international, of this project. The advantages which its realization would bring to each prince, to each nation, to the whole of Europe, are immense, manifest, incontestable; and nothing could be more solid or more precise than the arguments which the author employs to prove them. Realize his commonwealth of Europe for a single day, and you may be sure it will last forever; so fully would experience convince men that their own gain is to be found in the good of all. For all that, the very princes who would defend it with all their might, if it once existed, would resist with all their might any proposal for its creation; they will as infallibly throw obstacles in the way of its establishment as they would in the way of its abolition. Accordingly Saint-Pierre's book on *A Lasting Peace* seems to be ineffectual for founding it and unnecessary for maintaining it. 'It is then an empty dream,' will be the verdict of the impatient reader. No: it is a work of solid judgement, and it is of the last importance for us to possess it.

IMMANUEL KANT

IMMANUEL KANT was born on 22 April 1724 in Königsberg, then in East Prussia, the son of a harness maker. He thus came from a poor family, though one marked by exceptional religious belief. Both his parents died early (his mother when he was fourteen) but his precocious intellectual gifts were swiftly recognized and he entered the University of Königsberg, where he had a brilliant undergraduate career. In 1755, after the fashion of German universities of the time, Kant was granted the right to lecture as a *privatdozent*, that is, an unsalaried lecturer who depended on his lecture fees for his income. Kant thus lectured frequently and on a wide variety of topics, merely to earn a living. That same year he began his scholarly career with a treatise on *The General History of Nature and Theory of the Heavens*, and for a while his main interests were in the theory and philosophy of science. Kant remained a *privatdozent* until 1770 when at last he won the coveted position of *ordinariius*, or full-tenured professor, at Königsberg. Kant was, by all accounts a lively, provocative, and powerful lecturer, a fact recognized by the university (even before his growing scholarly fame outshone it) by raising his stipend. Kant was also a very popular figure and became rector of the university (the highest position in the German university system) on several occasions. His real philosophical breakthrough came with the publication of the *Critique of Pure Reason* in 1781 (a second edition was produced in 1787), which marked the real beginning of Kant's development of what became known as the "critical philosophy," which eventually encompassed not only science and cosmology but also theology, ethics, law, history, and politics. His political writings properly so-called were mainly written towards the end of his life, but they form a natural outgrowth of his more general philosophical and moral positions. By the end of his life Kant had become a major figure on the European intellectual scene, much sought out, though he had rarely moved from Königsberg in the whole of his long life. His fixed routine was as famous as it was inviolable; it was said that he had only ever missed his fabled afternoon walk once (the reason was that he was reading Rousseau's novel *Emile*). Despite this he was an avid socializer and a keen student of the practical politics and political foibles of his own day, as his lectures (more than his formal publications) reveal. He died on 12 February 1804, at the age of eighty.

From *Essay on Theory and Practice*

On the relationship of theory to practice in international
right, considered from a universally philanthropic,
i.e. cosmopolitan point of view

...

[The] hope for better times to come, without which an earnest desire to
do something useful for the common good would never have inspired the
human heart, has always influenced the activities of right-thinking men. And
the worthy [Moses] Mendelssohn must himself have reckoned on this, since
he zealously endeavoured to promote the enlightenment and welfare of the
nation to which he belonged. For he could not himself reasonably hope to do
this unless others after him continued upon the same path. Confronted by
the sorry spectacle not only of those evils which befall mankind from natural
causes, but also of those which men inflict upon one another, our spirits
can be raised by the prospect of future improvements. This, however, calls
for unselfish goodwill on our part, since we shall have been long dead and
buried when the fruits we helped to sow are harvested. It is quite irrelevant
whether any empirical evidence suggests that these plans, which are founded
only on hope, may be unsuccessful. For the idea that something which has
hitherto been unsuccessful will therefore never be successful does not justify
anyone in abandoning even a pragmatic or technical aim (for example, that
of flights with aerostatic balloons). This applies even more to moral aims,
which, so long as it is not demonstrably impossible to fulfil them, amount to
duties. Besides, various evidence suggests that in our age, as compared with
all previous ages, the human race has made considerable moral progress, and
short-term hindrances prove nothing to the contrary. Moreover, it can be
shown that the outcry about man's continually increasing decadence arises
for the very reason that we can see further ahead, because we have reached a
higher level of morality. We thus pass more severe judgements on what we are,
comparing it with what we ought to be, so that our self-reproach increases
in proportion to the number of stages of morality we have advanced through
during the whole of known history.

If we now ask what means there are of maintaining and indeed acceler-
ating this constant progress towards a better state, we soon realise that the
success of this immeasurably long undertaking will depend not so much upon
what *we* do (e.g. the education we impart to younger generations) and upon
what methods *we* use to further it; it will rather depend upon what human
nature may do in and through us, to *compel* us to follow a course which we
would not readily adopt by choice. We must look to nature alone, or rather

to *providence* (since it requires the highest wisdom to fulfil this purpose), for a successful outcome which will first affect the whole and then the individual parts. The schemes of men, on the other hand, begin with the parts, and frequently get no further than them. For the whole is too great for men to encompass; while they can reach it with their ideas, they cannot actively influence it, especially since their schemes conflict with one another to such an extent that they could hardly reach agreement of their own free volition.

On the one hand, universal violence and the distress it produces must eventually make a people decide to submit to the coercion which reason itself prescribes (i.e. the coercion of public law), and to enter into a *civil* constitution. And on the other hand, the distress produced by the constant wars in which the states try to subjugate or engulf each other must finally lead them, even against their will, to enter into a *cosmopolitan* constitution. Or if such a state of universal peace is in turn even more dangerous to freedom, for it may lead to the most fearful despotism (as has indeed occurred more than once with states which have grown too large), distress must force men to form a state which is not a cosmopolitan commonwealth under a single ruler, but a lawful *federation* under a commonly accepted *international right*.

The increasing culture of the states, along with their growing tendency to aggrandise themselves by cunning or violence at the expense of the others, must make wars more frequent. It must likewise cause increasingly high expenditure on standing armies, which must be kept in constant training and equipped with ever more numerous instruments of warfare. Meanwhile, the price of all necessities will steadily rise, while no-one can hope for any proportionate increase in the corresponding metal currencies. No peace will last long enough for the resources saved during it to meet the expenditure of the next war, while the invention of a national debt, though ingenious, is an ultimately self-defeating expedient. Thus sheer exhaustion must eventually perform what goodwill ought to have done but failed to do: each state must be organised internally in such a way that the head of state, for whom the war actually costs nothing (for he wages it at the expense of others, i.e. the people), must no longer have the deciding vote on whether war is to be declared or not, for the people who pay for it must decide. (This, of course, necessarily presupposes that the idea of an original contract has already been realised.) For the people will not readily place itself in danger of personal want (which would not affect the head of state) out of a mere desire for aggrandisement, or because of some supposed and purely verbal offence. And thus posterity will not be oppressed by any burdens which it has not brought upon itself, and it will be able to make perpetual progress towards a morally superior state. This is not produced by any love on the part of earlier ages for later ones, but only by the love of each age for itself. Each commonwealth, unable to harm the others by force, must observe the laws on its own account, and it may reasonably hope that other similarly constituted bodies will help it to do so.

But this is no more than a personal opinion and hypothesis; it is uncertain, like all judgements which profess to define the appropriate natural cause of an intended effect which is not wholly within our control. And even as such, it does not offer the subject of an existing state any principle by which he could attain the desired effect by force (as has already been demonstrated); only the head of state, who is above coercion, can do so. In the normal order of things, it cannot be expected of human nature to desist voluntarily from using force, although it is not impossible where the circumstances are sufficiently pressing. Thus it is not inappropriate to say of man's moral hopes and desires that, since he is powerless to fulfil them himself, he may look to *providence* to create the circumstances in which they can be fulfilled. The end of *man* as an entire species, i.e. that of fulfilling his ultimate appointed purpose by freely exercising his own powers, will be brought by providence to a successful issue, even although the ends of *men* as individuals run in a diametrically opposite direction. For the very conflict of individual inclinations, which is the source of all evil, gives reason a free hand to master them all; it thus gives predominance not to evil, which destroys itself, but to good, which continues to maintain itself once it has been established.

Nowhere does human nature appear less admirable than in the relationships which exist between peoples. No state is for a moment secure from the others in its independence and its possessions. The will to subjugate the others or to grow at their expense is always present, and the production of armaments for defence, which often makes peace more oppressive and more destructive of internal welfare than war itself, can never be relaxed. And there is no possible way of counteracting this except a state of international right, based upon enforceable public laws to which each state must submit (by analogy with a state of civil or political right among individual men). For a permanent universal peace by means of a so-called *European balance of power* is a pure illusion, like Swift's story of the house which the builder had constructed in such perfect harmony with all the laws of equilibrium that it collapsed as soon as a sparrow alighted on it. But it might be objected that no states will ever submit to coercive laws of this kind, and that a proposal for a universal federation, to whose power all the individual states would voluntarily submit and whose laws they would all obey, may be all very well in the theory of the Abbé St Pierre or of Rousseau, but that it does not apply in practice. For such proposals have always been ridiculed by great statesmen, and even more by heads of state, as pedantic, childish and academic ideas.

For my own part, I put my trust in the theory of what the relationships between men and states *ought to be* according to the principle of right. It recommends to us earthly gods the maxim that we should proceed in our disputes in such a way that a universal federal state may be inaugurated, so that we should therefore assume that it *is possible* (*in praxi*). I likewise rely (*in subsidium*) upon the very nature of things to force men to do what they do not willingly choose (*fata volentem ducunt, nolentem trahunt*). This involves human nature, which is still animated by respect for right and duty. I therefore cannot and will not see it as so deeply immersed in evil that practical moral reason will not triumph in the end, after many unsuccessful attempts, thereby showing that it is worthy of admiration after all. On the cosmopolitan level too, it thus remains true to say that whatever reason shows to be valid in theory, is also valid in practice.

From *Perpetual Peace: A Philosophical Sketch*

'The perpetual peace'

A Dutch innkeeper once put this satirical inscription on his signboard, along with the picture of a graveyard. We shall not trouble to ask whether it applies to men in general, or particularly to heads of state (who can never have enough of war), or only to the philosophers who blissfully dream of perpetual peace. The author of the present essay does, however, make one reservation in advance. The practical politician tends to look down with great complacency upon the political theorist as a mere academic. The theorist's abstract ideas, the practitioner believes, cannot endanger the state, since the state must be founded upon principles of experience; it thus seems safe to let him fire off his whole broadside, and the *worldly-wise* statesman need not turn a hair. It thus follows that if the practical politician is to be consistent, he must not claim, in the event of a dispute with the theorist, to scent any danger to the state in the opinions which the theorist has randomly uttered in public. By this saving clause, the author of this essay will consider himself expressly safeguarded, in correct and proper style, against all malicious interpretation.

First section

WHICH CONTAINS THE PRELIMINARY ARTICLES OF A PERPETUAL PEACE BETWEEN STATES

1 . 'No conclusion of peace shall be considered valid as such if it was made with a secret reservation of the material for a future war.'

For if this were the case, it would be a mere truce, a suspension of hostilities, not a *peace*. Peace means an end to all hostilities, and to attach the adjective 'perpetual' to it is already suspiciously close to pleonasm. A conclusion of peace nullifies all existing reasons for a future war, even if these are not yet known to the contracting parties, and no matter how acutely and carefully they may later be pieced together out of old documents. It is possible that either party may make a mental reservation with a view to reviving its old pretensions in the future. Such reservations will not be mentioned explicitly, since both parties may simply be too exhausted to continue the war, although they may nonetheless possess sufficient ill will to seize the first favourable opportunity of attaining their end. But if we consider such reservations in themselves, they soon appear as Jesuitical casuistry; they are beneath the dignity of a ruler, just as it is beneath the dignity of a minister of state to comply with any reasoning of this kind.

But if, in accordance with 'enlightened' notions of political expediency, we believe that the true glory of a state consists in the constant increase of its power by any means whatsoever, the above judgement will certainly appear academic and pedantic.

2 . 'No independently existing state, whether it be large or small, may be acquired by another state by inheritance, exchange, purchase or gift.'

For a state, unlike the ground on which it is based, is not a possession (*patrimonium*). It is a society of men, which no-one other than itself can command or dispose of. Like a tree, it has its own roots, and to graft it on to another state as if it were a shoot is to terminate its existence as a moral personality and make it into a commodity. This contradicts the idea of the original contract, without which the rights of a people are unthinkable. Everyone knows what danger the supposed right of acquiring states in this way, even in our own times, has brought upon Europe (for this practice is unknown in other continents). It has been thought that states can marry one another, and this has provided a new kind of industry by which power can be increased through family alliances, without expenditure of energy, while landed property can be extended at the same time. It is the same thing when the troops of one state are hired to another to fight an enemy who is not common to both; for the subjects are thereby used and misused as objects to be manipulated at will.

3 . 'Standing armies (*miles perpetuus*) will gradually be abolished altogether.'

For they constantly threaten other states with war by the very fact that they are always prepared for it. They spur on the states to outdo one another in arming unlimited numbers of soldiers, and since the resultant costs eventually make peace more oppressive than a short war, the armies are themselves the cause of wars of aggression which set out to end burdensome military expenditure. Furthermore, the hiring of men to kill or to be killed seems to mean using them as mere machines and instruments in the hands of someone else (the state), which cannot easily be reconciled with the rights of man in one's own person. It is quite a different matter if the citizens undertake voluntary military training from time to time in order to secure themselves and their fatherland against attacks from outside. But it would be just the same if wealth rather than soldiers were accumulated, for it would be seen by other states as a military threat; it might compel them to mount preventive attacks, for of the three powers within a state – the *power of the army*, the *power of alliance* and the *power of money* – the third is probably the most reliable instrument of war. It would lead more often to wars if it were not so difficult to discover the amount of wealth which another state possesses.

4 . 'No national debt shall be contracted in connection with the external affairs of the state.'

There is no cause for suspicion if help for the national economy is sought inside or outside the state (e.g. for improvements to roads, new settlements, storage of foodstuffs for years of famine, etc.). But a credit system, if used by the powers as an instrument of aggression against one another, shows the power of money in its most dangerous form. For while the debts thereby incurred are always secure against present demands (because not all the creditors will demand payment at the same time), these debts go on growing indefinitely. This ingenious system, invented by a commercial people in the present century, provides a military fund which may exceed the resources of all the other states put together. It can only be exhausted by an eventual tax-deficit, which may be postponed for a considerable time by the commercial stimulus which industry and trade receive through the credit system. This ease in making war, coupled with the warlike inclination of those in power (which seems to be an integral feature of human nature), is thus a great obsta-cle in the way of perpetual peace. Foreign debts must therefore be prohibited by a preliminary article of such a peace, otherwise national bankruptcy, in-evitable in the long run, would necessarily involve various other states in the resultant loss without their having deserved it, thus inflicting upon them a public injury. Other states are therefore justified in allying themselves against such a state and its pretensions.

5 . 'No state shall forcibly interfere in the constitution and government of another state.'

For what could justify such interference? Surely not any sense of scandal or offence which a state arouses in the subjects of another state. It should rather serve as a warning to others, as an example of the great evils which a people has incurred by its lawlessness. And a bad example which one free person gives to another (as a *scandalum acceptum*) is not the same as an injury to the latter. But it would be a different matter if a state, through internal discord, were to split into two parts, each of which set itself up as a separate state and claimed authority over the whole. For it could not be reckoned as interference in another state's constitution if an external state were to lend support to one of them, because their condition is one of anarchy. But as long as this internal conflict is not yet decided, the interference of external powers would be a violation of the rights of an independent people which is merely struggling with its internal ills. Such interference would be an active offence and would make the autonomy of all other states insecure.

6 . 'No state at war with another shall permit such acts of hostility as would make mutual confidence impossible during a future time of peace. Such acts would include the employment of *assassins* (*percussores*) *or poisoners (venefici), breach of agreements, the instigation of treason (perduellio)* within the enemy state, etc.'

These are dishonourable stratagems. For it must still remain possible, even in wartime, to have some sort of trust in the attitude of the enemy, otherwise peace could not be concluded and the hostilities would turn into a war of extermination (*bellum internecinum*). After all, war is only a regrettable expedient for asserting one's rights by force within a state of nature, where no court of justice is available to judge with legal authority. In such cases, neither party can be declared an unjust enemy, for this would already presuppose a judge's decision; only the *outcome* of the conflict, as in the case of a so-called 'judgement of God', can decide who is in the right. A war of punishment (*bellum punitivum*) between states is inconceivable, since there can be no relationship of superior to inferior among them. It thus follows that a war of extermination, in which both parties and right itself might all be simultaneously annihilated, would allow perpetual peace only on the vast graveyard of the human race. A war of this kind and the employment of all means which might bring it about must thus be absolutely prohibited. But the means listed above would inevitably lead to such a war, because these diabolical arts, besides being intrinsically despicable, would not long be confined to war alone if they were brought into use. This applies, for example, to the employment of spies (*uti exploratoribus*), for it exploits only the dishonesty of others (which can never be completely eliminated). Such practices will be carried over into peacetime and will thus completely vitiate its purpose.

All of the articles listed above, when regarded objectively or in relation to the intentions of those in power, are *prohibitive laws* (*leges prohibitivae*). Yet some of them are of the *strictest* sort (*leges strictae*), being valid irrespective of differing circumstances, and they require that the abuses they prohibit should be abolished *immediately* (Nos. 1, 5, and 6). Others (Nos. 2, 3, and 4), although they are not exceptions to the rule of justice, allow some *subjective* latitude according to the circumstances in which they are applied (*leges latae*). The latter need not necessarily be executed at once, so long as their ultimate purpose (e.g. the *restoration* of freedom to certain states in accordance with the second article) is not lost sight of. But their execution may not be *put off* to a non-existent date (*ad calendas graecas*, as Augustus used to promise), for any delay is permitted only as a means of avoiding a premature implementation which might frustrate the whole purpose of the article. For in the case of the second article, the prohibition relates only to the *mode of acquisition*, which is to be forbidden hereforth, but not to the present *state of political possessions*. For although this present state is not backed up by the requisite legal authority, it was considered lawful in the public opinion of every state at the time of the putative acquisition.

Second section

WHICH CONTAINS THE DEFINITIVE ARTICLES OF A PERPETUAL PEACE BETWEEN STATES

A state of peace among men living together is not the same as the state of nature, which is rather a state of war. For even if it does not involve active hostilities, it involves a constant threat of their breaking out. Thus the state of peace must be *formally instituted*, for a suspension of hostilities is not in itself a guarantee of peace. And unless one neighbour gives a guarantee to the other at his request (which can happen only in a *lawful* state), the latter may treat him as an enemy.

First definitive article of a perpetual peace: The civil constitution of every state shall be republican

A *republican constitution* is founded upon three principles: firstly, the principle of *freedom* for all members of a society (as men); secondly, the principle of the *dependence* of everyone upon a single common legislation (as subjects); and thirdly, the principle of legal *equality* for everyone (as citizens). It is the only constitution which can be derived from the idea of an original contract, upon which all rightful legislation of a people must be founded. Thus as far as right is concerned, republicanism is in itself the original basis of every kind of civil constitution, and it only remains to ask whether it is the only constitution which can lead to a perpetual peace.

The republican constitution is not only pure in its origin (since it springs from the pure concept of right); it also offers a prospect of attaining the desired result, i.e. a perpetual peace, and the reason for this is as follows. – If, as is inevitably the case under this constitution, the consent of the citizens is required to decide whether or not war is to be declared, it is very natural that they will have great hesitation in embarking on so dangerous an enterprise. For this would mean calling down on themselves all the miseries of war, such as doing the fighting themselves, supplying the costs of the war from their own resources, painfully making good the ensuing devastation, and, as the crowning evil, having to take upon themselves a burden of debt which will embitter peace itself and which can never be paid off on account of the constant threat of new wars. But under a constitution where the subject is not a citizen, and which is therefore not republican, it is the simplest thing in the world to go to war. For the head of state is not a fellow citizen, but the owner of the state, and a war will not force him to make the slightest sacrifice so far as his banquets, hunts, pleasure palaces and court festivals are concerned. He can thus decide on war, without any significant reason, as a kind of amusement, and unconcernedly leave it to the diplomatic corps (who are always ready for such purposes) to justify the war for the sake of propriety.

The following remarks are necessary to prevent the republican constitution from being confused with the democratic one, as commonly happens. The various forms of state (*civitas*) may be classified either according to the different persons who exercise supreme authority, or according to the way in which the nation is governed by its ruler, whoever he may be. The first classification goes by the form of sovereignty (*forma imperii*), and only three such forms are possible, depending on whether the ruling power is in the hands of an *individual*, of *several persons* in association, or of *all* those who together constitute civil society (i.e. *autocracy*, *aristocracy* and *democracy* – the power of a prince, the power of a nobility, and the power of the people). The second classification depends on the form of government (*forma regiminis*), and relates to the way in which the state, setting out from its constitution (i.e. an act of the general will whereby the mass becomes a people), makes use of its plenary power. The form of government, in this case, will be either *republican* or *despotic. Republicanism* is that political principle whereby the executive power (the government) is separated from the legislative power. Despotism prevails in a state if the laws are made and arbitrarily executed by one and the same power, and it reflects the will of the people only in so far as the ruler treats the will of the people as his own private will. Of the three forms of sovereignty, *democracy*, in the truest sense of the word, is necessarily a *despotism*, because it establishes an executive power through which all the citizens may make decisions about (and indeed against) the single individual without his consent, so that decisions are made by all the people and yet not by all the people; and this means that the general will is in contradiction with itself, and thus also with freedom.

For any form of government which is not *representative* is essentially an *anomaly*, because one and the same person cannot at the same time be both the legislator and the executor of his own will, just as the general proposition in logical reasoning cannot at the same time be a secondary proposition subsuming the particular within the general. And even if the other two political constitutions (i.e. autocracy and aristocracy) are always defective in as much as they leave room for a despotic form of government, it is at least possible that they will be associated with a form of government which accords with the *spirit* of a representative system. Thus Frederick II at least *said* that he was merely the highest servant of the state, while a democratic constitution makes this attitude impossible, because everyone under it wants to be a ruler. We can therefore say that the smaller the number of ruling persons in a state and the greater their powers of representation, the more the constitution will approximate to its republican potentiality, which it may hope to realise eventually by gradual reforms. For this reason, it is more difficult in an aristocracy than in a monarchy to reach this one and only perfectly lawful kind of constitution, while it is possible in a democracy only by means of violent revolution. But the people are immensely more concerned with the mode of government than with the form of the constitution, although a great deal also depends on the degree to which the constitution fits the purpose of the government. But if the mode of government is to accord with the concept of right, it must be based on the representative system. This system alone makes possible a republican state, and without it, despotism and violence will result, no matter what kind of constitution is in force. None of the so-called 'republics' of antiquity employed such a system, and they thus inevitably ended in despotism, although this is still relatively bearable under the rule of a single individual.

Second definitive article of a perpetual peace: The right of nations shall be based on a federation of free states

Peoples who have grouped themselves into nation states may be judged in the same way as individual men living in a state of nature, independent of external laws; for they are a standing offence to one another by the very fact that they are neighbours. Each nation, for the sake of its own security, can and ought to demand of the others that they should enter along with it into a constitution, similar to the civil one, within which the rights of each could be secured. This would mean establishing a *federation of peoples*. But a federation of this sort would not be the same thing as an international state. For the idea of an international state is contradictory, since every state involves a relationship between a superior (the legislator) and an inferior (the people obeying the laws), whereas a number of nations forming one state would constitute a single nation. And this contradicts our initial assumption, as we are here considering the right of nations in relation to one another in so far as they are a group of separate states which are not to be welded together as a unit.

We look with profound contempt upon the way in which savages cling to their lawless freedom. They would rather engage in incessant strife than submit to a legal constraint which they might impose upon themselves, for they prefer the freedom of folly to the freedom of reason. We regard this as barbarism, coarseness, and brutish debasement of humanity. We might thus expect that civilised peoples, each united within itself as a state, would hasten to abandon so degrading a condition as soon as possible. But instead of doing so, each *state* sees its own majesty (for it would be absurd to speak of the majesty of a *people*) precisely in not having to submit to any external legal constraint, and the glory of its ruler consists in his power to order thousands of people to immolate themselves for a cause which does not truly concern them, while he need not himself incur any danger whatsoever. And the main difference between the savage nations of Europe and those of America is that while some American tribes have been entirely eaten up by their enemies, the Europeans know how to make better use of those they have defeated than merely by making a meal of them. They would rather use them to increase the number of their own subjects, thereby augmenting their stock of instruments for conducting even more extensive wars.

Although it is largely concealed by governmental constraints in law-governed civil society, the depravity of human nature is displayed without disguise in the unrestricted relations which obtain between the various nations. It is therefore to be wondered at that the word *right* has not been completely banished from military politics as superfluous pedantry, and that no state has been bold enough to declare itself publicly in favour of doing so. For Hugo Grotius, Pufendorf, Vattel and the rest (sorry comforters as they are) are still dutifully quoted in *justification* of military aggression, although their philosophically or diplomatically formulated codes do not and cannot have the slightest *legal* force, since states as such are not subject to a common external constraint. Yet there is no instance of a state ever having been moved to desist from its purpose by arguments supported by the testimonies of such notable men. This homage which every state pays (in words at least) to the concept of right proves that man possesses a greater moral capacity, still dormant at present, to overcome eventually the evil principle within him (for he cannot deny that it exists), and to hope that others will do likewise.

Otherwise the word *right* would never be used by states which intend to make war on one another, unless in a derisory sense, as when a certain Gallic prince declared: 'Nature has given to the strong the prerogative of making the weak obey them.' The way in which states seek their rights can only be by war, since there is no external tribunal to put their claims to trial. But rights cannot be decided by military victory, and a *peace treaty* may put an end to the current war, but not to that general warlike condition within which pretexts can always be found for a new war. And indeed, such a state of affairs cannot be pronounced completely unjust, since it allows each party to act as judge in its own cause. Yet while natural right allows us to say of men living in a lawless condition that they ought to abandon it, the right of nations does not allow us to say the same of states. For as states, they already have a lawful internal constitution, and have thus outgrown the coercive right of others to subject them to a wider legal constitution in accordance with their conception of right. On the other hand, reason, as the highest legislative moral power, absolutely condemns war as a test of rights and sets up peace as an immediate duty. But peace can neither be inaugurated nor secured without a general agreement between the nations; thus a particular kind of league, which we might call a *pacific federation* (*foedus pacificum*), is required. It would differ from a *peace treaty* (*pactum pacis*) in that the latter terminates *one* war, whereas the former would seek to end *all* wars for good. This federation does not aim to acquire any power like that of a state, but merely to preserve and secure the *freedom* of each state in itself, along with that of the other confederated states, although this does not mean that they need to submit to public laws and to a coercive power which enforces them, as do men in a state of nature. It can be shown that this idea of *federalism*, extending gradually to encompass all states and thus leading to perpetual peace, is practicable and has objective reality. For if by good fortune one powerful and enlightened nation can form a republic (which is by its nature inclined to seek perpetual peace), this will provide a focal point for federal association among other states. These will join up with the first one, thus securing the freedom of each state in accordance with the idea of international right, and the whole will gradually spread further and further by a series of alliances of this kind.

It would be understandable for a people to say: 'There shall be no war among us; for we will form ourselves into a state, appointing for ourselves a supreme legislative, executive and juridical power to resolve our conflicts by peaceful means.' But if this state says: 'There shall be no war between myself and other states, although I do not recognise any supreme legislative power which could secure my rights and whose rights I should in turn secure', it is impossible to understand what justification I can have for placing any confidence in my rights, unless I can rely on some substitute for the union of civil society, i.e. on a free federation. If the concept of international right is to retain any meaning at all, reason must necessarily couple it with a federation of this kind.

The concept of international right becomes meaningless if interpreted as a right to go to war. For this would make it a right to determine what is lawful not by means of universally valid external laws, but by means of one-sided maxims backed up by physical force. It could be taken to mean that it is perfectly just for men who adopt this attitude to destroy one another, and thus to find perpetual peace in the vast grave where all the horrors of violence and those responsible for them would be buried. There is only one rational way in which states coexisting with other states can emerge from the lawless condition of pure warfare. Just like individual men, they must renounce their savage and lawless freedom, adapt themselves to public coercive laws, and thus form an *international state* (*civitas gentium*), which would necessarily continue to grow until it embraced all the peoples of the earth. But since this is not the will of the nations, according to their present conception of international right (so that they reject *in hypothesi* what is true *in thesi*), the positive idea of a *world republic* cannot be realised. If all is not to be lost, this can at best find a negative substitute in the shape of an enduring and gradually expanding *federation* likely to prevent war. The latter may check the current of man's inclination to defy the law and antagonise his fellows, although there will always be a risk of it bursting forth anew. *Furor impius intus – fremit horridus ore cruento* (Virgil).

Third definitive article of a perpetual peace: Cosmopolitan right shall be limited to conditions of universal hospitality

As in the foregoing articles, we are here concerned not with philanthropy, but with *right*. In this context, *hospitality* means the right of a stranger not to be treated with hostility when he arrives on someone else's territory. He can indeed be turned away, if this can be done without causing his death, but he must not be treated with hostility, so long as he behaves in a peaceable manner in the place he happens to be in. The stranger cannot claim the *right of a guest* to be entertained, for this would require a special friendly agreement whereby he might become a member of the native household for a certain time. He may only claim a *right of resort*, for all men are entitled to present themselves in the society of others by virtue of their right to communal possession of the earth's surface. Since the earth is a globe, they cannot disperse over an infinite area, but must necessarily tolerate one another's company. And no-one originally has any greater right than anyone else to occupy any particular portion of the earth. The community of man is divided by uninhabitable parts of the earth's surface such as oceans and deserts, but even then, the *ship* or the *camel* (the

ship of the desert) make it possible for them to approach their fellows over
these ownerless tracts, and to utilise as a means of social intercourse that *right
to the earth's surface* which the human race shares in common. The inhospitable
behaviour of coastal dwellers (as on the Barbary coast) in plundering ships on
the adjoining seas or enslaving stranded seafarers, or that of inhabitants of the
desert (as with the Arab Bedouins), who regard their proximity to nomadic
tribes as a justification for plundering them, is contrary to natural right. But
this natural right of hospitality, i.e. the right of strangers, does not extend
beyond those conditions which make it possible for them to *attempt* to enter
into relations with the native inhabitants. In this way, continents distant from
each other can enter into peaceful mutual relations which may eventually be
regulated by public laws, thus bringing the human race nearer and nearer to
a cosmopolitan constitution.

If we compare with this ultimate end the *inhospitable* conduct of the
civilised states of our continent, especially the commercial states, the injustice which they display in *visiting* foreign countries and peoples (which in
their case is the same as *conquering* them) seems appallingly great. America, the
negro countries, the Spice Islands, the Cape, etc. were looked upon at the
time of their discovery as ownerless territories; for the native inhabitants
were counted as nothing. In East India (Hindustan), foreign troops were
brought in under the pretext of merely setting up trading posts. This led to oppression of the natives, incitement of the various Indian states to widespread
wars, famine, insurrection, treachery and the whole litany of evils which can
afflict the human race.

China and Japan (Nippon), having had experience of such guests, have
wisely placed restrictions on them. China permits contact with her territories,
but not entrance into them, while Japan only allows contact with a single
European people, the Dutch, although they are still segregated from the
native community like prisoners. The worst (or from the point of view of
moral judgements, the best) thing about all this is that the commercial states
do not even benefit by their violence, for all their trading companies are on the
point of collapse. The Sugar Islands, that stronghold of the cruellest and most
calculated slavery, do not yield any real profit; they serve only the indirect
(and not entirely laudable) purpose of training sailors for warships, thereby
aiding the prosecution of wars in Europe. And all this is the work of powers
who make endless ado about their piety, and who wish to be considered as
chosen believers while they live on the fruits of iniquity.

The peoples of the earth have thus entered in varying degrees into a
universal community, and it has developed to the point where a violation of
rights in *one* part of the world is felt *everywhere*. The idea of a cosmopolitan
right is therefore not fantastic and overstrained; it is a necessary complement
to the unwritten code of political and international right, transforming it

into a universal right of humanity. Only under this condition can we flatter ourselves that we are continually advancing towards a perpetual peace.

First supplement: On the guarantee of a perpetual peace

Perpetual peace is *guaranteed* by no less an authority than the great artist *Nature* herself (*natura daedala rerum*). The mechanical process of nature visibly exhibits the purposive plan of producing concord among men, even against their will and indeed by means of their very discord. This design, if we regard it as a compelling cause whose laws of operation are unknown to us, is called *fate*. But if we consider its purposive function within the world's development, whereby it appears as the underlying wisdom of a higher cause, showing the way towards the objective goal of the human race and predetermining the world's evolution, we call it *providence*. We cannot actually observe such an agency in the artifices of nature, nor can we even *infer* its existence from them. But as with all relations between the form of things and their ultimate purposes, we can and must *supply it mentally* in order to conceive of its possibility by analogy with human artifices. Its relationship to and conformity with the end which reason directly prescribes to us (i.e. the end of morality) can only be conceived of as an idea. Yet while this idea is indeed far-fetched in *theory*, it does possess dogmatic validity and has a very real foundation in *practice*, as with the concept of *perpetual peace*, which makes it our duty to promote it by using the natural mechanism described above. But in contexts such as this, where we are concerned purely with theory and not with religion, we should also note that it is more in keeping with the limitations of human reason to speak of *nature* and not of *providence*, for reason, in dealing with cause and effect relationships, must keep within the bounds of possible experience. *Modesty* forbids us to speak of providence as something we can recognise, for this would mean donning the wings of Icarus and presuming to approach the mystery of its inscrutable intentions.

...

We now come to the essential question regarding the prospect of perpetual peace. What does nature do in relation to the end which man's own reason prescribes to him as a duty, i.e. how does nature help to promote his *moral purpose*? And how does nature guarantee that what man *ought* to do by the laws of his freedom (but does not do) will in fact be done through nature's compulsion, without prejudice to the free agency of man? This question arises, moreover, in all three areas of public right – in *political, international* and *cosmopolitan right*. For if I say that nature *wills* that this or that should happen, this does not mean that nature imposes on us a *duty* to do it, for duties can only be imposed by practical reason, acting without any external constraint. On the contrary, nature does it herself, whether we are willing or not: *fata volentem ducunt, nolentem trahunt.*

1. Even if people were not compelled by internal dissent to submit to the coercion of public laws, war would produce the same effect from outside. For in accordance with the natural arrangement described above, each people would find itself confronted by another neighbouring people pressing in upon it, thus forcing it to form itself internally into a *state* in order to encounter the other as an armed *power*. Now the *republican* constitution is the only one which does complete justice to the rights of man. But it is also the most difficult to establish, and even more so to preserve, so that many maintain that it would only be possible within a state of *angels*, since men, with their self-seeking inclinations, would be incapable of adhering to a constitution of so sublime a nature. But in fact, nature comes to the aid of the universal and rational human will, so admirable in itself but so impotent in practice, and makes use of precisely those self-seeking inclinations in order to do so. It only remains for men to create a good organisation for the state, a task which is well within their capability, and to arrange it in such a way that their self-seeking energies are opposed to one another, each thereby neutralising or eliminating the destructive effects of the rest. And as far as reason is concerned, the result is the same as if man's selfish tendencies were non-existent, so that man, even if he is not morally good in himself, is nevertheless compelled to be a good citizen. As hard as it may sound, the problem of setting up a state can be solved even by a nation of devils (so long as they possess understanding). It may be stated as follows: 'In order to organise a group of rational beings who together require universal laws for their survival, but of whom each separate individual is secretly inclined to exempt himself from them, the constitution must be so designed that, although the citizens are opposed to one another in their private attitudes, these opposing views may inhibit one another in such a way that the public conduct of the citizens will be the same as if they did not have such evil attitudes.' A problem of this kind must be soluble. For such a task does not involve the moral improvement of man; it only means finding out how the mechanism of nature can be applied to men in such a manner that the antagonism of their hostile attitudes will make them compel one another to submit to coercive laws, thereby producing a condition of peace within which the laws can be enforced. We can even see this principle at work among the actually existing (although as yet very imperfectly organised) states. For in their external relations, they have already approached what the idea of right prescribes, although the reason for this is certainly not their internal moral attitudes. In the same way, we cannot expect their moral attitudes to produce a good political constitution; on the contrary, it is only through the latter that the people can be expected to attain a good level of moral culture. Thus that mechanism of nature by which selfish inclinations are naturally opposed to one another in their external relations can be used by reason to facilitate the attainment of its own end, the reign of established right. Internal and external

peace are thereby furthered and assured, so far as it lies within the power of the state itself to do so. We may therefore say that nature *irresistibly wills* that right should eventually gain the upper hand. What men have neglected to do will ultimately happen of its own accord, albeit with much inconvenience. As Bouterwek puts it: 'If the reed is bent too far, it breaks; and he who wants too much gets nothing.'

2. 'The idea of international right presupposes the separate existence of many independent adjoining states. And such a state of affairs is essentially a state of war, unless there is a federal union to prevent hostilities breaking out. But in the light of the idea of reason, this state is still to be preferred to an amalgamation of the separate nations under a single power which has overruled the rest and created a universal monarchy. For the laws progressively lose their impact as the government increases its range, and a soulless despotism, after crushing the germs of goodness, will finally lapse into anarchy. It is nonetheless the desire of every state (or its ruler) to achieve lasting peace by thus dominating the whole world, if at all possible. But *nature* wills it otherwise, and uses two means to separate the nations and prevent them from intermingling – *linguistic* and *religious* differences. These may certainly occasion mutual hatred and provide pretexts for wars, but as culture grows and men gradually move towards greater agreement over their principles, they lead to mutual understanding and peace. And unlike that universal despotism which saps all man's energies and ends in the graveyard of freedom, this peace is created and guaranteed by an equilibrium of forces and a most vigorous rivalry.

3. Thus nature wisely separates the nations, although the will of each individual state, even basing its arguments on international right, would gladly unite them under its own sway by force or by cunning. On the other hand, nature also unites nations which the concept of cosmopolitan right would not have protected from violence and war, and does so by means of their mutual self-interest. For the *spirit of commerce* sooner or later takes hold of every people, and it cannot exist side by side with war. And of all the powers (or means) at the disposal of the power of the state, *financial power* can probably be relied on most. Thus states find themselves compelled to promote the noble cause of peace, though not exactly from motives of morality. And wherever in the world there is a threat of war breaking out, they will try to prevent it by mediation, just as if they had entered into a permanent league for this purpose; for by the very nature of things, large military alliances can only rarely be formed, and will even more rarely be successful.

In this way, nature guarantees perpetual peace by the actual mechanism of human inclinations. And while the likelihood of its being attained is not sufficient to enable us to *prophesy* the future theoretically, it is enough for practical purposes. It makes it our duty to work our way towards this goal, which is more than an empty chimera.

Second supplement: Secret article of a perpetual peace

In transactions involving public right, a secret article (regarded objectively or in terms of its content) is a contradiction. But in subjective terms, i.e. in relation to the sort of person who dictates it, an article may well contain a secret element, for the person concerned may consider it prejudicial to his own dignity to name himself publicly as its originator.

The only article of this kind is embodied in the following sentence:

'The maxims of the philosophers on the conditions under which public peace is possible shall be consulted by states which are armed for war.'

Although it may seem humiliating for the legislative authority of a state, to which we must naturally attribute the highest degree of wisdom, to seek instruction from *subjects* (the philosophers) regarding the principles on which it should act in its relations with other states, it is nevertheless extremely advisable that it should do so. The state will therefore invite their help *silently*, making a secret of it. In other words, it will *allow them to speak* freely and publicly on the universal maxims of warfare and peace-making, and they will indeed do so of their own accord if no-one forbids their discussions. And no special formal arrangement among the states is necessary to enable them to agree on this issue, for the agreement already lies in the obligations imposed by universal human reason in its capacity as a moral legislator. This does not, however, imply that the state must give the principles of the philosopher precedence over the pronouncements of the jurist (who represents the power of the state), but only that the philosopher should be given a *hearing*. The jurist, who has taken as his symbol the scales of right and the sword of justice, usually uses the latter not merely to keep any extraneous influences away from the former, but will throw the *sword* into one of the *scales* if it refuses to sink (*vae victis!*). Unless the jurist is at the same time a philosopher, at any rate in moral matters, he is under the greatest temptation to do this, for his business is merely to apply existing laws, and not to enquire whether they are in need of improvement. He acts as if this truly low rank of his faculty were in fact one of the higher ones, for the simple reason that it is accompanied by power (as is also the case with two of the other faculties). But the philosophical faculty occupies a very low position in face of the combined power of the others. Thus we are told, for instance, that philosophy is the *handmaid* of theology, and something similar in relation to the others. But it is far from clear whether this handmaid bears the torch before her gracious lady, or carries the train behind.

It is not to be expected that kings will philosophise or that philosophers will become kings; nor is it to be desired, however, since the possession of power inevitably corrupts the free judgement of reason. Kings or sovereign peoples (i.e. those governing themselves by egalitarian laws) should not, however, force the class of philosophers to disappear or to remain silent, but should allow them to speak publicly. This is essential to both in order that light may be thrown on their affairs. And since the class of philosophers is by nature incapable of forming seditious factions or clubs, they cannot incur suspicion of disseminating propaganda.

...

2. We now come to *international right.* – We can speak of international right only on the assumption that some kind of lawful condition exists, i.e. that external circumstances are such that a man can genuinely be accorded his rights. For as a form of public right, it implies by definition that there is a general will which publicly assigns to each individual that which is his due. And this *status iuridicus* must be derived from some sort of contract, which, unlike that from which a state originates, must not be based on coercive laws, but may at most be a state of *permanent and free association* like the above-mentioned federation of different states. For without some kind of *lawful condition* which actively links together the various physical or moral persons (as is the case in the state of nature), the only possible form of right is a private one. This again involves a conflict between politics and morality (the latter in the shape of a theory of right). The criterion of publicness in the relevant maxims can, however, once again be easily applied, but only on condition that the contract binds the states for the single purpose of preserving peace amongst themselves and in relation to other states, and on no account with a view to military conquest. We can thus envisage the following instances of an antinomy between politics and morality, along with the appropriate solution in each case.

(*a*) 'If one of these states has promised something to another, whether it be assistance, cession of certain territories, subsidies, or the like, it may be asked whether this state, on occasions when its own welfare is at stake, may free itself from the obligation to keep its word, maintaining that it ought to be regarded as a dual person – on the one hand, as a *sovereign* who is not responsible to anyone within the state, and on the other, merely as the highest political *official* who is responsible to the state; and the conclusion to be drawn from this is that the state (or its ruler) can be exempted in the latter capacity from obligations it incurred in the first.' But if the ruler of a state were to let it be known that this was his maxim, everyone else would naturally flee from him, or unite with others in order to resist his pretensions; which proves that such a system of politics, for all its cunning, would defeat its own purpose if it operated on a public footing, so that the above maxim must be wrong.

(*b*) 'If a neighbouring power which has grown to a formidable size (*potentia tremenda*) gives cause for anxiety, can one assume that it will *wish* to oppress other states because is *is able* to do so, and does this give the less powerful party a right to mount a concerted attack upon it, even if no offence has been offered?' If a state were to *let it be known* that it affirmed this maxim, it would merely bring about more surely and more quickly the very evil it feared. For the greater power would anticipate the lesser ones, and the possibility that they might unite would be but a feeble reed against one who knew how to use the tactics of *divide et impera*. Thus this maxim of political expediency, if acknowledged publicly, necessarily defeats its own purpose and is consequently unjust.

(*c*) 'If a smaller state, by its geographical situation, constitutes a gap in the territory of a larger state, and this larger state requires the intrusive territory for its own preservation, is not the larger state justified in subjugating the smaller one and in annexing its territory?' One can easily see that the larger state must on no account let it be known that it has adopted such a maxim. For the smaller states would either unite in good time, or other powerful states would quarrel over the proposed prey, so that the plan would be rendered impracticable if it were made public. This is a sign that it is unjust, and it would in fact be an injustice of very great magnitude; for the fact that the object of an injustice is small does not mean that the injustice done to it may not be very great.

3 . As for *cosmopolitan right*, I pass over it here in silence, for its maxims are easy to formulate and assess on account of its analogy with international right.

In the principle that the maxims of international right may be incompatible with publicity, we thus have a good indication that politics and morality (in the sense of a theory of right) are *not in agreement*. But it is also necessary that we should know what the condition is under which its maxims will agree with international right. For we cannot simply conclude by a reverse process that all maxims which can be made public are therefore also just, because the person who has decisive supremacy has no need to conceal his maxims. The condition which must be fulfilled before any kind of international right is possible is that a *lawful state* must already be in existence. For without this, there can be no public right, and any right which can be conceived of outside it, i.e. in a state of nature, will be merely a private right. Now we have already seen above that a federative association of states whose sole intention is to eliminate war is the only *lawful* arrangement which can be reconciled with their *freedom*. Thus politics and morality can only be in agreement within a federal union, which is therefore necessary and given *a priori* through the principles of right. And the rightful basis of all political prudence is the founding of such a union in the most comprehensive form possible; for without this aim, all its reasonings are unwisdom and veiled injustice. This kind of false politics has its own *casuistry* to match that of the best Jesuit scholars. For it includes the *reservatio mentalis* whereby public contracts are formulated in terms which one can interpret to one's own advantage as required (for example, the distinction between the *status quo* of fact and the *status quo* of right); it also includes the *probabilismus*,

§ 54

The elements of international right are as follows. Firstly, in their external relationships with one another, states, like lawless savages, exist in a condition devoid of right. Secondly, this *condition* is one of war (the right of the stronger), even if there is no actual war or continuous active fighting (i.e. hostilities). But even although neither of two states is done any injustice by the other in this condition, it is nevertheless in the highest degree unjust in itself, for it implies that neither wishes to experience anything better. Adjacent states are thus bound to abandon such a condition. Thirdly, it is necessary to establish a federation of peoples in accordance with the idea of an original social contract, so that states will protect one another against external aggression while refraining from interference in one another's internal disagreements. And fourthly, this association must not embody a sovereign power as in a civil constitution, but only a partnership or *confederation*. It must therefore be an alliance which can be terminated at any time, so that it has to be renewed periodically. This right is derived *in subsidium* from another original right, that of preventing oneself from lapsing into a state of actual war with one's partners in the confederation (*foedus Amphictyonum*).

...

§ 57

The most problematic task in international right is that of determining rights in wartime. For it is very difficult to form any conception at all of such rights and to imagine any law whatsoever in this lawless state without involving oneself in contradictions (*inter arma silent leges*). The only possible solution would be to conduct the war in accordance with principles which would still leave the states with the possibility of abandoning the state of nature in their external relations and of entering a state of right.

No war between independent states can be a *punitive* one (*bellum punitivum*). For a punishment can only occur in a relationship between a superior (*imperantis*) and a subject (*subditum*), and this is not the relationship which exists between states. Nor can there be a *war of extermination* (*bellum internecinum*) or a *war of subjugation* (*bellum subiugatorium*); for these would involve the moral annihilation of a state, and its people would either merge with those of the victorious state or be reduced to bondage. Not that this expedient, to which a state might resort in order to obtain peace, would in itself contradict the rights of a state. But the fact remains that the only concept of antagonism which the idea of international right includes is that of an antagonism regulated by principles of external freedom. This requires that violence be used only to preserve one's existing property, but not as a method of further acquisition; for the latter procedure would create a threat to one state by augmenting the power of another.

The attacked state is allowed to use any means of defence except those whose use would render its subjects unfit to be citizens. For if it did not observe this condition, it would render itself unfit in the eyes of international right to function as a person in relation to other states and to share equal rights with them. It must accordingly be prohibited for a state to use its own subjects as spies, and to use them, or indeed foreigners, as poisoners or assassins (to which class the so-called sharpshooters who wait in ambush on individual victims also belong), or even just to spread false reports. In short, a state must not use such treacherous methods as would destroy that confidence which is required for the future establishment of a lasting peace.

It is permissible in war to impose levies and contributions on the conquered enemy, but not to plunder the people, i.e. to force individual persons to part with their belongings (for this would be robbery, since it was not the conquered people who waged the war, but the state of which they were subjects which waged it *through them*). Bills of receipt should be issued for any contributions that are exacted, so that the burden imposed on the country or province can be distributed proportionately when peace is concluded.

...

Section III: Cosmopolitan right

§ 62

The rational idea, as discussed above, of a *peaceful* (if not exactly amicable) international community of all those of the earth's peoples who can enter into active relations with one another, is not a philanthropic principle of ethics, but a principle of *right*. Through the spherical shape of the planet they inhabit (*globus terraqueus*), nature has confined them all within an area of definite limits. Accordingly, the only conceivable way in which anyone can possess habitable land on earth is by possessing a part within a determinate whole in which everyone has an original right to share. Thus all nations are *originally* members of a community of the land. But this is not a *legal community* of possession (*communio*) and utilisation of the land, nor a community of ownership. It is a community of reciprocal action (*commercium*), which is physically possible, and each member of it accordingly has constant relations with all the others. Each may *offer* to have commerce with the rest, and they all have a right to make such overtures without being treated by foreigners as enemies. This right, in so far as it affords the prospect that all nations may unite for the purpose of creating certain universal laws to regulate the intercourse they may have with one another, may be termed *cosmopolitan* (*ius cosmopoliticum*).

The oceans may appear to cut nations off from the community of their fellows. But with the art of navigation, they constitute the greatest natural incentive to international commerce, and the greater the number of neighbouring coastlines there are (as in the Mediterranean), the livelier this commerce will be. Yet these visits to foreign shores, and even more so, attempts to settle on them with a view to linking them with the motherland, can also occasion evil and violence in one part of the globe with ensuing repercussions which are felt everywhere else. But although such abuses are possible, they do not deprive the world's citizens of the right to *attempt* to enter into a community with everyone else and to *visit* all regions of the earth with this intention. This does not, however, amount to a right to *settle* on another nation's territory (*ius incolatus*), for the latter would require a special contract.

But one might ask whether a nation may establish a *settlement alongside another nation* (*accolatus*) in newly discovered regions, or whether it may take possession of land in the vicinity of a nation which has already settled in the same area, even without the latter's consent. The answer is that the right to do so is incontestable, so long as such settlements are established sufficiently far away from the territory of the original nation for neither party to interfere with the other in their use of the land. But if the nations involved are pastoral or hunting peoples (like the Hottentots, the Tunguses, and most native American nations) who rely upon large tracts of wasteland for their sustenance, settlements should not be established by violence, but only by treaty; and even then, there must be no attempt to exploit the ignorance of the natives in persuading them to give up their territories. Nevertheless, there are plausible enough arguments for the use of violence on the grounds that it is in the best interests of the world as a whole. For on the one hand, it may bring culture to uncivilised peoples (this is the excuse with which even Büsching tries to extenuate the bloodshed which accompanied the introduction of Christianity into Germany); and on the other, it may help us to purge our country of depraved characters, at the same time affording the hope that they or their offspring will become reformed in another continent (as in New Holland). But all these supposedly good intentions cannot wash away the stain of injustice from the means which are used to implement them. Yet one might object that the whole world would perhaps still be in a lawless condition if men had had any such compunction about using violence when they first created a law-governed state. But this can as little annul the above condition of right as can the plea of political revolutionaries that the people are entitled to reform constitutions by force if they have become corrupt, and to act completely unjustly for once and for all, in order to put justice on a more secure basis and ensure that it flourishes in the future.

CONCLUSION

If a person cannot prove that a thing exists, he may attempt to prove that it does not exist. If neither approach succeeds (as often happens), he may still ask whether it is *in his interest to assume* one or other possibility as a hypothesis, either from theoretical or from practical considerations. In other words, he may wish on the one hand simply to explain a certain phenomenon (as the astronomer, for example, may wish to explain the sporadic movements of the planets), or on the other, to achieve a certain end which may itself be either *pragmatic* (purely technical) or *moral* (i.e. an end which it is our duty to take as a maxim). It is, of course, self-evident that no-one is duty-bound to make an *assumption* (*suppositio*) that the end in question can be realised, since this would involve a purely theoretical and indeed problematic judgement; for no-one can be obliged to accept a given belief. But we can have a duty to act in accordance with the idea of such an end, even if there is not the slightest theoretical probability of its realisation, provided that there is no means of demonstrating that it cannot be realised either.

Now, moral-practical reason within us pronounces the following irresistible veto: *There shall be no war*, either between individual human beings in the state of nature, or between separate states, which, although internally law-governed, still live in a lawless condition in their external relationships with one another. For war is not the way in which anyone should pursue his rights. Thus it is no longer a question of whether perpetual peace is really possible or not, or whether we are not perhaps mistaken in our theoretical judgement if we assume that it is. On the contrary, we must simply act as if it could really come about (which is perhaps impossible), and turn our efforts towards realising it and towards establishing that constitution which seems most suitable for this purpose (perhaps that of republicanism in all states, individually and collectively). By working towards this end, we may hope to terminate the disastrous practice of war, which up till now has been the main object to which all states, without exception, have accommodated their internal institutions. And even if the fulfilment of this pacific intention were forever to remain a pious hope, we should still not be deceiving ourselves if we made it our maxim to work unceasingly towards it, for it is our duty to do so. To assume, on the other hand, that the moral law within us might be misleading, would give rise to the execrable wish to dispense with all reason and to regard ourselves, along with our principles, as subject to the same mechanism of nature as the other animal species.

It can indeed be said that this task of establishing a universal and lasting peace is not just a part of the theory of right within the limits of pure reason, but its entire ultimate purpose. For the condition of peace is the only state in which the property of a large number of people living together as neighbours under a single constitution can be guaranteed by *laws*. The rule on which this constitution is based must not simply be derived from the experience of those who have hitherto fared best under it, and then set up as a norm for others. On the contrary, it should be derived *a priori* by reason from the absolute ideal of a rightful association of men under public laws. For all particular examples are deceptive (an example can only illustrate a point, but does not prove anything), so that one must have recourse to metaphysics. And even those who scorn metaphysics admit its necessity involuntarily when they say, for example (as they often do): 'The best constitution is that in which the power rests with laws instead of with men.' For what can be more metaphysically sublime than this idea, although by the admission of those who express it, it also has a well-authenticated objective reality which can easily be demonstrated from particular instances as they arise. But no attempt should be made to put it into practice overnight by revolution, i.e. by forcibly overthrowing a defective constitution which has existed in the past; for there would then be an interval of time during which the condition of right would be nullified. If we try instead to give it reality by means of gradual reforms carried out in accordance with definite principles, we shall see that it is the only means of continually approaching the supreme political good – perpetual peace.

8

State and nation in nineteenth-century international political theory

Both the "state" and, perhaps less obviously, the "nation" are terms which recur in international political theory; nonetheless, both terms came to have rather different meanings from past usage in the course of the period from the end of the eighteenth century to the outbreak of the First World War. Moreover, the two meanings became interwoven one with another, such that in the course of our own century it has become common to regard them as almost synonymous, or at least both incorporated in the composite term "nation-state" – even though it is very difficult to arrive at a substantive definition of a nation which would allow more than a minority of the actual states of today to qualify, for all their membership of the United *Nations*. The purpose of the texts which follow this introduction is to set out the international implications of these changes in meaning.

If one were to attempt to encapsulate as simply as possible the nature of these changes, it would be by noting the emergence of the idea of an "ethical" state and the principle of national sovereignty. In past thinking – at least in the Christian era – the state had been understood as an institution which was either a necessary evil, as a partial antidote to human sinfulness, or a clever, contracted, solution to the problem of the egoism generated by the human condition in a state of nature. But, from the end of the eighteenth century onwards, a number of different movements in thought converged on the proposition that the state could be a positive force for good, indeed that an ethical life actually required the existence of a particular kind of state. Moreover, although this thought was initially heavily influenced by, and envious of, classical Greek or Roman republicanism, in its most important manifestation in the writings of Hegel and his followers it came to be seen that there were specific characteristics of the modern state which made it an even more suitable carrier of the ethical idea than had been Athens or Rome. Again, whereas, in past thinking, a nation had been understood in rather loose terms as a "people" (*gens*), or even a wider grouping – as at the University of Paris in medieval times when the "English Nation" was a body of students who incorporated a number of different modern nationalities, some unconnected to England or even the British Isles – in the course of the nineteenth century it became widely believed that the world (or at least the "civilized" world) was naturally divided into nations, and that such nations formed the only legitimate foundations upon which a state could be built. Sovereignty came to be seen as something that grew out of, was exercised on behalf of, the "nation," which ultimately meant the "people" – hence the revolutionary symbolism of the change of title between Louis XVI, who was king of France (a place), and Napoleon I who was emperor of the French (the people).

In the nineteenth century both the ethical state and national sovereignty were resisted by powerful forces; utilitarians and "Manchester School" liberals (see chapter 9) resisted the idea that the state could be anything other than a neutral force in society, anything more than a resolver of the dilemmas of collective action, while dynastic legitimists inevitably opposed the national principle. These movements of opposition continued into the twentieth century, but with rather less effect. The triumph of the national principle has been noted already; national self-determination has become one of the "settled norms" of international society (Frost, 1996). Much the same might be said of the idea of an ethical state; although the term itself is rarely used today, the idea that the state exists to promote in a positive way the good life for its citizens is more widely held now than it was in the last century. In short, when we study the emergence of these ideas in the nineteenth century, we are studying forces of great significance for our own era.

One preliminary point needs to be made. This chapter examines state and nation in nineteenth-century international relations, while the next, chapter 9, traces the impact of the emergence of industrial society on the international relations of the period. Although this division makes sense in presentational terms it is, nonetheless, artificial – one of the reasons for the emergence of new notions of the state and nation was the simultaneous emergence of industrial society; moreover, the chain of causation went in both directions, and the new national states which emerged then were critical for the spread of industrialism. In terms of the themes which run through this book, these two sides of the coin of nineteenth-century international relations – industrialism and the nation-state – largely pull in opposite directions. As we shall see, the dominant, liberal, view of industrial society, prefiguring later theories of "globalization," held that it was breaking down barriers between "insiders" and "outsiders," that it would provide a foundation upon which a truly cosmopolitan world order could be constructed. The theorists of state and nation whose work will be discussed in this chapter dispute this trajectory, arguing instead that the demands of the new nation-state, legitimized by the people, told in favor of a more particularistic account of politics. In so far as the particularistic community has moral value its putative replacement by wider, more inclusive, structures cannot be seen as unproblematic. For most of the writers discussed in both chapters, the line between universal and particular was less clear cut than this account would imply, but the tension remains. In short, chapters 8 and 9 need to be read together as accounts of different aspects of the same broad story, rather than as discrete narratives.

The ethical state and its external environment

Political legitimacy and the role of the state was an important issue in Enlightenment thinking but the positive value attached to these notions is a function of *post*-Enlightenment thought. The great thinkers of the Enlightenment either despised patriotism and the claims of the state – Hume, Voltaire, and Mozart – or valued it by reference to dubiously appropriate models drawn from Greece and Rome – as with the French Encyclopaedists and revolutionaries, and, perhaps, Rousseau himself. At best, and building on the contract tradition, there might be Kant's acknowledgement of the potential role of the state in overcoming humanity's "unsocial sociability." None of these authors welcomed the idea of popular participation in politics, much less democracy, unless, as in the revolutionary tradition, the people could first be turned into good republican citizens. Politics was widely regarded as the realm of irrationality and unenlightenment, and at the international level much of the thought of the period revolved around schemes of "Perpetual Peace" which were designed to overcome the impact of irrational particularistic identifications. Meanwhile, personal satisfaction was to be gained from "cultivating one's garden" (Voltaire's *Candide*) or contemplating the moral law and the wonders of nature (Kant) – two extreme expressions of the importance of a private life and a life of the mind. Only Rousseau – whose thought is notoriously difficult to classify – envisages the good life as a life lived publicly as a citizen; however, the terms under which he believed this to be possible, small autarchic face-to-face communities, had, as he acknowledged, gone for ever. After his death, revolutionary France with its mix of mob-rule and elitism parodied the classical tradition and demonstrated the unviability of that kind of republican life.

It was inevitable that this cosmopolitanism would provoke a reaction. For many involved in the "romantic" movement of the end of the eighteenth century, even revolutionary chaos seemed preferable to the desiccated rationalism of the Enlightenment. Drawing inspiration from folklorists such as J. G. Herder or the (possibly fake) Scots bard Ossian, and from their sense of the lost warmth of the communities of the ancient world, these writers developed a compelling critique of Enlightenment, but not a viable account of politics and the state. Part of the problem was that although they were critical of the rationalism and individualism of the Enlightenment, they were, in effect, a product of what they condemned; it was only because they were actually rational, self-determining individuals and not, in fact, defined by all-encompassing affective communities that they were able to critique the former and advocate the latter. What was required to escape this contradiction was a politics which preserved the notion of the self-determining individual, the Enlightenment's greatest achievement, while embedding this person in an affective community which could provide the warmth and sense of belonging banished by Enlightenment rationalism. It was this combination that G. W. F. Hegel (1770–1831) claimed to be able to provide (Avineri, 1972; C. Taylor, 1975; Plant, 1983).

Hegel is a notoriously difficult writer who offers a very ambitious system which claimed to comprehend everything of philosophical significance. Of particular importance to us are his *Philosophy of History* (Hegel, 1956) and his *Elements of the Philosophy of Right* (Hegel, 1991), lectures which give the fullest account of his notions of ethics and politics. Hegel understands history as the growing self-understanding of *Geist* which takes place through the emergence of ever more complex and ethically rich institutions and ideas, culminating in the rational, ethical state of the modern age – *Geist* is best translated as Spirit, although Mind would also be acceptable; the term has strong religious connotations. How Spirit or Mind can be said to achieve self-understanding has puzzled many very capable thinkers, and it is fortunate that it is possible to present an account of Hegel which does not rely too heavily on this notion. We can instead think of his work as an account of the development of freedom and the conditions required to create autonomous, self-determining individuals – it is because of the richness of his thought understood in these terms that he became, and remains, one of the most influential of all political philosophers.

For the emergence of free individuals, Hegel argues, three dimensions of ethical life are necessary. The ethical family provides unconditional love, a context within which the individual comes to have a sense of his or her own worth. This is a necessary foundation for autonomy but not sufficient; individuals must leave this arena of unconditional affection and make their way in a wider world in which they must earn respect. In this wider world, which Hegel terms "civil society," individuals encounter each other as potential opponents and rivals, but also as rights-holders in a context where relations are governed by law. In civil society are to be found many of the institutions that from the perspective of Anglo-American liberalism are thought of as part of the state – public administration and the judicial system, for example, or "the police and the corporation" as Hegel puts it. But, just as the family needs to be accompanied by civil society because autonomous individuals cannot be created in a world governed by unconditional love, so civil society on its own would be a realm of strife and tension were it not to be accompanied by a third ethical institution, the state. For Hegel, the state is not to be understood primarily as the site of decision-making on policy matters, which is its role in conventional liberal thought; instead the role of the state is to reconcile individuals to each other. As members of civil society individuals compete fiercely – albeit under terms governed by law – and inequality and a degree of civil strife is the inevitable result, but as fellow citizens they meet as equals and differences are reconciled; such at least is Hegel's claim.

Before moving to consider the implications of this position for international relations one or two points need to be clarified. First, this set of institutions – family, civil society, and the state – is, in their ethical forms, a product of modernity. In the world of classical Greece, freedom was available in the *polis*, but for some only and in an unreflective form. The Romans created universal legal categories but under the empire free institutions disappeared and the Roman family was based, indefensibly, on the untrammeled power of the father. It is only in the modern, post-Reformation, post-Enlightenment world that all the preconditions of freedom come together. At times Hegel seems to suggest that a fully ethical state has been achieved already, and "Right Hegelians" draw conservative lessons from this position; "Left Hegelians" argue – with at least equal plausibility – that Hegel's thought offers not a defense of the *status quo* but a call to reform; the ethical community is a possibility towards which we should strive rather than an achievement to be defended.

A second, very important, point concerns the nature of the state itself. Hegel regards the state as a critically important institution which overshadows every other aspect of communal life, in the process using language which has led many to accuse him of worshipping the state, and of preparing the way for totalitarianism. However, what is crucial to remember here is that Hegel's ethical state is characterized by the rule of law and the separation of powers. Hegel favors monarchy, but always constitutional monarchy in a *Rechtstaat* – a state governed by law and devoted to justice.

What kind of international relations might one expect to find in a world of Hegelian states? The first text presented in this chapter provides the answer, reproducing those sections of the *Philosophy of Right* on international law (§§ 330–40) (pp. 470–5 below). It will be noted that Hegel believes that states need other states in order to function properly; just as individuals cannot develop their individuality except by rubbing against other individuals (metaphorically speaking) so states can only develop their individuality by living in a world of other states; whether this is a helpful analogy can be disputed, but for Hegel it follows that states cannot surrender their sovereignty, that, therefore, war must always remain a possibility and schemes of "Perpetual Peace" – he mentions Kant in particular – cannot succeed. They rely on states limiting themselves and any agreement of self-limitation will always be "tainted with contingency." Moreover, Hegel is prepared to envisage a positive role for war in providing a context within which individuals can demonstrate self-sacrifice and the civic virtues – although it will be noted that he sees war as a public act in which harm to civilian life and property is excluded.

Is Hegel what has come to be called in twentieth-century International Relations theory a "realist"? One thing is clear – he most certainly does not believe that "might is right." The judgement of history is an important notion here – world history is a kind of world court, it is the place wherein the destiny of nations is determined in accordance with *Geist*. Nothing of significance happens by accident, simply because of the application of force. Hegel is content to see war as an instrument available to states – in the manner theorized by his near-contemporary, Clausewitz – and, in any event, his account of sovereignty means that the possibility of war can never be eliminated from the system, but this is a different matter from an explanation of the causes of any particular war (Clausewitz, 1976; Suganami, 1996). He refers elsewhere in the *Philosophy of Right* to the expansionist tendency of states (§ 246) but it is noteworthy that this tendency is rooted in the economy and civil society rather than in the state as such. Some later Hegelians, such as the British Idealists, have resisted the idea that war is an incorrigible feature of international relations, as we shall see below.

Nationalism and international society

Interestingly, the Hegelian ethical state is not necessarily a national state – it is the ethical nature of the institutions which make up the community that is central, not their national quality. Although Hegelian ideas do feed into nineteenth-century nationalist thought, the initial impetus for nationalism comes from elsewhere, from the folklorism of Herder, and the political experiences of the Revolutionary and Napoleonic wars. Nowhere was this latter experience felt more deeply than in Italy – which was divided amongst a number of small, generally oppressive states, and dominated by the Habsburg empire which, post 1815, still owned Lombardy and Venice – and no-one expressed this kind of nationalism more passionately than the Italian revolutionary and thinker, Giuseppe Mazzini (1805–72).

As Mack Smith has demonstrated, there was a time when Mazzini was regarded as one of the most important political thinkers of the nineteenth century (Mack Smith, 1994: 151). Partly this was because of his romantic life as an

Italian revolutionary, fighting on behalf of a cause which was held dear by right-thinking people everywhere, but it also rested on the popularity of his writings, in particular of the articles collected and published in 1840 as *On the Duties of Man* (Mazzini, 1907). This work went through a great many editions and translations in the nineteenth century, but more or less disappeared in the twentieth. The reason for its popularity then is clear enough, and is the same reason for its disappearance today. Mazzini gives a passionate account of the affective qualities of the national community and ties nationalism into all the good things life has to offer – but he has precious little sense of the difficulties of the notion, difficulties which have become all too apparent in the twentieth century. The flavor of Mazzini's thought is well captured in an early, messianic, text, *Faith and the Future* (1835):

We believe therefore in the HOLY ALLIANCE OF THE PEOPLE as the broadest formula of association possible in our age – in the *liberty* and *equality* of the peoples, without which association has no true life – in *Nationality*. Which is the conscience of the peoples, which assigns to them their share of work in the association, their office in HUMANITY, and hence constitutes their mission on earth, their *individuality*: for without Nationality neither liberty nor equality is possible – and we believe in the holy *Fatherland*, that is, the cradle of nationality, the altar and patrimony of the individuals that compose each people. (Mazzini: 1907, italics in original)

The Holy Alliance of the People is to be set against the reactionary Holy Alliance of Empires. The national principle is in no sense in contradiction to universal principles; all nations can and should live in harmony, one with another. Political freedom is enhanced by the national principle, democracy and nationalism go together.

These positions are developed at greater length in *On the Duties of Man*. This book begins with an invocation to the Italian working man, but immediately moves to God and the Law. Sections of the next two chapters "Duties to Humanity" and "Duties to Country" are reproduced below (pp. 476–85). It will be noted that for Mazzini duties to humanity come before duties to country both in the text and in life ("You are *men* before you are *citizens* or *fathers*") but, what is rather more to the point, there is little sense that there might be a contradiction here. That there is, in fact, at least a potential contradiction is clear enough. Mazzini argues for a redrawing of the map of Europe on national lines to create states based on Countries of the People and "between these Countries there will be harmony and brotherhood." However, his account of the borders of Italy ("the best-defined country in Europe") suggests that this would be an implausible outcome. Along with assigning Corsica to Italy, he suggests that a semicircle drawn with Parma as the base and the mouths of the Var and the Isonzo as starting and end points will mark the frontier that God has given Italy. The reader is invited to try this, and contemplate the reaction of the gods of France, Switzerland, and Slovenia.

A rather more thoughtful justification of liberal nationalism is offered by John Stuart Mill (1806–73), albeit in less inclusive terms and without solving the underlying dilemma. Rather than approach problems of nationality from the perspective of an account of pre-given nationhood, Mill sees the issue in terms of "self-determination" – the right of a people to determine their own form of government. In *Considerations on Representative Government* he endorses this right in terms which make it clear that the national principle rests upon popular will:

Where the sentiment of nationality exists in any force, there is a *prima facie* case for uniting all the members of a nationality under the same government, and a government to themselves apart. This is merely saying that the question of government ought to be decided by the governed. One hardly knows what any division of the human race should be free to do if not to determine with which of the various collective bodies of human beings they choose to associate themselves. (Mill, 1972: 361)

However, in the same paragraph, he adds a different and stronger claim – "Free institutions are next to impossible in a country made up of different nationalities." This is highly revealing – perhaps unintentionally – because it clarifies somewhat the meaning for Mill of nationality. Since virtually no countries are actually mono-national this would seem to be a counsel of despair, but since Mill clearly does not believe that free institutions are next to impossible in, for example, multi-national Great Britain, what it actually suggests is that he is working on a more restrictive account of nationality than might at first seem to be the case. It is only some "divisions of the human race" that ought to be free to determine their own fate.

This point becomes clearer when one examines Mill on the subject of the reverse side of the coin to the principle of self-determination, the principle of non-intervention. Mill's essay of 1859, "A Few Words on Non-Intervention," extracted below (pp. 486–93), sets out the case for the general principle of non-intervention, and for the necessary exceptions to the rule, employing arguments some of which have been re-employed in the late twentieth century by writers such as Michael Walzer. According to Mill, non-intervention is generally the right policy because it is not possible for outsiders to create free states; peoples have to take freedom for themselves, they cannot be given it, and the exceptions to this rule largely concern circumstances where intervention would be, in effect, counter-intervention – action taken in order to counter the prior intervention of an oppressing power. However, it will be noted that these principles apply only to cases where the nations concerned are of the same, or roughly the same, level of civilization. The rules of ordinary international morality imply reciprocity, but barbarians will not reciprocate. The underdeveloped barbarian mind is incapable of growth without the assistance of the higher civilizations. Thus it is that British imperialism in India, or French in Algeria, is justified in its acts of intervention in a way that, say, Russian intervention on behalf of Austria against the Hungarians in the rising of 1848/9 is not. Much of the beginning of this essay is devoted to showing that those who describe this attitude as hypocritical are missing the point.

Mill's Eurocentric account makes uncomfortable reading a hundred and fifty years later, but a number of points need to be made, if not in mitigation, then at least in order to provide a context. First, Mill in these comments was doing no more than express both the norms of international society in the nineteenth century, and the common viewpoint of the vast majority of educated Europeans. As to the first, full membership of International Society was largely restricted to European states and ex-colonies, and the notion of the "Standards of Civilization" codified the idea that certain kinds of socio-economic and legal norms needed to be met before membership could be granted (Gong, 1984). As to the second, it is far more difficult to find prominent nineteenth-century Europeans who were *not* convinced of the superiority of European civilization than it is to find the opposite. Mill was one of the foremost liberals of the day but conservative thinkers were even more dismissive of non-European values, while, to move further to the left, the terms with which Marx and Engels dismissed non-European civilizations are if anything more patronizing and hostile than those of Mill – "barbarian egotism ... undignified, stagnatory and vegetative life ... man, the sovereign of nature, fell down on his knees in adoration of Kanuman the monkey, and Sabbala, the cow" is Marx's account of life in India before the impact of British rule, which is motivated by selfish greed but has beneficial effects nonetheless (Marx, 1973: 306). A further point may be made on Mill's behalf; for all that his reasoning is offensive, he does at least understand that there is a real issue here, that it is not possible simply to endorse all nationalisms in the manner of Mazzini. From the perspective of the twentieth century this is refreshingly realistic, even if Mill's attempt to distinguish between "good," progressive nations and "bad," backward-looking nations cannot be allowed to stand.

Power and the nation-state

As suggested above, Hegel was not a believer in "power-politics" and his defense of the state is cast in ethical terms. Clearly neither Mazzini nor Mill fit the bill here either; Mazzini's faith in the universal brotherhood and harmony links him to later liberal internationalist thought, while Mill's commitment to a norm-governed international society is also incompatible with power-politics or any other crude version of realism. To find a true nineteenth-century precursor of the "realist paradigm" it is necessary to refer to the works of the German political scientist Heinrich von Treitschke (1834–96). Von Treitschke was born a Saxon, but, as a professor in Berlin, made himself the foremost intellectual defender of Prussian expansionism. His work was enormously influential in Germany at the end of the last century, and had a major, albeit indirect, influence on at least some currents of twentieth-century realism.

Like Mazzini, but for very different reasons, Treitschke largely ceased to exert direct influence after the First World War. Whereas Mazzini's optimism seemed out of place in the post-war world, in Treitschke's case it was the more overtly nationalist, reactionary, anti-Semitic, and sexist nature of his writing which has made him intellectually *persona non grata*. There is a sense in which Treitschke represents the dark side of the realist approach to international relations; when junior students (and some of their senior colleagues) produce caricatured accounts of realism, accounts which implicitly describe such profoundly moral human beings as Hans Morgenthau or George Kennan as ruthless power-worshippers, we rightly condemn them, but were their fire to be directed at Treitschke it would come closer to the mark. Moreover, his writings are characterized by an unpleasant moralizing: thus, his Christian principles are repeatedly invoked to explain why an immoral foreign policy is unacceptable – which is said to be in contrast with Machiavelli's instrumentalism and Hegel's supposed deification of the state – while the body of his work makes it plain that in his case the shackles of any kind of morality are worn very loosely, if at all.

In the circumstances, it might be asked why his writings are being presented here at all, given these faults. The answer is because, for all these sins of omission and commission, he is one of the clearest and most intelligent defenders of a full-blown, unapologetic account of the sovereign state as a power-based institution which is inevitably drawn into conflict with other states and which can brook no restrictions. He puts into words what many others in his century and ours have believed, but generally have not dared to make explicit. For this, at least, he deserves our thanks – but beyond this grudging praise, it will also be clear from his writings that Treitschke possessed a subtle intelligence, and a very good grasp of the diplomatic realities of his age. We may not like the picture he paints, but it is largely drawn from life.

In *Politics* Treitschke begins by defining the state as "the people, legally united as an independent entity" (Treitschke, 1916: 3). The state protects the people, the state is power, it demands obedience. The state is, and must be, sovereign. Restraints on states can only be self-imposed and can only apply *rebus sic stantibus* – so long as circumstances do not change. Sovereign states must be self-sufficing as far as possible – only the great powers are truly sovereign – indeed, small states are lacking in "that capacity for justice which characterizes their greater neighbors." What is interesting about these positions is, first, the way in which they draw on writers such as Hegel and Herder, while subverting their purposes, and second, the extent to which they are devoid of the kind of theological justifications common among the "righteous realists" of the twentieth century (M. J. Smith, 1986; Rosenthal, 1991). Original sin and human frailty do not feature here – the state is simply power and the will to prevail.

The conduct of war is a prime role of the state and war is the one remedy for an ailing nation. There is no apology here for its destructiveness, none of the qualifications that Hegel attached to his own account of the positive role of warfare. The extracts from Book II of *Politics* presented below set out in more detail Treitschke's view of the comity of nations and international law (pp.494–505). Although he endorses a number of procedural principles such as diplomatic immunity he is deeply skeptical of more substantive attempts to circumscribe state behavior. In his account, much of this kind of international law represents the will of the powerful – the argument here will be repeated by Carr in 1939; "haves" make the law, and it is futile to blame the "have-nots" for refusing to accept its legitimacy (Carr, 1939).

The First World War and the ethical state

Treitschke's book was first translated into English in 1916, in the midst of the First World War, and was, with some justification, employed to demonstrate the evils of German militarism. Certainly, Bethmann-Holweg's famous remark to the effect that the treaty guaranteeing Belgian neutrality was a mere "scrap of paper" whose violation could not justify Britain's intervention against Germany was totally in keeping with Treitschke's views. What was rather less intellectually justifiable was the tarnishing of all German philosophy, and especially Hegelianism, with the same, militarist, brush. Unfortunately such blackguarding became common and unexceptionable; L. T. Hobhouse's attribution of responsibility for German air raids to the "Hegelian theory of the god-state" was treated far more seriously than it deserved (Hobhouse, 1918: 6). This was hardly a reasonable attack on Hegel – although as we have seen he does lay himself open to misunderstanding in his enthusiasm for the ethical state and in his account of the role of war – but it was particularly inappropriate as a critique of the British Idealists, each of whom had rejected key elements of Hegel's view of war. The Idealists fought back, but it is fair to say that Hegel's reputation within the

English-speaking countries went into a decline after 1914 from which it did not recover until the 1960s and 1970s, and only then largely on the back of Western Marxism.

Much of this Idealist fight back was in reply to direct criticism by liberals such as Hobhouse – several examples are given in a recent collection of texts by the British Idealists (Boucher, 1997). However, the final reading in this section was written before the anti-Hegelian storm broke, and is, accordingly, rather less apologetic in tone. "Patriotism in the perfect state" by Bernard Bosanquet (1848–1923) is the text of a lecture delivered early in 1915 (pp. 506–17 below); Bosanquet provides a short but penetrating account of Hegel, identifying those elements of his thought that have misled the unwary, and a much briefer denunciation of the true power-worshippers such as Treitschke, but the bulk of the essay is an account of the way in which the patriotism that the perfect state requires in order to exist is in no sense incompatible with a commitment to humanity and a rejection of war. The state rests on popular will, and no state can judge another or surrender its sovereignty to another – until a universal will develops, international government is not a possibility – but war, far from being necessary for the health of a nation, is itself a sign of disease, a symptom not the cure.

In this text, an occasional work by a great philosopher, categories break down. The particularism associated with the Hegelian notion of an ethical state is revealed to be compatible with a wider universalism – we are both human beings and citizens, cosmopolitans and members of a particular community. We participate in the universal through our membership of particular communities. The line between internal and external must be clearly drawn if our communities are to work, but this is not a line that runs through our moral life in such a way that on one side – the outside – there are no moral obligations at all. On the contrary our obligations to humanity are part and parcel of our obligations to our fellow citizens. International society is composed of states, but these states are not simply the concentrations of sovereign power envisaged by Treitschke. The state is the way in which we express our universal aspirations, and its external conduct cannot be exempt from the moral law, nor should we wish it to be. There is clearly an element of utopianism about this, and as between Treitschke and Bosanquet it is the former who is a forerunner of realism and has probably had the greater indirect influence – but it may be as unrealistic to think that power is all-important as it is to believe that the universal and the particular can be reconciled in this way. Certainly one could have wished that Bosanquet's vision of the future had had more impact and influence than it did. The liberal internationalists of the post-1914–18 era could have used this particular form of Idealism more constructively than they did. In any event, it is to the forerunners of these liberal internationalists that we now turn.

FURTHER READING

The recent revival of Hegel studies owes a great deal to Charles Taylor's outstanding and monumental general study (1975), but rather more accessible for the beginner are Shlomo Avineri's account of Hegel's theory of the modern state (1972), and Raymond Plant's introductory volume (1983). Until recently, the most sustained work by Hegelians in English was produced by the British Idealists of the late nineteenth, early twentieth century. Bernard Bosanquet (1965), F. H. Bradley (1988), and T. H. Green (1941) are the key names here; David Boucher's recent collection of *The British Idealists* (1997) contains a good selection of writings by these and other authors, and Andrew Vincent and Raymond Plant have produced a good survey volume (1984). Modern Hegel-influenced writers on international political theory include John Charvet (1981, 1995) and Mervyn Frost (1996). The literature on nationalism is very extensive. Elie Kedourie (1960) regards nationalism as a doctrine invented at around the time of the French Revolution; Anthony Smith (1998) sees primordial ethnic identities lying behind modern nations, while Ernest Gellner (1983) and Benedict Anderson (1991) understand nationalism as a response to industrialism and the destruction of traditional societies. J. S. Mill's variant of liberal nationalism is ably represented today by Michael Walzer (1977, 1983) and David Miller (1995). The statism of von Treitschke is placed in a wider context by Friedrich Meinecke in his monumental study of Machiavellianism (1957). The gap between the ideas of twentieth-century realists and von Treitschke's 'power politics' is set out in studies by Michael J. Smith (1986), Joel Rosenthal (1991), and Alastair Murray (1997).

SOURCES

G. W. F. Hegel, from *Elements of the Philosophy of Right* (1821), ed. Allen Wood (Cambridge: Cambridge University Press, 1991), §§ 330–40, pp. 366–71.

G. Mazzini, "On the Duties of Man" (1840) in *Mazzini's Essays* (London: Everyman's Library, Dent, 1907), pp. 41–5, 49–59.

J. S. Mill, from "A Few Words on Non-Intervention" (1959), in *Collected Works of John Stuart Mill*, vol. xxi: *Essays on Equality Law and Education* (Toronto: University of Toronto Press, 1984) – italicized editorial matter then pp. 376–84.

H. von Treitschke, from *Politics* (1897) (London: Constable, 1916), vol. ii, pp. 587–620, extracts.

B. Bosanquet, "Patriotism in the Perfect State" (1915), in *The International Crisis in its Ethical and Psychological Aspects*, by Eleanor M. Sidgwick, Gilbert Murray, A. C. Bradley, L. P. Jacks, G. F. Stout, and B. Bosanquet (Oxford: Oxford University Press, 1915).

HEGEL

G.W.F. HEGEL (1770–1831), along with Kant the most important of German philosophers. Hegel's idealism – his belief that ideas, in particular the notion of *Geist* (spirit), shaped reality – was highly influential throughout the nineteenth century partly in its own terms, but also in stimulating critics such as Marx and Nietzsche. Through most of the twentieth century Hegel's influence waned; he was regarded (quite wrongly) as a supporter of German militarism and forerunner of fascism, and best known as the philosopher whom Marx "stood on his head" by demonstrating the material basis of thought. However, with the ending of communism, Hegel's idea of civil society as a set of institutions to be distinguished from both the family and the state and which form the basis for human freedom became very influential, and he has now regained his place as one of the greatest of political philosophers. *Elements of the Philosophy of Right* was published in 1821; it is a set of lecture notes setting out the way in which the individual is formed by the family, civil society, and the state. In the extract printed below, the relations of states are described.

From *Elements of the Philosophy of Right*

International Law *(Das äußere Staatsrecht)*

§ 330

International law (*das äußere Staatsrecht*) applies to the *relations* between independent states. What it contains *in and for itself* therefore assumes the form of an *obligation*, because its actuality depends on *distinct and sovereign wills*.

Addition (H). States are not private persons but completely independent totalities in themselves, so that the relations between them are not the same as purely moral relations or relations of private right. Attempts have often been made to apply private right and morality to states, but the position of private persons is that they are subject to the authority of a court which implements what is right in itself. Now a relationship between states ought also to be inherently governed by right, but in worldly affairs, that which has being in itself ought also to possess power. But since no power is present to decide what is right in itself in relation to the state and to actualize such decisions, this relation (*Beziehung*) must always remain one of obligation. The relationship between states is a relationship of independent units which make mutual stipulations but at the same time stand above these stipulations.

§ 331

The nation state (*das Volk als Staat*) is the spirit in its substantial rationality and immediate actuality, and is therefore the absolute power on *earth*; each state is consequently a sovereign and independent entity in relation to others. The state has a primary and absolute entitlement to be a sovereign and independent power *in the eyes of others*, i.e. *to be recognized* by them. At the same time, however, this entitlement is purely formal, and the requirement that the state should be recognized simply because it is a state is abstract. Whether the state does in fact have being in and for itself depends on its content – on its constitution and [present] condition; and recognition, which implies that the two [i.e. form and content] are identical, also depends on the perception and will of the other state.

Without relations (*Verhältnis*) with other states, the state can no more be an actual individual (*Individuum*) than an individual (*der Einzelne*) can be an actual person without a relationship (*Relation*) with other persons (see § 322). On the other hand, the legitimacy of a state, and more precisely – in so far as it has external relations – of the power of its sovereign, is a purely *internal* matter (one state should not interfere in the internal affairs of another). On the other hand, it is equally essential that this legitimacy should be *supplemented* by recognition on the part of other states. But this recognition requires a guarantee that the state will likewise recognize those other states which are supposed to recognize it, i.e. that it will respect their independence; accordingly, these other states cannot be indifferent to its internal affairs. – In the case of a nomadic people, for example, or any people at a low level of culture, the question even arises of how far this people can be regarded as a state. The religious viewpoint (as in former times with the Jewish and Mohammedan nations (*Völkern*) may further entail a higher opposition which precludes that universal identity that recognition requires.

Addition (G). When Napoleon said before the Peace of Campo Formio "the French Republic is no more in need of recognition than the sun is," his words conveyed no more than that strength of existence (*Existenz*) which itself carries with it a guarantee of recognition, even if this is not expressly formulated.

§ 332

The immediate actuality in which states coexist is particularized into various relations which are determined by the independent arbitrary wills of both parties, and which accordingly possess the formal nature of *contracts* in general. The subject-matter (*Stoff*) of these contracts, however, is infinitely less varied than it is in civil society, in which individuals (*die Einzelnen*) are mutually interdependent in innumerable respects, whereas independent states are primarily wholes which can satisfy their own needs internally.

§ 333

The principle of *international law* (*Völkerrecht*), as that *universal* right which ought to have international validity in and for itself (as distinct from the particular content of positive treaties), is that *treaties*, on which the mutual obligations of states depend, *should be observed*. But since the sovereignty of states is the principle governing their mutual relations, they exist to that extent in a state of nature in relation to one another, and their rights are *actualized* not in a universal will with constitutional powers over them, but in their own particular wills. Consequently, the universal determination of international law remains only an *obligation*, and the [normal] condition will be for relations governed by treaties to alternate with the suspension (*Aufhebung*) of such relations.

There is no praetor to adjudicate between states, but at most arbitrators and mediators, and even the presence of these will be contingent, i.e. determined by particular wills. Kant's idea (*Vorstellung*) of a *perpetual peace* guaranteed by a federation of states which would settle all disputes and which, as a power recognized by each individual state, would resolve all disagreements so as to make it impossible for these to be settled by war presupposes an *agreement* between states. But this agreement, whether based on moral, religious, or other grounds and considerations, would always be dependent on particular sovereign wills, and would therefore continue to be tainted with contingency.

§ 334

Consequently, if no agreement can be reached between particular wills, conflicts between states can be settled only by *war*. Since the sphere of the state is extensive and its relations (*Beziehungen*) through its citizens are extremely varied, it may easily suffer injuries (*Verletzungen*) on many occasions. But which of these injuries should be regarded as a specific breach of treaties or as an injury to the recognition and honour of the state remains *inherently* (*an sich*) indeterminable; for a state may associate its infinity and honour with any one

of its individual interests, and it will be all the more inclined to take offence
if it possesses a strong individuality which is encouraged, as a result of a long
period of internal peace, to seek and create an occasion (*Stoff*) for action
abroad.

§ 335

Furthermore, the state, as a wholly spiritual entity, cannot confine itself simply
to noting that an *injury* has actually taken place. On the contrary, a further
cause of discord arises in the *idea* (*Vorstellung*) of such an injury as a *danger*
threatening from another state, in changing estimates of greater and lesser
degrees of probability, in conjectures as to the other state's intentions, etc.

§ 336

The relationship of states to one another is a relationship between independent entities and hence between *particular* wills, and it is on this that the very
validity of treaties depends. But the *particular will* of the whole, *as far as its content is concerned*, is its own *welfare* in general. Consequently, this welfare is the
supreme law for a state in its relations with others, especially since the Idea
of the state is precisely that the opposition between right as abstract freedom
and the particular content which fills it, i.e. the state's own welfare, should be
superseded within it, and it is on this Idea as a *concrete* whole that the initial
recognition of states is based (see § 331).

§ 337

The substantial welfare of the state is its welfare as a *particular* state in its specific
interest and condition and in its equally distinctive external circumstances in
conjunction with the particular treaties which govern them. Its government
is accordingly a matter of *particular wisdom*, not of universal providence (cf.
Remarks to § 324), just as its end in relation to other states and its principle
for justifying wars and treaties is not a universal (philanthropic) thought, but
its actually offended or threatened welfare in *its specific particularity*.

There was at one time a great deal of talk about the opposition between morality
and politics and the demand that the latter should conform to the former. In the
present context, we need only remark in general that the welfare of a state has
quite a different justification from the welfare of the individual (*des Einzelnen*). The
immediate existence (*Dasein*) of the state as the ethical substance, i.e. its right, is

directly embodied not in abstract but in concrete existence (*Existenz*), and only this
concrete existence, rather than any of those many universal thoughts which are held
to be moral commandments, can be the principle of its action and behaviour. The
allegation that, within this alleged opposition, politics is always wrong is in fact based
on superficial notions (*Vorstellungen*) of morality, the nature of the state, and the state's
relation to the moral point of view.

§ 338

The fact that states reciprocally recognize each other as such remains, *even
in war* – as the condition of rightlessness (*Rechtlosigkeit*), force, and contingency – a *bond* whereby they retain their validity for each other in their being
in and for themselves, so that even in wartime, the determination of war is
that of something which ought to come to an end. War accordingly entails
the determination of international law (*Völkerrecht*) that it should preserve the
possibility of peace – so that, for example, ambassadors should be respected
and war should on no account be waged either on internal institutions and
the peace of private and family life, or on private individuals.

ADDITION (G)

Modern wars are accordingly waged in a humane manner, and persons do not
confront each other in hatred. At most, personal enmities will arise at military
outposts, but in the army as such, hostility is something indeterminate which
takes second place to the duty which each respects in the other.

§ 339

Otherwise, the conduct of states towards one another in wartime (e.g. in the
taking of prisoners), and concessions of rights in peacetime to the citizens of
another state for the purpose of private contacts, etc. will depend primarily
on national *customs*, for these are the universal aspect of behaviour which is
preserved under all circumstances.

ADDITION (G)

The European nations (*Nationen*) form a family with respect to the universal
principle of their legislation, customs, and culture (*Bildung*), so that their
conduct in terms of international law is modified accordingly in a situation
which is otherwise dominated by the mutual infliction of evils (*Übeln*). The
relations between states are unstable, and there is no praetor to settle disputes;
the higher praetor is simply the universal spirit which has being in and for
itself, i.e. the world spirit.

§ 340

Since states function as *particular* entities in their mutual relations, the broadest view of these relations will encompass the ceaseless turmoil not just of external contingency, but also of passions, interests, ends, talents and virtues, violence (*Gewalt*), wrongdoing, and vices in their inner particularity. In this turmoil, the ethical whole itself – the independence of the state – is exposed to contingency. The principles of the *spirits of nations* (*Volksgeister*) are in general of a limited nature because of that particularity in which they have their objective actuality and self-consciousness as *existent* individuals, and their deeds and destinies in their mutual relations are the manifest (*erscheinende*) dialectic of the finitude of these spirits. It is through this dialectic that the *universal* spirit, *the spirit of the world*, produces itself in its freedom from all limits, and it is this spirit which exercises its right – which is the highest right of all – over finite spirits in *world history* as the *world's court of judgement* (*Weltgericht*).

GIUSEPPE MAZZINI

G IUSEPPE MAZZINI (1805–72), Italian patriot, liberal, revolutionary, and nationalist. At one time considered one of the most important thinkers of nineteenth-century Europe, Mazzini is now little known outside of his homeland. His very successful set of homilies *On the Duties of Man* was originally published in 1840, going through many editions. In the extracts printed below the importance of love of country is stressed, but so also is the compatibility of this patriotism with a love of humanity. Mazzini's is a world in which nationalisms are in conflict with multi-national empires rather than with each other – which perhaps explains why his influence declined in the twentieth century.

From *On the Duties of Man*

Duties to humanity

Your first duties, first not in point of time but of importance – because without understanding these you can only imperfectly fulfil the rest – are to Humanity. You have duties as citizens, as sons, as husbands, as fathers – sacred, inviolable duties of which I shall presently speak at length; but what makes these duties sacred and inviolable is the mission, the *duty*, which your nature as *men* imposes on you. You are fathers in order that you may educate *men* to worship and to unfold God's law. You are citizens, you have a country, in order that in a limited sphere, with the concourse of people linked to you already by speech, by tendencies, and by habits, you may labour for the benefit of all *men* whatever they are and may be in the future – a task which each one could ill do by himself, weak and lost amid the immense multitude of his fellow-men. Those who teach morality, limiting its obligations to duties towards family or country, teach you a more or less narrow *egoism* and lead you to what is evil for others and for yourselves. Country and family are like two circles drawn within a greater circle which contains them both; like two steps of a ladder without which you could not climb any higher, but upon which it is forbidden you to stay your feet.

You are *men*; that is, *rational* and *social* creatures *capable, by means of association only, of a progress* to which no one may assign limits; and this is all that we know to-day of the law of life given to Humanity. These characteristics constitute *human nature*, which distinguishes you from the other beings around you and which is entrusted to each of you as a seed to bring to fruit. All your life should tend to the exercise and the regular development of these fundamental faculties of your nature. Whenever you suppress one of these faculties or allow it to be suppressed wholly or in part, you fall from the rank of men to the level of the inferior animals and violate the law of your life, the Law of God.

You fall to the level of the brutes and violate God's Law whenever you suppress, or allow to be suppressed, one of the faculties which constitute human nature in yourself or in others. What God wills is not only that his Law should be fulfilled in you as individuals – had He willed this only, He would have created you solitary – but that it should be fulfilled in the whole earth, among all the beings whom He created in His own image. What He wills is that the Idea of perfectibility and of love which He has given to the world should reveal itself in ever-increasing glory, ever more adored and better manifested. Your earthly and individual existence within its narrow limits of time and of capacity can only manifest it most imperfectly and by flashes. Humanity alone, continuous through the generations and through the general intellect fed by the individual intellect of each of its members, can gradually unfold that divine idea and apply or glorify it. Life, then, was given you by God that you might use it for the benefit of humanity, that you might direct your individual faculties to the development of the faculties of your fellow-men, and that you might contribute by your work some portion to that collective work of improvement and that discovery of the truth which the generations slowly but continuously carry on.

...

A people, Greek, Polish, Circassian, raises the banner of the Fatherland and of Independence, fights, conquers, or dies for it. What is it that makes your hearts beat at the story of its battles, which makes them swell with joy at its victories, and sorrow over its defeats? A man, perhaps your fellow-countryman, perhaps a foreigner, rises amid the universal silence, in some corner of the earth, gives utterance to certain ideas which he believes to be true, maintains them in persecution and in chains, and dies, still constant to them, upon the scaffold. Why do you honour him with the name of Saint and of Martyr? Why do you respect and teach your children to respect his memory?

And why do you eagerly read the miracles of patriotic love recorded in Greek story, and repeat them to your children with a feeling of pride, almost as if they were stories of your own fathers? These deeds of the Greeks are two thousand years old, and belong to an epoch of civilisation which is not and never can be yours. That man whom you call martyr died perhaps for ideas which you do not hold, and anyhow by his voluntary death he cut short his individual progress here below. That people whom you admire in victory and in defeat is a people foreign and perhaps almost unknown to you; speaking a different language, and with a manner of life which has no visible influence upon yours; what matters it to you whether it is dominated by the Sultan or the King of Bavaria, by the Russian Czar or by a government springing from the common will of the nation? But in your heart a voice cries, Those men of two thousand years ago, those far-off peoples that fight to-day, that martyr to ideas for which you would not die, were and are your brothers: brothers not only by community of origin and nature, but community of work and of purpose. Those ancient Greeks passed away; but their work did not pass away, and without it you would not possess to-day that degree of intellectual and moral development which you have reached. Those peoples consecrate with their blood an idea of national liberty for which you too are fighting. That martyr proclaimed by his death that man must sacrifice all things, and if needs be life also, for that which he believes to be the Truth. It is of little importance that he and all who seal their faith with their blood cut short their own individual development here upon earth; God provides elsewhere for them. But the development of Humanity is of importance. It is of importance that the coming generation, taught by your combats and your sacrifices, should rise higher and grow mightier than you in the understanding of the Law, in the adoration of the Truth. It is of importance that human nature, fortified by example, should become better, and realise more and more God's will upon earth. And wherever human nature grows better, wherever a new truth is won, wherever a step forward is taken on the path of education, of progress, and of morality, it is a step, a gain, which will bear fruit sooner or later for the whole of Humanity. You are all soldiers of an army which moves by diverse ways, divided into different bands, to the conquest of a single enterprise. At present you only look to your immediate leaders; different uniforms, different words of command, the distances which separate the operating corps, the mountains which conceal them from one another, make you often forget this truth, and fix your attention exclusively upon the end which is closest to you. But there is One above you all who sees the whole and directs all the movements. God alone has the secret of the battle, and will be able to gather you all together into one camp and under one banner.

...

There is no hope for you except in universal reform and in the brotherhood of all the peoples of Europe, and through Europe of all humanity. I charge you then, O my brothers, by your duty and by your own interest, not to forget that your first duties – duties without fulfilling which you cannot hope to fulfil those owed to family and country – are to Humanity. Let your words and your actions be for all, since God is for all, in His Love and in His Law. In whatever land you may be, wherever a man is fighting for right, for justice, for truth, there is your brother; wherever a man suffers through the oppression of error, of injustice, of tyranny, there is your brother. Free men and slaves, YOU ARE ALL BROTHERS. Origin, law, and goal are one for all of you. Let your creed, your action, the banner beneath which you fight, be likewise one. Do not say, *The language which we speak is different*; tears, actions, martyrdom form a common language for all men, and one which you all understand. Do not say, *Humanity is too vast, and we are too weak*. God does not measure powers, but intentions. Love Humanity. Ask yourselves whenever you do an action in the sphere of your Country, or your family, *If what I am doing were done by all and for all, would it advantage or injure Humanity?* and if your conscience answers, *It would injure Humanity*, desist; desist, even if it seem to you that an immediate advantage for your Country or your family would ensue from your action. Be apostles of this faith, apostles of the brotherhood of nations, and of the unity of the human race – a principle admitted to-day in theory, but denied in practice. Be such apostles wherever and in whatever way you are able. Neither God nor man can demand more of you. But I say to you that by becoming such apostles – even to yourselves only, when you are not able to do more – you will advantage Humanity. God measures the degrees of education which he allows the human race to ascend by the number and the purity of the believers. When you are pure and numerous, God, who numbers you, will open for you the way to action.

Duties to country

Your first Duties – first, at least, in importance – are, as I have told you, to Humanity. You are *men* before you are *citizens* or *fathers*. If you do not embrace the whole human family in your love, if you do not confess your faith in its unity – consequent on the unity of God – and in the brotherhood of the Peoples who are appointed to reduce that unity to fact – if wherever one of your fellow-men groans, wherever the dignity of human nature is violated by falsehood or tyranny, you are not prompt, being able, to succour that wretched one, or do not feel yourself called, being able, to fight for the purpose of relieving the deceived or oppressed – you disobey your law of life, or do not comprehend the religion which will bless the future.

But what can *each* of you, with his isolated powers, *do* for the moral improvement, for the progress of Humanity? You can, from time to time, give sterile expression to your belief; you may, on some rare occasion, perform an act of *charity* to a brother not belonging to your own land, no more. Now, *charity* is not the watchword of the future faith. The watchword of the future faith is *association*, fraternal cooperation towards a common aim, and this is as much superior to *charity* as the work of many uniting to raise with one accord a building for the habitation of all together would be superior to that which you would accomplish by raising a separate hut each for himself, and only helping one another by exchanging stones and bricks and mortar. But divided as you are in language, tendencies, habits, and capacities, you cannot attempt this common work. The *individual* is too weak, and Humanity too vast. *My God*, prays the Breton mariner as he puts out to sea, *protect me, my ship is so little, and Thy ocean so great!* And this prayer sums up the condition of each of you, if no means is found of multiplying your forces and your powers of action indefinitely. But God gave you this means when he gave you a Country, when, like a wise overseer of labour, who distributes the different parts of the work according to the capacity of the workmen, he divided Humanity into distinct groups upon the face of our globe, and thus planted the seeds of nations. Bad governments have disfigured the design of God, which you may see clearly marked out, as far, at least, as regards Europe, by the courses of the great rivers, by the lines of the lofty mountains, and by other geographical conditions; they have disfigured it by conquest, by greed, by jealousy of the just sovereignty of others; disfigured it so much that to-day there is perhaps no nation except England and France whose confines correspond to this design. They did not, and they do not, recognise any country except their own families and dynasties, the egoism of caste. But the divine design will infallibly be fulfilled. Natural divisions, the innate spontaneous tendencies of the peoples will replace the arbitrary divisions sanctioned by bad governments. The map of Europe will be remade. The Countries of the People will rise, defined by the voice of the free, upon the ruins of the Countries of Kings and privileged castes. Between these Countries there will be harmony and brotherhood. And then the work of Humanity for the general amelioration, for the discovery and application of the real law of life, carried on in association and distributed according to local capacities, will be accomplished by peaceful and progressive development; then each of you, strong in the affections and in the aid of many millions of men speaking the same language, endowed with the same tendencies, and educated by the same historic tradition, may hope by your personal effort to benefit the whole of Humanity.

To you, who have been born in Italy, God has allotted, as if favouring you specially, the best-defined country in Europe. In other lands, marked by more uncertain or more interrupted limits, questions may arise which the pacific vote of all will one day solve, but which have cost, and will yet perhaps cost, tears and blood; in yours, no. God has stretched round you sublime and indisputable boundaries; on one side the highest mountains of Europe, the Alps; on the other the sea, the immeasurable sea. Take a map of Europe and place one point of a pair of compasses in the north of Italy on Parma; point the other to the mouth of the Var, and describe a semicircle with it in the direction of the Alps; this point, which will fall, when the semicircle is completed, upon the mouth of the Isonzo, will have marked the frontier which God has given you. As far as this frontier your language is spoken and understood; beyond this you have no rights. Sicily, Sardinia, Corsica, and the smaller islands between them and the mainland of Italy belong undeniably to you. Brute force may for a little while contest these frontiers with you, but they have been recognised from of old by the tacit general consent of the peoples; and the day when, rising with one accord for the final trial, you plant your tricoloured flag upon that frontier, the whole of Europe will acclaim re-risen Italy, and receive her into the community of the nations. To this final trial all your efforts must be directed.

Without Country you have neither name, token, voice, nor rights, no admission as brothers into the fellowship of the Peoples. You are the bastards of Humanity. Soldiers without a banner, Israelites among the nations, you will find neither faith nor protection; none will be sureties for you. Do not beguile yourselves with the hope of emancipation from unjust social conditions if you do not first conquer a Country for yourselves; where there is no Country there is no common agreement to which you can appeal; the egoism of self-interest rules alone, and he who has the upper hand keeps it, since there is no common safeguard for the interests of all. Do not be led away by the idea of improving your material conditions without first solving the national question. You cannot do it. Your industrial associations and mutual help societies are useful as a means of educating and disciplining yourselves; as an economic fact they will remain barren until you have an Italy. The economic problem demands, first and foremost, an increase of capital and production; and while your Country is dismembered into separate fragments – while shut off by the barrier of customs and artificial difficulties of every sort, you have only restricted markets open to you – you cannot hope for this increase. To-day – do not delude yourselves – you are not the working-class of Italy; you are only fractions of that class; powerless, unequal to the great task which you propose to yourselves. Your emancipation can have no practical beginning until a National Government, understanding the signs of the times, shall, seated in Rome, formulate a Declaration of Principles to be the guide for Italian progress, and shall insert into it these words, *Labour is sacred, and is the source of the wealth of Italy*.

Do not be led astray, then, by hopes of material progress which in your present conditions can only be illusions. Your Country alone, the vast and rich Italian Country, which stretches from the Alps to the farthest limit of Sicily, can fulfil these hopes. You cannot obtain your *rights* except by obeying the commands of *Duty*. Be worthy of them, and you will have them. O my Brothers! love your Country. Our Country is our home, the home which God has given us, placing therein a numerous family which we love and are loved by, and with which we have a more intimate and quicker communion

of feeling and thought than with others; a family which by its concentration
upon a given spot, and by the homogeneous nature of its elements, is destined
for a special kind of activity. Our Country is our field of labour; the products
of our activity must go forth from it for the benefit of the whole earth: but
the instruments of labour which we can use best and most effectively exist
in it, and we may not reject them without being unfaithful to God's purpose
and diminishing our own strength. In labouring according to true principles
for our Country we are labouring for Humanity; our Country is the fulcrum
of the lever which we have to wield for the common good. If we give up this
fulcrum we run the risk of becoming useless to our Country and to Humanity.
Before *associating* ourselves with the Nations which compose Humanity we
must exist as a Nation. There can be no association except among equals; and
you have no recognised collective existence.

Humanity is a great army moving to the conquest of unknown lands,
against powerful and wary enemies. The Peoples are the different corps and
divisions of that army. Each has a post entrusted to it; each a special operation
to perform; and the common victory depends on the exactness with which
the different operations are carried out. Do not disturb the order of the battle.
Do not abandon the banner which God has given you. Wherever you may be,
into the midst of whatever people circumstances may have driven you, fight
for the liberty of that people if the moment calls for it; but fight as Italians,
so that the blood which you shed may win honour and love, not for you only,
but for your Country. And may the constant thought of your soul be for Italy,
may all the acts of your life be worthy of her, and may the standard beneath
which you range yourselves to work for Humanity be Italy's. Do not say *I*;
say *we*. Be every one of you an incarnation of your Country, and feel himself
and make himself responsible for his fellow-countrymen; let each one of you
learn to act in such a way that in him men shall respect and love his Country.

Your Country is one and indivisible. As the members of a family cannot
rejoice at the common table if one of their number is far away, snatched from
the affection of his brothers, so you should have no joy or repose as long as
a portion of the territory upon which your language is spoken is separated
from the Nation.

Your Country is the token of the mission which God has given you to
fulfil in Humanity. The faculties, the strength of *all* its sons should be united
for the accomplishment of this mission. A certain number of common duties
and rights belong to every man who answers to the *Who are you?* of the other
peoples, *I am an Italian*. Those duties and those rights cannot be represented
except by one *single* authority resulting from your votes. A Country must have,
then, a single government. The politicians who call themselves federalists,
and who would make Italy into a brotherhood of different states, would
dismember the Country, not understanding the idea of Unity. The States

into which Italy is divided to-day are not the creation of our own people; they are the result of the ambitions and calculations of princes or of foreign conquerors, and serve no purpose but to flatter the vanity of local aristocracies for which a narrower sphere than a great Country is necessary. What you, the people, have created, beautified, and consecrated with your affections, with your joys, with your sorrows, and with your blood, is the City and the Commune, not the Province or the State. In the City, in the Commune, where your fathers sleep and where your children will live, where you exercise your faculties and your personal rights, you live out your lives as *individuals*. It is of your City that each of you can say what the Venetians say of theirs: *Venezia la xe nostra: l'avemo fatta nu.*[1] In your City you have need of *liberty* as in your Country you have need of *association*. The Liberty of the Commune and the Unity of the Country – let that, then, be your faith. Do not say Rome and Tuscany, Rome and Lombardy, Rome and Sicily; say Rome and Florence, Rome and Siena, Rome and Leghorn, and so through all the Communes of Italy. Rome for all that represents Italian life; your Commune for whatever represents the *individual* life. All the other divisions are artificial, and are not confirmed by your national tradition.

A Country is a fellowship of free and equal men bound together in a brotherly concord of labour towards a single end. You must make it and maintain it such. A Country is not an aggregation, it is an *association*. There is no true Country without a uniform right. There is no true Country where the uniformity of that right is violated by the existence of caste, privilege, and inequality – where the powers and faculties of a large number of individuals are suppressed or dormant – where there is no common principle accepted, recognised, and developed by all. In such a state of things there can be no Nation, no People, but only a multitude, a fortuitous agglomeration of men whom circumstances have brought together and different circumstances will separate. In the name of your love for your Country you must combat without truce the existence of every privilege, every inequality, upon the soil which has given you birth. One privilege only is lawful – the privilege of Genius when Genius reveals itself in brotherhood with Virtue; but it is a privilege conceded by God and not by men, and when you acknowledge it and follow its inspirations, you acknowledge it freely by the exercise of your own reason and your own choice. Whatever privilege claims your submission in virtue of force or heredity, or any right which is not a common right, is a usurpation and a tyranny, and you ought to combat it and annihilate it. Your Country should be your Temple. God at the summit, a People of equals at the base. Do not accept any other formula, any other moral law, if you do not want to dishonour your Country and yourselves. Let the secondary laws for the

---

1 Venice is our own: we have made her.

gradual regulation of your existence be the progressive application of this supreme law.

And in order that they should be so, it is necessary that *all* should contribute to the making of them. The laws made by one fraction of the citizens only can never by the nature of things and men do otherwise than reflect the thoughts and aspirations and desires of that fraction; they represent, not the whole country, but a third, a fourth part, a class, a zone of the country. The law must express the general aspiration, promote the good of all, respond to a beat of the nation's heart. The whole nation therefore should be, directly or indirectly, the legislator. By yielding this mission to a few men, you put the egoism of one class in the place of the Country, which is the union of *all* the classes.

A Country is not a mere territory; the particular territory is only its foundation. The Country is the idea which rises upon that foundation; it is the sentiment of love, the sense of fellowship which binds together all the sons of that territory. So long as a single one of your brothers is not represented by his own vote in the development of the national life – so long as a single one vegetates uneducated among the educated – so long as a single one able and willing to work languishes in poverty for want of work – you have not got a Country such as it ought to be, the Country of all and for all. *Votes, education, work* are the three main pillars of the nation; do not rest until your hands have solidly erected them.

And when they have been erected – when you have secured for every one of you food for both body and soul – when freely united, entwining your right hands like brothers round a beloved mother, you advance in beautiful and holy concord towards the development of your faculties and the fulfilment of the Italian mission – remember that that mission is the moral unity of Europe; remember the immense duties which it imposes upon you. Italy is the only land that has twice uttered the great word of unification to the disjoined nations. Twice Rome has been the metropolis, the temple, of the European world; the first time when our conquering eagles traversed the known world from end to end and prepared it for union by introducing civilised institutions; the second time when, after the Northern conquerors had themselves been subdued by the potency of Nature, of great memories and of religious inspiration, the genius of Italy incarnated itself in the Papacy and undertook the solemn mission – abandoned four centuries ago – of preaching the union of souls to the peoples of the Christian world. To-day a third mission is dawning for our Italy; as much vaster than those of old as the Italian People, the free and united Country which you are going to found, will be greater and more powerful than Cæsars or Popes. The presentiment of this mission agitates Europe and keeps the eye and the thought of the nations chained to Italy.

Your duties to your Country are proportioned to the loftiness of this mission. You have to keep it pure from egoism, uncontaminated by falsehood and by the arts of that political Jesuitism which they call diplomacy.

The government of the country will be based through your labours upon the worship of principles, not upon the idolatrous worship of interests and of opportunity. There are countries in Europe where Liberty is sacred within, but is systematically violated without; peoples who say, *Truth is one thing, utility another: theory is one thing, practice another*. Those countries will have inevitably to expiate their guilt in long isolation, oppression, and anarchy. But you know the mission of our Country, and will pursue another path. Through you Italy will have, with one only God in the heavens, one only truth, one only faith, one only rule of political life upon earth. Upon the edifice, sublimer than Capitol or Vatican, which the people of Italy will raise, you will plant the banner of Liberty and of Association, so that it shines in the sight of all the nations, nor will you lower it ever for terror of despots or lust for the gains of a day. You will have boldness as you have faith. You will speak out aloud to the world, and to those who call themselves the lords of the world, the thought which thrills in the heart of Italy. You will never deny the sister nations. The life of the Country shall grow through you in beauty and in strength, free from servile fears and the hesitations of doubt, keeping as its *foundation* the people, as its *rule* the consequences of its principles logically deduced and energetically applied, as its *strength* the strength of all, as its *outcome* the amelioration of all, as its *end* the fulfilment of the mission which God has given it. And because you will be ready to die for Humanity, the life of your Country will be immortal.

JOHN STUART MILL

JOHN STUART MILL (1806–73) was a leading philosopher, political economist, and social critic of mid-Victorian Britain. His essay "A Few Words on Non-Intervention" (1859) was largely designed to contest the view that non-intervention was, for Great Britain, a self-serving policy which either betokened indifference to suffering, or was downright hypocritical in so far as the British empire was very obviously the product of active intervention in the affairs of the rest of the world. In the following extended extract, Mill sets out the reasons why non-intervention is generally a principled policy, but also why it is not necessarily appropriate when dealing with "primitive" peoples.

From "A Few Words on Non-Intervention"

[*The first half of this essay is devoted to explaining Britain's policy of non-intervention and defending it from those foreign critics who simply cannot understand that a great nation should devote its efforts not to self-aggrandizement but to the good of mankind. Britain's reputation for craftiness and hypocrisy rests partly on the way in which her statesmen characteristically justify non-intervention in terms of Britain's interests, thereby giving an impression of selfishness. We might note that this was written in 1859, before the scramble for Africa and the wave of imperialism that swept Britain in the later years of the century – however, the suppression of rebellion in India, war with China, and various other imperial enterprises conducted at the time by Britain perhaps explain the unwillingness of Britain's neighbours to accept this picture of moral rectitude.*]

There seems to be no little need that the whole doctrine of non-interference with foreign nations should be reconsidered, if it can be said to have as yet been considered as a really moral question at all. We have heard something lately about being willing to go to war for an idea. To go to war for an idea, if the war is aggressive, not defensive, is as criminal as to go to war for territory or revenue; for it is as little justifiable to force our ideas on other people, as to compel them to submit to our will in any other respect. But there assuredly are cases in which it is allowable to go to war, without having been ourselves attacked, or threatened with attack; and it is very important that nations should make up their minds in time, as to what these cases are. There are few questions which more require to be taken in hand by ethical and political philosophers, with a view to establish some rule or criterion whereby the justifiableness of intervening in the affairs of other countries, and (what is sometimes fully as questionable) the justifiableness of refraining from intervention, may be brought to a definite and rational test. Whoever attempts this, will be led to recognise more than one fundamental distinction, not yet by any means familiar to the public mind, and in general quite lost sight of by those who write in strains of indignant morality on the subject. There is a great difference (for example) between the case in which the nations concerned are of the same, or something like the same, degree of civilization, and that in which one of the parties to the situation is of a high, and the other of a very low, grade of social improvement. To suppose that the same international customs, and the same rules of international morality, can obtain between one civilized nation and another, and between civilized nations and barbarians, is a grave error, and one which no statesman can fall into, however it may be with those who, from a safe and unresponsible position, criticise statesmen. Among many reasons why the same rules cannot be applicable to situations so different, the two following are among the most important. In the first place, the rules of ordinary international morality imply reciprocity. But barbarians will not reciprocate. They cannot be depended on for observing any rules. Their minds are not capable of so great an effort, nor their will sufficiently under the influence of distant motives. In the next place, nations which are still barbarous have not got beyond the period during which it is likely to be for their benefit that they should be conquered and held in subjection by foreigners. Independence and nationality, so essential to the due growth and development of a people further advanced in improvement, are generally impediments to theirs. The sacred duties which civilized nations owe to the independence and nationality of each other, are not binding towards those to whom nationality and independence are either a certain evil, or at best a questionable good. The Romans were not the most clean-handed of conquerors, yet would it have been better for Gaul and Spain, Numidia and Dacia, never to have formed part of the Roman Empire? To characterize any conduct whatever towards a barbarous people as a violation of the law of nations, only shows that he who so speaks has never considered the subject. A violation of great principles of morality it may easily be; but barbarians have no rights as a *nation*, except a right to such treatment as may, at the earliest possible period, fit them for becoming one. The only moral laws for the relation between a civilized and a barbarous government, are the universal rules of morality between man and man.

The criticisms, therefore, which are so often made upon the conduct of the French in Algeria, or of the English in India, proceed, it would seem, mostly on a wrong principle. The true standard by which to judge their proceedings never having been laid down, they escape such comment and censure as might really have an improving effect, while they are tried by a standard which can have no influence on those practically engaged in such transactions, knowing as they do that it cannot, and if it could, ought not to be observed, because no human being would be the better, and many much the worse, for its observance. A civilized government cannot help having barbarous neighbours: when it has, it cannot always content itself with a defensive position, one of mere resistance to aggression. After a longer or shorter interval of forbearance, it either finds itself obliged to conquer them, or to assert so much authority over them, and so break their spirit, that they gradually sink into a state of dependence upon itself: and when that time arrives, they are indeed no longer formidable to it, but it has had so much to do with setting up and pulling down their governments, and they have grown so accustomed to lean on it, that it has become morally responsible for all evil it allows them to do. This is the history of the relations of the British Government with the native States of India. It never was secure in its own Indian possessions until it had reduced the military power of those States to a nullity. But a despotic government only exists by its military power. When we had taken away theirs, we were forced, by the necessity of the case, to offer them ours instead of it. To enable them to dispense with large armies of their own, we bound ourselves to place at their disposal, and they bound themselves to receive, such an amount of military force as made us in fact masters of the country. We engaged that this force should fulfil the purposes of a force, by defending the prince against all foreign and internal enemies. But being thus assured of the protection of a civilized power, and freed from the fear of internal rebellion or foreign conquest, the only checks which either restrain the passions or keep any vigour in the character of an Asiatic despot, the native Governments either became so oppressive and extortionate as to desolate the country, or fell into such a state of nerveless imbecility, that every one, subject to their will, who had not the means of defending himself by his own armed followers, was the prey of anybody who had a band of ruffians in his pay. The British Government felt this deplorable state of things to be its own work; being the direct consequence of the position in which, for its own security, it had placed itself towards the native governments. Had it permitted this to go on indefinitely, it would have deserved to be accounted among the worst political malefactors. In some cases (unhappily not in all) it had endeavoured to take precaution against these mischiefs by a special article in the treaty, binding the prince to reform his administration, and in future to govern in conformity to the advice of the British Government. Among the treaties in which a provision of this sort had been inserted, was that with Oude. For fifty years and more did the British Government allow this engagement to be treated with entire disregard; not without frequent remonstrances, and occasionally threats, but without ever carrying into effect what it threatened. During this period of half a century, England was morally accountable for a mixture of tyranny and anarchy, the picture of which, by men who knew it well, is appalling to all who read it. The act by which the Government of British India at last set aside treaties which had been so pertinaciously violated, and assumed the power of fulfilling the obligation it had so long before incurred, of giving to the people of Oude a tolerable government, far from being the political crime it is so often ignorantly called, was a criminally tardy discharge of an imperative duty. And the fact, that nothing which had been done in all this century by the East India Company's Government made it so unpopular in England, is one of the most striking instances of what was noticed in a former part of this article – the predisposition of English public opinion to look unfavourably upon every act by which territory or revenue are acquired from foreign States, and to take part with any government, however unworthy, which can make out the merest semblance of a case of injustice against our own country.

But among civilized peoples, members of an equal community of nations, like Christian Europe, the question assumes another aspect, and must be decided on totally different principles. It would be an affront to the reader to discuss the immorality of wars of conquest, or of conquest even as the consequence of lawful war; the annexation of any civilized people to the dominion of another, unless by their own spontaneous election. Up to this point, there is no difference of opinion among honest people; nor on the wickedness of commencing an aggressive war for any interest of our own, except when necessary to avert from ourselves an obviously impending wrong. The disputed question is that of interfering in the regulation of another country's internal concerns; the question whether a nation is justified in taking part, on either side, in the civil wars or party contests of another; and chiefly, whether it may justifiably aid the people of another country in struggling for liberty; or may impose on a country any particular government or institutions, either as being best for the country itself, or as necessary for the security of its neighbours.

Of these cases, that of a people in arms for liberty is the only one of any nicety, or which, theoretically at least, is likely to present conflicting moral considerations. The other cases which have been mentioned hardly admit of discussion. Assistance to the government of a country in keeping down the people, unhappily by far the most frequent case of foreign intervention, no one writing in a free country needs take the trouble of stigmatizing. A government which needs foreign support to enforce obedience from its own citizens, is one which ought not to exist; and the assistance given to it by foreigners is hardly ever anything but the sympathy of one despotism with another. A case requiring consideration is that of a protracted civil war, in which the contending parties are so equally balanced that there is no probability of a speedy issue; or if there is, the victorious side cannot hope to keep down the vanquished but by severities repugnant to humanity, and injurious to the permanent welfare of the country. In this exceptional case it seems now to be an admitted doctrine, that the neighbouring nations, or one powerful neighbour with the acquiescence of the rest, are warranted in demanding that the contest shall cease, and a reconciliation take place on equitable terms of compromise. Intervention of this description has been repeatedly practised during the present generation, with such general approval, that its legitimacy may be considered to have passed into a maxim of what is called international law. The interference of the European Powers between Greece and Turkey, and between Turkey and Egypt, were cases in point. That between Holland and Belgium was still more so. The intervention of England in Portugal, a few years ago, which is probably less remembered than the others, because it took effect without the employment of actual force, belongs to the same category. At the time, this interposition had the appearance of a bad and dishonest backing of the government against the people, being so timed as to hit the exact moment when the popular party had obtained a marked advantage, and seemed on the eve of overthrowing the government, or reducing it to terms. But if ever a political act which looked ill in the commencement could be justified by the event, this was; for, as the fact turned out, instead of giving ascendancy to a party, it proved a really healing measure; and the chiefs of the so-called rebellion were, within a few years, the honoured and successful ministers of the throne against which they had so lately fought.

With respect to the question, whether one country is justified in helping the people of another in a struggle against their government for free institutions, the answer will be different, according as the yoke which the people are attempting to throw off is that of a purely native government, or of foreigners; considering as one of foreigners, every government which maintains itself by foreign support. When the contest is only with native rulers, and with such native strength as those rulers can enlist in their defence, the answer I should give to the question of the legitimacy of intervention is, as a general rule, No. The reason is, that there can seldom be anything approaching to assurance that intervention, even if successful, would be for the good of the people themselves. The only test possessing any real value, of a people's having become fit for popular institutions, is that they, or a sufficient portion of them to prevail in the contest, are willing to brave labour and danger for their liberation. I know all that may be said. I know it may be urged that the virtues of freemen cannot be learnt in the school of slavery, and that if a people are not fit for freedom, to have any chance of becoming so they must first be free. And this would be conclusive, if the intervention recommended would really give them freedom. But the evil is, that if they have not sufficient love of liberty to be able to wrest it from merely domestic oppressors, the liberty which is bestowed on them by other hands than their own, will have nothing real, nothing permanent. No people ever was and remained free, but because it was determined to be so; because neither its rulers nor any other party in the nation could compel it to be otherwise. If a people – especially one whose freedom has not yet become prescriptive – does not value it sufficiently to fight for it, and maintain it against any force which can be mustered *within* the country, even by those who have the command of the public revenue, it is only a question in how few years or months that people will be enslaved. Either the government which it has given to itself, or some military leader or knot of conspirators who contrive to subvert the government, will speedily put an end to all popular institutions: unless indeed it suits their convenience better to leave them standing, and be content with reducing them to mere forms; for, unless the spirit of liberty is strong in a people, those who have the executive in their hands easily work any institutions to the purposes of despotism. There is no sure guarantee against this deplorable issue, even in a country which has achieved its own freedom; as may be seen in the present day by striking examples both in the Old and New Worlds: but when freedom has been achieved *for* them, they have little prospect indeed of escaping this fate. When a people has had the misfortune to be ruled by a government under which the feelings and the virtues needful for maintaining freedom could not develope themselves, it is during an arduous struggle to become free by their own efforts that these feelings and virtues have the best chance of springing up. Men become attached to that which they have long fought for and made sacrifices for; they learn to appreciate that on which their thoughts have been much engaged; and a contest in which many have been called on to devote themselves for their country, is a school in which they learn to value their country's interest above their own.

It can seldom, therefore – I will not go so far as to say never – be either judicious or right, in a country which has a free government, to assist, otherwise than by the moral support of its opinion, the endeavours of another to extort the same blessing from its native rulers. We must except, of course, any case in which such assistance is a measure of legitimate self-defence. If (a contingency by no means unlikely to occur) this country, on account of its freedom, which is a standing reproach to despotism everywhere, and an encouragement to throw it off, should find itself menaced with attack by a coalition of Continental despots, it ought to consider the popular party in every nation of the Continent as its natural ally: the Liberals should be to it, what the Protestants of Europe were to the Government of Queen Elizabeth. So, again, when a nation, in her own defence, has gone to war with a despot, and has had the rare good fortune not only to succeed in her resistance, but to hold the conditions of peace in her own hands, she is entitled to say that she will make no treaty, unless with some other ruler than the one whose existence as such may be a perpetual menace to her safety and freedom. These exceptions do but set in a clearer light the reasons of the rule; because they do not depend on any failure of those reasons, but on considerations paramount to them, and coming under a different principle.

But the case of a people struggling against a foreign yoke, or against a native tyranny upheld by foreign arms, illustrates the reasons for non-intervention in an opposite way; for in this case the reasons themselves do not exist. A people the most attached to freedom, the most capable of defending and of making a good use of free institutions, may be unable to contend successfully for them against the military strength of another nation much more powerful. To assist a people thus kept down, is not to disturb the balance of forces on which the permanent maintenance of freedom in a country depends, but to redress that balance when it is already unfairly and violently disturbed. The doctrine of non-intervention, to be a legitimate principle of morality, must be accepted by all governments. The despots must consent to be bound by it as well as the free States. Unless they do, the profession of it by free countries comes but to this miserable issue, that the wrong side may help the wrong, but the right must not help the right. Intervention to enforce non-intervention is always rightful, always moral, if not always prudent. Though it be a mistake to *give* freedom to a people who do not value the boon, it cannot but be right to insist that if they do value it, they shall not be hindered from the pursuit of it by foreign coercion. It might not have been right for England (even apart from the question of prudence) to have taken part with Hungary in its noble struggle against Austria; although the Austrian Government in Hungary was in some sense a foreign yoke. But when, the Hungarians having shown themselves likely to prevail in this struggle, the Russian despot interposed, and joining his force to that of Austria, delivered back the Hungarians, bound hand and foot, to their exasperated oppressors, it would have been an honourable and virtuous act on the part of England to have declared that this should not be, and that if Russia gave assistance to the wrong side, England would aid the right. It might not have been consistent with the regard which every nation is bound to pay to its own safety, for England to have taken up this position single-handed. But England and France together could have done it; and if they had, the Russian armed intervention would never have taken place, or would have been disastrous to Russia alone: while all that those Powers gained by not doing it, was that they had to fight Russia five years afterwards, under more difficult circumstances, and without Hungary for an ally. The first nation which, being powerful enough to make its voice effectual, has the spirit and courage to say that not a gun shall be fired in Europe by the soldiers of one Power against the revolted subjects of another, will be the idol of the friends of freedom throughout Europe. That declaration alone will ensure the almost immediate emancipation of every people which desires liberty sufficiently to be capable of maintaining it: and the nation which gives the word will soon find itself at the head of an alliance of free peoples, so strong as to defy the efforts of any number of confederated despots to bring it down. The prize is too glorious not to be snatched sooner or later by some free country; and the time may not be distant when England, if she does not take this heroic part because of its heroism, will be compelled to take it from consideration for her own safety.

HEINRICH VON TREITSCHKE

HEINRICH VON TREITSCHKE (1834–96) was the leading historian and political scientist of Imperial Germany in the late nineteenth century. An apologist for force and an ardent anti-Semite, he is the supreme exponent of "power politics" and (unlike Hegel) can reasonably be seen as a forerunner of German militarism and National Socialism in the twentieth century. The following extracts are taken from his *Politics*, which was translated in Britain in the middle of the First World War in order to elucidate the roots of German "frightfulness."

From *Politics*

International law and international intercourse

When we ask, does an international law exist at all? we are met by two extreme and contradictory conceptions, both alike untenable, of the international life of States. The first, the naturalistic, whose chief champion we already know to be Machiavelli, starts from the principle that the State is absolute power, and may do anything which serves its ends, consequently it can bind itself by no law in its relations with other States, which are determined by purely mechanical considerations of proportionate strength. This is an idea which can only be disproved by its own arguments. We must admit that the State is absolute physical power, but if it insists upon being that, and nothing else, unrestrained by conscience or reason, it will no longer be able to maintain itself in a position of security.

...

Taken without qualification, the doctrine of Power, as such, is quite empty of meaning, and unmoral as well, because it can find no justification within itself.

It is opposed by another, as false as itself, the moralizing doctrine of Liberal theorists. Here we find the State regarded as if it were a good little boy, who should be washed, and brushed, and sent to school, who should have his ears pulled to keep him obedient; he, on his side, is expected to be grateful and good, and God knows how much else.

...

We must recognize, then, that these extreme views are both of them untenable, but we need not despair of establishing a doctrine of international law which is workable, because based upon the facts of history. In doing so it is above all important not to make greater demands upon human nature than its frailty can satisfy. The idealist who loses sight of this principle may all too easily become a disappointed enthusiast. One may be sure that any one who declaims that brute force is the only arbiter in the rivalries of nations is one of the sentimentalists undeceived who once smoked the Pipe of Peace, and who now, having seen that his dreams cannot be realized in this world, has rushed to the other extreme, and sees a crude cynicism in everything. It is true that all the really great political thinkers do cherish a cynical contempt for mankind in general, and with justice, provided it is not carried too far. Those who do not ask too much of human nature are the most successful in calling forth the really great gifts which it possesses admidst all its bestiality and liability to err. Therefore we must start from the historical standpoint, and take the State as it really is; physical power indeed, but also an institution designed to co-operate in the education of the human race. As physical power, its natural inclination will be to seize as many of the necessaries of life as it thinks useful to itself; it is acquisitive by nature. Every State, however, will of its own accord pay a certain respect to the neighbouring Powers. A more definite feeling of law will be evolved by time out of the dictates of reason and a mutual recognition of personal advantage. Every State will realize that it is an integral part of the community of other States in which it finds itself placed, and that it must live with them on some kind of terms, bad or good, as the case may be. These reflections will arise from very real considerations of reciprocity, and not from love to mankind.

The formal side of international law, dealing with such matters as the inviolability of the person of Ambassadors, and the ceremonial therewith connected, was fixed comparatively early, and in modern Europe diplomatic rights are absolutely settled. It is safe to say that this department of the law of nations is much less often infringed than the internal legal ordinances of the average State. Nevertheless the existence of international law must always be precarious, and it cannot cease to be a *lex imperfecta*, because no power higher than the States themselves can be called upon to arbitrate. Everything has to depend upon a mutual give-and-take, and, since the supreme compelling authority is lacking, the co-operation of science, and above all, the force of public opinion, will have an important influence. Savigny declared that international law was no *strictum jus*, but continually in process of development. But this is a long way from asserting the impotence of the law of nations, for changeful as it is, its influence is palpable, and we can follow its consequences step by step at the present day. There is no doubt that the development of modern international law has been quite particularly modified by Christianity, and the cosmopolitanism, in the noble sense of the word, which Christianity has introduced, and which goes beyond and above the State. It was therefore quite reasonable and logical to exclude the Porte, for many hundreds of years, from the scope of European international law. The government of the Sultan had no claim to a full share in its benefits so long as the Porte was dominated by a Mohammedan civilization. Only in later times, when Christianity had gained strength enough in the Balkan Peninsula to drive Mohammedanism somewhat into the background, was Turkey included in the international negotiations of Europe.

History shows us how great States spring to life from the ashes of their smaller brethren. These great States finally attain to a measure of strength which enables them to stand upon their own feet and to become sufficient for themselves. When they have reached this point they are anxious to secure peace, for the safety of their own existence and the civilization of which they are the guardians. Thus an organized comity of nations, or so-called system of States, arises out of the mutual guarantee of law. This necessarily presupposes the existence of at least an approximate balance of power between the States. We have seen how very mechanical this idea became at one time in its application to European polities, but nevertheless it contains a kernel of truth. We cannot think of it as a *trutina gentium* with its scales exactly suspended, but any organized system of States must assume that no one State is so powerful as to be able to permit itself any license without danger to itself. Here the superiority of Europe to the unripe political world of America at once becomes apparent. Nothing obliges the Union to place any restraint upon its actions, and the small South American Republics have only been spared a direct interference with their affairs because the connexion between them and their greater neighbour is still slight.

Gortschakoff was perfectly right when he said that the last International Congress would promote the interests neither of the nations which always fear attack, nor of those unduly powerful countries which believe themselves strong enough to take the offensive The observation hit the mark, as may be proved by an actual example. Countries like Belgium and Holland, which, to the great detriment of that science, have unfortunately so long been the home of international jurisprudence, adopted a sentimental view of it, because they lived in constant fear of aggression. In the name of humanity, demands were made upon the victor which were unnatural, and unreasonable, and irreconcilable with the power of the State. The Peace Treaties of Nymegen and Ryswyk both show how Holland was regarded in the seventeenth century as the arena of *la haute politique*. Switzerland held the same position later, and few persons nowadays reflect how ludicrous it is for Belgium to look upon herself as the chosen centre for the science of international law. As it is certain that all such law must be grounded upon practice, so it is equally certain that a State whose position is abnormal will also be the occasion for an abnormal misconstruction of the principles which should govern it. Belgium is a neutral State, therefore incomplete by its very nature; how is it possible to expect a sound and healthy law of nations to proceed from such a source? I must ask you all to keep this in mind when in time to come you are confronted with the voluminous Belgian literature on this subject. There is, on the other hand, a State in our midst to-day which believes itself to be always in the position of the assailant, and which is consequently the fountain-head of barbarism in international law. It is the fault of England, and of England only, that in time of war the maritime law of nations continues on the level of privileged piracy. Thus we see that, between nations, all law is grounded upon mutual give-and-take, and that it is useless to hold up the phrases and doctrines of a vaguely general humanity for the edification of the countries concerned. In this matter theory must be rooted in practice, and practice presupposes a real reciprocity, or, in other words, a real balance of power.

In order to make no mistake as to the real meaning of international law, we must always remember that it must not run counter to the nature of the State. No State can reasonably be asked to adopt a course which would lead it to destroy itself. Likewise every State in the comity of nations must retain the attributes of sovereignty whose defence is its highest duty even in its international relations. We find the principles of international law most secure in that department of it which does not trench upon questions of sovereignty; that is in the domain of etiquette and of international civil law.

In times of peace these agreements are seldom encroached upon, or if they are, the offence is expiated at once. Any insult offered, even if only outwardly, to the honour of a State, casts doubt upon the nature of the State. We mistake the moral laws of politics if we reproach any State with having an over-sensitive sense of honour, for this instinct must be highly developed in each one of them if it is to be true to its own essence. The State is no violet, to bloom unseen; its power should stand proudly, for all the world to see, and it cannot allow even the symbols of it to be contested. If the flag is insulted, the State must claim reparation; should this not be forthcoming, war must follow, however small the occasion may seem; for the State has never any choice but to maintain the respect in which it is held among its fellows.

From this it follows that all the restraints to which States bind themselves by treaty are voluntary, and that all treaties are concluded on the tacit understanding *rebus sic stantibus*. No State ever has, or ever will exist, which is willing to hold to all eternity to the agreements which it signs. No State will ever be in a position to pledge its whole hereafter to a treaty, which cannot fail to be a limitation of its sovereignty; it always intends that the contract shall eventually be annulled, and shall only apply so long as the present circumstances are not totally altered. This principle is often called inhumane, but its logical conclusion shows it to be the contrary. Only if the State is aware that all its treaties only apply conditionally will it go to work prudently in the making of them. History is not meant to be looked at from the point of view of a judge hearing a civil suit.

...

Politics must never discount the free moral forces in the national life. No State in the world may renounce the "I" in its sovereignty. If conditions are imposed upon it which impinge upon this, and which it is unable to prevent, then "the breach is more honoured than the observance." It is one of the fine things about history that we see nations more easily consoled for their material losses than for injuries to their honour.

...

When a State recognizes that existing treaties no longer express the actual political conditions, and when it cannot persuade the other Powers to give way by peaceful negotiation, the moment has come when the nations proceed to the ordeal by battle. A State thus situated is conscious when it declares war that it is performing an inevitable duty. The combatant countries are moved by no incentives of personal greed, but they feel that the real position of power is not expressed by existing treaties and that they must be determined afresh by the judgment of the nations, since no peaceful agreement can be reached. The righteousness of war depends simply and solely upon the consciousness of a moral necessity. War is justified because the great national personalities can suffer no compelling force superior to themselves, and because history must always be in constant flux; war therefore must be taken as part of the divinely appointed order. Of course it is possible for a Government to be mistaken about the necessity which drives them to declare it; "War creates no right which was not already existing," as Niebuhr truly said, and, for this very reason, isolated deeds of violence are justified by their successful accomplishment, witness the achievement of German and Italian unity. On the other hand, since not every war is caused by an inward necessity, the historian must keep his vision clear, and remember that the life of States is counted in centuries. The proud saying of the defeated Piedmontese, "We are beginning again," will always have its place in the chronicles of noble nations.

No Courts of Arbitration will ever succeed in banishing war from the world. It is absolutely impossible for the other members of the group of nations to take an impartial view of any questions vitally affecting one of their number. Parties there must be, if only because the nations are bound together, or driven apart by living interests of the most various kinds. What European country could have taken a totally unbiassed attitude towards the question of Alsace and Lorraine, supposing that Germany had been foolish enough to submit it to an Arbitration Court? The wildest imagination cannot picture a detached Tribunal in this instance. Here we have the explanation of the well-known fact, that international Congresses are quite capable of finding legal formulae for the results of a war, but that they can never avert the outbreak of it. A foreign State can only pronounce impartial judgment on matters of third-rate importance.

We have already seen that war is both justifiable and moral, and that the ideal of perpetual peace is not only impossible but immoral as well. It is unworthy of man's reason to regard the impracticable as feasible, but a life of pure intellect is all too often enervating to the reasoning faculty. War cannot vanish from the earth as long as human sins and passions remain what they are. It is delightful to observe how the feeling of patriotism breaks involuntarily through the cosmopolitan phrases even of the apostles of perpetual peace. The prophet Joel prayed that before its day should dawn Israel might call all the heathen to a bloody reckoning in the valley of Jehoshaphat, and Victor Hugo likewise demanded that the Germans should get their drubbing first. Yet again we must repeat – the arbitrament of force is the logical outcome of the nature of the State. The mere fact of the existence of many States involves the necessity of war. The dream of eternal peace – said Frederick the Great – is a phantom, which each man rejects when the call of war rings in his own ears. It is impossible to imagine – he went on to say – any balance of power which can last.

War, however, is the very sphere in which we can most clearly trace the triumph of human reason. All noble nations have felt that the physical forces which war unchains require to be regulated, and thus an international military law has been developed, based upon mutual interests. This department of international jurisprudence, which fools dismiss as unworthy of a civilized people, is where the science has achieved the most; in modern days we rarely see crude violations of the laws of war. There is nothing in international law more beautiful, or showing more unmistakably the continual progress of mankind, than a whole series of principles, grounded only upon *universalis consensus* and yet as firmly established as those of the Common Law of any given country. It is evident that the law of nations must always lag a few steps behind the law of the individual States, for certain principles of civilization and law must first be developed at home before they can be put in practice in intercourse abroad. Thus it was impossible to have international legislation against slavery until respect for the individual had become as universal as our century has made it. In the course of centuries the instinct for justice between countries has become so strong, that at any rate the formal side of international law may be looked upon as quite secured.

...

We will now examine a few of the fundamental principles which have been legally defined primarily by the peaceful intercourse of nations. Every people without exception must nowadays be allowed to pursue uninterruptedly the trade and commerce, the arts and sciences, which are such a bond between different countries. The races of antiquity sometimes forbade other nations to practise some particular industry, whose secrets they looked upon as their own private possession. Even in the time of the later Roman Empire it was forbidden to instruct the barbarians in the art of shipbuilding, and similar monopolies were still practically enforced at the date of the Hanseatic League. In modern days this could no longer happen. No State may deny free competition in trade to its fellows, and this principle is guarded by a system of treaties.

In ancient times, moreover, almost every nation laid claim to some sort of monopoly with regard to the navigation of a sea. In later days it was still held that particular seas, which were not exactly the ocean itself, belonged to certain States, as the Adriatic to the Venetian Republic, the Ligurian Sea to Venice, the Gulf of Bothnia to Sweden, and so forth. Now the sea is only the property of the countries upon its shores as far as their military domination of it extends, that is, within cannon range from the shore, and this limit has been altered again quite recently by the advance of technical science. All such questions are finally decided, however, by the realities of power; if a State is in a position to dominate any sea, no amount of well-meant theorizing will make that sea free. The Caspian is nominally controlled by two States which border it, Russia and Persia, but the power of the former is such that we may call the Caspian a Russian Sea. If a Government were established in Constantinople which was really able to shut the Bosphorus against every Navy, it could mock at all the declamations which might be hurled against it. For the rest, the ocean is free to every ship sailing under legitimate colours. The policing of the high seas is provided by the Navies of every country, for every ship of war has the right to stop a merchant vessel and inspect her papers. This is the result of an endlessly long and difficult process of development, but all the Powers are now agreed that an occasional inconvenience to their merchantmen is a lesser evil than sea-piracy.

All international rights are guaranteed by treaties between States. It is clear that these must differ in many ways from the contracts of civil law.

The first distinction is that they can only be concluded upon a basis of faith and loyalty, as there is no judge who can enforce their observance. The Athenians were guided by a true instinct when they contracted their agreements only for a limited time. Christian nations think otherwise, and make their treaties for eternity, but, as we have seen, they are made on the understanding that they are only to endure while the conditions of power between the contracting parties are not totally altered. The more this is insisted upon, and the more soberly each State reflects upon it, the more secure will their treaties be.

There are, furthermore, such things as compulsory treaties. No agreement made by sovereign States in time of peace can ever be so described – little Switzerland, for instance, is perfectly at liberty to make or to refuse a peaceful treaty with ourselves – but, on the other hand, every peace imposed by the victor on the vanquished must be compulsory. Here again we are confronted with the question of who can be arbiter endowed with legal authority to pronounce whether a treaty is freely made.

...

The process of time has connected a reciprocal support in the prosecution of criminals with the mutual defence of civil law, and with it a whole series of the most difficult problems have come into being. It is easy enough to state the theory that the whole human race is concerned in prosecuting crime, and among noble nations this principle presents no difficulties until we come to the definition of what crime is. The distinction between ordinary and political crime at once becomes of primary importance. Every State must make the prosecution of persons accused of high treason by another Government dependant upon its own interests. A state of war may be latent between two countries who are outwardly friendly, as is the case with France and Germany at the present time. Again, it may often happen that a man whom the law of his own country regards as a political traitor may be the welcome guest of another nation, and it would be unreasonable to require that they should deliver him up. Agreements can be made in respect of the extradition of common offenders, though no State will engage itself to refuse its protection to political criminals, but will always reserve the right of judgment for each case. This applies to political offences in general, although there are certain bomb-throwing Anarchists pure and simple about whom a mutual arrangement might be possible.

The exact degree of ordinary crime which involves extradition can, of course, only be settled by positive treaties; but it should in any case be limited to really serious offences. The great differences of legal procedure in the various countries make it imperatively necessary to try offenders as much as possible by their own laws, and experience has shown that this expansion of the powers of courts, as far as can be managed, has had good results.

Out of the joint maintenance of law has sprung an ordered comity of nations, or system of States, which has also received its settled outward forms. The disputes over etiquette in the seventeenth century which seem so ludicrous to us now had the right idea at the back of them in spite of their lack of good taste. Even to-day a difference exists between royal majesty and petty princes, and none the less because unwritten, between the Great Powers and second- or third-rate States. A State may be defined as a Great Power if its total destruction would require a coalition of other States to accomplish. The preponderance of Great Powers is felt on all hands to-day, yet it has been the very means of ensuring a certain security in international traffic. The Congress of Aix-la-Chapelle in 1818 set diplomatic relations on so firm a footing that all civilized countries now differentiate exactly between the various classes of diplomats. Another result of the undue preponderance of the leading European Powers in modern history has been to exclude the smaller States from taking a part in Congresses unless they are directly concerned in a disputed point. If, however, one of these small countries is consulted, its opinion is given the same weight as that of one of the Great Powers. Moreover, a Congress is not ruled by a majority, but by the *liberum veto* of natural Law. I have spoken already about the unreasonableness of deciding by the vote of a majority when the question at issue is not one of power in which physical strength supports the decision by the many against the few. It is not logical to proceed on this basis in a Congress which is not waging war, but is formulating the results of war, and of whom unanimity must consequently be demanded.

It is not possible to lay down any fixed principles for international policy, for, as we have seen, the unconditional doctrine of intervention is as false as its antithesis. Every State may be placed in a position where the party strifes of another country are a menace to its own freedom. Thus we may find that a cosmopolitan party at the helm of a neighbouring State may lead to consequences so important for ourselves that we are bound for our own sake to interfere. Such intervention is always fraught with danger, for the worship of national independence has waxed so strong in our own day that any meddling with it will produce a strong reaction in other countries beyond the one directly concerned. Stern experience has taught modern States to hold themselves aloof as much as possible from the private affairs of their neighbours. No dogmas can decide these problems, but when its own safety is at stake a State should, and will, take action.

When a war is actually in progress its guiding political idea is to bring about new conditions of international law which will express the real relative strength of the contending parties and be recognized by both of them. It is, therefore, perfectly equitable to wage war in the most effective manner possible, so that its goal of peace may be reached as quickly as may be. For this reason the blow must be aimed at the enemy's heart, and the use of the most formidable weapons is absolutely justifiable, provided that they do not inflict needless suffering on the wounded. Philanthropists may declaim as much as they like against explosive shells fired into the powder magazines of wooden battle-ships, but still facts remain unchanged. States in conclave have decided what weapons are to be forbidden; the use of explosive bullets for small arms was prohibited at the instance of Russia. It is permissible to take advantage of all the enemy's weak points, and a State may turn treason and mutiny within its enemy's borders to serve its own ends. Nothing but the rapid march of events prevented us in Prussia from making a compact with Hungary in 1866.

It is equally impossible to deny to a belligerent State the right of employing all its troops in the field, whether they be savages or civilized men. It is important to take an unbiassed view of ourselves in this question, in order to guard against prejudice in respect of other nations. The Germans raised a fearful outcry against the French for letting loose the Turcos against a civilized nation in the last war. It was a natural accusation in the passion of the moment, but our calmer judgment can find no violation of international law in what was done. The principle stands that a belligerent State may, and must, throw all its troops and all its physical resources into the struggle. Where is it possible to draw the line? Which of the charming races which make up its Empire is Russia to withhold from the field? A State is obliged to make the fullest use of all its material strength, but it must do so in accordance with the honourable usages which have been settled by the long experience of war. Yet with all this, the employment of the Turcos places the claim of France to be the leader of civilization in a peculiar light. Thus a whole series of complaints arise because demands are made upon a State which it cannot possibly satisfy. In the national wars of the present day every honest subject is a spy, and therefore the banishment of 80,000 Germans from France in 1870 was not in itself a violation of the law, but was only indefensible because it was carried out with a certain brutality.

There is one rule of humanity in war which is theoretically of universal application, although it is only practically recognized in land campaigns; namely, that it is States who are fighting, and not their individual citizens. Certain definite signs there must be, therefore, to distinguish those persons who are entitled to fight by authority of the State, and who are to be treated as soldiers. It is an ugly gap in international law that no universal agreement has as yet been reached on this point, although it is the foundation of all humanity in war. A solider must feel that he has no foe but the soldiers of the enemy, and that he need not fear that the peasant who has met him in peaceful fashion will be shooting at him half an hour later from behind a bush. The behaviour of soldiery in an enemy's country is sure to be unfeeling and cruel if they do not know who they should treat as soldiers like themselves, and who as highway robbers. No one can be recognized as a soldier unless he has taken the oath of allegiance, stands under the Articles of War, and wears some kind of badge which need not be exactly a full uniform. It goes without saying that the irregular levies who hover round the enemy, and do not stand under the Articles of War, should be treated with unrelenting severity. It is urgently necessary that an international agreement should be come to over the forms which make an armed person a real member of a lawful army. The question was discussed in Brussels in 1874, when the difference of interests at once became apparent. Small States like Switzerland had no desire to bind themselves by any obligations.

···

No one contests the right of every State not only to make war, but to declare itself neutral in the wars of others, in so far as material conditions allow. It is mere boasting when a State declares a neutrality which it is not in a position to uphold, for neutrality needs defence as much as does participation with one of the belligerents. The neutral State must disarm every solider who crosses its frontier, and should it fail to do so the belligerents are justified under some circumstances in refusing to recognize its neutrality, even if it has only permitted the armed enemy to enter a single one of its villages.

Unhappily the laws of war are still very differently interpreted on land and on the seas, and it is here that the mischievous influence of English power over civilization and universal law cannot fail to strike any one who chooses to see it. The melancholy saying of Schiller still holds good:

> Auf den Wellen ist alles Welle,
> Auf dem Meer ist kein Eigentum.

> (There is nothing stable among the waves,
> Where no man calls anything his own.)

Deeply mortifying as this is to our pride, it is true, because even to-day there is no balance of power at sea, and for this we have no one to blame but England. Her superiority is so immeasurable that she can do whatever she pleases. A balance of naval power must be brought to pass before the ideals of humanity and international law can hope to be realized upon the seas. The modern infatuation of public opinion is often astonishing; again and again the countries are belauded which are following false paths; again and again the sentimentalities of Belgian teachers of international law and the barbarisms of the English maritime code are held up to admiration. Every other State would be ready, under certain conditions, to respect merchant shipping in time of war, but England alone holds by the principle that at sea there is no distinction to be made between the property of the State and the property of the individual. So long as one State takes its stand upon this all the others must imitate its barbarism. Of course maritime conditions cannot be quite the same as those on land, because there are many commodities which serve the purposes of war. Therefore freedom for private property cannot be so widely extended at sea, but this is no reason why ocean warfare should to all eternity remain ocean piracy, or why belligerents should be authorized to despoil one another of all merchandise without distinctions made.

···

From whatever angle we view political science we find that its proper function lies in dealing with that only true humanity which is rooted in the actual facts of history, and that the dreams of fancy are beyond its scope. The destinies of States are accomplished by processes of attraction and repulsion whose final consummation is hidden from mortal eyes, and whose tendencies can only be dimly guessed at. There is no need for us to become critics of history, for the real point is to understand how the Divine plan has unfolded itself little by little in all the variety of actual existence. A practical politician is great if he can read the signs of the times, and foresee more or less the trend of history at a given moment. No quality beseems him better than modesty. He must not stray with blind uncertainty among the many complex circumstances which he has to handle, but he must concentrate upon the attainable and keep his goal clearly before him. It is my hope that you may have learned from these lectures how many factors go to the making of history and how carefully considered all our political judgments should therefore be. If what I have said has taught you this modesty of true science, I shall be well content.

BERNARD BOSANQUET

B ERNARD BOSANQUET (1848–1923), English Idealist (i.e. Hegelian) philosopher, highly influential, along with his colleagues T. H. Green and F. H. Bradley, in the last quarter of the nineteenth and first quarter of the twentieth century, author of *The Philosophical Theory of the State* (1899), the most important work of Hegelian political philosophy published in English. With the outbreak of war in 1914, German philosophy came to be suspect in England, with Hegelianism seen as supportive of German militarism. Bosanquet's "Patriotism in the perfect state" (printed below) offers another point of view; in the process, Bosanquet provides one of the best brief introductions to Hegelian political philosophy available.

"Patriotism in the perfect state"

The quality of patriotism is determined by what we desire for our country, as the quality of friendship is determined by what we desire for our friend. And this question – the question what it is that we desire for our country – is of supreme moment to-day, because in the answer given to it, whether by practice or in principle, are rooted the permanent underlying conditions of war and peace.

Assuming then that what is true of principles is true of the corresponding practice, whether or no the actors understand what they are doing, I will ask you to consider with me three typical ideas expressive of what men desire for their country, each of them bearing a distinctive relation to the causes and customs of war, and to the permanent basis of peace.

And in this consideration I hope that we shall also be elucidating an interesting question in the history of recent thought. We shall see how the splendid political philosophy of Germany a hundred years ago has passed on the one hand into her intoxication of to-day, while on the other hand, elsewhere, in face of a more liberal experience, it has found a decisive completion in a human and democratic sense. The three conceptions to which I refer have very much in common, and a great part of the interest of our inquiry, and also perhaps a little practical value which it might possess, depends on noticing very precisely the points at which distinctions become blurred, and the ideas, mostly by mere omission, are apt to slide into one another.

Let us make a beginning, then, with Hegel's political thought, the German thought of a hundred years ago. At that time the idea of a man's country, as focussed in the state, was a glorious vision, stimulated largely by Greek conceptions and drawing something from English constitutional experience; while in the existing reality of the Prussian system there was little to catch the eye, and little power, therefore, to narrow the outlook.

Now the essential point for us here to grasp firmly, if we wish to enter into the truth of the matter and its adjacent fallacies, is that Hegel means by the state, not the machine of government, but all that fulfils, in the actual community, the individual's mind and will. The individual is supposed to see in it the form of life, and more than that, the particular form of sentiment and volition, which his nation has so far worked out for itself, and in which he, the private person, finds the substance of his own mind, and what unites him with others. It includes, of course, the ethical tradition of the society, with the observances and institutions in which it is embodied and preserved; and more especially it is identified with the general will as expressed in the laws and the political constitution. The state, in short, is the ark in which the whole treasure of the individual citizen's head and heart is preserved and guarded within a world which may be disorderly and hostile.

One may naturally ask, where then does humanity come in, and how recognize the claims of other nations and persons? This is exceedingly important, but not difficult. Your country is held to express the whole form of life for which you stand, and therefore, within that, your moral attitude to humanity and the world in general. If you are an Englishman, you probably object to slavery. But that attitude is not a thing of chance, in which you stand outside your age and country. It is part of the outlook at which, on the whole, England had at a certain time arrived, and which came to individual Englishmen through their participation in the national mind. Here is a point at which a slide into fallacy is too possible. That moral view of the world which you and your state stand up for is one thing. A moral view which considers only your own and your state's immediate interests is quite another thing; but it is very easy to confuse the two, both in practice and in controversy.

We have said enough to indicate the value which, according to such ideas, the private individual, in theory or by practice, recognizes in his state. Looked at in this way, our country, the state, is simply all we have. Innumerable claims may come to us from outside, but they all come through it and subject to it; just as they all come to us through our own feelings and our own beliefs. Without the state we are nothing and nobody. It is for us the vehicle of the value of the world. It stands for our contribution to the general sum of what humanity has achieved and what makes any life worth living.

So far what we desire for our country, our view of its mission, is to achieve the very best we all are capable of becoming. But there is another side to this same set of ideas.

Obviously, to fulfil this, its necessary mission, the state needs above all things to be *strong*. Men who had lived through Napoleonic times could have no doubt about that. Who indeed was to help a state if it could not help itself? War, then, was the inevitable arbiter, and by the test of war the state must stand or fall. Hegel is primarily appealing to facts when he says that outside the several communities there is no general will. As yet there could not be; for the general will *is* the will of a community, backed by its whole body, mind, and sentiment. Thus, no one can possibly dictate into what demands separate states shall throw their ultimate honour and self-assertion; and if in these they conflict there is no ultimate solution but war. On one side, we have seen, the state is akin to art, philosophy, and religion; it is mind in a concentrated form. But between it and these other shapes of mind there is the one fundamental distinction. The state is mind 'in the world'. It is not only our treasure, but it is the ark which carries our treasure. 'In the world' right can only prevail through might. Strength in war is therefore the first condition of the state's fulfilment of its function; and being the first condition, and a condition peculiar to the state among the forms of mind, it is too easily taken as the aim and whole upshot of the state. This again, as we shall see, is a point at which one idea is apt to slide into another.

Therefore, since as yet there can be, outside and above the several states, no general will with a common heart and force, no 'praetor' – judge representing power – but only at best an 'arbitrator,' all international laws, treaties, and usages are, at bottom, only agreements of a number of particular wills, the wills of absolute independent bodies. *So far* nations are to one another, as older writers had said, in a state of nature, like the supposed (but quite imaginary) individuals before Society was invented. Hegel does not say that there cannot be, and are not, humane usages, conventions, rules, and treaties. The whole of international law rests on the principle that treaties are to be observed. But behind all this there is the sheer fact of the separate individual powers, each absolute in its limited area; so that, at bottom, the whole fabric of international rules and customs is just an agreement of separate wills, and not an expression of a single general will. Ultimately, or fundamentally, each of these separate wills is and must be determined by its own conception of its own welfare. This is the difficulty I think in the way of leagues and federations in favour of peace as suggested by Kant and by Norman Angell. They are purely *de facto*. They do not rest upon the spirit of a solid community; and every powerful league tends *ipso facto* to raise up a powerful counterleague against it, with grave risk of war.

It follows from this that there is a fundamental distinction between the moral position of the private individual who works out the detail of his duty on the basis of recognized rights within a previously ordered and organized society, and that of the state, which has 'in the world' to provide and sustain, at all hazards, the organized society within which the individual is to live. The tasks of morals and of international politics are different in principle, though the end to which they co-operate is the same. The immediate task of morals is to live a life, that of international politics is to provide a world within which life can be lived.

The same distinction must be pushed beyond the difference of the tasks into the difference of their possibility. For the private individual it is fairly easy, in the main, at least to *know* what he should do, and what he should not. He lives within a scheme of recognized rights and obligations; and, starting from his legal position and accepted duties, he can tell whether he is behaving selfishly or generously, rudely or courteously, kindly or unkindly. His lawyer will tell him his legal rights; and it is for him to insist upon them or to surrender them. But in principle the state has no such guide. It is not living out an ordered life, within a recognized scheme. It cannot tell whether it is being less than just, or merely just, or kind and generous. For it every case is under altering conditions and new, and it is sole judge in its own cause. A state may think that it is behaving with superhuman generosity, while its antagonist may think it is behaving like a bandit. There is no complete or detailed scheme and scale of conduct and sentiment to operate as a norm of feeling and judgement. Of course this language may seem exaggerated in face of the well-established usages of international law, and the existence of treaties. But the difference we have mentioned affects them all. *Ultimately*, to reiterate that terrible adverb, which governs the whole argument, it is as we say. A private person has the letter and spirit of his moral world to live up to, and on the main lines and choices of life there is a wealth of recognized obligations which, I do not say tell him what to do, but certainly warn him what he is doing. A state is sailing a sea but slightly charted, and what marks the charts do furnish are mostly recent and depend on a revocable consent. As a supreme power, it has a responsibility for every choice, of which no precedents nor external recommendations can divest it. At every step it is making a new world.

Thus, in such an idea of patriotism as we have been describing, the attitude to war is favourable on the whole. There is, it suggests, an element in the world which is transitory and accidental, the element of temporal life and temporal goods. It is natural and necessary that accident should prey upon the accidental, and that contingent values should thus be distinguished from substantial. War is the fiery test of reality, and the maker of nations. 'In the world' accident is necessary and has its good. Here is a striking passage; not a complete survey of the question, but, I think, requiring consideration, and showing the conviction embodied in the attitude we have tried to portray:

Of course, war brings insecurity of possessions, but this actual insecurity is only a necessary movement. We hear from the pulpit so much of the uncertainty, vanity, and fickleness of temporal things; but every one thinks as he hears it, however touching may be the eloquence, "*I* shall manage to keep what is mine." But now if this uncertainty confronts them in grim earnest in the shape of hussars with naked sabres, then the touching spirit of edification, in the face of the very thing it foretold, betakes itself to hurling curses at the victors. But in spite of all, wars take place when the occasion demands it; the crops grow again; and babble is mute before the grim iterations of history.[1]

Before leaving these ideas of a hundred years ago, it is worth while to note the general temper of intellectual Germany in that great age. It was full, no doubt, of self-assertion, not unbecoming to a nation conscious of immense capacities. But it was sympathetic and receptive. No men ever worked harder to educate themselves in the widest experience of humanity than Goethe and his contemporaries. Their feeling is fairly expressed in some verses addressed by Schiller to Goethe, on the exceptional occasion of a play by Voltaire being performed at the Weimar theatre. We see in them the delicate balance of self-assertion and receptivity. Here is a rough version:

> To home-born art this stage is consecrated,
> No more are stranger idols worshipped here;
> The laurel we display with heart elated
> On *our* poetic mount its growth did rear;
> To art's high fane, himself initiated,
> Boldly the German genius has drawn near;
> And on the track of Briton and of Greek
> Has set his face a purer fame to seek.

The Briton and the Greek are Shakespeare and Aristotle, or perhaps the Greek Tragedians. And the same types of experience, English and Hellenic, were at work in the conception of patriotism we have portrayed. It is not, Hegel says, emphatically, the mere occasional readiness for extreme sacrifices. It is the recognition of the community as our substance throughout all the detailed functions of life. We shall further see the supreme value of this apparently prosaic view.

Now we need not add many words in explaining how this attitude of the great time has degenerated into the creed of violence and self-interest of which we hear to-day. It is essentially the passage of a large and many-sided philosophical doctrine into the hands of ignorant and biased amateurs, soldiers, historians, politicians. Well, all philosophy is dangerous, for it blinks no side of the truth, and any one of its statements, taken by itself and with bias, may act as a mighty strong wine or as a high explosive.

---

1   Hegel, *Philosophy of Right*, s. 324.

It is enough to recall the two points in the great German philosophy at which we noted how readily one idea slides into another. One is where it says that a state is and can be determined only by its own good. We tried to explain that the thing is a truism. Its good is the form of life and feeling which it has made and chosen, and includes its relations to others. But if for good (Wohl) you read exclusive self-interest, the thing is done. A great idea slides before your eyes into the meanest of worldly maxims. So with the other point. As guardian of a treasure, the state must be strong in war. But it is different when you say that its strength in war sets it free to sully at its will the treasure it has to guard.

To make these two transitions is the same thing as to drop out from the conception of patriotism all that we said about the positive values of which the state is guardian. In a huge country, intoxicated with its new material prosperity, and even in the realm of intellect so busy with myriad specialities as to be deafened to voices from without by the clamour of its own contending schools, such a transition seems almost natural.

But yet, when this transition is made, the public conscience, the compass of the difficult voyage, is gone. Everything depended on its recognition of the supreme values within its own good; and the change leaves them as mere names for whatever can be effected by force. And now, all the *de facto* truths which the great philosophy conceded with regard to international conventions return upon us with crushing force. You can find parallels in Hegel, as we saw, for much of the language, e.g., of the *Book of War*, about mere usages and conventions. The only difference is that the national conscience – which makes Hegel say, for instance, that Europe is in actual humane behaviour a single family – the national conscience is now deleted from the theory.

So by mere omission and exaggeration, this great idea of patriotism is totally perverted, and we are brought to the point that what a man desires for his country is military supremacy to be used without scruple in the promotion of its exclusive interest.

This was the second of the three attitudes or ideas of patriotism which we meant to consider. We have observed how it might arise by a heated and narrowed conception of the first, under the intoxication of new achievements, leading to new temptations and ambitions.

But now, recurring for a moment to the philosophy of the great time, let us consider a third expression of patriotism, to which it has given rise in a wholly different atmosphere.

It was a conviction, held in common by the two forms of patriotism we have been considering, that war is a necessary accident, arising out of the very nature of the state as a separate sovereign power exposed to accident, and therefore, something to which a state is liable because and in as far as it is what a state should be. Now a great deal in this idea may seem to us a truism.

States *are* particular independent bodies, themselves sole ultimate judges of their differences and their honour. No independent state (as Pericles said) *will* brook an order from another state; if it does, its independence is gone. And on such a point there can be no arbitration. War *is* the ultimate arbiter, and therefore springs from this very nature of states; and it *does* behove states to be strong. And for war, as for all other evils and accidents, there *is* a good deal to be said. Each of them by itself is clearly a thing to be fought against, but without any of them at all – well, life would very soon generate new ones.

But a further question has been raised, and seems worth pursuing. Is not a wrong done somewhere, when lives are sacrificed in war? Certainly it is not murder, for it is not unlawful killing; but again, it is not merely like an earthquake. It comes from human conduct somewhere and somewhen. We may not be able to apportion the guilt of it, but it might be worth inquiry whether the conduct could not be changed. Perhaps our analysis has hitherto not gone far enough. *After* differences have broken out between independent sovereign states all we have said holds good – the separate wills of separate bodies, the mere outward agreements with no deep-seated impartial will and power behind them, the usages and rules at the mercy of the individual conscience of states, which in some cases appears to be an absent factor.

Well, but cannot we go further back? *Is* it in the nature of states that differences should constantly be arising between them? The state is there to be the condition of organized good life for the inhabitants of a certain territory. Is it a property of this function that different states should be continually liable to be at variance? Is tendency to war really a feature of states in respect of what they are as states? Or is it not rather perhaps a feature of them in so far as they fail to be states? To organize good life in a certain territory seems to have nothing in it prima facie which should necessitate variance between the bodies charged with the task in one place and in another.

When, in the light of this question, we look closer at the facts, what stares us in the face is that the cause of external conflict as a rule is not internal organization, but internal disorganization. The quarrelsome man is not well organized in his mind; he is ill organized – certainly in mind, probably in body. Plato indeed laid his finger on the place, though you might criticize his explanation in some particulars. The origin of war, he says, is when states become internally diseased; the more they are distracted within, the more they come into conflict without.

Let us think further of this. People who are satisfied do not want to make war; and in a well-organized community people are satisfied. War must arise from dissatisfied elements in a community; people who have not got what they want within (or have it but are afraid of losing it) and so look for profit or for security in adventures without. War belongs to a state, then, ultimately, not in so far as it is a state, but in so far as it is not a state.

All sorts of causes of dissatisfaction or alarm lead to external conflict. There may be privileged classes directly interested in resisting the better organization of the community; in maintaining, for instance, an obsolete franchise and the power of a military caste. There may be oppressed religious persuasions, oppressed nationalities, provinces torn from the allegiance they prefer. All of these are likely to throw their hopes and ambitions outside the state which formally includes them, and to produce resentments against it in other groups. Then, more subtle and more modern, there are the whole set of restrictions upon human intercourse which depend on the idea that the gain of one community is the loss of another. All of these make doubly for war; they make privileges at home, which turn the mind of the privileged class away from internal organization and towards external aggression; and they make exclusions abroad, turning the mind of the excluded classes to retaliation both in kind and by arms. Exclusion reaches the climax of its vicious effect when it becomes an affair of what I shall call for short 'passive markets' – such, that is, as raise the problem of the prior possession of uncivilized regions which the white man can exploit at pleasure, and at pleasure close against others.

I must not pause to analyse at length the claims supported by that blessed word 'expansion'. So good a historian as Dr. Holland Rose seems to accept the increase of Germany's population by 50 per cent. in one generation as a sufficient reason for a vigorous expansion policy. But surely we must distinguish between the duties really imposed upon a state by such an increase with a view to organization of life, and the adventures and exclusive exploitations for which it may be the pretext, but which do nothing serious to aid the work of organization, while they fill the world with monopolies and with terrors of aggression.

And again, it appears only just to remark, following for example a recent article by Sir Harry Johnston, confirmed in this respect by Mr. Morel, that when in a huge world-empire there is advocated a policy of commercial exclusion directed against other countries, these countries will anticipate being gravely prejudiced in their legitimate foreign trade. Then follows the desire on their part to possess themselves of exclusive markets, and unending fears and resentments are bred on every side. That the practical and theoretical inspiration of the policy so advocated had its source in some of the countries threatened by it, would have made it, if carried out, an interesting retribution, but would not have diminished its danger.

Surely, for the legitimate expansion demanded by increase of population the 'open door' is the right and effective principle. It will meet both the need of trade, and in the last resort, the need of space and elbow-room for population. Under it no one's expansion can be a threat to any one, or produce monopolies which will hinder social organization, and turn men's minds to aggression. And it must also be noted that the loss of citizen population, which is sometimes complained of, is not really met by mere increase of territorial possessions. It is largely due to the very military system which is relied on to remedy its causes – in a word, to defective social organization, which lays unwelcome burdens on the ordinary citizen, and even fails to utilize territorial expansion as an outlet for population.

It must be borne in mind, however, that the exclusive policy advocated within our Empire was decisively rejected, and the open door, the main thing demanded by expansion elsewhere, was as decisively maintained. Even territorial acquisition in tropical regions, though it has practically been of little value to the increasing populations of European countries, this country has not obstructed, and I hope and trust that it will maintain its unenvious policy in this respect up to the limits of possibility in the settlement after the war.

I have no right to lecture on economics, but the general principles which I have been advocating, of absence of monopoly at home, and the 'open door' abroad, fall, I think, within the competence of a student of politics. Restrictions on human intercourse are prima facie injurious, and demand the very strongest justification if they are to be tolerated.

And on a kindred point, really beyond my competence, I will merely put a question. Presupposing a sufficiency of external trade to pay for food and raw materials, is not the home market the most important and the most secure? When it is not so, is not the purchasing power of the most numerous classes short of what it should be? And through directing the minds of the leaders of trade to external adventure, is not such a state of things a constant incentive to exclusive exploitation and to war?

I will end by summarizing as shortly as I can the conclusions which follow from our argument – both what we must admit, and what we are anxious to maintain.

(1) We must admit that states, in consequence of their separateness and absoluteness, are *so far* in a relation of nature to each other, though this is mitigated by humane conventions and usages. If differences arise, the ultimate arbiter is war, which is therefore necessary to the function of states as now existing. While this is so, international politics must differ from individual morality as maintaining a world differs from living in one.

(2) We must admit that when, on this basis, it is attempted to secure peace according to the rule *Si vis pacem, para bellum*, the project is self-contradictory. As principles are the same for all parties, it implies the condition of securing peace to be that of any two opponent powers each must be at the same time stronger than the other. This contradiction is the root of the race in armaments.

(3) We must admit that, on this basis, no league or federation *ad hoc* can secure peace. Every such league must, sooner or later (being a mere

convention of separate wills) arouse a counter-league. Such arrangements, I believe, are fertile of wars.

(4) We maintain that the fundamental root of peace lies in the recognition that war belongs to states not in as far as they are states, but in as far as they are not states; granted that their actual defects to-day make the reverse of this appear to be the truth.

(5) We maintain that the patriotism which is the source of peace therefore lies in a thorough everyday loyalty to the state as a means of harmonious internal organization excluding privilege and monopoly, and in our desire for our country of those supreme goods which are not diminished by sharing. Trade and industry, though acquisitions of material wealth, take on this character when conducted on an impartial and rational basis. This view agrees with the great German philosophy in its estimate of true patriotism, but goes further in analysing the relation of such patriotism to the causes of war.

(6) We maintain that in a group or world of states, possessed by such a patriotism, and therefore organized so as to be free from causes of resentment, and united in aims and methods which admit of harmony, it is conceivable that a true general will (not a mere external convention) might grow up which should be solidly supported by the body, spirit, and sentiment of all the communities. In such a case a genuine international moral world would be created, and international politics would approach more nearly to the nature of private morality, though they could never be the same. In some respects, indeed, the state, as more impartial, might maintain a higher standard than the individual, as happens on occasion even to-day.

(7) We maintain that the patriotism which is the desire for our country of those supreme goods which are not diminished by sharing, is a guarantee of a right estimate of values, and therefore of justice and reasonable organization in dealing with wealth and power both at home and abroad.

Such a patriotism, desiring and sustaining the perfection of the state in its organizing functions as a state, is the only force which is essentially directed to destroying the causes of war. Even those intangible springs of hostility, the jealousy and vanity of nations, cannot ultimately exist in the same world with such a patriotism.

This temper of mind offers the only prospect of a solid general will including groups of states. As its expression, but not without it, leagues of states for the enforcement of peace might do good service. Its detailed operation in such a crisis as will confront the nations of Europe at the close of the war, will consist in a sincere and persevering effort to secure everywhere the removal of all such causes of internal distraction as have been specified above.

By the merest accident in the world, the last word in this course of lectures has fallen to me. And I feel irresistibly impelled to use the opportunity, well knowing how inadequately, in making an appeal to you in the spirit of a conviction which more and more possesses my mind.

I will try to explain it thus.

It was proposed some weeks ago that there should be a day of national humiliation. The highest authority in the land rejected that form of expression, and I believe that we all approved of the rejection.

No, we do not want a day of national humiliation. If ever it is right for a country to hold up its head, it is right for our country to-day. But nevertheless there is something, not wholly different from this, for which in the spirit of our argument I would earnestly appeal. There is a way in which every one of us can do something, and even can do much, to promote the solid foundations of a stable peace. I repeat that we do not want a national humiliation. But we at least who must stay at home have a need and duty of individual and national self-examination. It cannot indeed be a duty incumbent on the men at the front – they have other matters to attend to – but, most remarkably, the evil temper against which it is directed is not on the whole the temper of the men at the front. But for us – it is a thing we can do, and a thing we should do. We should examine ourselves – is our patriotism such as to lead towards the perfectly organized state? Do we desire for our country and ourselves only the best things we know, beauty and truth and love and wholesome living? Do we seek, by this infallible criterion of values, to guarantee both ourselves and our country against the corrupt self-seeking which is the ultimate cause of war?

Right as our cause is to-day, has not the wrong which we are labouring to undo been fostered by ourselves as by others, if not in our case by direct international action, yet by the exhibition of a jealous and menacing spirit of rivalry? Do we not constantly endeavour to lower other nations in our private and public talk, in the world of letters, and in trade? Is our journalism, is our literature of the war – though I gladly acknowledge some most excellent things in both – yet are they on the whole such as we can look upon with satisfaction?

I am entirely without sympathy for the attempts made by a few among our learned men, and by very many who are far from learned, to belittle the intellectual and moral debt of Europe to Germany, and to prove for instance that Goethe – *Goethe* – was a great exemplar of selfishness. And horrible things as I believe her armies have done in the war, yet the attitude which demands that when peace returns Germany or Prussia should be intentionally humiliated and excluded from the European family of nations, to my own feeling is actually repellent, and to my judgement is an attitude of self-satisfaction, morally dangerous in the extreme, and politically absurd. Surely, whatever others may do, we on our side should fight our terrific battle like gentlemen, without rancour or venom, and with eagerness, above all, when the fight is done, to recognize the merits of our adversary which both his passion and ours have for the moment travestied, and to renew the international bonds of commerce, science, art, and philosophy. We ought not to fall below the standard set us by our private soldiers upon Christmas Day, and indeed, as we hear, upon every day of the war.

Punishment and humiliation let us leave to consequences and to history. Belligerents are not good moral judges of each other. Much of what we hear to-day in anticipation of the sequel of the war brings irresistibly to my mind the profound wisdom of George Meredith's warning against the ridiculous attempt at a union of ill temper and policy.

The patriotism we have attempted to portray implies and demands that we should desire for our country, not a triumph of vanity and self-interest, but a share in such a solid work of organization as shall be most favourable to the performance of a true state's function in *every* community of Europe. Thus alone can we deserve well of our country, and our country of the world.

9

International relations
and industrial society

The emergence of new ideas on state and nation in the early years of the nineteenth century cannot be understood in isolation from the socio-economic changes which were also characteristic of that era. The term "industrial revolution" is no longer widely used by economic historians who, today, point to the slow and uneven nature of change in the period, but, nonetheless, it can hardly be denied that major changes were taking place in the productive capacities of societies and the lives of ordinary people. First the factory system and the application of steam power to production, then, later in the nineteenth century, industrialism and mass production proper, transformed, directly or indirectly, the lives of most of the inhabitants of the planet. Part of this "Great Transformation" involved increasing importance for trade and international financial transactions (Polanyi, 1975). Whereas before the nineteenth century foreign trade in bulk goods such as foodstuffs rarely accounted for more than a small percentage of domestic consumption, by 1900 a full-scale international division of labor had been established, with a number of countries specializing in manufacturing products and no longer capable of feeding themselves without imports. That this became a possibility reflected the revolution in transportation and communication during the period, in particular the development of the electric telegraph, the steam ship, and techniques of refrigeration. Britain in particular had ceased to be a pre-dominantly agricultural country in the middle of the nineteenth century, and by 1914 was living off the earnings of her manufacturing sector and the interest on her enormous portfolio of foreign investment. Her rather more successful industrial competitors, the United States and Germany, still had large agri-cultural sectors, and most other European and non-European economies had experienced even less the great domestic changes of the Transformation, but all alike – "developed" and "underdeveloped" – found themselves caught up in the new global economy.

What would be the implications of this new situation for the general conduct of international relations? In the pre-industrial world, international economic activity had been judged largely from the perspective of the power of the state. The underlying assumption of this world was that trade always produced winners and losers, and that states should manage their international activities with a view to ending up as the former. Generally this meant having a positive trade balance and an inflow of gold, although some argued that any flow of goods out of the country, even if paid for in bullion, represented a weakening of the state. Either way, from this mercantilist perspective, the emergence of higher levels of trade and a global division of labor could only be regarded as a source of potential dissension.

One of the major achievements of liberal political economy was to undermine the intellectual foundations of this approach. The process was begun by David Hume, who, in a short essay, "Of the Balance of Trade," showed that the desire for a continuing trade surplus and inflow of bullion was self-defeating; inflows of gold would raise price levels and cut exports and make imports more attractive (Hume, 1987). Adam Smith continued the process by demonstrating the value of an extended division of labor, suggesting that, in principle at least, trade could be beneficial for all parties – see pp. 532–4 below (A. Smith, 1954). However, the figure who put the crucial building block of liberal trade theory into place was David Ricardo (1772–1823). Ricardo's great achievement in his *Principles of Political Economy and Taxation* was to demonstrate that trade could raise the general level of welfare even under circumstances which appear to make this outcome highly unlikely (pp. 535–7 below). Everyone can imagine that in some circumstances trade will be beneficial; if one country is better than another at producing one good, while the situation is reversed for another good, the benefits of trade are obvious. Ricardo demonstrates that trade is beneficial not just under those conditions, but even when one country is more efficient at producing *all* goods than another. All that is required is that a country should have a *comparative* advantage in the production of one product or another – hence this is often termed the Law of Comparative Advantage (or Comparative Costs). In practice this means that trade will always raise the general level of welfare, since it is highly unlikely that comparative costs will be identical in two or more different countries.

Ricardo's law does not guarantee that trade relations will be harmonious. Although he shows that the general welfare is served by trade, the division of the gains from trade remains indeterminate, and there is certainly no guarantee that any particular exchange will produce equal benefits. Moreover, although this is one of the few propositions of this era which still commands support amongst modern economists, the current version of Ricardo's law is surrounded by so many qualifications as to dampen its revolutionary impact. Still, the achievement remains of great consequence, and modern trade theory – especially the neo-liberal orthodoxy promoted by institutions such as the IMF (International Monetary Fund) – rests on its foundations; the underlying assumption of the contemporary trade regime, that free trade is a desirable state of affairs, is Ricardian. All in all, his work is still at the heart of cosmopolitan readings of the international implications of industrial society, and thus deserves to be studied at its source.

Free trade and liberal internationalism

David Ricardo did not attempt to work through the wider implications of his account of the gains from trade. Most likely his views on these wider issues would have echoed those of Adam Smith, who was always conscious of the need to moderate the cosmopolitan policy implications of the laws of political economy by giving due weight to the requirement to preserve national power. From neither Smith nor Ricardo is it possible to see a sense in which the whole nature of international relations has been changed by the new economic order. To find the view that such a change had taken place elaborated at length we have to turn to Richard Cobden, the most intellectually powerful propagandist for free trade of the age. It was Cobden who asked the key question:

Can the "States System" which was applicable to the international affairs of Europe a century ago be suited to the circumstances of today? – or, on the contrary, do not those portentous events which have intervened – in the rise and paramount commercial importance of free America, the downfall of the colony system, and the applications of the doctrines of free trade – demand reforms of proportionate magnitude in the foreign policy of Great Britain? (Cobden, 1836/1903)

Cobden (1804–65) was a self-made man who put his formidable intellect at the service of the newly important manufacturing interests of the North of England. These interests came to be summarized by the name of the town at the center of manufacturing, Manchester, whence the "Manchester School." Cobden's most prominent campaign, in and out of parliament, was to bring about the repeal of the Corn Laws, protectionist legislation which served the interests of agriculture by limiting the import of grain from abroad, thereby keeping the price of bread high – and, of course, requiring Manchester to pay higher wages to its workers. The campaign was successful in 1846 but Cobden remained active in public affairs, promoting the cause of free trade in general – and negotiating a free trade treaty with France in 1860 in particular – and also as a leading light of the mid-nineteenth-century peace movement in Britain.

The great cause with which this peace movement was primarily engaged concerned Britain's involvement in the so-called Eastern Question, that is to say, the complex political ramifications of the steady collapse of Ottoman power in the Balkans. To put the matter in a nutshell, the official line, promulgated by most of the political class, and especially by Lord Palmerston who dominated British foreign policy from the early 1830s to the mid 1860s, was that Russia could not be allowed to take advantage of this collapse by extending her influence into the Balkans and capturing Constantinople and the Straits. Such a move would disrupt the balance of power in Europe and threaten British rule in India. The need was, therefore, to buttress Ottoman power and to resist Russian expansionism.

This position was popular with militant patriots and chauvinists, with those attracted by the exotic romance of the Levant, and with many progressives and radicals for whom Russia was the oppressor of Poles and Hungarians, the most reactionary power in Europe. Indeed, the great revolutionaries Marx and Engels were so committed to the anti-Russian cause that they were even prepared to give credence to the views of the pro-Turk enthusiast David Urquhart, whose particular contribution was to suggest that Palmerston was in the pay of the Russians, a view akin to the American militia movement's apparent belief that Ronald Reagan was an agent of a conspiracy to impose UN rule in the United States in the 1980s. Even the Soviet editors of volume XII of the *Marx–Engels Collected Works*, which covers these writings, felt obliged to distance themselves somewhat from Marx on this point, but, eccentricities aside, the idea that one should judge international events in terms of their impact on the revolutionary cause in general rather than from some other, less instrumental, viewpoint was, and is, basic to Marxist thinking on international relations (Marx and Engels, 1979; C. Brown, 1992).

The liberal peace movement, however, denounced the official line from the point at which it first emerged in the 1820s and 1830s right through to Gladstone's campaign against Turkish atrocities in the 1870s. One of the most vociferous advocates of peace was Cobden. Part of his argument, which is to be found in a number of speeches and pamphlets over a thirty-year period, consisted of a denunciation of Ottoman backwardness and vice and a corresponding whitewashing of the Russian record, the only excuse for which can be that it simply represented a turning on their head of the equally specious arguments of his opponents. However, the more thoughtful aspect of his case is to be found in his critique of the "balance of power" – that centerpiece of conventional international theory discussed in chapter 5 above – and of the notion that Britain's prosperity and security required her to pursue an active engaged foreign policy.

Cobden's views of the balance of power are known to international political theory in caricature form: his famous hyperbole to the effect that the balance of power "is not a fallacy, a mistake, an imposture; it is an undescribed, indescribable, incomprehensible nothing: mere words conveying to the mind not ideas but sounds" (Cobden, 1836: 200) is better known than the arguments with which he backed up this judgement. These words come from a pamphlet entitled *Russia, 1836*, the product of a war scare of that year. The first two chapters examine the issues of the day, Turkish iniquity described in detail, Russian behavior towards Poland – not to be excused of course, but the Poles were a troublesome, backward people – Russian power – always overstated in Britain for political reasons – and so on, but chapters III and IV, which are extracted extensively below (pp. 538–49), work at a different level. His aim in these two chapters is to challenge the two principles which underpinned British foreign policy, the balance of power and the protection of commerce. Chapter III on the balance of power sets out all the difficulties of defining the term, and has a great deal of fun with the various semantic traps into which statesmen regularly fall when they attempt to make sense of this protean term, while, at the same time, pointing out the serious consequences of attempts to put the notion to practical use. Chapter IV, on the protection of commerce, is, in some respects more interesting, for here is to be found virtually the whole array of intellectual weapons which liberal internationalists have deployed over the past hundred and fifty years. Commerce rests on the cheapness of commodities which is compromised by high spending on the military, war would be a disaster for the nation; many successful trading nations have very low military expenditures, we cannot be the policeman of the world; the most important way in which we can exercise influence is by being a moral example to the rest of the world, and so on – the sense of familiarity this document evokes is fascinating, given its early provenance.

Cobden is a supporter of non-intervention, and it is interesting to compare his defense of this principle with that of John Stuart Mill, which was set out in chapter 8. For Mill, the essential reason for a norm of non-intervention is that no people can be given freedom; they have to take it for themselves for it to be meaningful. This is an argument that centres on the victim of oppression, and takes seriously the notion of moral autonomy. Cobden is less concerned with such matters, more with the cost to the state that might actually do the intervention – thus he is prepared to ask "am I my brother's keeper" and to answer "no." As we have seen, Mill himself is highly selective in the causes he is prepared to support and is all too ready to defend British imperialism, but, nonetheless, there is a meanness of spirit about Cobden's argument which deserves the invective it attracted from his critics. Marx had his own reasons, domestic and foreign, for describing Cobden as applying his peace doctrines "with all the sharp ingenuity of the *monomaniac*, with all the contradictions of the *ideologue* and with all the calculating cowardice of the shop-keeper" but the latter taunt, at least, strikes home however much the first two seem like the pot calling the kettle black (Marx and Engels, 1979: 274).

The protectionist response

For Cobden, and Manchester more generally, the "states system" which nineteenth-century Europe had inherited was no longer capable of operating in the old ways. Cobden is a patriot, someone who desires to promote the interests of his country, but, as far as he is concerned, what this actually ought to involve is a passive foreign policy, or rather a foreign policy devoted to spreading the doctrines of free trade by word and deed. In his public writings at least, Cobden is more or less free of the kind of affective loyalties envisaged by the theorists of state and nation whose work was examined in the last chapter. In so far as Cobden expressed these kinds of feelings at all, they were directed towards the United States, which represented his ideal of a non-aristocratic commercial republic.

Interestingly, within the United States itself, the very people whom Cobden admired – the Yankee traders and manufacturers – were largely opponents of free trade, while its supporters – the aristocratic slaveowners of the cotton belt – were exactly the sort of people he despised in Britain. Although the former shared Cobden's values, more or less, their circumstances were different, and the policies they promoted differed accordingly. Given free access to American markets, the well-established industries of Manchester might well stifle at birth the newly emerging industrial strength of the manufactories of New England, with great implications for America's future role in the world. The point had been well taken in the early years of the Republic. Secretary of the Treasury Alexander Hamilton's "Report on the Subject of Manufactures" to the US Congress in 1791 set out in painstaking detail the basis for a policy of protecting some "infant industries" (A. Hamilton, 1966). However, the most fully developed critique of free trade came not from the United States but from the other great future industrial rival of Great Britain, Germany, and especially from the pen of Friedrich List.

List (1789–1846) was born in Würtemburg and was a successful bureaucrat in the local civil service until his involvement with liberal and revolutionary causes led to his exile first from Würtemburg, then from other German cities; he spent much of the 1820s in the United States where he developed excellent contacts with leading American politicians, and became involved in controversies over tariff policy. On his return to Europe and Germany in the 1830s, he became involved in similar controversies over the tariff policy of the *Zollverein* – the North German customs union which was centered on

Prussia. Partly in response to these controversies, List produced his major work *The National System of Political Economy* in 1841. *The National System* is a scholarly work but it is also a work of propaganda, designed to influence the policy of Germany's leaders in the direction of resistance to British industrial hegemony.

The book contains two sorts of argument, which work at different levels of generality. At the policy level, his most basic point is that Britain's own prosperity and dominance was not achieved by adopting the policies she now advocates for others; with a compelling metaphor he comments that:

It is a very common device that when anyone has attained the summit of greatness, he kicks away the ladder by which he has climbed up, in order to deprive others of the means of climbing after him ... Any nation which by means of protective duties and restrictions on navigation has raised her manufacturing power and her navigation to such a degree of development that no other nation can sustain free competition with her, can do nothing wiser than to throw away these ladders of her greatness, to preach to other nations the benefits of free trade, and to declare in penitent tones that she has hitherto wandered in the paths of error, and has now for the first time succeeded in discovering the truth. (List, 1966: 368)

This line of argument is, of course, extremely effective, and has been employed repeatedly since, usually by people who have never heard of List and have picked up his ideas at second or third hand.

List's more philosophical point is contained in his chapter xi, "Political and Cosmopolitan Economy" (pp. 550–60 below). The free traders from Adam Smith onwards – the "school" or the "popular school" as he calls them – advocate policies which would make a great deal of sense if we assume a universal union or confederation of all nations. In such circumstances we would be able to think of the benefits from free trade in terms of the interests of individuals and the world as a whole, and the arguments set out by the school would hold true. Moreover, it would be in everyone's interest were such a state of affairs to come about. The problem is that the popular school has assumed as "being actually in existence a state of things which has yet to come into existence." If free trade were to be adopted now, before the arrival of the universal federation, the result would be to preserve in place the power of England and to set up an international division of labor in which the rest of the world would be relegated to the role of hewers of wood and drawers of water for England. A *national* system of political economy, as opposed to the *cosmopolitan* system of Smith and the school, would recognize the importance of these facts and start from the world as it is rather than as it should be. Only once other nations have been raised by artificial measures to the stage of cultivation of England will it be possible for free trade to be adopted universally.

List's account does little justice to the sophistication of Smith's arguments but the general point is well taken. The root assumption of free trade theory is that the pattern of specialization produced by the operation of comparative advantage will be politically neutral, that is to say, there is no *prima facie* reason for preferring an advantage in one product as opposed to another. Obviously, looked at from the perspective of national power, this cannot be right. It should be noted that in the twentieth century dependency theorists and other followers of the Argentinian economist Raul Prebisch, have developed List's line of argument – usually without crediting him – to make the point that there is a long-term trend for the terms of trade to move against primary production and in favor of industrial goods; this has been used to justify policies of industrialization in the South, even in circumstances where comparative advantage would mandate specialization in agricultural goods (Prebisch, 1950). This is not quite List's actual argument, but, as the text makes clear, his general line of reasoning can be used to support this policy. Perhaps the difference is that List is quite explicitly statist, justifying his approach as underwritten by political as opposed to cosmopolitan political economy, while Prebisch's followers have mostly been of the left, and unwilling to acknowledge that what they are doing is advocating nationalist policies.

From competitive capitalism to cartels

Whether free trade or protectionist, the political economists of the first half of the nineteenth century shared some common assumptions about the nature of the new manufacturing interests. The most important of these assumptions was that the manufacturers would compete with each other for markets whether they were of the same nationality or not, and that the role of the state would be, at best, to provide a context in which this competition would take place, both by preserving the conditions for capitalist reproduction at home – that is, preserving the civil peace, establishing a framework of commercial law, providing services such as transport and mail systems, perhaps education – and, possibly, by opening markets abroad through the promotion of free trade, or, in the protectionist variant, by restricting entry to the market at home to local competitors only. Either way, no one manufacturer would have the kind of capacity to be able to suborn the state to act in its interests against its competitors, whether the latter were domestic or foreign.

This picture of capitalists as competitors was shared by liberals and the contemporary left. It is striking, for example, that Marx and Engels in their extensive journalism on international relations in general, and the Eastern Question in particular, rarely if ever try to explain events in terms that might imply, for example, that the capitalist state in Britain was acting on behalf of British capitalists. Instead, they employ the conventional categories of *Realpolitik* although, looking at things from their perspective as revolutionaries, they also hold cosmopolitan views about class loyalties crossing state boundaries as expressed in the famous words of "The Communist Manifesto," extracted briefly below. This consensus is not difficult to understand – it reflects the reality of the mid-nineteenth century when most firms were still comparatively small, and managed by their owners. However, in the late nineteenth century the picture changed somewhat; new technologies in chemicals and the steel industry made larger firms more viable than smaller, changes in company law and management techniques led to the emergence of joint-stock companies which operated on a larger scale than heretofore, and, in Germany and the United States in particular, banks became involved in industrial activity, often promoting cartels or trusts – agreements between firms to restrict their competitive activities, usually at the expense of the public and, in the United States, for that reason, regulated by Federal Anti-Trust legislation. Marxist writers refer to these trends as the development of monopolies; strictly speaking this is incorrect, as comparatively few industries were dominated by one producer, but the late nineteenth and early twentieth century certainly saw the emergence of oligopoly – a situation in which a small number of firms dominate a market and are able to be "price makers" as well as "price takers."

It would be plausible to expect that these changes would have an impact on international relations. Whereas previously no individual capitalist concern was capable of exerting sufficient power to change state policy, this could no longer be assumed to be the case; similarly, whereas previously the collective capitalist interest, if it could be discerned at all, lay in a passive foreign policy, this also could no longer be assumed to be so. However, thinking on these issues was somewhat confused by another change in international relations in the final third of the nineteenth century, the emergence of the so-called "new imperialism" and, in particular the scramble for Africa, in which the major European powers divided the continent up amongst themselves. Since this seemed to represent a shift from an earlier skepticism about the value of colonies, and since it took place contemporaneously with the trend towards increasing firm size and oligopoly, it was not surprising that some writers would attempt to link the two phenomena.

The English radical economist J. A. Hobson (1858–1940) made this connection in his book *Imperialism: A Study* (1902), which was written partly in response to the Anglo-Boer War of 1899 to 1902. Hobson regarded British policy in South Africa as being determined by the power of special economic interests – which was not an unreasonable point, although his use of anti-Semitic rhetoric in this context is highly distasteful – but he also developed a wider theory in which imperialism was linked to "under-consumptionism." His argument is that the rise of capitalist conglomerations led to the phenomenon of "surplus capital" – capital that could not find employment at home and therefore sought "vents" abroad, leading to imperialism and the conquest of territory wherein surplus capital could be deployed.

Hobson has been a very influential writer; his notions on the domestic economy influenced Keynes and Keynesianism, and his writings on imperialism influenced Lenin and the Bolsheviks. However, his arguments on the causes of imperialism have not stood the test of time. D. K. Fieldhouse has demonstrated that, with the partial exception of South Africa, capital did *not* flow to the new imperial possessions; British capital went to the United States, Argentina, India, and Australia; French capital to Russia and Eastern Europe; German to the Ottoman Empire and the Balkans (Fieldhouse, 1961). Others have challenged the notion that there was a new imperialism at the end of the last century; British imperial possessions increased throughout the "free trade" era, and were usually driven by security concerns or by local conditions rather than by the need to vent surplus capital (Gallagher and Robinson, 1953). In any event, it may be doubted whether there ever was such a phenomenon as "surplus capital"; in Britain at least, most foreign capital investments at the end of the century were actually re-investments of the earnings of early investments and throughout the period the returns on capital invested abroad were only marginally higher than returns on capital invested at home, the premium being more than accountable for by the higher risk of the former (Fieldhouse, 1961, 1973).

In short, the "economic theory of imperialism" in its usual form as an account of the new imperialism and the extension of formal rule, simply does not stand up to scrutiny; it survives largely because of the prestige in revolutionary circles of Lenin, whose 1917 work *Imperialism: Highest Stage of Capitalism* draws heavily on Hobson. The persistence of this error is particularly important since it has obscured the much more impressive contribution of other writers on the international relations of late-nineteenth, early-twentieth-century capitalism, in particular that of the Austrian Marxist Rudolf Hilferding (1877–1941). Hilferding's masterwork is his *Finance Capital*, which was published in 1910 and which dominated Marxist thinking on economics until its author was denounced by Lenin for his political sins as a social democrat – *pace* this denunciation, *Finance Capital* is the most impressive work of Marxist political economy of the twentieth century, and is extracted here (pp. 561–71 below), along with some characteristic comments from "The Communist Manifesto" (pp. 572–4 below), to show how far the argument has changed since the heyday of Marx and Engels (Hilferding, 1981; Marx, 1996).

Hilferding argues that industrial capital and bank capital have now fused together to create finance capital. The national economies of the advanced capitalist powers are now dominated by interlocking oligopolies in such a way that capitalists no longer compete with each other within the national economy, but instead compete predominantly with foreign capitals which have also formed into national blocks. The texts extracted below summarize this change, setting out the way in which commercial policy has been reoriented, and outlining the resulting international implications – the export of capital and the struggle for economic territory. The new monopolies are vulnerable only to external competition and they recruit the power of the state to restrict this competition via tariffs. At the same time, they seek to extend the area over which they can extract monopoly profits (their "economic territory") and this leads to "imperialism" in the sense of a general tendency to expand. It should be noted that a country's economic territory does not have to be under direct political control – Britain's "informal empire" might well at this stage have included countries not ruled from London, such as Argentina, or even, at an earlier period, the United States. It should also be noted that tariff policy is not seen simply as defensive in the manner of List, but also as a tool that can be employed aggressively to expand the national territory. Hilferding sees imperialism/expansionism as the foreign policy of finance capital, and, along with other Marxist writers of the time such as Rosa Luxemburg, is concerned by the increasing militarism of contemporary international relations (Luxemburg, 1913/1963: 454–69), a militarism that he sees as alien to the liberalism of the old competitive capitalist bourgeoisie. International conflict is more or less guaranteed – but it should be noted that, unlike Lenin, Hilferding does not assume that this conflict will always and necessarily lead to war.

Hilferding's account of the nature of the state and of international relations is rather more akin to that of some of the writers anthologized in chapter 8 than it is to that of either Cobden or List or the schools they represent. Hilferding's political values are, of course, very different from those of Treitschke, but the extent to which their accounts of the world can be made to mesh together in policy terms is striking. In effect, on Hilferding's account, in the age of finance capital the national state returns to center-stage, not as the representative of a community, but as the political expression of the capitalist syndicates. How well does his analysis stand the test of time? Clearly he exaggerates the importance of the trends he identifies; in most countries the growth of firm size and the process of cartelization had only just begun prior to 1914. By the end of the twentieth century average firm size has increased beyond his imagination – but what is rather more to the point is that many firms today can no longer be seen simply as national firms. The idea that national capitals compete with one another on the world stage may have had some resonance earlier in the century, but today the "internationalization" or "globalization" of capital is more noticeable. Moreover, in common with most Marxists of the period, Hilferding seems not to have understood just how resilient capitalism was; the general view was that capitalism was decadent, had reached the end of the line – virtually no-one foresaw the rise of new industries based on the motor car, "white goods," and, later, information technology. For all these weaknesses, his is an impressive achievement, unjustly neglected over the past century.

The phenomenon of imperialism and war was, of course, of concern in this era to non-Marxist as well as Marxist political economists, and the former were understandably keen to provide their own account of the relationship of these disasters to capitalism. The best such response to Marxist writings is an essay "The Sociology of Imperialisms" (1919) by the Austrian/American economist Joseph Schumpeter (1883–1950), selections of which are extracted below (pp. 575–84). Schumpeter's position is that imperialism is a phenomenon that can be found in all past epochs, and that its roots lie in the interests of the ruling classes of each age. Although he concedes that under capitalism particular groups will sometimes be able to hijack the state in their own interests, he regards the values of capitalist society as essentially anti-militarist and anti-imperialist. Instead, imperialism is atavistic in character. It is a surviving feature of an earlier age. It is not part of the inner logic of capitalism, even of the export-oriented monopolism which he concedes has emerged in some areas – instead such new features of capitalism have been harnessed by a war machine inherited from a previous age.

Thus, the period of the long nineteenth century ends as it begins, with supporters of the new way of life which has emerged from out of the Great Transformation insisting on its essentially peaceful character. Schumpeter is, in this respect, the natural descendant of Cobden and the Manchester School, although his awareness of the nature of modern capitalist society is more sociologically sophisticated than that of his predecessors. Schumpeter is surely right to note that all actually existing social formations are a mélange of different institutions and value-systems, and that abstractions such as the "capitalist" state (or "state-capitalism") are as liable to confuse as to illuminate. In so far as this is so, it may be a mistake to look for specific changes in international political theory and practice that can be traced directly to the emergence of industrial society, because "industrial society" can never be isolated from the pre-industrial forms within which it remains embedded. This is a sobering conclusion, given the faith that so many people had after 1914–18 that a new international order could be erected on liberal internationalist principles which owed a great deal to precisely the kind of belief undermined by this argument. The record of the liberal internationalist order of 1919 suggests that pessimism here may be justified – but that is another story, or a story for another anthology.

FURTHER READING

For the mercantilists and early liberal political economists, the standard histories of economic thought do a very good job – see, for example, Robert Heilbroner (1986), Mark Blaug (1985). On Richard Cobden and nineteenth-century radicals generally, A. J. P. Taylor's *The Trouble Makers* (1957) is still very valuable and an entertaining read. J. A. Hobson has recently attracted a good critical study by David Long (1996). Marxist approaches to the international relations of industrial society are surveyed in Chris Brown (1992). Karl Marx's writings on the Eastern Question (most of which, confusingly, were actually written by Frederick Engels) are collected in an 1890s volume, reprinted in 1969, edited by his daughter and son-in-law (E. Marx Aveling and E. Aveling, 1969). The best survey of "Marxist theories of imperialism" is that by Anthony Brewer (1990). As Brewer makes clear, the aim of these theories was not, as it is often taken to be, to explain the expansion of areas of European formal rule in Africa in the late nineteenth century, but rather to give an account of the dynamics of inter-capitalist relations; the rather different issue of "economic explanations for imperialism" has been explored profitably by a number of historians, most notably D. K. Fieldhouse (1961, 1973).

SOURCES

Adam Smith, from *Wealth of Nations* (London: Everyman edn., Dent, 1954), extracts pp. 381, 401, 402.

David Ricardo, from "On the Principles of Political Economy and Taxation," in *The Works and Correspondence of David Ricardo* vol. I, ed. Piero Sraffa (Cambridge: Cambridge University Press, 1951), pp. 133–7.

Richard Cobden, from *The Political Writings of Richard Cobden* (London: T. Fisher Unwin, 1903), pp. 196, 201, 203, 204, 216, 217–19, 220–2, 234–6, 253–5, footnotes excluded.

Friedrich List, from *The National System of Political Economy* (London: Frank Cass & Co., Reprints of Economic Classics, 1966), pp. 119–32.

Rudolf Hilferding, *Finance Capital*, ed. Tom Bottomore (London: Routledge and Kegan Paul, 1981), pp. 307, 308, 310, 321–5, 326–8, 331, 332, 334–6.

Karl Marx and Friedrich Engels, from "The Communist Manifesto," in *Marx: Later Political Writings*, ed. Terrell Carver (Cambridge: Cambridge University Press, 1996), pp. 2–5. extracts, pp 17–18.

Joseph Schumpeter, from *Imperialism and Social Classes* (New York: Augustus M. Kelly Inc., 1951), pp. 97–9, 104–7, 110, 111, 120–30.

ADAM SMITH

A DAM SMITH (1723–90), political economist, moral philosopher, and central figure in the Scottish Enlightenment. His *The Wealth of Nations* (1776) is a central document in liberal and political theory. The following brief extract sets out the case for an international division of labor.

From *The Wealth of Nations*

[*In Book IV of "The Wealth of Nations" – on systems of political economy – Smith first demolishes the mercantilist argument that there is some special merit to building up a national stock of precious metals.*]

A country that has no mines of its own must undoubtedly draw its gold and silver from foreign countries in the same manner as one that has no vineyards of its own must draw its wines. It does not seem necessary, however, that the attention of government should be more turned towards the one than towards the other object. A country that has wherewithal to buy wine will always get the wine which it has occasion for; and a country that has wherewithal to buy gold and silver will never be in want of those metals. They are to be bought for a certain price like all other commodities, and as they are the price of all other commodities, so all other commodities are the price of those metals. We trust with perfect security that the freedom of trade, without any attention of government, will always supply us with the wine which we have occasion for: and we may trust with equal security that it will always supply us with all the gold and silver which we can afford to purchase or to employ, either in circulating our commodities, or in other uses.

[*He then proceeds to attack the case for the protection of domestic industry, regarding this as simply one more example of the tendency of monopolists to seek special treatment at the public's expense.*]

To give the monopoly of the home market to the produce of domestic industry, in any particular art or manufacture, is in some measure to direct private people in what manner they ought to employ their capitals, and must, in almost all cases, be either a useless or a hurtful regulation. If the produce of domestic can be brought there as cheap as that of foreign industry, the regulation is evidently useless. If it cannot, it must generally be hurtful. It is the maxim of every prudent master of a family never to attempt to make at home what it will cost him more to make than to buy. The tailor does not attempt to make his own shoes, but buys them of the shoemaker. The shoemaker does not attempt to make his own clothes, but employs a tailor. The farmer attempts to make neither the one nor the other, but employs those different artificers. All of them find it for their interest to employ their whole industry in a way in which they have some advantage over their neighbours, and to purchase with a part of its produce, or what is the same thing, with the price of a part of it, whatever else they have occasion for.

What is prudence in the conduct of every private family can scarce be folly in that of a great kingdom. If a foreign country can supply us with a commodity cheaper than we ourselves can make it, better buy it of them with some part of the produce of our own industry employed in a way in which we have some advantage. The general industry of the country, being always in proportion to the capital which employs it, will not thereby be diminished, no more than that of the above-mentioned artificers; but only left to find out the way in which it can be employed with the greatest advantage. It is certainly not employed to the greatest advantage when it is thus directed towards an object which it can buy cheaper than it can make. The value of its annual produce is certainly more or less diminished when it is thus turned away from producing commodities evidently of more value than the commodity which it is directed to produce. According to the supposition, that commodity could be purchased from foreign countries cheaper than it can be made at home. It could, therefore, have been purchased with a part only of the commodities, or, what is the same thing, with a part only of the price of the commodities, which the industry employed by an equal capital would have produced at home, had it been left to follow its natural course. The industry of the country, therefore, is thus turned away from a more to a less advantageous employment, and the exchangeable value of its annual produce, instead of being increased, according to the intention of the lawgiver, must necessarily be diminished by every such regulation.

By means of such regulations, indeed, a particular manufacture may sometimes be acquired sooner than it could have been otherwise, and after a certain time may be made at home as cheap or cheaper than in the foreign country. But though the industry of the society may be thus carried with advantage into a particular channel sooner than it could have been otherwise, it will by no means follow that the sum total, either of its industry, or of its revenue, can ever be augmented by any such regulation. The industry of the society can augment only in proportion as its capital augments, and its capital can augment only in proportion to what can be gradually saved out of its revenue. But the immediate effect of every such regulation is to diminish its revenue, and what diminishes its revenue is certainly not very likely to augment its capital faster than it would have augmented of its own accord had both capital and industry been left to find out their natural employments.

[*Smith will accept special treatment for domestic industry only for reasons of national defence – for example the protection of shipping in Britain.*]

DAVID RICARDO

D AVID RICARDO (1772–1823), banker and political economist. Ricardo's *Principles of Political Economy and Taxation* (1817) is a foundation stone for contemporary economic theory. The following extract sets out his demonstration that there are gains to be made from trade even when one of the countries involved can make all the goods traded cheaper than can another; all that is required for there to be gains from trade is that comparative costs be different. This is one of the few theories of the nineteenth century which, suitably amended, is still part of twenty-first century economics; it remains the basis for liberal internationalism and the belief that trade promotes peace.

From "On the Principles of Political Economy and Taxation"

[*Ricardo's classic account of comparative costs*]

Under a system of perfectly free commerce, each country naturally devotes its capital and labour to such employments as are most beneficial to each. This pursuit of individual advantage is admirably connected with the universal good of the whole. By stimulating industry, by rewarding ingenuity, and by using most efficaciously the peculiar powers bestowed by nature, it distributes labour most effectively and most economically: while, by increasing the general mass of productions, it diffuses general benefit, and binds together by one common tie of interest and intercourse, the universal society of nations throughout the civilized world. It is this principle which determines that wine shall be made in France and Portugal, that corn shall be grown in America and Poland, and that hardware and other goods shall be manufactured in England.

In one and the same country, profits are, generally speaking, always on the same level; or differ only as the employment of capital may be more or less secure and agreeable. It is not so between different countries. If the profits of capital employed in Yorkshire, should exceed those of capital employed in London, capital would speedily move from London to Yorkshire, and an equality of profits would be effected; but if in consequence of the diminished rate of production in the lands of England, from the increase of capital and population, wages should rise, and profits fall, it would not follow that capital and population would necessarily move from England to Holland, or Spain, or Russia, where profits might be higher.

If Portugal had no commercial connexion with other countries, instead of employing a great part of her capital and industry in the production of wines, with which she purchases for her own use the cloth and hardware of other countries, she would be obliged to devote a part of that capital to the manufacture of those commodities, which she would thus obtain probably inferior in quality as well as quantity.

The quantity of wine which she shall give in exchange for the cloth of England, is not determined by the respective quantities of labour devoted to the production of each, as it would be, if both commodities were manufactured in England, or both in Portugal.

England may be so circumstanced, that to produce the cloth may require the labour of 100 men for one year; and if she attempted to make the wine, it might require the labour of 120 men for the same time. England would therefore find it her interest to import wine, and to purchase it by the exportation of cloth.

To produce the wine in Portugal, might require only the labour of 80 men for one year, and to produce the cloth in the same country, might require the labour of 90 men for the same time. It would therefore be advantageous for her to export wine in exchange for cloth. This exchange might even take place, notwithstanding that the commodity imported by Portugal could be produced there with less labour than in England. Though she could make the cloth with the labour of 90 men, she would import it from a country where it required the labour of 100 men to produce it, because it would be advantageous to her rather to employ her capital in the production of wine, for which she would obtain more cloth from England, than she could produce by diverting a portion of her capital from the cultivation of vines to the manufacture of cloth.

Thus England would give the produce of the labour of 100 men, for the produce of the labour of 80. Such an exchange could not take place between the individuals of the same country. The labour of 100 Englishmen cannot be given for that of 80 Englishmen, but the produce of the labour of 100 Englishmen may be given for the produce of the labour of 80 Portuguese, 60 Russians, or 120 East Indians. The difference in this respect, between a single country and many, is easily accounted for, by considering the difficulty with which capital moves from one country to another, to seek a more profitable employment, and the activity with which it invariably passes from one province to another in the same country.[1]

It would undoubtedly be advantageous to the capitalists of England, and to the consumers in both countries, that under such circumstances, the wine and the cloth should both be made in Portugal, and therefore that the capital and labour of England employed in making cloth, should be removed to Portugal for that purpose. In that case, the relative value of these commodities would be regulated by the same principle, as if one were the produce of Yorkshire, and the other of London: and in every other case, if capital freely flowed towards those countries where it could be most profitably employed, there could be no difference in the rate of profit, and no other difference in the real or labour price of commodities, than the additional quantity of labour required to convey them to the various markets where they were to be sold.

Experience, however, shews, that the fancied or real insecurity of capital, when not under the immediate control of its owner, together with the natural disinclination which every man has to quit the country of his birth and connexions, and intrust himself with all his habits fixed, to a strange government and new laws, check the emigration of capital. These feelings, which I should be sorry to see weakened, induce most men of property to be satisfied with a low rate of profits in their own country, rather than seek a more advantageous employment for their wealth in foreign nations.

1   It will appear then, that a country possessing very considerable advantages in machinery and skill, and which may therefore be enabled to manufacture commodities with much less labour than her neighbours, may, in return for such commodities, import a portion of the corn required for its consumption, even if its land were more fertile, and corn could be grown with less labour than in the country from which it was imported. Two men can both make shoes and hats, and one is superior to the other in both employments; but in making hats, he can only exceed his competitor by one-fifth or 20 per cent., and in making shoes he can excel him by one-third or 33 per cent.; – will it not be for the interest of both, that the superior man should employ himself exclusively in making shoes, and the inferior man in making hats?

RICHARD COBDEN

RICHARD COBDEN (1804–65), English publicist and politician. Although born in rural Sussex, Cobden became the leading figure in the "Manchester School" of liberalism, representing the interests of Lancashire manufacturers and industrialists, especially in the cotton industry. He was the leading publicist for the Anti-Corn Law League, which promoted free trade in agricultural products. A strong opponent of traditional diplomacy, Cobden regarded general free trade as the only route to international peace. The following extracts from a comparatively early pamphlet on *Russia* (1836) set out his opposition to the idea of balance of power and to any British intervention in overseas quarrels, and in the process lay out many of the themes which would be developed in twentieth-century liberal internationalism.

From *The Political Writings of Richard Cobden*

...

British intervention in the state policy of the Continent has been usually excused under the two stock pretences of maintaining the balance of power in Europe, and of protecting our commerce; upon which two subjects, as they bear indirectly on the question in hand, we shall next offer a few observations.

The first instance in which we find the "balance of power" alluded to in a king's speech is on the occasion of the last address of William III. to his Parliament, December 31, 1701, where he concludes by saying – "I will only add this – if you do in good earnest desire to see England *hold the balance of Europe*, it will appear by your right improving the present opportunity." From this period down to almost our time (latterly indeed, the phrase has become, like many other cant terms, nearly obsolete), there will be found, in almost every successive king's speech, a constant recurrence to the "balance of Europe;" by which, we may rest assured, was always meant, however it might be concealed under pretended alarm for the "equilibrium of power" or the "safety of the Continent," the desire to see England "hold the balance." The phrase was found to please the public ear; it implied something of equity; whilst England, holding the balance of Europe in her hand, sounded like filling the office of Justice herself to one half of the globe. Of course such a post of honour could not be maintained, or its dignity asserted, without a proper attendance of guards and officers, and we consequently find that at about this period of our history large standing armies began to be called for; and not only were the supplies solicited by the government from time to time under the plea of preserving the liberties of Europe, but in the annual mutiny bill (*the same in form as is now passed every year*) the preamble stated, amongst other motives, that the annual army was voted for the purpose of *preserving the balance of power in Europe.* The "balance of power," then, becomes an important practical subject for investigation. It appeals directly to the business and bosoms of our readers, since it is implicated with an expenditure of more than a dozen millions of money per annum, every farthing of which goes, in the shape of taxation, from the pockets of the public.

Such of our readers as have not investigated this subject will not be a little astonished to find a great discrepancy in the several definitions of what is actually meant by the "balance of power." The theory – or it has never yet been applied to practice – appears, after upwards of a century of acknowledged existence, to be less understood now than ever. Latterly, indeed, many intelligent and practical-minded politicians have thrown the question overboard, along with that of the balance of trade, of which number, without participating in their favoured attributes, we claim to be ranked as one. The balance of power, which has for a hundred years been the burden of kings' speeches, the theme of statesmen, the ground of solemn treaties, and the cause of wars; which has served, down to the very year in which we write, and which will, no doubt, continue to serve for years to come as a pretence for maintaining enormous standing armaments by land and sea, at a cost of many hundreds of millions of treasure – the balance of power is a chimera! It is not a fallacy, a mistake, an imposture, it is an undescribed, indescribable, incomprehensible nothing; mere words, conveying to the mind not ideas, but sounds like those equally barren syllables which our ancestors put together for the purpose of puzzling themselves about words, in the shape of *Prester John* or the *philosopher's stone!* We are bound, however, to see what are the best definitions of this theory.

"By this balance," says Vattel, "is to be understood such a disposition of things as that no one potentate or state shall be able absolutely to predominate and prescribe laws to the others." – *Law of Nations*, b. 3, c. 3, §47.

"What is usually termed a balance of power," says Gentz, "is that constitution subsisting amongst neighbouring states more or less connected with one another by virtue of which no one among them can injure the independence or essential rights of another without meeting with effectual resistance on some side, and, consequently, exposing itself to danger." – *Fragments on the Political Balance*, c. 1.

"The grand and distinguishing feature of the balancing system," says Brougham, "is the perpetual attention to foreign affairs which it inculcates, the constant watchfulness over every nation which it prescribes, the subjection in which it places all national passions and antipathies to the fine and delicate view of remote expediency, the unceasing care which it dictates of nations most remotely situated and apparently unconnected with ourselves, the general union which it has effected of all the European powers, obeying certain laws, and actuated in general by a common principle; in fine, the right of mutual inspection universally recognised among civilised states in the rights of public envoys and residents." – *Brougham's Colonial Policy*, b. 3, §1.

These are the best definitions we have been able to discover of the system denominated the balance of power. In the first place it must be remarked that, taking any one of these descriptions separately, it is so vague as to impart no knowledge even of the writer's meaning, whilst, if taken together, one confuses and contradicts another, Gentz describing it to be "a constitution subsisting among neighbouring states more or less connected with each other," whilst Brougham defines it as "dictating a care of nations most remotely situated and apparently unconnected with ourselves." Then it would really appear, from the laudatory tone applied to the system by Vattel, who says that it is "such a disposition of things as that no one potentate or state *shall be able* absolutely to predominate and prescribe laws to the others," as well as from the complacent manner in which Brougham states "the general *union which it has effected* of all the European powers, obeying certain laws, and actuated in general by a common principle," it would seem from such assurances as these that there was no necessity for that "perpetual attention to foreign affairs," or that "constant watchfulness over every nation," which the latter authority tells us the system "prescribes and inculcates." The only point on which these writers, in common with many other authors and speakers in favour of the balance of power, agree, is in the fundamental delusion that such a system was ever acceded to by the nations of Europe. To judge from the assumption by Brougham of a "general *union* among all the European powers;" from the allusion made by Gentz to "that *constitution* subsisting among neighbouring states;" or from Vattel's reference to "a *disposition of things*," &c., one might be justified in inferring that a kind of federal union had existed for the last century throughout Europe in which the several kingdoms had found, like the States of America, uninterrupted peace and prosperity. But we should like to know at what period of history such a compact amongst the nations of the Continent was entered into. Was it previously to the peace of Utrecht? Was it antecedent to the Austrian war of succession? Was it prior to the seven years' war or to the American war? Or did it exist during the French revolutionary wars? Nay, what period of the centuries during which Europe has (with only just sufficient intervals to enable the combatants to recruit their wasted energies) been one vast and continued battle-field, will

Lord Brougham fix upon to illustrate the salutary working of that "balancing system" which "places all national passions and antipathies in subjection to the fine and delicate view of remote expediency?"

Again, at what epoch did the nations of the Continent subscribe to that constitution "by virtue of which," according to Gentz, "no one among them can injure the independence or essential rights of another?" Did this constitution exist whilst Britain was spoiling the Dutch at the Cape or in the east? or when she dispossessed France of Canada? or (worse outrage by far) did it exist when England violated the "essential rights" of Spain by taking forcible and felonious possession of a portion of her native soil? Had this constitution been subscribed by Russia, Prussia, and Austria at the moment when they signed the partition of Poland? or by France when she amalgamated with a portion of Switzerland? by Austria at the acquisition of Lombardy? by Russia when dismembering Sweden, Turkey, and Persia? or by Prussia before incorporating Silesia?

So far from any such confederation having ever been, by written, verbal, or implied agreement, entered into by the "European powers, obeying certain laws, and actuated in general by a common principle;" the theory of the balance of power has, we believe, generally been interpreted, by those who, from age to age, have, parrotlike, used the phrase, to be a system invented for the very purpose of supplying the want of such a combination. Regarding it for a moment in this point of view, we should still expect to find that the "balancing system" had, at some period of modern history, been recognised and agreed to by all the Continental states; and that it had created a spirit of mutual concession and guarantee, by which the weaker and more powerful empires were placed upon a footing of equal security, and by which any one potentate or state was absolutely unable "to predominate over the others." But, instead of any such self-denial, we discover that the balance of Europe has merely meant (if it has had a meaning) that which our blunt Dutch king openly avowed as his aim to his parliament – a desire, on the part of the great powers, to "*hold the balance of Europe*." England has, for nearly a century, held the European scales – not with the blindness of the goddess of justice herself, or with a view to the equilibrium of opposite interests, but with a Cyclopean eye to her own aggrandisement. The same lust of conquest has actuated, up to the measure of their abilities, the other great powers; and, if we find the smaller states still, in the majority of instances, preserving their independent existence, it is owing, not to the watchful guardianship of the "balancing system," but to the limits which nature herself has set to the undue extension of territorial dominion – not only by the physical boundaries of different countries, but in those still more formidable moral impediments to the invader – the unity of language, laws, customs, and traditions; the instinct of patriotism and freedom; the hereditary rights of rulers; and, though last not least, that homage to the restraints of justice which nations and public bodies[1] have in all ages avowed, however they may have found excuses for evading it.

So far, then, as we can understand the subject, the theory of a balance of power is a mere chimera – a creation of the politician's brain – a phantasm, without definite form or tangible existence – a mere conjunction of syllables, forming words which convey sound without meaning.

...

We must not, however, pass over the "balance of power" without at least endeavouring to discover the meaning of a phrase which still enters into the preamble of an annual act of Parliament, for raising and maintaining a standing army of ninety thousand men. The theory, according to the historian Robertson, was first invented by the Machiavellian statesmen of Italy during the prosperous era of the Florentine (miscalled) republic; and it was imported into Western Europe in the early part of the sixteenth century, and became "fashionable," to use the very word of the historian of Charles V., along with many other modes borrowed, about the same time, from that commercial and civilised people. This explanation of its origin does not meet with the concurrence of some other writers; for it is singular, but still consistent with the ignis-fatuus character of the "balance of power," that scarcely two authors agree, either as to the nature or the precise period of invention of the system. Lord Brougham claims for the theory an origin as remote as the time of the Athenians; and Hume describes Demosthenes to have been the first advocate of the "balancing system" – very recommendatory, remembering that ancient history is little else than a calendar of savage wars! There can be little doubt, however, that the idea, by whomsoever or at whatever epoch conceived, sprang from that first instinct of our nature, fear, and originally meant at least some scheme for preventing the dangerous growth of the power of any particular state; *that power being always regarded, be it well remembered, as solely the offspring of conquest and aggrandisement*: notwithstanding, as we have had occasion to show in a former page of this pamphlet, in the case of England and the United States, that labour, improvements, and discoveries confer the greatest strength upon a people; and that, by these alone, and not by the sword of the conqueror, can nations, in modern and all future times, hope to rise to supreme power and grandeur. And it must be obvious that a system professing to observe a "balance of power" – by which, says Vattel, "no one potentate or state shall be able absolutely to predominate;" or, according to Gentz, "to injure the independence or essential rights of another;" by which, says Brougham, "a perpetual attention to foreign affairs is inculcated, and a

1 "Mankind, although reprobates in detail, are always moralists in the gross." – *Montesquieu.*

constant watchfulness over every nation is prescribed:" – it must be obvious that such a "balancing system" – if it disregards those swiftest strides towards power which are making by nations excelling in mechanical and chemical science, industry, education, morality, and freedom – must be altogether chimerical.

...

America, for fifty years at peace, with the exception of two years of defensive war, is a spectacle of the beneficent effects of that policy which may be comprised in the maxim – As little intercourse as possible betwixt the *Governments*, as much connection as possible between the *nations* of the world. And when England (*without being a republic*) shall be governed upon the same principles of regard for the interests of the people, and a like common sense view of the advantages of its position, we shall adopt a similar motto for our policy; and then we shall hear no more mention of that costly chimera, the balance of power.

Protection of commerce

[*Cobden uses an address to parliament by King William IV in 1836 to make his next point. King William is reported as saying:*]

"The necessity of maintaining the maritime strength of the country, and of giving adequate protection to the extended commerce of my subjects, has occasioned some increase in the estimates for the naval branch of the public service."

Now, if we felt some difficulty in apprehending the question of the "balancing principle," we confess ourselves to be much more at a loss to understand what is here meant by the protection of commerce through an increase in the navy estimates. Our commerce is, in other words, our manufactures; and the first inquiry which occurs necessarily is, Do we need an augmentation of the naval force, in order to guard our ingenious artisans and industrious labourers, or to protect those precious results of their mechanical genius, the manufactories of our capitalists? This apprehension vanishes, if we refer to the assurances held out in the above double guarantee for the continuance of peace, that our shores are safe from foreign aggression. The next idea that suggests itself is, Does piracy increase the demand for vessels of war? We, who write in the centre of the largest export trade in the world, have not heard of even one complaint of violence done to British interests upon the ocean; and probably there are not to be found a dozen freebooters upon the face of the aquatic globe. South America demands no addition to the force upon its coasts at the present moment, when those several Governments are more firmly organised, and foreign interests consequently more secure, than at any previous period. China presents no excuse; for her policy is, fortunately for her territorial integrity, invulnerable to foreign attempts at "intervention." The rest of Asia is our own. Where, then, shall we seek for a solution of the difficulty, or how account for the necessity which called for the increase of our naval strength?

The commerce of this country, we repeat, is, in other words, its manufactures. Our exports do not consist, as in Mexico or Brazil, of the produce of our soil and our mines; or, as in France and the United States, of a mixture of articles of agricultural and manufacturing origin: but they may be said to be wholly produced by the skill and industry of the manufacturing population of the United Kingdom.[2] Upon the prosperity, then, of this interest, hangs our foreign commerce; on which depends our external rank as a maritime state; our customs duties, which are necessary to the payment of the national debt; and the supply of every foreign article of our domestic consumption – every pound of tea, sugar, coffee, or rice, and all the other commodities consumed by the entire population of these realms. In a word, our national existence is involved in the well-doing of our manufacturers. If our readers – many of whom will be of the agricultural class, but every one of them nevertheless equally interested in the question – should ask, as all intelligent and reasoning minds ought to do, To what are we indebted for this commerce – we answer, in the name of every manufacturer and merchant of the kingdom – The *cheapness* alone of our manufactures. Are we asked, How is this trade protected, and by what means can it be enlarged? The reply still is, By the *cheapness* of our manufactures. Is it inquired how this mighty industry, upon which depends the comfort and existence of the whole empire, can be torn from use? – we rejoin, Only by the *greater cheapness* of the manufactures of another country.

...

But, if, instead of naming such causes and remedies as these, the Manchester Chamber of Commerce had stated in its report that the prints of Switzerland and the drills of Saxony (*the governments of which two countries do not together own a ship of war, as we believe*) were cheaper than the like articles fabricated here, *because the British navy was not sufficiently strong*, and had advised for relief that half a million a year should be added to the navy estimates – would not a writ *de lunatico inquirendo* have justly been issued against those intelligent Directors, the writer's colleagues, without further evidence of their insanity! Yet, having seen that the only way in which we can protect our commerce is the cheapness of our manufactures, what other object can be meant, when the Government calls for an augmentation of the navy, with a view to the protection of our

---

2   We stated this familiar fact in a former pamphlet; but it is one that cannot be too frequently placed broadly before the public eye.

commerce, but some plan, however inappreciable to common minds, for reducing the expenditure of the country, and thereby relieving us from some of the burdensome imposts with which our race of competition is impeded?

But there is, in the second passage which we have just quoted from his Majesty's speech, a part which tends to throw more light upon the whole – where it refers to the necessity of giving adequate protection to the "*extended*" commerce of the country. By which we are to infer that it is the principle of the government that the extension of our trade with foreign countries demands for its protection a corresponding augmentation of the royal navy. This, we are aware, was the policy of the last century, during the greater part of which the motto, "Ships, Colonies, and Commerce," was borne upon the national escutcheon, became the watchword of statesmen, and was the favourite sentiment of public writers; but this, which meant, in other words – "Men of war to conquer colonies, to yield us a monopoly of their trade," must now be dismissed, like many other equally glittering but false adages of our forefathers, and in its place we must substitute the more homely, but enduring maxim – *Cheapness*, which will command commerce; and whatever else is needful will follow in its train.

At a time when all beyond the precincts of Europe was colonial territory, and when the trade of the world was, with the exception of China, almost wholly forced into false channels, by the hand of violence, which was no sooner withdrawn than, by its own inherent law – the law of nature – it again sought its proper level course, the increase of the navy necessarily preceded and accompanied an extension of our commerce. The policy of nations, *then*, if judged by the standard which we apply to the conduct of individuals *now* – and there can be no exculpation in multitudinous immorality – was, to waylay their customers, whom they first knocked down and disabled, and afterwards dragged into their stores and compelled to purchase whatever articles they chose to offer, at such prices as they chose to ask! The independence of the New World has for ever put an end to the colonial policy of the Old, and with it that system of fraud and violence which for centuries characterised the commercial intercourse of the two hemispheres. And in that portentous truth, *the Americas are free*, teeming as it does with future change, there is nothing that more nearly affects our destiny than the total revolution which it dictates to the statesmen of Great Britain, in the commercial, colonial, and foreign policy of our Government. America is once more the theatre upon which nations are contending for mastery: it is not, however, a struggle for conquest, in which the victor will acquire territorial dominion – the fight is for commercial supremacy, and the battle will be won by the cheapest!

Whilst our trade rested upon our foreign dependencies, as was the case in the middle of the last century – whilst, in other words, force and violence were necessary to command customers for our manufactures – it was natural and consistent that almost every king's speech should allude to the importance of protecting the commerce of the country, by means of a powerful navy; but whilst, under the present more honest principles of trade, *cheapness* alone is necessary to command free and independent purchasers, and to protect our commerce, it must be evident that such armaments as impose the smallest possible tax upon the cost of our commodities must be the best adapted for the protection of our trade. But, besides dictating the disuse of warlike establishments, free trade (for of that beneficent doctrine we are speaking) arms its votaries by its own pacific nature, in that eternal truth – *the more any nation traffics abroad upon free and honest principles, the less it will be in danger of wars*.

...

It has been seen that armies and ships cannot protect or extend commerce; whilst, as is too well known, the expenses of maintaining them oppress and impede our manufacturing industry – two sufficient grounds for reducing both. There is another motive in the above facts. That feeling which was awakened by our overwhelming power at sea, at the conclusion of the war – the feeling of fear and mistrust lest we should be, in the words of the American state paper, just quoted, "apt to feel power and forget right" – is kept alive by the operation of the same cause, which tends still, as we have seen by the last debates in the French Chamber of Deputies, to afford excuses for perpetuating the restrictive duties upon our fabrics. The standing armies and navies, therefore, whilst they cannot possibly protect our commerce – whilst they add, by the increase of taxation, to the cost of our manufactures, and thus augment the difficulty of achieving the victory of "cheapness" – tend to deter rather than attract customers. The feeling is natural; it is understood in the individual concerns of life. Does the shopkeeper, when he invites buyers to his counter, place there, as a guard to protect his stock or defend his salesmen from violence, a gang of stout fellows, armed with pistols and cutlasses?

There is a vague apprehension of danger to our shores experienced by some writers, who would not feel safe unless with the assurance that the ports of England contained ships of war ready at all times to repel an attempt at invasion. This feeling arises from a narrow and imperfect knowledge of human nature, in supposing that another people shall be found sufficiently void of perception and reflection – in short, sufficiently mad – to assail a stronger and richer empire, merely because the retributive injury, thereby inevitably entailed upon themselves, would be delayed a few months by the necessary preparation of the instruments of chastisement. Such are the writers by whom we have been told that Russia was preparing an army of 50,000 men, to make a descent upon Great Britain to subjugate a population of twenty-five millions! Those people do not in their calculations award to mankind even the instinct of self-preservation which is given for the protection of the brute creation.

The elephant is not for ever brandishing his trunk, the lion closes his mouth and conceals his claws, and the deadly dart of the reptile is only protruded when the animal is enraged; yet we do not find that the weaker tribes – the goats, the deer, or the foxes – are given to assaulting those masters of the forest in their peaceful moods.

If that which constitutes cowardice in individuals, viz., the taking of undue and excessive precautions against danger, merits the same designation when practised by communities – then England certainly must rank as the greatest poltroon among nations. With twenty-five millions of the most robust, the freest, the richest, and most united population of Europe – enclosed within a smaller area than ever before contained so vast a number of inhabitants – placed upon two islands, which, for security, would have been chosen before any spot on earth, by the commander seeking for a *Torres Vedras* to contain his host – and with the experience of seven hundred years of safety, during which period no enemy has set foot upon their shores – yet behold the government of Great Britain maintaining mighty armaments, by sea and land, ready to repel the assaults of imaginary enemies! There is no greater obstacle to cheap and good government than this feeling of danger, which has been created and fostered for the very purpose of misgovernment.

...

Our object, however, in vindicating Russia from the attacks of prejudice and ignorance, has not been to transfer the national hatred to Turkey, but to neutralise public feeling, by showing that our only wise policy – nay, the only course consistent with the instinct of self-preservation – is to hold ourselves altogether independent of and aloof from the political relations of both these remote and comparatively barbarous nations. England, with her insular territory, her consolidated and free institutions, and her civilised and artificial condition of society, ought not to be, and cannot be, dependent for safety or prosperity upon the conduct of Russia or Turkey; and she will not, provided wisdom governs her counsels, enter into any engagements so obviously to the disadvantage of her people, as to place the peace and happiness of this empire at the mercy of the violence or wickedness of two despotic rulers over savage tribes more than a thousand miles distant from our shores.

...

In the name of every artisan in the kingdom, to whom war would bring the tidings, once more, of suffering and despair, in the behalf of the peasantry of these islands, to whom the first cannon would sound the knell of privation and death; on the part of the capitalists, merchants, manufacturers, and traders, who can reap no other fruits from hostilities but bankruptcy and ruin; in a word, for the sake of the vital interests of these and all other classes of the community, we solemnly protest against Great Britain being plunged into war with Russia, or any other country, in defence of Turkey – a war which, whilst it would inflict disasters upon every portion of the community, could not bestow a permanent benefit upon any class of it; and one upon our success in which no part of the civilised would have cause to rejoice. Having the *interests* of all orders of society to support our argument in favour of peace, we need not dread war. *These*, and not the piques of diplomatists, the whims of crowned heads, the intrigues of ambassadresses, or schoolboy rhetoric upon the balance of power, will henceforth determine the foreign policy of our government. That policy will be based upon the *bonâ fide* principle (not Lord Palmerston's principle) of *non-intervention in the political affairs of other nations*; and from the moment this maxim becomes the load-star by which our government shall steer the vessel of the state – from that moment the good old ship Britannia will float triumphantly in smooth and deep water, and the rocks, shoals, and hurricanes of foreign war are escaped for ever.

If it be objected, that this selfish policy disregards the welfare and improvement of other countries – which is, we cordially admit, the primary object of many of those who advocate a war with Russia, in defence of Turkey, and for the restoration of Poland – we answer, that, so far as the objects we have in view are concerned, we join hands with nearly every one of our opponents. Our desire is to see Poland happy, Turkey civilised, and Russia conscientious and free; it is still more our wish that these ameliorations should be bestowed by the hands of Britain upon her less instructed neighbours: so far the great majority of our opponents and ourselves are agreed; *how* to accomplish this beneficent purpose is the question whereon we differ. They would resort to the old method of trying, as Washington Irving says, "to promote the good of their neighbours, and the peace and happiness of the world, by dint of the cudgel." Now, there is an unanswerable objection to this method: experience is against it; it has been tried for some thousands of years, and has always been found to fail. But, within our own time, a new light has appeared which has penetrated our schools and families, and illuminated our prisons and lunatic asylums, and which promises soon to pervade all the institutions and relations of social life. We allude to that principle which, renouncing all appeals, through brute violence, to the mere instinct of fear, addresses itself to the nobler and far more powerful qualities of our intellectual and moral nature. This principle – which, from its very nature as a standard, tends to the exaltation of our species, has abolished the use of the rod, the fetters, the lash, and the strait-waistcoat, and which, in a modified degree, has been extended even to the brute creation, by substituting gentleness for severity in the management of horses and the treatment of dogs – this principle we would substitute for the use of cannon and musketry in attempting to improve or instruct other communities. In a word, our opponents would "promote the good of their neighbours by dint of the cudgel:" we propose to arrive at the same end by means of our own national example. *Their method,* at least, cannot be right; since it assumes that they are at all times competent to judge of what is good for others – which they are not: whilst, even if they were, it would be still equally wrong; for they have not the jurisdiction over other states which authorises them to do them even good by force of arms.

FRIEDRICH LIST

F RIEDRICH LIST (1789–1846), German political economist. A liberal nationalist, List was forced to flee Germany in the 1820s and during his exile in the United States he became acquainted with American ideas on political economy and the protection of "infant industries." Returning to Germany, he became an advocate of a customs union of the various German states, with a high external tariff. In the following extract from his masterwork, *The National System of Political Economy* (1841), he explains how free trade is a policy of the strong which works to the advantage of the more advanced economy, using arguments which have been repeated frequently in the last century and a half by opponents of liberal economic theory.

From *The National System of Political Economy*

Chapter XI

Political and cosmopolitical economy

Before Quesnay and the French economists there existed only a *practice* of political economy which was exercised by the State officials, administrators, and authors who wrote about matters of administration, occupied themselves exclusively with the agriculture, manufactures, commerce, and navigation of those countries to which they belonged, without analysing the causes of wealth, or taking at all into consideration the interests of the whole human race.

Quesnay (from whom the idea of universal free trade originated) was the first who extended his investigations to the whole human race, without taking into consideration the idea of the nation. He calls his work 'Physiocratie, ou du Gouvernement le plus avantageux au Genre Humain,' his demands being that we must imagine that *the merchants of all nations formed one commercial republic*. Quesnay undoubtedly speaks of *cosmopolitical* economy, i.e. of that science which teaches how the entire human race may attain prosperity; in opposition to political economy, or that science which limits its teaching to the inquiry how a *given nation* can obtain (under the existing conditions of the world) prosperity, civilisation, and power, by means of agriculture, industry, and commerce.

Adam Smith treats his doctrine in a similarly extended sense, by making it his task to indicate the cosmopolitical idea of the absolute freedom of the commerce of the whole world in spite of the gross mistakes made by the physiocrates against the very nature of things and against logic. Adam Smith concerned himself as little as Quesnay did with true political economy, i.e. that policy which each separate nation had to obey in order to make progress in its economical conditions. He entitles his work, 'The Nature and Causes of the Wealth of Nations' (i.e. of all nations of the whole human race). He speaks of the various systems of political economy in a separate part of his work solely for the purpose of demonstrating their non-efficiency, and of proving that 'political' or *national* economy must be replaced by 'cosmopolitical or world-wide economy.' Although here and there he speaks of wars, this only occurs incidentally. The idea of a perpetual state of peace forms the foundation of all his arguments. Moreover, according to the explicit remarks of his biographer, Dugald Stewart, his investigations from the commencement are based upon the principle that 'most of the State regulations for the promotion of public prosperity are unnecessary, and a nation in order to be transformed from the lowest state of barbarism into a state of the highest possible prosperity needs nothing but bearable taxation, fair administration of justice, and *peace*.' Adam Smith naturally understood under the word 'peace' the 'perpetual universal peace' of the Abbé St. Pierre.

J. B. Say openly demands that we should imagine the existence of a *universal republic* in order to comprehend the idea of general free trade. This writer, whose efforts were mainly restricted to the formation of a system out of the materials which Adam Smith had brought to light, says explicitly in the sixth volume (p. 288) of his 'Economie politique pratique:' 'We may take into our consideration the economical interests of the family with the father at its head; the principles and observations referring thereto will constitute *private economy*. Those principles, however, which have reference to the interests of whole nations, whether in themselves or in relation to other nations, form *public economy* (l'économie publique). *Political economy*, lastly, relates to the interests of all nations, to *human society in general*.'

It must be remarked here, that in the first place Say recognises the existence of a national economy or political economy, under the name 'économie publique,' but that he nowhere treats of the latter in his works; secondly, that he attributes the name *political* economy to a doctrine which is evidently of *cosmopolitical* nature; and that in this doctrine he invariably merely speaks of an economy which has for its sole object the interests of the whole human society, without regard to the separate interests of distinct nations.

This substitution of terms might be passed over if Say, after having explained what he calls political economy (which, however, is nothing else but cosmopolitical or world-wide economy, or economy of the whole human race), had acquainted us with the principles of the doctrine which he calls 'économie publique,' which however is, properly speaking, nothing else but the economy of given nations, or true political economy.

In defining and developing this doctrine he could scarcely forbear to proceed from the idea and the nature of the nation, and to show what material modifications the 'economy of the whole human race' must undergo by the fact that at present that race is still separated into distinct nationalities each held together by common powers and interests, and distinct from other societies of the same kind which in the exercise of their natural liberty are opposed to one another. However, by giving his cosmopolitical economy the name *political*, he dispenses with this explanation, effects by means of a transposition of terms also a transposition of meaning, and thereby masks a series of the gravest theoretical errors.

All later writers have participated in this error. Sismondi also calls political economy explicitly, 'La science qui se charge du bonheur de l'espèce humaine.' Adam Smith and his followers teach us from this mainly nothing more than what Quesnay and his followers had taught us already, for the article of the 'Revue Méthodique' treating of the physiocratic school states, in almost the same words: *'The well-being of the individual is dependent altogether on the well-being of the whole human race.'*

The first of the North American advocates of free trade, as understood by Adam Smith – Thomas Cooper, President of Columbia College – denies even the existence of nationality; he calls the nation 'a grammatical invention,' created only to save periphrases, a nonentity, which has no actual existence save in the heads of politicians. Cooper is moreover perfectly consistent with respect to this, in fact much more consistent than his predecessors and instructors, for it is evident that as soon as the existence of nations with their distinct nature and interests is recognised, it becomes necessary to modify the economy of human society in accordance with these special interests, and that if Cooper intended to represent these modifications as errors, it was very wise on his part from the beginning to disown the very existence of nations.

For our own part, we are far from rejecting the theory of *cosmopolitical* economy, as it has been perfected by the prevailing school; we are, however, of opinion that political economy, or as Say calls it 'économie publique,' should also be developed scientifically, and that it is always better to call things by their proper names than to give them significations which stand opposed to the true import of words.

If we wish to remain true to the laws of logic and of the nature of things, we must set the economy of individuals against the economy of societies, and discriminate in respect to the latter between true political or national economy (which, emanating from the idea and nature of the nation, teaches how a given *nation* in the present state of the world and its own special national relations can maintain and improve its economical conditions) and cosmo-political economy, which originates in the assumption that all nations of the earth form but one society living in a perpetual state of peace.

If, as the prevailing school requires, we assume a universal union or confederation of all nations as the guarantee for an everlasting peace, the principle of international free trade seems to be perfectly justified. The less every individual is restrained in pursuing his own individual prosperity, the greater the number and wealth of those with whom he has free intercourse, the greater the area over which his individual activity can exercise itself, the easier it will be for him to utilise for the increase of his prosperity the properties given him by nature, the knowledge and talents which he has acquired, and the forces of nature placed at his disposal. As with separate individuals, so is it also the case with individual communities, provinces, and countries. A simpleton only could maintain that a union for free commercial intercourse between themselves is not as advantageous to the different states included in the United States of North America, to the various departments of France, and to the various German allied states, as would be their separation by internal provincial customs tariffs.

In the union of the three kingdoms of Great Britain and Ireland the world witnesses a great and irrefragable example of the immeasurable efficacy of free trade between united nations. Let us only suppose all other nations of the earth to be united in a similar manner, and the most vivid imagination will not be able to picture to itself the sum of prosperity and good fortune which the whole human race would thereby acquire.

Unquestionably the idea of a universal confederation and a perpetual peace is commended both by common sense and religion.[1] If single combat between individuals is at present considered to be contrary to reason, how much more must combat between two nations be similarly condemned? The proofs which social economy can produce from the history of the civilisation of mankind of the reasonableness of bringing about the union of all mankind under the law of right, are perhaps those which are the clearest to sound human understanding.

History teaches that wherever individuals are engaged in wars, the prosperity of mankind is at its lowest stage, and that it increases in the same proportion in which the concord of mankind increases. In the primitive state

---

1 The Christian religion inculcates perpetual peace. But until the promise, 'There shall be *one fold and one shepherd*,' has been fulfilled, the principle of the Quakers, however true it be in itself, can scarcely be acted upon. There is no better proof for the Divine origin of the Christian religion than that its doctrines and promises are in perfect agreement with the demands of both the material and spiritual well-being of the human race.

of the human race, first unions of families took place, then towns, then confederations of towns, then union of whole countries, finally unions of several
states under one and the same government. If the nature of things has been
powerful enough to extend this union (which commenced with the family)
over hundreds of millions, we ought to consider that nature to be powerful
enough to accomplish the union of all nations. If the human mind were capable of comprehending the advantages of this great union, so ought we to
venture to deem it capable of understanding the still greater benefits which
would result from a union of the whole human race. Many instances indicate this tendency in the spirit of the present times. We need only hint at
the progress made in sciences, arts, and discoveries, in industry and social
order. It may be already foreseen with certainty, that after a lapse of a few
decades the civilised nations of the earth will, by the perfection of the means
of conveyance, be united as respects both material and mental interchange in
as close a manner as (or even closer than) that in which a century ago the various counties of England were connected. Continental governments possess
already at the present moment in the telegraph the means of communicating
with one another, almost as if they were at one and the same place. Powerful forces previously unknown have already raised industry to a degree of
perfection hitherto never anticipated, and others still more powerful have already announced their appearance. But the more that industry advances, and
proportionately extends over the countries of the earth, the smaller will be
the possibility of wars. Two nations equally well developed in industry could
mutually inflict on one another more injury in one week than they would
be able to make good in a whole generation. But hence it follows that the
same new forces which have hitherto served particularly for production will
not withhold their services from destruction, and will principally favour the
side of defence, and especially the European Continental nations, while they
threaten the insular State with the loss of those advantages which have been
gained by her insular position for her defence. In the congresses of the great
European powers Europe possesses already the embryo of a future congress
of nations. The endeavours to settle differences by protocol are clearly already prevailing over those which obtain justice by force of arms. A clearer
insight into the nature of wealth and industry has led the wiser heads of all
civilised nations to the conviction that both the civilisation of barbarous and
semi-barbarous nations, and of those whose culture is retrograding, as well
as the formation of colonies, offer to civilised nations a field for the development of their productive powers which promises them much richer and
safer fruits than mutual hostilities by wars or restrictions on trade. The farther we advance in this perception, and the more the uncivilised countries
come into contact with the civilised ones by the progress made in the means
of transport, so much more will the civilised countries comprehend that the

civilisation of barbarous nations, of those distracted by internal anarchy, or which are oppressed by bad government, is a task which offers to all equal advantages – a duty incumbent on them all alike, but one which can only be accomplished by unity.

That the civilisation of all nations, the culture of the whole globe, forms a task imposed on the whole human race, is evident from those unalterable laws of nature by which civilised nations are driven on with irresistible power to extend or transfer their powers of production to less cultivated countries. We see everywhere, under the influence of civilisation, population, powers of mind, material capital attaining to such dimensions that they must necessarily flow over into other less civilised countries. If the cultivable area of the country no longer suffices to sustain the population and to employ the agricultural population, the redundant portion of the latter seeks territories suitable for cultivation in distant lands; if the talents and technical abilities of a nation have become so numerous as to find no longer sufficient rewards within it, they emigrate to places where they are more in demand; if in consequence of the accumulation of material capital, the rates of interest fall so considerably that the smaller capitalist can no longer live on them, he tries to invest his money more satisfactorily in less wealthy countries.

A true principle, therefore, underlies the system of the popular school, but a principle which must be recognised and applied by science if its design to enlighten practice is to be fulfilled, an idea which practice cannot ignore without getting astray; only the school has omitted to take into consideration the nature of nationalities and their special interests and conditions, and to bring these into accord with the idea of universal union and an everlasting peace.

The popular school has assumed as being actually in existence a state of things which has yet to come into existence. It assumes the existence of a universal union and a state of perpetual peace, and deduces therefrom the great benefits of free trade. In this manner it confounds effects with causes. Among the provinces and states which are already politically united, there exists a state of perpetual peace; from this political union originates their commercial union, and it is in consequence of the perpetual peace thus maintained that the commercial union has become so beneficial to them. All examples which history can show are those in which the political union has led the way, and the commercial union has followed.[2] Not a single instance can be adduced in which the latter has taken the lead, and the former has grown up from it. That, however, under the existing conditions of the

2   This statement was probably accurate up to the period when List wrote, but a notable exception to it may now be adduced. The commercial union of the various German states under the Zollverein preceded by many years their political union under the Empire, and powerfully promoted it. – TR.

world, the result of general free trade would not be a universal republic, but, on the contrary, a universal subjection of the less advanced nations to the supremacy of the predominant manufacturing, commercial, and naval power, is a conclusion for which the reasons are very strong and, according to our views, irrefragable. A universal republic (in the sense of Henry IV. and of the Abbé St. Pierre), i.e. a union of the nations of the earth whereby they recognise the same conditions of right among themselves and renounce self-redress, can only be realised if a large number of nationalities attain to as nearly the same degree as possible of industry and civilisation, political cultivation, and power. Only with the gradual formation of this union can free trade be developed, only as a result of this union can it confer on all nations the same great advantages which are now experienced by those provinces and states which are politically united. The system of protection, inasmuch as it forms the only means of placing those nations which are far behind in civilisation on equal terms with the one predominating nation (which, however, never received at the hands of Nature a perpetual right to a monopoly of manufacture, but which merely gained an advance over others in point of time), the system of protection regarded from this point of view appears to be the most efficient means of furthering the final union of nations, and hence also of promoting true freedom of trade. And national economy appears from this point of view to be that science which, correctly appreciating the existing interests and the individual circumstances of nations, teaches how *every separate nation* can be raised to that stage of industrial development in which union with other nations equally well developed, and consequently freedom of trade, can become possible and useful to it.

The popular school, however, has mixed up both doctrines with one another; it has fallen into the grave error of judging of the conditions of nations according to purely cosmopolitical principles, and of ignoring from merely political reasons the cosmopolitical tendency of the productive powers.

Only by ignoring the cosmopolitical tendency of the productive powers could Malthus be led into the error of desiring to restrict the increase of population, or Chalmers and Torrens maintain more recently the strange idea that augmentation of capital and unrestricted production are evils the restriction of which the welfare of the community imperatively demands, or Sismondi declare that manufactures are things injurious to the community. Their theory in this case resembles Saturn, who devours his own children – the same theory which allows that from the increase of population, of capital and machinery, division of labour takes place, and explains from this the welfare of society, finally considers these forces as monsters which threaten the prosperity of nations, because it merely regards the present conditions of individual nations, and does not take into consideration the conditions of the whole globe and the future progress of mankind.

It is not true that population increases in a larger proportion than production of the means of subsistence; it is at least foolish to assume such disproportion, or to attempt to prove it by artificial calculations or sophistical arguments, so long as on the globe a mass of natural forces still lies inert by means of which ten times or perhaps a hundred times more people than are now living can be sustained. It is mere narrow-mindedness to consider the present extent of the productive forces as the test of how many persons could be supported on a given area of land. The savage, the hunter, and the fisherman, according to his own calculation, would not find room enough for one million persons, the shepherd not for ten millions, the raw agriculturist not for one hundred millions on the whole globe; and yet two hundred millions are living at present in Europe alone. The culture of the potato and of food-yielding plants, and the more recent improvements made in agriculture generally, have increased tenfold the productive powers of the human race for the creation of the means of subsistence. In the Middle Ages the yield of wheat of an acre of land in England was fourfold, to-day it is ten to twenty fold, and in addition to that five times more land is cultivated. In many European countries (the soil of which possesses the same natural fertility as that of England) the yield at present does not exceed fourfold. Who will venture to set further limits to the discoveries, inventions, and improvements of the human race? Agricultural chemistry is still in its infancy; who can tell that to-morrow, by means of a new invention or discovery, the produce of the soil may not be increased five or ten fold? We already possess, in the artesian well, the means of converting unfertile wastes into rich corn fields; and what unknown forces may not yet be hidden in the interior of the earth? Let us merely suppose that through a new discovery we were enabled to produce heat everywhere very cheaply, and without the aid of the fuels at present known: what spaces of land could thus be utilised for cultivation, and in what an incalculable degree would the yield of a given area of land be increased? If Malthus' doctrine appears to us in its tendency narrowminded, it is also in the methods by which it could act an unnatural one, which destroys morality and power, and is simply horrible. It seeks to destroy a desire which nature uses as the most active means for inciting men to exert body and mind, and to awaken and support their nobler feelings – a desire to which humanity for the greater part owes its progress. It would elevate the most heartless egotism to the position of a law; it requires us to close our hearts against the starving man, because if we hand him food and drink, another might starve in his place in thirty years' time. It substitutes cold calculation for sympathy. This doctrine tends to convert the hearts of men into stones. But what could be finally expected of a nation whose citizens should carry stones instead of hearts in their bosoms? What else than the total destruction of all morality, and with it of all productive forces, and therefore of all the wealth, civilisation, and power of the nation?

If in a nation the population increases more than the production of the means of subsistence, if capital accumulates at length to such an extent as no longer to find investment, if machinery throws a number of operatives out of work and manufactured goods accumulate to a large excess, this merely proves, that nature will not allow industry, civilisation, wealth, and power to fall exclusively to the lot of a single nation, or that a large portion of the globe suitable for cultivation should be merely inhabited by wild animals, and that the largest portion of the human race should remain sunk in savagery, ignorance, and poverty.

We have shown into what errors the school has fallen by judging the productive forces of the human race from a political point of view; we have now also to point out the mistakes which it has committed by regarding the separate interests of nations from a cosmopolitical point of view.

If a confederation of all nations existed in reality, as is the case with the separate states constituting the Union of North America, the excess of population, talents, skilled abilities, and material capital would flow over from England to the Continental states, in a similar manner to that in which it travels from the eastern states of the American Union to the western, provided that in the Continental states the same security for persons and property, the same constitution and general laws prevailed, and that the English Government was made subject to the united will of the universal confederation. Under these suppositions there would be no better way of raising all these countries to the same stage of wealth and cultivation as England than free trade. This is the argument of the school. But how would it tally with the actual operation of free trade under the existing conditions of the world?

The Britons as an independent and separate nation would henceforth take their national interest as the sole guide of their policy. The Englishman, from predilection for his language, for his laws, regulations, and habits, would wherever it was possible devote his powers and his capital to develop his own native industry, for which the system of free trade, by extending the market for English manufactures over all countries, would offer him sufficient opportunity; he would not readily take a fancy to establish manufactures in France or Germany. All excess of capital in England would be at once devoted to trading with foreign parts of the world. If the Englishman took it into his head to emigrate, or to invest his capital elsewhere than in England, he would as he now does prefer those more distant countries where he would find already existing his language, his laws, and regulations, rather than the benighted countries of the Continent.

All England would thus be developed into one immense manufacturing city. Asia, Africa, and Australia would be civilised by England, and covered with new states modelled after the English fashion. In time a world of English states would be formed, under the presidency of the mother state, in which the European Continental nations would be lost as unimportant, unproductive races. By this arrangement it would fall to the lot of France, together with Spain and Portugal, to supply this English world with the choicest wines, and to drink the bad ones herself: at most France might retain the manufacture of a little millinery. Germany would scarcely have more to supply this English world with than children's toys, wooden clocks, and philological writings, and sometimes also an auxiliary corps, who might sacrifice themselves to pine away in the deserts of Asia or Africa, for the sake of extending the manufacturing and commercial supremacy, the literature and language of England. It would not require many centuries before people in this English world would think and speak of the Germans and French in the same tone as we speak at present of the Asiatic nations.

True political science, however, regards such a result of universal free trade as a very unnatural one; it will argue that had universal free trade been introduced at the time of the Hanseatic League, the German nationality instead of the English would have secured an advance in commerce and manufacture over all other countries.

It would be most unjust, even on cosmopolitical grounds, now to resign to the English all the wealth and power of the earth, merely because by them the political system of commerce was first established and the cosmopolitical principle for the most part ignored. In order to allow freedom of trade to operate naturally, the less advanced nations must first be raised by artificial measures to that stage of cultivation to which the English nation has been artificially elevated. In order that, through that cosmopolitical tendency of the powers of production to which we have alluded, the more distant parts of the world may not be benefited and enriched before the neighbouring European countries, those nations which feel themselves to be capable, owing to their moral, intellectual, social, and political circumstances, of developing a manufacturing power of their own must adopt the system of protection as the most effectual means for this purpose. The effects of this system for the purpose in view are of two kinds; in the first place, by gradually excluding foreign manufactured articles from our markets, a surplus would be occasioned in foreign nations, of workmen, talents, and capital, which must seek employment abroad; and secondly, by the premium which our system of protection would offer to the immigration into our country of workmen, talents, and capital, that excess of productive power would be induced to find employment with us, instead of emigrating to distant parts of the world and to colonies. Political science refers to history, and inquires whether England has not in former times drawn from Germany, Italy, Holland, France, Spain, and Portugal by these means a mass of productive power. She asks: Why does the cosmopolitical school, when it pretends to weigh in the balance the advantages and the disadvantages of the system of protection, utterly ignore this great and remarkable instance of the results of that system?

RUDOLF HILFERDING

R UDOLF HILFERDING (1877–1941), Austrian-born Marxist political economist, whose *Finance Capital* (1910) has some claim to be considered the most important work of Marxist economic theory after Marx's *Capital* itself. His explanation of imperialism as the foreign policy of finance capital, which is extracted below, clearly provides the intellectual backbone of Lenin's theory of imperialism – although the latter was unwilling to admit this, since Hilferding was a democrat and anti-Bolshevik. An opponent of one tyranny, Soviet communism – and a Social Democrat Minister in the Weimar Republic – he was murdered by another, going into exile in 1933 and being found dead in a Nazi prison cell in Paris in 1941.

From *Finance Capital*

[*First, Hilferding establishes that the tariff policies of finance capital are different in intention and effect from those advocated by, for example, Hamilton or List.*]

The purpose of the old protective tariff, aside from compensating for various natural disadvantages, was to accelerate the emergence of industry within the protected borders. It was intended to guard the developing domestic industry against the danger of being stifled or destroyed by overwhelming competition from a well developed foreign industry. It needed only to be high enough to offset the advantages of foreign industry, and in no circumstances could it be prohibitive because domestic industry could not yet satisfy the entire demand. Above all it was not regarded as permanent. Once it had fulfilled its 'educational' function, and domestic industry had developed to the stage where it could both satisfy domestic demand and begin to think about exports, the protective tariff lost its meaning. It became an obstacle to export promotion, since it induced other nations to adopt similar policies. Under a system of free competition, it would cease to raise prices when the protected domestic industry could satisfy domestic demand and begin to export goods. The price on the protected market would then necessarily be the same as the price on the world market, because the saving of freight charges to more distant foreign markets would make sales on the domestic market more profitable than those abroad and the output of industry would equal or exceed domestic demand. The protective tariff, therefore, was intended to be both moderate and temporary, simply to help an infant industry overcome its initial difficulties.

But matters are different in the age of capitalist monopolies. Today it is just the most powerful industries, with a high export potential, whose competitiveness on the world market is beyond doubt and which, according to the old theory, should have no further interest in protective tariffs, which support high tariffs. If we assume the maintenance of free competition a protective tariff loses its power to raise prices once domestic industry fully satisfies domestic demand. But the protective tariff for industry was one of the most effective means of promoting cartels, first by making foreign competition more difficult, and second, because cartels provided an opportunity to take advantage of the tariff margin even when industry had become capable of exporting. By restricting production quotas for domestic consumption the cartel eliminates competition on the domestic market. The suppression of competition sustains the effect of a protective tariff in raising prices even at a stage when production has long since outstripped domestic demand. Thus it becomes a prime interest of cartelized industry to make the protective tariff a permanent institution, which in the first place assures the continued existence of the cartel, and second, enables the cartel to sell its product on the domestic market at an extra profit. The amount of this extra profit is given by the difference between the domestic price and the price on the world market. This difference, however, depends upon the level of the tariff, and so efforts to raise tariffs have become just as unrestrained as those to increase profits. Cartelized industry has therefore a direct and supreme interest in the level of the protective tariff. The higher the tariff, the more the domestic price can be raised above the price on the world market; and so the 'educational' tariff has evolved into a high protective tariff. The protagonist of friendly agreements and advocate of the gradual reduction of tariffs has become a fanatical high tariff protectionist.

···

With the development of export subsidies the function of the protective tariff has undergone a complete change, and indeed has turned into its opposite. From being a means of defence against the conquest of the domestic market by foreign industries it has become a means for the conquest of foreign markets by domestic industry. What was once a defensive weapon of the weak has become an offensive weapon in the hands of the powerful.

[*He then examines the forces which make the export of capital an important feature of finance capital and distinguishes them from earlier phases of capitalist development, stressing the way in which direct rule of colonies has now become necessary.*]

Since the new markets are no longer simply outlets for goods, but also spheres for the investment of capital, this has also brought about a change in the political behaviour of the capital-exporting countries. Trade alone, so far as it was not colonial trade which has always been associated with robbery and plunder, but comprised trade with relatively advanced white or yellow peoples who were capable of resistance, for a long time left the social and political relations in these countries basically undisturbed, and confined itself to economic relations. So long as there exists a state power which is capable of maintaining some kind of order, direct rule over these areas is less important. All this changes when the export of capital becomes predominant, for much more substantial interests are then at stake. The risks involved in building railways, acquiring land, constructing harbours, opening and operating mines, in a foreign country, are much greater than in the mere buying and selling of goods.

The backwardness of the legal system thus becomes an obstacle, and finance capital demands ever more insistently that it should be removed, even if that has to be done by force. This leads to increasingly acute conflicts between the advanced capitalist states and the state authorities of the backward areas, and to ever more pressing attempts to impose upon these countries legal systems appropriate to capitalism, regardless of whether the existing rulers are retained or destroyed. At the same time the competition for the newly-opened spheres of investment produces further clashes and conflicts among the advanced capitalist states themselves. In the newly-opened countries themselves, however, the introduction of capitalism intensifies contradictions and arouses growing resistance to the invaders among the people, whose national consciousness has been awakened, which can easily take the form of policies inimical to foreign capital. The old social relations are completely revolutionized, the age-old bondage to the soil of the 'nations without a history' is disrupted and they are swept into the capitalist maelstrom. Capitalism itself gradually provides the subjected people with the ways and means for their own liberation. They adopt as their own the ideal that was once the highest aspiration of the European nations; namely, the formation of a unified national state as an instrument of economic and cultural freedom. This independence movement threatens European capital precisely in its most valuable and promising areas of exploitation, and to an increasing extent it can only maintain its domination by continually expanding its means of coercion.

This explains why all capitalists with interests in foreign countries call for a strong state whose authority will protect their interests even in the most remote corners of the globe, and for showing the national flag everywhere so that the flag of trade can also be planted everywhere. Export capital feels most comfortable, however, when its own state is in complete control of the new territory, for capital exports from other countries are then excluded, it enjoys a privileged position, and its profits are more or less guaranteed by the state. Thus the export of capital also encourages an imperialist policy.

The export of capital, especially since it has assumed the form of industrial and finance capital, has enormously accelerated the overthrow of all the old social relations, and the involvement of the whole world in capitalism. Capitalist development did not take place independently in each individual country, but instead capitalist relations of production and exploitation were imported along with capital from abroad, and indeed imported at the level already attained in the most advanced country. Just as a newly established industry today does not develop from handicraft beginnings and techniques into a modern giant concern, but is established from the outset as an advanced capitalist enterprise, so capitalism is now imported into a new country in its most advanced form and exerts its revolutionary effects far more strongly and in a much shorter time than was the case, for instance, in the capitalist development of Holland and England.

The revolution in transport is a milestone in the history of capital exports. Railways and steamships in themselves are immensely important to capitalism because they reduce the turnover time. This releases circulation capital and then raises the rate of profit. The reduction in the price of raw materials lowers costs and increases consumption. Thus it is the railways and steamships which first create those large economic territories that make possible the giant modern concerns with their mass production. But above all the railways were the most important means of opening up foreign markets. Without them, it would have been impossible to distribute the products of these countries in such vast quantities throughout Europe and to expand the market so rapidly into a world market. Even more important, however, is the fact that the export of capital now became necessary on a vast scale in order to construct these railways, which have been built almost entirely with European, particularly English, capital.

The export of capital was, however, an English monopoly, and it secured for England the domination of the world market. Neither industrially nor financially had England any reason to fear competition from other countries, and so the freedom of the market remained its ideal. Conversely, England's supremacy necessarily made all other states even more determined to maintain and extend their rule over territories which they had already acquired, so that at least within their own borders they would be protected against the overwhelming competition of England.

The situation changed when England's monopoly was broken and English capitalism, which as a result of free trade had never been effectively organized, had to meet the superior competition of America and Germany. The development of finance capital created in these states a powerful drive towards the export of capital. As we have seen, the development of joint-stock companies and cartels generates promoter's profits which flow into the banks as capital seeking application. In addition, the protective tariff system restricts domestic consumption and makes it essential to promote exports. At the same time the export subsidies which are made possible by cartel tariffs provide a means for competing vigorously with England in neutral markets, and this competition is all the more dangerous because the newer large-scale industry of these countries is to some extent technically superior to that of England as a result of its more modern equipment. Export subsidies having become an important weapon in the international competitive struggle, they are all the more effective the larger they are. Their size depends upon the level of tariffs, and raising this level thus becomes a prime interest of the capitalist class in every nation. No one can afford to lag behind in this respect. A protective tariff in one country makes it essential for others to follow suit, and this is all the more certain to happen the more advanced capitalism is in this country and the more powerful and widespread its capitalist monopolies. The level of the protective tariff thus becomes the decisive factor in the international competitive struggle. If it is raised in one country, others must necessarily do the same if they are not to suffer from adverse conditions of competition and to be beaten on the world market. Thus the industrial tariff too becomes what the agrarian tariff is by its very nature, an endless spiral.

But the competitive struggle, which can only be waged by reducing the price of commodities, always threatens to bring losses or at least not to produce an average rate of profit, so that here too the elimination of competition has become the ideal of the large capitalist combines. All the more so because, as we have seen, exports have become an urgent necessity for them under any circumstances, as a result of technological conditions which make imperative the largest possible scale of production. But competition rules on the world market, and there is no alternative but to replace one type of competition by a less dangerous one; to substitute for competition on the commodity market, where the price of the commodity is the only determining factor, competition on the capital market in the provision of loan capital on condition that any loan will subsequently be used for obtaining goods from the country making it. The export of capital has now become a means of ensuring that the capital-exporting country will be the supplier of industrial goods. The customer has no choice; he becomes a debtor and hence a dependent who must accept the conditions imposed by his creditor. Serbia can obtain a loan from Austria, Germany or France only if it undertakes to buy its guns or its rolling-stock from Skoda, Krupp or Schneider. The struggle for markets for goods becomes a conflict among national banking groups over spheres of investment for loan capital, and since rates of interest tend to be equalized on the international market, economic competition is confined here within relatively narrow limits, so that the economic struggle quickly becomes a power struggle in which political weapons are employed.

From an economic standpoint the older capitalist states still retain an advantage in these conflicts. England possesses an old capital-satiated industry which was originally adapted to the needs of the world market in the days of England's monopoly and now develops more slowly than German or American industry, lacking their capacity for rapid expansion. On the other hand, its accumulated capital is extraordinarily large, and vast amounts of profit available for accumulation flow steadily back to England from its overseas investments. The proportion of the accumulated masses of capital to the volume of capital which can be invested internally is at its highest here, which explains why the pressure to invest capital abroad is strongest and the rate of interest lowest in England. The same situation had emerged in France for different reasons. Here also there is a store of old accumulated wealth which is centralized by the banking system (though it is somewhat less concentrated as a result of the property system in France) together with a steady flow of income from foreign investments, and on the other side a stagnation of industrial growth at home; hence a powerful tendency to export capital. The advantage which England and France enjoy can only be made effective politically through strong diplomatic pressure, which is a dangerous, and therefore limited, means, or else economically, by making sacrifices in respect of prices, which would outweigh a possible rise in the rate of interest.

But the intensity of competition arouses a desire to eliminate it altogether. The simplest way of achieving this is to incorporate parts of the world market into the national market, through a colonial policy which involves the annexation of foreign territories. Thus, while free trade was indifferent to colonies, protectionism leads directly to a more active colonial policy, and to conflicts of interest between different states.

[*The foreign policy of finance capital is then summarized, its potential for inducing intercapitalist struggles examined, along with some countervailing tendencies.*]

The policy of finance capital has three objectives: (1) to establish the largest possible economic territory; (2) to close this territory to foreign competition by a wall of protective tariffs, and consequently (3) to reserve it as an area of exploitation for the national monopolistic combinations. Such aims, however, were bound to come into the sharpest possible conflict with the economic policy which industrial capital carried to a state of classic perfection during its period of absolute rule (in the double sense that commercial and bank capital were subordinated to it, and that it had absolute control of the world market) in England. All the more so since the application of this policy of finance capital in other countries has also increasingly threatened the interests of English industrial capital. Indeed, the country of free trade was the natural target for attack by foreign competition, though of course 'dumping' also has certain advantages for English industry. The processing industry obtained cheaper raw materials as a result of cut-throat competition. But on the other hand this also hurt the raw material industries, and so, as cartelization advanced, as more stages of production were integrated, and as the system of export subsidies was extended, the hour was bound to strike for those English industries which had hitherto profited from 'dumping'. The most important factor, however, is that the tariff opens up the prospect of an era of rapid monopolization with its opportunities for extra profits and promoter's profits, which are a great enticement to English capital.

On the other hand, it would be entirely possible for England to enter into a customs union with her colonies. Most of the self-governing colonies are important primarily as suppliers of raw materials to England and purchasers of industrial products. The protective tariff policy adopted by other states, especially in agriculture, has in any case made England the principal market for the colonies. In so far as English industry could impede the development of their own industries these countries (in the British Empire) are still at the stage of the 'educational' tariff, that is to say at a stage which cannot tolerate a rise in tariffs above a certain level because importation of foreign industrial products is still absolutely essential to supply their own market. It would be quite easy, therefore, to establish a higher cartel tariff for the British Empire as a whole, while retaining the 'educational' tariffs within the empire; and the prospect of establishing such an economic territory, which would be strong enough both politically and economically to counter the expulsion of British industries as a result of other states raising their tariffs, is capable of uniting the whole capitalist class. Furthermore, by far the greater part of the capital used in the colonies is owned by English capitalists, for whom an imperial tariff is much more important than the larger increase that an independent colonial tariff would bring.

The United States is in itself a sufficiently large economic territory even in the age of imperialism, and the direction of its expansion is determined by geography. The Pan-American movement, which found its initial political expression in the Monroe Doctrine, is still in its beginnings and has immense potentialities because of the enormous predominance of the United States.

Things are different in Europe, where the division into independent states has given rise to conflicting economic interests, the elimination of which by means of a Central European customs union encounters very serious obstacles. Here, unlike the British Empire, it is not a matter of mutually complementary parts but of more or less identical, and hence competing, entities confronting each other in hostile fashion.

...

But here also there are opposing tendencies at work. The larger the economic territory and the greater the power of the state, the more favourable is the position of its national capital on the world market. That is why finance capital has come to champion the idea that the power of the state should be strengthened by every available means. But the greater the historically produced disparities between the power of difficult states, the more the conditions on which they engage in competition will vary, and the more bitter – because more rewarding – will be the struggle of the large economic territories to dominate the world market. This struggle is intensified the more developed finance capital is and the more vigorous its efforts to monopolize parts of the world market for its own national capital; and the more advanced this process of monopolization, the more bitter the struggle for the rest of the world market becomes. The English free trade system made this conflict bearable, but the transition to protectionism which is bound to occur very soon will necessarily exacerbate it to an extraordinary degree. The disparity which exists between the development of German capitalism and the relatively small size of its economic territory will then be greatly increased. At the same time as Germany is making rapid progress in its industrial development, its competitive territory will suddenly contract. This will be all the more painful because, for historical reasons which are irrelevant to present-day capitalism (indifferent to the past unless it is accumulated 'past labour') Germany has no colonial possessions worth mentioning, whereas not only its strongest competitors, England and the United States (for which an entire continent serves as a kind of economic colony), but also the smaller powers such as France, Belgium and Holland have considerable colonial possessions, and its future competitor, Russia, also possesses a vastly larger economic territory. This is a situation which is bound to intensify greatly the conflict between Germany and England and their respective satellites, and to lead towards a solution by force.

Indeed this would have happened long ago if there had not been countervailing forces at work. The export of capital itself gives rise to tendencies which militate against such a solution by force. The unevenness of industrial development brings about a certain differentiation in the forms of capital export. Direct participation in opening up industrially backward or slowly developing countries can be undertaken only by those countries in which industrial development has attained its most advanced form, both technically and organizationally. Among them are, first, Germany and the United States, and in the second place England and Belgium. The other countries of long-standing capitalist development take part in the export of capital rather in the form of loan capital than of capital for the construction of factories. This has as a consequence that French, Dutch, and even to a great extent English capital, for example, constitute loan capital for industries which are under German and American management. Various tendencies thus emerge which make for solidarity among international capitalist interests. French capital, in the form of loan capital, acquires an interest in the progress of German industries in South America, etc. Moreover, connections of this kind, which greatly enhance the power of capital, make it possible to open up foreign territories much more rapidly and easily as a result of the increased pressure of the associated states.

Which of these tendencies prevails varies from case to case and depends primarily upon the opportunities for profit which emerge in the course of the struggle. The same considerations which decide whether competition should continue in a given branch of industry, or should be eliminated for a longer or shorter period of time by a cartel or trust, play a similar role here at the international and inter-state level. The greater the disparities of power the more likely it is, as a rule, that a struggle will occur. Every victorious struggle, however, would enhance the power of the victor and so change the power relationships in his favour at the expense of all the others. This accounts for the recent international policy of maintaining the *status quo* which is reminiscent of the balance of power policy of the early stages of capitalism. Moreover, the socialist movement has inspired a fear of the domestic political consequences which might follow from a war. On the other hand the decision as to war or peace does not rest solely with the advanced capitalist states, where the forces opposing militarism are most strongly developed. The capitalist awakening of the nations of Eastern Europe and Asia has been accompanied by a realignment of power relations which, through its effect upon the great powers, may well bring the existing antagonisms to the point where they erupt in war.

[*Finally, the ideological shift towards a new, nationalist attitude on the part of the bourgeoisie is set out.*]

This ideology, however, is completely opposed to that of liberalism. Finance capital does not want freedom, but domination; it has no regard for the in-dependence of the individual capitalist, but demands his allegiance. It detests the anarchy of competition and wants organization, though of course only in order to resume competition on a still higher level. But in order to achieve these ends, and to maintain and enhance its predominant position, it needs the state which can guarantee its domestic market through a protective tariff policy and facilitate the conquest of foreign markets. It needs a politically powerful state which does not have to take account of the conflicting in-terests of other states in its commercial policy. It needs also a strong state which will ensure respect for the interests of finance capital abroad, and use its political power to extort advantageous supply contracts and trade agreements from smaller states; a state which can intervene in every corner of the globe and transform the whole world into a sphere of investment for its own finance capital. Finally, finance capital needs a state which is strong enough to pursue an expansionist policy and the annexation of new colonies. Liberalism opposed international power politics, and only wanted to secure its own rule against the old forces of aristocracy and bureaucracy by granting them the least possible access to state power, but finance capital demands unlimited power politics, and this would be the case even if military and naval expenditures did not directly assure the most powerful capitalist groups of important markets, which provide in most cases monopolistic profits.

The demand for an expansionist policy revolutionizes the whole world view of the bourgeoisie, which ceases to be peace-loving and humanitarian. The old free traders believed in free trade not only as the best economic policy but also as the beginning of an era of peace. Finance capital abandoned this belief long ago. It has no faith in the harmony of capitalist interests, and knows well that competition is becoming increasingly a political power struggle. The ideal of peace has lost its lustre, and in place of the idea of humanity there emerges a glorification of the greatness and power of the state. The modern state arose as a realization of the aspiration of nations for unity. The national idea, which found a natural limit in the constitution of a state based upon the nation, because it recognized the right of all nations to independent existence as states, and hence regarded the frontiers of the state as being determined by the natural boundaries of the nation, is now transformed into the notion of elevating one's own nation above all others. The ideal now is to secure for one's own nation the domination of the world, an aspiration which is as unbounded as the capitalist lust for profit from which it springs. Capital becomes the conqueror of the world, and with every new country that it conquers there are new frontiers to be crossed. These efforts become an economic necessity, because every failure to advance reduces the profit and the competitiveness of finance capital, and may finally turn the smaller economic territory into a mere tributary of a larger one. They have an economic basis, but are then justified ideologically by an extraordinary perversion of the national idea, which no longer recognizes the right of every nation to political self-determination and independence, and ceases to express, with regard to nations, the democratic creed of the equality of all members of the human race. Instead the economic privileges of monopoly are mirrored in the privileged position claimed for one's own nation, which is represented as a 'chosen nation'. Since the subjection of foreign nations takes place by force – that is, in a perfectly natural way – it appears to the ruling nation that this domination is due to some special natural qualities, in short to its racial characteristics. Thus there emerges in racist ideology, cloaked in the garb of natural science, a justification for finance capital's lust for power, which is thus shown to have the specificity and necessity of a natural phenomenon. An oligarchic ideal of domination has replaced the democratic ideal of equality.

While this ideal appears to embrace the whole nation in the sphere of international politics, it becomes transformed in domestic politics by emphasizing the point of view of the rulers as against the working class. At the same time the increasing power of the workers intensifies the efforts of capital to reinforce the power of the state as a bulwark against proletarian demands.

Thus the ideology of imperialism arises on the ruins of the old liberal ideals, whose naïvety it derides. What an illusion it is, in the world of capitalist struggle where superiority of weapons is the final arbiter, to believe in a harmony of interests. What an illusion to expect the reign of eternal peace and to preach international law in a world where power alone decides the fate of peoples. What stupidity to advocate the extension of the rule of law which prevails within nations beyond their frontiers, and what irresponsible interference with business this humanitarian fantasy which has turned workers into a labour problem, invented social reform at home, and now wants to abolish contract slavery in the colonies, the only possible form of rational exploitation. Eternal justice is a beautiful dream, but morality builds no railways, not even at home. How are we to conquer the world if we have to wait for competition to undergo a spiritual conversion?

But imperialism only dissolves the faded ideals of the bourgeoisie in order to put in their place a new and greater illusion. It is clear-headed and sober in evaluating the real conflicts among capitalist interest groups, and it conceives all politics as a matter of capitalist syndicates either fighting or combining with each other. But it is carried away and becomes intoxicated when it unveils its own ideal. The imperialist wants nothing for himself, but he is also no visionary and dreamer who would dissolve the tangled profusion of races at every level of civilization and of potentiality for further development, into the bloodless concept of 'humanity', instead of seeing them in all their colourful reality. He observes with a cold and steady eye the medley of peoples and sees his own nation standing over all of them. For him this nation is real; it lives in the ever increasing power and greatness of the state, and its enhancement deserves every ounce of his effort. The subordination of individual interests to a higher general interest, which is a prerequisite for every vital social ideology, is thus achieved; and the state alien to its people is bound together with the nation in unity, while the national idea becomes the driving force of politics. Class antagonisms have disappeared and been transcended in the service of the collectivity. The common action of the nation, united by a common goal of national greatness, has taken the place of class struggle, so dangerous and fruitless for the possessing classes.

KARL MARX AND FRIEDRICH ENGELS

KARL MARX (1818–83) and Friedrich Engels (1820–95), revolutionaries. "The Communist Manifesto" had little influence at its time of publication during the 1848 revolutions in Europe but has since become the most influential pamphlet of the nineteenth century. The short extracts printed below point to the international nature of capitalism and the way in which capitalism has, allegedly, undermined the notion of nationality – although it might be argued that the actual history of the last century and a half suggests that capitalism is more likely to promote than to undermine nationalist sentiment.

From "The Communist Manifesto"

[*"The Communist Manifesto" is one of the most famous documents in world history. Two aspects of this document are of particular interest to students of international political theory. First is Marx and Engels' description of capitalism as a "world-system" – this description was certainly overstated at the time, but chimes well with our current concerns about globalization.*]

The discovery of America and the voyages round Africa provided fresh territory for the rising bourgeoisie. The East Indian and Chinese market, the colonisation of America, the colonial trade, the general increase in the means of exchange and of commodities, all gave to commerce, to sea transport, to industry a boost such as never before, hence quick development to the revolutionary element in a crumbling feudal society.

. . .

But markets were ever growing and demand ever rising. Even small-scale manufacture no longer sufficed to supply them. So steampower and machinery revolutionised industrial production. In place of small-scale manufacture came modern large-scale industry, in place of the middle ranks of industry came industrial millionaires, the generals of whole industrial armies, the modern bourgeois.

Large-scale industry has established a world market, for which the discovery of America prepared the way. The world market has given an immeasurable stimulus to the development of trade, sea-transport and land communications. This development has produced in turn an expansion of industry, and just as industry, commerce, sea-trade and railways have expanded, so the bourgeoisie has developed, increased its capital, and pushed into the background all pre-existing classes from the middle ages onwards.

...

The need for a constantly expanding outlet for their products pursues the bourgeoisie over the whole world. It must get a foothold everywhere, settle everywhere, establish connections everywhere.

Through the exploitation of the world market the bourgeoisie has made the production and consumption of all countries cosmopolitan. It has pulled the national basis of industry right out from under the reactionaries, to their consternation. Long-established national industries have been destroyed and are still being destroyed daily. They are being displaced by new industries – the introduction of which becomes a life-and-death question for all civilised nations – industries that no longer work up indigenous raw materials but use raw materials from the ends of the earth, industries whose products are consumed not only in the country of origin but in every part of the world. In place of the old needs satisfied by home production we have new ones which demand the products of the most distant lands and climes for their satisfaction. In place of the old local and national self-sufficiency and isolation we have a universal commerce, a universal dependence of nations on one another. As in the production of material things, so also with intellectual production. The intellectual creations of individual nations become common currency. National partiality and narrowness become more and more impossible, and from the many national and local literatures a world literature arises.

[*The second feature of the "Manifesto" worthy of note is its cosmopolitanism, its insistence that the "working men have no country."*]

Workers have no nation of their own. We cannot take from them what they do not have. Since the proletariat must first of all take political control, raise itself up to be the class of the nation, must constitute the nation itself, it is still nationalistic, even if not at all in the bourgeois sense of the term.

National divisions and conflicts between peoples increasingly disappear with the development of the bourgeoisie, with free trade and the world market, with the uniform character of industrial production and the corresponding circumstances of modern life.

The rule of the proletariat will make them disappear even faster. United action, at least in the civilised countries, is one of the first conditions for freeing the proletariat.

To the degree that the exploitation of one individual by another is transformed, so will the exploitation of one nation by another.

As internal class conflict within a nation declines, so does the hostility of one nation to another.

[*However, it should be noted that the "Manifesto" also acknowledges that political action will necessarily be national in the first place, and the history of Marxist regimes in the twentieth century suggests that moving from national to international action presents almost insuperable problems.*]

JOSEPH SCHUMPETER

JOSEPH SCHUMPETER (1883–1950), Moravian-born American economist and social theorist. Schumpeter contributed to a number of areas of economic theory, and his *Capitalism, Socialism and Democracy* (3rd edn, 1950) is a sustained analysis of the relationship between political and economic forms. In the essay "The Sociology of Imperialisms" (1919) extracted below, he attempts to refute the notion that imperialism is connected in some way to capitalism.

From "The Sociology of Imperialisms"

[*Schumpeter begins by establishing that capitalists in general have an interest in peace; acknowledging Hilferding's argument, he accepts that monopolists are obliged to see things differently but finds countervailing tendencies even in such cases.*]

It is in the nature of a capitalist economy – and of an exchange economy generally – that many people stand to gain economically in any war. Here the situation is fundamentally much as it is with the familiar subject of luxury. War means increased demand at panic prices, hence high profits and also high wages in many parts of the national economy. This is primarily a matter of money incomes, but as a rule (though to a lesser extent) real incomes are also affected. There are, for example, the special war interests, such as the arms industry. If the war lasts long enough, the circle of money profiteers naturally expands more and more – quite apart from a possible paper-money economy. It may extend to every economic field, but just as naturally the commodity content of money profits drops more and more, indeed, quite rapidly, to the point where actual losses are incurred. The national economy as a whole, of course, is impoverished by the tremendous excess in consumption brought on by war. It is, to be sure, conceivable that either the capitalists or the workers might make certain gains as a class, namely, if the volume either of capital or of labor should decline in such a way that the remainder receives a greater share in the social product and that, even from the absolute viewpoint, the total sum of interest or wages becomes greater than it was before. But these advantages cannot be considerable. They are probably, for the most part, more than outweighted by the burdens imposed by war and by losses sustained abroad. Thus the gain of the capitalists as a class cannot be a motive for war – and it is this gain that counts, for any advantage to the working class would be contingent on a large number of workers falling in action or otherwise perishing. There remain the entrepreneurs in the war industries, in the broader sense, possibly also the large landowner – a small but powerful minority. Their war profits are always sure to be an important supporting element. But few will go so far as to assert that this element alone is sufficient to orient the people of the capitalist world along imperialist lines. At most, an interest in expansion may make the capitalists allies of those who stand for imperialist trends.

...

A protectionist policy, however, does facilitate the formation of cartels and trusts. And it is true that this circumstance thoroughly alters the alignment of interests. It was neo-Marxist doctrine that first tellingly described this causal connection (Bauer) and fully recognized the significance of the "functional change in protectionism" (Hilferding). Union in a cartel or trust confers various benefits on the entrepreneur – a saving in costs, a stronger position as against the workers – but none of these compares with this one advantage: a monopolistic price policy, possible to any considerable degree *only* behind an adequate protective tariff. Now the price that brings the maximum monopoly profit is generally far above the price that would be fixed by fluctuating competitive costs, and the volume that can be marketed at that maximum price is generally far below the output that would be technically and economically feasible. Under free competition that output *would* be produced and offered, but a trust cannot offer it, for it could be sold only at a competitive price. Yet the trust *must* produce it – or approximately as much – otherwise the advantages of large-scale enterprise remain unexploited and unit costs are likely to be uneconomically high. The trust thus faces a dilemma. Either it renounces the monopolistic policies that motivated its founding; or it fails to exploit and expand its plant, with resultant high costs. It extricates itself from this dilemma by producing the full output that is economically feasible, thus securing low costs, and offering in the protected domestic market only the quantity corresponding to the monopoly price – insofar as the tariff permits; while the rest is sold, or "dumped," abroad at a lower price, sometimes (but not necessarily) *below* cost.

What happens when the entrepreneurs successfully pursue such a policy is something that did not occur in the cases discussed so far – a conflict of interests between nations that becomes so sharp that it cannot be overcome by the existing basic community of interests. Each of the two groups of entrepreneurs and each of the two states seeks to do something that is rendered illusory by a similar policy on the part of the other. In the case of protective tariffs *without* monopoly formation, an understanding is sometimes possible, for only a few would be destroyed, while many would stand to gain; but when monopoly rules it is very difficult to reach an agreement for it would require self-negation on the part of the new rulers. All that is left to do is to pursue the course once taken, to beat down the foreign industry wherever possible, forcing it to conclude a favorable "peace." This requires sacrifices. The excess product is dumped on the world market at steadily lower prices. Counterattacks that grow more and more desperate must be repulsed on the domestic scene. The atmosphere grows more and more heated. Workers and consumers grow more and more troublesome. Where this situation prevails, capital export, like commodity export, becomes aggressive, belying its ordinary character. A mass of capitalists competing with one another has no means of counteracting the decline in the interest rate. Of course they always seek out the places where the interest rate is highest, and in this quest they are quite willing to export their capital. But they are unable to adopt a policy of forced capital exports; and where there is freedom of capital movement they also lack the motive. For any gaps which might be opened up at home would be filled by foreign capital flowing in from abroad, thus preventing a rise of the domestic interest rate. But *organized* capital may very well make the discovery that the interest rate can be maintained above the level of free competition, if the resulting surplus can be sent abroad and if any foreign capital that flows in can be intercepted and – whether in the form of loans or in the form of machinery and the like – can likewise be channeled into foreign investment outlets. Now it is true that capital is nowhere cartelized. But it is everywhere subject to the guidance of the big banks which, even without a capital cartel, have attained a position similar to that of the cartel magnates in industry, and which are in a position to put into effect similar policies. It is necessary to keep two factors in mind. In the first place, everywhere except, significantly, in England there has come into being a close alliance between high finance and the cartel magnates, often going as far as personal identity. Although the relation between capitalists and entrepreneurs is one of the typical and fundamental *conflicts* of the capitalist economy, monopoly capitalism has virtually fused the big banks and cartels into one. Leading bankers are often leaders of the national economy. Here capitalism has found a central organ that supplants its automatism by conscious decisions. In the second place, the interests of the big banks coincide with those of their depositors even less than do the interests of cartel leaders with those of the firms belonging to the cartel. The policies of high finance are based on control of a *large* proportion of the national capital, but they are in the actual interest of only a *small* proportion and, indeed, with respect to the alliance with big business, sometimes not even in the interest of capital as such at all. The ordinary "small" capitalist foots the bills for a policy of forced exports, rather than enjoying its profits. He is a tool; his interests do not really matter. This possibility of laying all the sacrifices connected with a monopoly policy on one part of capital, while removing them from another, makes capital exports far more lucrative for the favored part than they would otherwise be. Even capital that is independent of the banks is thus often forced abroad – forced into the role of a shock troop for the real leaders, because cartels successfully impede the founding of new enterprises. Thus the customs area of a trustified country generally pours a huge wave of capital into new countries. There it meets other, similar waves of capital, and a bitter, costly struggle begins but never ends.

...

Thus we have here, within a social group that carries great political weight, a strong, undeniable, economic interest in such things as protective tariffs, cartels, monopoly prices, forced exports (dumping), an aggressive economic policy, an aggressive foreign policy generally, and war, including wars of expansion with a typically imperialist character. Once this alignment of interests exists, an even stronger interest in a somewhat differently motivated expansion must be added, namely, an interest in the conquest of lands producing raw materials and foodstuffs, with a view to facilitating self-sufficient warfare. Still another interest is that in rising wartime consumption. A mass of unorganized capitalists competing with one another may at best reap a trifling profit from such an eventuality, but organized capital is sure to profit hugely. Finally there is the political interest in war and international hatred which flows from the insecure position of the leading circles. They are small in numbers and highly unpopular. The essential nature of their policy is quite generally known, and most of the people find it unnatural and contemptible. An attack on all forms of property has revolutionary implications, but an attack on the privileged position of the cartel magnates may be politically rewarding, implying comparatively little risk and no threat to the existing order. Under certain circumstances it may serve to unite all the political parties. The existence of such a danger calls for diversionary tactics.

Yet the final word in any presentation of this aspect of modern economic life must be one of warning against overestimating it. The conflicts that have been described, born of an export-dependent monopoly capitalism, may serve to submerge the real community of interests among nations; the monopolist press may drive it underground; but underneath the surface it never completely disappears. Deep down, the normal sense of business and trade usually prevails. Even cartels cannot do without the custom of their foreign economic kin. Even national economies characterized by export monopoly are dependent on one another in many respects. And their interests do not always conflict in the matter of producing for third markets. Even when the conflicting interests are emphasized, parallel interests are not altogether lacking.

...

[*How then is militarist behavior to be explained? The answer is that capitalism is not a "pure" social formation – it contains within itself pre-capitalist elements that are the source of imperialism and militarism.*]

Trade and industry of the early capitalist period thus remained strongly pervaded with precapitalist methods, bore the stamp of autocracy, and served its interests, either willingly or by force. With its traditional habits of feeling, thinking, and acting molded along such lines, the bourgeoisie entered the Industrial Revolution. It was shaped, in other words, by the needs and interests of an environment that was essentially noncapitalist, or at least precapitalist – needs stemming not from the nature of the capitalist economy as such but from the fact of the coexistence of early capitalism with another and at first overwhelmingly powerful mode of life and business. Established habits of thought and action tend to persist, and hence the spirit of guild and monopoly at first maintained itself, and was only slowly undermined, even where capitalism was in sole possession of the field. Actually capitalism did not fully prevail *anywhere* on the Continent. Existing economic interests, "artificially" shaped by the autocratic state, remained dependent on the "protection" of the state. The industrial organism, such as it was, would not have been able to withstand free competition. Even where the old barriers crumbled in the autocratic state, the people did not all at once flock to the clear track. They were creatures of mercantilism and even earlier periods, and many of them huddled together and protested against the affront of being forced to depend on their own ability. They cried for paternalism, for protection, for forcible restraint of strangers, and above all for tariffs. They met with partial success, particularly because capitalism failed to take radical action in the agrarian field. Capitalism did bring about many changes on the land, springing in part from its automatic mechanisms, in part from the political trends it engendered – abolition of serfdom, freeing the soil from feudal entanglements, and so on – but initially it did not alter the basic outlines of the social structure of the countryside. Even less did it affect the spirit of the people, and least of all their political goals. This explains why the features and trends of autocracy – including imperialism – proved so resistant, why they exerted such a powerful influence on capitalist development, why the old export monopolism could live on and merge into the new.

These are facts of fundamental significance to an understanding of the soul of modern Europe. Had the ruling class of the Middle Ages – the war-oriented nobility – changed its profession and function and become the ruling class of the capitalist world; or had developing capitalism swept it away, put it out of business, instead of merely clashing head-on with it in the agrarian sphere – then much would have been different in the life of modern peoples. But as things actually were, neither eventuality occurred; or, more correctly, both are taking place, only at a very slow pace. The two groups of landowners remain social classes clearly distinguishable from the groupings of the capitalist world. The social pyramid of the present age has been formed, not by the substance and laws of capitalism alone, but by two different social substances, and by the laws of two different epochs. Whoever seeks to understand Europe must not forget this and concentrate all attention on the indubitably basic truth that one of these substances tends to be absorbed by the other and thus the sharpest of all class conflicts tends to be eliminated. Whoever seeks to understand Europe must not overlook that even today its life, its ideology, its politics are greatly under the influence of the feudal "substance," that while the bourgeoisie can assert its interests everywhere, it "rules" only in exceptional circumstances, and then only briefly. The bourgeois outside his office and the professional man of capitalism outside his profession cut a very sorry figure. Their spiritual leader is the rootless "intellectual," a slender reed open to every impulse and a prey to unrestrained emotionalism. The "feudal" elements, on the other hand, have both feet on the ground, even psychologically speaking. Their ideology is as stable as their mode of life. They believe certain things to be really true, others to be really false. This quality of possessing a definite character and cast of mind as a class, this simplicity and solidity of social and spiritual position extends their power far beyond their actual bases, gives them the ability to assimilate new elements, to make others serve their purposes – in a word, gives them *prestige*, something to which the bourgeois, as is well known, always looks up, something with which he tends to ally himself, despite all actual conflicts.

The nobility entered the modern world in the form into which it had been shaped by the autocratic state – the same state that had also molded the bourgeoisie. It was the sovereign who disciplined the nobility, instilled loyalty into it, "statized" it, and, as we have shown, imperialized it. He turned its nationalist sentiments – as in the case of the bourgeoisie – into an aggressive nationalism, and then made it a pillar of his organization, particularly his war machine. It had not been that in the immediately preceding period. Rising absolutism had at first availed itself of much more dependent organs. For that very reason, in his position as leader of the feudal powers and as warlord, the sovereign survived the onset of the Industrial Revolution, and as a rule – except in France – won victory over political revolution. The bourgeoisie did not simply supplant the sovereign, nor did it make him its leader, as did the nobility. It merely wrested a portion of his power from him and for the rest submitted to him. It did not take over from the sovereign the state as an abstract form of organization. The state remained a special social power, confronting the bourgeoise. In some countries it has continued to play that role to the present day. It is in the *state* that the bourgeoisie with its interests seeks refuge, protection against external and even domestic enemies. The bourgeoisie seeks to win over the state for itself, and in return serves the state and state interests that are different from its own. Imbued with the spirit of the old autocracy, trained by it, the bourgeoisie often takes over its ideology, even where, as in France, the sovereign is eliminated and the official power of the nobility has been broken. Because the sovereign needed soldiers, the modern bourgeois – at least in his slogans – is an even more vehement advocate of an increasing population. Because the sovereign was in a position to exploit conquests, needed them to be a victorious warlord, the bourgeoisie thirsts for national glory – even in France, worshiping a headless body, as it were. Because the sovereign found a large gold hoard useful, the bourgeoisie even today cannot be swerved from its bullionist prejudices. Because the autocratic state paid attention to the trader and manufacturer chiefly as the most important sources of taxes and credits, today even the intellectual who has not a shred of property looks on international commerce, not from the viewpoint of the consumer, but from that of the trader and exporter. Because pugnacious sovereigns stood in constant fear of attack by their equally pugnacious neighbors, the modern bourgeois attributes aggressive designs to neighboring peoples. All such modes of thought are essentially noncapitalist. Indeed, they vanish most quickly wherever capitalism fully prevails. They are survivals of the autocratic alignment of interests, and they endure wherever the autocratic state endures on the old basis and with the old orientation, even though more and more democratized and otherwise transformed. They bear witness to the extent to which essentially imperialist absolutism has patterned not only the economy of the bourgeoisie but also its mind – in the interests of autocracy and against those of the bourgeoisie itself.

This significant dichotomy in the bourgeois mind – which in part explains its wretched weakness in politics, culture, and life generally; earns it the understandable contempt of the Left and the Right; and proves the accuracy of our diagnosis – is best exemplified by two phenomena that are very close to our subject: present-day nationalism and militarism. Nationalism is affirmative awareness of national character, together with an aggressive sense of superiority. It arose from the autocratic state. In conservatives, nationalism in general is understandable as an inherited orientation, as a mutation of the battle instincts of the medieval knights, and finally as a political stalking horse on the domestic scene; and conservatives are fond of reproaching the bourgeois with a lack of nationalism, which, from their point of view, is evaluated in a positive sense. Socialists, on the other hand, equally understandably exclude nationalism from their general ideology, because of the essential interests of the proletariat, and by virtue of their domestic opposition to the conservative stalking horse; they, in turn, not only reproach the bourgeoisie with an excess of nationalism (which they, of course, evaluate in a negative sense) but actually identify nationalism and even the very idea of the nation with bourgeois ideology. The curious thing is that both of these groups are right in their criticism of the bourgeoisie. For, as we have seen, the mode of life that flows logically from the nature of capitalism necessarily implies an antinationalist orientation in politics and culture. This orientation actually prevails. We find a great many antinationalist members of the middle class, and even more who merely parrot the catchwords of nationalism. In the capitalist world it is actually not big business and industry at all that are the carriers of nationalist trends, but the intellectual, and the content of *his* ideology is explained not so much from definite class interests as from chance emotion and individual interest. But the submission of the bourgeoisie to the powers of autocracy, its alliance with them, its economic and psychological patterning by them – all these tend to push the bourgeois in a nationalist direction; and this too we find prevalent, especially among the chief exponents of export monopolism. The relationship between the bourgeoisie and militarism is quite similar. Militarism is not necessarily a foregone conclusion when a nation maintains a large army, but only when high military circles become a political power. The criterion is whether leading generals as such wield political influence and whether the responsible statesmen can act only with their consent. That is possible only when the officer corps is linked to a definite social class, as in Japan, and can assimilate to its position individuals who do not belong to it by birth. Militarism too is rooted in the autocratic state. And again the same reproaches are made against the bourgeois from both sides – quite properly too. According to the "pure" capitalist mode of life, the bourgeois is unwarlike. The alignment of capitalist interests should make him utterly reject military methods, put him in opposition to the professional soldier. Significantly, we see this in the example of England where, first, the struggle against a standing army generally and, next, opposition to its elaboration, furnished bourgeois politicians with their most popular slogan: "retrenchment." Even naval appropriations have encountered resistance. We find similar trends in other countries, though they are less strongly developed. The continental bourgeois, however, was used to the sight of troops. He regarded an army almost as a necessary component of the social order, ever since it had been his terrible task-master in the Thirty Years' War. He had no power at all to abolish the army. He might have done so if he had had the power; but not having it, he considered the fact that the army might be useful to him. In his "artificial" economic situation and because of his submission to the sovereign, he thus grew disposed toward militarism, especially where export monopolism flourished. The intellectuals, many of whom still maintained special relationships with feudal elements, were so disposed to an even greater degree.

Just as we once found a dichotomy in the social pyramid, so now we find everywhere, in every aspect of the bourgeois portion of the modern world, a dichotomy of attitudes and interests. Our examples also show in what way the two components work together. Nationalism and militarism, while not creatures of capitalism, become "capitalized" and in the end draw their best energies from capitalism. Capitalism involves them in its workings and thereby keeps them alive, politically as well as economically. And they, in turn, affect capitalism, cause it to deviate from the cause it might have followed alone, support many of its interests.

Here we find that we have penetrated to the historical as well as the sociological sources of modern imperialism. It does not *coincide* with nationalism and militarism, though it *fuses* with them by supporting them as it is supported by them. It too is – not only historically, but also sociologically – a heritage of the autocratic state, of its structural elements, organizational forms, interest alignments, and human attitudes, the outcome of precapitalist forces which the autocratic state has reorganized, in part by the methods of early capitalism. It would never have been evolved by the "inner logic" of capitalism itself. This is true even of mere export monopolism. It too has its sources in absolutist policy and the action habits of an essentially precapitalist environment. That it was able to develop to its present dimensions is owing to the momentum of a situation once created, which continued to engender ever new "artificial" economic structures, that is, those which maintain themselves by political power alone. In most of the countries addicted to export monopolism it is also owing to the fact that the old autocratic state and the old attitude of the bourgeoisie toward it were so vigorously maintained. But export monopolism, to go a step further, is not yet imperialism. And even if it had been able to arise without protective tariffs, it would never have developed into imperialism in the hands of an unwarlike bourgeoisie. If this did happen, it was only because the heritage included the war machine, together with its socio-psychological aura and aggressive bent, and because a class oriented toward war maintained itself in a ruling position. This class clung to its domestic interest in war, and the pro-military interests among the bourgeoisie were able to ally themselves with it. This alliance kept alive war instincts and ideas of overlordship, male supremacy, and triumphant glory – ideas that would have otherwise long since died. It led to social conditions that, while they ultimately stem from the conditions of production, cannot be explained from capitalist production methods alone. And it often impresses its mark on present-day politics, threatening Europe with the constant danger of war.

This diagnosis also bears the prognosis of imperialism. The precapitalist elements in our social life may still have great vitality; special circumstances in national life may revive them from time to time; but in the end the climate of the modern world must destroy them. This is all the more certain since their props in the modern capitalist world are not of the most durable material. Whatever opinion is held concerning the vitality of capitalism itself, whatever the life span predicted for it, it is bound to withstand the onslaughts of its enemies and its own irrationality much longer than essentially untenable export monopolism – untenable even from the capitalist point of view. Export monopolism may perish in revolution, or it may be peacefully relinquished; this may happen soon, or it may take some time and require desperate struggle; but one thing is certain – it *will* happen. This will immediately dispose of neither warlike instincts nor structural elements and organizational forms oriented toward war – and it is to their dispositions and domestic interests that, in my opinion, much more weight must be given in every concrete case of imperialism than to export monopolist interests, which furnish the financial "outpost skirmishes" – a most appropriate term – in many wars. But such factors will be politically overcome in time, no matter what they do to maintain among the people a sense of constant danger of war, with the war machine forever primed for action. And with them, imperialisms will wither and die.

References

Adams, Robert P. (1962) *The Better Part of Valor: More, Erasmus, Colet, and Vives on Humanism, War, and Peace, 1496–1535* (Seattle: University of Washington Press).

Airaksinen, Timo and Martin A. Bertman, eds. (1989) *Hobbes: War among Nations* (Aldershot: Avebury).

Anderson, Benedict (1991) *Imagined Communities*, 2nd edn. (London: Verso).

Ashley, Richard K. (1989) "Living on Borderlines: Man, Poststructuralism and War," in James Der Derian and Michael Shapiro, eds., *International/Intertextual: Postmodern Readings in World Politics* (Lexington: Lexington Books).

Avineri, Shlomo (1972) *Hegel's Theory of the Modern State* (Cambridge: Cambridge University Press).

Barker, Ernest (1929) *The Political Theory of Plato and Aristotle* (New York: Dover).

(1955) *From Alexander to Constantine* (Oxford: Clarendon Press).

(1956) *Social and Political Thought in Byzantium From Justinian 1 to the Last Palaeologus* (Oxford: Clarendon Press).

(1959) *The Political Thought of Plato and Aristotle* (New York: Dover Publications).

Barnes, Jonathan (1982) "The Just War," in N. Kretzmann, A. Kenny, and J. Pinborg, eds., *The Cambridge History of Later Medieval Philosophy* (Cambridge: Cambridge University Press).

(1995) *The Cambridge Companion to Aristotle* (Cambridge: Cambridge University Press).

Barraclough, Geoffrey (1950) *The Medieval Empire: Idea and Reality* (London: G. Philip for the Historical Association).

Barry, Brian (1973) *The Liberal Theory of Justice* (Oxford: Clarendon Press).

Beck, Lewis White (1956) *Essays on Kant and Hume* (New Haven: Yale University Press).

Beiner, R. and Booth, W. J., eds. (1993) *Kant and Political Philosophy* (New Haven: Yale University Press).

Beitz, Charles R. (1979) *Political Theory and International Relations* (Princeton, NJ: Princeton University Press).

(1994) "Cosmopolitan Liberalism and the States System," in Chris Brown (1994).

Bentham, Jeremy (1789/1960) *Fragment on Government and Introduction to the Principles of Morals and Legislation* (Oxford: Basil Blackwell).

Beranger, J. (1973) *Principatus: Etudes de notion et d'histoire politiques dans l'Antique gréco-romaine* (Paris: Droz).

Berman, Marshall (1970) *The Politics of Authenticity* (London: Allen and Unwin).

Bernstein, Richard (1991) *The New Constellation* (Cambridge: Polity).

Black, Antony (1993) *Political Thought in Europe 1250–1450* (Cambridge: Cambridge University Press).

Blaug, Mark (1985) *Economic Theory in Retrospect*, 5th edn. (Cambridge: Cambridge University Press).

Bluhm, William (1965) *Theories of the Political System* (Englewood Cliffs, NJ: Prentice Hall).

Bodin, Jean (1992) *On Sovereignty: Four Chapters from the Six Books of the Commonwealth*, trans. J. H. Franklin (Cambridge: Cambridge University Press).

Bosanquet, Bernard (1915) "Patriotism in the Perfect State," in *The International Crisis in its Ethical and Psychological Aspects*, by Eleanor M. Sidgwick, Gilbert Murray, A. C. Bradley, L. P. Jacks, G. F. Stout, and B. Bosanquet (Oxford: Oxford University Press).

(1965) *The Philosophical Theory of the State*, 4th edn. (London: Macmillan).

Boucher, David (1997), ed. *The British Idealists* (Cambridge: Cambridge University Press).

(1998) *Political Theories of International Relations* (Oxford: Oxford University Press).

Bradley, F. H. (1988) *Ethical Studies* (Oxford: Oxford University Press).

Brewer, Anthony (1990) *Marxist Theories of Imperialism: A Critical Survey*, 2nd edn. (London: Routledge).

Brown, Chris (1992) "Marxism and International Ethics," in Terry Nardin and David Maple, eds., *Traditions of International Ethics* (Cambridge: Cambridge University Press).

(1994), ed. *Political Restructuring in Europe* (London: Routledge).

(1995) "International Theory and International Society: The Viability of the Middle Way?," *Review of International Studies*, vol. 21, no. 2.

Brown, Peter (1967) *Augustine of Hippo* (London: Faber).

Brown, S. C. (1979), ed. *Philosophers of the Enlightenment* (Brighton: Harvester Press).

Bull, Hedley (1966) "The Grotian Tradition in International Relations," in Herbert Butterfield and Martin Wight, eds., *Diplomatic Investigations* (London: Allen and Unwin).

(1977) *The Anarchical Society* (London: Macmillan).

Bull, Hedley, Kingsbury, Benedict, and Roberts, Adam (1990), eds. *Hugo Grotius and International Relations* (Oxford: Clarendon Press).

Burns, J. H. (1988), ed. *The Cambridge History of Medieval Political Thought* (Cambridge: Cambridge University Press).

Burns, J. H. with Goldie, Mark, eds. (1991) *The Cambridge History of Political Thought, 1450–1700* (Cambridge: Cambridge University Press).

Buzan, Barry (1996) "The Timeless Wisdom of Realism?," in Smith, Booth, and Zalewski (1996).

Canning, Joseph (1996) *A History of Medieval Political Thought, 300–1450* (London: Routledge).

Carlyle, A. J. and Carlyle, R. W. (1903–36) *A History of Medieval Political Theory in the West* (London and New York: Blackwood).

Carr, E. H. (1939) *The Twenty Years' Crisis* (London: Macmillan).

Cassirer, Ernst (1951) *The Philosophy of the Enlightenment* (Princeton: Princeton University Press).

Chadwick, Henry (1988) "Christian Doctrine," in Burns (1988).

Charvet, John (1981) *A Critique of Freedom and Equality* (Cambridge: Cambridge University Press).

(1995) *The Idea of an Ethical Community* (Ithaca, NY: Cornell University Press).

Cherniss, Harold (1945) *The Riddle of the Early Academy* (Oxford: Clarendon Press).

Church, W. F. (1972) *Richelieu and Reason of State* (Princeton: Princeton University Press).

Churchill, Winston (1948) *The Gathering Storm* (Boston: Houghton Mifflin).

Clausewitz, Carl von (1976) *On War* (Princeton: Princeton University Press).

Cobden, Richard (1836/1903) *The Political Writings of Richard Cobden* (London: T. Fisher Unwin).

Cohen, Joshua (1997), ed. *For Love of Country: Debating the Limits of Patriotism* (Boston: Beacon Press).

Coulter, James A. (1964) "The Relation of the Apology of Socrates to Gorgias' 'Defence of Palamedes', and Plato's Critique of Gorgianaic Rhetoric," *Journal of Politics*, vol. 54.

Der Derian, James (1987) *On Diplomacy: A Genealogy of Western Estrangement* (Oxford: Blackwell).

Donelan, Michael (1990) *Elements of International Political Theory* (Oxford: Clarendon Press).

Donnelly, Jack (1992) "Twentieth Century Realism," in Nardin and Mapel (1992).

(2000) *Realism and International Relations* (Cambridge: Cambridge University Press).

Doyle, Michael (1997) *Ways of War and Peace* (New York: Norton).

(1983) "Kant, Liberal Legacies and Foreign Policy," Parts I and II, *Philosophy and Public Affairs*, vol. 12, 205–35 and 323–53.

Dunne, Timothy (1998) *Inventing International Society: A History of the English School* (London: Macmillan).

Dyson, Robert (1998), ed. *The City of God Against the Pagans by Augustine of Hippo* (Cambridge: Cambridge University Press).

Elshtain, Jean Bethke (1995) *Augustine and the Limits of Politics* (Notre Dame, IN: Notre Dame University Press).

Enayat, Hamid (1982) *Modern Islamic Political Thought* (London: Macmillan).

Euben, Peter (1990) *The Tragedy of Political Theory: The Road Not Taken* (Princeton: Princeton University Press).

Fernández-Santamaría, J. A. (1977) *The State, War and Peace: Spanish Political Thought in the Renaissance, 1516–1599* (Cambridge: Cambridge University Press).

Fieldhouse, David K. (1961) "Imperialism: An Historiographical Revision," *Economic History Review*, 2nd series, vol. 14, no. 2

(1973) *Economics and Empire: 1830–1914* (London Weidenfeld and Nicholson)

Finnis, John (1996) "The Ethics of War and Peace in the Catholic Natural Law Tradition," in Terry Nardin (ed.), *The Ethics of War and Peace: Religious and Secular Perspectives* (Princeton: Princeton University Press).

(1998) *Aquinas: Moral, Political, and Legal Theory* (Oxford: Oxford University Press).

Fliess, Peter (1966) *Thucydides and the Politics of Bipolarity* (Baton Rouge: University of Louisiana Press).

Forbes, Duncan (1975) *Hume's Philosophical Politics* (Cambridge: Cambridge University Press).

Forde, Steve (1992) "Classical Realism," in Nardin and Mapel (1992).

Forsyth, M., Keen-Soper, M., and Savigear, P. (1970), eds. *The Theory of International Relations* (London: Allen and Unwin).

Freidrich (1962) *Inevitable Peace* (Harvard: Harvard University Press).

Friedman, Milton (1966) "The Methodology of Positive Economists," *Essays in Positive Economics* (Chicago: University of Chicago Press).

Fritz, Kurt Von (1975) *The Theory of the Mixed Constitution in Antiquity* (New York: Arno Press).

Frost, Mervyn (1996) *Ethics in International Relations* (Cambridge: Cambridge University Press).

Gadamer, Hans G. (1980) *Dialogue and Dialectic: Eight Hermeneutical Studies of Plato* (New Haven: Yale University Press).

Gallagher, J.and Robinson, R.E.(1953) "The Imperialism of Free Trade," *Economic History Review*, 2nd. series, vol. 6, no. 1.

Gay, Peter (1959) *Voltaire's Politics* (Princeton: Princeton University Press).

(1970) *The Enlightenment: An Interpretation*. Vol. i: *The Rise of Modern Paganism*; vol. ii: *The Science of Freedom* (New York: Wildwood House).

Gellner, Ernest (1983) *Nations and Nationalism* (Oxford, Blackwell).

George, Jim (1994) *Discourses of Global Politics* (Boulder: Lynne Rienner).

Gilbert, Felix (1973) "Machiavellism," in Philip P. Wiener, ed., *Dictionary of the History of Ideas*, vol. iii (New York: Charles Scribner's Sons).

Gilpin, Robert (1984) "The Richness of the Tradition of Political Realism," in Keohane (1984).

Gomperz, Heinrich (1912) *Sophistik und Rhetorik* (Leipzig: Verlag).

Gong, G. C. (1984) *The Standard of "Civilization" in International Society* (Oxford: Oxford University Press).

Grayeff, Felix (1974) *Aristotle and his School* (London: Duckworth).

Green, T. H. (1941) *Lectures on the Principle of Political Obligation* (London: Longman).

Grene, David (1965) *Greek Political Theory* (Chicago: University of Chicago Press).

Grimsby, Ronald (1979) "Jean-Jacques Rousseau, Philosopher of Nature," in S.C.Brown (1979).

Griswold, Charles (1988) *Platonic Writings, Platonic Readings* (London: Routledge).

Grotius, Hugo (1925) *On the Law of War and Peace*, trans. Francis W. Kelsey (Oxford: Clarendon Press).

(1950) *Commentary on the Law of Prize and Booty*, trans. Gladys L. Williams (Oxford: Clarendon Press).

Gulick, Edward Vose (1955) *Europe's Classical Balance of Power* (Ithaca: Cornell University Press).

Guthrie, W. K. C. (1969) *A History of Greek Philosophy*, vol. iii (Cambridge: Cambridge University Press).

Haakonssen, Knud (1996) *Natural Law and Moral Philosophy: From Grotius to the Scottish Enlightenment* (Cambridge: Cambridge University Press).

Hadot, Pierre (1995) *Philosophy as a Way of Life* (Oxford: Blackwell).

Haggenmacher, Peter (1983) *Grotius et la doctrine de la guerre juste* (Paris: Presses Universitaires de France).

(1990) "Grotius and Gentili: A Reassessment of Thomas E. Holland's Inaugural Lecture," in Bull, Kingsbury, and Roberts (1990).

Hale, John (1994) *The Civilization of Europe in the Renaissance* (New York: Atheneum).

Hamilton, Alexander (1966) "Report on the Subject of Manufactures, 1791," *The Papers of Alexander Hamilton* (New York: Columbia University Press).

Hamilton, Bernice (1963) *Political Thought in Sixteenth-Century Spain: A Study of the Political Ideas of Vitoria, De Soto, Suárez, and Molina* (Oxford: Clarendon Press).

Hampson, Norman (1968) *The Enlightenment* (Harmondsworth: Penguin Books).

Hanke, Lewis (1949) *The Spanish Struggle for Justice in the Conquest of America* (Philadelphia: American Historical Association).

(1959) *Aristotle and the American Indians: A Study in Race Prejudice in the Modern World* (Chicago: Henry Regnery).

Hay, Denys (1968) *Europe: The Emergence of an Idea*, rev. edn. (Edinburgh: Edinburgh University Press).

Hegel, G. F. W. (1956) *Philosophy of History* (New York: Dover Books).

(1991) *Elements of the Philosophy of Right*, ed. Allen Wood (Cambridge: Cambridge University Press).

Heilbroner, Robert (1986) *The Worldly Philosophers*, 6th edn. (New York: Simon and Schuster).

Hilferding, Rudolf (1981) *Finance Capital*, ed. Tom Bottomore (London: Routledge and Kegan Paul).

Hinsley, F. H. (1963) *Power and the Pursuit of Peace* (Cambridge: Cambridge University Press).

Hobhouse, L. T. (1918) *The Metaphysical Theory of the State* (London: George Allen and Unwin).

Hobson, J. A. (1902) *Imperialism: A Study* (London: Nisbet and Co.).

Hoffmann, Stanley (1981) *Duties beyond Borders* (Syracuse, NY: Syracuse University Press).

Hoffmann, Stanley and Fidler, David P. (1991), eds. *Rousseau on International Relations* (Oxford: Clarendon Press).

Holbraad, Carsten (1970) *The Concert of Europe: A Study in German and British International Theory, 1815–1914* (London: Longman).

Hollis, Martin and Smith, Steve (1991) *Explaining and Understanding International Relations* (Oxford: Clarendon Press).

Holzgrefe, J. L. (1989) "The Origins of Modern International Relations Theory," *Review of International Studies*, vol. 15.

Hornblower, S. (1987) *Thucydides* (London: Duckworth).

Hourani, Albert (1991) *A History of the Arab Peoples* (London: Faber).

Hulliung, Mark (1983) *Citizen Machiavelli* (Princeton: Princeton University Press).

Hume, David (1987) *Essays: Moral, Political and Literary* (Indianapolis: Liberty Classics).

Hurrell, Andrew (1990) "Kant and the Kantian Paradigm in International Relations," *Review of International Studies*, 16, 3.

(1996) "Vattel: Pluralism and its Limits," in Ian Clark and Iver B. Neumann, eds., *Classical Theories of International Relations* (London: Macmillan).

Johnson, James Turner (1975) *Ideology, Reason, and the Limitation of War: Religious and Secular Concepts, 1200–1740* (Princeton: Princeton University Press, 1975).

Kant, Immanuel (1982), *Critique of Pure Reason*, edited and translated by Norman Kemp Smith (London: Macmillan).

Kedourie, Elie (1960) *Nationalism* (London: Hutchinson).

Keohane, R. (1984), ed. *Neorealism and its Critics* (New York: Columbia University Press).

Keohane, Robert and Nye, Joseph (1977) *Power and Interdependence* (Boston: Little Brown).

Kerferd, G. B. (1955) "Gorgias on Nature or That Which is Not," in *Phronesis*, vol 11.

Klosko, G. (1986) *The Development of Plato's Political Theory* (London: Methuen).

Knight, W. S. M. (1925) *The Life and Works of Hugo Grotius* (London: Sweet and Maxwell).

Knutsen, Torbjold (1992) *A History of International Relations Theory* (Manchester: Manchester University Press).

Kramer, H. J. (1990) *Plato and the Foundations of Metaphysics*, trans. John Catan (New York: State University of New York Press).

Kratochwil, Friedrich (1989) *Rules, Norms and Decisions* (Cambridge: Cambridge University Press).

Kraut, Richard (1989) *Aristotle on the Human Good* (Princeton: Princeton University Press).

Krieger, Leonard (1965) *The Politics of Discretion: Pufendorf and the Acceptance of Natural Law* (Chicago: University of Chicago Press).

Lapid, Yosef (1989) "The Third Debate: On the Prospects of International Theory in a Post-Positivist Era," *International Studies Quarterly*, vol. 33.

Leibniz, Gottfried Wilhelm (1988) *Leibniz: Politial Writings*, trans. and ed. Patrick Riley, 2nd. edn. (Cambridge: Cambridge University Press).

Lerner, Ralph and Mahdi, Mushin (1963), eds. *Medieval Political Philosophy* (Ithaca: Cornell University Press).

Lewis, Ioan and Mayall, James (1996) "Somalia," in J. Mayall, ed., *The New Interventionism: 1991–94* (Cambridge: Cambridge University Press).

Linklater, Andrew (1990) *Men and Citizens in the Theory of International Relations*, 2nd. edn. (London: Macmillan).

(1998) *The Transformation of Political Community* (Cambridge: Polity Press).

List, Friedrich (1966) *The National System of Political Economy* (London: Frank Cass and Co.).

Lloyd-Jones, Hugh (1983) *The Justice of Zeus* (Berkeley: University of California Press).

Long, A. A. (1986) *Hellenistic Philosophy* (London: Duckworth).

Long, David (1996) *Towards a New Liberal Internationalism: The International theory of J. A. Hobson* (New York: Cambridge University Press).

Luther, Martin (1991) "On Secular Authority," in Harro Höpfl, ed., *Luther and Calvin on Secular Authority* (Cambridge: Cambridge University Press).

Luxemburg, Rosa (1913/1963) *The Accumulation of Capital* (London: Routledge and Kegan Paul).

Mack Smith, Denis, (1994) *Mazzini* (New Haven: Yale University Press).

Mahdi, Muhsin (1963) "Al-Farabi," in Strauss and Cropsey (1963).

Mansfield, Jr., Harvey (1979) *Machiavelli's New Modes and Orders* (Ithaca: Cornell University Press).

Mapel, David and Nardin, Terry (1998), eds. *International Society: Diverse Ethical Perspectives* (Princeton: Princeton University Press).

Markus, R. A. (1970) *Saeculum: History and Society in the Theology of St. Augustine* (Cambridge: Cambridge University Press).

(1988) "The Latin Fathers," in Burns (1988).

Marx, Karl (1969) *The Eastern Question*, ed. E. Marx Aveling and E. Aveling (London: Cass).

(1973) "The British Rule in India," in David Fernbach, ed., *Surveys from Exile: Political Writings*, vol. II (Harmondsworth: Penguin Books).

Marx, Karl and Friedrich Engels (1979) *Collected Works*, vol. XII (Moscow: Progress Publishers).

(1996) "The Communist Manifesto," in Terrell Carver, ed., *Marx: Later Political Writings* (Cambridge: Cambridge University Press).

Masters, Roger (1990) *The Nature of Politics* (New Haven: Yale University Press).

Mattingly, Garrett (1955) *Renaissance Diplomacy* (New York: Houghton-Mifflin).

Mazzini, G. (1907) "On the Duties of Man," in *Mazzini's Essays* (London: Dent).

Meinecke, Friedrich (1957) *Machiavellism: The Doctrine of Raison d'Etat and its Place in Modern History*, trans. Douglas Scott (London: Routledge and Kegal Paul).

Mill, John Stuart (1972) *Utilitarianism, On Liberty and Representative Government* (London: Dent).

(1984) "A Few Words on Non-Intervention," in *Collected Works of John Stuart Mill*, vol. XXI. *Essays on Equality, Law and Education* (Toronto: University of Toronto Press).

Miller, David (1995) *On Nationality* (Oxford: Oxford University Press).

Momigliano, Arnaldo (1963a), ed. *The Conflict between Christianity and Paganism in the Fourth Century* (Oxford: Clarendon Press).

(1963b) "Pagan and Christian Historiography in the Fourth Century," in Momigliano (1963a).

Moravscik, Gy (1949) *Constantine Porphyrogenitus: De Administrando Imperio*. Corpus Fontium Historiae Byzantinae (Dumbarton Oaks: Center for Byzantine Studies).

Mossner, E. C. (1980) *The Life of David Hume* (Oxford: Clarendon Press).

Murray, Alastair (1997) *Reconstructing Realism* (Edinburgh: Keele University Press).

Nagel, Thomas (1972) "War and Massacre," *Philosophy and Public Affairs*, vol. 1, no. 2.

Nardin, Terry (1983) *Law, Morality and the Relations of Nations* (Princeton: Princeton University Press).

Nardin, Terry and Mapel, David (1992), eds. *Traditions of International Ethics* (Cambridge: Cambridge University Press).

Nelson, Janet (1988) "Kingship and Empire," in Burns (1988).

Neufeld, Mark (1995) *The Restructuring of International Relations Theory* (Cambridge: Cambridge University Press).

Nicol, D. M. (1988) "Byzantine Political Thought," in Burns (1988).

Nussbaum, Arthur (1954) *A Concise History of the Law of Nations*, rev. edn. (New York: Macmillan).

Nussbaum, Martha (1986) *The Fragility of Goodness: Luck and Ethics in Greek Tragedy and Philosophy* (Cambridge: Cambridge University Press).

(1994) *The Therapy of Desire: Theory and Practice in Hellenistic Ethics* (Princeton: Princeton University Press).

(1996) *The Therapy of Desire* (Princeton: Princeton University Press).

(1997) "Patriotism and Cosmopolitanism," in Cohen (1997).

Nussbaum, Martha and Sen, Amartya (1993), eds. *The Quality of Life* (Oxford: Clarendon Press).

O'Neill, Onora (1989) *Constructions of Reason: Explorations of Kant's Practical Philosophy* (Cambridge: Cambridge University Press).

(1996) *Beyond Justice and Virtue: Towards a Constructive Account of Practical Reason* (Cambridge University Press).

Onuma, Yasuaki (1993), ed. *A Normative Approach to War: Peace, War, and Justice in Hugo Grotius* (Oxford: Oxford University Press).

Orwin, Clifford (1994) *The Humanity of Thucydides* (Princeton: Princeton University Press).

Ostrogorsky, George (1968 [1940]) *History of the Byzantine State* (New York: Rutgers University Press; 1968 edn, Oxford: Basil Blackwell).

Pagden, Anthony (1986) *The Fall of Natural Man: The American Indians and the Origins of Comparative Ethnology*, 2nd edn. (Cambridge: Cambridge University Press).

(1987) "Dispossessing the Barbarian: The Language of Spanish Thomism and the Debate over the Property Rights of the American Indians," in Anthony Pagden, ed., *The Languages of Political Theory in Early-Modern Europe* (Cambridge: Cambridge University Press).

Pangle, Thomas (1973) *Montesquieu's Philosophy of Liberalism* (Chicago: University of Chicago Press).

(1987), ed. *The Roots of Political Philosophy* (Ithaca: Cornell University Press).

Pangle, Thomas and Ahrensdorf, Peter (1999) *Justice Among Nations: On the Moral Basis of Power and Peace* (Lawrence, KA: University Press of Kansas).

Parkinson, Fred (1977) *The Philosophy of International Relations* (Beverly Hills: Sage Publications).

Pieper, Josef (1962) *Guide to Thomas Aquinas*, trans. Richard and Clara Winston (Notre Dame, IN: University of Notre Dame Press).

Plamenatz, John (1963) *Man and Society*, vols. I and II (London: Longman).

Plant, Raymond (1983) *Hegel: An Introduction* (Oxford: Basil Blackwell).

Pocock, J.G.A. (1975) *The Machiavellian Moment: Florentine Political Thought and the Atlantic Republican Tradition* (Princeton: Princeton University Press).

Polanyi, Karl (1975) *The Great Transformation* (Boston: Beacon Books).

Porter, Roy and Teich, Miklaus (1981), eds. *The Enlightenment in National Context* (Cambridge: Cambridge University Press).

Prebisch, R. (1950) *The Economic Development of Latin America and its Principal Problems* (New York: United Nations).

Press, Gerald (1993) *Plato's Dialogues: New Studies and Interpretations* (Princeton: Princeton University Press).

Pufendorf, Samuel (1934/1991) *On the Law of Nature and Nations* (Oxford: Oxford University Press).

(1991) *On the Duty of Man and Citizen according to Natural Law*, ed. James Tully, trans. Michael Silverthorne (Cambridge: Cambridge University Press).

Rawls, John (1971) *A Theory of Justice* (Oxford: Oxford University Press).

(1993) "The Law of Peoples," in Stephen Shute and Susan Hurley, eds., *On Human Rights* (New York: Basic Books).

Reale, Giovanni (1990) *The Schools of the Imperial Age* (New York: State University of New York).

Reiss, Hans (1970), ed. *Kant's Political Writings* (Cambridge: Cambridge University Press).

Rengger, N. J. (1995) *Political Theory, Modernity and Postmodernity: Beyond Enlightenment and Critique* (Oxford: Basil Blackwell).

Ricardo, David (1951) "Principles of Political Economy and Taxation," in *The Works and Correspondence of David Ricardo*, vol. I, ed. Piero Sraffa (Cambridge: Cambridge University Press).

Roelofsen, C. G. (1990) "Grotius and the International Politics of the Seventeenth Century," in Bull, Kingsbury, and Roberts (1990)

Rosenberg, Justin (1994) *The Empire of Civil Society* (London: Verso).

Rosenthal, Joel (1991) *Righteous Realists* (Baton Rouge, LA: University of Louisiana Press).

Ruggie, John G. (1998) *Constructing the World Polity* (London: Routledge).

Russell, Frederick H. (1975) *The Just War in the Middle Ages* (Cambridge: Cambridge University Press).

Saxonhouse, Arlene (1992) *Fear of Diversity: The Birth of Political Science in Ancient Greek Thought* (Chicago: University of Chicago Press).

Schiffer, Walter (1954) *The Legal Community of Mankind* (New York: Columbia University Press).

Schmidt, Brian C. (1998) *The Political Discourse of Anarchy: A Disciplinary History of International Relations* (Albany: State University of New York Press).

Schumpeter, J. (1951) *Imperialism and Social Classes* (New York: Augustus M. Kelly).

Shklar, Judith (1969) *Men and Citizens: A Study of Rousseau's Political Theory* (Cambridge: Cambridge University Press).

(1987) *Montesquieu* (Oxford: Oxford University Press).

Sinclair, T. A. (1967) *A History of Greek Political Thought* (London: Routledge).

Skinner, Quentin (1978) *The Foundations of Modern Political Thought*, 2 vols. (Cambridge: Cambridge University Press).

(1981) *Machiavelli* (New York: Hill and Wang).

(1989) "The State," in T. Ball, J. Farr, and R. L. Hanson, eds., *Political Innovation and Conceptual Change* (Cambridge: Cambridge University Press).

Smith, Adam (1954) *Wealth of Nations* (London: Dent).

Smith, Anthony D. (1998) *Nationalism and Modernism* (New York: Routledge).

Smith, Michael J. (1986) *Realist Thought from Weber to Kissinger* (Baton Rouge, LA: University of Louisiana Press).

Smith, Steve, Booth, Ken, and Zalewski, Marysia (1996) eds. *International Theory: Positivism and Beyond* (Cambridge: Cambridge University Press).

Southern, R. W. (1953) *The Making of the Middle Ages* (London: Hutchinson).

Strauss, Leo (1968) *The City and Man* (Chicago: Chicago University Press).

Strauss, Leo and Cropsey, Joseph (1963) *A History of Political Philosophy* (Chicago: Chicago University Press).

Suárez, Francisco (1944) "On Laws and God the Lawgiver," in *Selections from Three Works*, trans. Gwladys L. Williams (Oxford: Clarendon Press).

Suganami, Hidemi (1996) *On the Causes of War* (Oxford: Oxford University Press).

Swanson, Judith (1992) *The Public and the Private in Aristotle's Political Philosophy* (Ithaca: Cornell University Press).

Taylor, A. J. P. (1957) *The Trouble Makers: Dissent over Foreign Policy 1792–1939* (London: Hamish Hamilton).

Taylor, Charles (1975) *Hegel* (Cambridge: Cambridge University Press).

Tesón, Fernando R. (1988) *Humanitarian Intervention: An Inquiry into Law and Morality* (Dobbs Ferry: Transnational Publishers).

(1998) *The Philosophy of International Law* (Boulder, CO: Westview Press).

Tierney, Brian (1997) *The Idea of Natural Rights: Studies on Natural Rights, Natural Law and Church Law, 1150–1625* (Atlanta: Scholars Press).

Todorov, Tzvetan (1999) *The Conquest of America: The Conquest of the Other*, trans. Richard Howard, with a new foreword by Anthony Pagden (Norman: University of Oklahoma Press).

Toynbee, Arnold (1973) *Constantine Porphyrogenitus and his World* (Oxford: Oxford University Press).

Treitschke, Heinrich von (1916) *Politics* (London: Constable).

Tuck, Richard (1987) "The 'Modern' Theory of Natural Law," in Anthony Pagden, ed., *The Languages of Political Theory in Early-Modern Europe* (Cambridge: Cambridge University Press).

(1989) *Hobbes* (Oxford: Oxford University Press).

(1999) *The Rights of War and Peace: Political Thought and the International Order from Grotius to Kant* (Oxford: Oxford University Press).

Tully, James (1988) *Meaning and Context: Quentin Skinner and his Critics* (Cambridge: Polity Press).

Ullmann, Walter (1975) *Medieval Political Theory* (Harmondsworth: Penguin Books).

Untersteiner, Mario (1954) *The Sophists*, trans. Kathleen Freeman (Oxford: Blackwell).

Vattel, E. de (1916) *The Law of Nations or Principles of Natural Law*, trans. Charles G. Fenwick (Washington, DC: Carnegie Institution).

Vincent, Andrew and Plant, Raymond (1984) *Philosophy, Politics and Citizenship* (Oxford: Basil Blackwell).

Vitoria, Francisco de (1991) *Political Writings*, ed. Anthony Pagden and Jeremy Lawrance (Cambridge: Cambridge University Press).

Voegelin, Eric (1952) *The New Science of Politics* (Chicago: University of Chicago Press).

Walker, R. B. J. (1992) *Inside/Outside: International Relations as Political Theory* (Cambridge: Cambridge University Press).

Waltz, Kenneth (1959) *Man, the State and War* (New York: Columbia University Press).

(1962) "Kant, Liberalism and War," *American Politial Science Review*, vol. 56, 331–40.

(1979) *Theory of International Politics* (Reading, MA: Addison Wesley).

(1997) "Evaluating Theories," *American Political Science Review*, vol. 91, no. 4.

Walzer, Michael (1974) *Regicide and Revolution: Speeches at the Trial of Louis XVI* (Cambridge: Cambridge University Press).

(1977) *Just and Unjust Wars* (New York: Basic Books).

(1983) *Spheres of Justice* (New York: Basic Books).

Welsh, Jennifer M. (1995) *Edmund Burke and International Relations* (London: Macmillan).

Wendt, Alexander (1992) "Anarchy is What States Make of It: The Social Construction of Power Politics," *International Organization*, vol. 46.

(1999) *Social Theory of International Relations* (Cambridge: Cambridge University Press).

White, Ian (1979) "Condorcet: Politics and Reason," in S. C. Brown (1979).

Wight, M. (1991), in G. Wight and B. Porter, eds., *International Theory: The Three Traditions* (Leicester: Leicester University Press).

Wight, Martin (1966) "Why is There No International Theory?," in Herbert Butterfield and Martin Wight, eds., *Diplomatic Investigations* (London: Allen and Unwin).

Williams, Howard (1983) *Kant's Political Philosophy* (Oxford: Blackwell).

(1992) *International Relations as Political Theory* (Milton Keynes: Open University Press).

Williams, Howard, Wright, Moorhead, and Evans, Tony (1992), eds. *A Reader in International Relations and Political Theory* (Buckingham: Open University Press).

Winch, Donald (1978) *Adam Smith's Politics: An Essay in Historiographic Revision* (Cambridge: Cambridge University Press).

Winkleman, F. (1975), ed. *In Praise of Constantine: A Historical Study and New Translation of Eusebius' Tricennial Orations* (Berkeley: University of California Press).

Wolff, Christian von (1934) *The Law of Nations Treated According to the Scientific Method*, trans. Joseph H. Drake (Oxford: Oxford University Press).

Wood, Neal (1988) *Cicero's Social and Political Thought* (Berkeley: University of California Press).

Wright, Moorhead (1975), ed. *Theory and Practice of the Balance of Power, 1486–1914* (London: Dent).

Yack, Bernard (1993) *The Problems of a Political Animal* (Berkeley: University of California Press).

Zouche, Richard (1650/1911) *An Exposition of Fecial Law and Procedure*, trans. J. L. Brierly (Washington, DC: Carnegie Institution).

Index

absolutism, and sovereignty, 248–9
Abstract and Judgement of Saint-Pierre's Project for Perpetual Peace (Rousseau), 386, 416, 425–7
Academy, 61, 90–1
Active Intellect, role in the perfectability of man, al-Farabi on, 149–51
Adages (Erasmus), 185
Adeodatus (Augustine of Hippo's son), 101, 119
affinity, as expression of fellowship between individuals, Marcus Aurelius on, 88–9
Agis (king of Sparta), 267
agricultural production, and population increases, List on, 556–8
Al-Farabi, Abu Nasr Muhammad, 107–8, 148–69, 170
al-Mulk, Nizam, *Book of Government*, 109
Alcibiades, views of domestic and foreign politics, 22
Alexander the Great, 24, 27, 61, 124
alienation, Rousseau on, 385, 386
alliances, essential nature in the face of territorial ambitions of universal monarchy, Fénelon on, 301–6
Allies, bombing policies in the Second World War, and the just-war theory, 184
ambassadors
    diplomatic immunity: Montesquieu on, 406; under *ius gentium* transferred to Spaniards in the New World, 237
    qualities, Callières on, 280
    role: Callières on, 277; sixteenth–eighteenth centuries, 244
    see also diplomacy
Ambrose (bishop of Milan), 100–1, 119
American Indians, classified as barbarians, 186–9, 231
ancient Greeks, 4, 9, 14
ancient world

attitudes to international political theory, 17–20: Aristotle, 23–7, 32; Plato and Platonism, 30–2; Stoics, 27–30; Thucydides, 20–3, 32, 34–60
angels, as celestial intelligences, Dante on, 200
Anglo-German conflict, inevitability because of trade rivalries, Hilferding on, 568
Answer to the Question "What is Enlightenment?" (Kant), 380, 389
Antioch (Syria), Constantine I the Great's building activities, 117
apostates, as citizens of virtuous cities, al-Farabi on, 167
Apuleius, *De mundo*, quoted by Augustine, 121–2
Arabs, as seekers of pleasure in base cities, al-Farabi on, 165
arbitration
    preferable to just war, Erasmus on, 228–30
    and war, Pufendorf on, 344, 345
    Arete (virtue), 19
aristocracies
    Aristotle on, 70
    John of Paris on, 191–2
    see also nobility
Aristotle, 61–2
    Erasmus' criticisms, 225–6
    international political theory, 23–7, 32
    Islamic attitudes towards, 107
    rediscovery in thirteenth-century Europe and its effects on Christian political thought, 178
    responsibility of rulers seen as involving the waging of war, 183
    The Politics, 62–82
armies *see* standing armies
arms race, Bosanquet on, 514
associations *see* cities
atheism, Burke on, 295

Athens
    attitudes to justice, in Thucydides, 21, 22, 23
    attitudes to military security compared to
        those of other states, 38
    attitudes towards the neutrality of Melos,
        Peloponnesian War, 53–9
    citizenship, 7, 8
    sovereignty, as delegated to the archon, 271–2
Augustine of Hippo, 5, 96, 101–4, 105, 119–35
    war as the consequence of sin, 183, 184
Augustinianism, Aristotle's effects upon in
        thirteenth-century Christendom, 178
authority
    identification in just-war theory, 183, 185
    and sovereignty, 249–50
Avicenna (Abu Ali Al Husayn Ibn Sina),
        The Healing, 109, 170–3

balance of Europe see balance of power
balance of power, 244, 254–5, 307–10, 379
    Cobden's criticisms, 522–3, 538–43
    Hume on, 407–9
    Vattel on, 323
balance of trade, and British–Portuguese trade,
        Smith on, 411–15
banking industry, and protectionism,
        Schumpeter on, 577–8
baptism, lawful administration to children of
        unbelievers questioned by Vitoria, 231
barbarians
    Byzantine and Chinese views, 99
    Christian relations with in the New World,
        177–8, 186–9, 231–41
    definition in the ancient Greek world, 9
    distinguished from civilized nations
        in the waging of war, Mill on, 487–9
    and Greeks, Aristotle on, 63
Barraclough, Geoffrey, 104
base cities
    al-Farabi on, 156–7, 165–6
    see also cities
Basil of Caesarea, attitudes to military force, 98
Beccaria, Cesare de, marchese de, 381
Belgium, political position in relationship to
        international law, Treitschke's views,
        496–7, 504
ben Maimon, Moshe (Moses Maimonides),
        174–5
benevolence, duty, Pufendorf on, 317
Bentham, Jeremy, and international law, 6
bodies, and souls, Aristotle on, 66–8
Bodin, Jean
    concept of sovereignty, 248–9, 270–5
    and ius gentium, 319

Boekelen, Christian Otho of, exceptions to
        the observance of treaties, 282, 284
Boniface VIII (pope), "tow-swords" theory, 179
Book of Government (Nizam al-Mulk), 109
booty, Pufendorf on, 318, 348
Bosanquet, Bernard, and patriotism, 468,
        506–17
Boucher, David, history of international
        thought, 12
bourgeoisie
    and capitalism: Hilferding on, 570–1;
        Marx and Engels on, 572–3
    ineffectiveness in opposition to war,
        Hilferdings on, 580–2
British–Portuguese trade and the balance of
        trade, Smith on, 411–15
Brougham and Vaux, Henry Peter Brougham,
        1st Baron, definition of balance of power,
        539–40, 541, 542–3
Brown, Christopher, 178
Brown, Peter, 100
Buddhists, Islamic attitudes towards, 9
Bulgarians, relations with the Byzantine
        Empire and other nations, 139–40
bullion trade, and the balance of trade,
        Smith on, 411–15
Burgundy, possession by Charles V or by
        the French defensible in a just war, Vitoria
        on, 236
Burke, Edmund, attitude to French Revolution,
        253–4, 292–300
Buzan, Barry, 3
Bynkershoek, Cornelius van (1673–1743), and
        diplomacy, 251–2, 281–5
Byzantium, 96
    Byzantine thought and international
        political theory, 99–100, 115, 136–47
    relations with non-Roman peoples,
        Constantine VII Porphyrogenitus on, 137,
        138–46

Caesar, Julius, 246
caliphate, 105, 106
    Avicenna on, 170–1, 173
Callières, François de, and diplomacy, 251–2,
        276–80
cannibalism, practice by American Indians, 239
capital flows, and protectionism, Schumpeter
        on, 577–8
capital investments, and trade agreements,
        Hilferding on, 565–6
capitalism
    competitive capitalism: effects of new
        imperialism, 527–8; and nationalism,

capitalism (cont.).
Hilferding on, 529–30, 561–71; and the state, nineteenth century, 526–7
effects on the bourgeosie, Hilferding on, 570–1
and imperialism: Hilferding on, 562–5, 568–71; Schumpeter on, 530, 575–84
and internationalism, Marx and Engels on, 572–4
see also imperialism
Carlyle, A. J., 104
Carlyle, R. W., 104
Carneades, argues for the non-existence of the law of nature, Grotius on, 325–6, 328, 329
cartels see tariff policies
Cassirer, Ernst, 391
Catherine the Great, influence of Montesquieu, 381
Chadwick, Henry, early Christian attitudes to government, 96
chance killings, culpable nature, Thomas Aquinas on, 219–20
Charles V (Holy Roman Emperor), 302
and the European balance of power, Montesquieu on, 408
rights to Burgundian possessions defensible in a just war, Vitoria on, 236
Charles V the Wise (king of France), and regency, 272
Chersonites, relations with the Byzantine Empire and other nations, 140
China, attitudes to foreigners, 442
choice, in man, al-Farabi on, 150–2
Christendom
coterminous with Europe, Fénelon on, 303
emergence in Europe, 177
government, 179–80
international political theory and the regulation of relations between states, 177–83
political thought affected by rediscovery of Aristotle in the thirteenth century, 178
unity destroyed by divisions betwen western and eastern churches, 180
Christian gospel, contamination by the philosophers, Erasmus on, 226–7
Christianity
Augustine defends against its critics at the time of the Vandal attacks against Rome in, 405, 120–5

importance for the development of international law in Europe, Treitschke on, 496
and international political theory: early Christianity, 96–8, 111–14; late antiquity and early middle ages, 95–6, 96–8
Christians
capable of righteous living without secular law, Luther on, 206–7, 208–9, 210–11, 212
duty to serve the secular authorities, Luther on, 209–10, 211–12
Islamic attitudes towards, 9
Chrysippus, 328
church
Augustine's views, influence, 103
government, challenged by Lutheranism, 182, 204
political authority in relation to authority of the secular state, 179–81
and Roman Empire, 101, 102, 116–18
Cicero, Marcus Tullius, 107, 247, 255
cosmopolitanism, 29
first principles of nature and laws in conformity with reason as principles of action in relation to was, 333–4
and honour, 284
On Duties, 83–5
cities
governance, Maimonides on, 175
ranking, al-Farabi on, 155–66
ruling ranks, 152–3
see also collectivities; states; virtuous cities
citizens and citizenship
classes in virtuous cities, Weeds, al-Farabi on, 155, 166–9
in Rome and Athens, 7, 8
City of God, peace, seen by Augustine as the perfection of the saints, 125–6, 129–30, 131–5
City of God against the Pagans, The (Augustine of Hippo), 102, 103, 105, 119–35
civic humanism, 244
civil law
concept, 311
distinguished from international law, Rachel on, 321, 353–5
Hobbes on, 320
and liberty, Montesquieu on, 405
manipulation by debtors, 377
rejection as basis of morality, Grotius on, 312
see also law
civil society
effects on the individuality of human beings, Hegel on, 460–1
evolution, Kant on, 389, 390

Grotius' understanding, 314–15
Hobbes on, 317, 335
and the state of war, Rousseau on, 425–6
see also society
civilization, expansion through trade, List on,
    554–5
civilized nations, distinguished from barbarians
    in the waging of wars, Mill on, 487–9
civitas maximus (supreme state), Wolff on, 321–2,
    360–7, 368
Clausewitz, Karl von, role of war, 462
Cleomedes (Athenian general), Melian
    dialogue, 53–9
Cleomenes (king of Sparta), 267
Cleon, relationships between collectivities,
    views expressed during the Mytilenian
    debate, in Thucydides, 45–9
clergy, no right to kill in self-defense, Aquinas
    on, 218
Cobden, Richard
    advocates peace in the Eastern Question,
        522–4, 547–9
    and the balance of power, 522–3, 538–43
    views about free trade, 521, 524, 542–6
collectivities
    relations between, 6, 10–12: as the basis of
        international political theory, 6–8, 11–12;
        Stoics on, 28–30; Thucydides on, 21–3,
        35–6, 37–40
    relations with individuals, 6, 8–10, 11–12:
        Thucydides on: during the Athenian
        plague, 42–44; Pericles' funeral oration,
        39–42
    relationship between collectivities,
        Thucydides on, in the Melian dialogue,
        53–60
see also cities; states
colonialism and colonization
    advantages for the annexation of states,
        Machiavelli on, 259–60
    British colonialism, Cobden's criticisms,
        545–6
    effects on English trading policies,
        Hilferding on, 567
    legal constraints to avoid war, 453–4
    management of colonies in a European
        union, Saint-Pierre on, 397
combatants, legal distinctions between
    members of armed forces and irregular
    troops
    Treitschke on, 503–4
commerce *see* trade
commonwealths
    Bodin on, 270

Burke's definition, 293
Europe as a commonwealth, Burke on,
    297
"Communist Manifesto, The" (Marx and
    Engels), capitalism and internationalism,
    572–4
communitarianism (particularism)
    in Greek thought, 18, 18–19
    and international political theory, 9, 11
communities *see* states and collectivities
Comparative Advantage (Comparative Costs),
    Law (Ricardo), 520–1
conflict, in politics, Aristotle on, 25, 26
conflict resolution, monarchy essential to,
    Dante on, 202
congresses, states' participation in and
    operation on voting rights, Treitschke on,
    501–2
conquest, right of conquest, Montesquieu on,
    402–5
consensus, as basis of morality, Grotius on,
    313
conservatives, and nationalism, Schumpeter
    on, 581
Considerations on the Government of Poland
    (Rousseau), 387, 416
Considerations on Representative Government
    (Mill), 464
Constantine I, the Great (Roman emperor),
    98–9, 115–18, 142, 143, 144, 145
Constantine VII, Porphyrogenitus, *De
    Administrando Imperio*, 96, 99–100, 136–47
Constantinianism, and international political
    theory, 98–9, 115–18
Constantinople, Constantine the Great's
    building activities, 117
Constitutional Project for Corsica (Rousseau), 387
constitutions, Aristotle on, 69, 70
contract, and law, Bodin on, 275
convention (*nomos*), 19–20
conversion, Islamic attitudes towards, 106
Corn Laws, repeal, 521, 538
cosmopolitanism
    in Greek thought, 19
    Marx and Engels on, 573–4
    Stoics on, 28–30
costs, comparative costs, and trading profits,
    Ricardo on, 535–7
crime, discrimination between ordinary and
    political crime and international law,
    Treitschke on, 501
Critias (Athenian oligarch disobeyed by
    Socrates), 90
Critique of Pure Reason (Kant), 388

Cromwell, Oliver, preserves England's honour as a state under the Commonwealth, Vattel on, 371

cross (Saving Trophy), used by Constantine I the Great in establishing his rule over the Roman Empire, 115, 116, 117

custom, as the origin of the law of nations, Rachel on, 352–3

customary law, Wolff on, 368

daily life, attainment of virtue, Avicenna on, 173

Dante Alighieri (1265–1321), understanding of monarchy, 181–2, 198–203

Dar al harb (world of war), 108

Dar al Islam (world of Islam), 108

David (king of Israel), 246, 267–8

De Administrando Imperio (Constantine VII Porphyrogenitus), 96, 99–100, 136–47

De Ceremoniis Aulae Byzantinae (Constantine VII Porphyrogenitus), 136

De la manière e négocier avec les Souverains (Callières), 252, 276–80

de las Casas, Bartolomé, 187

De mundo (Apuleius), quoted by Augustine, 121–2

De Thematibus (Constantine VII Porphyrogenitus), 136

death, way, *Didache*, 111, 113

debtors, manipulation on civil law, 377

democracy
    Aristotle's views, 69, 70–1
    as despotism, Kant on, 437–8
    Plato's dislike, 90
    Thucydides on, in Pericles' funeral oration, 37–8
    within the supreme state, Wolff on, 365–6

democratic cities, al-Farabi on, 163–6

despotic cities, al-Farabi on, 159–63

despotism, Kant on, 437–8

devil, nature, 130

Dialogues Concerning Natural Religion (Hume), 407

Didache, 95, 97, 111–14

Diderot, Denis, 379, 384, 416

Diodotus
    relationship of individuals with their collectivities, in Thucydides, 22, 23, 49–50
    relationships between collectivities, views expressed during the Mytilenian debate, in Thucydides, 50–2

Diogenes the Cynic, cosmopolitanism, 28

Dionysius II (tyrant of Syracuse), views repudiated by Plato, 31

diplomacy
    diplomatic relations between states, Callières's views, 251–2, 276–80

evolution, 244, 250–5
    see also ambassadors

diplomatic immunity, 251

direct rule, advantages for the annexation of states, Machiavelli on, 259

"Discourse on the Arts and Sciences" (Rousseau), 384

Discourses on the First Ten Books of Livy (Machiavelli), 245, 246–7, 257, 262–9

disputes between states, resolution in any European union, Saint-Pierre on, 396

dogmatism, as basis of morality, Grotius on, 313

domination
    as associated with despotic cities, al-Farabi on, 159–63
    as associated with ignorant cities, al-Farabi on, 157–8, 159–60

double effect, principle, 184, 218

Doyle, Michael, 3, 386, 391

dulce bellum inexpertis (Erasmus), 221–30

dumping, 567
    Schumpeter on, 576, 577, 578

Dunne, Tim, 12

Dutch East India Company, engage Grotius to defend their rights to prize, 312–14

duties, degrees and importance in fellowship, Cicero's views, 83–5

Eastern Question, 521–3, 527, 547–9

Elements of the Philosophy of Right (Hegel), 460, 461, 462, 470–5

Elizabeth I (queen of England), 302

Elshtain, Jean Bethke, 103

Emile (Rousseau), 384, 385, 416

empire
    concept, during the period of Latin Christendom, 104
    Dante's understanding, 198, 201

Engels, Friedrich
    superiority of European civilization assumed, 465
    support for British policy in the Eastern Question, 522, 527

Engels, Friedrich (1820–95), capitalism and internationalism, 572–4

England *see* Great Britain

English Nation, concept in the University of Paris in medieval times, 457–8

Enlightenment, 379–80
    international political theory, 380–2
    political legitimacy and the role of the state, 459
    Rousseau's criticisms of political thought, 384–7

Enquiry Concerning Human Understanding (Hume), 382, 407

Enquiry Concerning the Principles of Morals (Hume), 382, 407

equality
   civil equality, Gentz on, 308
   equality of states, Gentz on, 255, 307–10
   within the supreme state, Wolff on, 364–5

Erasmus, Desiderius, and just-war theory, 185–6, 221–30

erring cities, al-Farabi on, 166

eschatology, *Didache*, 97, 114

Essay on Theory and Practice (Kant), 429–32

Essays, Moral and Political (Hume), 407

eternal life, as the peace of the City of God, Augustine's views, 125–6, 129–30, 131–5

Euben, Peter, 22

Europe
   balance of power: Montesquieu on, 408–9;
      seen as being controlled by England,
      Cobden on, 538–43
   as a commonwealth, Burke on, 297
   coterminous with Christendom, Fénelon
      on, 303
   economic union, affected by nationalism,
      Hilferding on, 567–8
   intervention of states in internal affairs of
      European states justified, Mill on, 490
   potential to become a universal republic,
      List on, 554

European civilization, superiority assumed
   in the nineteenth century, 465

European nations
   colonization of other peoples regarded
      as inhospitable, Kant on, 442
   conduct of war modified by civilized
      cultures, Hegel on, 474
   as the expression of God's will, Mazzini
      on, 463, 480

European union, proposals for, Saint-Pierre
   on, 394–8

Eusebius Pamphili (bishop of Caesarea),
   Constantinianism, 98–9, 100, 115–18

evil, voluntary evil in man, al-Farabi on, 151

executioners, culpability when ordered to
   execute the innocent, Thomas Aquinas
   on, 216, 217

existence, transient nature, Marcus Aurelius
   on, 86–7

expediency, as the basis of law, Grotius on,
   326, 328

extradition, Treitschke on, 501

extraterritoriality, 251

Faith and the Future (Mazzini), 463

families
   Aristotle on, 63, 65
   effects on the individuality of human beings,
      Hegel on, 460–1
   paternal authority in the Roman world, 461

fate, as productive of perpetual peace, Kant
   on, 444

fathers, authority over families in the Roman
   world, 461

Federalist, The, 286

federations
   as the means to state security, Kant on,
      438–41, 445
   see also states

fellowship, expressed through affinity between
   individuals, Marcus Aurelius on, 88–9

fellowships, Cicero on, 83–5

Fénelon, François de Salignac de la Mothe,
   (1651–1715), foreign policy and the balance
   of power, 254–5, 301–6

"Few Words on Non-Intervention, A" (Mill),
   464, 486–93

Fieldhouse, D. K., 528

finance capital
   aims and effects on English capital
      investment, Hilferding on, 566–7
   and industrialization, Hilferding on, 568–9
   and nationalism, Hilferding on, 568, 569–71

finance capitalism, *see also* capitalism

first principles, importance for deductive
   arguments, Dante on, 198–9

First World War, and the ethical state, 467–8

Fliess, Peter, 4

Forde, Steve, 22

foreign policy
   and balance of power, 254–5, 301–6
   in a European union, Saint-Pierre on,
      397, 398
   see also international relations

Fox, Charles James, foreign policy during
   French revolutionary wars, 253, 254

France
   and capital investment, Hilferding on, 566
   claims to statehood as a republic, Napoleon's
      observation, 471
   "sovereignty", concept, 248, 250
   sovereignty as exercised during a regency, 272
   see also French Revolution

Francis I (king of France), 302

Franco-Prussian War, France's conduct
   codemned, Treitschke on, 503

Franks, relations with the Byzantine
   Empire, 144

free trade
  English policies, Hilferding on, 564–5, 566,
    567
  inviolability and control by treaties,
    Treitschke on, 500
  and liberal internationalism, 521–4
  List on, 550–60
  protectionist criticisms, 525–6
  Smith on, 383, 532–4
  see also trade
freedom
  concept, 461
  and self-determination in multi-national
    states, Mill on, 464
Freedom of the Seas (Grotius), 313
French Revolution
  effects on diplomatic policies, 252–4, 286–91
  and the renunciation of international law by
    France, Burke on, 293–300
  see also France
friendship
  Cicero on, 85
  philia, Aristotle on, 26

Gay, Peter, 380–1
Geist (Spirit), Hegel's concept, 460, 462
Gelasius I (pope), 101
general will, Rousseau on, 385
Gentz, Friedrich von, and the balance of power,
    255, 307–10, 539, 540, 541, 542
Germany
  and capitalism, Hilferding on, 564–5, 566, 568
  expansion justified as necessity, Treitschke
    on, 498
  international standing, Bosanquet supports,
    516–17
  nationalism, during the First World War, 467
  philosophical climate and effects on ideas of
    patriotism, 510–11
gladiators, revolt under Spartacus against the
    Roman Empire, 124–5
globalization, 530
God
  assists in the expansion of the Roman
    Empire, Augustine on, 122–3
  as Creator of all natures whether good or
    evil, Augustine on, 130–1
  law, and the law of nature in the Old
    Testament, 332
  man's relationship with, Pufendorf on, 341, 343
  as origin of the law of nature, Grotius on, 327,
    328
  purposes in creation to produce intellectual
    activity in man, 199–200

will: for the benefit of humanity rather than
    that of the individual, Mazzini on, 476–7,
    478
gods, relationship with the Universe, Marcus
    Aurelius on, 87
good
  as the aim of the state, Aristotle on, 62
  existence in sinners leads to awareness of
    loss of salvation, Augustine on, 130–1
  voluntary good in man, al-Farabi on, 151
goods
  temporal goods and their proper use,
    Augustine on, 131
  types and desirability for both individuals
    and states, Aristotle on, 77–9
governed, distinguished from the rulers,
    Aristotle's views, 62–3
government, importance of philosophy for
    good government, 92–3
governments
  desirable forms, Aristotle on, 73–7, 79
  type: Aristotle on, 68–71; Montesquieu, 400–1
gratitude, questionable nature in international
    relations, 290
Great Britain
  accused of piracy in international relations
    during wartime, Treitschke on, 497, 504
  and the balance of power in Europe, Cobden
    on, 538–43
  foreign policy during French revolutionary
    wars, 253
  free trade policies: criticized by List, 525–6;
    Hilferding on, 564–7
  honour retained by Cromwell under the
    Commonwealth, Vattel on, 371
  maintenance of the balance of power in
    Europe, Hume on, 408–9
  nationalism, as basis of free trade, List on,
    558–9
  navy, taxation for its maintenance for the
    protection of trade attacked by Cobden,
    543–7
  non-intervention policy, Mill on, 464–5,
    486–93
  policy towards the government of India, Mill
    on, 487–9
  trade policies, and peace-making, Bosanquet
    on, 513
Greek fire, 143
Greek philosophy, influence, on Islam and
    Judaism, 106–7
Greeks, and barbarians or non-Greeks,
    Aristotle on, 24, 27, 63
Gregory I, the Great (pope) (540–604), 105

Grotius, Hugo
criticized for failure to derive the laws of
nations from the concept of the supreme
state, Wolff on, 361
differences between the law of nations and
natural law, 366
and *ius gentium*, 319
Kant's criticisms, 439
and natural law, 312–17, 325–34, 349, 350
treaty-making, 251
voluntary law of nations, 367, 377
Guide of the Perplexed (Maimonides), 174
Gustavus Adolphus (king of Sweden), 278

Hagia Sophia (Constantinople), 142, 143, 144
Hamilton, Alexander, 252–3, 286–91
impressions of Montesquieu, 381
"Report on the Subject of Manufactures",
and protectionism, 524
happiness, al-Farabi on, 150, 151–2, 153, 154, 166, 167
Healing, The (Avicenna), 109, 170–3
Hegel, G. W. F.
concept of the state, 457
and German nationalism during the First
World War, 467, 468, 470
philosophical system and international
political theory, 460–2, 465, 470–5
the state and war, 508, 509–10, 511
Hegelianism, Bosanquet's defence, 506–17
Herder, J. G., 459
hereditary states, Machiavelli on, 257–8
Hierocles, cosmopolitanism, 29
Hilferding, Rudolf (1877–1941), *Finance Capital*,
528–30, 561–71
Hindus, Islamic attitudes towards, 9
history, Hegel's concept, 460, 462
History of England (Hume), 383, 407
Hobbes, Thomas
ius gentium, 320
law of nations and natural law, 354
and natural law, 316–17, 320, 335–40
views of war as universal, 416–17, 424
Hobhouse, L. T., German militarism blamed on
Hegelianism, 467
Hobson, J. A., *Imperialism*, effects of new
imperialism on competitive capitalism,
527–8
Holland, political position in relationship to
international law, Treitschke on, 496
Holy Roman Emperor, honour due, Vattel on,
371–2, 373
Holy Roman Empire, 180–1
Italian city-states achieve independence, 244
sovereignty, 250

Holy Scriptures, rejection of the Scriptures as
basis of morality, Grotius on, 313
Homer, importance for international political
theory, 18
honour, importance to the state, Bynkershoek
on, 283–4
honourableness, supremacy in fellowship
between men, Cicero on, 84–5
hospitality, cosmopolitan hospitality and
universal rights, Kant on, 441–3
Hourani, Albert, 105, 106, 107–8
households
governance: Aristotle on, 64–6, 69;
Maimonides on, 175
human beings
cognition and imagination, 153–5, 166
concern for humanity expressed through
nationalism, Mazzini on, 479–85
depravity revealed in international relations,
Kant on, 439
inclination to war, Kant on, 430, 431
individuality, Hegel's concept, 460–1
moral imperfections work against the
creation of states, Kant on, 444–5
personhood, Hegel on, 471
purpose to engage in intellectual activity,
Dante on, 199–200
relationships between individuals subject to
civil laws, Hegel on, 470–1
responsibility for fellow human beings to
take precedence over nationalism, Mazzini
on, 463, 476–80
social nature, al-Farabi on, 148
and the state, Hegel on, 508–9
human nature
Aristotle on, 24, 25–6
Mazzini on, 476–7
moral improvement dependent upon, Kant
on, 429–30
human sacrifice, practice by American
Indians, 239
humanity
corruption by society, Rousseau on, 384–6
division between Christians and
non-Christians necessitates the
existence of secular authorities for
the rule of non-Christians, Luther on,
205–9
Hume, David, 379, 380, 381, 384, 407–9
"Of the Balance of Trade", attacks on
mercantilist perceptions of trade, 520
origins of the concept of balance of power,
542
political writings, 382–3

Ibn Sina, Abu Ali Al Husayn (Avicenna),
    The Healing, 109, 170–3
Idea for a Universal History (Kant), 389–90, 392–3
idealism, Hegel on, and influence, 470
ignorant cities, al-Farabi on, 159–66
imams, 106
    Avicenna on, 171, 172–3
immaturity, Kant's views, 380
immoral cities, al-Farabi on, 166
immorality, as the key to the maintenance of
    power by rulers, Machiavelli on, 261
imperial vestments, sacred nature in Byzantine
    Empire, 142–3
imperialism
    and capitalism, Schumpeter on, 530, 575–84
    effects with the growth of capitalism,
        Hilferding on, 562–5, 568–71
    new imperialism, effects on competitive
        capitalism, 527–8
    see also capitalism
Imperialism (Hobson), effects of new
    imperialism on competitive capitalism,
    527–8
Imperialism (Lenin), 528
impiety, as the contradiction of the Nature of
    the Universe, Marcus Aurelius on, 88
Incarnation, dependence on unity of the
    Roman Empire under Augustus in
    justification of monarchy, Dante on,
    202–3
India, Great Britain's policy towards, Mill on,
    487–9
indispensible cities, al-Farabi on, 156
individuals
    affinity as the expression of fellowship
        between individuals, Marcus Aurelius on,
        88–9
    goods, and their desirability, 77–9
    and law, 311
    relations with collectivities, 6, 8–10, 11–12:
        Thucydides on, 21, 21–3: during the
        Athenian plague, 42–4; expressed by
        Diodotus during Mytilenian debate, 50–2;
        Pericles' funeral oration, 39–42
    relations with the Universe, Marcus Aurelius
        on, 88, 89
    and the state: fellowship between, Cicero on,
        84; happiness common to both, Aristotle
        on, 79–82; Plato on, 93
industrialization
    and finance capital, Hilferding on, 568–9
    and international political theory,
        519–30
    and international relations, nineteenth
        century, 458

injustice
    effects, Grotius on, 330
    Marcus Aurelius on, 88
    quality appropriate only to civil society,
        Grotius on, 338
innocents
    defense against tyranny, as justification of
        Spanish colonization of the New World,
        239–40
    killing, Thomas Aquinas on, 215–17
insiders and outsiders *see* collectivities
Institutes (Justinian), 312
intellect, seen as the highest human capacity
    and to be used at its best in tranquillity for
    the well-being of the world, Dante on, 181
intellectual activity, as the purpose of human
    activity, Dante on, 199–200
intellectuals, and nationalism, Schumpeter on,
    582, 583
intermarriage, forbidden between Byzantine
    rulers and other nations, 144–5
international law
    based on observance of treaties, Hegel on,
        472–3
    concept, and its development, 311–23
    distinctions between political and ordinary
        crimes and states' attitudes towards,
        Treitschke on, 501
    Hegel on, 461–2
    as obligations and contracts between states,
        Hegel on, 470–2
    renunciation by France during the French
        Revolution, Burke on, 293–300
    and the role of the state, Treitschke on,
        495–9
    Vattel on, 322–3, 370–8
    see also law; law of nations; laws; natural law
international legal positivism, 281
International Monetary Fund (IMF), 521
international political theory
    ancient world's attitudes to, 17–20: Aristotle,
        23–7, 32; Plato and Platonism, 30–2; Stoics,
        27–30; Thucydides, 20–3, 32, 34–69
    approaches towards, 12–14
    Augustine of Hippo's influence, 101–4, 105,
        119–35
    in Christendom, and the regulation of
        relations between states, 177–83
    Constantinianism and Byzantine thought,
        98–100, 115–18, 136–47
    defined, 1
    development in late antiquity and the early
        middle ages, 95–6
    and early Christianity, 96–8, 111–14
    Enlightenment, 380–2

and the evolution of European states, 243–55
Hobbes on, 317, 320, 335–40
Hume's commitment to, 383
and industrialization, 519–30
and Islam, 105–9, 170–3
and Judaism, 109, 174–5
Kant on, 389–93
and Latin Christendom, 104–5
literary canon, 2–6
Montesquieu on, 382
Rousseau on, 386
themes: collectivities and their rights and
    duties, 6, 10–12; relations between
    individuals and their collectivity, 6, 8–10,
    11–12; relationship between collectivities,
    6–8, 11–12
international society, and nationalism,
    nineteenth century, 462–5
international state, concept a nonsense, Kant
    on, 439, 441, 445
international thought, histories, 12–13
international trade
    growth in the nineteenth century, 519
    validity allowed in the case of Spanish
        colonization of the New World, Vitoria
        on, 235–6, 241
    see also trade
internationalism
    and capitalism, Marx and Engels on, 572–4
    liberal internationalism, and free trade, 521–4
intervention and non-intervention, Treitschke
    on, 502
investiture dispute, 179
Irving, Washington, 548
Islam
    expansion threatens Christendom, 177
    and international political theory, 105–9,
        170–3: late antiquity and the early middle
        ages, 95, 96
    particularism and universalism, 9
    as the reason for Turkey's exclusion from
        international negotiations in Europe,
        Treitschke on, 496
    rise, Constantine VII Porphyrogenitus on,
        146–7
Isocrates, pan-Hellenism, 18–19
Italy
    Italian city-states, evolution and use of
        power, 244–7
    nationalism: as the expression of God's will,
        Mazzini on, 480–5; nineteenth century,
        462–3
ius
    as basis of natural law, Grotius'
        understanding, 314

Hobbes' concept as right, 339
    and lex, 319
ius feciale, 320, 355
ius gentium see law of nations
ius inter gentes, and ius gentium, 320
Ius inter gentes (Zouche), 351

Jacobinism, Burke on, 294–5
Japan (Nippon), attitudes to foreigners, 442
Jay, John, 286
Jerusalem, Constantine I the Great's building
    activities, 117
Jews, Islamic attitude towards, 9
John of Paris, argues for secular rule rather
    than spiritual rule, 180, 191–7
Judaism
    and Greek philosophy, 106–7
    and international political theory 109, 174–5:
        late antiquity and the early middle ages,
        95, 96
judgement, powers, inherent within man,
    Grotius on, 327
judges, culpability when the innocent are
    condemned, Thomas Aquinas on, 216, 217
Jupiter, as origin of the concept of ius, Grotius
    on, 328
jurists, pronouncements more effective than
    those of philosophers in advising the state
    on the promotion of war, Kant on, 446
just cause, and just-war theory, 183–4
just war, see also war
just wars, 183–6, 213–20, 221–30
    al-Farabi on, 108
    Augustine on, 103–4
    Pufendorf on, 345, 347
    Rachel on, 355
    seen as support for Spanish colonization
        of the New World, Vitoria on, 236–9
justice
    administration dependent on the secular
        authorities, Luther on, 204–5, 207–9
    Aristotle on, 26, 71–2
    effects, Grotius on, 330
    essential to the well-being of kingdoms, 123–4
    as the good, Aristotle on, 76–7
    as the mean in life, Avicenna on, 173
    perversion, Erasmus' definition, 226
    quality appropriate only to civil society,
        Grotius on, 338
    Thucydides' concerns with, 20, 21–3, 56, 57
    war as the means to international justice,
        Burke on, 296–7, 299–300
Justin, treaty observance among the Parthians,
    281
Justinian, Institutes, 312

Kant, Immanuel, 428–55
    definition of Enlightenment, 380
    general philosophy, 387–9
    international political theory, 389–93
    role of the state, 459
kingdoms
    superiority over the other forms of
        government, John of Paris on, 191–3
    territorial ambitions, Fénelon on, 301–6
kings and kingship
    Aristotle on, 63, 70
    and oligarchy, John of Paris on, 180
    political position in Sparta, 263
    see also monarchy; rulers

labour, international division, Smith's
        arguments for, 532–4
Lactantius, Rome's cosmopolitanism, 29
languages, differences as working against
        perpetual peace, Kant on, 445
Latin Christendom, and international
        political theory, 104–5
law
    and contract, Bodin on, 275
    enforcement upon individual nations in
        the supreme state, Wolff on, 363
    in international relationships, Bynkershoek
        on, 282–3
    lex, Hobbes' concept, 339
    nature, Grotius on, 326–7
    and sovereignty, Bodin on, 249, 273–5
    see also civil law; international law; law of
        nations; laws
law codes, establishment by imams, under
        Islam, Avicenna on, 172–3
law of nations, 311
    arguments against Rachel on, 351–5
    customary law of nations, Wolff on, 368
    definition: Rachel on, 350–1; Wolff on,
        356
    dependence on treaties, 349–50
    distinguished from law of nature, Grotius
        on, 331–2
    Grotius on, 329–31
    ius gentium, 6, 7, 319–20: Vitoria on, 234–5, 236,
        237
    lack of observance, Rachel on, 353
    and natural law: Rachel on, 349, 353–4; Wolff
        on, 357–8, 366
    necessary law of nations: Vattel on, 376, 377–8;
        Wolff views, 358, 369
    origins, in custom, Rachel on, 352–3
    positive laws of nations, Wolff on, 368–9
    Rachel on, 320–1, 349–55
    and sociality, Wolff on, 359–60

stipulative law of nations, Wolff on, 367–8,
    369
voluntary law of nations: operation in war,
    Vattel on, 375–8; Wolff on, 367, 368
Wolff on, 321–3, 356–69, 370
    see also internatioal law; laws; natural law
Law of Nations, The (Vattel), 370–8, 379
law of nature
    denial of its existence shown to be false,
        Grotius on, 325–6
    distinguished from law of nations, Grotius
        on, 331–2
    Hobbes on, 339
    as origin of municipal laws, Grotius on, 328
    origin, Grotius on, 326–8
    and war, Grotius on, 333–4
Law of Prize, The (Grotius), 312–13
Law of War and Peace, The (Grotius), 315–16,
    325–34
laws
    attitudes to among founders of states,
        Machiavelli on, 246–7, 265–7
    civil vicinity, as applied to international
        political theory, Burke on, 298–300
    and diplomatic immunity, Montesquieu
        on, 406
    justice, Aristotle on, 76
    municipal laws and their origins in the law
        of nature, Grotius on, 328
    nature, Montesquieu on, 401
    origins in war, Montesquieu on, 400
    prohibitive laws relating to war, Kant on,
        432–6
    see also international law; law; law of nations;
        natural law
Laws of Nations Treated According to the Scientific
    Method (Wolff), 356–69
legality, within the supreme state, Wolff on,
    365
legislation, as the responsibilty of all the
    inhabitants of a country for the realization
    of nationhood, Mazzini on, 484
Leibnitz, Gottfried Wilhelm, ius feciale, 320
Lenin, Vladimir Ilyich, Imperialism, 528
Lentulus, Cyriacus, and honour, 284
Lentulus, Lucius, 247, 268
Leo V (Byzantine emperor), 143, 144
Lerner, Ralph, 106–7
Letters of Pacificus (Hamilton), 253, 286–91
Letters on a Regicide Peace (Burke), 253–4, 292–300
Leviathan (Hobbes), 335–40
lex
    Hobbes' concept as law, 339
    and ius, 319
liberalism, Hilferding on, 570

liberty
  Hobbes on, 339
  as the result of civil laws, Montesquieu
    on, 405
life, way, *Didache*, 111–13
List, Friedrich, and protectionism, 524–6,
  550–60
Livy, Titus, use by Machiavelli, 246
Logic (Maimonides), 174–5
logos, embodiment in the universe, Stoics on, 28
Long, A. A., Stoicism and its importance, 28
Louis XII (king of France), annexation of Milan,
  258–9
love, of God and neighbour as the way to peace,
  132–3, 135
Luther, Martin, spiritual and secular
  government, 182–3, 204–12
Lycurgus (Spartan lawgiver), 263, 267

Machiavelli, Niccolò, 3, 5, 245–7, 255, 257–69
  allows lawfulness of treachery for princes,
    281, 282
  realism in international relations, 10
  The Prince, 99, 244, 245, 247, 257–61
Mack Smith, Denis, 462
Madison, James, 286
madmen, legal rights, Vitoria on, 232
Mahdi Muhsin, 106–7
Mahomet, origins and teachings, Constantine
  VII Porphyrogenitus, 146–7
Maimonides, Moses (Moshe ben Maimon), 109,
  174–5
Malthus, Thomas Robert, 556, 557
Manchester School liberals, 521, 538
  concept of the state, 458
Manicheanism, 101, 119
Mansfield, Jr., Harvey, 246
Manzikert, battle (1071), 95, 99
Marcus Aurelius Antoninus, 30, 107
  cosmopolitanism, 29
  Meditations, 86–9
Markus, R. A., 100, 102
Marx, Karl
  attacks Cobden's support for
    non-intervention, 523–4
  capitalism and internationalism, 572–4
  criticisms of Hegel, 470
  superiority of European civilization
    assumed, 465
  support for British policy in the Eastern
    Question, 522, 527
Mary I (queen of England), 302
Mary, Queen of Scots, 302
masters, and slaves, Aristotle on, 65, 66–8,
  69, 80

Mattingly, Garrett, diplomacy, 250–1
Mazzini, Giuseppe, (1805–72), nationalism,
  462–3, 465, 466, 476–85
Meditations (Marcus Aurelius Antoninus), 86–9
Melian dialogue, relationships between
  collectivities, Thucydides on, 53–60
mental incapacity, barbarians in the New
  World, seen as justification of Spanish
  colonization, 240–1
mercantilism, 383
merit, as associated with ignorant cities,
  al-Farabi on, 157–8
Metaphysical Elements of Right, The (Kant), 450–5
Metaphysics of Morals, The (Kant), 388, 389
middle ages
  international political theory, 5
  universalism, 9, 9–10
  universities, inter-national relations between
    groups of students, 7
Milan, annexation by Louis XII of France,
  Machiavelli on, 258–9
militarism
  Augustine on, 103
  and nationalism, Schumpeter on, 582–3
military force, early Christian attitudes
  towards, 97–8
military intervention, advantages for the
  annexation of states, Machiavelli on, 260
Mill, John Stuart, (1806–73)
  nationalism, and self-determination, 464–5
  non-intervention: basis on moral autonomy,
    523; and nationalism, 486–93
  non-intervention and nationalism, 464–5,
    486–93
mirror for princes literature, 99
missionary work, as justification for Spanish
  colonization of the New World, Vitoria
    on, 238–9, 241
mixed states
  Machiavelli on, 258–60
  see also states
monarchy
  absolute monarchy, Fénelon opposes, 301
  Dante's understanding, 181–2, 198–203
  Hegel on, 461
  temporal monarchy, Dante's understanding,
    198, 201
  universal monarchy, limitations essential,
    Fénelon on, 301–6
  see also kings and kingship; rulers
Monarchy (Dante), 181–2
Monica (Augustine of Hippo's mother), 101, 119
Montesquieu, Charles de Secondat, Baron de la
  Brede et de, 399–406
  influence, 379, 380, 381–2

moral habits, Maimonides on, 174
moral perfection, realization in the universal
    state, Kant on, 429–32
morality
    bases, Grotius on, 313–14
    basis on speculative reason, Kant on, 388
    lack of agreement with politics except in
        federations, Kant on, 448–9
Moravscik, J., 100
multi-national states, and freedom of
    self-determination, Mill on, 464
Mytilenian debate
    relationship between collectivities,
        Thucydides on, 44–53
    relationship of individuals with their
        collectivities, in Thucydides, 22, 23,
        49–50

nation-states
    concept, 457–9: Hegel on, 471
    and patriotism, Bosanquet on, 468, 506–17
    and power, nineteenth century, 465–7
national debts, use for war to be prohibited,
    Kant on, 434
National System of Political Economy, The (List),
    and protectionism, 525–6, 550–60
nationalism
    effects on European economic union,
        Hilferding on, 567–8
    as the expression of concern for humanity,
        Mazzini on, 479–85
    and finance capitalism, Hilferding on, 568,
        569–71
    and international society, nineteenth
        century, 462–5
    Schumpeter on, 581–4
    subordination to the individual's
        responsibility to fellow human beings,
        Mazzini on, 463, 476–80
nations
    common will within the supreme state,
        Wolff on, 366
    concept, nineteenth century, 457–9
    definition, Wolff on, 357
    economics, and effects on free trade, List on,
        553, 556–7
    equality of rights, Vattel on, 322–3, 370–8
    honours due, Vattel on, 370–4
    as the most perfect association of men,
        al-Farabi on, 148–9
    relationship within the supreme state, Wolff
        on, 363–4
    rights, secured through federations, Kant on,
        438–41, 445

natural law
    and antipathy to war, Rousseau on, 417–18,
        424–5
    and international law: Rachel on, 321, 353–5;
        Vattel on, 322–3; Wolff on, 321
    and law of nations: Rachel on, 349, 353–4;
        Wolff on, 357–8, 366
    and national rights, Grotius on, 311–17,
        325–34
    and natural rights, Hobbes' understanding,
        316–17
    Pufendorf on, 317–18, 341–8, 349
    relationship to peace, Pufendorf on, 345
    and sovereigns, 319–20
    see also international law; law of nations; laws
natural liberty, Pufendorf on, 343
natural state, and international relations,
    Pufendorf on, 341–5
nature, as productive of perpetual peace, Kant
    on, 443–5
necessity, and justice, in Thucydides, 21, 23
Nelson, Janet, 104
Neoplatonism, 32
neutrality
    and national security, 253: United States at
        the time of the French revolutionary
        wars, Hamilton on, 286–91
    Treitschke on, 504
New Testament
    Grotius' use in identifying those laws
        applicable to Christians and
        distinguishable from the law of nature,
        332–3
    quotation by Machiavelli, 246, 268
New World, Christian relations with the
    barbarian inhabitants, 177–8, 186–9, 231–41
Nicaea, Council (AD 325), 115
Nichol, D. M., barbarians' views of the
    Byzantine Empire, 99
Nippon (Japan), attitudes to foreigners, 442
nobility
    Aristotle on, 68
    persistence of warlike attitudes and
        influence on capitalist societies,
        Schumpeter on, 579–80
    political position in Sparta, 263
    see also aristocracies
nomadic peoples, statehood, Hegel on, 471
nomos (convention), 19–20
non-Christians, incapable of righteous living
    without secular law, Luther, 207–9
non-Greeks, and Greeks, Aristotle on, 24, 27
non-intervention
    Cobden's support for, 523–4, 547–9

Hegel on, 471
and nationalism, Mill on, 464–5, 486–93
non-Roman peoples, relations with Byzantium,
    Constantine VII Porphyrogenitus on, 137,
    138–46
noumenal world, and phenomenal world,
    Kant on, 388, 392–3
La Nouvelle Héloïse (Rousseau), 384
Nussbaum, Martha, 28–9

oathtaking, Luther on, 211
Of the Balance of Power (Hume), 407–9
"Of the Balance of Trade" (Hume), attacks on
    mercantilist perceptions of trade, 520
Old Testament, and the law of nature, Grotius
    on, 332
Oldenbarnevelt, Johan van, 312
oligarchies
    Aristotle on, 69, 70–1
    and kingship, John of Paris on, 180
    Plato's dislike of, 90
oligopoly, 527
"On the American Indians" (Vitoria), 188–9,
    231–41
"On Dietary Laws, or Self-Restraint" (Vitoria),
    187
On Duties (Cicero), 83–5
On the Duties of Man and Citizen (Pufendorf), 318,
    341–8
On the Duties of Man (Mazzini), 463, 476–85
"On the Law of Nations" (Rachel), 349–55
On the Law of Nature and of Nations (Pufendorf),
    318
On the Necessity of Forming Alliances (Fénelon),
    301–6
On Royal and Papal Power (John of Paris), 191–7
On Secular Authority (Luther), 182–3, 204–12
opportunists, as citizens of virtuous cities,
    al-Farabi on, 166–7
Origen, attitudes to military force, 98
Orwin, Clifford, 20, 21, 22
Ossian, 459
Ostrogorsky, George, 99
outsiders and insiders *see* collectivities
ownership, and natural law, Grotius on, 314–16

pacifism
    Christian pacifism, attitudes towards
        universalism, 11
    Erasmus' support for, 221–30
pacts, as stipulative law of nations. Wolff on,
    367–8
pagan gods, seen as enemies to the Roman
    Empire by Augustine, 124–5

pain, Marcus Aurelius on, 88
Palmerston, Lord, and the Eastern Question,
    521–2, 548
papacy
    as an expression of internationalism for
        Europe, Mazzini on, 484
    claim to appoint sovereigns, Vattel on, 373–4
    power over secular rulers, 179: John of Paris
        on, 195–7
    and sovereignty, 250
papal states, Italian city-states achieve
    independence, 244
Paris, University of
    concept of the English Nation in medieval
        times, 457–8
    inter-national nature of political relations
        between groups of student, 7
Parthians, failure to keep treaties, 281
particularism (communitarianism)
    in Greek thought, 18–19
    and international political theory, 9, 11
passions, control, Seneca on, 30
patriotism
    Enlightenment views, 459
    Hegel on, 510–11
    and the nation-state, Bosanquet on, 468,
        506–17
"Patriotism in the Perfect State" (Bosanquet),
    506–17
Patzinacia, relations with the Byzantine
    Empire, 140
Paul, St. (apostle), 97
peace
    contrast with truces, Kant on, 432–3
    desirablilty for self-preservation, Hobbes
        on, 339–40
    as eternal life in the City of God, Augustine
        on, 125–6, 129–30, 131–5
    as part of natural law, Pufendorf on, 345
    promotion by trade, Ricardo on, 535
    universal desire for and as the object of
        creation, Augustine on, 126–30, 131–5
    and war, Pufendorf on, 348
    see also perpetual peace
peace-making, Bosanquet on, 514–15
Pechenegs, relations with the Byzantine
    Empire and other peoples, 138–41
Peloponnesian War, realist accounts, 4
Pericles, funeral oration, 21, 22, 36–42
perpetual peace
    as the effect of nature, Kant on, 443–5
    Enlightenment views, 459
    establishment as the moral aim, based upon
        reason, Kant on, 454–5

perpetual peace (cont.).
Hegel's criticisms, 462
immorality and futility, Treitschke on, 499
Kant on, 392
List on, 551, 553n
presupposed agreements between states,
Kant on, 472
Rousseau's views of Saint-Pierre's proposals,
426–7
Saint-Pierre on, 380, 392, 394–8
see also peace
Perpetual Peace (Kant), 389, 391–2, 432–50
Persian Letters (Montesquieu), 399
persons, rights, Grotius' understanding, 315
phenomenal world, and noumenal world,
Kant on, 388, 392–3
philia (friendship), Aristotle on, 26
Philip II (King of Macedon), 61
Philip II (king of Spain), territorial ambitions
opposed, 302–3
Philip IV the Fair (king of France), attitude
to papacy, 179, 180
Philip of Macedon, 246, 268
Philosophical Theory of the State, The (Bosanquet),
506
philosophy
importance: for good government, 92–3; as
guide in life, Marcus Aurelius on, 86–7
Philosophy of History (Hegel), 460
physiocrats, 383, 410
piracy, British piracy during wartime,
Treitschke on, 497, 504
Pitt, William, foreign policy during the French
revolutionary wars, 253, 254
plague, public behaviour during the Athenian
plague, as illustration of relationships
between individuals and collectivities,
Thucydides, 42–4
Plato, 90–1
and Aristotle, 23
connections with Aristotle, 61
international political theory, 30–2
Seventh Letter, 91–3
views of the *polis*, 19
writings available to Islamic world, 107
pleasure
Marcus Aurelius on, 88
pursuit in base cities, al-Farabi on, 156–7,
165–6
plebeians, political position in Sparta, 263
Plotinus, 32
Plutarch, cosmopolitanism, 29
polis, 4, 5, 8, 18–19
Aristotle's views, 24, 25, 26, 178, 179

Political Discourses (Hume), 383, 407
political economy, Say's understanding
criticized by List, 551–2
political legitimacy, and the role of the state,
459–62
Political Regime, The (al-Farabi), 148–69
political regimes
al-Farabi's classification of political regimes,
107–8, 148–9
Aristotle's view, 26
political science, Maimonides on, 174
Political Theory, 1
viewed as ineffective by political realists,
Kant on, 432
politics
Aristotle on, 25
lack of agreement with morality except
in federations, Kant on, 448–9
Plato's attitude towards, 91–3
Politics, The (Aristotle), 62–82
Politics (Treitschke), 466–7, 494–505
polycratia, John of Paris on, 192
polytheism, as the cause of conflict between
the two cities, Augustine on, 134
population increases, and agricultural
production, List on, 556–8
Porphyry, 32
Porter, Roy, 381
Portuguese–British trade and the balance
of trade, Smith on, 411–15
poverty, as democracy, Aristotle on, 71
power
absolute power distinguished from
sovereignty, Bodin on, 270–2, 272–4
and nation-states, nineteenth century, 465–7
use by Italian city-stats, 244–7
Prebisch, Raul, continuation of List's
protectionist arguments, 526
pride, opposition to God's peace, Augustine
on, 128
Prince, The (Machiavelli), 244, 245, 247, 257–61
Principles of Political Economy and Taxation
(Ricardo)
trade and increases in welfare, 520–1
trading profits and comparative costs, 535–7
prisoners of war, treatment, 351
private citizens, property open to seizure
in time of war, Pufendorf on, 347–8
Private International Law, 6
prize, 312–13
professional classes, ineffectiveness in
opposition to war, Hilferding on, 580
Project for settling an everlasting peace in Europe, A
(Saint-Pierre), 394–8

property, importance in households, 65–6
protectionism
  Schumpeter on, 576–8, 583–4
  Smith's opposition to, 532–4
  and tariff policies, Hilferding on, 561–2,
    565, 567
  see also tariff policies; trade
providence
  moral improvement dependent upon,
    Kant on, 429–30, 431
  as productive of perpetual peace, Kant
    on, 443–5
Public International Law, 6–7
public law of Europe, 311
Pufendorf, Samuel
  Kant's criticisms, 439
  and natural law, 317–18, 341–8, 349, 354

Quaestionum Juris Publici (Bynkershoek), 252,
    281–5
Quesnay, François, and free trade, 550, 551, 552

Rachel, Samuel, and the law of nations, 320–1,
    349–55
realism
  rights and duties of collectivities, 10
  in Thucydides, 20
  and use of canonical texts, 3–4
reason
  laws and the first principles of nature in
    relation to war, Grotius on, 334–5
  speculative reason, Kant on, 388
reason of state, 245–7, 254, 257, 265–7
  ratio status, Bynkershoek on, 282
rebellions, Kant on the purpose of rebellions,
    390
Reflections on the Revolution in France (Burke), 292
regencies, and sovereignty, Bodin on, 272
regicide, Burke on, 294
regimes see political regimes
Reiss, Hans, 389, 390–1
relativism, as basis of morality, Grotius on, 313
religions
  al-Farabi on, 154
  differences as working against perpetual
    peace, Kant on, 445
religious coercion, 103
Remus (brother of Romulus), 246, 265, 266,
    267
"Report on the Subject of Manufacturers"
    (Hamilton), and protectionism, 524
reprisals, Pufendorf on, 347
republicanism
  as basis for perpetual peace, Kant on, 436–7

growth to lead to increasing opposition to
    war, Kant on, 392–3
  Kant on, 437, 438, 440, 444
republics, governments best based upon that of
    the Roman Republic, Machiavelli on, 262–5
revolution, unlawful nature, Machiavelli on, 246
Ricardo, David, Principles of Political Economy and
    Taxation
  trade and increases in welfare, 520–1
  trading profits comparative costs, 535–7
Richelieu, Armand Jean Duplessis, Duc de,
    Cardinal Richlieu, establishment of
    foreign and diplomatic corps at the court
    of Louis XIII, 252, 277–8
right intention, just-war theory, 184–5, 214, 215,
    218
right on nature, Hobbes on, 316, 339
rights
  cosmopolitan rights, Kant on, 452–4
  cosmopolitan rights and universal
    hospitality, Kant on, 441–3
  international right, and the right of states
    with regard to war, Kant's views, 450–2
  nations' rights secured through federations,
    Kant on, 438–41
rights on nations, Montesquieu on, 400
Roman Empire
  as an example of internationalism for
    Europe, Mazzini on, 484
  assisted by God rather than pagan gods,
    Augustine on, 122–3, 124–5
  attitudes to barbarians in the waging of war,
    Mill on, 487
  and the church, 101, 102, 116–18
  cosmopolitanism, and Stoicism, 29
  unity under Augustus as justification of
    monarchy, Dante on, 202–3
  see also Byzantium
Roman Law, ius gentium, 6, 7
Roman Republic, as the form of government
    best suited to that of a republic,
    Machiavelli on, 262–5
Romans
  distinctions between ius and lex, 319
  ius feciale, 320
Romanticism, reaction against the
    Enlightenment, 459–60
Romanus I Lecapenus (Byzantine emperor),
    144–5, 145–6
Romanus II (Byzantine emperor), 99, 100, 136–8
Rome
  citizenship, 7, 8
  foundation, seen as illustrative of reasons of
    state by Machiavelli, 246, 265–7

Romulus, 246, 265, 266, 267
Rousseau, Jean-Jacques
concept of the private life, 459
concept of the state, 459
corruption of international society, 386
opposition to mainstream Enlightenment
thought, 384–5
and the universal state, 431
rulers
in democratic cities, al-Farabi on, 163–4
in despotic cities, al-Farabi on, 160, 161
distinguished from the governed, Aristotle
on, 62–3
in ignorant cities, al-Farabi on, 164–5
in indispensible cities, al-Farabi on, 156
lack of liberty and subjection to force,
Montesquieu on, 405
maintenance of power through immoral
actions, Machiavelli on, 261
as objects of war, Pufendorf on, 347
responsibilities, 152–3
rights to wage war: Pufendorf's views, 346–7,
348; Thomas Aquinas on, 214–15, 218
sovereignty, Bodin on, 271
in timocratic cities, al-Farabi on, 157–9
types, Aristotle on, 62, 63
in vile cities, al-Farabi on, 156
in virtuous cities, al-Farabi on, 168
see also kings and kingship; monarchy;
sovereigns; sovereignty
Russell, Frederick H., 185
Russia (Cobden), 523, 538–49
Russians, relations with the Byzantine Empire
and other nations, 138–9

saeculum, 97
Saint-Pierre, Abbé de, 551, 556
and perpetual peace, 380, 392, 394–8:
Rousseau on, 426–7
and the universal state, 431
Saving Trophy (the Cross), use by Constantine
the Great in establishing his rule over the
Roman Empire, 115, 116, 117
Say, J. B., and free trade, List's criticisms, 551
Schmidt, Brian, 12
Schumpeter, Joseph (1883–1950), "The Sociology
of Imperialism", 530, 575–84
Scotland, sovereignty as exercised during a
regency, 272
seas, control and freedom, Treitschke on, 500,
504
secular authorities, seen as essential for
the administration of justice, Luther
on, 204–5, 207–9

secular government, Luther on, 182–3
secular power, relation to spiritual power,
John of Paris on, 193–5
self-determination, and nationalism, Mill
on, 464–5
self-preservation
as basis of morality, Grotius on, 313–16
for individuals and for nations, Wolff's
views, 357
as justification for war, 184, 217–19
and natural law: Grotius on, 314–16;
Hobbes on, 316–17
Pufendorf on, 317, 318, 343, 344–5, 346
as reason for non-observance of treaties,
United States concerns, Hamilton on,
286–91
Seneca
on the control of the passions, 30
cosmopolitanism, 29
treaty observance, 281, 284, 285
Sepúlveda, Juan Ginés de, 187, 189
Seventh Letter (Plato), 91–3
Sforza, Ludovico, the Moor (Duke of Milan), 258
Sharrock, Robert, Law of nations and natural
law, 354
Sinclair, T. A.
Homer's importance for political thought
in classical Greece, 18
the Sophists, 19
sinners, awareness of loss of salvation through
goodness inherent in their natures,
Augustine's views, 130–1
Six Books on the Commonwealth (Bodin), concept
of sovereignty, 248–9, 270–5
skepticism, and self-preservation as the basis
for morality, Grotius on, 314
slaves and slavery
al-Farabi on, 155
Aristotle's views applied to European
attitudes towards American Indians,
188, 232, 234, 241
early Christian attitudes towards, 97
and masters, Aristotle on, 65, 66–8, 69, 80
as a result of conquest, Montesquieu
on, 402–4
Smith, Adam, 379, 380, 383, 410–15, 522
advocacy of free trade criticized by List,
525–6, 551, 552
attacks on mercantilist perceptions of
trade, 520
Wealth of Nations, The, international division
of labour, 532–4
sociableness, as part of men's nature, Grotius
on, 326, 327

Social Contract, The (Rousseau), 384, 385, 416
socialists, and nationalism, Schumpeter
    on, 581–2
sociality
    Grotius' understanding, 315
    and laws of nations, Wolff on, 359–60
    Pufendorf on, 317, 341–2, 343–4
societies, classification, al-Farabi on, 148–9
society
    corruption of humanity, Rousseau on, 384–6
    international society, corruption, Rousseau
        on, 386
    war's origins in society, Montesquieu on,
        399–400
    see also civil society
"Sociology of Imperialism, The" (Schumpeter),
    530, 575–84
Socrates
    death, 62
    influence, over Plato, 90, 91–2
    views expressed through Plato, 30–1
soldiers
    culpability in war, Grotius on, 316
    identification and legal standing in war,
        Treitschke on, 503–4
Somalia, mono-nationality, 7–8
Sophists, political thought, 19–20
souls, and bodies, Aristotle on, 66–8
South Africa, British imperialism criticized by
    Hobson, 527–8
South American states, political relationship
    with the United States of America,
    Treitschke on, 496
Southern, R. W., 109
sovereigns
    conduct in waging of war, Vattel on, 375–7
    honours due as representative of their states,
        Vattel on, 370, 371, 372, 373–4
    influence over the development of the
        modern state opposed to that of the
        bourgeosie in attitudes to war,
        Schumpeter on, 580–2
    and natural law in international relations,
        319–20
    power to make war: condemned by Kant, 437,
        439; Rousseau's views, 418, 422
    rights to declare war to be abrogated,
        Kant on, 430
    roles, Kant on, 389
    see also rulers; sovereignty
sovereignty, 247–50, 270–5
    barbarians' sovereignty over their possessions
        in the New World, Vitoria, 231–4
    Bodin's views, 270–5

consolidation after revolution best by
    completely new government, Machiavelli
    on, 267–8
and diplomatic immunity, 251
distinguished from absolute power,
    Bodin on, 270–2, 272–4
establishment best through sole rule,
    Machiavelli on, 265–7
as exercised by the nation, 458
external sovereignty, 250
inviolable nature in any European union,
    Saint-Pierre on, 394–5
Kant on, 437, 438
and law, Bodin on, 273–5
precludes the operation of international law,
    Treitschke on, 497–8
within the supreme state, Wolff on, 364–5,
    366–7
see also rulers; sovereigns
Spanish empire, policy towards native
    Americans in the sixteenth century,
    186–9, 231–41
Sparta
    attitudes to justice: in Thucydides, 21, 23
    attitudes to military security, 38
    republican government considered as a
        possible form for successful government,
        Machiavelli on, 262, 263, 264, 267
    virtue, Aristotle's condemnation, 27
Speusippus (Plato's nephew), 32, 61
    and Aristotle, 23
spies, Kant on, 435, 452
Spirit (*Geist*), Hegel's concept, 460, 462
Spirit of the Laws, The (Montesquieu), 399–406
    international political theory, 381–2
spiritual government, existence possible only
    where the world is Christian, Luther on,
    206–7, 208–9
spiritual power, relations to secular power,
    John of Paris on, 193–5
standing armies
    abolition desirable to abolish war, Kant on,
        433–4
    in a European union, Saint-Pierre on, 397
    maintenance justified for England's policy of
        dominating the balance of power in
        Europe, Cobden's criticisms, 539, 542,
        546–7
state
    concept, 247: Bosanquet on, 468; Hegel on,
        507–8; nineteenth century, 457–9;
        Treitschke on, 466–7, 494–5
    effects on the individuality of human beings,
        Hegel on, 461

state (cont.).
    European state, concept based on Aristotle's
        polis, 178, 179
    and individuals, Plato on, 93
    role, in international law, Hegel on, 461–2
    status, Pufendorf on, 341–2
    "two-swords theory", 178–80
    and war: Bosanquet's views, 511–15; Hegel on,
        508, 511
    see also states
state of nature, and war, Hobbes on, 335–8,
    339–40
State of War, The (Rousseau), 385, 416–25
states
    annexation, Machiavelli on, 258–60
    Aristotle on, 25–6
    civil states, and the origins of war,
        Rousseau on, 417, 418–25
    community and international political
        theory, 11
    and competitive capitalism, nineteenth
        century, 526–7
    composition, Kant on, 450
    confederations and the development of
        international law, Treitschke on, 496
    creation of states the result of war,
        Kant on, 444
    definition, Kant on, 388–9
    establishment best through sole rule,
        Machiavelli on, 265–7
    ethical states, and the First World War,
        467–8
    European states, evolution and international
        political theory, 243–55
    evolution and aims, Aristotle on, 62–4, 69,
        72–3, 77–8
    foreign policies and diplomatic relations,
        250–5
    goods, and their desirability, 77–9
    government, Montesquieu on, 400
    independence, as guarantee of lack of
        interference in internal affairs by other
        states, Kant on, 434–5
    independence precludes states being
        annexed, Kant on, 433
    and individuals: Aristotle on, 64; fellowship
        between, Cicero on, 84; happiness
        common to both, Aristotle on, 79–82;
        Hegel on, 508–9
    and international law, 177–83, 311–12
    international relations: based on obligations
        or contracts, Hegel on, 470–2, 508;
        Bosanquet's views, 514; in international
        congresses, Treitschke on, 501–2
    natural rights, Grotius' understanding, 315–16

prosecution of war only to be made after
        consultation with philosophers,
        Kant on, 446–7
    role, and political legitimacy, 459–62
    secular states, political authority in relation
        to church authority, 179–81
    security to be maintained by any
        expediency, 268–9
    self-preservation, Pufendorf on, 318
    Stoics on, 26
    supreme state (civitas maximus), Wolff on,
        321–2, 360–7, 368
    types: Kant on, 437–8; Machiavelli on, 257–60
    will, aimed at welfare of the state and its
        maintenance through treaties,
        Hegel on, 473–4
    see also cities; collectivities; federations;
        governments; nations; state
Stoics
    community, 26
    influence over Marcus Aurelius, 86
    international political theory, 27–30
    and self-preservation as the basis for morality
        Grotius on, 313–14
    universalism, 9
Suárez, Francisco
    and ius gentium, 320
    understanding of ius, 314
Swanson, T. A., 27
Switzerland, political position in relationship
        to international law, Treitschke on, 496

tacit truces, Pufendorf on, 348
Tacitus, 247
tariff policies
    Hilferding on, 562, 565
    and limitations on competitive capitalism,
        527
    and protectionism: Hilferding on, 561–2,
        565, 567; Schumpeter on, 576–8
    see also protectionism
territorial acquisitions, forbidden in any
        European union, Saint-Pierre on, 395–6
Tertullian, 97
theatre, Augustine condemns their immorality,
    121
Theory of Moral Sentiments, The (Smith), 383, 410
Theory and Practice (Kant), 389
Thomas Aquinas (c., 1225–74)
    just-war theory, 183–5, 213–20
    "two-swords" theory, 178–9
Thoughts on French Affairs (Burke), 292
Thucydides
    international political theory, 20–3, 32, 34–60
    Peloponessian War, 34–5

realism in international relations, 10
  use by realist International Relations
    theorists, 3, 4
timocratic cities, al-Farabi on, 157–9
Tisias (Athenian general), Melian dialogue, 53–9
tournaments, outlawed by the church, 213
trade
  Britain, naval defence of her trading interests
    attacked by Cobden, 543–6
  economics, Smith on, 410–15
  low costs seen as essential for the protection
    of British trade, Cobden on, 544–6
  mercantilist perceptions, pre-nineteenth
    century, 520
  productive of perpetual peace, Kant on, 445
  promotion of peace, Ricardo on, 535
  protectionism, 524–6: Cobden's arguments
    for, 523–4
  and war, Kant on, 453
  see also free trade; international trade;
    protectionism
trade agreements, capital investment,
    Hilferding on, 565–6
trade policies, and peace-making, Bosanquet
    on, 513–14
trading profits, and comparative costs, Ricardo
    on, 535–7
transport, development and effects under
    capitalism, Hilferding on, 564
travel, international travel, validity allowed
    in the case of Spanish colonization of the
    New World, Vitoria on, 234–5, 236
treachery
  in non-observance of treaties: Bynkershoek
    on, 282; Machiavelli, 281, 282
treaties, 251, 252
  conditional nature, Treitschke on, 497–8,
    500–1
  nature, Rousseau on, 421
  observance essential, Bynkershoek on, 281–5
    Rachel on, 349, 349–50
  see also truces; war
Treatise on Human Nature (Hume), 382, 407
Treitschke, Heinrich Von (1834–96), realist
    nationalism, 466, 467, 468, 494–505
Triakontaeterrikos (Tricennial Orations) (Eusebius),
    Constantinianism, 98–9, 115–18
truces
  contrast with peace, Kant on, 432–3
  Pufendorf on, 348
  see also treaties; war
True Concept of a Balance of Power, The (Gentz),
    307–10
truth, perceptions among Weeds in virtuous
    cities, 167–9

Turks
  exclusion from international negotiations in
    Europe, Treitschke on, 496
  relations with the Byzantine Empire and
    other nations, 139, 141
  as seekers of pleasure in base cities, al-Farabi
    on, 165
two cities
  Augustine on, 102–3, 105, 133–5
  "two-swords" theory, 101, 179–80
two ways, Didache, 111–14
tyrannies
  al-Farabi on, 108
  Aristotle on, 70: quoted by John of Paris,
    192–3
  defense of the innocent against tyranny as
    justification of Spanish colonization of
    the New World, 239–40

'ulama (men of religious learning), 106
umma (community of religious believers), 106
"underconsumptionism", 528
United Provinces, honoured as a republic,
    Vattel on, 371
United States of America
  and capitalism, Hilferding on, 564–5, 566,
    567, 568
  neutrality, French revolutionary wars, 252–3,
    286–91
  political relationship with South American
    states, Treitschke on, 496
  and protectionism, 524
universal state
  existence demanded by free trade, List on,
    551–6, 558–60
  ultimate desirability as the aim of moral
    perfection, Kant on, 429–32
universalism, and international political
    theory, 9, 11
Universe
  relationship with individuals, Marcus
    Aurelius on, 88, 89
  Stoics on, 28
unjust wars, Grotius, 316
utilitarianism, 255
  concept of the state, 458

Varro, 120–1
Vattel, Emmerich de, 379
  definition of balance of power, 539, 540,
    542
  exceptions to the observance of treaty
    obligations, 288
  and international law, 322–3
  Kant's criticisms, 439

Venice
    honoured as a republic, Vattel on, 371
    republican government considered as a
        possible form for successful government,
        Machiavelli on, 262–3, 264
vile cities, al-Farabi on, 156
villages, evolution, Aristotle on, 63
violence, justification by reasons of state,
    Machiavelli on, 266, 268
virtue, attainment in daily life, Avicenna on, 173
virtue (Arete), 19
virtuous cities, 152–3, 155
    and democratic cities, al-Farabi on, 164, 165
    and timocratic cities, al-Farabi on, 159
    Weeds as citizens, al-Farabi on, 155, 166–9
    see also cities
virtuous regime, al-Farabi on, 107, 108
Vitoria, Francisco de
    Christian relations with native Americans
        and the waging of war, 186–9, 231–41
    and ius gentium, 319
Voltaire, 180, 379, 381, 384
    concept of the private life, 459

war
    as affected by international right, Kant on,
        450–2
    al-Farabi on, 108
    and arbitration, Pufendorf on, 344, 345
    Aristotle on, 27
    and capitalism, Schumpeter on, 575–6, 578,
        579–84
    and civil society, Rousseau on, 425–6
    and commerce, Kant on, 453
    conduct: Treitschke on, 502–4; Vattel on, 323,
        375–8
    costs, levying on states no populations, Kant
        on, 452
    culpability in war, Pufendorf on, 347
    duties to wage war, Avicenna on, 170–1, 171–2
    effects, to establish ultimate universal peace,
        Kant on, 430
    ending, as the moral aim based upon reason,
        Kant on, 454–5
    forbidden activities in the prosecution of
        war, Kant on, 435, 452
    Hilferding's attitudes towards, 529
    inevitability, Rousseau on, 387
    justice during, Grotius on, 330–1
    justification: Grotius on, 312–14, 315–16, 325,
        333–4; in inevitability and divine nature,
        Treitschke on, 498–9; motivation for
        righteousness the only justification for
        war, Thomas Aquinas on, 214, 215, 218; only

by the need to punish the guilty, Thomas
    Aquinas on, 214, 215; Pufendorf on, 318;
    Rachel on, 355
justification for killing of the innocent,
    Thomas Aquinas on, 215–17
and the law of nature, Grotius on, 333–4
List's opposition to, 553–4
as the means of asserting a state's rights,
    Kant on, 440, 441
as the means of settling disputes between
    states as a result of the non-observance
    of treaties, Hegel on, 472–3
as the means to international justice,
    Burke on, 296–7, 299–300
as natural defence, Montesquieu on, 402
nature, Bosanquet on, 514, 514–15
non–justifiable and justifiable causes,
    Mill on, 486–7, 489–91
origins in insults to national sovereignty,
    Treitschke on, 497
origins and nature, Rousseau on, 416–25
origins in society, Montesquieu on, 399–400
and peace, Pufendorf on, 348
peace as the object of war, Augustine
    on, 126, 130
perpetual readiness for war as a means of
    self-preservation for the state, Pufendorf
    on, 344–5
popularity to decrease as republicanism
    grows, Kant on, 392–3
pressures of war result in the creation of
    states, Kant on, 444
as the prime role of the state, Treitschke
    on, 467
prohibitive laws relating to, Kant on, 432–6
promotion of war by ancient states, 80
regarded as disease, Bosanquet on, 468
as the result of development in international
    capitalism, 568–9
and right of conquest, Montesquieu on,
    402–4
role, Hegel on, 462, 467
and the state: Bosanquet on, 511–15;
    Hegel on, 508, 509–10, 511
and the state of nature, Hobbes on, 335–8,
    339–40
treatment of the conquered, Pufendorf
    on, 348
unjust wars, Pufendorf on, 345–6
waging of war: between civilized and
    barbarian peoples, Mill on, 487–9; by
    any European union, Saint-Pierre on, 396,
    397; Hegel on, 474; Pufendorf on, 346–7
see also just war; treaties; truces

Washington, George, declares American neutrality in French revolutionary wars, 252–3, 289

wealth
acquisition, in vile cities, al-Farabi on, 156
as oligarchy, Aristotle on, 71, 72

Wealth of Nations, The (Smith), 383, 410–15
international division of labour, 532–4

Weeds (citizens), position in the virtuous city, al-Farabi on, 155, 166–9

welfare, increases, and trade, Ricardo on, 520–1

Westphalia, Peace of, and sovereignty, 250

Wight, Martin, history of international thought, 12

William III (king of Great Britain), references to the balance of Europe, 538, 541

William IV (king of Great Britain), and taxation for the maintenance of the British navy, 543, 545

wisdom, Avicenna on, 173

Wolff, Christian von (1679–1554), and the law of nations, 321–2, 356–69, 370

women
early Christian attitudes towards, 97
roles, in base cities, al-Farabi on, 165–6

workers, powers, opposed to the capitalist state, Hilferding on, 571

world, well-being served by monarchy, Dante on, 201–2

world court, desirability under international law, Rachel on, 321, 355

world of Islam (*Dar al Islam*), 108

world order, early Christian views, 98, 111–14

world state, Kant's opposition to, 391, 392

world of war (*Dar al harb*), 108

Zeno of Citium, 28

Zouche, Richard
international law and civil law, 320
law of nations, 351